I0093806

DeKalb County, Alabama, Wills and Estates, 1836-1929

Volume I
A - J

Transcribed and Compiled by
Dorothy Smith Duff

CLEARFIELD

Printed for Clearfield Company by
Genealogical Publishing Company
Baltimore, Maryland
2010

Set ISBN: 978-0-8063-5487-3
ISBN, Volume I: 978-0-8063-5488-0

Made in the United States of America

Contents

Surnames	Page
A	1
B	17
C	53
D	87
E	117
F	129
G	139
H	199
J	243
All Name Index	265

Introduction

The wills and estate records for DeKalb County, Alabama from 1838-1929 have been reviewed. All probate records of wills and estate settlements for this period have been listed by the Estate Record Name as it appears in the court records. From the probate records, the estate record name, the box number, the file number, and the year of probate have been abstracted. In addition, other names in the file are listed as they appear in the court records and in many cases the role of that person is listed; these names include administrators, guardians, heirs, attorneys, appraisers, debtors, creditors and others.

The original probate records are stored in the DeKalb County Courthouse in Fort Payne, Alabama. The records are referenced by the estate name, box number, and file folder number in the box. In 2003-2004, the Utah Genealogical Society microfilmed the probate court records. The original records and the microfilms are my source for transcribing the names in the wills and estate records of DeKalb County, Alabama.

Dekalb County was formed in 1836 from Cherokee Lands; therefore, the records herein are the earliest probate records for the county. Volume I, covers Surnames A-J. No records were found for Surname I. More than 18,000 name entries are included in this volume.

Abbreviations

adm., admin.	administrator
admx.	administratrix
adv.	advertise
atty.	attorney
bro-i-law	brother-in-law
c/o	child of
comm.	commissioner
dau.	daughter
dec., decd., dec'd,	deceased
depos.	deposition
et al	and others
exec.	executor
f/o	father of
g/c	grandchild
g/dau	grandaughter
g/son	grandson
guar.	guardian
guar.ad litem	guardian ad litem
h/o	husband of
hus.	husband
JP	Justice of Peace
m/o	mother of
m-i-l	mother in law
NP	Notary Public
parenthesis, estate sale	item purchased
parenthesis, name	alternative interpretation
purch.	purchased
question mark ?	questionable entry
tax coll.	tax collector, tax collected
w/o	wife of
wit.	witness

A

Estate Record Name

Abercrombie, Erb
Box 2, File 1 1925
Names in File:
Abercrombie, Martha J.(mother)
Abercrombie, J. M.
Abercrombie, Ohpelia
Gravitt, Claris
Williams, J. D.

Abercrombie, John
Box 1, File 2 1904-1913
Names in File:
Abercrombie, W. S.(guardian)
Abercrombie, Ruthie(minor)
Abercrombie, Jonnie (minor)
Black, J. H.
Heaton, S. L.
Croley, J. A. (Judge)

Abercrombie, John
Box 2, File 3 1907
Names in File:
Croley, James A.
Campbell, H. B.
Isbell, John B.
Davis, Reuben (JP)
Berry, Minnie (Commissioner)
Copeland, A. C.
Abercrombie, Ruthy (minor)
Abercrombie, John (minor)
Abercrombie, Mary Jane,(widow)
Abercrombie, W. S. (guardian)
Black, J. H.
Cash, James
Bobo, Janey
Abercrombie, Mary Susan
Henry, Nannie

Adams, A.H.
Box 2, File 4 1902-1903
Names in File:

Estate Record Name

Adams, A.H. (Cont.)
Adams, Mary
Adams, Eunica
Adams, ?
Adams Willie
Culver, N. L.
Caryle, J. J.
Culver, N. L.
Caryle, J. J.
Russell, W.W.
Hall, J. A.
Traylor, G. R.
Haralson, W.R.
Hall, J. D.
Green, P. B. (M.D.)
Workman, S. D.
Mc _____, J. M.
Stone, B. C.
Shankles, G. W.
Graves, H. L.
Shankles, Geo. W.
Marshall, Hugh
Carnes, James
Dobbs, W. W
Presley, I. M.
Sales of Estate Property:
Bailey, J. T.
Caryle, L. L.
Adams, W. H.
Maton, J. T.
Rose, B. D.
King, Tom
Jacoway, W. V.
Wooten, J. J.
Robertson, J. A.
Bucks, J. T.
DeShields, Lee
Jones, G. H.

Estate Record Name

Adams, A.H. (Cont.)
Farris, M. D.
Foster, W. H.
Moody, T. E.
Hall, J. H.
Love, J. W.
Paid:
King, Tom
Green, P. B. (Dr.)
Dean, J. E.
Traylor, T. M.
McCluskey, J. W.
Jones, G. R.
Culver, N. L.
Russell, W. W.
Adams, Marie (minor)
Box 2, File 5 1916-1930
Names in File:
Jenkins, Bessie M.
Wade, Marie
Higdon, G. C.
Jenkins, R. R.
Land, S. J.
Johnson, J. A.
Rose, R. F.
Jacoway, W. W.
Biddle, W. R.
Miller, S. W.
Adkins, Benjamin F. (B. F.)
Box 2, File 6 1906-1909
Names in File:
Adkins, Smith
Adkins, Nancy
Adkins, M. V.
Adkins, Geo. (Leo)
Jenkins, Margaret
Blevins, Lorene
Blevins, Lennie
Adkins, Morris
Adkins, Mary
Adkins, E. B.

Estate Record Name

Adkins, Benjamin F. (B.F.) (Cont.)
Adkins, George W.
Blevins, F. M.
Cook, W.C.D., Atty.
Adkins, Smith, (Adm.)
Austin, M. L.
Blevins, G. L.
Adkins, J. G.
Case, James R.
Austin, H. D.
Lusk, W. D.
Austin, W. L.
Adkins, J. C.
Garron, Geo.
Austin, W. B.
Blevins, H. W.
Blevins, F. M.
Young, J. W.
Smith, W. H.
Slaughter, W. L.
Mathes, Alex
Adkins, D. L. G.
Evans, J. H.
Simpson, Jim
Steel, James
Blevins, Laura (Launa) E.
Steel, W. A.
Fisher, G. A.
Adkins, Mary
Cunton, W. C.
Jenkins, Joe
Adkins, Smith (Adm.)
Adkins, Nancy (wife of Dock)
Adkins, Dock (Hus. of Nancy)
Tinker, Malvina
Tinker, M. V.
Adkins, George W.
Jenkins, Margaret
Jenkins, W.J.N. (h/o Margaret)
Blevins, Launa (w/o F.M.)
Blevins, F. M. (h/o Launa)

Estate Record Name
Adkins, Benjamin F.(B. F.)(Cont.)
Blevins, Tenie
Blevins, F. M.
Adkins, Mary
Adkins, Morris
Adkins, Enoch B.
Cook & Presley, Atty.
Adkins, G. W.
Smith, Loney
Harris, William
Adkins, J. C.
Sale of Inventory
Austin, M. L. (wagon)
Blevins, G. J. (wagon)
Blevins, H. E. (hand saw)
Adkins, J. F. C. (hand saw)
Case, H, R, (brace & bit)
Austin, H. D. (4-augers)
Lusk, W. D. (knife & saw)
Austin, W. L. (box of tools)
Adkins, J. C. (wagon repairs)
Adkins, Alvin (mowing blade)
Gearrin, G. W. (grain cradle)
Blevins, G. J. (grain cradle)
Adkins, Jess (grain cradle)
Adkins, J. C. (grind rock)
Austin, M. L. (wagon hubs)
Adkins, W. B. (work bench)
Austin, M. L. (bins & rye)
Austin, J. C. (wagon plunder)
Case, J. R. (wheel barrow)
Blevins, H. W. (mattock, hoe)
Blevins, F. M. (blacksmith tools)
Adkins, J. F. (double shovel)
Young, J. W. (plow stock)
Smith, W. H. (plow stock)
Slaughter, W. L. (corn drill)
Austin, J. C. (2-horse plow)
Young, J. W. (plows)
Austin, J. C. (log chain)
Blevins, G. J. (wagon)

Estate Record Name
Adkins, Benjamin F.(B. F.)(Cont.)
Adkins, J. C.(white oak lumber)
Blevins, F. M. (boards)
Mathis, Alex (bull)
Austin, W. B. (corn sheller)
Adkins, D. L. G.
Blevins, G. J. (2-baskets)
Adkins, J. C. (pr. mules)
Adkins, J. C. (wagon)
Evans, J. H. (wash pot)
Simpson, James (18 hogs)
Austin, W. L. (10 stands bees)
Austin, W. L. (5 stands bees)
Adkins, Smith (feather bed)
Steel, James (feather bed)
Blevins, G. J. (3 quilts)
Blevins, G. J. (2 quilts)
Steel, James (counterpins)
Blevins, L. E. (11 chairs)
Steel, W. H. (mirror)
Evans, J. H. (mirror)
Blevins, L. E. (1-lot dishes)
Blevins, Laura (1 safe)
Adkins, Alvin (2 baskets)
Fisher, G. A.. (basket)
Evans, G. H. (basket)
Adkins, Mary (willow basket)
Evans, G. H. (basket)
Blevins, L. E. (table cloth)
Blevins, L. E. (table)
Blevins, L. E.(flour chest)
Cureton, W. C. (bee bellows)
Austin, W. B. (spinning wheel)
Blevins, Teny (1 chest)
Blevins, Teny (1 trunk)
Austin, J. C. (suit case)
Blevins, F. M. (bowl)
Case, J. R. (set shoe tools)
Austin, W. B. (2 large jars)
Blevins, Teny (jars)
Jenkins, Joe (jars)

Estate Record Name

Adkins, Benjamin F.(B. F.)(Cont.)
 Blevins, Oscar (cooking utensils)
 Blevins, L. E. (irons & keg)
 Blevins, L. E. (bed stead)
 Blevins, Oscar (lamp & tongs)
 Cureton, W. C.(crosscut saw)
 Adkins, J. (tooth pullers)
 Blevins, Teny (window shades)
 Simpson, James (grass seeds)
 Adkins, J. C. (grinds stone)
 Simpson, James (The Farm)

Adkins, G. W.
 Box 2, File 7 1886
 Names in File:
 Adkins, Charlotte W.(widow)
 Widow Exemption
 Adkins, D. L. (minor)
 Blevins, R. M. (JP)
 Countiss, John B., Sr. (adm.)
 Payne, Thomas (adm.)
 Franklin, John M., Judge
 Adkins, Dock
 Adkins, G. M.

Adkins, J. D.
 Box 2, File 8 1899-1904
 Names in File:
 Adkins, J. C. (adm.)
 Holland, Jesse
 Harris, William
 Adkins, J. C.
 Adkins, A. J.
 Austin, W. M.
 Austin, J. F.
 Austin, J. L.
 Cook, W.C.D.
 Clark, E. J.
 Adkins, James C.
 Smith, Loney
 Adkins, Lottie
 Adkins, Ollie
 Pruett, Rebecca

Estate Record Name

Adkins, J. D. (Cont.)
 Hamrick, W. X.
 Scott, J.W.T.
 Hawkins, James C.
 Adkins, Samuel
 Blevins, G. J.
 Dodd, B. W.
 Heirs:
 Adkins, J. C.
 Adkins, John F.
 Adkins, W. H.
 Adkins, Samuel
 Prewitt, Rebecca
 Adkins, Lottie
 Adkins, Ollie
 Steel, Malvina
 Steel, Isaac
 Steel, Claude
 Steel, Maude
 Steel, Amanda J.
 Ellis, Ginty
 Ellis, Minnie
 Adkins, Ben
 Adkins, H. G.

Adkins, Lottie
 Box 2, File 9 1901-1904
 Names in File:
 Adkins, Charlotte (minor)
 Adkins, Ollie (minor)
 Adkins, James C.
 Young, G. L.
 Blansit, R. L.
 Lusk, W. D.
 Cook, W.C.D., (Judge)
 Adkins, Olie
 Smith, Loney

Adkins, S. G.
 Box 2, File 10 1906-1910
 Names in File:
 Adkins, M. E. (w/o S.G.)
 Widow Exemption

Estate Record Name
Adkins, S. G.
Adkins, M. E., Mrs.
Fischer, D. S.
Baker, J. H.
Croley, James A., Judge
Akins, John W.
Box 2, File 11 1866
Names in File:
Nicholson, D.L.
Beeson, J. G.
Slone, Jesse
Allen, Crosby
Box 2, File 12
Names in File:
Brandon, P. A.
Grider, W. M., (Adm.)
Bynum, R. H,
Ryan, S.
Franklin, John N.
McNutt, R. C.
Hunt & Tally (Attys.)
Kyle, Nelsen
Judge Jackson County
Allen, Hiram
Box 2, File 13 1865-1874
Names in File:
Peacock, Henry
Brock, Wilborn
White, J. G.
White, Wm. H.
Allen, Ruth
Brock, Andrew
McSpadden, C. A.
Allen, W. T.
Brandon, , P. A.
Franklin, John
Malone, G. W.
Horton, A. J.
Allen, Joseph A.
Smith, Thomas H.
Dobbs, L. A.

Estate Record Name
Allen, Hiram (Cont.)
Haralson, W. R.
Davenport, N. S.
Allen, Jefferson D. (minor)
Campbell, H. B.
Copeland, A. C.
Allen, John W.
Box 2, File 14 1859-1869
Names in File:
Nicholsen, D. L. (Admin.)
Branden. P. A.
Cox, T.G.A.
Lambert, Thomas
Randall, John
Cox, Thomas G. A.
Allen, Rubie (minor)
Box 2, File 15 1914-1922
Names in File:
Allen, A. A.
O'Shields, H. H.
Bishof, W.W.
Allen, M. J., Mrs.
Wright, W. I. (Dr.)
Gilbert, E. N.
Harris, W. M.
Gilbert, E. N.
Allen, Rubie, (minor)
Allen, William F.
Box 2, File 16 1875-1879
Names in File:
Frazier, P. B.
Brock, Wilburn
Brandon, P. A., Judge
Spring, David
Allen, Edward F (minor)
Allen, Nancy (minor)
Poe, W. R.
McSpadden, Hiram A.(adm)
Allen, Sarah A.
Allen, Benjamin
Hill, Margaret

Estate Record Name
Allen, William F. (Cont.)
Hill, John
Mahan, Susan
Allen, Hiram A.
McSpadden, Mary(w/o H.A.)
Allen, John V.
Allen, Sally
McSpadden, H. A. (Admin.)
Allen, Ben
Jacoway, J. G.
Henegar, Moses
Clayton, Tom
Davenport, W. S.
Davenport, Frank
Laramore, V. C.
Allen, Berry J.
Allen, Sarah
Allen, Joe
Long, James
Mahan, S.V.
Allen, H. R.
Allen J.A.Q.
McSpadden, M.J.
Allen, S. A.
Allen, N. T.
Allen, W. F.
Allen, E. F.
Franklin, Jno. N.
Allison, W. M.
Box 2, File 17 1907
Names in File:
Allison, A. B. (Admin.)
Brown, C. J.
O'Rear, Samuel
Amos (Amus)(Aamus), M.
Box 2, File 18 1866-1867
Names In File:
Amos, Milton Hames
Amos, M.
Aamus, M.
Amus, M.

Estate Record Name
Amos (Amus)(Aamus), M.
Amos, John, (guardian)
Amos (Amus)(AaMus), M.
Aminer, July (Julia)Amos
Amos (Amus) Julia (Minor)
Amos, John F.
Amos, Madason
Hawkins, James
Franklin, J. N., Judge
Amus, John
Hames, Reba Cash Milton
Amos (Minor Children)
Anderson, Ida M.
Box 2, File 19 1893
Names in File:
Anderson, Edward
Anderson, R. E.
Anderson, Lora
Anderson, Reulla
Cook, W. C. D., Judge
Johnson, C. C.
Pope, W. E.
?, W. H. H.
Ansley (Ausley), James A.
Box 2, File 20 1883-1897
Names in File:
Ansley, Mattie J. (widow, adm)
Ansley,W. J. (child)
Ansley, James M.(child)
Ansley, Edward J.(child)
Ansley, Heulet L.(child)
Ansley (Ausley)
Payne, H. G., (JP)
Russell, James E.
Clayton, C. P.
Campbell, Lewis
Franklin, John N. (Judge)
Ansley, W. J., (Adm.)
Cochran, L. L. (Judge)
Harrison, W. J.
Killian, E. S.

Estate Record Name

Ansley (Ausley), James A. (Cont.)
Rooney, J. D.
D. B. Loverman & Co.
Jeffins & Payne
Gannett, Thomas
Gilbert, W. P.
Killian, A. C.
Russell, J. E.
Lanthom, Nettie
C. S. Williams & Co.
Green, A. B.
Key & Richmond, Atty.
Smith, Thomas N.
Ausley (Ansley)
Ansley, W. J., (adm.)
Collins, O. H.
Howard, J. M.
Stewart, Thomas G.
Campbell, J.
Harlston, Davis
Davis, George H., Jr.
Davis & Haralson, Attys.
Poe, W. R.
Johnson, R. C.
Ellis, A. J.
Quin, W. E.
Johnson, R.
McCurdy, J. A.
Fort Payne Herald
Stewart, Thomas G.
Dobbs & Howard
Gilespie & Smyne
Franklin, John N.
Baxter, F. M.
Williams, D. C.
Williams, DeWitt C.
Ausley, Mattie J. (Adm.)
West, James
Durham, James M.
Ausley, Wm. J., (Adm.)
Campbell, H. B.

Estate Record Name

Applewhite, J. T.
Box 2, File 21 1910-1912
Names in File:
DeKalb Co. Bank
Haralson, J. B. (Adm.)
Bohling, J. G.
De Shields, J. G.
Wedgworth, H. C.
Croley, J.A., Judge
Downs, T. L.
Wood, Emma, (dau.)
Wood, Emma, (wife of Wm.)
Wood, William
Kennedy, Sarah E. (dau)
Jones, Minnie, (w/o Bird Jones)
Jones, Bird
Tuggle, Jessie (w/o Will)
Tuggle, Will
Hall, R. C.
Miller, G. W.
Hawkins, N. T.
Ward, C. G.
Wood, T. J.
Gullegr, Jesse, Dr., (paid)
Gulledger, Jesse
Scott, J. H., (paid)
McSpadden, B. J.
Herren Bros. (casket & hearse)
Patterson & Herrin, (paid)
Ruskin, J. T., Dr., (paid)
Brown, W. R., (Note)
Jones, B. G., Mrs.
Jones, B. G.
Miller, G. W.
Rice, John & Martha
Lindsey, A. C. (Waiver Note)
Glasby, J. A.
Glasby, J. L.
Hale, P. C.
Hawkins, N.
Ward, C. G.

Estate Record Name
Applewhite, J. T. (Cont.)
Presley, J. M. (Atty.)
Smith, G. H.
Armstrong, James
Box 2, File 22 1887
Names in File:
Gilreath, M. M. (Admin.)
Brandon, P. A., Judge
McMahan, S. W., Sheriff
Armstrong, James C.
Box 2, File 23 1862-1868
Names in File:
Mary A. Armstrong
M. M. Gilbreath (Adm)
Armstrong, John H.
Slone (Stone) Jesse
Cox, James
Armstrong, Mary Ann (guar.)
Bone, James H.
Haralson, W. J.
Wright, Elizabeth
Horton, A. J., Judge
Nichols, D. L.
Foster, John, (atty)
Hoge, John K.
Franklin, John N., Judge
Kirk, W. P. (sheriff)
Roden, W. W.
Nicholsen & Collins
Collins, J. B.
Armstrong, L. D.
Franklin, J. N.
King, J. R.
Gilbreath, M. M.
Warren, N. M.
Gilbreath, S. E.
Bray, Shadrack
Crabtree, J. W.
Shankles, George
Shankles, Nancy Ann
Samples, B.

Estate Record Name
Armstrong, James C. (Cont.)
Armstrong, John
Armstrong, William
Armstrong, Sarah
Sampley, Nancy Ann
Sampley, Bradford, (h/o N.)
Smith, Rufina
Smith, William, (h/o Rufina)
Fricks, Y. A.
Igou, A. J.
King, R.
King, W. F.
King, W. H.
Dobbs, L. A.
Cardan, H. W.
Lea, James
Shelton, A. W. (sheriff)
Pierce, John A.
Cox, James
Smith, W. H.
Smith, L.
Hoge, J. K., Judge
Armstrong, James H.
Haralston & Haralston
Sampley, B. H.
Hearn, John T.
Staton, G. W.
Lea, Allen
McDaniel
McClain
McCommack, Albert
Hannan, B. G., (J.P.)
Cox, James
Collins, T. B.
Fullerton, T. C. (atty.)
Dobbs, L. A.
Cardan, Hugh W.
Wright, Elizabeth
Ryon, Thomas
Kirkland, G. H.
Guest, G. B.

Estate Record Name
Armstrong, James C. (Cont.)
Light, Meredith (JP)
Armstrong, James H.
Box 2, File 24 1867
Names in File:
Franklin, John
Gilbreath, M. M.
See File 23, James C.
Ashberry, William
Box 2, File 25 1851-1863
Names in File:
Shasteen, Jno.
Franklin, J. W.
Ashberry, Joseph
Shasteen, John
Estes, Burham
Ashberry, A.B.
Ashberry, Loucinda
Ashberry, Rufus
Bryant, Wm.
Bryant, Eliza
Ashberry, Eliza
Williams, J. A.
Estes, Reuben
Shankles, Jno.
Gibson, J. W.
Shankles, Robt.
Shankles, July
Grider, C.
Rink, Jno. F.
Strother, James
Stafford, Mahlon
John Shasteen (guardian)
Minors: Joseph & Julia
Minors, Eliza & Jane
Ashberry, Joseph Andrew
Risk, John R.
Estes, Reuben, Judge
Ashberry, Julian
Ashberry, Jane
Ashburn, Martin

Estate Record Name
Ashburn, Martin
Box 2, File 26 1860-1880
Names in File: Folder 1 of 2
Dunlap, R. A.
Horton, A. J.
Collins, T. B.
Ashburn, Bob
Dobbs, Dunlap
Dobbs, L. A.
Ashburn, S. B.
Ashburn, R. T.
Austin, S. B. (Admin)
Stewart, Samuel
Brown, Golston
Cook, B. F.
Driskill, W. L.
White, Thomas
Brown, M. S.
Ashburn, Robert T.
Ashburn, ?
Lowry, Adam
Austin, Stephen B.
Swader, Margaret
Swader, A. J.
Dunlap & Dobbs &Jacoway
Stewart, Margaret
Ashburn, Robert
Jacoway, Henry J.
Ashburn, Isaac
White, Thomas H.
White, Mary E.
Hanna, A. B.
Cook, B. F.
Hawkins, Preston
Hawkins, Jas. M.
Stone, W. J.
Street, A.
Payne, Thomas
Tatum, R. H.
Blevins, Jonathan
Smith, Henry

Estate Record Name
Ashburn, Martin (Cont.)
Dorsey, J. R.
Dorsey, A. J.
Ashburn, William L.
Ashburn, Susan
Franklin, J. N.
Dobbs, L. A.
Bouldin, E.
Painter, Hardy
Chitwood, R.
Richolson, ?
Brandon, P. A.
Lowes, Adam
Hawkins, Raugley, Jr.
Cagle, Charles
Cagle, Malinda
Smith, Lucinda C.
Smith, W. O.
Blevins, Robert
Blevins, Marg. L.
Blevins, James
Cagle, Wm. J.
Cagle, Geo. M.
Cagle, Stephen J.
Cagle, Robert L.
Mason, Sarah A.
Mason, James W.
Hess, Willis
Blansit,
Austin, S. B.
Abbott, Tobias
Becown (Becom), Louisa
Becom, Medow
Becom, James
Bush, Alley
Cooper, Jackson
Frost, Henry
Gatlin, Wm.
Johnson, Wm.
Henegar, Sham I.
McHaffey, Wm.

Estate Record Name
Ashburn, Martin (Cont.)
Tiege, Delila
Keath, Rufus
Wood, G. W.
Whitehead, John G.
Wilson, John P.
Wilkinson, Wm.
Woodall, Andrew
Wilbanks, E.
Warren, Joseph
Warren, Charles
Young, S. C.
Young, M.
Young, W.
Smith, Wm.
Smith, Hiram
Smith, Daniel
Sisemore, A. G.
Stone, W. F.
Sisemore, Richland
Dorsey, A. J.
Cooper, Jackson
Cooper, Gaines
Cook, James W.
Cook, James
Cook, P. A.
Cook, John
Crow, Isaac
Cross, Andrew
Clark, John
Crae, J. C.
Crae, Isaac
Cook, Robert M.
Cook, J. W
Deathridge, G. R.
Doyle, C. C.
Durham, Madison,
Earp, Thos.
Frost, Henry
Forester, Peter, (JP)
Fry, Joe

Estate Record Name
Ashburn, Martin (cont.)
Frizell, Carlton
Fletcher, James
Francis, Josiah
Hartline, W. A.
Jones, Asa, (JP)
Adkins, William
Anderson, Joseph
Allen, John
Adkins, Madison
Akins, Joseph
Abbot, Allen
Adkins, William
Austin, J. A.
Atkins, W. W.
Blevins, Jas.
Blevins, Jessie
Blevins, Jessie B.
Blevins, Richard
Blevins, Jackson
Blevins, John
Brown, James
Bryant, Joe
Blevins, W.
Brown, Jas. G.
Beckom, George
Pearson, W. K.
Panther, C.
Paxton, John
Palmore, I. H.
Porter, Brad
Rockhall, H.
Rode, G. W.
Russell, Matilda J.
Steel, John
Steel, Christopher
Steel, Ransom
Smith, Grey
Scruggs, John
Smith, Hiram
Smith, Henry

Estate Record Name
Ashburn, Martin (cont.)
Smith, Carroll
Smith, Jey
Simpson, Cummings
Smith, Jackson
Smith, David
Slaton, C. G. (T.G.)
Smith, C. G.
Sizemore, A. J.
Smith, B.
Stafford, N. A.
Sizemore, I. H.
Sizemore, A. G.
Sizemore, Richard
Saterwhite, David
Taylor, Jesse
Tulley, S.
Wilkerson, Wm.
Warren, R. I. (R.J.)
Warren, R. J.
Warren, Wm.
Jones, Asa
Jones, Joseph
Jones, Albert
Jones, Jas. Wm.
Igou, J. N.
Igou, A. I. (A. J.)
Morris, Thomas A.
Milligan, James
Milligan, M.
Morgan, W.A.
Milligan, James
Milligan, Wm.
Melton, John
Milligan, Lory
Melton, H W.
Mahaffey, Richard
Melton, Wm. P
McDaniel, Wm.
Mahaffey, Wm.
McCampbell, R.

Estate Record Name

Ashburn, Martin (Cont.)
Box 2, File 26 1860-1880
Mason, J. E. J.
Morgan, Wm.
Millican, Lory
Lea, James
Lusk, Josiah
McKagg, Hugh
Lowry, Lony (Lory)
Marshall, Lolis
O'Neal, Alfred
O'Neal, H. A.
O'Neal, James
O'Neal, A. C.
Painter, Hardy
Painter, Alexander
Two Large Files
See File 27

Ashburn, Martin
Box 2, File 27 1860-1880
Names in File: Folder 2 of 2
See File 26
Cooper, Jackson
Blancit, A. D.
Jacoway, J. G.
Bouldin, E.
Lowery, Adams
Cook, B. F.
Jacoway, John G.
Dobbs, L. A.
Brandon, P. A.
Blevins, Rufinna
Bouldin, Elijah
Ashbury, Mary
Austin, S. B.
Blevins, Calvin
Cagle, Malinda
Tax Assessment List
Dunlap, R.A.D.
Dobbs, L. F.
Griffin, Wm.

Estate Record Name

Ashburn, Martin (Cont.)
Austin, Robert
Ashburn, Robert T. (adm.)
Franklin, John N., Judge
Collins, T. B.
Masters, J M.
Hoge, John K.
Accounts Due Estate:
Bush, Olive
Cooper, Jackson
Frost, Henry
Gray, John
Johnson, William
Henegar, Isam
Stoner, Randolph
Welch, Samuel
Gatlin, Jane
Cooper, Manora
Ashburn, Franklin
Farmer, __
Sizemore, Allen
Winters, J. W.
Blevins, Calvin
Austin, Jonathan
Tankersly, Daniel
Blansit, A. D.
Slattan, Thomas
Hughes, J.
Hartline, A.
Swafford, John
Blevins, James
Tatum, Pierce
Crow, Isaac
Branam, Jacob
Raper, Sarah
Whited, Abraham
Halloway, James
Roseborough, S. B.
Rawlston, Alex
Street, E. O.
Frederick, George

Estate Record Name
Ashburn, Martin (Cont.)
Crabtree, Russell
Streets, Martha
Roberts, Thomas
Haney, Wm.
Lusk, Josiah
McDaniel, Alexander
Bryant, Henry
Hughes, Jim
Hughes, Cash
Wilson, John
Panther, Alex.
Kilgore, James
Blevins, Richard
Bouldin, Elijah
Tate, John
Oyler, George
Smith, Hiram
Smith, Henry
Millican, Wm.
Oyler, Daniel
Stephens, Willis
Easley, Jack
Forister, Elisha
Cooper, James
Holloway, Newton
Holloway, Jackson
Blevins, Norris
Woodall, Georga
Hartline, J. A.
Hunter, Julius
Cook, Lemuel
Highfield, Jonathan
Wade, R. P.
Millican, Andrew
Brown, M. S.
Accounts Due Estate:
Gifford, R.
Potter, Richard
Cooke, B. F.
Bennett, Mitchell

Estate Record Name
Ashburn, Martin (Cont.)
Box 2, File 27 1860-1880
Russell, Mathew
Clark, Shade
Wilburn, Alfred
Anderson, Joseph
Hughes, Martha
Young, Benjamin
Sweet, Jane
Sitton, John
Lowry, Levi
Oyler, Frederick
Blevins, Stephens
Blevins, John L.
Street, Alfred
Worley, Winston
Worley, Lank
Warren, Samuel
Warren, John
Slatton, Carrison
Watt, Louisa
Hawkins, Benjamin
Jones, Wm. C.
Hazelnut, George
Sizemore, Richard
Hawkins, Mary Ann
Hawkins, John
Sadler, Keziah
Saterwhite, David
Stoner, Caldean
Brown, W. E.
Stephens, Mary
Preswood, Wilson
Atkins, W. W.
Presswood, Francis M.
Frost, John
Wingfield, M. A.
Whited, James
Cooke, James
Bouldin, George W.
Accounts Due Estate:

Estate Record Name
Ashburn, Martin (Cont.)
Accounts Due Estate:
Jones, Asa
Frizell, Widow
Bata, William
Easley, Charles
Cox, James
Cox & Crannell
Warren, Lot
Millican, Andrew
Lolis, Marshall
Marshall, Lolis
Branom, Richard
King, James
Cooper, Hammon
Russell, Miles R.
Painter, Jackson
Abbitt, A. B.
Ballenger, Pheba
Highfield, Malinda
Bryant, James R.
Blansit, Widow
Blansit, A. D.
Smith, John
Harris, Samuel
Morrison, A. R.
Jones, Joseph
Palmore, Widow
Herrin, James
McCoy, Hughey
Bryant, Elijah
Steel, Isaac
Steel, Levi
Stafford, Anderson
Harris, Samuel
Morris, A. R.
Ivins, Leonidas
Stafford, N. A.
Grimes, Thomas
Smith, William
Harris, James

Estate Record Name
Ashburn, Martin (Cont.)
Henegar, George
Cooper, Polly Ann
Mahon, Archibald
Abbott, William
Abraham & Co.
Bryant, James
Groves, Bert
Forester, Rebecca
Lewis, Jonathan
O'Neal, Zachariah
Igou, J.S. N.
Steel, Isaac
Grayson, Cyntha
Gilliam, Wm.
O'Neal, John W.
O'Neal, John W.& Mother
Blevins, William
Taylor, Jesse
Abbott, Huts? (Cuts?)
McDaniel, Elizabeth M.
Chambers, John
Stewart, Robert
Lewis, Mary
Durham, Philip
Easley, Benjamin
Ballenger, William
Robinson, Hiram
Easley, Dick
Hall, Calvin
Steel, Isaac
Atkins, Morris
Box 2, File 28 1882-1889
Names in File:
Atkins, George
Atkins, B. F.
Atkins, Ben
Atkins, Calvin
Young, Samuel
Blevins, R. M.
Atkins, Charlotte

Estate Record Name
Atkins, Morris (Cont.)
Atkins, Jesse
Adkins, A. J. (adm)
Davis, Jno. A.
Atkins, Calon
Franklin, Jno. N.
Dobbs & Howard
Cochran, L. L.
Cuzzort, Catherine
Cuzzort, Benjamin
Barnes, Edgar
Harralson, W. W.
Blevins, Calvin
Cauntis, John
Austin, James
Gulon, James
Brandon, P. A.
Smith, Loney
Gardener, J. G.
Atkins, J. C.
Blansit, A. D.
Brown, M. S.
Young, Nancy
Young, Samuel
Terrell, T. J.
Rodgers, R. S.
Atkins, Gaines W.
Purcell, Mary
Fitzpatrick, H. A.
Frazier, R. L.
Gibson, B. F.
Atkins, Alvin
Hatfield, W. H.
Atkins, Jessey
Blevins, J. T.
Allison, H. R.
Jenkins, G. W.
Ginn, W. P.
Hundley, James
Steel, Isaac
Steel, W. A.

Estate Record Name
Atkins, Morris (Cont.)
Steel, James
Rogers, A. W.
Slaton, Robert
Sormond, J. M.
Dunagin, W. H.
Case, Mrs.
Green, Jacob
Lumpkin, T. J.
Thurman, I. S. N.
Lawrence, Lee
Atkins, Ezekiel
Gooch, W. T.
Dodd, Neal
Atkins, Samuel
Buttrum, Jonathan
Buttram, Ferby
Lowe, John E.
Ashberry, A. H.
York, John
Jones, Johnson
Gibson, George
Olyer, Smith
Oyler, Samuel
Oyler, James
Oyler, Elizabeth
Kelsoe, Allison
Rogers, A. M.
Fuller, W. T.
Cooper, Morris
Heirs:
Butrum, Ferby (Fanby)
Atkins, Samuel
Atkins, Morris
Atkins, Ezekiel
Lawrence, Rebecca (w/o Lee)
Lawrence, Lee
Cazort, Catherine (w/o Benj.)
Cazort, Benjamin
Young, Nancy (w/o Samuel)
Young, Samuel

Estate Record Name
Atkins, Morris (Cont.)
Adkins, Jesse
Adkins, Alvin
Adkins, Calvin
Adkins, B. F. (grandchild)
Adkins, Gaines (grandchild)
Prenell, Mary (grandchild)
Oyler, Smith
Oyler, Samuel
Oyler, James (minor)
Oyler, A. J.
Atkins (Adkins)
Austin, Daniel
Box 2, File 29 1850-1853
Names in File:
Austin, Jamima
Austin, Jno D.
Estes, Reuben
Painter, Hardy
Alfred, William (guardian)
Clayton, Sampson
Austin, John A. (minor)
Austin, David (minor)
Ayers, Albert K.
Box 2, File 30 1888-1895
Names in File:
Ayers, John G. (minor)
Ayers, Ada (minor)
Ayers, Ida (minor)
Howard, J. M.
Hasley, G. R.
Davis, R. C.
Stephens, J. R. T

Estate Record Name
Ayers, Albert K. (Cont.)
Norwood, Jno. C.
Waters, W. R. (guardian)
Davis & Haralson
Russ, C. C.
Camp, S. M.
England, M. W.
Hall, James H.
Cochran, L. L., Judge
Campbell, H. B.
Cook, W.C.D., Judge
DeShields, John G.(sheriff)
Fuller, W. T.
Clayton, C. C.
Forrester, James
Thompson, W. F.
Thompson, J. W.
Waters, William R.
Ayers, Alda
Box 2, File 31 1896-1897
Ayers, John G.
Bates, J. D.
Waters, W. R.
Davis, Reubin C. (guardian)
Ayers, Ada
Cook, W.C.D., Judge
England, M. V.
Ayers, J. G.
Ayers, A. K.
Ayers, J. G. (minor)
Bates, Ida Ayers (minor)
Ayers, Ada (minor)

B

Estate Record Name
Bagle, Joseph H.
Box 2, File 32 1898
Names in File:
Bagle, H. C. (guardian)
Bagle, Ethel P.
Bagle, Alice E.
Bagle (Bogle)
Campbell, H. B. (guardian)
Bagle, Joseph H. (minor)
Davenport, J. G.
Davenport, Bles
Davenport, B. C.
Cook, W. C. D., Judge
Bailey, A. K.
Box 2, File 33 1911-1913
Names in File:
Bailey, M. A., Mrs.
Homestead Exemption
Parliwood, W. J.
Meadows, P. J.
Croley, James A., Judge
Marshall, P. G. (JP)
Bailey, William P.
Box 2, File 34 1891-1892
Names in File:
Bailey, Eliza J. (widow)
Cochran, L. L., Judge
Bailey, A. K.
Little, Marion
Upton, Robert
Bailey, William W.
Box 2, File 35 1906
Names in File:
Bailey, Annie A., (adm.)
Hill, Mose
Bailey, J. A.
Croley, K. A., Judge
Hewitt, F. A., Jr.

Estate Record Name
Bailey, William W.
Daugette, Palmer P., Atty.
Baker, Ellen
Box 2, File 36 1908-1913
Names in File:
Maxwell, L. O.
Haralson, W. W.
Keith, Josie
Parker, Cicero
Harris, T., (sheriff)
Adams, S. B. (S. D.)
Lea, W. A.
Bohanan, J. B.
Keith, Thomas
Maxwell, Louie O.
Riders, F. M.
Baker, James R.
Box 2, File 37 1903
Names in File:
Cook, W. C. D., Judge
Baker, Frances (widow)
Wright, J. W.
Walker, E. J.
Edmondson, W. E. (JP)
Baker, Woodrow Wilson (minor)
Box 2, File 38 1915-1924
Names in File:
Baker, J. F. (guardian)
Wood, Pluma (mother)
Pressley, I. M.
McSpadden, B. A.
Ballard, James A. (guardian)
Box 2, File 39 1870
Names in File:
Ballard, G. F. (minor)
Horton, A. J., Judge
Ballard, Mirah
Box 2, File 40 1909

Estate Record Name

Ballard, Mirah
- Box 2, File 40 1909
- Names in File:
- Biddle (Riddle)
- Biddle, William R.
- Croley, Jas. A.
- Riddle (Biddle), Minnerva
- Johnson, Ann
- Smith, Jane
- Riddle (Biddle), William H.
- Troxtel, J. R.
- Crow, E. D.
- White, L. W.
- Riddle, Thomas
- Johnson, Nute
- Smith, Joseph

Barksdale, S. W.
- Box 2, File 41 1895
- Names in File:
- Barksdale, E. J. (adm.)
- McWhorter, H. A.
- Cochran, L. L., Judge

Barnard, Lou W.
- Box 2, File 42 1890
- Names in File:
- Cochran, L. L. (Judge)
- Barnard, Lucy
- Quin, W. E.
- Souwell, G. W.
- Barnard, Ethel

Barnes, John
- Box 2, File 43 1877-1878
- Names in File:
- Stuart, John
- Hammons, B. G. (adm.)
- Brandon, P A.
- Wells, Franklin
- Wells, Andrew
- Lea, George
- Lea, William
- Lea, A. B.

Estate Record Name

Barnes, John (Cont.)
- Nichelson, Doc
- Woodall, T. I.
- Keith, Tobe
- Barnes, G. W.
- Slaton, B.F.
- White, I. L.
- Lea, Walter
- Brown, William
- Hill, Eli
- Dean, William
- Blaylock, William
- Shankle, Lesa
- Lea, Allen
- Moore, James
- Biddle, John
- Haralson & Haralson
- Barnes, John
- Ferguson, W. S.
- Ferguson, W. D.
- Keith, Marshall
- Keath, Marteal (coffin)
- Long, James
- Paine, B. F., Dr.(medicine)
- Slatton, E. A.
- Smith, Thomas H. (adv.)
- Fort Payne Journal
- Dobbs, W. W.
- McNutt, R. C. (sheriff)
- Hill, Robert L.
- Paine, Ben F.
- Stuart, John
- Wells, Andrew
- Dodds, L. A., (Atty.)
- Holleman, E. J. (sheriff)
- **Heirs:**
- Slaton, Jane (w/o B.F.)
- Slaton, B. F.
- Clark, Alpha (husband dec.)
- Barnes, Elizabeth
- Hill, Eliza (w/o Ely Hill)

Estate Record Name
Barnes, John (Cont.)
Hill, Ely
Lea, Sarah (w/o Walter Lea)
Lea, Walter
Barnes, G. W.
Barnes, James
Barnes, Abner
Barnes, John
Evans, Vina Barnes, (hus.dec.)
Inventory Sales:
Clark, Alfa (kittle)
Barnard, J. L. (scales)
Smith, William (wash tub)
Wells, Andrew (hand saw)
Wells, Andrew (drawer knife)
Woodall, A. J. (square)
Woodall, A. J. (hoe)
Smith, William (auger & chisel)
Lea, William (cutting blade)
Woodall, A. J. (1-ax)
Blaylock, William (hatchet)
Lee, William (l-lug)
Keith, Tobe (l-bucket)
Keith, Tobe (1-wash pan)
Keith, Tobe (1-header bucket)
Lea, Walter (1-pitcher)
Blaylock, William (knives/forks)
Lea, Walter (Lge Brass Cittle)
Dean, William (2-buckets)
Barnard, J. L. (pr.fire dogs)
Lea, Walter (pr. fire dogs)
Igo, George (mattock)
Lea, Walter (1-brier cythe)
Woodall, A. J. (1-hoe)
Lea, Walter (long hand shovel)
Hoge, John (lock chain)
Bennett, Samford (sho?box)
Lea, Geo. (2-pots)
Lea, William (smoldering iron)
Nickelson, Doc. (1-cittle)
Woodall, A. J. (1-skillet)

Estate Record Name
Barnes, John (Cont.)
Keith, Tobe (oven & hooks)
Keith, Tobe (check real)
Wells, Andrew (1-pare?)
Lead Ab (1-pare/lare?)
Barnes, W. G. (book)
Slaton, B. F. (book)
Hammon, B. G. (book)
White, J. L.
Barnes, W. G. (1-lock)
Lea, Ab (1-fire shovel)
Lea, William (grime stone)
Lea, William (1-pot rack)
Dean, William (1-table)
Lea, Walter (1-meal tub)
Lea, Walter (table)
Keith, Tobe (8-chairs)
Lea, Walter (Loom & 3?)
Hill, Eli (bed & clothes)
Lea, Ab (1-looking glass)
Nicklson, Doc. (1-book shelf)
Lea, Ab (Bare of Lead)
Dean, William (1-chest)
White, J. L. (1-cag/keg?)
Blaylock, William (1-cag)
Shankle, Jesa
Lea, William (1-box)
Lea, William (4-planks)
Lea, William (1-sack cotton)
Lea, William (1-barel)
Woodall, A. J. (1/3 bar.salt)
Biddle, John (1-cock)
Biddle, John (1-hog)
Lewis, __ (3-hogs)
Bass, Jesse
Box 2, File 44 1836
Names in File:
Bates, Jesse (adm.)
Estes, R., Judge
Edwards, J. (sheriff)
Bates, Pink

Estate Record Name
Bates, Pink
Box 2, File 45 1906-1913
Names in File:
Mattox, Ethel
Bates, I.R. (widow)
Bates, Jesse (minor)
Bates, Willie (minor)
Bates, Alvis (minor)
Bates, Irby (minor)
Bates, Esther (minor)
Pendergrass, Nora
Campbell, H. B.
Bobo, Johnnie G. C.
Isbell, John B.
Croley, J. A., Judge
Berry, Minnie
Copeland, A. C.
Pruett, S. L.
Cant, R. L. (NP)
Bauldin, Hilley
Box 6, File 46 1860
Names in File:
Estes, R.
Bauldin, Noble (guardian)
Bauldin, Giden
Bauldin, Hilley (minor)
Bauldin, Gidean
Baxter, Francis Marion (F. M)
Box 2, File 47 1909
Names in File:
Jacoway, W. V.
Baxter, J. R., (son)
Croley, Jas. A., Judge
Jacoway, Mary Elizabeth, (dau.)
Jacoway, Wm. V., (g-son)
Jacoway, Benjamin J., (g-son)
Baxter, J. B., (son) (exec.)
Jacoway, Wm. V., (exec.)
Haralson, W. W., (witness)
Jacoway, Alice, (witness)
Couch, W. G., (witness)

Estate Record Name
Baxter, Francis Marion (F. M)(Cont.)
Down, T. T., (sheriff)
Baxter, J. J.
Box 2, File 48 1909-1919
Names in File:
Baxter, Susan A., (widow)
Baxter, Martin, (minor)
Baxter, Julia, (minor)
Sargent, Julia Baxter
Gilbert, B. F., (NP)
Gilbert, M. P., (witness)
Croley, Jas. A., Judge
Evans, Wilt
Gilbert, Ben F.
Johnson, J. E., (NP)
Homestead Exemption
Gipson, M. C.
Allen, M. A.
Sargent, G. D.
Baxter, J. W. (Willis)
Box 2, File 49 1909-1910
Names in File:
Baxter, S. J., Mrs., (widow)
Baxter, Dollie, (minor)
Baxter, Lonie, (minor)
Baxter, May, (minor)
Baxter, Erskine, (minor)
Baxter, Lena, (minor)
Croley, Jas. A., Judge
Baxter, O. B.
Baxter, Thomas, (son)
Baxter, T. C., (son) (adm)
Brock, H. B., (burial goods)
Pressley & Isbell, Atty.
McBroom & Malone
Campbell, H. B.
Copeland, C. C.
Peak, J. S. (Cofffin)
Warren, W.D., Dr. (services)
Lively, W. C.
Downs, T. L.

Estate Record Name

Baxter, J. W. (Willis) (Cont.)
Quin & Wright
McSpadden, H. A., (Tax Coll.)
Smith, Thomas H. (editor)
Fort Payne Journal, (adv)
Copeland, A. C.
Edmondson, W. E.
Browder, J. T.
Heirs:
Baxter, Lucy
Baxter, George
Edmondson, S. J.
Cunningham, Mary
Lyons, Ellen
Baxter, Willis
Baxter, T.C.
Edmondson, Sarah Jane
Baxter, Lucy
Baxter, Oscar
Baxter, Dollie
Baxter, Lonnie
Baxter, May
Baxter, Erskine
Baxter, Lena
Sale of Inventory:
Little, Dick (2-plows)
Burgess, J. A. (plow stock)
Jacoway, W. V. (log chain)
Burgess, J. A. (plows)
Lively, M. C. (hames,chain)
Jacoway, W. V., (cant hook?)
Moody, J. T. (scrap iron)
Guest, R. J. (1-shovel)
Moody, J. T. (double tree)
Warren, W. E. (2-cow bells)
Jacoway, W. V., (wheel barrow)
Little, Dick, (1-shoat)
Frazier, R. W. (1-shoat)
Little, Belden (1-shoat)
Jacoway, W. V., (spring seat)
Lowery, Adam (1-saw)

Estate Record Name

Baxter, J. W. (Willis) (Cont.)
Jacoway, W. V., (cow & calf)
Jacoway, W. V., (cow & calf)
Templeton, J. F.,(halter & chain)
Jacoway, W. V., (1-horse)
Baxter, James
Box 2, File 50 1896
Names in File:
Baxter, E. D. (widow)
Baxter, E. D. M.
Hester, Frank
Eidson, Robert
Eidson, R. W.
Baxter, James
Box 2, File 51 1853-1879
Names in File:
Winston, John G.
Ward, John D.
Malone, G. L. (Judge)
Bearden, Frances
Dooley, J. G.
Cook, W.C.D., Judge
Barbour, Margarett
Barbour, William
Ingram, Fannie
Tatum, Ann
Tatum, Bradford
Porter, Jane
Porter, James
Withrow, Nancy
Burns, J. B.
Inventory Appraisal List
Winston, Wm. O.
Burns, John B. (Estate)
Bibbs, James M.
Reeves,
Wilks, Washington B.
Walder, J. B.
May, W. H.
Accounts Due:
Blackburn, Elijah

Estate Record Name
Baxter, James (Cont.)
Clayton, S.
Clayton, Daniel
Walker, Peter T.
Estes, R.
Walls, B.
Dobb, Elijah
Cholson, James
Reeves, F. Hugh
George, C. D.
Porter, B. F.
Mitchell, Wm.
Ward, A. I.
Stiff, Edward
Jett, Joseph M.
McNaron, Abner
Newkirk, Hiram
Burshire, James
Wright, Freeman
Brock, Harris
Wilson, William
Chastain, Jesse
Previtt, Calvin
Lovern, John
Ryan, Amos
Colbert, __
Ryan, Seaman
Swofer, M.
Humphries, John T.
Isell, John
Carrie, Peter
Estes, W.
Haralson, J. S.
Pratt, John
Malone, John
Rhodes, W.
Burt, Elijah
Ward, S. (widow)
Hulgan, Robert
Little, Isaac
Williams, Jas.

Estate Record Name
Baxter, James (Cont.)
Box 2, File 51 1853-1879
Blanton, Whit
Majors, Elisha
Bryant, Vesten (Westen)
Hawes, Samuel
Segmire, Sam'l.
Hyler, Wm. L.
Hopkins, C. F.
Burt, Ryal
Baxter, Jesse
Reed, James
Baxter, Willis
Clayton, Solomon, Sr.
Ward, John D.
Edwards, Joseph
Frazier, Robert
Bruce, John M.
Nicholson, William
Williams, Henry
Cunningham, John
Tiner, Rachael, Mrs.
Clayton, David, Sr.
Roberts Richard
Machey, Alex
Wadkins, John A.
Hibbs, Jermiah
Lewis, Burrell
Newman, Widow
Harris, Larkin
Nicholson, Warren D.
Warren, Edward
Barkley, Wm.
Chitwood, Clement
Holloway, Jesse
Driscill, Tobia
Counts, Isaac
Dobbs, Elijah
Seymore, Saml.
Wilkes, R. W..
Adams, Ambrose

Estate Record Name
Baxter, James (Cont.)
Roberts, Isham B.
Baxter, James, Jr.
Snodgrass, Alexander
George, Thos. H.
Ryan, Wm.
Wilson, Wm.
Darting, Wm.
Ryan, Marshall
Ward, Isaac G.
May, W. H.
Majors, A. W..
Spangler, Isaac
Malone, Henry
Frazier, Dorcas
Callaham, Wm.
Frazier, John B.
Murphy, Robert
Gregory, Robert
Tyner, Stephen J.
Paden, Robert
Clayton, Sampson
McNaran, Abner
Hoge, Joseph
Chitwood, Andrew
Morgan, John B.
Ryan, Amos
Coggins, Vestly
Rocter, Elijah
Davidson, Solomon
Estes, Wm.
Oliver, James H
Grady, A. E.
Chitwood, Richard
Mays, Fletcher
Walden, J. B.
McBroom, Stephen
Dobbs, J.
Frazer, Robert
Cunningham, John
Adkinson, John

Estate Record Name
Baxter, James (Cont.)
Accounts Due (Cont.)
Frazer, Dorcas
Morris, Thomas
Withrow, Mary A.
Reed, Amy
Frazer, John
Spangler, Gidean
Clayton, W.. H.
May, W. H.
McCampbell, Frank
Ragland, Patrick
Phillips, Caleb
Morgan, David
Spangler, Martha
McElvay,__
Haralson, W. I.
Ward, John D.
Ryan, Wm.
Natt, W. J.
Cunningham, Jesse
Cunningham, N. l.
Fike, Mrs.
Brandon, Wm.
Bearden, O. J.
Box 2, File 52 1907
Names in File:
Bearden, Frances (widow)
Bearden, Willie (minor)
Bearden, Alma (minor)
Bearden, Sherman (minor)
Croley, Jas. A., Judge
Black, John H., Dr.
Cash, James M.
Milwee, James A. (JP)
Phillips, Sam'l (witness)
Hooper, E. S., (witness)
Hooper, A. B., (NP)
Beck, Thomas
Box 2, File 53 1854-1890
Names in File:

Estate Record Name

Beck, Thomas
Box 2, File 53 1854-1890
Beck, Lucinda (widow)
Shankles, Hannah
Smith, Sarah T.
Smith, J.
Smith, Jane
Smith, David
Davis, Polly Ann
Davis, J. H.
Durham, Polly Ann
Durham, __
Beck, William
Cochran, L. L. (Judge)
Durham, John J. (Admin)
Campbell, Isaac
Fossett, Jackson
McCurdy, John A.
Webb, G. W.
Dennis, E. A.
Hawkins, John N., Judge
Smith, D.M.
Smith, Jane
Smith, J. L.
Smith, S. J.
Shankles, B. R.
Smith, Jeptha
Franklin, Jackson
Durham, John J., (Adm.)
Dennis, Joel
Marshall, Hugh S.
Campbell, Isaac
Fossitt, Jackson
Stewart, Thos. G.
Haralson & Son, Atty.
Franklin, A. G. (sheriff)
Shankles, Hanner
Beck, William
Appleton, W. H.
Fossett, Jackson
Smith, J. L.

Estate Record Name

Beck, Thomas (Cont.)
Smith, Sarah T.
Shankles, B. R.
Fort Payne Journal
Durham, J. J., (adm.)
Hawkins, H. A.
Shankles, Jesse
Stout, Zeno
Dennis, O. A.
Nix, Joe J. (burial clothes)
Hill, Joseph, (JP)
Taylor, E. N.
Smith, Thomas A., (adv.)
Jacoway, Wm.
Jacoway, J. P.
Lyons, Thomas
Stewart Thomas G.
Brandon, P. A., Judge
McHan, E. A.
Davis & Haralson, Atty.
Davis, J. H.
Smith , S. L.
Beck, Lusinda, Miss
Shankles, Hanner
Notes Due:
Browder, Albert
Franklin, Jas.
West, Jas.
Beck, W. W.
Taylor, E. N.
Cushen, J. W. E.
McCurdy, W. A. & W. B.
Hughes, J. B.
Lyons, Thomas
Huckaby, H. C.
Jacoway, Wm. & J. P.
Jacoway, J. G.
Smith, Elisha

Beene, Jacob
Box 2, File 54 1883
Names in File:

Estate Record Name
Beene, Jacob
Box 2, File 54 1883
Names in File:
Beene, W. J. (son) (Adm.)
Beene, Nancy, (widow)
Beene, Jacob T., (son)
Morgan, Amanda J., (dau.)
Crow, Mary Ann, (dau.)
Beene, John P., (son)
Morgan, Maria S., (g-dau.)
Miller, Nancy E., (g-dau.)
Hawkins, Cornelia, (g-dau.)
Hawkins, Margaret, (g-dau.)
Hawkins, Hattie, (g-dau.)
Hawkins, Huldah, (g-dau.)
Hawkins, Maria, (g-dau.)
Hawkins, Belle, (g-dau.)
Hawkins, Alice V., (g-dau.)
Hawkins, Alex.
Hawkins, James T.
Hawkins, Wm. J.
Beene, Wm. J.
Beene, Samuel
Box 2, File 55 1872
Names in File:
Beene, Wm., (Adm.)
Horton, A. J., Judge
Phillips, Abner
Temmemas?, Wm., (sheriff)
Beene, W. J.
Beeson, Jesse B.
Box 2, File 56 1877
Names in Files:
Green, Grief S.
Brandon, P. A, (JP)
Beeson, Jesse G.
Box 2, File 57 (1 of 3) 1857-84
Names in File:
Green, Fannie S.
Bryan, James M.
Bryan, Tabitha

Estate Record Name
Beeson, Jesse G. (Cont.)
Bryan, Wilbourne N.
Bryan, James S.
Bryan, Effie M
Bryan, Wm. E.
Bryan, Charles M.
Bryan, Marion
Green, G.A.
Brock, Wilburn
Duncan, R. D.
Campbell, Lewis
Long, James
Reese, Andrew
McCurdy, John A.
Kean, John P.
Nicholson, D. L.
Beeson, Henry C.
Haralson, W.J.
Haralson, Henry C.
Haralson, Ella V.
Horton, A. J. (Judge)
Bogle, J. C.
Jack, Elizabeth L.Mickler
Brock, Andrew
Brock, Wilborn
Jack, E. L.
Jack, Thomas M.
Nickolson, Mary
Phillips, C. J.
Chitwood, Wm.
Mickler, Jacob
Costello, Frank
Frazier, John
Bradon, P. A.
May, William R.
Hoge, John K.
Clayton, C. P.
Phillips, Corinna J.
Johnson, C. P.
Moragne, Eula
Moragne, John

Estate Record Name

Beeson, Jesse G. (Cont.)

Geruthaur, Cosinna J.
Granthaur, Thomas
Green, Grief S.
Dunlap, R.A.D.
Beeson, V. Bell
Beck, Ester
Miler, Chamberlain
Webb, G. W.
Mickler, E. L.
Lyons, Thomas
Gipson, I. C.
Smith, B. F.
Miler, Judy Chamberlain
Beeson, Lula
Beeson, Jepe (Jesse)
Beeson, Eula L.
Jack, Betty
Raley, Matthias
Hess, I. A.

Sale of Inventory

Green, T. S.
Nicholson, M. H.
Beeson, H. C.
Michler, E. L.
Nicklson, D. L.
Dunlap, James
Green, F. S.
Hammack, Thos.
Phillips, P. S.
Dunlap, R. A.
Hollemon, F.
Belcher, J. B.
Scott, Thomas
Hagler, C. H.
Reece, I. (J.)
Estes, R.
Gipson, J. C.
White, W.
Dobbs, L. A.
Killian, Dan

Estate Record Name

Beeson, Jesse G. (Cont.)

Hagler, C. S.
Wooten, W.
Clayton, Sol
Webb, C. W.
Banter, M.
Griffin, Wm.
Phillips, P. D.
Evett, James
Franklin, John
Betcher, Jno.
Lankford, J. B.
Baxter, Pat
Wootern, W. I (J.)
Slayton, E. A.
Arledge, Eli
Laramore, V. C.
Davenport, R. R.
Bagley, N.
Rhodes, Wm.
Reese, W. S.
May, W. H.
Garrett, H.
Hunter, Casper
Jacoway, J. C.
Beeson, H. C., (adm)
Green, G. S., (adm)
Brandon, P. A., Judge
McNutt, R. C., (sheriff)
Chitwood, Wm.
Long, James
Morgan, Eula
Payne, A. F.
See File #58 & File #59

Beeson, Jesse G.

Box 2, File 58 (2 of 3) 1868-87
Names in File:
Green, Fannie S., (adm.)
McCurdy, J. A.
Green, G. S.
Costello, Frank

Estate Record Name
Beeson, Jesse G. (Cont.)
Kean, W. C.
Horton, A. J., Judge
Costello, Frank
Fisher, Geo.
Johnson, Robert
McSpadden, Allen
McCrasy, Robert
Browder, P, H.
Stuart, B. S.
Haralson, W. J.
Mechler, Husten
Castleton?, N. F.
Laramore, V. C.
Green, G. S.
McSpadden, S. D.
Bidle, James
Dye, James
Barnard, John
Franklin, John
Gibson, Jacob
Chitwood, R.
Jack, Thomas M.
Brandon, H. H.
Lelleman, E. F.
McNutt, R. C.
McCrary, R. C.
Cunningham, John
Hendrix, Jas. M.
See File #57 & File #59
Beeson, Jesse G.
Box 2, File 59 (3 of 3) 1857-91
1857-1891
Names in File:
Green, Fannie S. (Admin.)
Grantham, Corinne J.
Grantham, Thomas
Locks, J. H.
Gentry, J. L.
Moragne, J. B.
Moragne, Eulale (Eulah)

Estate Record Name
Beeson, Jesse G.
Box 2, File 59 (3 of 3) 1857-91
Chandler, Wm.
Cochran, L. L.
Jack, Elizabeth L.
Jack, Thomas
Beeson, Fannie S. (wife)
Nicholson, Mary
May, William R.
Smith, M. V.
See Files No. 57 & 58
Belcher, Joseph
Box 2, File 60 1835
Names in File:
Lankford, J. M.
Lankford, A. E.
Lusk, J. M.
Willis, W. F.
Lankford, Jim
Garrett, Thomas
Andrew, Matthew V.
Bell, James W.
Box 2, File 61 1871
Names in File:
Bell, James W. (deceased)
Bell, Charles
Bell, Charley, (son), (adm.)
Cain, W. C.
Raley, W. C
Bell, J. R.
Box 2, File 62 1906
Names in File:
Croley, J. A.
Bell, A. M., (adm.)
Crane, J. J.
Crane, J. F.
Palner, F. V.
Bell, Maudie
Ellis, C. T.
Bell, Lillie
Bell, R. W.

Estate Record Name

Bell, R. W.
Box 2, File 63 1907
Names in File:
Dawson, A. F.
Sears, J. W.
Dawson, Alverice (Alverine) F.
Bell, W. J.
Sears, J. M.
Bell, R. W., Mrs. (widow)

Berry, A. J., Sr.
Box 2, File 64 1885-1888
Names in File:
Berry, Winnifred (widow)
Widow Exemption
Tiner, James C.
Vann, A. J.
Ward, N. W. (JP)
McWhorter, H. P.
Berry, Winnie

Berry, Hugh
Box 2, File 65 1858-1874
Names in File:
Berry, A. J. (adm.)
Berry, Eliza
Francis, Coleman
Spears/Span
Berry, Jeptha
Berry, Robert Wilson
Berry, Mary (Erwin)
Erwin, John A.
Span, (Spear) Emily
Span, (Spear) William
Ingle, Sarah Elizabeth Berry
Children of Sarah Berry Ingle:
Ingle, Peter M. (minor)
Ingle, Sarah E. (minor)
Ingle, Malachi C. (minor)
Ingle, Wilson A. (minor)
Ingle, Mary E. (minor)
Ingle, Hugh A.J. (minor)
Berry, William

Estate Record Name

Berry, Hugh (Cont.)
Berry, Major
Morgan, Eliza J. (Berry)
Morgan, John
Berry, James
Children of James Berry:
Berry, F. M. (g/c of Hugh)
Berry, John W. (g/c of Hugh)
Berry, A.J. (g/c of Hugh)
Berry, ? (g/c of Hugh)
Petty, Thomas
Dobbs, L.A. (attorney)
Brandon, P. A. (clerk)
Ingle, Sarah (deceased)
Ingle, William
Williams, Ruthy, (w/o T.)
Williams, Thomas
Frances, Malvina, (w/o Hugh)
Frances, Hugh
Ingle, William Alonza
Ingle, Mary Eliza
Berry, Robert Wilson
Berry, Coleman Frances
Berry, Andrew Jackson
Berry, Elizabeth
Berry, Nancy Adeline
Berry, Sarah
Berry, James Washington
Berry, John Wesley
Berry, A. J. (adm)

Bethune, Elmer, et al
Box 2, File 66 1903-1905
Names in File:
DeShields, J. G., (guar.ad litem)
Bethune, C. L., Mrs. (guardian)
Bethune, Elmer, (minor)
Bethune, Vinnie, (minor)
Bethune, Clara, (minor)
Bethune, D. L. (witness)
Bethune, O. L., (witness)
Huckaby, W. T.

Estate Record Name
Bethune, Elmer, et al (Cont.)
Huckaby, W. P.
Hamrick, J. D.
Burke, O. T. (JP)
Croley, J. A., Judge
Cook, W. C. D.
Bethune, John T.
Box 2 File 67 1907
Names in File:
Bethune, C. L., Mrs.
Bethune, Carrie L, (widow)
Bethune, John E. (minor)
Bethune, Vennie L., (minor)
Bethune, Clarra L. (minor)
Wilson, M. M., (comm.)
Richey, Wm., (comm)
Hall, J. A., (Justice of Peace)
Wilson, Mack
Bethune, W. T.
Box 2 File 68 1900
Names in File:
Cook W. S. D., Judge
Dawson, A. F., (JP)
Bethune, Adeline V., (widow)
Widow's Exemption
Bethune, Effie L., (minor)
Morrison, John, (comm.)
Bell, Wm.. (comm.)
Bethune, William A., (minor)
Bethune, Maude V., (minor)
Birk (Burk), M. O.
Box 2 File 69 1863
Names in File:
Birk (Burk), Yancy
Burk (Birk)
Rex?, J. D.
Franklin, John N., Judge
Blackwell, B. H.
Box 2 File 70 1907-1908
Names in File:
Blackwell, Sallie, Mrs. (guar.)

Estate Record Name
Blackwell, B. H. (copy)
Blackwell, Sallie, (mother)
Blackwell, Walter, (minor)
Blackwell, John H., (minor)
Brock, H. B., (bond)
Dwyer, John J., (bond)
Blackwell, John G.
Croley, Jas. A., Judge
Roberts, Calvin
Roberts, J. W.
Appleton, C. C.
Blackwell, Nancy S.
Box 2 File 71 1868
Names in File:
Blackwell, T. J., (estate)
Blackwell, Nancy S. (guardian)
Horton, A. J., Judge
Brock, William, (adm)
Brock, Andrew
Franklin, J.
Blackwell, Thomas
Blackwell, Bagley H.
Hammack, Thomas
Estes, Rueben
Spring, I. W.
Blake, Fanny
Box 2 File 72 1902-1903
Names in File:
Blake, Fannie B., (petitioner)
Blake, L. M.
Blake, B. P.
Lankford, Sallie
Lankford, P. H. (hus.of Sallie)
Blake, Isaac
Frost, Mary
Frost, Pat, (hus.of Mary)
Isbell, J. B.
Isbell, Howard
Cook, W. C. D.
Howard & Isbell, (atty)
Blake, J. B.

Estate Record Name

Blake, J. B.
Box 2 File 73 1901
Names in File:
Blake, Margaret N., (widow)
Widow's Exemption
Kerby, L. B. (comm.)
Crow, G. B. (comm.)
Culberson, (Notary Public)
Crow, Green

Blalock, David S.
Box 2 File 74 1911
Names in File:
Blalock, Nannie H., (widow)
Widow's Exemption
Blalock, Joseph D.
Blalock, Taylor E.
Gray, Flavie Blalock
McCowan, James
Davenport, E. T.
McKown, J. M.
Davis & Pope, (atty)
Culberson, C. Y., (Notary)

Blalock, Lula
Box 2 File 75 1924
Names in File:
Blalock, Lula (minor)
Argo, J. H., (guardian release)
Malone, G. L., Judge
Stoner, W. E., (witness)
Whitmire, J. G., (witness)

Blancitt, C. C.
Box 2 File 76 1881
Names in File:
Blancitt, William A., (adm)
Howard, Eliza J. Blancitt
Dean, Elisa J. Blancitt
Blancitt, Eliza J.
Lea, William, (guardian)
Blancitt, Clement C., (minor)
Blancitt, John C., (minor)
Blancitt, America L., (minor)

Estate Record Name

Blancitt, C. C. (Cont.)
Blancitt, James N., (minor)
Blancitt, Wm. A.
Dean, Leander
Howard, Henry
Lee, John
Shaffer, Samuel
Small, Mathew
Johnson, Jefferson
Bouldin, E., (bond)
Beene, Jacob, (bond)
Cunningham, J. D., (bond)
Lea, Allen, (bond)
Hoge, John F., (witness)
Branden, P. A., Judge
Lee, Allen
Crow, James, (bond)

Blansit, James N.
Box 2 File 77 1923
Names in File:
Blansit, James N., (will)
Blansit, Chester A., (executor)
Blansit, Nancy A., (widow)
Koger, Wm.
Humble, D. M., (witness)
Koger, R. H., (witness)
Bailey, H. T., (guardian)
Blansett, Georgia, (minor)
Blansett, Kate, (minor)
Blansett, Nellie, (minor)
Blansett (Blansit) (Blansitt)
Blansit (Blansitt) (Blansett)
Blansett, Oscar
Haney, Nettie, Mrs.
Key, America Mrs.
Steele, Daisy, Mrs.
Blansitt, Jim
Blansett, Tom
Blansett, John
Hickson, Lynday, Mrs.
Hixon, Linday (Linda)

Estate Record Name

Blansit, James N. (Cont.)
- Haney, Myrtle, Mrs.
- Bailey, J. H. T.
- Blansitt, Ned
- Blansit, Nonnie, Mrs.
- Malone, G. L., Judge
- Biddle, W. R., (sheriff)
- Culberson, J. N., (adm)

Blansit, Joseph P.
- Box 2 File 78 1916-1907
- Names in File:
- Blansit, Lillie M., (minor)
- Guffey, Lillie M. Blansit
- Blansit, Elizabeth, (minor)
- Blansit, Leona, (minor)
- McClain, Leona Blansit
- Blansit, Wm., (minor)
- Blansit, Robert L., (minor)
- Blansit, D. M.
- Blansit, Nancy J.
- Workman, Samuel D., (guardian)
- Culver, N. L., (bond)
- Kenemore, M. T., (bond)
- DeShields, J. G., (witness)
- Durham, John J., (witness)
- DeShields, W. L.
- Guest, J., (bond)
- Traylor, G. R., (bond)
- Campbell, H. B.
- Isbell, John B.
- Hairston, Bell
- Malone, J. A.
- Malone, G. L.
- Davis, John A., (witness)
- DeShields, J. A., (witness)
- Campbell, H. B.,(guar.ad litem)
- Dobbs, Cordie, (comm)
- Dobbs, Frank, (comm.)
- Isbell & Presley, (atty)
- Payments made:
- Cook, W. C.D. (court)

Estate Record Name

Blansit, Joseph P.
- Guest, J. H. E.
- Croley, Jas. A., (court cost)
- Workman, S. D., (services)
- Haiston, R. M.
- Minors, (sales of land)
- Stout, R., (mule for minors)
- Young, B. F., (groceries)
- Malone Gen.Store, (mdse)
- Adams, W. H., (pork for minors)
- Kennedy, D. L., (moving minors) from Jackson Co.to DeKalb
- DeShields, W. L., (purch.land)
- McCamy, J. A., (supplies)
- McCamy, J. N.
- Curry, M. F.(H), (tax on land)
- Benson, John, (tax)

Blansitt (Blancit), William
- Box 2 File 79 1851-1855
- Names in File:
- Blancit, Elizabeth, (wife)
- Cooper, Nicholson
- Estes, Rueben, Judge
- Blancit, A. D., (executor)
- Lawful Heirs-filed
- Blancit, George H.
- Beene, Nancy
- Blancit, A. D.
- Blancit, James P
- Blancit, John C.
- Blancit, C. C.
- Blancit, J. N.
- Hawkins, Sarah Ann
- Blancit, M. M.
- Blancit, Leanah J.
- Blancit, William, (will)
- Blancit, Elizabeth, (wife)
- Rena, Negro Woman
- Harriet, Negro Girl
- Price, R. L., (witness)
- Blancit, G. H., (witness)

Estate Record Name

Blansitt (Blancit), William (Cont.)
- Hoge, D. S., (witness)
- Hull & Spencer
- Phillips, Abner, (JP)
- Brainerd, Addison, (agent)
- Sale of Inventory-1851
- Blancit, Elizabeth,(yoke/steers)
- Blancit, Elizabeth (horse)
- Grayson, Thomas, (cattle)
- Blancit, A. D., (stack of oats)
- Blancit, Elizabeth, (cupboard)
- Blancitt, Elizabeth, (9-chairs)
- Blancit, A. D., (dining table)
- Blancitt, C. C., (mattock & hoe)

Blancit, Elizabeth, (estate)
- In file with William Blancit
- Box 2 File 79 1855
- Names in File:
- Blansitt, Archibald (adm.)
- Blansitt, B., (bond)
- White, John S., (bond)
- Blancitt, John C., (bond)
- Lee, Allen, (appraiser)
- Bolin, E., (appraiser)
- Tanter, James, (appraiser)
- Sale of Inventory Nov. 13, 1855
- Beene, Jacob, (1-saw)
- Hawkins, John, Sr., (7-hogs)
- Blansitt, Jasper H., (1-horse)
- Morgan, William D., (horse colt)
- Blancitt, John, (1-young mare)
- Blancitt, A. D., (2-steers)
- Blansitt, Leann. (1-yearlin)
- Blansitt, Missiniah (1-yearlin)
- Blancitt, C. C., (cow)
- Ashburn, Martin, (1-cow)
- Gardner, Marion (1-yoke oxen)
- Hill, Eli, (1-cow)
- Blancitt, N. D. (cow & calf)
- Brown, T. W. (10 barrels corn)
- Blancitt, A. D., (10 barr.corn)

Estate Record Name

Blancit, Elizabeth, (estate) (Cont.)
- Blake, J. G. , (10 barr.corn)
- York, Enoch, (1-wagon)
- Hughes, A. A., (1-oat stack)
- Gardner, Marion (1-oat stack)
- McCenless, (1-sheep)
- Blancitt, A. D., (potatoes)
- Blancitt, Missianah (1-bed)
- Price, R., (10 bu.wheat)
- Milican, Levi, (10-bu.wheat)
- Hughes, A. A., (10 bu.wheat)
- Blancitt, A. D., (sythe & cradle)
- Blancitt, A. D., (10 bu.wheat)
- Blancitt, A. D., (1-sack cotton)
- Blancitt, A. D., (1-pr scales)
- Blancitt, Geo.(5-bunches thread)
- Corvin, H. Sebird, (pr.steelyard)
- Painter, James (1-lot tools)
- Blancitt, George, (1-lot tools)
- Blancitt, A. D., (1-pc. iron)
- Blancitt, George, (1- pr strechers)
- Blancitt, Missiniah, (2-trunks)
- Blancitt, A. D., (1-table)
- Blancitt, A. D., (1-cupboard)
- Blancitt, Missiniah (spin. wheel)
- Blancitt, A. D., (spinning wheel)
- Blancit, A. D., (ovens, etc.)
- Blancitt, George, (1-spider)
- Hughes, A. R., (sheep shears)
- Blancitt, George, (sheep shears)
- Alfred, William, (1-pot)
- Craze, James, (1-bell)
- Blancitt, A. D., (churn, etc.)
- Blancitt, Missiniah (1-loom)
- Miligan, Levi, (1-bee gum)
- Elis, James, (horse gearing)
- Blancitt, George, (plows, etc.)
- Beene, Jacob, (5-hoes)
- Blancitt, A. D., (churn, etc.)
- Blancitt, A. D., (1-lot poultry)
- Blancitt, A. D., (1-check reel?)

Estate Record Name

Blancit, Elizabeth, (estate) (Cont.)
Blancitt, John J., (1-jug)
Blancitt, Leanah, (1-bed)
Blancitt, J. N., (bee stand)
Blancitt, J. C., (hammer)
Thomason, G.
Lilas, Negro Boy
Jane, Negro Girl
Lorene, Negro Woman
Blancitt, J. N., (200 ac.land)
Bouldin, Elijah, (appraiser)
Cook, B. F., (appraiser)
Beene, Jacob, (JP
Cooper & Nicholsen, (attys)

Blevins, E. B.
Box 2 File 80 1909
Names in File:
Blevins, Emily, (widow, adm.)
Howard, M. W., (bond)
Hunt, Luther P., (bond)
Howard, C. G.
Blevins, Emily, Mrs.
Howard & Hunt, (attys)
Blevins, H. W.
Blevins, J. A.
Heirs:
Blevins, Emily
Blevins, Calvin
Blevins, James
Blevins, Amos (Amon)
Blevins, Gaines
Cagle, Eliza J.
Boyston, Judie
Blevins, John
Blevins, Hardie
Cagle, Melvina

Blevins, Gaines
Box 2 File 81 1864-1886
Names in File:
Blevins, Richard M., (adm)
Blevins, Nancy (widow)

Estate Record Name

Blevins, Gaines (Cont.)
Burkhalter, D, B., (witness)
Driskill, W. L., (witness)
Cook, B. F., (witness)
Payne, Thomas, (witness)
Horton A. G.
Cochran, L. L.
Collins, T. B.
Blevins, O. M.
Blevins, H. T.
Heirs:
Steel, Millie Blevins
Steele, John (h/o Millie)
Boyston, Jane Blevins
Boydston, A. C., (h/o Jane)
Blevins, John L., (adm)
Gibson, Sarah Blevins
Gibson, F. P. (h/o Sarah)
Condra, Nancy J. Francis
Condra, W. H., (h/o Nancy J.)
Francis, Polly Ann Blevins
Blevins, H. T., (minor)
Blevins, Martin, (minor)
Blevins, Rebecca, (minor)
Howard, John Calvin, (minor)
Howard, Polly Ann Francis
Howard, B. M., (h/o Polly)
Blevins, R. M., (adm)
Blevins, W. H., (deceased)
Griffin, Wm., (sheriff)
Masters, J. M., (surveyor)
Payne, S. F.
Dobbs, L. A., (atty)
Smith, Lomey
Blevins, O. M.
Sale of Property 3-27-1869
Steel, John, (1/2 int. in Thresh)
Blevins, R. M., (1-cart)
Blevins, R. M., (cutting knives)
Blevins, J. L., (blacksmith tools)
Steel, John (kettle)

Estate Record Name

Blevins, Gaines (Cont.)
Blevins, John L., (1-bee stand)
Sells, A. A., (1-stand bees)
Blevins, H. T., (1-stand bees)
Sells, A. A., (1-stand bees)
Blevins, Calvin, (1-stand bees)
Blevins, J. L., (1-stand bees)
Blevins, H. T., (chain & fork)
Blevins, R. M., (tools,grindstone)
Adkins, Morris (1-wire sive?)

Blevins, Hardy W.
Box 2 File 82 1906
Names in File:
Blevins, Hardy W., (guardian)
Blevins, A. L., (minor)
Blevins, O. D., (minor)
Blevins, A. D., (minor)
Blevins, Minnie, (minor)
Blevins, J. E., (minor)
Blevins, Bonnie, (minor)
Steele, W. A., (bond)
Blevins, G. J., (bond)
Violette, Benjamin, (JP)

Blevins, Henry
Box 2 File 83 1853-1857
Names in File:
Blevins, Henry
Blevins, Ammilla, (widow)
Blevins, James, (adm)
Blevins, Jonathan, (JP)
Burkhalter, F. B., (appraiser)
Cagle, Charles, (appraiser)
Tinker, B., (appraiser)
Blevins, James
Butram, Ephraim
Butram, Laurahamy
Huckely, John
Huckley, Ester
Blevins, Calvin
Blevins, Gains
Puckett, Elizabeth

Estate Record Name

Blevins, Henry (Cont.)
Blevins, Sarah
Burkhalter, D. B. (note)
Hersey, H., (note)
Blevins, V.
Blevins, John, (horse)
Huckley, Ester, (bed & furn.)
Blevins, Martha Ann, (bed)
Blevins, Martha Ann, (furniture)
Blevins, James, (horse)
Blevins, James, (cow)
Estes, R., Judge
See File 84

Blevins, Henry
Box 2 File 84 1853-1857
Names in File:
Blevins, James, (adm)
Blevins, Amilla (widow)
Blevins, Calvin
Huckabee, Ester
Puckett, Silas
Puckett, Elizabeth, (w/o Silas)
Blevins, Manilla Ann (widow)
Estes, R., Judge
Blevins, V. M.
Burton, E.
Chadwick, Agnatha
Shadwick, James
Blevins, Jonathan, (witness)
Simpson, Cummings(witness)
Burkhalter, D. B., (witness)
Smith, James
Blevins, Gaines
Nicholson & Higgins, (atty)
Franklin, J. N., (sheriff)
Shadwick (Chadwick)
Shadwick, James
Shadwick, Agenetta
Sale of Inventory:
Blevins, Melia, (1-horse)
Steel, Alexander, (black horse)

Estate Record Name
Blevins, Henry (Cont.)
Box 2 File 84 1853-1857
Sale of Inventory:
Blevins, Melia, (mare)
Caperton, Wm., (mule colt)
Blevins, Milly, (black colt)
Blevins, Milly, (sheep)
Adkins, Washington,(raw hides)
Steel, John, (2-yearlins)
Sizemore, A. G., (9-hogs)
Blevins, Milly, (1-clock)
Steel, Alexander,(mare,saddlery)
Adkins,Washington, (saddle)
Blevins, Millie, (side saddle)
Blevins, Wm., Jr., (1-Sithe)
Blevins, Milly. (cow & calf)
Austin, J. A., (wagon)
Blevins, Milly, (1-grindstone)
Steel, Alexander, (1-matick)
Blevins, James, (1-lot tools)
Steel, Alexander, (1-bell)
Blevins, Embeeson (smith tools)
Blevins, Milly, (1-lot tools)
Whited, William
Blevins, James, (1-plane)
Huckaby, John, (1-iron wedge)
Brown, Steve, (yoke oxen)
Blevins, Calvin, (cow)
Adkins, Washington, (cow)
Blevins, William J., (cow)
Cooper, Jackson, (cow)
Slatton, John (2-steers)
Steel, Alexander, (2-seers)
Adkins, Washington, (2-steers)
Alford, William (1-steer)
Blevins, Gains, Jr., (2-heifers)
Huckaby, John, (1-calf)
Blevins, Calvin, (1-yearlin)
Allison, Robert, (1-lot chain)
Blevins, J. F.
Box 2 File 85 1910

Estate Record Name
Blevins, J. F. (Cont.)
Names in File:
Blevins, J. F., (estate)
Blevins, Rufus, (guardian)
Blevins, Rufus, (bro./minors)
Blevins, Jesse, (minor)
Blevins, James, (minor)
Blevins, Ida May, (minor)
Brown, S. W, (bond)
Blevins, J. M.
Blevins, Emily
Malone, G. J.
Blevins, J. R.
Box 2 File 86 1911
Names in File:
Blevins, J. M., (adm.)
Adkins, J. C., (bond)
York, Moses, (bond)
Blevins, J. M., (brother or J. R.)
Blevins, Melvina V., (widow)
Blevins, M. V., (widow)
Francis, J. M. (witness)
Emmett, R. W.
Croley, Jas. A., Judge
Blansit, R. L.
Brown, L. R., (Justice Peace)
Marona, J. F.
Brown, Annie John, (witness)
Brown, Edith R., (witness)
Smith, Hardy
Smith, Levosa (w/o Hardy)
Hunt & Wolfes, (atty)
Presley, I. M.,(guar.ad litem)
Barnes, W. H., (witness)
Heirs:
Weldon, Lula
Weldon, George, (h/o Lula)
Weldon, Laura
Weldon, Sandford, (h/o Laura)
Blevins, Virgil
Blevins, Joe

Estate Record Name

Blevins, J. R. (Cont.)
York, Rosa
York, Moses, (h/o Rosa)
Blevins, Jack W.
Blevins, Malinda, (minor)
Blevins, Gaines, (minor)
Blevins, Harry, (minor)
Blevins, Richard, (minor)
Blevins, James, (minor)
Blevins, Henry (Harry)
Blevins, Melvina V.
Blevins, V. B.
Blevins, J. W.
Slone, S. B., (guar.ad litem)
Blevins, M. V., (Homestead)
Emmett, R. N., (comm)
Adkins, J. C., (comm)
Marona, G. F., (JP)
Brown, L. R., (witness)
Harris, T. G., (sheriff)
Blevins, J. M., (dep.sheriff)
Scott, John, (Rock Quarry)
Smith, Hardy', (Place)
Blevins, Jesse R., (pur.40-ac.land)
Blancitt, R. L., (pur.40-ac.land
Blevins, Virgil, (pur.40-ac.land)

Bogle, Joseph R.
Box 2 File 87 1878
Names in File:
Roberts, F. M., (bond)
McNutt, R. C., (bond)
Roberts, F. M., (guardian)
Roberts, J. R., (minor)
Roberts, Minervia, (minor)
Roberts, W. G., (minor)
Roberts, Eva, (minor)
Brandon, P. A., Judge

Bohling, Henry
Box 2 File 88 1904-1909
Names in File:
Holmes, William A. (exec)

Estate Record Name

Bohling, Henry (Cont.)
Koerner, Wm. F., (bro-i-law)
Koerner, Lillian M. (witness)
Koerner, Wm. F., MD, (exec)
Raymond, Walter B., (witness)
McCartney, C. H., (appraiser)
Quin, Jos. J., (appraiser)
Dobbs, W. W., (appraiser)
Williams, Geo.C., Jr.,(God-child)
Williams, Estelle (God-child)
Williams, Grace, (God-child)
Williams, Dorothy L.,(God-child)
Williams, Emma, (sister)
Bohling, John, (father)
Boling, Henry, (brother)
Koerner, William, (b-i-l)
Koerner, Lilliam M., (sister)
Koerner, (resident of NY)

Bolton, J. M.
Box 2 File 89 1910
Names in File:
Ross, Lem C., (estate)
Bolton, J. M., (guardian)
Bolton, J. M., (father of minors)
Yarbrough, J. T., (bond)
Sims, W. N., (bond)
Bolton, Nora, (minor)
Bolton, Bertie, (minor)
Bolton, Willie, (minor)
Bolton, Carl, (minor)
Bolton, Johnnie, (minor)

Boozer, C. C.
Box 2 File 90 1901-1906
Names in File:
Boozer, C. C., (petitioner)
Boozer, John W.
Boozer, George W. (H.)
Hodge, Elizabeth
Hodge, A. J., (h/o Elizabeth)
Boozer, P.
Boozer, Elijah

Estate Record Name
Boozer, C. C. (Cont.)
Boozer, Taylor
Boozer, Carter
Boozer, Daniel
Boozer, Wesley
Estes, Lutitia M.
Estes, T. N., (h/o Lutitia)
Gipson, Elizabeth, (Eliza)
Gipson, Melton,(h/o Elizabeth)
Edmondson, W. E., (JP)
Isbell, John B.
Boozer, Z. T.
Boozer, Henry, (father of Z.T.)
Boozer, Christopher
Myricks, Richard, (witness)
Harris, Ben, (witness)
Blackwell, T. Y., (witness)
Howard & Isbell, (atty)
Chitwood, W. J., (sheriff)
Cain, Wall, (deputy sheriff)
Webb, J. M., (sheriff)
Farmer, T. F. (Jackson Co sheriff)
Howard, M. W., (Agent)
Isbell, Zona M., (purch.land)
Howard, Sallie A., (purch.land)
Gipson, William
Hodge, A. J.
Estes, J. N.
Boozer, Henry, (estate)
Boozer, Peter
Handage, Elizabeth
Bouldin, Elijah
Box 2 File 91 1883-1894
Names in File:
Painter, Nancy, (w/o Alexander)
Painter, Alexander
Phillips, Elizabeth
Phillips, John
Whited, Frances
Whited, John
Bouldin, Elijah Jackson

Estate Record Name
Bouldin, Elijah (Cont.)
Bouldin, John Franklin
Bouldin, Abe L.
Bouldin, Wm. Grant
Bouldin, Mariah (widow)
Lea, Mariah Bouldin
Lea, Wm., (hus.of Mariah)
Crow, James M.
Blansit, James N.
Bouldin, William J.
Green, A. B., Dr.
York, John C.
Lea, Allen
Bouldin, Richard Grant
Franklin, John N., Judge
Craze, George W., (h/o America)
Craze, Union America
Koger, Margaret, dau.
Koger, William, (h/o Margaret)
Koger, Margaret, (m/o minors)
Koger, Syntha, (minor)
Koger, Robert, (minor)
Koger, Charles, (minor)
Koger, Sarah, (minor)
Koger, Margaret, (minor)
Koger, Nancy A.
Koger, Meary
Koger, Wm., (Petitioner)
Koger, Wm., (adm.de borius)
Crow, Sarah, (dau.)
Crow, Calvin, (h/o Sarah)
Crow, Sarah, (m/o minors)
Crow, Ollie, (minor)
Crow, John, (minor)
Crow, Elijah, (minor)
Phillips, M. E., (w/o John)
Whited, Maranda F., (w/o John)
Craze, America
Bouldin, Wm. Grant, (minor)
Bouldin, Abraham L., (Texas)
Hammock, Mary S.

Estate Record Name
Bouldin, Elijah (Cont.)
Hammond, William, (h/o Mary)
Koger, William, (adm)
Bouldin, Wm. G,
Craze, U. A.
Roberts, Syntha
Smith, Henry H., (JP)
Bouldin, John F.
Beane, T. J., (set dower land)
Lowery, S. C., (set dower land)
Ellis, A. J. , (set dower land)
Willis, Green, (set dower land)
Chadwick, A. J., (set dower land)
Nicholsen, E. P., MD
Cochran, L. L., Judge
McNutt, R. C., (sheriff)
Elllis, Wm.
Hammock, W.
Bouldin, John F., (pd.burial exp.)
Davenport, Paine & Lowery
Stewart, Thos. G., (comm.)
Smith, Thomas H., (advertise)
Fort Payne Journal
Dobbs & Howard, (atty)
Blancit, A. D., (juror paid)
Willis, W. G.
Beene, J. T., (juror paid)
Hardy, Gaines A., (auctioneer)
Ellis, Abner J., (juror paid)
Davis, R. C., (tax collector)
Franklin, A. G., (sheriff)
Lowery, Samuel C., (juror pd.)
Holloman, E. T., (witness)
Humble, J. T., (comm.)
Beene, Geo T., (services)
Fuller, W. T., (atty)
Whited, John, (expenses pd.)
Hammock, W., (guar.fee paid)
Campbell, Isaac, (witness)
Stewart, Thomas G., (guar.fee)
Sanford, John A.

Estate Record Name
Bouldin, Elijah (Cont.)
Lowry, Geo. M.
Hammock, Vaney
Whitehead, M. Frances
Blancit, A. D., (appraiser)
Lowery, Samuel C.,(appraiser)
Smith, Thomas H., (register)
Painter, Nancy Serena
Crow, Calvin M.
Lee, Mariah A.
Craze, G. W.
Craze, U. A.
Bouldin, E. J.
Lee, William
Koger, Wm., (adm.bond)
York, F. M., (adm bond)
Smith, Henry H., (adm.bond)
York, John C. (adm.bond)
Last File in Box 2
Bowen, Archie
Box 3 File 1 1883-1885
Names in File:
Owens, John T., (adm)
Painter, M. H., (bond)
Miller, J. B., (bond)
Nelson, C. L., (bond)
Forrester, J. J., (bond)
Bearden, James, (witness)
Franklin, John N., Judge
Copeland, Alex C., (witness)
Haralston & Haralston, (atty)
Haralston, H. C.
Haralston, J. W.
Smith, Thomas H., (adv.)
Kean, J. P., (notary public)
Hawkins, John N., Judge
Cochran, L, L, Judge
Franklin, A. G., (sheriff)
Waller, E. M., (JP)
Davis, Rueben C. (tax coll.)
McCurdy, J. A. (tax coll-1866)

Estate Record Name

Bowen, Archie (Cont.)
- Ferguson, W. L., (tax coll-1875)
- Sander, C., (tax coll. -1857)
- Snider, C., (tax coll.-1860)
- Wright, L. T., (tax coll.-1859)
- Belshire, J. B., (tax coll.-1861)

Bowen, John T. (Will)
- Box 3 File 2 1915-1925
- Names in File:
- Bowen, Marcus E., (exec.)
- Lackey, G. W., (bond)
- Miller, Frank, (bond)
- Bowen, Slety A., (widow)
- Bowen, Thomas L.
- Bearden, Alice
- Nailer, Riller
- Nailer, L. J., Mrs.
- Naler, Nailor, Nalor
- Bowen, Madison C.
- Bowen, Marcus E.
- Broadwell, Annie
- Duncan, Arlevia (Arlene)
- Bowen, John L.
- Jolly, B. P. (appraiser)
- Naler, L. J., (appraiser)
- Malone, G. L., Judge
- Bowen, M. E.
- Bowen, J. L.
- Bowen, M. C.
- Brown, Joseph C., (atty fee)
- Bailey & Weaver, (atty)
- Wolfes, C. A., (atty)
- Lyons, Wallace
- Bowen, John T., (Will)
- Owen, M. T., (wit. to will)
- Owen, Billie, (wit. to will)

Bowens, Sallie
- Box 3 File 3 1907-1908
- Names in File:
- Bowens, Sallie, (petitioner)
- Deerman, M. A., Mrs., (estate)

Estate Record Name

Bowens, Sallie (Cont.)
- Deerman, Martha
- Deerman, Fletcher, (minor)
- Deerman, Robert, (minor)
- Deerman, Mary Lou, (minor)
- Deerman, Safa, (minor)
- Deerman, Wyley
- Roberts, Emma, (w/o Charles)
- Roberts, Charles
- Jenkins, Rachel, (w/o John)
- Jenkins, John
- Deerman, Martha, (w/o Scott)
- Deerman, Scott
- Moman, Zolly, (w/o Chas.)
- Moman, Charles
- Cook, Pearl, (w/o Spurgeon)
- Cook, Spurgeon
- Staples, John L., (sher.-Jackson)
- Nichols, R. A., (dep.sheriff)
- Presley, I. M., (comm)
- Perry, R. M., (JP)
- Berry, Minnie, (took deposition)
- Pharr, G. W., (deposition)
- Roberts, C. Y., (h/o E. F.)
- Roberts, E. F., (proceeds)
- Cook, T. J.
- Carter, H., (purchased land)

Boyd, John H.
- Box 3 File 4 1890
- Names in File:
- Boyd, S. C., (widow)
- Boyd, Belzona, (minor)
- Widow Exemption
- Bell, C. M., (comm)
- Campbell, Isaac, (comm.)
- West, James, (comm)
- McCurdy, J. A.

Boyd, Robert
- Box 3 File 5 1909
- Names in File:
- Kirby, Rockey, (Admx.)

Estate Record Name
Boyd, Robert (Cont.)
Kirby, Rockey, (sister)
Sou. Railway Co. Claim
Leatherwood, R. L., (bond)
Leatherwood, Agnes F.,(bond)
Blake, Jane, (witness)
Wistan, W. H., (notary pub.)
Croley, Jas. A., Judge
Brackett, Laura A. & Francis V.
Box 3 File 6 1906
Names in File:
Windsor, N. E., Mrs., (guar.)
Windsor, N. E., Mrs., (mother)
Davis, Rueben, (bond)
Naler, C. C., (bond)
Croley, Jas. A., Judge
Brackett, Laura A., (minor)
Brackett, Francis V., (minor)
Milwee, James A., (JP)
Brandon, Hugh T., et al
Box 3 File 7 1919-1910
Names in File:
Brandon, Hugh T. (petitioner)
Sale for Division of Land
Casey, Andrew M.
Casey, Amanda E.
Whatley, Harriett
Tate, D. M.
Evans, Elizabeth J.,
Evans, R. M., (h/o Elizabeth J.)
Dobbs, Robert
Dobbs, Hardy
Dobbs, Stephen
Dobbs, Cordie
Dobbs, Otto
Fox, Salethy
Tracey, Minnie
Bain, Ethel
Tate, A. W.
Ueasy, Corinna Tate
Tate, Willie

Estate Record Name
Brandon, Hugh T., et al (Cont.)
Tate, Early
Tate, Altha
Killian, G. W., (purchased land)
Croley, Jas. A., Judge
Davis & Pope
Davis, John A., (atty)
Fort Payne Journal
Pope, J. D., (comm)
Pope, Jesse D.
McBroom, A. M., (deposition)
Killian, E. S., (deposition)
Campbell, H. B., (take depos.)
Presley, I. M., (guar.ad litem)
Dodds, Stephen, (minor)
Dodds, Cordia, (minor)
Dodds, Otto, (minor)
Dodds, Charley, (minor)
Tate, Early, (minor)
Tate, Altha, (minor)
Brandon, John W.
Box 3 File 8 1884-1892
Names in File:
Frazier, P. M., (adm)
Heirs:
Brandon, David
Hurst, Caroline
Hurst, Joseph
Brandon, Lela
Brandon, Johnie Lou
Cochran, L. L., Judge
Singer Mfg. Co.
Hurst, J. S.
Russell, J. E.
Brandon, D. A., (adm)
Hurst, J. S. (Adm)
Cooper, L. E., Mrs.
Cooper, T. T., (h/o L. E.)
Cooper, L. E., Mrs. (Texas)
Brandon, P. A., (atty)
Haralson, W. C., (comm.)

Estate Record Name
Brandon, John W. (Cont.)
Killian, John, (deposition)
Newkirk, James F., (deposition)
Fort Payne Journal
Smith, Thos. H., (adv.)
Hurst, J. I.
Davis, R. C., (tax coll. 1884-85)
Quin, W. E.
Guin (Quin)
DeShields, J. G., (sheriff-1892)
W. D. Webster Co
Nixon & Webster Co.
Brandon, D. A., (resigned adm)
Hurst, Joseph, (resigned adm)
Brandon, P. A., (purch. land)
Green, A. B., (purchased land)
Frazier, P. M., (adm.)
Fuller, W. T., (clerk)
Greyton, George
Greyton, Mary, (w/o George)
Haralston, Wallace, (guardian)
Brandon, Lela, (minor)
Brandon, Jonnie Lou, (minor)
Franklin, J. N., Judge
Franklin, A. G., (sheriff)
Haralston, W. C., (comm.)
Dodds, L. A., (atty)
Hurst, J. S.
Baxter, Jesse
Quin, W. E.
Webb, J. W., (clerk)
Hurst, Caroline E.
Brandon, Johnnie L.
Cleveland, G. H., (witness)
Pickens, D. F., (witness)
Twitty, J. W., (notary public)
Hurst, J. S., (bond)
Brandon, P. A., (bond)
Quin, W. E., (bond)
Hogler, I. W., (appraiser)
Hagles (Hogles) (Hogler)

Estate Record Name
Brandon, John W. (Cont.)
Newkirk, James F., (appraiser)
Killian, John, (appraiser)
Harrelson, W. C., (JP)
Hurst, J. S., (adm)
Foster?, C. C., (sheriff)
Sale of Property Inventory:
Jack, Thos. M., (tools)
Horn, Thos., (tools)
Brandon, Dave, (tools)
Brandon, P. A.,(hand saw,etc.)
Killian, W. T., (tools)
Herst, (hammer)
Killian, E., (machine plains)
Haralson, W. C.,(box&contents)
Killian, W. T., (vice & bench)
Killian, D. J., (double plow)
Jack, Thos., (bench screws)
Newkirk, J. F., (Grindstone)
Brandon, P. A., (wagon tong)
Hurst, Jos. (plow stock)
Brandon, Dave, (loom)
Hurst, Jos., (mare)
Brandon, Dave, (2-mule colts)
Haralson, W. C., (cow)
Burt, R. A., (2-yearlings)
Jacoway, H. J., (11-sheep)
Hurst, Jos., (3-hogs)
Brannon, Daniel
Box 3 File 9 1906
Names in File:
Lawrence, J. P., (adm)
Brannon, Ella, (widow)
Name Unknown, (1-minor)
Croley, Jas. A., Judge
Lan? Iron Mountain Co.
Batella, Alabama
Allen, E. L., (atty), B'ham
U. S. Fidelity & Guar. Co.
Bray, Houston, et al
Box 3 File 10 1907-1922

Estate Record Name
Bray, Houston, et al (Cont.)
Bray, M. E., Mrs., (guardian)
Bray, Houston, (minor)
Bray, D. H., (minor)
Bray, William, (minor)
Bray, J. B., (minor)
Bray, M. E., Mrs., (mother)
Elrod, J. G. (bond)
Head, G. W., (bond)
Harden, H. D., (bond)
McMahan, C. B., (bond)
Croley, Jas. A., Judge
Haralson, W. W., Judge
Bouldin, Thos., (receipts)
Stone, Virgil, (receipts)
Walker, M., (receipts)
Gravitt, W. J., (court cost)
Bristow, E. T.
Box 3 File 11 1870-1873
Names in File:
Tabor, F. M., (adm)
Dunlap, Dobbs & Jacoway
McCurdy, J. A.
Griffin, William
Chitwood, R., (register)
Smith, P. J., (editor)
Republican Union Newspaper
Chitwood, Joel
Payne, A. F.
Cunningham, John, (guar.ad litem)
Bristow, Elisha
Bristoe (Bristow) (Bristo)
Dobbs, L. A., (atty)
Cain, R. W.
Griffin, Perry, (JP)
Tabor, F. M., (adm.bond)
Lovins, L. B. (adm.bond)
Johnston, W. S., (adm.bond)
Heirs:
Tabor, Mary E., (w/o F. M.)
Bristoe, Sarah M.

Estate Record Name
Bristow, E. T. (Cont.)
Campbell, Jane, (w/o Bethel)
Campbell, Bethel
Wommack, Nancy C.
Wommack, R. J., (h/o Nancy C.)
Wammock (Wommack)
Bristoe, Warrick, (estate)
Bristoe, Samuel I., (deceased)
Bristoe, Elizabeth T, (widow)
Bristoe, Elizabeth, (adm)1852
Bristow, Warrick
Box 3 File 12 1854
Names in File:
Bristow, Elisha, (adm)
Estes, Mary, heir
Estes, John W., heir
Walden, L. B., (atty)
Cunningham, John,(guar.ad litem)
Higgins, Robert W.
Sibert, John, (witness)
Walder, J. B.
Johnson, C. Pickney, (witness)
Estes, R., Judge
See File 11
Brock, Isaiah H. (Will)
Box 3 File 13 1900-1902
Names in File:
Brock, I. H., (estate)
Brock, William H., (minor)
Brock, Albert F., son
Copeland, Florence E., (dau)
Longshore, Marietta E., (dau)
No widow
Ward, N. A., (exec.)
Boyd, E. D., (witness)
Guin, G. A., (witness)
Slay, J. M., (witness)
Campbell, H. B., (guar.ad litem)
Cook, W. C. D., Judge
Brassell, Josie Brock, (dau)
Brock, Josie, (by first wife)

Estate Record Name
Brooks, Aaron
Box 3 File 14 1843-1844
Names in File:
Wasa, John, (Adm)
Ward, John,, (adm)
Brooks?, Elizabeth, (guardian)
Brooks?, James, (guardian)
Brooks, Sarah, (minor)
Brooks, Susan, (minor)
Brooks, John, (minor)
Brooks, Elizabeth, (minor)
Patrick, Thos. A.
Naylor, Poly
Grant, T. I.
Grant, J. F.
Kirby, S. W.
Berry, A. I.
Berry, A. J.
Boyd, James
Browder, E. J.
Box 3 File 15 1912-1914
Names in File:
Browder, T. E., (widow)
Homestead Exemption
No minor children
Blake, B. P., (appraisal)
Lyons, Wallace, (appraisal)
Croley, Jas. A., Judge
Brown, C. C.
Box 3 File 16 1914
Names in File:
Brown, S. E., Mrs., (adm)
Brown, S. E., Mrs., (bond)
Smith, Bonnie M. Brown, (bond)
Brown, Mary Maude, (bond)
Brown, C. R., (bond)
Jones, Bertie, Mrs. (bond)
Tucker, Inez, Mrs., (bond)
Brown, Jimmie M., (bond)
Brown, Evie Ruth, (bond)
Brown, Willis, (bond)

Estate Record Name
Brown, C. C. (Cont.)
Croley, Jas. A., Judge
Smith, Marinda, (receipts)
Chatman, A. A., (receipts)
York, Elijah, (receipts)
Holtzclaw, Dr., (receipts)
Maxwell & Jones
Davenport & Co.
Burgiss, G. A.
Smith, T. H.
Jones, Hardie
Mallicott, L. A., Dr.
Jones, D. A.
Hollerman, R. E.
Sharf, D. J. & Co.
Nicholson, Wm. P., Dr.
Herman, H. A.
Heirs:
Brown, S. E., Mrs.
Brown, Maude
Brown, C. R.
Jones, Bertie, Mrs.
Brown, Jimmie
Brown, Willie
Smith, Bonnie, Mrs.
Tucker, Inez, Mrs.
Brown, Evie Ruth, Miss
Jones, Fred, (hus./o Bertie)
Smith, W. J., (h/o Bonnie)
Tucker, J. M., (hus/o Inez)
Brown, Rufus (Will)
Box 3 File 17 1880
Names in File:
Resident of NJ, Land in Dekalb
Brown, Affa E. (widow, Admx)
Brown, Affa E., (residing NJ)
Cochran, L. L., Judge
Follett, Martha E., (witness,NJ)
Brown, Andrew J., (register,NJ)
No Names with Ala. Address
Brown, Abraham R., (brother)

Estate Record Name
Brown, Rufus (Will) (Cont.)
Sanborn, George W. (nephew)
Sanborn, Betsy Brown
Brown, Charles R., (nephew)
Brown, Frank W., (nephew)
Brown, Gilman A., (nephew)
Medbury, Mary C., (cousin)
Brown, Able, (cousin)
Brown, Abby, (w/o cousin)
Murphey, Alice Ann
Murphey, Patrick, (h/o Alice)
Nelson, Joseph G., (witness/will)
Merrill, John B., (witness/will)
Merrill, Brandman, (witness/will)
Merrill, Charles E.
Wiggins, Joseph F.
Moulton, William P.
Chase, Amos C.
Follett, John A., Dr.
Moulton, Martha C.
Brown's Academy, (NJ)
Bruce, Bailey
Box 3 File 18 1886-1892
Names in File:
Bruce, W. F., (executor)
Bruce, Benjamin F., (executor)
Baxter, F. M., (adm. bond)
Hughes, D. D., (adm. bond)
Jackaway, Henry, (adm. bond)
Killian, Mary A.
Killian, D. S. (hus. of Mary)
Majors, Fannie E.
Majors, Sam (hus. of Fannie)
Brock, S. Allie
Brock, Rufus H., (hus. of S.A.)
Davis, Abe, (guardian)
Bruce, William.(minor)
Bruce, John B. (minor)
Bruce, Thomas, (minor)
Arthur, W. H.
Majors, N. S.

Estate Record Name
Bruce, Bailey (Cont.)
Majors, F. E.
Brock, R. H.
Brock. A. S.
Williams, Mary A.
Davis, Abe, (guar.ad litem)
Deshields, J. G., (sheriff)
Estes, John, (dep. sheriff)
Campbell, H. B., (guar.ad litem)
Brock, Alabama S, (gr.dau)
Bruce, Bailey, (will)
Mary Dawson, (note)
Austin, J. A., (note)
Collett, Green C. (note)
McNutt, J. I., (note)
Lann, J. M. (note)
Thompson, J. D., (note)
Barber, W. H., (note)
McNutt, John W., (note)
Dutton, M. I., (note)
Hoge, Lemuel?, (note)
Baxter, T. J., (note)
Stewart, Thomas G, (paid)
Davis, R. C., (taxes)
Steele, W. A. (taxes)
Hobbs & Howard, (paid)
Haralson & Son, (paid)
Cochran, L. L. (paid)
Haralson, W. W., (paid)
Killian, Mollie
Bruce, B. F.
Majors, Fannie
Brock, Ala
Davis, C. C., (guar.)
Bruce, J. B.
Bruce, T. D.
Bruce, J. D.
Bruce, H. G
Major, S. N.
Bruce, William F.
Bruce, John B.

Estate Record Name
Bruce, John B.
Box 3 File 19 1886-1890
Names in File:
Bruce, Harris
Bruce, Bailey
Bruce, John B., minor
Bruce, Thomas D., minor
Bruce, William, minor
Davis, C. C. (guar.ad litem)
Cochran, L. L., Judge
Majors, S. N. (rent rec'd)
Bruce, W. F., (acct. rec'd)
Davis, John A.
Davis, C. C. (guar.ad litem)
Hamond, J. M., (tax coll)
Steele, W. A., (tax coll.)
Fuller, W. T.
Hawkins, John N., Judge
Bruce, W. F.
Sarton, Johnson
Franklin, John N., Judge
Davis & Haralson, Atty
Bruce, Mary
Box 3 File 20 1905-1906
Names in File:
Bruce, Mary, (petitioner)
Bruce, Bertha A., (minor)
Bruce, J. H.
Roe, Robert
Copeland, A. C., (guar. a l)
Milwee, Jas. A., (comm.)
Hale, P. C.
Davis, Rueben E., (Jus.P.)
Croley, J. A., Judge
Bruce, Rufus
Box 3 File 21 1901-1906
Names in File:
Bruce, Bertha A., (minor)
Wilson, Bertha A Bruce
Bruce, Mary A., (guardian)

Estate Record Name
Bruce, Rufus (Cont.)
Bruce, Mary A., (mother)
Bruce, J. H.
Croley, Jas. A.
Copeland, A. C.
Roe, R. B.
Davis, J. R.
Cook, W. C. D.
Harris, T. G. (sheriff)
Bryan, James M.
Box 3 File 22 1892
Names in File:
Bryan, Talitha C. (petitioner)
Bryan, Talitha (T. C.) (widow)
Bryan, Winbourne N., (minor)
Bryan, James J., (minor)
Bryan, Effie M., (minor)
Bryan, William E., (minor)
Bryan, Charles M., (minor)
Bryan, Marion, (minor)
Killian, H. E., (comm.)
Dutton, Abe, (comm)
Cochran, L. L., Judge Probate
Evans, J. M., (acct. due)
Works, W., (acct. due)
Steavens, C. H., (acct. due)
Clayton, L. J., (acct. due)
Bryce, William
Box 3 File 23 1890
Names in File:
Durham, John T., (adm, creditor)
Stanley, J. T., (adm bond)
Durham, J. M., (adm bond)
Cochran, L. L., Judge
Bryce, Sarah F., (widow)
Bryce, James
Bryson, Ruth K.
Box 3 File 24 1878
Names in File:
Bryson, Nelson M., (husband)
Bryson, N. M., (estate)

Estate Record Name

Bryson, Ruth K. (Cont.)
- Chitwood, Richard
- Burkhalter, D. B.
- McCartnery, A. P.
- Powell, Jno. S.
- Powell, J. S.
- Hawkins, J. J.
- Riley, J. M.
- Ferguson, W. L., (tax coll)
- Bradford
- Kully?, James M.
- Haralsen, W. J., (atty)
- Branden, P. A., Judge

Bunden, James
- Box 3 File 25 1896-1902
- Names in File:
- Bunden, James B.
- Kerby, Hugh H., (adm.)
- Kerby, Hugh H., (son-in-law)
- Kerby, J. S., (adm. Bond)
- Bookout, W. L., (adm bond)
- Kerby, John W., (adm bond)
- Kerby, H. H., (adm)
- Cook, W. C. D.
- Smith, Thomas, (ad)
- *The Fort Payne Journal*
- DeShields, J. G., (guardian)
- Heirs:
- McDaniel, Mary J.
- Fry, Hestor Ann
- Bunden, John W.
- Kerby, Louisa E.
- Bundren, James B.
- Bundren, Napolian
- Sizemore, Tennessee Agnes
- Preswood, Sarah J.
- Bauerlee, I. Victoria
- Cooper, Nancy E., (deceased)
- Wells, Sarah
- Shrader, Fenie
- Cooper, Mary

Estate Record Name

Bunden, James (Cont.)
- Cooper, James
- Peek, Lavada
- Cooper, T. G.
- Cooper, Dolf
- Cooper, Lillie Mae, (minor)

Burgess, Thomas B.
- Box 3 File 26 1910-1913
- Names in File:
- Burgess, Mollie Amella
- Burgess, Mollie, (minor)
- Burgess, Henry Richard, (min)
- Burgess, Thomas Ed, (minor)
- Burgess, Lilly May, (minor)
- Burgess, Alice Gerturde,(minor)
- Horton, P. T.
- Horton, J. P.
- Horton, W. A.
- Hulgan, S. N.
- Green, G. W. (guardian)
- Kelton, Jno. F., Judge Blount Co

Burk, M. D.
- Box 3 File 27 1863
- Names in File:
- Gilliland, W. B., (appraiser)
- Gilliland, D. M., (appraiser)
- McBrayer, J. T., (appraiser)
- Brothers, W. W.
- Franklin, J. N.
- Walters, R., (note)
- Burnett, John, (note)
- Fletcher, W. S., (note)
- Edwards, Jesse. (note)
- Gray, Jacob, (note)
- Gardener, Mary, (note)
- Burk, Yancy, (note)
- Brothers, N. W., (note)

Burkhalter, D. B.
- Box 3 File 28 1903-1915
- Names in File:
- Burkhalter, Daniel B., Estate

Estate Record Name

Burkhalter, D. B. (Cont.)
- Burkhalter, E. M., (adm.)
- Burkhalter, N. J., (widow)
- Blevins, R. M., (appraiser)
- Blevins, F. M., (appraiser)
- Adkins, D. L. G., (appraiser)
- Burkhalter, David B
- Campbell, H. M.
- Burkhalter, I.N.F.
- Croley, J. A., Judge
- Cook, W. C. D., Judge
- Davis, John A., (notary public)
- Adkins, B. F., (witness)
- Blevins, R. M., (witness)
- Deshields, J. G., (guar.ad litem)
- Austin, William, (minor)
- Blevins, Marion
- Austin, J. C., (purch. land)
- Austin, W. L., (purch. land)
- Burkhalter, D. C., (purch.land)
- Adkins, D. L. G., (adm. bond)
- Blevins, R. M., (adm. bond)
- Adkins, B. F., (adm. Bond)
- Smith, Lomey, (adm. Bond)
- Forester, Joshua, (witness)
- Austin, D. O., (sheriff)
- Burkhalter, N. J., (widow exemption)
- Heirs:
- Burkhalter, G. W.
- Burkhalter, Alex
- Austin, Jasper
- Austin, Rebecca
- Austin, Jasper
- Austin, George
- Austin, Fannie
- Austin, Belle
- Austin, Willie, (minor)
- Austin, Margaret
- Burkhalter, George
- Burkhalter, J. D.
- Burkhalter, E. M., (adm.)

Estate Record Name

Burkhalter, D. B. (Cont.)
- Burkhalter, T. E.
- Burkhalter, G. H.
- Burkhalter, B. K.
- Burkhalter, N. L.
- Burkhalter, N. S.
- Gillis, Sarah
- Burkhalter, James
- Shivers, Nettie
- Burkhalter, D. C.
- Austin, Willie
- Deceased Children of D. B.:
- Burkhalter, John
- Burkhalter, Nancy Ann
- Austin, Rebecca
- Burkhalter, Andrew
- Burkhalter, James Polk
- Burkhalter, Daniel
- End of Microfilm Roll No. 62

Burns, T. C.
- Box 3 File 29 1910-1911
- Names in File:
- Burns, S. M., Mrs., (widow)
- Widow Exemption
- Croley, Jas. A., Judge
- Walker, S. W., (set exemption)
- Southerlin, Charley, (set exemp.)
- Southerlin, C. E.
- Sparks, N. O., (JP)
- Mann, G. W., (Notary Public)
- Ventuas, Thomas, (Not. Pub.)
- Children:
- Burns, Jerry, (deceased)
- Burns, George
- Burns, Zeal
- Whitt (White), Eliza

Burnside, Delos
- Box 3 File 30 1881-1885
- Names in File:
- Keith, Colonel C., (adm)
- Keith, C. G.

Estate Record Name
Burnside, Delos (Cont.)
Keith, William R., (adm)
Keith, W. R.
Keath (Keith)
Keith (Keath)
Crow, Thomas J., (appraiser)
Kirby, H. H., (appraiser)
Kirby (Kerby)
Kerby (Kirby)
Clark, E. F., (appraiser)
White, J. T., (JP)
Bray, William C., (witness)
Biddle, John V., (witness)
Keath, C. G.
Keath, William R.
McCurdy, Nathaniel W., (bond)
Durham, J. M.
Shankles, Jesse, (witness)
Paine, Mearia L.
Keith, M.
Olds, C. P., Dr.
Webb, G. W., (clerk)
Heirs:
Burnside, Levie L., Mrs.
Burnside, DeWitt C. (minor)
Burnside, Ella , (minor)
Burnside, Jessie J., (minor)
Burnside, Franklin, (minor)
Burnside, Lyllis, (minor)
White, James T., (JP)
Keith, W. R., (guardian ad litem)
Keith, C. G., (guardian ad litem)
Davis, John A.
Dobbs, J.
Paine, Benjamin F.
Burnside, D.
Haralson & Haralson
Davis, Reuben C., (tax collector)
Shankles, Jesse
Burnside, J. D.
Smith, Thomas H.

Estate Record Name
Burnside, Delos (Cont.)
Fort Payne Journal
Sale of Personal Property:
Chambers, A. B., (door latches)
Walter, (bits and file)
Moore, F. A., (box)
Tankersley, J. F., (chest)
Biddle, T. W., (scales & padlocks)
Crabtree, G. W., (bedstead&table)
Tankersley, J. F., (spade & iron)
Lea, Walter, (scrap iron)
Nelson, J. S., (tools, oil can)
Moore, F. A., (auger)
Lea, Walter, (keg & beehive)
Nelson, J.S., (looking glass)
Burt, James
Box 3 File 31 1903-1907
Names in File:
Bryant, W. E., (adm)
Isbell, John B., (bond)
Bryant, W. E., ((bond)
DeShields, J. G.. (bond)
Burt, James, (deceased)
Croley, Jas. A., Judge
Heirs:
Bishop, Minnie, (1/5)
McClintock, Ella, (1/5)
Roberts, Dalllis, (1/5)
Roberts, Kent, (1/10)
Roberts, Bertha, (1/10)
Hazelett, Etta, (1/20)
McClintock, Clarence, (1/20)
McClintock, Walter, (1/20)
Leanard, Ora, (1/20)
Presley, I. M., (guar.ad litem)
Frazier, Walter, (minor)
Frazier, Wyatt, (minor)
Frazier, Lela, (minor)
Frazier, Ida, (minor)
Frazier, Jennie, (minor)
Burt, Bessie, (minor)

Estate Record Name

Burt, James (Cont.)
- Burt, Rube, (minor)
- Burt, Jos., (minor)
- Burt, Gain, (minor)
- Bryant, Daily, Mrs.
- Bryant, Des, Mrs.
- Burt, Marion
- Burt, Rube
- Chitwood, Emma
- Frazier, Walter
- Frazier, Wyatt
- Frazier, Lela
- Frazier, Ida
- Frazier, Jennie
- Wallace, Ella, Mrs.
- Wallas, Ella, Mrs.
- Stafford, Jennie, Mrs.
- Burt, Bain
- Burt, Bessie
- Burt, Rube
- Burt, Joe
- Roberts, Calvin
- Bishop, Minnie
- Burt, Geo., Estate
- Chitwood, W. J. (adm)
- Cain, Wall, (tax collector)
- Moore, W. E., Dr.
- Quin & Co., (med. Bills)
- Nappier, T. S. (JP)
- Jacoway, T. R.
- Black Diamond Roofing
- Bush, G. V., MD
- Edmondson, W. E., (JP)
- Duff & Quin, Doctors
- Duff, W. S., MD (services)
- Berry, Minnie, Miss (comm)
- Jacoway, T. R. (Purch. Land)

Burt, Mary, et al
- Box 3 File 32 1906-1908
- Names in File:
- Chitwood, W. J. , (adm)

Estate Record Name

Burt, Mary, et al (Cont.)
- Jacoway, W. V., (appraiser)
- Killian, W. T. (appraiser)
- Croley, Jas. A., Judge
- Burt, George
- Burt, Mary
- Campbell, H. B., (adm.ad litem)
- Simpson, W. H., (Chancellor)
- Cochran, Earl, (register)
- Burt, Mary, (mother of Geo.)
- Brandon, H. H., Mrs.
- Carrol, R. M.
- Burt, M.
- Chitwood, Mary C.
- Howard & Hunt
- Cochran, Earl, (register)
- Burt, R. A., (comm)
- Killian, W. S., (comm.)
- Carroll, R. M., (comm)
- Hannah, Josie, (witness)
- Burt, J. T.
- Dobbs, S. A.
- Dobbs, L. A.
- Brandon, H. H.
- Baxter, T. C.
- Whiteside, W. W., (chancellor)
- Simpson, N. H. (chancellor)
- Downs, T. L., (sheriff)
- Smith, Jesse
- Dixon, James
- Privett Heirs:
- Hill, Adeline
- Bohanon, Lucinda
- Privett, Frank
- Privett, Napolean
- Clayton, Martha
- Gross, Adeline
- Fossitt, Addie
- Long, Jennie
- Privett, George
- Reeves, Julia

Estate Record Name

Burt, Mary, et al (Cont.)

Privett, Charlie
Privett, Lillian
Privett, Fred
Privett, Glenn
Mitchell, Alice
Mitchell, Hugh
Miller, Lucy
Miller, William
Miller, Luella
Miller, Ette
Coleman, Minervie
Coleman, W. L.
Coleman, George
Coleman, Robert
Coleman, Elizabeth
Jaco, Martha
Privett, Pleasant
Privett, Joseph
Privett, Pleasant
McDowell, Martha
Privett, Eliza
Privett, Charles
McDowell, Mary
Privett, Elisha
Campbell, Louise
McDowell, Julia
Campbell, Amanda
Privett, Ervin
James, Luella
Privett, William
Previtt, Henley
Privett, Sally
Adams, Molly
Privett, Jessie
Privett, Thompson
Burt, Margaret
Couch, Pattie
Baxter, Angie
Baxter, Angie
Baxter, Oscar

Estate Record Name

Burt, Mary, et al (Cont.)

Privett Heirs (cont.):
Baxter, Houston
Chitwood, Mary
Burt, Henry
Burt, M.
Burt, Elisha
Busbee, Nancy
Busbee, John Burns
Lax, Mary
Lax, Jas.
Dobbs, Dora
Lax, E. T.
Lax, Thomas
Lax, Lou
Burt, James
Bohannon, Daisy
Burt, Reuben
Bryant, E. Z.
Burt, Marion
Bryant, Daily
Burt, Billy
Wallace, Ella
Burt, Bain
Stafford, Jennie
Stafford, Bessie
Burt, Reuben
Burt, Joe
Frazier, Lucinda
Frazier, Wyeth
Frazier, Walter
Chitwood, Emma
Frazier, Ida
Frazier, Lela
Frazier, Jennie
Burt, Calvin
Burt, John Tom
Burt, Tom
Burt, Elisha
Burt, John
Burt, Robert

Estate Record Name
Burt, Mary, et al (Cont.)
Burt, Henry
Burt, Fred
Dobbs, Neely
Burt, Pally (Polly)
Burt, Joe
Burt, Carl
Baxter, Eliza
Baxter, Willis
Edmondson, Sarah Jane
Cunningham, Mary
Lyons, Ellen
Baxter, Lucy
Baxter, George
Baxter, Thomas
Burt, Polly
Box 3 File 33 1906
Names in File:
Burt, Henry
Creole Marble Co.
Burt, J. W.
Higgins, W. V.
Burt, Mack
Malone, G. L., (deposition)
Chitwood, W. J., (comm)
Privett S. L.
Davis, John A.
Busbee, John
Major Brothers
Isbell, John
DeShields, J. G., (guar.ad litem)
Fossett, Addie
Cunningham,
Holbrook, W. L., (deposition)
Burt, Joe
Burt, Bessie
Burt, Reuben
Frazier, Walter
Frazier, Wyatt
Frazier, Lela
Frazier, Ida

Estate Record Name
Burt, Polly (Cont.)
Frazier, Jennie
Burt, Polley
Lax, Mary
Baxter, J. Willis
Berry, Minnie
Burt, Pallie
Burt, M.
Burt, Henry
Burt, Elisha
Chitwood, Mary C.
Burt, John T.
Burt, Marion
Wallace, Ella
Stafford, Jennie
Burt, Bain
Chitwood, Emma
Burt, Elisha
Burt, John
Burt, Robert
Burt, Fred
Burt, Henry
Dobbs, Cornelia
Burt, Palley
Baxter, Thomas C.
Edmondson, Sarah J.
Cunningham, Mary
Baxter, Lucy
Lyons, Ellen
Baxter, Geo.
Bohannon, Daily
Burt, Elijah
Burt, H.
Parish, S. L., (purchased land)
Parrish/Parish
Bynum, John W.
Box 3 File 34 1854-1858
Names in File:
Bynum, Rachel, (widow)
One Son
Two Daughters

Estate Record Name

Bynum, John W. (Cont.)
- Easley, Solomon, (adm)
- Bynum, John W., (adm)
- May, Wm. H., (guar.ad litem)
- Gublett, J. G., (sheriff)
- Walden, J. B., (atty)
- Porter, Benj. J., (witness)
- Estes, R., Judge
- Horton, J. B.,
- Horton, Jesse B.
- Nelson, J. M.
- Nelson, Pleasant M.
- Higgins, Robert
- Dixon, J. G., Judge
- McCurdy, Macklin

Byrd, James (J. M.)
- Box 3 File 35 1899-1900
- Names in File:
- See File 36 (J. M.. Byrd)
- Fuller, W. T., (guardian)
- Byrd, W. F., (minor)
- Byrd, Maude S., (minor)
- Byrd, Thomas C., (minor)
- Byrd, Alma C., (minor)
- Nations, W. T., (bond)
- Fuller, W. T., (bond, guardian)
- Stinson, J. F., (bond)
- Haralson, W. W., (bond)
- Dobbs, R. L., (bond)
- Ferguson, James B., (guar.ad l.)
- Chitwood, W. J., (sheriff)
- Frazier, R. W., (sheriff)
- Nations, W. T., (dep.sheriff)
- DeShields, J. G., (guar.ad litem)
- Cook, W. C. D., Judge
- Byrd, J. B., (exp. for minors)
- Byrd, Webb
- Byrd, Thomas C.
- Davis, John A., (NP)
- Stinson, S. M.
- Lowry, S. C.

Estate Record Name

Byrd, James (J. M.) (Cont.)
- Bell, C. N.
- Davenport, N. S. (school books)
- Nicholson, E. P., MD
- See File 36 (J. M.. Byrd)
- Hammonds
- Davenport & Crabtree
- Keith, John
- Smith, Thomas
- Quin, W. E., Dr.
- Campbell, A. L.
- Russell, W. W.
- Davenport & Co.
- Reed, W. D., (tax coll-1899)
- Graves, N. L. (tax coll.-1900)

Byrd, James M. (J. M.)
- Box 3 File 36 1899
- Fuller, W. F., (adm)
- Byrd, W. F.
- Byrd, Maud (Maude)
- Byrd, Thomas C.
- Byrd, Alma C.
- Lyons, W. W., (appraiser)
- Larmore, G. J., (appraiser)
- Hamman, W. J., (appraiser)
- Winston, J. N., Dr.
- Byrd, Webb
- Byrd, Weaver R.
- Schwelz Bros.
- Barnard, F. C., (comm)
- Johnson, J. Samuel, (comm)
- Warren, F. M., (comm)
- Barnard, Frank
- Fuller, W. F., (bond)
- Green, P.M., (bond)
- Haralson, W. W., (bond)
- Heirs:
- Holleman, E. J.
- Hamman, Idella
- Byrd, C. B.
- Byrd, J. B.

C

Estate Record Name
Cagle, J. L., Administrator
Cagle, S. A., Mrs., Estate
Box 3 File 37 1904-1914
Names in File:
Cagle, Jasper L., (adm)
Cagle, J. L., (oldest son)
Cagle, S. A., Mrs., Estate
White, J. H., (bond)
Dutton, S. L., (bond)
Burt, R. A., (bond)
Cagle, J. L., (bond)
White, James H., (appraiser)
Berryhill, L. C., (appraiser)
Thompson, D. R., (appraiser)
Berry, Minnie, (took deposition)
Copeland, A. C., (guar.ad litem)
Cagle, Vastie, (dau.)
Teague, Dora Cagle, (dau)
Cagle, Laura, (dau.)
Cagle, J. L., (son)
Cagle, John R.,
Cagle, Dora
Cagle, Della
Teague, Dora Cagle, (dau)
Cagle, A. L.
Hicks, T. E., (purchased land)
Cagle, Laura, (minor)
Smith, Thos. H., (bond)
Heirs in Adm.Papers:
Cagle, J. R.
Manley, Vastie Cagle
Cagle, John R.,
Teague, James M.
Webb, Lavina, Mrs.
Cagle, Della
Webb, Laura, Mrs.
Cagle, J. L.
Cagle, Ellen, Mrs.

Estate Record Name
Cagle, S. A., Mrs., (Cont.)
Killian, S. A.
Killian, H. E.
Cagle, Luke
Foys, Melia, Mrs.
Webb, S. N., Jr.
Teagues, Dorah
Miller, D. M.
Killian, Hugh
Smith, Thomas
Burt, W. C.
Boyd, J. G., (tax coll-1905)
Cain, Wall, (tax coll -1905)
Brisendine, E. (burial expense)
Thompson, D. B.
White, J. H.
Berryhill, L. C., Mrs.
Killian & Co.
Killian, G. W.
Berry, Minnie,(comm)
Davis, John A., (NP)
Cagle, S. A., Mrs.
Box 3 File 38 1905-1907
Names in File:
Guardianship of Laura Cagle
White, J. H., (guardian)
Cagle, J. L., (guar. bond)
Cagle, John
Cagle, Laura, (minor)
Cagle, John
Webb, Laura
Webb, S. N, Jr., (witness)
Teague, Dora
Cagle, Vasti
Flarity, J. T., (witness)
Croley, J. A.
Brock, H. B.
Franklin, Joe S., (teacher)

Estate Record Name

Cagle, S. A., Mrs.
Nowlin, B. S. Co.,(school books)
Burt, W. C.
Lowry, C. L.
Dutton, S. L.
Cagle, Laura, (minor)
Webb, Laura Cagle
Cain, Wall, (tax coll-1906)
Killian, H. H.
So. Railroad Co.

Callan, S. E. (Sallie)
Box 3 File 39 1872-1892
Names in File:
Callan, Sallie E., (guardian)
Callan, Sallie E., Mrs., (mother)
Callan, Lizzie, (minor)
Callan, Annie, (minor)
Callan, N. J., (minor)
Callan J. B., (minor)
Callan, H. H., (minor)
Callan, S. F., (minor)
Callan, James A., Estate
Haralson, W. W.., (bond)
Marsh, J. B., (bond)
Cochran, L. L., Judge

Campbell, A. L.
Box 3 File 40 1894
Names in File:
Train, Annie V.
Train, A. W.
Campbell, A. L. (purch. land)
Campbell, H. B.
McCarty, A. P.
Cochran, Earl
Hemphill, W. P.
Hawkins, R. H.
Cochran, L. L., (atty)

Campbell, G. H. (Guardian)

Campbell, Martha, Mrs., Estate
Box 3 File 41 1908
Names in File:

Estate Record Name

Campbell, Martha, Mrs., (Cont.)
Campbell, G. H., (guardian)
Campbell, G. H., (father/minors)
Campbell, Luther, (minor)
Campbell, Rufus, (minor)
Campbell, Walter, (minor)
Campbell, Ambe (Amby),(minor)
Campbell, Amos, (minor)
Campbell, Mary, (minor)
Campbell, George, (minor)
Campbell, Paul, (minor)
Monroe, J. D., (bond)
McClain, B. H., (bond)
Pope, J. D., (guardian ad litem)
Croley, Jas. A., Judge
Bowman, A. R.
Moore, W. J.
Allen, L. B.
Smith, W. L.
Kerby, M. M., Mrs.
Smith, John T.

Campbell, Isaac
Box 3 File 42 1905
File show #12 should be #42
Names in File:
Sales of Land for division
Campbell, John N.
Gibbs, Sally
Scott, Roxie
Campbell, J. N.
Campbell, Martha
Campbell, Lewis
Campbell, Isaac
Campbell, Louis, (minor)
Presley, I. M., (guar.ad litem)
Campbell, J. M.
Dean, Martha Campbell
Campbell, Laura
Lewis, W. E.
Hatton, Thompson
McCartney, C. H.

Estate Record Name

Campbell, Isaac (Cont.)
- Sampley, Samuel
- McCartney, John H., (witness)
- Dobbs, W. H., (witness)
- Isbell, John B., (atty)
- Dobbs, W. N.
- Berry, Minnie, (took deposition)
- Croley, J. A., Judge
- Dobbs, W. W., (witness)
- Isbell, John B., (purchased land)
- Sampley, Theodore
- Sampley, Oliver
- Quin, W. E., (witness)
- Gibbs, Sallie
- Brock, H. B., (witness)
- Thompson, (witness)
- Campbell, John H.
- Samuel Scroggins Place

Campbell, Lewis
- Box 3 File 42A 1869
- Names in File:
- Indentured Deed with Trust
- Davenport, R. R.
- Horton, A. J., Judge
- Long, James, Trustee
- Davenport, Radolphus R.
- Crow, G. W.
- Campbell, Isaac, (witness)
- Davenport, Nick S., (witness)
- Brandon, J. L., (JP)
- Branden, T. A., Trustee

Campbell, Manassa
- Box 3 File 43 1861
- Names in File:
- Campbell, Manassy, Estate
- Luth, Inman, (Executor)
- Luth, Emmon
- Luth, B. T., (bond)
- Walker, Jeremiah, (bond)
- Smith, A. B.
- Estes, R., Judge

Estate Record Name

Campbell, Manassa (Cont.)
- **Appraisement of Notes Due:**
- Smith, A. B.
- Dalrymple, J. D.
- Crump, James T.
- Reeves, E (C). R.
- Horton, P. J.
- Ramy, John
- Crump, J. W.
- Green, John
- Murdock, T. H.
- Williamson, D. C.
- Burgess, T. P.
- Stevens, Levi
- Ward, O. W.
- Penn, Stephen
- Taylor, John
- Williamson, D. C.
- Teague, Joshua
- Campbell, John
- Tow, John
- Banister, Thomas
- Reeves, T. W.
- Horton, S. W.
- Thompson, John L.
- Leath, Susanah
- Leath, Wm. J.
- Leath, B. T.
- Murdock, T. W.
- Malone, Wm.
- Ward, L. P.
- Gilbreath, A. A.
- McDaniel, Wm.
- Campbell, B. P.
- Yancy, Wm. A.
- Crump, M. W.
- Vaughn, James
- Pain, John
- Edwards, Jeptha
- Horton, A. B.
- Walker, Jeremiah

Estate Record Name

Campbell, Manassa (Cont.)
  Milwee, George
  Walker, Jeremiah (appraiser)
  Horton, A. B., (appraiser)
  Amos, James, (appraiser)
  Lankford, T. R.
  Moore, L. P.
  Burgess, T. J.
  M___, C. J.
  Ward, L. P.
  Thompson, John F.

Campbell, Rebecca
  Box 3 File 44 1879
  Names in File:
  Campbell, Rebecca, Estate
  Dobbs, Stephen E., (adm)
  Brandon, P. A., Judge

Capshaw, Thomas
  Box 3 File 45 1857
  Names in File:
  Capshaw, Elizabeth, (widow)
  Capshaw, William, (son, minor)
  Williams, William G., (adm)
  Shook, O. S., (atty)
  Gilbert, J. B., (JP)
  Estes, Reuben, Judge
  Williams, W. G., (adm)
  Chitwood, Rebecca, (comm)
  Light, Miley, (petitioner)
  May, Daniel, (appraiser)
  Houston, Jas. C., (appraiser)
  May, Robert, (appraiser)
  Capshaw, Thomas
  Chitwood, Richard
  Capshaw, Benjamin
  Light, Wiley
  Houston, Idene
  Houston. James
  Nicholsen, D. L., (guar.ad litem)

Carden, Christopher C.
  Box 3 File 46 1868-1870

Estate Record Name

Carden, Christopher C. (Cont.)
  Carden, Rebecca, (widow)
  Appleton, Hariett, (dau.)
  Carden, Hugh
  Carden, Laura
  Carden, Sally, (minor)
  Winston, John G., (deposition)
  Winston, J. G., (friend)
  Winston, William O., (witness)
  Roberts, William J.
  Griffin, (sheriff)
  Brandon, P. A., (guar.ad litem)
  Lowrence, G. A.,(Marshall Co.)
  Horton, A. J., Judge
  Franklin, John N., Judge

Carnes, David R.
  Box 3 File 47 1887
  Carnes, Martha, (widow)
  Homestead Exemption
  Carnes, D. R., (deceased)
  No Minor children
  Gilbreth, M. N., (comm)
  Gilbreth, Madison H., (comm)
  DeShields, J. S., (JP)
  Yarbrough, J. C., (witness)
  Cochran, L. L., Judge

Carpenter, Y.
  Box 3 File 48 1908
  Names in File:
  Guardianship of Minors
  Conway, W. F., Mrs., (guardian)
  Conway, W. F., Mrs.,(mother)
  Carpenter, Docia, (minor)
  Carpenter, Margie, (minor)
  Carpenter, Frankie, (minor)
  Carpenter, Eldridge, (minor)
  Carpenter, Willie B., (minor)
  Carpenter, John F., (minor)
  Minor Children of Y. Carpenter
  Croley, Jas. A., Judge
  Conway, W. F., Mrs., (bond)

Estate Record Name
Carpenter, Y. (Cont.)
Conway, J. A., (bond)
Russell, W. W., (bond)
Presley, I. M., (guar.ad litem)
Isbell & Presley, (atty)
Carr, John
Box 3 File 49 1904
Names in File:
Carr, E. W., (adm., father)
Carr, Martha, (mother)
Carr, E. W., (adm bond)
Carr, Geo. H., (adm bond)
John Carr, (Unmarried man)
Ala. Great So RR Co., (claim)
Carter, H.
Box 3 File 50 1915-1918
Names in File:
Carter, C. L., (adm)
Carter, Sarah, (widow)
Croley, Jas. A. Judge
Carter, C. L., (adm)
Carter, Sarah, (widow)
Children:
Carter, C. L.
Carter, J. S.
Carter, W. T.
Summerville, S. L.
Carter, H. J.
Carter, R. G.
Carter, Mary A.
Monroe, T. L., (appraiser)
Graham, W. S., (appraiser)
Brumbeloe, J. S., (appraiser)
Carter, C. L., (adm bond)
Monroe, T. L., (adm. bond)
Graham, W. S., (adm bond)
Worthy, Clifford
Bowens, J. B.
Guice, Y. Y.
Harris, W. R.
Rucks, J. W.

Estate Record Name
Carter, H. (Cont.)
Fuller, B. B.
Brumbeloe, J. H., (NP)
Smith, T. H.
Presley, I. M., (atty fee)
Powell, J. C., (hauling seeds)
Inventory Notes Due Estate:
Lybrand, Walter
Lybrand, G. W.
Wearthy, A. C.
Wearthy, W. C.
Willoughby, J. O.
Fuller, B. B.
Yancy, W. J.
Dallas, Sam
Fuller, W. L.
Monroe, T. L.
Owens, G.
Owens, G. W.
Carter, C. L.
Pickens, J. M.
Pickens, J. F.
Yarbrough, W. C.
Harris, M. H.
James, M. J., Mrs.
Marks, C. C.
Mosley, S. W.
Carter, J. L.
Carter, J. S.
Saffolds, L. L.
Carter, W. T.
Harralsen Co. Ga-160 acres
Eaves, W. T., (Ga. Ordinary)
Edwards, W. F., (clerk, GA)
Farmer & Citizen Bank, GA
Fulton Co. GA Tax, 1914
Case, Davy C.
Box 3 File 51 1907-1912
Names in File:
Case, Josie. (widow)
Case, Josie, Mrs., (exec.)

Estate Record Name
Case, Davy C. (Cont.)
Case, Joseph L., (bond, son)
Case, Oscar V., (bond. son)
Case, Lora D., (bond, dau.)
Williams, Nena Nicholson, (wit.)
Case, D. C., Mrs., (exec.)
Croley, Jas. A., Judge
Case, John W.
Box 3 File 52 1884
Names in File:
Case, John W., (will)
Case, Mary Jane, (widow)
Case, James, (son)
Blevins, R. M., (witness)
Payne, Thomas, (witness)
Tatum, M. A. B., (witness)
Casey, Joel
Box 3 File 53 1879-1880
Names in File:
Casey, J. L.
Casey, W. L.
Thiver, M. E.
Cooper, Armiza
William, P. J.(F.)
McNutt, R. C., (adm)
Lucas, J.
Wallace, S. M.
Franklin, J. H.
Brandon, P. A., Judge
Lowndes Co.
Cash, L.
Box 3 File 54 1914-1915
Names in File:
Cash, Josie, (widow)
Homestead Exemption
Cash, Jesse, (minor)
Cash, Della O., (minor)
Cash, Alfred E., (minor)
Cash, Stella E., (minor)
Cash, L, (father of minors)
Milwee, James A., (JP)

Estate Record Name
Cash, L. (Cont.)
Drain, J. D., (appraiser)
Anderson, W. N., (appraiser)
Notes Due:
Tidwell, C. N.
Tidwell, J. C.
Cash, Reuben
Caverly, Charles M.
Box 3 File 55 1891-1892
Names in File:
Frazier, P. M., (Ex Off.Adm.)
Frazier, P. M., (sheriff)
Kennedy, F. H., (rent)
Dobbs & Howard, (attys)
Newmans, C. S.
Green, P. B. (Physician)
Cochran, L. L., Judge
DeShields, J. G., (sheriff)
Dobbs & Ewing, (attys)
Paid:
Baxter, F. M.
Nicholson, B. H.
Durham, J. J.
Davenport, J. G.
Fuller, W. F.
Johnson, H.
Ide, D. M.
Lively
Newkirk, James
Killian, A. F. (T.)
Spaulding,
Driskill, Wm.
Shepard,
Malone, Jim
Killian, A. F.
Monroe, S. D.
McHan, E. A., Mgr.
Fort Payne Journal
Chadwick, A. M.
Box 3 File 56 1870
Names in File:

Estate Record Name
Chadwick, A. M. (Cont.)
Chadwick, Isaac, (adm)
Chadwick, Isaac, (bond)
Chadwick, William, (bond)
Lankford, Y. M., (bond)
Hoge, John R., Judge
Warren, Eliza, (w/o Reuben)
Warren, Reuben, (resides TN)
Chadwick, Mauda, (w/o Harman)
Chadwick, Harman, (res. GA)
Chadwick, Wm., (resides TN)
Chadwick, James
Chadwick, Benjamin, (minor)
Chadwick, Wm., (minor)
Chadwick, Lafayette, (minor)
Chadwick, James
Anderson, Catherine
Anderson, Biddie, (minor)
Jones, Elizabeth, (w/o Geo. W.)
Jones, Geo. W., (resides in KY)
David, Matilda, (w/o Benj.)
David, Benj., (resides GA)
Chadwick, Isaac
Roe, John, (note)
Shelton, W. T., (note)
Chadwick, James, (note)
Penager, John C.
Vantanden, J. E.
Jones, G. W., (note)
Ellis, John, (note)
Chadwick, J. W., (note)
Duggan, Julius, (note)
Smith, Robert
Warren, John
Quillen, Manervia
Stubblefield, Melvinia
Ray, Elizabeth
McMillon, Elijah
Pack, Johnson
Howard, Emmie
Russ, Wm.

Estate Record Name
Chadwick, A. M. (Cont.)
Howard, Benj.
Howard, Marthy
Howard, John G.
Pack, G. C.
Duggan, J. H.
Harvey, Jefferson
Porter, Nancy
Reeves, Smith
Taylor, C. C. R.
Warren, William
Warren, Ara
Warren, Rebecca
Bryant, John
Bryant, Sarah
Back, Catherine
Lively, Emery
O'Neal, Evaline
Lively, John
Bryant, Emley
Bryant, George
Jones, G. W.
Jackson Co. School Fees
Smith, Peter
Warren, John
Quillen, Manervy
Stubblefield, Melviry
Ray, Elizabeth
McMillon Elijah
Pack, Johnson
Howard, Emma
Reese, William
Howard, Benjamin
Howard, Martha
Howard, John G.
Back, G. C.
Dugger, J. L.
Haney, Jefferson
Porter, Nancy
Reeves, Sintha
Horton, A. J., Judge

Estate Record Name
Chadwick, A. M. (Cont.)
Chadwick, A. M.
Honorable Discharge-1864
Griffin, W., (sheriff)
Chadwick, A. M.(teacher)
Chadwick, A. M., Papers
Curtis, N.
Rutledge, W.
Riley, John
Beldin, Cason B.
Cunningham, J. W.
Jenkins, John
Magratt, Thomas
Bean, William
Bowker, J. A.
Canoyer, Capt.
Zimmerman, Henry
Ross, J. W.
Davis, C. L.
Ross, John
Compton, John
Humble, B. H.
Jones, J. A.
Lett, James
Hulsey, J. H. (F.)
Pay, Fillip
Gossett, James
Todd, John H.
Warnock, H.
Spangler, A.
Pettitt, H.
Marfit, John
Burns, John
McGlothling, John
Gatling, B. T.
Croak, Mikel
Moore,
Nance, James
Wellborn, D. A.
Daniel, R. G.
Mosley, J. N.

Estate Record Name
Chadwick, A. M. (Cont.)
Therman, J. T.
Tipton, T. C.
Brown, C. H.
Bird, Wm. G
Fellers, A. A.
Pellers, A. A.
Vanderworker, John
Jay, Rubin
Bird, S. M.
Towers, Wm.
Norvel, W. C.
Ayers, W. G.
Ellison,
McGraw, James
Mires, Jacob
Peak, Isaac
Vanderbirgh, John
McKinzie, J. A.
Williams, Sampson
Stintson, Robert
Willson, H.
Black, J. P.
Chadwick, R. D.,
Box 3 File 57 1911-1912
Names in File:
Culberson, C. Y, (adm.,friend)
Jones, E. N., (bond)
Maxwell, A., (bond)
Heirs:
Chadwick, B. F.
Chadwick, H. D.
Chadwick, Hellen
Chadwick, Annie
Croley, Jas. A., Judge
Smith, Thomas S.
Fort Payne Journal
Presley, I. M.
Christian, T. S. Jr. Gen Mdse
Aldrich, J. H. (T. H.)
Aldrich, Anna M., Trustee

Estate Record Name
Chadwick, R. D. (Cont.)
Aldrich, Herbert, (atty)
Shaw, H. E.
Chadwick, William
Box 3 File 58 1889-1904
Names in File:
Chadwick, W. A., (adm)
Chadwick, J. B., (adm)
Chadwick, Geo. R.
Harris, Sarah, (dau.)
Chadwick, T. J.
Chadwick, Samuel M.
Chadwick, A. J.
Lowry, Elizabeth, (dau.)
Chadwick, Charles W.
Payne, Amanda J., (dau)
Chadwick, Thomas J., (son)
Chadwick, William A., (son)
Chadwick, Andrew J.,(son)
Chadwick, John B. (son)
Davenport, G. W.
Holmes, T. C., (witness)
McDonough, Wood, (witness)
Holmes, J. T., (witness)
Faust, John Emory, (witness)
Lowry, C. E., (Elizabeth)
Lowry, J. M., (h/o Elizabeth)
Chadwick, C. W.
Chadwick, Samuel
Payne, Amanda
Payne, Thomas
Blake, T. B.
Reed, W. D.
Payne, W. H., Jr., (NP)
Prigmore, E. M., (NP)
Davis, K. D., MD
Smith, Thomas H.
Chadwick, Wm.
Graves, W. L.
Payne & Payne, (atty)
Fricks, A. T.

Estate Record Name
Chadwick, William (Cont.)
Chapman, Harry E., Dr.
Smith, S. M.
Carter, A. U.
Harris, S. A.
Harris, Sarah J.(w/o G.W.)
Harris, G. W.
Lowry, Chevy Elizabeth, Mrs.
Chadwick, T. J.
Payne, Amond J.
Holmes, Thomas W.
Payne, Thomas, (h/o Amanda)
Heirs of Geo. R., (deceased):
Hawkins, Bettie
Chadwick, Wm. R.
Chadwick, Thomas
Chadwick, James
Cordell, Ella
Vandergriff, Eva
Bolin, Mattie
Chadwick, Wm. A. (adm.bond)
Chadwick, J. B., (adm.bond)
Chadwick, C. W., (adm. Bond)
Smith, W. F., (adm. bond)
Harris, S. A., (adm bond)
Payne, A. J., (adm bond)
Lowry, C. E., (adm bond)
Payne, Thomas, (adm bond)
Lowry, J. M., (adm bond)
Bryan, C. A., (Dade Co tax)
Graves, H. L., (Dekalb Tax)
Graves, H. L., (tax coll-1901)
Smith, Thomas H., (adv.)
Fort Payne Journal
Reed, W. D., (tax coll-1899)
Blake, T. B.
Davenport, George G., (pd note)
Street, A. M., (pd. interest)
Pettitt, W. P., (pd note)
Chapman, A. E., (funeral exp)
Davis, K. D., Dr.. (medical)

Estate Record Name
Chadwick, William (Cont.)
Chadwick & Crow (fence work)
Driskill, Charles, (farm work)
Foust, A. L., (atty)
Rent from Farm $3535.
Chandler, James M.
Box 3 File 59 1913
Names in File:
Chandler, Ellen L., (widow)
Chandler, Minnie, (minor dau.)
Homestead Exemption
Roberts, Joe G., (comm)
Ryan, Robert, (comm)
Ryan, R. M.
Anderson, John C., (JP)
Croley, Jas. A. Judge
Chappell, Mary A.
Box 3 File 60 1904-1919
Names in File:
Graves, H. L., (adm)
Graves, H. L., (nephew by marr.)
Gravitt, W. J., (adm. bond)
Graves, W. V., (adm. bond)
Heirs, 2-sisters, 6-brothers:
White, Fannie, Mrs.
Guest, Mattie, Mrs.
Chappell, W. T.
Chappell, James
Chappell, Robert
Chappell, George
Chappell, H. B.
Chappell, John
Heirs of Fannie White:
White, H. R.
White, J. B.
Graves, Nora, Mrs.
Siniard, Mattie, Mrs.
McGee, E. C., (witness)
Brown, J. A., (witness)
Hughs, D. B., (payment)
Elrod, W. A., (medical aid)

Estate Record Name
Chappell, Mary A. (Cont.)
Thomas, J. R., MD, (medical)
Hunt & Wolfes, (atty)
Gadsden Marble & Stone Co
Tombstone-Mary A. Chappell
Tombstone-Robert Chappell
Gillespie, M. L., (Gen. Mgr.)
White, H. R., (burial expenses)
Murdock, A. O., (tax coll-1917)
McAbee, T. A.,
(hauling tombstone)
Guest, Robert, (h/o Mattie)
White, H. R., (Purch. Land)
20 Acres for $565.00
Chastain, George W., et al
Box 3 File 61 1909-1920
Names in File:
Wallace, J. O., (guardian)
Wallace, J. O.,(uncle of minors)
Chastain, George W., (minor)
Chastain, Zanie, (minor)
Chastain, Beadie, (minor)
Chasteen/Chastain
Wallace, J. O., (bond)
Roden, W. V., (bond)
Jones, E. B., (bond)
Kemp, S. A. (bond)
Chastain, J. B.
Box 3 File 62 1908
Names in File:
Chastain, J. B., Agent
National Marble Mills
Roden, James, (Monument $18.)
Amos, Ollie, Mrs., (purchaser)
Childs, Walter H.
Box 3 File 63 1909
Names in File:
Vermont Will Probate
Childs, Walter H., (will)
Childs, Charles Frederick, (son)
Childs, George Arthur, (son)

Estate Record Name
Childs, Walter H. (Cont.)
Property in DeKalb Co.
Sawyers, Chas. M. T., (atty)
Chitwood, Elizabeth
Box 3 File 64 1909-1910
Names in File:
Chitwood, M. A., (adm, son)
Chitwood, James N.
Russell, W. W., (bond)
Killian, S. F., (bond)
Gilbreath, Stant, (appraiser)
Sargent, S. D. (appraiser)
Boggs, Anderson, (appraiser)
Croley, Jas. A., Judge
Presley, I. M., (guar.ad litem)
Hilyer, Johnie. (minor)
Downer, Ethel, (minor)
Downer, Luther, (minor)
Downer, Elmer, (minor)
Downer, Ollie, (minor)
Chitwood, Henry B., (minor)
Chitwood, M. A.
Chitwood, James N.
Chitwood, W. W.
Payne, Eliza J., (w/o F.M.)
Chitwood, R. J.
Chitwood, R. H.
Chitwood, Walter S.
McNaron, Sarah, (w/o W. R.)
Andrew, Ennis (Emmir)
Bates, Belle, (w/o Ollie)
Downer, Charles
Downer, Lillie
Chitwood, Henry Bradford
Payne, F. M., (h/o Eliza)
McNaron, W. R.. (h/o Sarah)
Andrews, James, (h/o Emmir)
Bates, Ollie, (h/o Belle)
Hilyer, John, (h/o Johnnie)
Downer, Charles, (guardian)
Etherly, Cora, (minor)

Estate Record Name
Chitwood, Elizabeth (Cont.)
Jackson, Luther, (minor)
Downer, Horace, (minor)
Downer, Ollie, (minor)
Downer, Addie
Davis & Pope, (atty)
Ware, Beulah Lacy, (guardian)
Gilbreath, Stant
Mitchell, W. J.
Bynum, Sam
Pickens, J. M.
Boggs, William
Jacoway, Bob
Downer, Charley
Estes, John
Robbins, Walker
Collins, J. P.
Mikels, C. C., (tombstone $21.)
Warren, F. M., (tax coll-1909)
Downer, W. C.
Gilbert, J. G.
Chitwood, M. A., (adm)
Chitwood, Reuben & William
Box 3 File 65 1867
Names in File:
Frazier, P. B., (guardian)
Sheffard, James M., (bond)
Slone, Jesse, (bond)
Chitwood, Reuben, (minor)
Chitwood, William P., (minor)
Chitwood, Pleasant, (heirs)
Choate, Austin
Box 3 File 66 1861-1871
Names in File:
Griffin, Wm., (Ex Off.Adm.)
Nicholsen, D. L., (atty)
Griffin, R., (witness)
Eldridge, Wm. H., (due note)
Carmichael, G. J., (due note)
Gray, J. B., (due note)
Horton, A. J., Judge

Estate Record Name

Choate, Austin (Cont.)
Hayden, Thomas
Moon, A. W.
Worthington, L.
Chote/Choat/Choate

Clarkson, D. J.
Box 3 File 67 1832
Names in File:
Lamar, James, (guardian, atty)
Lameri/(Lamar
Clarkson, Lucy, (minor)
Clarkson, Sarah, (minor)
Taylar, Elizabeth, (minor)
Clarkson, Susan, (minor)
Ward, O. W., (appraiser)
Callins, Alfred, (appraiser)
Value of 6-Negroes
Moses & Alby
Letin & Sandy
Louise & Jonnah

Clary, David A.
Box 3 File 68 1891-1901
Names in File:
Massachusetts Will
Reister, John Edwards
Clary, Kate L., (widow)
Clary, David Gordon Hull
Clary, Gordon McKay (son)
Clary, David A., (grandson)
Patridge, Harvey W., (exec)
Clary, Kate L., (exec.)
Gleason, Monroe, (witness)
Haight, Jonathan, (witness)
Waterman, A. J., (witness)
Kennedy, Alex
Bowerman, Gratia E.
Robinson, J. T., (Judge Mass.)
Shocum, E. T., (Reg. Mass)
Will filed in DeKalb Co. AL

Clayton, M. A.
Box 3 File 69 1896

Estate Record Name

Clayton, M. A. (Cont.)
Names in File:
DeShields, J. G., (adm de bouis)
Clayton, Nannie, (widow)
Clayton, Sampson, (son)
Clayton, Clifford, (son)
Clayton, Fannie,(dau.)
Clayton, Hoss, (son)
Stewart, Thos. G., (adm)
Cook, W. C. D., Judge
Cochran, L. L.
The Coosa River News
Jackson, James, (lot near)
Jackson, Martha J.(Purch.lot)
Stewart, Thomas G., (purch land)
Fort Payne Journal
Reece, Dovine, (land known as)
Stewart, Thomas G., (purch.lot)
DeShields, John G., (Adm)

Clayton, Stephen C
Slayton, Stephen C.
Box 3 File 70 1904
Names in File:
Wrong Name on Folder
Chitwood, Rebecca J., (exec)
Slayton, Stephen C.
Chitwood, W. P., (bond)
Warren, C. W., (bond)
Siniard, Palistine
Croley, Jas. A. Judge

Clayton, M. L.
Box 3 File 71 1909
Names in File:
Clayton, Mollie B., (widow)
Clayton, Mollie B., (adm)
Crump, J. C., (bond)
Crump, C. J., (bond)
Croley, Jas. A., Judge
Clayton, Ona L., (minor)
Clayton, Carl, (minor)
Clayton, James, (minor)

Estate Record Name
Clayton, M. L. (Cont.)
Clayton, Mary O., (minor)
Clayton, Arlie Jay, (minor)
Clayton, Jesse
Clayton, Baxter L., (minor)
Clayton, Floriene, (minor)
Clayton, M. L., (minor)
Clayton, Mollie B., (guardian)
Clayton, Mollie B., (mother)
Clayton, A. L., (guar.bond)
Clayton, O. W., (guar.bond)
Clayton, B. M., (guar.bond)
Clayton, M. B., (Mollie)
Owens, E. M., (NP)
Pope, J. D., (guar.ad litem)
Clayton, M. L., (minor heirs)
Jones, E. B., (purch. land)
80 acres - $422.00
Clayton, W. W.
Box 3 File 72 1876-1877
Names in File:
Heirs:
Clayton, Robert B., (adm)
Smith, Nancy M., (w/o A.P.)
Bradley, Mary P., (w/o W. S.)
Clayton, W. C.
Coffie, Lucinda S., (w/o W.H..)
Clayton, Cash M., (minor)
Clayton, Monah L., (minor)
Clayton, Martha, (minor)
Smith, A. P., (h/o Nancy)
Bradley, W. S., (h/o Mary P.)
Coffie, W. H., (h/o Lucinda S.)
Smith, M. L. (w/o William)
Smith, William, (h/o M. L.)
Clayton, William
Smith, Charles W., (appraiser)
Black, Geo. W., (appraiser)
Cochran, W. W., (appraiser)
Brandon, P. A., Judge
Elrod, W. A., (paid)

Estate Record Name
Clayton, W. W. (Cont.)
Webb, Henry, (paid)
Sale of Property:
Bradley, W. S., (house)
Clayton, R. B., (wagon)
Clayton, R. B., (Buggy)
Smith, A. P., (sorrel mare)
Clayton, R. B., (sorrel mule)
Clayton, Wm. B., (mule colt)
Frazier, Levi, (Black Ox)
Clayton, R. B., (yellow cow)
Smith, A. P., (hog)
Bradley, W. S., (hog)
Clayton, R. B., (hog)
Clayton, L. S., Miss, (wash pot)
Frazier, Levi, (saddle)
Smith, A. P., (shovel & spade)
Bradley, W. S., (saw & auger)
Clayton, R. B., (2-axes)
Clayton, R. B., (bridle)
Wilbanks, James, (bridle)
Smith, A. P., (shovel plow)
Clayton, Wm. C. (shovel plow)
Morris, J. W., (Log chain)
Cook, J. W., (plow stock)
Smith, A. P., (pr. harness)
Bradley, W. S. (plow,chains)
Clayton, W. C., (hames)
Clayton, R. B.,(cow bell)
Clayton, W. C., (hames)
Clayton, W. C., (cobbler last)
Smith, A. P., (spinning wheel)
Black, E. W., Clerk
Rucks, E. P., Clerk
Cochran, L. L.
Box 3 File 73 1912
Names in File:
Cochran, Maggie M., (exec)
Cochran, Maggie M., (widow)
3-children:
Cochran, Earl

Estate Record Name

Cochran, L. L. (Cont.)
McCartney, Maggie, Mrs.
Cochran, Lucian, Jr., (minor)
Presley, I. M., (guar.ad litem)
Haralson, J. B., (witness)
Cook, T. C., (witness)
McCartney, C. H., (h/o Maggie)
Croley, Jas. A., Judge
Cochran, M. M., (adm)

Coker, William D., Sr.
Box 3 File 74 1902-1910
Names in File:
Coker, Margaret, (widow)
Coker, W. D., Jr., (exec)
Coker, Lee R., (exec)
Sons of deceased:
Coker, W. D., Jr.
Coker, Lee
Coker, O. D.
Coker, J. D.
Coker, Walter
Coker, Paul
Coker, H. P.
Daughters of deceased:
Nave, Lizzie, (w/o J. P.)
Tidmore, Mollie, (w/o W. H.)
Dobbs, Jennie, (w/o Frank)
Smith, Julia, (w/o Houston)
Tidmore, Emmer, (w/o J. P.)
Coker, Jessie, (minor)
Coker, Margaret, (guardian)
Coker, Margaret, (mother)
Croley, Jas. A., Judge
Nave, J. P., (h/o Lizzie)
Tidmore, W. H., (h/o Mollie)
Dobbs, Frank, (h/o Jennie)
Smith, Houston, (h/o Julia)
Tidmore, J. P., (h/o Emma)
Dobb, R. F.
Tidmore, William H.
Nave, James P.

Estate Record Name

Coker, William D., Sr. (Cont.)
Nave, S. E.
Coker, J. W.
Tidmore, Emmer Van
Coker, J. C.
DeShields, (guar.ad.litem)
Small, Henry, (appraiser)
Cochran, T. F., (appraiser)
Tidmore, Jas. W.
Payments:
Halls, Dry Goods
Miller, J. F., (physician)
Roberts, G. W., Sr.
Smith, R. H., (JP)
Appleton, T. H.
Warren, F. M., (tax coll-1910)
Myers, T. F.
Presley, I. M.
Bartlett, John T.
Roberts, J. W.
Graves, W. L. (tax coll-1904)
Cain, Wall, (tax coll-1905)
Receipts from Notes:
McKenzie, W.
Jolly, L. M.
Copeland, S. H.
Johnson, David
Morgan, S. J.
Roberts, W. R.
Dobbs, R. F.
Croley, J. A.
Miller, J. T.
Tidwell, J. W.
Tidwell, W. J.
Coker, J. D.
Warren, S. D.
Receipts from Notes (cont.):
Chitwood, C. C.
Morgan, J. A.
Roberts, Chas.
Watson, G. M.

Estate Record Name

Coker, William D., Sr. (Cont.)
Dobbs, Frank
Morgan, John
Roberts, W. R.
Roberts, Chas.
Roberts, Nannie
Lowry, T. C.
Lowry, C. W.
Bates, Geo.
Tyler, W. W.
Kuykendale, T. A.
Coker, Walter, (purch.land)
Coker, L. R., (purch.land)

Coleman, Elizabeth H.
(Widow of John Coleman)
Box 3 File 75 1908
Names in File:
Massachusetts Will
Coleman, John
Coleman, James W., (son)
Coleman, Walter G., (son)
Rogers, William E.
McIntire, Charles F.
Cutting, Fannie Coleman
Cutting, Elizabeth Swanton
Cutting, Henry
Cutting, Herbert
Newel, Emily, Mrs.
Kerr, Maggie
Smith, Mary Amelia
Williams, Harriet
Garrington, Harry A.
Cutting, Harper
Cutting, Ida May
Coleman, Sara J.
Harlow, Ella Elizabeth, Mrs.
Wheeler, Lilla Valentine, Mrs.
Coleman, Eva Frances
Newell, Emily, Mrs.
Rowe, Charles P.
Prouty, James L, Jr.

Estate Record Name

Coleman, Elizabeth H. (Cont.)
Jose, Edwin H.
Sawyers, Chas. M. T., (atty)

Coleman, Thomas A.
Box 3 File 76 1885-1886
Names in File:
Coleman, Thomas A., Estate
Coleman, Sarah Ann, (widow)
Johnson, Mary Jane, (petition)
Children named in will:
Coleman, James G., (son)
Johnson, Mary Jane, (dau.)
Johnson, Samuel, (h/o Mary J.)
Stovall, Martha Victory, (dau)
Stovall, Eugene, (h/o Martha)
Lacky, Rebecca Malinda, (dau)
Lacky, Levi, (h/o Rebecca)
Loveless, Mary Jane, (g-dau)
Hodges, J. W. (wit. to will)
Lusk, T. B., (witness to will)
Alexander, P. M., (witness)
Coleman, R. T., (witness)
Coleman, J. C.
Coleman, G. H.
Loveless, Green B.
Lacky, Victor L,(g.-son)
Stovall, R. E.
End of Microfilm Roll No. 63

Collins, Alfred
Box 3 File 77 1879-1882
Names in File:
Collins, J. H., (adm)
Collins, Mahala, (widow,adm)
Heirs:
Collins, Mahala E.
Collins, James H.
Roberts, Sallie E.,(w/o G. W.)
Roberts, G. W.
Collins, Tipton B.
Collins, N. S.
Kirby, Julia E., (w/o M. W.)

Estate Record Name
Collins, Alfred (Cont.)
Kirby, M. W.
Reed, Cornelia C., (w/o Wm. D.)
Reed, William D.
Collins, John W.
Collins, F. C.
Collins, Mahala E. (bond)
Collins, J. H. (bond)
Collins, Tipton B., (bond)
Collins, F. C., (bond)
Collins, J. W., (bond)
Reed, W. D., (bond)
Reed, C. C., (bond)
Collins, W. S., (bond)
Roberts, Sallie E., (w/o G. W.)
Smith, George S., (bond)
Williams, Dewitt C., (bond)
Jordan, Henry R., (bond)
Reed. James P., (bond)
Petty, W. D., (bond)
Hall, O. L., (bond)
Brandon, P. A., Judge
Franklin, John N., Judge
Petty, Wiley D., (appraiser)
Jordan, H. D., (appraiser)
Roberts, W. J., (appraiser)
Brandon, Phillip A., Judge
Hall, J. M., (comm.)
Hall, Bryan, (comm)
Williams, D. C., (comm)
Mackey, A. H., (comm)
Watts, L. B., (comm)
McNutt, R. C., (sheriff)
McNutt, J. I. (dep.sheriff)
Notes Due:
Tiner, James C.
Roberts, M. J.
Chaney, John
Chaney, A. G.
Reed, W. D.
Long, W. R.

Estate Record Name
Collins, Alfred (Cont.)
Collins, N. S.
Keener, P.
Cooper, G. W.
Bishop, R. S.
Chitwood, R.
Carr, Peter
Bidwell, S. W.
Roberts, W. P.
Roberts, J. W.
Petty, W. D.
Fenney?, J. E.
Heard, J. T.
Roberts, W. T.
Kirby, M. W.
George, C. D., Estate
Estes, Ruben
Payments:
Daley, P. C.(2 marble stones)
Collins, Alfred & Mahala
Ferguson, W. L., (tax coll 1879)
Davis, R. C., (tax coll. 1880)
Winston, J. M., MD (medical)
Stuart, John, (JP)
Petty, W. S.
Jorden, H. R.
Vann, A. P.
Lynch, Newton
Land, T. B.
Heard, J. T.
Williams, D. C.
Malone, R. J.
Cain, R. W.
Wright, Jas. W.
Masters, J. M., (surveyor)
Cooper, G. W.
Fielder, N. W.
Dobbs, L. A.
Fischer & Bros.
Smith & Roberts
Yarbrough, J. W.

Estate Record Name
Collins, Alfred (Cont.)
Williams, D. C.
Hall, Mackey & Co.
Collins, S. W.
Goen, A. B.
Tiner, James A.
Malone, George W.
Payne, H. P.
Green, A. B.
Lynch, Newton
Hall, O. L., (agent)
Tiner, J. C.
Dodds, L. A.
Fishel & Bros., Nashville
Payne, A. F.
Coker, J. W.
Chitwood, R., (register)
Frazier, P. M.
Turnley, M. J.
Malon, R. J.
Clayton, M. A., (JP)
Malone, Leo W.
Malone, E. H.
Collins, Mollie
Collins, F. C.
Box 3 File 78 1875-1885
Names in File:
Collins, N. S., (adm)
Kirby, M. W., (adm)
Collins, Mahala E.
Collins, James H.
Collins, Alfred, (estate)
Kirby, M. W., (bond)
Collins, N. S., (bond)
Reed, W. D., (bond)
Collins, J. H. (bond)
Collins, John W., (bond)
Liner, James, (NP)
Meeks, M. M., (adv.)
Gadsden Times
Heirs:

Estate Record Name
Collins, F. C. (Cont.)
Collins, J. H.
Collins, N. S.
Collins, T. B.
Collins, John W.
Roberts, Sallie E.
Kirby, Julia E. Collins
Reed, Cornelia C., (dec'd.)
Reed, Carrie, (minor)
Reed, Emma L., (minor)
Reed, Walter T., (minor)
Reed, W. D., (guar.of minors)
Roberts, G. W.,(h/o Sallie E.)
Roberts, S. E., (Sallie)
Kirby, M. W., (h/o Julia)
Collins, Tipton B., (T. B.)
Hall, O. S., (witness)
Williams, D. C., (witness)
Tiner, J. C., (comm.)
Sales of property:
Roberts, Sallie,(curtians & shades)
Collins, N.S., (scrap iron)
Watson, G. M., (blacksmith tools)
Roberts, G. W., (land $2114.50)
(Alfred Collins Homestead)
Watson, G. M., (pur. land $156.75)
Robinson, Andy,(purch.land $51.)
Roberts, George W.
Notes Due:
Burnette, W. T.
Hairell, John
Boyd, John W.
Nicholson, B. H.
Nicholson, W. D.
Kirby, M. W.
Reed, W. D.,
Collins, J. H.
Strickland, Barbara
George, Ellen
George, James
George, Mary

Estate Record Name
Collins, F. C. (Cont.)
Edwards, John
Edwards, Nettie
Malone, George W.
Winston, John W.
George, Robert
Franklin, John, Judge
Spencer, G. M. D. (taxes)
Fielder, George W.
Ford, J. L.
Dobbs, L. A., (atty)
Smith, Thomas, (adv.)
Fort Payne Journal
Collins, Mary
Box 3 File 79 1893-1895
Names in File:
Collins, J. H., (adm)
Pope, W. E., (bond)
Collins, J. Alfred, (minor)
Collins, W. S., (minor)
Collins, Della A., (minor)
Collins, Frank C., (minor)
Collins, J. H., (guardian)
Collins, Willie
Kirby, Fannie
Reed, Sarah C. (estate)
Collins, Mary, (g.-dau.)
Collins, M. A., (dec'd.)
Allen, Douglass
Cook, W. C. D., Judge
Conaway, John W.
Box 3 File 80 1865-1870
Names in File:
Conway/Conaway
McLeod/ McCland, Mary
McCland/ McLeoad, Mary
Gasque, Martha
Gasque, Milton
Gasque, William
Conaway, Margaret
Conaway, Sarah

Estate Record Name
Conaway, John W. (Cont.)
Conaway, Elizabeth
Conaway, James
Conaway, Joshua
Evett (Everett)
Evett, E.
Evett, W. H.
Conaway, Rachel
Conaway, Wm.
Conaway, John, (dec'd.)
Conaway, R. P., (adm)
Gasque, John M., (adm)
Kean, Jane
Slaton, Susan
Slaton, Elisha
Slaton, Polly Ann
Smith, Salley
Everett, Elizabeth, (w/o W.M.)
Gasque, Milton, (h/o Martha)
Green, Grief F., (witness)
Kean, Elcanay, (witness)
Dunlap & Dodds, (attys.)
Chitwood, Joel, (coroner)
Smith, Sally
Hoge, John K.
Haralson, W. J.
Griffin, Wm., (sheriff)
Haralson & Collins, (attys.)
Haralson, Wm. J. (pur.land)
Gibson, Jacob, (pur. land)
Cunningham, John, (pur.land)
Griffin, Wm.
Lewis, John, (estate)
Green, G. S., (appraiser)
Thomason, J. F., (appraiser)
King, James R., (appraiser)
Lyons, Thomas, (JP)
Griffin, Wm.,(Adm. ex.off.)
Horton, A. J., Judge
Sale of Personal Property:
Rachel Conway, (wash pot)

Estate Record Name

Conaway, John W. (Cont.)
McCland, Polly, (oven)
Conway, R. P., (Wagon)
Conway, R. P., (Log chain)
McCland, (2-sheep)
Lankford, P. G., (2-sheep)
Lillie, T. J., (2-sheep)
Conway, Sarah
Conway, Joshua, (1-steer)
Conway, Joshia,(augers. hand saw)
Conway, Joshia, (drawing knife)
Lankford, W. A., (2-single trees)
Lankford, J. N., (1-double tree)
Conway, Joshua, (axe)
Holburra, Sarah, (pail)
Carson, Wm., (hames & grubbing)
Lyons, Thomas, (square & spade)
Duncan, R. D., (chain & pin)
Conway Joshua, (clevis iron)
Dooly, Isaih, (1-single tree)
Conway, Joshua, (hammer)
Conway, R. P., (syth & blade)
Duncan, R.. D., (1-box sundries)
Lankford, W. A., (pr.chains)
Conway, Joshua (pr.hames)
Lankford, W. A. (pr. iron chains)
Staton, Elisha, (2-plow stocks)
Shankles, Elizabeth (1-plow stock)
Everett, Wm., (rent of land)

Condra, Emma M.

Condra. Lula E.

Condra, George E.
Box 3 File 81 1884-1890
Names in File:
Condra, B. C., (children)
Condra, Emma M., (minor)
Condra, Lula E., (minor)
Condra, George E., (minor)
Condra, Benj. C. heirs
Brock, Wilburn, (guardian)
Fuller, W. T. (Guardian ad litem)

Estate Record Name

Condra, George E. (Cont.)
Frazier, P. M., (sheriff)
Slone, Lula Condra
Slone, Sam C.
McSpadden, Hiram A., (bond)
Frazier, Polland B., (bond)
Dobbs & Howard, (atty.)
Cochran, L. L.

Condra, Charley & George
Box 3 File 82 1890
Names in File:
Condra, B. C., Heirs
Condra, Charley, (minor)
Condra, George, (minor)
Condra, Emma, (guardian)
Conda, Emma, (sister of minors)
Nix, Joe J., (bond)
Killian, E. S., (bond)

Cook, Benjamin F.
Box 3 File 83 1886
Names in File:
Cook, W. C. D., (Exec.)
Cook, Lemuel A.
Lowry, Manora A.
Lowry, F. M.
Driskill, Maggie
Driskill, Sanford
Cochran, L. L., Judge
Durham, Benj. D., (JP)
Hill, R. L., (witness)
Cook, W. C.
Cook, L. A.
Welch, P. L., (witness)
Rice, Walter, (witness)
Driskill, S. C.
Painter, A. J., (witness)
Blancit, R. L., (witness)
Blanset, A. D., Jr., (witness)
Cochran, R. L., Judge

Cook, Ida C.
Box 3 File 84 1892

Estate Record Name

Cook, Ida C. (Cont.)
- Cook, Ida C., (minor)
- Martin, Amanda, (mother)
- Martin, James C.,(guardian)
- Clardy, Norman S. (heir of)
- Cook, Joshua W., (bond)
- Howard, James M., (bond)
- Rucks, E. P., (witness)
- DeShields, J. G., (sheriff)
- Cook, W. C. D.
- Cochran, Earl
- Pickens, A. W.
- Cook, Alta, Mrs. (Adm.)

Cook, J. W.
- Box 3 File 85 1906-1919
- Names in File:
- Cook, T. J., (adm.)
- Cook, Sarah A., (widow)
- Croley, Nancy E. (w/o W.O.)
- Croley, W. O.
- Phillips, Hattie P.,(w/o W.F.)
- Phillips, W. F.
- Nichols, Callie, (Mrs. P. C.)
- Nichols, P. C.
- Lowery, Lou, (dec'd.)
- Lowery, Hattie P., (minor)
- Lowrey, Ocie, (minor)
- Lowrey, Orien, (minor)
- Lowery D. R., (guardian)
- Pruett, S. L., (guard.ad litem)
- Black, J. E., (appraiser)
- Pruett, S. L., (appraiser)
- Nichols, W. N., (appraiser)
- Houston, A. W., (witness)
- Copeland, A. C., (witness)
- Slone, S. B., (took depositions)
- Cook, S. A.
- Croley, J. A., Judge
- Nichols, C. L.
- Croley, W. C.
- Cook, T. J., (adm., bond)

Estate Record Name

Cook, J. W. (Cont.)
- Cook, W. C. D., (bond)
- Haralson, J. B., (bond)
- Slone, S. B. (bond)
- Homestead Exemption
- Phillips, Hattie M. (pur.land)
- Croft, W. B., (purchased land)
- Phillips, H. M.
- Croley, N. E.
- Phillips,W. F., (pur.land)
- **Notes Due:**
- Cook, T. C.
- Croft, T. W.
- Dalrumple, J. B.
- Denton, B. F.
- Daughtry, J. M.
- Dollar, J. C.
- Copeland, M. W.
- Crumbley & Son
- Coker, W. D.
- Erwin, L. F.
- Fuller, W. R..
- Elrod, H. W.
- Graham, F. C.
- Haynie, E. N.
- Gaines, R. A.
- Graham, H. M.
- Hurt, W. E.
- Gibbs, J. M.
- Harrison, J. J.
- Ivey, N. T.
- Jolly, L. M.
- Lassater, W. J.
- Law, C. J.
- Lowry, D. R.
- Litsey, W. F.
- McMahan, J. W.
- McDavid, J. M.
- Pruett, J. M.
- Peace, D. J.
- Sparks, J.

Estate Record Name
Cook, J. W. (Cont.)
Stephens, J. M.
Stevens, J. W.
Smalley, G. M.
Tidmore, M. J., Mrs.
Williams, J. H.
Crumly, M. J.
Allen, B. L.
Bruce, Bolus
Nichols, C. F.
Spencer, J. C,
Ridgeway, W. M.
Mauer, T. A.
Copeland, A. B.
Waller, John
Truce, Baylus
Nichols, C. L.
Copeland, J. B.
Fuller, P. N.
Monroe, T. F.
Cook & Presley, (attys)
Cain, Wall
Cook, W. C. D.
Box 3 File 86 1907-1908
Names in File:
Cook, Alta, Mrs., (widow)
Homestead Exemption
Cook, William B., (minor)
Cook, Clarra G., (minor)
Cook, Sarah G., (minor)
Cook, Joe W., (minor)
Cook, Ruth G., (minor)
Cook, Alta, (admx.)
Brock, H. B., (comm.)
Banning, H. M., (comm.)
McCartney, John H., (comm.)
Copeland, A. C., (guar.ad litem)
Cook, B. H.
Cook, J. M.
Lawrence, Florence, Mrs.
Cook, Maggie

Estate Record Name
Cook, W. C. D. (Cont.)
Cook, Jas. W.
Cook, Len D.
Cook, William B.
Moore, Ida, Mrs. (dec'd)
Moore, Willie (minor)
Moore, Alvin, (minor)
Moore, Viola. (minor)
Moore, Lola, (minor)
Moore, Harris, (minor)
Cook, T. J., (bond)
Jacoway, W. V., (bond)
Russell, W. W. (bond)
Downs, T. L., (sheriff)
Nations, W. T. (dep.sheriff)
McSpadden, H. A., (witness)
Presley, I. M., (witness)
Vann, S. J., (purch.farm)
Campbell, H. B.
DeShields, J. G., (witness)
Berry, Minnie,(took depositions)
Isbell & Presley, (attys)
Sales of Personal Property:
Jacoway, W. V., (binder)
Fisher, Wm., (disc plow)
Jacoway, Fred (2-horse wagon)
Jacoway, W. V., (turning plow)
Young, G. T., (2-horse wagon)
Jacoway, W. V., (mower)
Fisher, Wm., (plow stock)
Warren, F. M.,(plow stock)
Vann, S. J., (plow stock)
Wean, Walter, (plows)
Presswood, Will, (harrow)
Warren, F. M., (scythe blade)
Vann, S. J., (scythe blade)
Pell, Jas., (collar)
Scott, G. W., (buggy)
Hall, T. H., (harrow)
Jacoway, W. V., (cow)
Presswood, Will, (heifer)

Estate Record Name
Cook, W. C. D. (Cont.)
Jacoway, W. V., (yearling)
Scott, G. V., (disc harrow)
Warren, F. M., (plow)
Cain, Wall, (tax pd.-1907)
Brandon Bros. (pd.for casket)
Insolvency-Creditors:
Dobbs, Laura A.
Cunningham, J.
DeKalb Co. Bank
White Star Market
Peek, L. H.
Brock, H. B.
Malone, G. L.
Fort Payne Water Co.
Wade, Henry
McKinnon, A.
Warren, W. E.
Williams & Tiner
Dobbs, Emma
Russell, W. W.
State of Alabama
Cook, Alta
Campbell & Lankford
Quin, W. E.
McCartney & Co
Smith, Thomas H.
Cooper, E. C., Mrs.
Box 3 File 87 1910
Names in File:
Tumlin, T. J., (Exec.)
Ryan, W. T., (Exec.)
Dickerson, J. N., (witness)
Liles, L. A., (witness)
Jackson, Nealy
McGhee, Rosan
Williams, Mattie, (dec'd)
Williams, James H.
Jarmon, Lula
Jarmon, Caloin, (minor)
Jarmon, Lyman, (minor)

Estate Record Name
Cooper, E. C., Mrs. (Cont.)
Jarmon, Herman, (minor)
Jarmon, Alice, (minor)
Jarmon, W. T., (guardian)
Jarman (Jarmon)
Trible, W. H.
Trible, M. H.
Parsons, L. L., (JP)
Howard & Hunt, (attys)
Notes & Personal Estate:
Trible, W. H.
Trible, M. F.
Jaco, Jasper
Coleman, W. L.
Gravitt, L.
Dalrymple, J. B.
Williams, H. B.
Baker, M. W.
Wilks, J. T.
Adams, W. A.
Stackman/Stockman, R. L.
Light, L. L.
Partwood, W. J.
Bailey, W. H.
Thomas, R. L.
Yancy, Delana
Southerland, W. A.
Curtis, W. B.
Lee, A. B.
Uptan, David
Cash - Merchants Bank
Cooper, James H.
Box 3 File 88 1887
Names in File:
Cooper, Sallie C., (widow)
Homestead Exemption
Lay, Nancy W.
Campbell, Martha A.
Haygood, Thomas C.
Adams, Sallie
Adams, George W., (guar.)

Estate Record Name

Cooper, James H. (Cont.)
Clayton, Dow (L. D.), (comm)
King, Samuel, (comm.)
New, Luke L., (JP)
Bradford, Wm.
Norris, Jack
Clayton, Mrs.
Beck, E. H., (atty, JP)

Cooper, William
Box 3 File 89 1909-1911
Names in File:
Cooper, E. C., Mrs., (widow)
Homestead Exemption
Ryan, W. T., (adm) (friend)
Tumlin, T. J., (adm) (friend)
Cooper, Joseph
Williams, J. H.
Jarman, W. T., (guardian)
Jarman, Lula, Mrs.
Howard, M. W. (bond)
Cook, T. J., (bond)
Young, B. B., (appraiser)
Thomas, Rich, (appraiser)
Kelley, Joe, (appraiser)
Cooper, W. K., (B'ham.)
Gary, Wm. H.
Cooper, Julius B.
Gaudin Undertaking Co.
Gaudin, Jas. T., (B'ham.)
Un-named 3-Brothers
Jarmon, Lula, (witness)
Yancy, T. P., (NP)
Haralston, P. P.
Fort Payne Journal
Young, J. B.
Thomas, R. L.
Howard, M. W., Mrs.
Kelly, J. T.
Cooper, William, (dec'd)
Evans, W. D., (paid)
Kirkland, R., (paid)

Estate Record Name

Cooper, William (Cont.)
Brown, Joe, (paid)
Cooper, W. K., (paid)
Cooper, Julius B, Physician
Oliver & Hunt Co., (paid)
Hall, O. L. (Jobber)
Oliver Hall Co., (retail merch)
Brindley, V. M., (NP)
Hall, Irby C.
Jarman, Lula, (Minor Heirs)
Cooper, Frances, (summons)
Strickland, L. M., (sheriff)
Lantham, E. E., (sheriff)
Sale of Personal Property:
Britt, Henry, (scratcher)
DeBerry, J. A., (plow stock)
Brooks, Will, (Irons)
Brooks, Will, (buggy &harness)
Lee, R. E., wagon)
Bailey, G. P., (blacksmith tools)
Kirkland, Reuben, (clerk)
Brown, Josiah, (cashier)
Eason, O. B., (feather bed)
Hall, J. O., (watch)
Jarmon, Lula, (feather bed)
Stapp, Jno., (shovel)
Downs, T. L., (guano distr.)
Jones, B. C., (plow stock)
Carson, J. L., (hoe)
Britte, H. L.
Smith, Wilbur, (hand saw)
Fossatt, G. B., (square)
Harris, E. A., (spoke auger)
Hall, O. L., (1-broad ax)
Strickland, B. J,, (planes)
Blackwell, T. H., (draw knife)
Downs, T. L., (2-augers)
Kelly, J. T., (monkey wrench)
Kelly, J. T., (1-gun)
Gilbert, Longs, (2-chairs)
Stapp, Jno., (2-chairs)

Estate Record Name

Cooper, William (Cont.)
- Kelly, J. T., (2-chairs)
- Cannon, J. L., (2-chairs)
- Gilbert, G. W., Mrs., (desk)
- Cannon, G. L., (table)
- Kirkland, G. H., (Iron bedstead)
- Myricks, R. G., (1-auger)
- Wilson, H. B., (brace & bit)
- Curtis, W. B., (fiddle)
- Blackwell, R. F., (1-bureau)
- Baley, J. S., (rocking chair)
- Jones, B. C., (rocking chair)
- McBrayer, (1-safe)
- Thomas, Bell, (sewing machine)
- Cannon, J. L., (1-table)
- Murdock, J. O., (bedstead)
- Godwin, C. B., (bedstead)
- Fossett, G. B.
- Hall, J. W.
- **Notes Due:**
- Wright, J. W. J.
- Trible, W. H.
- Trible, M. F.
- Jaco, W. L.
- Gravitt, L.
- Dalrymple, J. B.
- Wilson, H. B.
- Baker, M. W.
- Wilks, J. T.
- Adams, W. A.
- Stockman, R. L.
- Light, L. L.
- Partwood, W. J.
- Bailey, W. H.
- Coleman, W. L.
- Thomas, R. L.
- Yancy, Delana
- Southerland, H. A.
- Curtis, W. B.
- Lee, A. B.
- Uptain, David

Estate Record Name

Cooper, William (Cont.)
- First National Bank, B'ham.
- Cooper, William
- Cooper, Julius
- Kelly, J. T.
- Baxter, J. W.
- Land, 200 acres

Copeland, James A.
- Box 3 File 90 1880-1888
- Names in File:
- Copeland, A. C., (adm.)
- Copeland, Nancy, (widow)
- Copeland, Samuel H.
- Copeland, John T.
- Copeland, William L.
- Copeland, W. L.
- Cook, Sarah A.
- Cook, J. W., (h/o Sarah A.)
- Graham, Mary J.
- Graham, W. B., (h/o Mary J.)
- Crumley, Margaret E.
- Crumley, A. C., (h/o Margaret)
- Bryant, Ella M.
- Bryant, J. W., (h/o Ella M.)
- Bryant, Harriet A.
- Bryant, J. F., (h/o Harriet A.)
- Copeland, Alexander A., (Adm)
- Morris, J. W., (appraiser)
- Jones, E. B., (appraiser)
- Croft, J. H., (appraiser)
- Bryan, Nancy L.
- Small, Henry
- Nicholson, M. M.
- Haralson, W. H., (guardian)
- Franklin, A. G., (sheriff)
- Haralson, W. W.,(guar.ad litem)
- Hall, Mackey & Co
- Nicholson & Howard
- Howard, M. W., (atty.)
- Smith, Thos. H.
- *Fort Payne Journal*

Estate Record Name
Copeland, James A. (Cont.)
Rape, W. M.
Dodds, L. A., (atty.)
Nicholson, B. H., (atty)
Russell, A. G., (Landers Adm.)
Landers, T. F., (estate)
Small, W. A.
Revel, E. R., (atty)
Crumley, M. E.
Clayton, C. C.
Tidwell, C. N.
Tidwell, William
Cochran, L. L., Judge
Lowrey, Alva
Bryant, Nancy L.
Davis, Reuben C., (tax-1883)
Williams, D. C., (burial exp.)
Carter, C. L., (clerk at sale)
Chastain, John B., (clerk at sale)
Nunn, John R., (note pd.)
Nicholson, B. H., (legal ser.)
McClain, M. S.
Black, E. W., (comm.)
Nicholsen, L. S., (comm)
Frazier, P. M.
Henry, A. G.
Fricks Bros.
Notes Due:
Tidwell, C. W.
Crumley, J. C.
Crumley, T. J.
Coker, W. D.
Coker, T. H.
Hodges, B. E.
Copeland, Pinkney
Mills, W. K.
Copeland, J. C.
Talley, John
Self, J. C.
Nicholson, B. H.
Copeland, A. C.

Estate Record Name
Copeland, James A. (Cont.)
Bryant, J. F.
Cochran, W. W.
Mathen, J. H.
Caldwell, C. A.
Copeland, James
Croft, Joseph H.
Payments:
Scott, Calvin
Copeland, Wm. L. (mail business)
Tidwell, C. N. (mail business)
Morton, J. M.
Nunn, John F.
Copeland, Alexander C.
Crumly, J. C., (work on house)
Crumly, T. J., (work on house)
Graham, W. B.
Crumly, Jane
Beasley, Samuel B.
Croft, F. W.
Croft, Lucinda
Copeland, Wm. L., (mail carrier)
(Mail services 8-28-1884)
Franklin, A. G., (sheriff)
Davis, Reuben C., (tax-1884)
Nicholson, B. H., (atty)
Graham, W. B.
Graham, T. D.
Hays, J. H.
Hays, Georgia
Davis, R. C., (tax coll. -1885)
Steel, W. A., (tax coll.-1886)
Copeland, James H., (estate)
Graham, R. H., (engine repairs)
Pace, J. L., (JP)
Duncan, R. D., Mrs.
Long, Charles
Sparks, R.
Duncan, J. W.
Bileups, John A.
Swann, John

Estate Record Name

Copeland, James A. (Cont.)
- Brandon, H. H.
- Graham, W. B.
- Dobbs, S. E.
- Bryan, Nancy
- Lowrey, J. A.
- Small, M. L., (tuition-1883)
- Tiner, James
- Stewart, Thomas G.
- Ashberry, A. H.

Cordell, Isaac
- Box 3 File 91 1879
- Names in File:
- Hawk, James M., (adm)
- Allison, Joseph, (bond)
- Cordell, Kimsey, (bond)
- Cordell, Nancy, (widow)
- Cordell, Mary C., (over 21)
- Cordell, Susan E., (minor)
- Cordell, Jospeh Edwin, (minor)
- Cordell, Charlsie A., (minor)
- Cochran, L. L., Judge
- Brandon, P. A. Judge

Cordell, J. E., et al
- Box 3 File 92 1905
- Names in File:
- Sale of Land for Division
- Cordell, J. E.
- Cordell, Lizzie
- Cordell, Charlsie
- Ellis, Mary E., (dec'd)
- Ellis, Minnie E., (minor)
- Ellis, Ora May, (minor)
- Ellis, Laura A., (minor)
- Ellis, Charles T.
- Ellis, J. C., (guardian)
- DeShields, J. G., (guar.ad litem)
- Davenport, E. T., (witness)
- Faulkner, J. N. B., (JP)
- Ellis, C. T., (deposition)
- Culberson, C. Y., (take depos.)

Estate Record Name

Cordell, J. E., et al (Cont.)
- Crow, G. W., (purch.land)
- Presley, I. M., (comm.)

Cordell, J. E., et al
- Box 3 File 93 1909
- Names in File:
- Sale of Land for Division
- Cordell, J. E., (petitioner)
- Russell, Sam, (minor)
- Russell, C. H., (minor)
- Russell, Kate, (minor)
- Russell, H. C.
- Russell, J. H.
- Russell, M. L.
- Russell, B. J.
- Russell, B. Y.
- Russell, R. M.
- Cargile, M. V.
- Cargile, R. E.
- Cargile, R. L., (minor)
- Cargile, J. M.
- Hunt, Luke P., (guardian)
- Isbell & Presley, (attys)
- Crane, J. J., (deposition)
- Biddle, T. J., (deposition)
- Hall, P. C. (took testimony)
- Presley, I. M.
- Howard, M. W.
- Pope, J. D.
- Cargile, Russell, (heirs)
- Cordell, J. E., (purch. land)

Cotnam, Fannie
- Box 3 File 94 1896
- Names in File:
- Sale of Land for Division
- Malone, G. W., (estate)
- Cotnam, Fannie
- Malone, George L.
- Chitwood, Zoe
- Burnett, Lizzie
- Malone, Wallace C.

Estate Record Name
Cotnam, Fannie (Cont.)
Estes, Mary C.
Estes, John R.
Coleman, Fannie
Chitwood, R. J.
Chitwood, J. C.
Burnett, J. B.
Malone, S. J., (guardian)
Malone, George W.
Chitwood, Joel, (witness)
Horton, J. B.
Garrett, W. W., (comm)
Moore, Lance, (commissioner)
Collins, O. H., (atty)
Wills Creek
McCampbell's House
Cook, W. C. D., Judge
Cochran, L. L.
Couch, Eli
Box 3 File 95 1855
Names in File:
Newman, Moses C., (adm)
Paden, Robert, (bond)
Paden, John, (bond)
Baden (Paden)
Estes, R., Judge
Cox, E. C.
Box 3 File 96 1901-1902
Names in File:
Sale for Division of Land
Cox, Ida M. , (widow, plaintiff)
Cox, L. M., (plaintiff)
Hermes, Frank
Cox, Lela, (minor)
Cox, Wm. H., (minor)
Presley, I. M., (guar.ad litem)
Cox, Ida, vs: Hermes F.
Cox, Willie
Cox, Lelah
Cox, E. C., (dec'd.)
Isbell, John B., (commissioner)

Estate Record Name
Cox, E. C. (Cont.)
Nichols, John
Howard, Samuel, (deposition)
Dean, Thomas, (take deposition)
Howard & Isbell, (attys.)
Dean, Thomas S, (comm.)
Howard, S. M. J., (witness)
Cook, John M., (purch.land)
Crabtree, G. W.
Box 4 File 1 1902-1912
Names in File:
Crabtree, Jas. A., (adm.)
Thompson, Letha Ann Crabtree
Crabtree, Velma, (minor)
Crabtree, Eula, (minor)
Corbin, Bonnie, (minor)
Corbin, Dexter, (minor)
Phillips, Paul Corbin, (minor)
Presley, I. M., (guar.ad litem)
Crabtree, Permelia
Crabtree, Thomas
Crabtree, Samuel A.
Phillips, Margaret Crabtree
Lea, Samantha Crabtree
Crabtree, Martin
Crabtree, Ben
Crabtree, Andrew
Crabtree, Ellen
Bean, Samira Crabtree
Crabtree, Charlie, (bond)
Crabtree, Alphi
Crabtree, Elmire
Crabtree, F. M.
Crabtree, Alf
Crabtree, Susan
Crabtree, Henry
Jones, Eliza, Mrs.
Stalvey, Lizzie, Mrs.
Stalvey, George
Crabtree, Rufus
Thomas, James, (bond)

Estate Record Name
Crabtree, G. W. (Cont.)
Phillips, Ellis, (bond)
Beane, J. T., (bond)
Crabtree, (bond)
Tatum, Elisha
Kerley, James
Rogers, America Crabtree
Crabtree, Emily
Crabtree, F. M.
Thompson, L. T.
Thomas, Permelia Crabtree
Thomas, John
Lea, Abner, (summons)
Jones, Charley
Lea, George
Moore, Ellen Crabtree
Bean, Tol
Crabtree, Lucy
Corbin, Perlina Crabtree
Corbin, Davis
Slone, S. B., (guar.of minors)
Lea, Samatha Crabtree
Moore, Ellen
Bean, Samina
Crabtree, Charley
Tatum, Elisha, (appraiser)
Kirby, James, (appraiser)
Igou, George, (appraiser)
Stelvey/Stalvey)
Crabtree, James, (adm.)
Jones, C. J.
Stalvey, G. W.
Campbell, H. B., (Comm.)
Day, W. J, (testimony)
Kirby, Tom, (testimony)
Receipts to Estate:
Moore, Mrs.
Bloom, Ellen
Crabtree, R. A.
Igou, A. M.
Phillips, Ellis

Estate Record Name
Crabtree, G. W. (Cont.)
Kirby, H. J. (I)
Crabtree, C. H.
Biddle, R. R.
Smith, John, (note for mare)
Smith, D. R.
Bean, J. G.
Moore, Ellen, Mrs.
Cash, Ellis
Tatum, Elisha
Hall,
Rent from Farm, 1910 & 1911
Keith, Ben
U. S. Pensions-Warrant
Keith, Willie
Davenport & McKowan,
(Purchased Land $985.00)
Tatum, Elisha,
(Purchased Land $191.00)
Smith, E. P.
Smith, M. V.
Smith, P. L.
Payments:
Warren, F. M., (tax 1910-1911)
Keith, G. A., (monument)
Payne, H. C., (making coffin)
Igou & Tatum, (burial supplies)
Hicks, G. L., (services)
Kirby, James, (appraiser)
Breland, A. F. & Co.
Floid, M. I., Dr., (medical)
Day, W. J., (pension matter)
Callah, J. H., (services)
Williams, Zilmon, (services)
McQuire, Geo. S., (selling R.E.)
Day, W, J., (witness)
Kirby, Thomas, (Land sale exp.)
Howard & Hunt
Crabtree, G. W., (17-children)
Crabtree, G. W., Jr., (dec'd)
Rogers, America Crabtree,(widow)

Estate Record Name

Crabtree, G. W. (Cont.)
- Crabtree, Emily/Emmie, (dau.)
- Crabtree, F. M.,(dec'd, no widow)
- Crabtree, James A. (c/o F.M.)
- Thompson, Letha Ann
- Thomas, Permelia C.,(w/o John)
- Phillips, Margaret C., (w/o Ellis)
- Lea, Mary C, (w/o Abner)
- Lea, Samantha C., (w/o George)
- Crabtree, Martin
- Crabtree, Ben
- Crabtree, Andrew
- Moore, Ellen Crabtree
- Bean, Samira C., (w/o Tol Bean)
- Crabtree, Charley
- Crabtree, Rufus, (dec'd.)
- Corbin, Permelia C., (dec'd.)
- Corbin, Davis, (h/o Permelia)
- Crabtree, Alf

Crabtree, G. W.
- Box 4 File 2 1910-1915
- Names in File:
- Crabtree, James A., (adm)
- Crabtree, C. H., (bond)
- Vinson, S. G., (witness)
- Phillips, Ellis
- Phillips, Margaret
- Been, Smiry
- Thomas, Permelia Jane
- Koger, William, (witness)
- Phillips, M. E. (witness)
- Crabtree, Alfred W.
- Davis, John A. (atty)
- Davis & Pope, (atty)
- Crabtree, Henry
- Lincoln, B. A.
- Callaham, J. F.
- Day, W. J.
- Breland, A. F.
- Kirby, J. N.
- Payne, H. C.

Estate Record Name

Crabtree, G. W. (Cont.)
- Box 4 File 2 1910-1915
- Williams, Zilmon
- Tolbert, J. J.
- Kerby, J. N.
- York, W. E.
- Tatum, E.
- Moore, Ellen
- Crabtree, B. F.
- Thurman, Palmer
- Harris, W. S.
- Hackworth, J. B.
- Stalvey, Lizzie
- Crabtree, Martin
- Lea, Samanthy
- Lea, G. W.
- Bean, S. M.
- Hunt, R. H.
- Roden, J. M.
- Presley, I. M., (guar.ad litem)
- Crabtree, Velma
- Crabtree, Vina
- Lawson, A. J., (witness)
- Warren, F. M., (tax collector)
- Keith, G. A.
- Blevins, J. T., (witness)
- Crabtree, A. J.
- McGuire, Geo. S.
- Keith, J. A.
- Hicks, G. L.
- Igou, G. A.
- Smith, H. H., (estate)
- Campbell, I.
- Igou & Tatum, (burial supplies)

Crane, J. E.
- Box 4 File 3 1905
- Names in File:
- Sale of Land for Division
- Crane, J. E., (joint owner)
- Dumbach, William
- Dumbach, Rosa

Estate Record Name

Crane, J. E. (Cont.)
- Dumbach, John
- Dumbach, Lawrence
- Dumbach, Charles
- DeShields, J. G., (guar.ad litem)
- Hall, Newton, (testimony)
- Underwood, D. M., (testimony)
- Chitwood, W. J., (comm.)
- Collins, O. H., (take testimony)
- Davis, John A., (atty)
- Crane, J. E., (purchased land)

Craze, Daniel
- Box 4 File 4 1912
- Names in File:
- Craze, Martha, (widow)
- Craze, Dewey, (minor)
- Craze, Rosa Belle, (minor)
- Craze, Eva, (minor)
- Craze, Daniel, Jr., (minor)
- Craze, Meta, (minor)
- Keith, C. G., (set exemption)
- Clark, J. B., (set exemption)
- Dean, W. T., (JP)

Crow, Calvin M.
- Box 4 File 5 1887-1893
- Names in File:
- Crow, Sarah Jane, (dec'd.)
- Crow, Elijah B., (minor)
- Crow, Ollie Isbell, (minor)
- Crow, John L., (minor)
- Crow, Calvin, (guardian)
- Crow, C. M., (father of minors)
- Webb, Garrett W., (guar.ad litem)
- Crow, J. M., (bond)
- Koger, William, (bond)
- Poe, W. R., (guar.ad litem)
- Lea, J. B.
- Bouldin, Elijah, (estate, land)
- Bouldin, Sarah Jane, (dau)
- Crow, Sarah Jane Bouldin
- Aiken, James, (atty)

Estate Record Name

Crow, Calvin M. (Cont.)
- Noble, Samuel, (purchased iron) ore and lead ore mining rights)

Crow, Isaac
- Box 4 File 6 1883
- Names in File:
- Minor Children Apprenticed
- Crow, Mary, (mother)
- Crow, Isaac, (father)
- Crow, Roma R., (minor)
- Crow, W. J.
- Crow, Ida M., (minor)
- Crow, W. D.
- McCurdy, (bond)
- Franklin, John N., Judge

Crow, Margaret
- Box 4 File 7 1887
- Names in File:
- Crow, Margaret, (dec'd.)
- Crow, Prudence D. (minor)
- Crow, James E., (minor)
- Crow, Wm. F., Jr., (minor)
- Crow, Chesley M., (minor)
- Crow, John M., (minor)
- Crow, Wm. F., (guardian)
- Crow, Wm. F. (father)
- Campbell, A. L., (bond)
- Campbell, Isaac, (bond)

Crow, Thomas
- Box 4 File 8 1907-1908
- Names in File:
- Crow, C. M., (adm.)
- Crow, W. A.
- Medlock, L. L.
- Hicks, Annie
- Crow, George G.
- Crow, J. S. O.
- Litlejohn, Lillian
- Trussell, Hester
- Taylor, Carie J.
- Littlejohn, J.F., (bond)

Estate Record Name

Crow, Thomas (Cont.)
- Crow, J. M., (Bond)
- Nichols, C. L., (bond)
- Gibbs, W. E., (bond)
- Lane, C. T., (bond)
- Crumley, Lizzie,
- Harris, W. A., (attest)
- Elrod, S. M., (attest)
- Wellborn, R. G.
- Elrod, A. W., (drilling well)
- Harrison, J. J., MD, (medical)
- Black, J. E., (Mortgage)
- Cain, Wall, (taxes 1907 & 1908)
- Martin, C. S., (JP)
- Elrod, J. G.
- Medlock, Lizzie
- Crow, Bill
- Taylor, Carry
- Hicks, Ann
- Crow, Sam
- Hall, P. C., (took testimony)
- Martin, C. S., (witness)
- Spencer, W. A., (witness)
- Cook & Presley, (atty)
- Littlejohn, W. S., (purch.land)

Crow, N. D.
- Box 4 File 9 1892
- Names in File:
- Homestead Exemption
- Crow, Mary Ann, (widow)
- Crow, Dyse B., (minor)
- Crow, Belia A., (minor)
- Crow, Ella O., (minor)
- York, F. M., (appraiser)
- Ragan, John C., (appraiser)
- Phillips, Pleasant D., (JP)

Crumley, George W.
- Box 4 File 10 1898-1908
- Names in File:
- Crumley, A. C.. (adm)
- Crumley, Charlsie, (minor)

Estate Record Name

Crumley, George W. (Cont.)
- Smith, Sam P., Dr., (guardian)
- Jones, E. B., (bond)
- Black, John E., (bond)
- Fuller, W. T., (guar.ad litem)
- DeShields, J. G.,(guar.ad litem)
- Chitwood, W. J., (sheriff)
- Cain, Wall, (dep.sheriff)
- Gravitt, L., (Justice Peace)
- Crumley, Elizabeth, Mrs.

Crump, J. F.
- Box 4 File 11 1898
- Names in File:
- Crump, J. F., (minor heirs)
- Crump, Charles, (minor)
- Crump, Minnie, (minor)
- Crump, Robert H., (minor)
- Crump, M. J., Mrs.(mother)
- Crump, M. J., Mrs., (guardian)
- Crump, R. M., (bond)
- Russell, C. A., (bond)
- Crump, M. W., (estate)
- DeShields, J. G., (guar.ad litem)
- Chitwood, W. J., (sheriff)
- Cain, Wall, (dep.sheriff)
- End of Microfilm Roll 64

Crump, John W.
- Box 4 File 12 1866-1877
- Names in File:
- Humphries, J. T., (adm.)
- Humphries, Amanda, (adm.)
- Crump, Amanda, (widow)
- Humphries, Amanda Crump
- Brandon, P. A., Judge
- Crump, Nora Elizabeth (minor)
- Crump, R. C.,(guardian)
- Shuffield, J., (adm.bond)
- Edwards, Joseph, (adm.bond)
- Carter, C. T., (appraiser)
- Humphries, J. T., (appraiser)
- Work, Nelson, (witness)

Estate Record Name
Crump, John W. (Cont.)
McClendon, James, (appraiser)
White, S. M., (commissioner)
Dobbs, L. A., (atty.)
Nicholson, D. L., (atty.)
Davidson, A. B., (pur.land)
Burns, Samuel, (prop.line)
Smith, Thomas H. (notice)
Hazle, Nora Crump
Hazle, Samuel, (h/o Nora)
Patrick, J. M., (tax.coll. 1877)
Pruett, A. S., Capt.
Louins, W. H., (sheriff)
Sale of Inventory:
McClendon, James(blacksmith tools)
Whitt, Wm. T., (harrow)
Crump, R. C., (yearling)
Shuffield, J., (buggy & hog)
Land, A. J., (scrap iron)
Carter, C. T., (cow & calf)
Atkins, A. W.
Hammett, James, (log chain & hogs)
Thomas, John, (plow stock)
Adair, A. P., (cow & calf)
McDaniel, Wm. M., (3-shoat hogs)
McDaniel, Wm. M., (12-pork hogs)
Relly, C., (3-pork hogs)
Bouth, T. J.
Work, N.
Nobles, William
Engle, Alford, (1-calf skin)
Edwards, J., (pr. gear, iron)
Edwards, Margaret, (3-pork hogs)
Crump, Martha
Box 4 File 13-A 1854-1856
Names in File:
Petition for Sale of Land
Reeve, Hester A., (dau.)
Reeve, James A., (h/o Hester)
Ward, Lewis P., (joint owner)
Hammock, Thos., (joint owner)

Estate Record Name
Crump, Martha (Cont.)
Reeve, Hester
Crump, Henry T.
Mathis, DeAnn, (w/o Samuel)
Mathis, Samuel
Reeve, Julia A., (w/o Daniel)
Reeve, Daniel M.
Crump, William, (minor)
Crump, Charity, (minor)
Crump, Harriet, (minor)
Crump, Bethel, (father, guar.)
Walden, J. B., (atty.)
Crump, R. C. (Rolin C.)
Box 4 File 13 1901-1903
Names in File:
Crump, J. C., (adm.)
Erwin, M. B., (adm.bond)
Crump, Ira J., (adm.bond)
Cook, W. C. D., Judge
Erwin, Marcus B., (witness)
Crosley, E., (witness)
Holsomback, W. J., (witness)
Crump, T. J., (attest)
Davis & Haralson, (attys.)
Holsonback, J. N., (appraiser)
Hazle, Oliver, (appraiser)
Gilbreath, B. N., (appraiser)
Yeuell, Claris, (editor)
The DeKalb Times, (notice)
The Fort Payne Journal
Meigs, J. H., (proprietor)
The Marshall Banner, (notice)
Copeland, A. C., (pur.land)
Crump, Ira J., (purch. Land)
Smith, S. P., (purch.land)
Edwards, Margaret
Crump, W. B.
Crump, J. C.
Erwin, Adalia
Keener, Mary
Hazle, Nora

Estate Record Name

Crump, R. C. (Rolin C.) (Cont.)
- Howard, Laura
- Carter, T. J.
- Gerard, Cornelia, (dec'd.)
- Keener, Beuna
- Crump, Anna
- Crump, Robert
- Crump, Allie
- Durham, Rosa
- Crump, Marcus
- Crump, Rolin C., (will)
- Crump, Rhoda E. (wife)
- Erwin, Macus B.,(named exec.)
- Waller, Edgar M., (witness)
- Erwin, Marcus B. (witness)
- Erwin, Marcus B. (h/o Adelia)
- Bradley, William A., (witness)
- Edwards, J., (h/o Margaret)
- Keener, J. P., (h/o Mary)
- Hazle, Samuel (h/o Norah)
- Gerard, Will, (h/o Cornelia)
- Keener, Buena
- Keener, John, (h/o Buena)
- Durham, William, (h/o Rosa)
- Howard, F. M., (attest)
- Durham, J. M.
- Durham, Nora L.
- Keener, Mary F.
- Carter, Thoms J.
- Hazel (Hazle)
- Girard (Gerard)
- Garrard (Gerard)
- Crump, G. Anna
- Kenner, Buna C.
- Burt, R. A., (witness)
- Garrard, William, (guar.)
- Garrard, Cornelia
- Hazel, Nora
- Crump, Allie, (niece of J. C.)
- Garrard, Melia
- Benjen, (sheriff-Jefferson Co.)

Estate Record Name

Crump, R. C. (Rolin C.) (Cont.)
- Box 4 File 13 1901-1903
- Mills, J. W.
- Copeland, A. C., (JP)
- Holsonback, W. J., (witness)
- J. C. Crump & Son
- J. C. Crump & Co. (Gen.Mdse)
- Sherman, John, MD, (med.)
- Chastain, J. B.,(tombstone)
- Sherman, James R., (med.ser.)
- Graves, H, L., (tax coll. 1902)
- Davis, R. C.
- Clayton, John J.
- Hall, J. A. (dental work)

Culberson, A. B.
- Box 4 File 14 1913-1918
- Names in File:
- Sale for Division of Land
- Culberson, C. Y., (adm.,brother)
- Culberson, Mary A., (widow)
- Culberson, Alonzo B, (minor)
- Culberson, Vernon V., (minor)
- Johnson, J. A., (guar.ad litem)
- Davenport, E. J., (bond)
- Jones, E. N., (bond)
- Jones, D. L., (witness)
- Perkins, W. C., (witness)
- Smith, Thom., (newspaper notice)
- Croley, Jas. A., Judge
- Bank of Valley Head
- Green, Frank, (purch.land)

Cunningham, John
- Box 4 File 15 1877
- Names in File:
- Malone, Geo.W., Estate vs:
- Cunningham, John, Estate
- Nicholson, J. A., (adm)
- Estes, Jno. R., (juror)
- Brandon, P. A., Judge
- Payne, A. H., (clerk)
- Malone, E. H.

Estate Record Name

Cunningham, John (Cont.)
Malone, R. W.
Receipts for purchase of land

Cunningham, N. L.
Box 4 File 16 1890-1893
Names in File:
Cunningham, Mary E., (widow)
Frazier, P. M., (ex-officio adm'r)
Frazier, P. M., (sheriff)
Yates, Jesse A., (creditor)
Cunningham, M. E. V. (widow)
Chitwood, R., (commissioner)
Johnson, Jas. R., (commissioner)
Fuller, W. T., (clerk Circuit Ct.)
Chitwood, Richard

Estate Record Name

D

Estate Record Name
Dalrymple, H. H.
Box 4 File 17 1874
Names in file:
Dalrymple, Annie
Dalyrmple, Sallie
Roberts, F. M., (guardian)
Coats, Henry (bond)
Horton, A. J., Judge
Dalrymple, I. B.
Box 4 File 18 1878-1880
Names in file:
Dalrymple, H. B.
Dalyrymple, N. J.
Dalyrmple, I. B., (guardian)
Dalrymlple, Henry H., (dec'd.)
Dalrymple, Naomi J.
Brandon, P. A., Judge
Dobbs, L. A., (atty.)
Dalrymple, John W.
Box 4 File 19 1856-1885
Names in file: See File 20
Dalrymple, Sarah A. C. (widow)
Dalrymple, John W. (will)
Dalrymple, Thomas, (guardian)
Dalryrmple, Linda/Lida (minor)
Waldrop, Samuel, (guar.bond)
Coats, Henry, (guar.bond)
Estes, Reuben, Judge
Franklin, John N., Judge
Stott, D. M., (adm.)
Stott, Drayton M., (exec.)
Dalrymple, Sarah A. C., (admx.)
Dalrymple, John W.
Box 4 File 20 1882-1884
Names in file: See File 19
Dalrymple, Sarah A. C., (widow)
Dalrymple, John B., (minor)
Dalrymple, Elizabeth, (minor)

Estate Record Name
Dalrymple, John W. (Cont.)
Dalrymple, Carrie, (minor)
Dalrymple, L. J., (minor)
Dalrymple, James, (minor)
Dalrymple, Richard, (minor)
Dalrymple, Minnie, (minor)
Dalrymple, Lizzie
See File 19
Dalrymple, John W., (will)
Masters, Ben
Masters, B. F.
Slater, P. L.
White, M. G.
Howard, M. W., (guar.ad litem)
Campbell, Isaac (guar.ad litem)
Frazier, P. M., (sheriff)
Stott, Drayton, (exec.)
Stott, L. M., Jr.
Franklin, J. N., Judge
Franklin, A. G., (sheriff)
Stott, Drayton E.
Martin, J. C., (appraiser)
Johnson, Daniel, (appraiser)
Masters, B. T., (appraiser)
Rucks, C. P., (JP)
Black, John (bought mule)
Dalrymple, Nancy
Box 4 File 21 1863
Names in File:
Dalrymple, Ludy, (adm.)
Dalrymple, Luda
Dalrymple, M. J., (adm.)
Dalrymple, Lindy/Leuda
Norman, Henry, (adm.bond)
Johnson, C. P., (appraiser)
Norman, Henry, (appraiser)
Lovins, Lemuel, (bond)
Lovins, L. B.

Estate Record Name
Dalrymple, Nancy (Cont.)
  Milwee, G. W., (JP)
  Hoge, John K.,(NP)
Dalrymple, Stephen H.
  Box 4 File 22 1874
  Names in File:
  Coats, Henry, (guardian)
  Dalrymple, Stephen, (minor)
  Dalrymple, H. H. (grandfather)
  Dalrymple, H. H.
  Dalrymple, I. B., (bond)
  Roberts, F. M.
  Horton, A. J., Judge
  Dalrymple, P. B. (I. B.)
Darby, W. F.
  Box 4 File 23 1904-1919
  Names in File: (1 of 2 folders)
  Sale of Land for Division
  Darby, Lula V., (widow)
  Darby, Lula V., (admx.)
  Darby, Eunice E. (minor)
  Darby, Idella J., (minor)
  Darby, Lela, (minor)
  Darby, Ernest F., (minor)
  Darby, Edgar W. (minor)
  Darby, Willie, (minor)
  Wright, W. I., (adm.bond)
  Cochran, J. J., (adm.bond)
  Pickens, J. M., (adm.bond)
  Cook, T. J., (appraiser)
  Wall, Jesse , (appraiser)
  Copeland, Mack, (appraiser)
  Copeland, H. C., (appraiser)
  Isbell & Presley, (attys.)
  Copeland, A. C., (guar.ad litem)
  Berry, Minnie, (take deposition)
  Cook, T. J., (deposition)
  Pharr, G. W., (deposition)
  Ward, C. G., (prop.line)
  Coe (Cox), (prop.line)
  Coe (Cox), W. A., (prop.line)

Estate Record Name
Darby, W. F. (Cont.)
  Cox (Coe)
  Heaton, Louis, (purch.land)
  Stephenson, J. M., (purch.land)
  Ward, C. G., (adm.)(uncle)
  Wright, W. J., (adm.bond)
  Patty, R. J., (adm.bond)
  Loyd, J. W., (adm.bond)
  Nicholson, C. R., (note paid)
  Garrett, J. R., (note paid)
  Hamdey, W. D., (land note pd)
  Isbell & Scott, (atty.)
  Smith, Thos. H., (adv.notice)
  Erwin, L. H., Dr., (dental exp.)
  Wright, W. I., Dr., (med.exp.)
  Presley, I. M., (guar.ad litem)
  Kirby, A. C., (sheriff)
  Stapp, Eunice
  Cochran, Lela
  Darby, Willie
  Darby, Lula
  Accounts Due Estate:
  Ward & Pickens, (goods)
  Bobo, C. C., (goods)
  Loyd, J. W., (goods)
  Johnson, W. R., (boiler, etc.)
  Cox, W. A., (land)
  Cochran, J. J., (warehouse)
  Ryon, W. C., (warehouse)
  Pickens, J. M., (real estate)
  Bates, L. F., (supplies)
  Appleton, Alf & Harriet,(horse)
  Clayton, S. W. (guano)
  Barrett, J. D., (guano)
  May, J. B., (guano)
  Williams, J. T., (guano)
  Gilbert, L. D., (guano)
  Reeves, C. C., (guano)
  McDaniel, J. T., (guano)
  Lee, A. B., (guano)
  Nichols, J. B., (guano)

Estate Record Name
Darby, W. F. (Cont.)
Pointer, Joshua, (guano)
Jackson, C. P., (guano)
Rone, J. F., (guano)
Richey, A. P., (guano)
Bobo, C. C., (guano)
Griffin, J. H., (note)
Griffin, J. T., (note)
Pickens, J. M., (mortgage)
Nelson, F, W, & David, (mortgage)
Satterfield, J. E., (mortgage)
Harris, E. L., (note)
Nicholson, C. R., (note)
Black, W. R., (note)
Accounts Due Estate:
Williams, C. D., (note)
Nelson, Geo., (note)
Garrett, J. R., (mortgage)
Garrett, W. R., (mortgage)
Rave, C, W., (mortgage)
Rane/Rave
Garrett, J. R., (2-land notes)
Willoughby, T. A., (mortgage)
Powell, W. H., (note)
Gilbert, A. J. (note)
Garrett, J. R. & W. R., (note)
Loyd, J. W., (note)
Machinery: Saw mill, cotton gin, plainer, boiler and engine
Machinery moved to Lydia, AL
Davis, John A., (atty.)
Isbell, John B., (atty)
Harvey, W. O., Gin Land
Harvey, W. O., (purch.land)
Dugan House & Land
Wade House & Land
Harvey House & Land
Friendship Church
Fairview Church
Machinery: Grist Mill
McGill Hardware

Estate Record Name
Darby, W. F. (Cont.)
Ward & Loyd
Ward, C. G., (bought.mach.)
Cochran, John J. (purch.land)
Dobbs, Cordia, (take despos.)
Dobbs, Frank, (take depos.)
Copeland, A. C., (deposition)
Cook, T. J., (deposition)
Cook, John M., (take depos.)
McSpadden, H. A., (guar.ad lit.)
McDaniel, W. S.,(bought land)
Darby, Della
Stapp, Eunice E.
Cochran, Lela F.
Darby, Ernest F.
Darby, Edgar W.
Campbell, H. B., (guar.ad litem)
Darby, Willie
Batson, J. B., (sheriff)
Patterson, T. P., (dep.sheriff)
Darby, W. F.
Box 4 File 23 1904-1919
Names in File: (2 of 2 folders)
Howard & Hunt, (atty)
Ward, C. G., (adm)
Harvey, W. O.
Wright, W. I.
Ward & Darby
Dekalb Co. Bank
Cochran, J. J.
Paid from Estate:
Graves, H. L., (tax coll. 1904)
Isbell, J. B., (atty.)
Wallis, John
Jackson, C. B. (saw mill exp.)
Cook, W. C. D.
American Carriage Co.
O'Shields, H. H.
Claiborne, Tate & Cowan
J. W. Cavenger & Co.
DeShields, J. G.

Estate Record Name
Darby, W. F. (Cont.)
Pickens, J. M.
Ward & Loyd
Erwin, L. F., DDS, (dental)
Darby, Lula V., (widow)
Darby, Emma E., (minor)
Darby, Idella J., (minor)
Darby, Leila G., (minor)
Darby, Ernest F., (minor)
Darby, Edgar W. (minor)
Chitwood, W. J., (sheriff)
Pharr, G. W.
Darby, Ernest F., (minor)
Darby, Edgar W. (minor)
Chitwood, W. J., (sheriff)
Pharr, G. W.
Pickens, J. M.
Cook, T. J., (appraiser)
Wall, Jesse , (appraiser)
Wall, J. L.
Copeland, Mack, (appraiser)
Copeland, H. C.
Stevenson, J. M. & S. A.
Ward & Darby
Notes Collected:
Jackson, Neal
Babb, C. C.
Cochran
Mergan
Henderson
Houston, Bill
Williams
Jones
Nichols, H.
Babbs
Babo
Turner, W. A.
Glascue
Johnson, Len
Leak, M. A.
Ward, Darby & Loyd

Estate Record Name
Darby, W. F. (Cont.)
Store Notes & Accounts:
Leak, M. A.
Bailey, Aaron
Smith, Frank
Pope, J. E.
Thacker, John
Heftinstall, J. C.
Black, S. M.
Bentley, S. H.
Owens, W. L.
Stone, W. B.
Hall, T. H.
Pickens, A. M.
Wester, Thomas
Harper, Zeke
Clay, J. W.
Fuller, B. B. .
Douglas, S. S.
Lackey, V. L.
Deuton, Isaac
Russell, A. G.
Simpson, W. A.
Pickens, J. M., Jr.
Phillips, A. E.
Hurst, Lonie
O'Shield, H. H.
Russell, A. G.
Black, W. R.
Rains, Robert
Meader, A. L.
Johnson, L. F.
Smith, James
Ridway, W. F.
Holcomb, W. T.
Matthews, W. M.
Turner, W. C.
Pickens, J. M., Jr.
Turner, W. A.
Pickens, Frank
Cobie, T. N.

Estate Record Name

Darby, W. F. (Cont.)

Box 4 File 23 1904-1919

Everett, G. A.
Harvey, W. H.
Deuton, S. R.
Hanes, S. H.
Croft, J. I.
Peraley, J.
Wright, W. I., Dr.
Patty, R. J., Dr.
Griggle, G. W.
Harvey, W. O.
Masters, Ella, Mrs.
Staff, James
Dillashaw, John
Nicholson, M. M.
Webb, Washington
Lutterell, B. G.
Harper, E. L.
Harris, T. N.
Marshall, Ida, Mrs.
Lowry, C. W.
Darby, W. F.
Clay, J. W.
Stone, O. D.
Wright, W. I.
Deuton, S. R.
Crump, C. J.
Hall, T. H.
Howard, W. L.
Mosley, M.
Traffinsteet,
Shelley, W. L.
Harris, T. N.
Pope, J. E.
Medlock, H. H.
Gilbert, B. F.
Hall, T. H.
Kuykendall, T. A.
Tumlin, J. M.
Fuller, J. B.

Estate Record Name

Darby, W. F. (Cont.)

Howard, W. L.
Blackwell, H. L.
Head, J. W.
Smith, P. C.
Hill, M. J.
Meaders, A. L.
Graham, W. S.
Davis, S. L.
Wright, W. H.
Shelley & Taffanstatt
Jolley, L. M.
Everitt, G. A.
Phillips, A. P.
Bishop, J. H.
Wester, Thomas
Fincher, A. J.
Williams, W. J.
Stephens, W. C.
Crouch, W. H.
Barnett, J. P.
Tidmons, Tom
Meaders, R. C.
Nunn, J. F.
Stone, B. W.
Tucker, J. W.
Morgan, T. S.
McMahan, J. W.
Nichols, M. C., Mrs.
O'Shields, H. H.
Owen, W. L.
Williams, J. T.
Nicholson, Charlie
Wright, J. W.
Stone, B. W.
Saye, J. H., Mrs.
Hill, R. L.
Nunn, J. F.
Deaton, L. F.
Turner, W. A.
Spears, W. T.

Estate Record Name

Darby, W. F. (Cont.)
 Johnson, W. R.
 Shirly, M. L.
 Deckerson, J. C.
 Spears, W. L. & O. L.
 Hall, H. M.
 Ridgeway W. P.
 Nickson, Isaac
 Shirly, M. L.
 Bryan, T. M.
 Jones, L. M.
 Sparks, J. F.
 Deaton, S. H.
 Bates, G. W.
 Carter, O. D.
 Clay, J. W.
 Houston, W. I.
 Glascon, J. T.
 Wilbanks, W. C.
 Nichols, H. H.
 Harvey, W. H.
 Frazier, J. A.
 Clay, J. W., et all
 Johnson, L. T.
 Houston, W. I.
 Bobo, C. C.
 Norton, E. H.
Davenport, David B, et al
 Box 4 File 25 1879-1892
 Names in File:
 Davenport, Rodolphus B., (guardian)
 Davenport, David B, (minor)
 Davenport, Ida M., (minor)
 Davenport, Joseph H., (minor)
 Davenport, Rodolphus R., Estate
 Davenport, R. B.
 Davenport, Nicholas S., (guardian)
 Stuart, John, (bond)
 Davenport, Erskine T.
 Brandon, Phillip A., Judge
 Davenport, N. S., (guardian)

Estate Record Name

Davenport, David B, et al (Cont.)
 Davenport, Joe H., (minor)
 Davenport, Ida, (minor)
 Davenport, D. B., (minor)
 Davenport, R. R.. (heirs of)
 Lowry, Geo. M. D., (depos.)
 Price, James M., (depos.)
 Davenport, E. T., (despos.)
 Davenport, Cicero, (bond)
 Rice, C. M., (commissioner)
 Campbell, H. B., (guar.ad litem)
 Hanna, A. B., (witness)
 Maffett, J., (witness)
 Emerson, T. H., (witness)
 Davis, G. W., (guar.ad litem)
 Webb, G. W., (Clerk Cir.Court)
 Callan & Hoge
 Callan, W. J., (tuition-Joe H.)
 Sulphur Springs, Ala.
 Cochran, L. L., Judge
 Winston, J. N., (medical)
 Davis, R. B. (tax coll. 1881)
 Ferguson, W. L., (tax coll 1879)
 Davis, R. C., (tax coll. 1880)
 Franklin, J. N., Judge
Davenport, O. J.
 Box 4 File 26 1869-1883
 Names in File:
 Davenport, Orville J., (guard.)
 Davenport, W. O., (minor)
 Davenport, Elizabeth (minor)
 Davenport, Cicero, (minor)
 Davenport, F. M.,(minor)
 Davenport, John H., (minor)
 Davenport, Taylor, (minor)
 Davenport, J. G., (minor)
 Davenport, O. J., (f/o minors)
 Grant, William, Estate
 Minors, heirs of William Grant
 Davenport, Casius
 Davenport, Erskine T.

Estate Record Name
Davenport, O. J. (Cont.)
Davenport, Joseph G.
Davenport, Lizzie
Davenport, Wheeler
Daveport, Ida
Davis, John A.
Horton, A. J., Judge
Jacoway, J. G., (bond)
Malone, Geo. W., (bond)
Davenport, M. C., Mrs., (guar.)
Davenport, N. A., (minor)
Davenport, Henry D.,(minor)
Davenport, Seaborn, (minor)
Price, R. S., (JP)
Davidson, Henry
Box 4 File 27 1910-1911
Names in File:
Davidson, Matilda, (widow)
Homestead Exemption
Davidson, Mary, (minor)
Campbell, H. B., (comm.)
McCartney, J. H., (comm.)
Davidson, Joseph
Box 4 File 28 1861-1888
Names in File:
Davidson Joseph, (will-1861)
Wesson, J. W., (witness)
Smith, J. W., (witness)
Holcomb, Wm., (witness)
Driskell, Warner L., (exec.)
Dobbs, Silas T., (witness)
Ward, John D., (witness)
Davis, Elizabeth
Davidson, Wm.
Davidson, Lucinda
Davidson, John
Davidson, Frances
Lankford, R. T., (guardian)
Davidson, Permelia (minor)
Davidson, Allen, (minor)
Vaughn, Chessie

Estate Record Name
Davidson, Joseph (Cont.)
McBee, Chessie L.
Davidson, J. B., Mrs.
Davidson, J. M., (guardian)
Tyner, S.
Estes, R., Judge
Lamar, James, (note)
Bibb, James M. (note)
Davis, C. C.
Box 4 File 29 1902-1908
Names in File:
Davis, John A., (adm.., brother)
Davis, Tennie, (widow)
Roberts, Nancy J., (w/o Charles)
Roberts, Charles
Reed, Mary, (w/o Walter)
Reed, Walter
Davis, James W., (minor)
Davis, John C., (minor)
Davis, Charlsie G., (minor)
Davis, William C., (minor)
Davis, Leila S., (minor)
Davis, Abraham, (minor)
Davis, George, (minor)
Davis, Christopher C.
Davis, Tennessee/Tennie/A.T.
Davis, A. T., (widow)
Homestead Exemption
Heard, Salon E., (appraiser)
Wheeler, T. D., (appraiser)
Killian, W. E., (appraiser)
McDonough, R. N.(purch. land)
Burt. W. C. (purch.. land)
Wheeler, T. D., (deposition)
Sawyer, Chas. M. T., (depos.)
Killian, D. S., Mrs. (paid note)
Jordan, C. C., (paid acct.)
Halls Dry Goods Co., (pd acct.)
Brinkley, V. M.
Killian, B., (paid acct.)
Hall, Vann

Estate Record Name
Davis, C. C. (Cont.)
Masters, J. M.
Chitwood, D.C., (pd acct.)
Novelle, Jannette, (pd on mortgage)
Robinson, Andy
Burt, W. C., (paid note)
Chitwood, Joel
Graves, H. L., (tax coll. 1903-4)
Sims, Jesse, (labor)
Sibert, Jadie/Josie. (paid note)
Hall, J. A., (paid note)
Novelle, Fannetta, (bal.on mortgage)
Heard, Solon E., (pd.comm.)
Turnipseed, W. E., (pd.note)
Presley, I. M., (fees paid)
McBroom, A. M.
McWhorter, H. P., (pd on acct.)
Smith, R. H., (pd.note)
Clayton, Sherman W., (pd acct.)
Marsh, W. C., (paid acct.)
Ryon, W. C., (paid acct.)
Keener, Geo. W., (pd.acct.)
Miller, J. R., MD, (pd. medical)
Gibson, J. C., (paid account)
Holbrooks, G. W.
Majors, S. N.
Cagle, Luke
Wheeler, T. D.
Nicholson, L. S.(notary public)
Lackey, J., (paid note to Lackey)
Vann, A. J., (paid note to Vann)
Rogers, Elijah & Davis, (pd.note)
Hairell, John, (paid note)
Receipts:
Edmondson, John R., (2-Notes)
McDonough, R. N., (Land $900.)
Copeland, J. R., (cotton rent)
Edmondson, John R.., (note)
Majors, S. N., (fodder rent)
Burt, W. C., (farm $2000.)
Baxter, Oscar, (house rent)

Estate Record Name
Davis, C. C. (Cont.)
Holbrooks, (hay)
Cagle, Luke, (corn)
Lovewell, G. W., (corn)
Lankford, J. D., (corn)
Majors, S. N., (corn)
Sibert, Josie, Mrs., (overpay.)
Rogers, Wm., (house rent)
Baxter, Jesse
Sims, Jesse M., Jr.
Smith, Thos. H., (adv.notice)
Lackey, J. W.
Miller, J. T.
Burt, J. W.
Fuller, P. N.
Southerland, M. E.
Lively, M. C.
Kelley, Thomas B.
Edmondson, John R.
Rich, T. M.
Morgan, W. H.
Chitwood, I. Y. & S. J.
Buddie, W. H.
O'Shields, J. G., (guar.ad litem)
Butler, S. G.
Heaton, Jack
Nappier House Rent
Stephens, Walter, (timber)
Slone, S. B. (land receipts)
DeKalb Co. Bank, (interest)
Cain, Wall, (tax coll. 1905-1908)
Warren, F. M., (tax 1909-1912)
Jordan, C. C.
Campbell, H. B., (guar.ad litem)
Wheeler, Thos. D.
Sawyer, C. M. T.
Reeves, J. L.
Miller, T. J., MD
Davis, A. T., (widow)
Edmondson, W. E. (debt)
Blanton, J. W.
Southerland, M. E.

Estate Record Name
Davis, C. C. (Cont.)
Southerland, M. E.
Southerland, R. J. & R. B.
Berry, J. A.
O'Shieds, H. H.
Woodward, W. K.
Freeman, R. F.
Roberts, J. W., (tax 1913-14)
Davis, A. T., (grave stone)
Reed, Julian, (son of Mary)
Davis, Cary
Davis, A. T., (guardian)
Vann Hall Grave Yard
Pyron, W. C.
Merchant and Cotton Buyer
Davis, A. T. (placing monument)
Davis, P. P., (adm.bond)
Davis, J. L. (adm.bond)
Haralson, J. B., (adm.bond)
Haralson, W. W., (adm.bond)
Newman, J. W., (adm.bond)
Davis, James
Box 4 File 30 1850-1869
Names in File: John Davis, Estate
Davis, James, (adm.) VS
Heirs of John Davis, (1869)
Horton, A. J. , Judge
Brandon, P. A., (commissioner)
Dunlap & Dodds
Burt, Elijah, (witness)
Davis, John, (estate)
Baxter, F. M., (witness)
Davis, Elizabeth, (widow)
Chitwood, Sarah, (w/o Joel)
Chitwood, Joel
Chitwood, Mary J., (w/o Clement)
Chitwood, Clement C.
Davis, Abraham
Hoge, John K., (guar.ad litem)
Davis, William
Green, George

Estate Record Name
Davis, James (Cont.)
Davis, George
Busby, Samuel
Griffin, W. R. (sheriff)
Killian, William T., (purch.land)
Chitwood, Andrew C., (bond)
Malone, G. W., (bond)
Davis, James, (bond)
Davis, James, (adm.)
Dunlap, Dodds & Jacoway
Sale of Personal Prop.:
Davis, G. (yearling)
Davis, Elizabeth,(yoke of oxen)
Franklin, J. N., (mule)
Davis, James, (mare)
McCamby, Alex (corn)
Davis, William, (corn)
Winston, J. G. (heaffer)
Chitwood, C. C. (plains)
Davis, A., (plains)
Davis, William, (4-augers)
Jett, Samuel
Lutterel, John, (saw)
Davis, A., (2-gouges)
Lewis, John, (2-chisels)
Chitwood, C. C., (3-chisels)
Davis, William, (lot of tools)
Chitwood, R.
Davis, Wm., (plain & chisels)
Davis, A., (bits, chisels, etc.)
Lutterel, John, (1-axe)
Winston, J. G., (saw & plain)
Davis, G., (1-broad ax)
Davis, Wm., (screws & clevis)
Davis, James, (sundreys)
Chitwood, Joel, (square, etc.)
Roberts, Isham, (saw)
Roberts, I. B., (tran square)
Davis, A., (hand saw)
Cunningham, L., (mallet, stone)
Estes, W. N., (1-ox banes)

Estate Record Name

Davis, James (Cont.)

Chitwood, Joel, (bridle blinders)
Cunningham, Jesse
Roberts, I. B., (lathe)
Chitwood, C. C., (grindstone)
Roberts, R. (lot of ?)
Hoge, Thomas, (1 pr. hames)
Bynum, Wm., (1-plain)
Farmer, Wm., (100 lb.bacon)
Davis, James, (1-pr chains)
Davis, William, (1-claw hamer)
Davis, Nancy, (widow of Wm. P)
Davis, William, W. P.
Davis, Sarah, (minor)
Davis, George, (minor)
Chitwood, Mary Jane
Davis, Joel, (minor)
Davis, Green, (minor)
Chitwood, M. J.
Davis, W. J.
Chitwood, Mat
Phillips, H. P.
Malone, George W.
Malone, G. W.
Majors, Samuel, (JP)
Majors, A. W.
Estes, R., Judge
Dary, William P.
Carithers, James G.
Hoge, John K., (guar.ad litem)
McCurdy, J. A.
Hoge, J. K.
Belsher, J. B.
Cunningham, Blankin & Jno.
Lankford, P. H.
Lankford, I. M.
Jack, T. I.
Stewart, J. I.
Caythers, J. T.
Caster, A. W.
Ryan, Wm.

Estate Record Name

Davis, James (Cont.)

Dobbs, L. A.
Lyon, Wm.
Cunningham, John
Jack, J. N.
Bogle, J. C., (appraiser)
Chitwood, Mattias, (appraiser)
Malone, G. J., (appraiser)
Winston, J. G., (lumber)
Lewis, John, (lumber)
McCawley, Alex, (corn)
Lewis, Ben, (spoke)
Roberts, R. M., (set plains)
Jack, Thomas J.
Nicholson, D. L.
McCampbell, Soloman
Hunter, J. P.
Stewart, J. L.
Findley, I.B.
Carter, Andrew W.
Stewart, John J.
Frazier, P. M.
Lankford, John M.
Cunningham, Jesse
Franklin, John N.
Snider, Cornelius
Parker, James
Estes, W. N.
McCampbell, E. A.
Hayes, W. I.
Walden, J. B.
Blanton, Whitman
Hughes, D. D.
May, Stephen
Chitwood, Mathias
Estes, Ruben

Davis, R. C.

Box 4 File 31 1904-1908
Names in File:
Widow's Exemption
Davis, Sallie M., (widow)

Estate Record Name

Davis, R. C. (Cont.)
- Davis, P. H., (minor)
- Gorham, Alma
- Roden, Walsie
- Roden, W. V.
- Cash, Emaline
- Daniel, May
- Bates, Alabama
- Dodd, Missouri
- Cash, Decie
- Davis, Gilbert
- Davis, R. E., (adm., nephew)
- Davis, Ruben E.
- Roden, Wm. G., (adm.bond)
- Smith, S. P., (adm.bond)
- Berry, H., (adm.bond)
- Crump, I. J., (adm.bond)
- McMahan, J. W., (adm.bond)
- Berry, H., (set homestead)
- Black, J. H., (set homestead)
- Milwee, H. H., (set homestead)
- Milwee, James A., (JP)
- Croley, Jas. A., Judge
- *DeKalb Record,* Newspaper
- Smith, Echols, Brunett Hdwe Co.
- Fletcher, J. H., Boaz,(debt acct.)
- J. F. Hooper Bank, Albertville
- Cain, Wall, (tax due)
- Farmers & Merchants Bank Boaz
- Milwee, W. T., (sureties)
- Willimson, E. G., (sureties)
- Black, J. H., Dr.
- Gadsden, Natl. Bank
- Notice of Insolvency
- Cain, Wall, (tax coll. 1907)
- Smith, Chas. W.
- Hooper, J. F., (banker)
- McNaron, T. B.
- McCord, E. O.
- Fletcher, J. H.

Notes Due R. C. Davis Estate:

Estate Record Name

Davis, R. C. (Cont.)
- Berry, H.
- Beard, A. J.
- Chandler, J. M.
- Swann, W. B.
- Dodd, O. L.
- Bates, F. M.
- Davis, N. G.
- Davis, N. E., Mrs.
- Ramsey, John
- North, T. J.
- Nelson, W. J., (note)
- Elrod, J. G.
- Trussell, A. L., (mortgage)
- Gilbreath, C. N.
- Sauls, O. N.
- Kidd, J. J.
- Green, W. L., (note)
- Naler, C. C.
- Graves, H. T.
- Brandon, J. A.
- Gilbreath, J. A.
- GA.Agriculture Works-Mach.
- Sparks, Howell O., (JP)
- Middlebrooks, J. T., (note)

Notes Due R. C. Davis Estate:
- Bradley, Frank, (note)
- Scotts, Lizzie, (note)
- Nailer, M. H., (note)
- Benefield, J. R., (note)
- Baker, M. M., (note)
- Gober, G. J., (note)
- Smith, John F., (note)
- Kidd, E. G., (note)
- Waller, C. J. M., (note)
- Templeton, J. C., (note)
- Branden, J. M., (note)
- Yancy, J. E., (note)
- Gibson, J. P., (note)
- Heatley, J. H. (note)
- Williams, L. I. (T,), (note)

Estate Record Name
Davis, R. C. (Cont.)
Roden, J. E., (note)
Moore, Jas. H., (note)
Washburn, T. S., (note)
Scott, G. B., (note)
Stott, W. M., (note)
Norton, E. H., (note)
Nailer, C.F., (note)
McDowell, E. L., (note)
Gregg, C. W., (note)
McConnell, O. L., (note)
Burns, Susan, (note)
Hall, Jane D., Mrs., (note)
Turner, R. J., (note)
Wesser, W. P., (note)
Bolden, L. B., (note)
Israell, J. M. , (note)
Graves, H. J., (note)
Gilbreath, V. J., (note)
Cash, J. M., (note)
Ramsey, H. R., (note)
Lisscomb, L. J., (note)
Graves, H. J., (note)
Daniel, R. I., (acct.)
Candler,J. M., (acct.)
Walls, L. K., (note)
Isbell & Presley, (attys)
Marion Bros. Gen. Mdse, Boaz, AL
Guano (fertilizer) R.C.Davis Acct.
Fletcher, J. H., agent for R.C.Davis
Williamson, E. G.
More, John
Scott, Dave
Roden, R. B.
Finch, J. H.
Beard, Rusel
Mayes, J. H.
Nales, G. J.
Green, G. W.
Jordan, J.
Williamson, J. W.

Estate Record Name
Davis, R. C. (Cont.)
Malone, T. P., Mrs.
Talley, J. H.
White, T. H.
Beavers, R. C.
Windsor, H.
Naler, J. N.
Garrard, W. F.
Johnson, J. S.
Justice, W. L.
Uptain, R. L.
Green, J. H.
Elrod, J. G.
Simpson, M. W.
Naler, W. A.
Roden, G. W.
Roden, H. E.
Davis, J. D.
Milner, F. M..
Roden, H. E.
Fletcher, M. M.
Davis, G. W.
Elrod, Grif, Dr.
Murdock, R. W.
Archer, F. N.
Israel, J. W.
Burns, S. M., Mrs.
Garrard, A.
Sauls, John
Williams, E. W.
Amos, S. D.
Marion Bros. Gen. Mdse, Boaz
Guano(fertilizer) R.C.Davis Acct.
Stott, W. M.
Simpson, M. W.
Nales, C. F.
Scott, D. A.
Davis, J. D.
Rush, W. D.
Malone, T. C.
Plunket, G. T.

Estate Record Name

Davis, R. C. (Cont.)

Box 4 File 31 1904-1908

Baits, L. H.
Wear, Suear
Burns, Zeal
Bishop, G. W.
Jordan, J.
Wear, Suear
Henry, G. W.
Baits, L. A.
Williams, S.
Lipscomb, L. J.
Otinger, L. F.
Jacobs, S. H.
Scott, J. M.
Nales, G. J.
Stott, W. M.
Scott, D. O.
Mulinax, Tine
Wallace, S. W.
Simpson, M. W.
Malone, T. P.
Turner, J. W.
Roden, W. L.
Graves, H. T.
Williamson, J. H.
Windsor, H. H.
Williams, S.
Henry, W. E.
Milwee, J. A.
Peppers, D. L.
Slaton, J. F.
Israel, J. W.
Jones, J. W.
Davis, J. D.
Scott, D. A.
Green, G. W.
Worley, S. R.
Gann, J. M. W.
Israel, J. M..
Israel, L..

Estate Record Name

Davis, R. C. (Cont.)

Bloodworth, H. F.
Roden, W. N., Dr.
More, L. O.
Walker, J. W.
Kilpatrick, J. A.
Davis, Rastes
McCollough, F. F.
Wallis, L. M.
Isdel, Jem
Barksdale, W. S.
Johnson, F. F.
Davis, J. R.
Dodd, W. R.
Dodd, M. H.
Wallace, J. S.
Milner, J. A.
Milwee, H. H.
Griffin, J. H.
Underwood, G. W.
Pack, G. M.
Davis, A.
Hall, J. H.
Roden, Geo.
Naler, C. C.
Peppers, S. W.
Naler, G. J.
Strawn, R. S.
Watts, G. M.
Cash, R. A.
Baker, M. M.
McPherson, J. L.
Malone, T. C.
Collier, T. T.
Bearden, J. M.
Windsor, W. F.
Mullinax, T. W.
Dickson, James
Williams, J. W.
Martin, J. M.
Graves, T. T.

Estate Record Name
Davis, R. C. (Cont.)
- Sauls, O. N.
- Stephens, J. R.
- Jacoups, S. H.
- Pugh, A.
- Milner, F. M.
- Lipscomb, L. J.
- Murdock, R. W.
- Campbell, G. H.
- Head, G. W.
- Harris, Delfry
- Swan, W. B.
- Greer, L. J.
- Green, J. W.
- Malone, T. C.
- Gaskin, J. W.
- Leeth, C. J.
- Elrod, W. J.
- Simpson, M. W.
- Windsor, Billy
- Nelson, P. J.
- Naler, G. J.
- Windsor, H. H.
- Logan, R. M.
- Beavers, R. C.
- Fielders, John
- Bruce, W. M.
- Roe, R. B.
- Kidd, W. A.
- Waller, P. J. M.
- Black, Sam
- Amos, S. D.
- McPherson, W. A.
- Bearden, F. M.
- Walice, S. W.
- Burns, Zeal
- Williams, C. H.
- Naler, C. F.
- Thrasher, T. J.
- Bouldin, E. L.
- Wheeler,

Estate Record Name
Davis, R. C. (Cont.)
- Edmondson, J. B.
- Byars, T. L.
- Roden, J. W.
- Leath, B. L.
- Henry, W. H.
- Brown, T. J.
- Garrett, J.
- Walker, G. W.
- Plunket, G. T.
- Worley, W. L.
- Naler, J. R.
- Nix, L. E.
- Naler, J. W.
- Gipson, J. P.
- Bruce, W. A.
- Davis, B. F.
- Plunket, G. T.
- Dickson, J. A. W.
- Baker, M. M., Mrs.
- McLeod, W. A.
- Nix, L. E.
- Edmondson, G. H.
- Huff, C. D.
- Naler, S. J.
- Davis, R. E.
- Roden, H. E.
- Worley, S. R.
- Walker, J W.
- Barksdale, J. H.
- Phillips, J. W.
- Nichols, C. L.
- Rector, J. A.
- Davis, P. I. (J.)
- Barksdale, S. W.
- Yancy, J. E.
- Green, H. N.
- Cash, C. C.
- Gann, J. M. W.
- Haygood, J. B.
- Griffin, H. W.

Estate Record Name
Davis, R. C. (Cont.)
Moore, L. O.
Worley, S. R.
Jones, G. W.
Davis, W. H.
Plunket, G. T.
McPherson, E. E.
Nichols, C. L.
Jackson, G. H.
Justice, G. W.
Jackson, G. H.
Roe, J. B.
Davis, W. N.
Williams, Stephen
Baker, M. M., Mrs.
Simmons, H. P.
Jacoups, S. H.
Barrett, H. J.
Davis, W. W.
Martin, J. M.
Davis, G. W.
Williams, J. W.
Byars. T. L.
Justice, J. H.
Wallace, L. P.
Uptain, R. L.
Williams, W. J.
Stott, W. M.
Wester, W. P.
Wester, F. H.
Elrod, W. T.
Fletcher, M. M.
Middlebrooks, J. T.
McCormick, J. V.
McCormick, J. P.
Gibson, J. P.
Nelson, C. J.
Logan, R. M.
Peppers, D. L.
Thomas, Ped
Garrard, A.

Estate Record Name
Davis, R. C. (Cont.)
Justice, J. N.
Norton, E. H.
Roe, J. W.
Dodd, M. H.
Israel, J. M.
Bell, L. D.
Swann, W. B.
Leeth, M. P.
Rubedont, Nanne
Walls, L. K.
Davis, P. J.
Barksdale, J. A.
Mafield, W. A.
Croley, W. O.
Justice, W. L.
Wood, J. N.
Stonicher, T. W.
West, J. R.
Pack, G. F.
Strowd, J. D.
Peppers, A. L.
Abercrombie, John
Marson, M. R.
Marson, J. T.
Barksdale, W. S.
Milwee, W. E.
Brown, T. J.
Edmondson, J. B.
Brown, Jeff
Rollins, J. C.
Roden, H. E.
Nichols, C. L.
Lipscomb, T. H.
Griffin, J. H.
Norton, E. H.
Leeth, G. A.
Walker, J. N.
Jordan, T. J.
Battles, J. N.
Jones, E. B.

Estate Record Name

Davis, R. C. (Cont.)

Brown, Early
McLeod, W. A.
Leeth, G. A.
Byars, T. J.
Naler, J. R.
Nix, L. E.
Garrett, J.
Green, H. N.
Justice, W. L.
Yancy, J. E.
Naler, S. J.
McPherson, Arch
McPherson, J. L.
Bouldin, E. L.
Bruce, D. B.
Thrasher, G. W.
Barclay, G. T., (acct.)
Henry, W. H., (acct)
McCormac, O. L. (acct.)
Dodd, Oliver, (acct.)
Harris, J. W. (acct.)
Stancil, J. M. (acct.)
Hall, J. H., (acct.)
Long, H. M. (acct.)
Cash, L., (acct.)
Barksdale, John W., (acct.)
Hall, W. T., (acct.)
Clayton, A. L., Dr., (acct.)
Wallace, S. J., (acct.)
Harden, H. D., (acct.)
Barksdale, Walt, (acct.)
Brown, F. M., (acct.)
Gilbreath, W. B., (acct.)
Beck, T. J., (acct.)
Barksdale, W. J., (acct.)
Cash, Van, (acct.)
Cash, W. C., (acct.)
Black, J. H., (acct.)
Davis, U. G., (acct.)
Middlebrooks, T. J., (note)

Estate Record Name

Davis, R. C. (Cont.)

Wester, W. P., (note)
Morrison, J. T., (note)
Greer, J. A., (note)
Belcher, W. T., (note)
Chambers, C. W., (note)
Gilbert, C. N., (note)
Hayes, J. M., (note)
Taylor, W. W., (note)
Logan, W. L., (note)
Powell, J. E., (note)
Sparks, Manda, (note)
Hall, J. D., (note)
Ramsey, H., (mortgage)
Walker, J. W., (mortgage)
Israel, J. M., (mortgage)
Israel, L., (mortgage)
Barksdale, W. J., (mortgage)
Wallis, L. M., (mortgage)
Slaten, J. F., (mortgage)
Worley, S. R., (mortgage)
Dollar, Jno. C., (mortgage)
Worley, T. H., (mortgage)
Rains, J. P., (mortgage)
Israel, Jas. W., (mortgage)
Burns, Zealos (mortgage)
Burns, Sallie, (mortgage)
Burns, Zealos & Sallie,(mort.)
Gilbreath, V. J., (mortgage)
Amos, J. F., (note)
Gilbreath, W. J. (note)
Sparks, Samuel, (note)
Wagencroft, L. L., (note)
Powell, B. M., (note)
Fielders, John, (note)
Hall, G. B., (note)
Johnson, R. B., (note)
Harris, E. F., (note)
Sparks, W. A., (note)
Bright, R. M., (note)
Smith, W. A., (note)

Estate Record Name

Davis, R. C. (Cont.)
Jackson, J. H., (note)
Gilbreath, John A., (mortgage)
Gilbreath, Martha C., (mort.)
Hooper, J. F., (cash)
Roden, H. E., (acct.)
McCormick, O. L., (acct.)
Graves, H. F., (acct.)
Lipscomb, T. H., (acct.)
Swann, W. B., (acct.)
Cash, J. M., (acct.)
Wallace, J. S., (acct.)
McPherson, E. E., (acct.)
Milwee, W. E., (acct.)
Beck, T. J., (acct.)
Barksdale, W. S., (acct.)
Barksdale, W. J., (acct.)
Cash, Nan, (acct.)
Ramsey, John, (acct.)
Beck, T. J., (note)
Elrod, J. T., (note)
Gibson, J. R., (note)
Bearden, A. J., (mortgage)
Graves, H. T., (mortgage)
Kidd, E. H., (mortgage)
Hall, J. B., (note)
McNaron,
Sparks, S., (note)
Wazencraft, L. L., (note)
Powell, R. M., (note)
Taylor, W. M., (note)
Walter, C. J. M., (note)
Templeton, S. C., (note)
Bearden, J. M., (note)
Pugh, A., (note)
Brannon, J. A., (note)
Nalor, M. F., (mortgage)

Dean, William
Box 4 File 32 1901-1906
Names in File:
Dean, Margaret E., (widow)

Estate Record Name

Dean, William (Cont.)
Widow's Exemption
Dean, Allen
Dean, Thomas S.
Dean, W. E.
Dean, N. S.
Dean, Henry
Dean, B. P.
Dean, Jesse M.
Dean, Charles, (minor)
Dean, M. E., (widow)
Guest, J. H. E., (adm)
Green, A. B., adm.bond)
Green, P. M., (adm.bond)
Campbell, I., (adm.bond)
Quin, W. E., (adm.bond
Croley, Jas. A., Judge
Haralson, W. W., (witness)
Houston, A. W., (appraiser)
Minott, W. H. H., (appraiser)
Pendergrass, Porter G., (appr.)
Isbell, John B., (atty.)
The DeKalb Record
Yeuell, Claris, (newspaper)
Howard & Isbell, (attys.)
Davis & Haralson, (attys.)
Ala. Great Sou. Railroad
Chitwood, W. J., (sheriff)
Howard, M. W.
Blacksmith Tools
Dean, Ed
Dean, Nich
Dean, Berry
Dean, Charles P.

Dearman, M. A., Mrs.
Box 4 File 33 1908-1915
Names in File:
Jenkins, Rachael R.
Momar, Zollie
Jenkins, J. T.
Dearman, Sallie

Estate Record Name

Dearman, M. A., Mrs. (Cont.)
- Dearman, V. S.
- Roberts, E. J.
- Roberts, C. Y.
- Roberts, Emma
- Cook, Pearl
- Cook, H. S., (guar., bro-in-law)
- Dearman, Mary Lou, (minor)
- Dearman, Sophia, (minor)
- Bowen/Bowers, Sallie
- Dearman, Fletcher
- Dearman, Robert
- Coker, E. D. , (guardian bond)
- Coker, L. R., (guardian bond)
- Deerman, J. D., (note)
- Wills, J., (note)
- Pharr, G. W., (guar.ad litem)
- Dearman, Wiley
- Dearman, Martha, Mrs.
- Roberts, Emma, Mrs.
- Jenkins, Rachel

Deaton, Henry
- Box 4 File 34 1853
- Names in File:
- Deaton, William, (guardian)
- Murry, Lelitha (bond)
- Kilgore, James (bond)
- Evatt, W. L. (bond)
- Estes, Reubin, Judge
- Thomason, Z., (bond)
- Deaton, Joseph, (bond)
- Murray, Telitha Deaton, (guar.)

Dennis, E. A.
- Box 4 File 35 1891-1894
- Names in File:
- Widow's Exemption
- Dennis, Margaret J., (widow)
- Dennis, Joel T.
- Dennis, James L.
- Dennis, Tina W.
- Dennis, Elijah A.

Estate Record Name

Dennis, E. A. (Cont.)
- Dennis, Texas A.
- Dennis, Julia R.
- Hunter, Mary J., (w/o Mosley)
- Hunter, Mosley
- Dennis, William F.
- Gibson, J. C., (comm.)
- Stoner, W. C., (comm.)
- Sampley, Jesse C. (JP)
- Cochran, L. L., Judge

Dennis, Joel T.
- Box 4 File 36 1896
- Names in File:
- Seeking Bond
- Bouldin, Virgil, (atty)
- Hunt, R. C., (solicitor, Jack. Co.)
- Talley & Procter, (attys.)
- Frazier, Robert W., (sheriff)
- Thomas, D. A., (sheriff)

Denson, George Erskin
- Box 4 File 37 1911-1912
- Names in File:
- Denson, Geo. W., (adm.,father)
- Denson, Mrs. Geo. W.,(mother)
- Scott, J. C., (atty.)
- Croley, Jas. A., Judge
- Keef, John, (claim against)
- Stafford, J. M., (adm.bond)
- Denson, Bogue, (adm.bond)
- Isbell, John, (witness)

Denton, James G.
- Box 4 File 38 1912-1914
- Names in File:
- Denton, J. H., (adm., son)
- Denton, J. H., (adm.bond)
- Denton, B. F., (adm.bond)
- Denton, Dora, (adm.bond)
- Denton, B.F., heir
- Turner, J. E.,Mrs.
- Turner, Jane Denton
- Turner, L. C.

Estate Record Name

Denton, James G. (Cont.)
Denton, George R.
Denton, Dora, (daughter)
Denton, Luke
Denton, Sam
Denton, S. D.
Summerville, Josie D., (dec'd.)
Summerville, James
Summerville, Glen
Summerville, Watson
Summerville, George
Alsman, Lena, (heir of Josie)
Alsman, W. H.
Owens, Sophia D., (dau., dec'd.)
Owens, Albert, (heir of Sophia)
Owens, Luther, (heir of Sophia)
Owens, Charley, (heir of Sophia)
Owens, Roy, (heir of Sophia)
Horton, Mattie, (dau. dec'd.)
Horton, Francis
Horton, Harry
Horton, G. R., (h/o Mattie)
Denton, G. R.
Turner, E. J.
Denton, J. L.
No Widow
Chitwood, A. G., (deposition)
Warren, F. M., (deposition)
Hale, P. C., (take deposition)
Presley, I. M., (guar.ad litem)
The Sand Mountain News
Sylvania, Alabama
Grandchildren: Summerville
Owens & Horton

Dobbins, Jesse A.
Box 4 File 39 1914-1918
Names in File:
Dobbins, Charles A., (son)
Balletine, Elizabeth F., (dau)
Ballentine, Martin Luther
Young, Margaret D., (dau.)

Estate Record Name

Dobbins, Jesse A. (Cont.)
Young, Bird, (h/o Margaret)
Tibbitts, Florence, (dau)
Tibbitts, W. G.,(h/o Florence)
Dobbins, Jesse A., (will)
Nicholson, L. S., (witness)
Nicholson, Louise, (witness)
Dobbins, Charles A., (adm.)
Ballentine, Elizabeth, (adm.)
Young, Margaret D., (adm.)
Tibbitts, Florence, (contested)
Tibbitts, G. W., (contested)
Gaines, J. T., Dr., (deposition)
Pope, Jesse D.,(take depos.)
Baker, Lee S., (atty.)
Baker & Baker, (attys.)
Croley, Jas., A. Judge
Taylor, R. M., (witness)
Taylor, T. E., (witness)
Honea, J. T., (witness)
Wolf, E. R., (witness)
Grooms, Dan, (witness)
Kimsey, G. W., (witness)
Kuykendall, Lesser, (witness)
Saye, W. W., (note)
Grooms, Dan, (note)
Grooms, M. J., (note)
Lybrand, T. B., (note)
Saye, H. P.
Fowler, John A.
Ballentine, Elmer
Taylor, T. E.
Wright, W. I., Dr.
Gains, Tom, Dr.
Driskell, Glen
Taylor, Sam
Kimsey, G. W.
Hemphill, J. P.
Pruett, P. D.
Wolf, E. R.
Kirby, H. C., (sheriff)

Estate Record Name
Dobbins, Jesse A. (Cont.)
Gilbert, S. W., (dep.sheriff)
Cochran, J. J.
Driskill, Jess
Harvy, Benson
O'Shields, Felix
Johnson, D. J., (dep.sheriff)
Bartlett, John F., (casket)
Murdock, A. O., (tax 1917-18)
Smith, Thomas S., (editor)
Fort Payne Journal, (notice)
Justice, G. W.
Hicks, P., Dr.
Presley, I. M., (atty)
Dobbins, C. A.
Young, M. D., Mrs.
Ballentine, E. F., Mrs.
Driskill, J. W.
Kuykendal, W. L.
Honey, J. T.
Harvey, R. B.
Honea, J. G., (witness)
Brombelow, (monument)
Hunt & Wolfes, (attys.)
Cantrell, N. L., (dep.sheriff)
McCord, Col.
Bynum, Mr.
Kirby, A. C.
King, O. D., (Notary Public)
Bowling, C. E., Mrs.
Dobbins, Alf, Mrs.
Brumbeloe, J. H., (JP)
Dobbins, Manervia
Box 4 File 40 1909-1910
Names in File:
Sale of Land for Division
Dobbins, Manervia, Petitioner
Bowling, Ida C.,(sister,minor)
Dobbins, Alf M. (h/o Manervia)
Bowling, C. E., (h/o Ida C.)
guardian, Marshall Co.

Estate Record Name
Dobbins, Manervia (Cont.)
Amos, R. L., (deposition)
Luther, T. B., (deposition)
Croley, Jas. A., Judge
Worthy, B. J., (JP)
Bynum, B. C., (comm.)
McCord, E. O. M., (atty)
Hawkins, A. E., (atty)
Warren, F. M., (tax. Coll 1909)
DeKalb Record (notice)
Peppers, J. L., (purch.land)
Scott, J. M., (place-prop.)
Howard, J. M., (JP)
Miller, J. B., (sheriff)
Dobbs, Earl
Box 4 File 41 1901-1908
Names in File:
Dobbs, Laura G., (guardian)
Dobbs, Lillian Earl, (minor)
Dobbs, Eugenia Ruth, (minor)
Dobbs, Laura G., (mother)
Presley, I. M., (guar.ad litem)
US Fidelity & Guaranty,(bond)
Walker, Wm., (atty.)
Colwick, Louis N, (agent)
O'Shields, J. G., (guar.ad litem)
Cook, W. C. D., (bro-in-law)
Sawyer, C.T.M, (special judge)
Cochran, Earl, (register)
Dobbs, Eugene
Box 4 File 42 1904
Names in File:
Sale for Division of Land
Campbell, H. B., (petitioner)
Cook, John M., (witness)
Jacoway, William V., (witness)
Howard & Hunt, (atty)
Heirs of S. E. Dobbs
Campbell, H. B., (1/5 interest)
Quin, W. E., (1/5 interest)
Dobbs, S. R., (1/5 interest)

Estate Record Name
Dobbs, Eugene (Cont.)
McArver, J. B., (1/5 interest)
Others share 1/5 interest
Dobbs, W. M.
Dobbs, W. W.
Dobbs, Laura
Dobbs, Cicero
Dobbs, Alice
Dobbs, Eugenia (minor)
Dobbs, Earl, (minor)
Minot, Lucy, (w/o Harry)
Minot, Harry
Dobbs, Mittie, (widow of S. H.)
Dobbs, S. H.
Dobbs, Edna, (dau.of Mittie)
Killian, Wallace
Randolph, Jennie
Randolph,
Killian, Josephine, (w/o Jim)
Killian, Jim
Killian, Zoe, (minor)
Killian, Ida, (minor)
Nix, Ella G.
Nix, Ella
Nix, Joe
Nix, Winter
Nix, Ruby, (minor)
Nix, N. B.
Nix, A. J.
Quin, Mary J., (w/o W. E)
McSpadden, H. A., (guar.ad lit)
Chitwood, W. J., (sheriff)
Dobbs, L. A.
Box 4 File 43 1892-1898
Names in File:
Dobbs, James G., (adm.,son)
Dobbs, Nannie M., (widow)
Dobbs, Nannie M., (adm.)
Dobbs, Cordie, (heir)
Dobbs, Ora, (heir)
Dobbs, Frankie, (minor)

Estate Record Name
Dobbs, L. A. (Cont.)
Dobbs, John, (minor)
Dobbs, Thomas, (minor)
Dobbs, Olena, (minor)
Dobbs, Ella, (minor)
Dobbs, Nina, (minor)
Campbell, H. B., (guar.ad litem)
Baxter, F. M., (adm.bond)
Frazier, P. M., (adm.bond)
Norwood, S. W., (adm.bond)
Campbell, Henry B.
Howard, M. W. C.,(deposition)
Kelley, Thomas B.,(deposition)
James, Albert, (deposition)
Poe, W. R., (take deposition)
Nix, Joe J.. (deposition)
Dobbs, R. L., (deposition)
Fortner, Archibald,(deposition)
Haralson, W. W., (deposition)
Dobbs, R. L., (adm.bond)
Farris, R. M., (appraiser)
Homestead Exemption
Baxter, J. R & F. M. (note)
Norwood, S. W., (note)
Gibson, B. F., (note)
Hopkins, M. E., (note)
Hicks, A. L. (note)
Franklin, J. N., (note)
Keele, E. R., (receipts)
Anderson, R. Y., (receipts)
Garrett Estate, (receipts)
Godfrey, (receipts)
Cunningham, (receipts)
Hall, Prescott, (receipts)
Slone House Rent, (receipts)
Russell, Amelia
Chihester&Yancy, B'ham,(paid)
Lunsford, W. G. Co., (paid)
Fort Payne Bldg. Co., (paid)
Stanley, J. P., (paid)
Evans, Pattie, (paid)

Estate Record Name

Dobbs, L. A. (Cont.)
- *Age-Herald*, B'ham, (paid)
- Barnes, J. E., B'ham, (paid)
- Harvey, Charles, (paid)
- Durham, J. J., (paid)
- Poe, W. R., (pd.deposition)
- Pressgrove, J. S., (paid)
- Warnock, Robt., (B'ham tax)
- Butler, J. S., (bldg.repairs)
- Dobbs Brick Bldg., Ft.Payne
- Lawenthal, H., (paid)
- Durham, J. M., (lumber)
- Woodward, Robert, (paid)
- Howard, M., (bldg.repair)
- Eustins, Geo., (B'ham taxes)
- Hewitt, R. G., (Jefferson Co tax)
- Campbell, H. B., (tax coll 1898)
- Francis, J. B., (Jeff.Co.Tax-1897)
- Reed, W. D., (tax coll. 1897)
- Fortner, A. H., (note)
- Howard, J. M., (tax coll.1896)
- Nix & Campbell, (paid)
- Doe & Erwin, (paid)
- Shepherd, Dr., (paid)
- Spence, Hellen, (paid)
- Majors, John, (paid)
- McWhorter, Dr., (med.ser.)
- Gale, Dr., (paid)
- Quin, W. E. & Co., (drug bill)
- City Drug Store, (drug bill)
- Franklin Lumber Co., (paid)
- City of Birmingham
- Cochran, L. L., (paid)
- Blakemon, John T., (paid)
- Smith, T. H., Mrs., (paid)
- Fortner, Arch, (paid)
- Frazier, P. M., (paid)
- Choate, John, (paid)
- Stewart, Thomas, (paid)
- Brick Bldg. Expense
- Frame Bldg. Expense

Estate Record Name

Dobbs, L. A. (Cont.)
- Blakemon, John T., (paid) (Children's tuition 1891-92)
- Collins, O. H., (Tax 1893)
- Davis & Haralson, (attys.)
- Nix & Campbell, (coffin & box)
- Smith, Chichester & Young
- Yancy, J. L.
- Howard, J. M., (tax 1895)
- Loveman, Joseph & Leob (Purchased land)
- Loveman, A. B., B'ham.
- Joseph, M. V., B'ham.
- Loeb, Emil, B'ham.
- Fuller, W. T., (clerk Cir. Ct.)
- Cuningham, Jonathan,(pur.land)
- L. A. Dodds & M. W. Howard
- Koalin Prop. Dekalb Co.
- Keolin Clay Mfg. (property)
- Hawkins, James, (land)
- Jett, D. P., (land)
- Hartline, J. A., (property line)
- Hartline, J. P., (property line)
- Phillips, P. D., (property line)
- Hawkins, James, (prop. line)
- Crabtree, Warren, (prop.line)
- Rogers, Reece, (prop.line)
- Microfilm Roll 65 end

Dobbs, Stephen E.
- Box 4 File 44 1889-1906
- Names in File:
- Dobbs, Laura, Widow
- Dobbs, W. M., (adm., son)
- Sawyer, Charles, (Sp. Judge)
- Dobbs, W. L.
- Dobbs, W. M.
- Dobbs, S. R.
- Dobbs, Lucy
- Dobbs, Alice
- Dobbs, Lillian Earl
- Dobbs, Jeannie

Estate Record Name
Dobbs, Stephen E. (Cont.)
Dobbs, Eula
Killian, Wallace
Killian, Jeanie
Killian, Zorah
Killian, Ida
Payne, John L, (guar.ad litem)
Killian, Wallace, (minor)
Killin, Jeanie, (minor)
Killian, Zora, (minor)
Killian, Ida, (minor)
Killian Josephine, (dec'd.)
Dobbs, Edna, (minor)
Dobbs, S. H., (dec'd.)
Dobbs, S. R., (adm. bond)
Davis, C. C., (adm. bond)
Heard, G. S. V., (adm.bond)
McWhorter, H. P., (adm.bond)
Frazier, P. M., (adm.bond)
Cook, W. C. D., Judge
Campbell, H. B., (guard.ad litem)
Dobbs, Edna, (minor)
Dobbs, Earl, (minor)
Dobbs, Jennie, (minor)
Killian, Ida, (minor)
Dobbs, Lucy, (minor of S. E.)
Dobbs, Alice, (minor of S. E.)
Dobbs, Lillian Earl, (minor)
Dobbs, Jeanie, (minor of S. E.)
Chitwood, W. J., (sheriff)
Dobbs, S. R., (note)
Horton, R. R., (mortgage)
First Natl. Bank, Chatt., (cert.)
Whittle, J. W., (note)
Reece, A. D., (note)
Phillips, A. J., (note)
Dobbs, S. H., (note)
Dobbs, W. W., (note-good)
City of Ft. Payne, (warrants)
Tenn. Land Dev., (bonds)
King, Joe, (acct.)

Estate Record Name
Dobbs, Stephen E. (Cont.)
Ala. State Treas., (warrants)
Fike, David, (note)
Receipts:
McCartney, W. A., (house rent)
Carroll, A., (cotton rent)
Dobbs, C. L., (cotton rent)
Spears,W. H.,(rent Cherokee Co.)
Hawkins, Chas., (house rent)
Franklin,Thos., (house rent)
Dobbs, S. R., (house rent)
Hoge, Lem, (house rent)
Hoge, J. M., (shucks)
Killian, M. H. (corn sold)
Carroll, R., (corn sold)
Dobbs, W. W., (Boatwright Pl.)
White, Mrs., (house rent)
Nowlin, B. A., (fodder sold)
Cross, F. W., (corn sold)
Love, Mrs., (house rent)
Bunt, R. A., (corn sold)
Jones, Sam, (corn sold)
Russell, W. W., (city warrants)
Chandler, Jesse, (corn sold)
Brock, Henry, (house rent)
Renfroe, Bob, (corn & tops)
Simpson, Mack, (cotton rent)
Dobbs, C. L., (cotton rent)
Stinson, __, (house rent)
Spears, Will, (house rent)
Bell Telephone Co.(right of way)
Rogers, Will, (house rent)
Rider, __, (cotton rent)
Copeland, Jack, (cotton rent)
Haralson, W. W., (town lot)
Dobbs, W. W., (town lot)
Peek, Oscar, (town lot)
Spears, W. H., (rent)
Cook, W. C. D., (land)
Killian, B. B., (house rent)
Rider, F. M., (cotton rent)

Estate Record Name

Dobbs, Stephen E. (Cont.)

Rutledge, M. J., (land sold)
Rothell, __, (fodder sold)
Copeland, et al, (cotton rent)
Rothell, __, (cotton rent)
Payne, W. D. M., (land sold)
Stephens, E. G. H., (land sold)
Farrar, Sarah
Killian, W. E. & B., (land)
Dobbs, W. W. (land)
Sizemore, W. H., (cotton rent)
Spears, Mrs., (rent)
Morris, Pierce, (corn)
Fike, Dave, (acct.)
Howard, John, (corn)
Teague, J. M., (timber)
Hawkins, Chas., (house rent)
PAID:
Sawyer, C. M., (ins., paid)
Cunningham, F. M., (paid)
Killian, E. S., (paid)
Davis & Haralson, (attys.)
Shepherd, G. W. J., (paid)
Gaines Marble Co., (monument)
Cochran, Earl, (adv., paid)
Payne, J. L., (paid)
Tuition for Lucy (paid)
Reed, W. D., (tax coll.1899)
Campbell, H. B., (tax coll,1901)
Grave, H. L., (tax coll. 1900)
W. W. Dobbs Gen Hdwe.
Burial Expense (paid)
McWhorter, H. M., (paid)
Abernathy, M. J. (Cherokee Co tax)
Melton, W. G., (paid)
Tusculossa Female College
Dobbs, Lucy, Tuition (paid)
Blackburn, W. F., (tax 1901-2)
McSpadden, H. A., (tax 1904)
Lawrence, Jas. R., (Cherokee tax)
Cain, Wall, (tax 1905)

Estate Record Name

Dobbs, Stephen E. (Cont.)

H. B. Brock Co. (windows)
Smith, T. H., Mrs. (adv.)
Fort Payne Journal (adv.)
Davis, John A., (NP)
Stewart, R. A. (auctioneer)
Smith, Thomas H., (adv.)
Brock, H. B., (house repairs)
Nichols, Thomas, (appraiser)
Houston, A. W., (appraiser)
Sherherd, G. W. T., (appraiser)
Harris, J. D.
Houston, Billy
Lively, W. C.
McWhorter, H. P., Dr.
DeShields, J. G.
Frazier, R. W.
Smith & Malone
Malone, James
Cochran, Earl
Taylor, J. N.
Quin, W. E., (physician)
Russell, W.
Dobbs, Laura G.
Randolph., Jennie
Dobbs, Sam R.
Dobbs, Samuel R.
Yarny, Ida
Miller, Zoe
Minot, Lucy
Farrar, Sarah E., (guardian)
Killian, Joe
Killian, Zoe
Dobbs, Sarah Alice
Ferguson, J. B., (guar.ad litem)
Penn, J. W., (Gadsden Judge)

Dobbs, W. W.

Box 4 File 45 1891
Names in File:
Dobbs, James D., (minor)
Collins, Eliza M., (minor)

Estate Record Name

Dobbs, W. W. (Cont.)
- Dobbs, W. W., minor heirs
- Dobbs, S. L., (guardian)
- Dobbs, S. L., (guar. bond)
- Dobbs, R. L., (guar.bond)
- Dobbs, S. E., (guar.bond)
- Cochran, L. L, Judge

Dobbs, W. W.
- Box 4, File 46 1890-1907
- Dobbs, L. A., (adm.)
- Dobbs, R. L., (adm.)
- Campbell, Ike
- Arthur, Ruth J.
- Arthur, Polk, (h/o Ruth)
- Wade, Mary
- Wade, Henry, (h/o Mary)
- Garrett, Tina (Nina)
- Garrett, William S. (h/o Tina)
- Collins, Liza
- Collins, Wallin, (h/o Lisa)
- Johnson, Cornelia A.
- Johnson, Thomas, (h/o Cornelia)
- Dobbs, Lucinda
- Dobbs, James
- Dobbs, James G.
- Dobbs, Cordie
- Dobbs, Ara
- Dobbs, Frankie
- Dobbs, John
- Dobbs, Alma
- Dobbs, Ella
- Dobbs, Nina
- Dobbs, Dorcus/Darius
- Dobbs, Angeline Collett
- Dobbs, James M.
- Dobbs, Franklin
- Houston, Caroline
- Houston, Edley, (h/o Caroline)
- Dobbs, James G.
- Fuller, W. T., (Guar.ad litem)
- Dobbs, Thomas, (minor)

Estate Record Name

Dobbs, W. W. (Cont.)
- Dobbs, Olena, (minor)
- Dobbs, Ella, (minor)
- Dobbs, Nine, (minor)
- Dobbs, Ira F.
- Dobbs, R. L.
- Dobbs, L. A.
- Dobbs, D. P.
- Dobbs, Thomas
- Dobbs, Laura
- Dobbs, Mary
- Dobbs, C. L.
- Dobbs, Frank
- Dobbs, John
- Dobbs, Eliza M.
- Dobbs, W. L.
- Dobbs, S. E.
- Dobbs, James M.
- Dobbs, Pauline Collett
- Dobbs, S. L.
- Dobbs, Nannie
- Dobbs, Jas. S.
- Dobbs, Sarah H.
- Houston, T. C., Mrs.
- Houston, E. M.
- Dobbs, Ira R.(F), (brother)
- Dobbs, Robert L., (brother)
- Dobbs, L. A., (brother)
- Dobbs, James M., (brother)
- Dobbs, S. E., (brother)
- Dobbs, C. L., (brother)
- Houston, Caroline, (sister)
- Dobbs, Angeline Collett, (sister)
- Dobbs, Dorcus C., (sister)
- Dobbs, Mary, (sister)
- Collett, Angeline
- Howard, M. W., (witness)
- Nix, Joe J., (witness)
- Payne, A. F., (comm.)
- Dobbs, Nannie M., (adm. L.A.)
- Dobbs, James G., (adm. L.A.)

Estate Record Name
Dobbs, W. W. (Cont.)
Russell, W. W.
Cochran, L. L.
Cook, W. C. D.
Chitwood, W. J.
White, Joseph A.
McClung, Mary E.
Dobbs, Lucinda C.
Collins, O. H.
Campbell, A. L., (witness)
Chitwood, W. J., (sheriff)
Frazier, P. M., (sheriff)
National Bank, (receipts)
First Natl.Bank, (receipts)
Howard, M. W., (note)
Bradley, (note)
Warren, F. M., (note)
Fuller, W. T., (note)
Franklin, James R., (note)
Campbell, Isaac, (note)
Chitwood, R. O., (note)
Kirkendal, T. A., (note)
Howard, S. O., (note)
Campbell, W. H., (note)
Baxter, James, (note)
Franklin, J. N., (note)
Durham, J. M., (note)
Winoche, Geo., (note)
Stamps, E. R., (note)
Payments from Estate:
Payne, A. F.
Campbell & Killian
Kramer & Graves, (lumber)
Ft. Payne Hdwe.
Frost, John
Nix & Campbell
Carriage & Mill, (buggy parts)
L. J. Sharp & Co.
Crowder, E. S.
Ft. Payne C & I
Ft. Payne Coal & Iron, (water)

Estate Record Name
Dobbs, W. W. (Cont.)
Ft. Payne CT Mill
New England Drug Store,(med.)
Bell, C. M., (carriage repair)
Tygert, Wm., (harness, etc.)
Green, Blev., (stables)
Ft. Payne Journal, (adv.)
Evans, Calvin
Howard, J. M., (tax 1890-92)
Bates, A. W., (tax coll. 1890)
Kelley & Davenport
DeKalb Livery & Stable
Campbell, Killian & Russell
Spaulding, J. S., (water)
Ft. Payne Plumbing, (pipes)
Crowder, E. S.
Ft. Payne Hdwe & Mining
Franklin, J. B., (receipts)
Dobbs, Isa F.
Dobbs, Dorcus
Collett, Angeline
Dobbs, Silas P.
Dobbs, S.L.
Garret, Sarah
Collins, Nina
Troutt, John, (marble monument)
Drain, John
Box 4 File 47 1857-1858
Names in File:
Drain, Geo. D., (minor)
Snider, C., (guardian)
Snider, Cornelius H.
Estes, Reuben, Judge
Driskell, A. Jackson (A. J.)
Box 4 File 48 1874
Names in File:
Driskell/Driskell
Driskill, Mary, (minor heir)
Driskill, Andrew, (minor heir)
McNearon, William, (guardian)
McNaron/McNearon

Estate Record Name
Driskell, A. Jackson (A.J.) (Cont.)
McNaron, William C. (bond)
Slone, William, (bond)
Bailor, W. H., (bond)
Horton, A. J., Judge
Duncan, Nancy K.
Box 4 File 49 1888-1889
Names in File:
Will of Nancy Duncan
Pickens, Henry W., (witness)
Hagler, C. S., (witness)
Tallman, James A., Judge Etowah Co
Dunlap, R. A. D.
Duncan, R. D., (husband)
Richards, Maggie, (g-dau.)
Richards, Mary Lilly, (g-dau.)
Beeson, Belle, (dau.)
Duncan, John W., (son, exec.)
Duncan, Robert H., (son)
Duncan, F. P., (son)
Duncan, Matilda
Duncan, John W., (guardian)
Dunson, R. E.
Box 4 File 50 1913
Names in File:
Dunson, R. E., (minor)
Dunson, Charles Richard, (minor)
Dunson, Dortha E. (minor)
Dunson, M. M., (guardian)
Dunson, M. M., (father)
Coe, W. A., (bond)
Cochran, J. J., (bond)
Croley, Jas. A., Judge
Dutton, David
Box 4 File 51 1850-1869
Names in File:
Crow, George W., (adm)
Dutton, Francis, (widow)
Dutton, William
Dutton, Thomas
Dutton, Lavica

Estate Record Name
Dutton, David (Cont.)
Crow, Amanda,(w/o Geo. Crow)
Spangler, Martha, (w/o Isaac)
Spangler, Isaac
Crow, Malina, (w/o Michael)
Crow, Michael K.
Dutton, Malinda Dutton
Dutton, Michael
Lane, Vadney Jane Dutton
Crow, Washington
Dutton, Sara, (dec'd.) heirs
Dutton, James William
Dutton, Mallissa
Dutton, Martha
Dutton Thomas
Dutton, Luettean
Dutton, Lavice
Dutton, Melissa, (minor)
Crow, Michael K., (guardian)
Crow, Geo. W., (guar.bond)
Spangler, Isaac, (guar.bond)
Crow, M. K.
Roberts, Richard, (appraiser)
Thomas, Martha
Dutton, Louisa
Bogles, Joseph C.
Walden, John
Harlson, Wm. J.
Cunningham, John
Estes, Reuben, Judge
Goggin, Edmond T., (witness)
Tucker, James, (witness)
Cooper & Baines, (attys.)
Bogle, J. C., (appraiser)
Brooks, Benj., (JP)
Lewis, W. L.
Lewis, J. L.
Dutton, Thomas, (minor)
Slone & Hawkins
Franklin, J. N., Judge
Majors, A. W.

Estate Record Name
Dutton, David (Cont.)
Winston, John G., (paid)
Hogue, D. S.
Hammack, Thomas, (paid)
Hammack, W.
Cunningham, Jesse, (JP)
Poe, James C., (paid)
Clayton, Daniel, (paid)
Brandon, Margaret, (paid)
Garrett, W. B., (JP)
Brandon, C. F., (JP)
Carter, A. W., (paid)
Dobb, J. G.
Dobb, James G.
Jack, Allen
Williams, James
Dutton, Samuel
Parkes, Wm.
Harvey, Lewis
Perry?, Noah, Estate
Harvey, Lewis, (adm)
N. Phillips & Co. (paid)
Hudson, T. W., (JP)
Phillips, R. D.
Brandon,
Crow, G. W.
Majors, A. W.
Horton, A. J.
Count, J. P.
Livingston, E. F.
Clayton, Perry
Majors, Samuel
Jacoway, W. A., (paid)
Rupell, (tuition)
Small, (tuition)
Parker, James
Garrett, Thomas (JP)
Clayton, Solmon, (pd./coffin)
Driskill, W. L., (JP)
May, Wm. H. (cutting coats)
Graham Beat Tax

Estate Record Name
Dutton, David (Cont.)
Cohen, J. J., (Rome, Ga.)
Barsoms?, James, 1853 tax
Sullivan, F. J., (cloth & thread)
Johnson, William, (JP)
Sullivan, Francis J.
Sullivan, F. J.
Blanton, Whitman, (paid)
Malone, G. W., (paid)
Dutton, Francis (84 ac. dower)
Hammock, Thomas
Brandon, H. H.
Goggin, E. T.(appraiser)
Frazier, John
Clayton, Daniel
Lainbeath, Jesse
Winston, John W., (paid)
Winston & Hoge, (mdse)
Hoge, John K.
Carden, J. W., (medicine)
Winston, J. G., (medicine)
Beesan & Phillips
Beeson, Jesse G.
Brock, Andrew, (witness)
Findley, John B.
Findley, J. B., (acct.due)
Killian, Elias (blacksmith)
Buntern, L. W., (JP)
Cave, James, (2-gal.whiskey)
Parkes, William
Comer, A. F. (Floyd Co.Ga.)
Parsons, T. C., (1851 tax)
Mackey, A. H., (paid)
Ward, A. J., (paid)
Newmin, M. C., (JP)
Gibert, J. W., (1850 tax)
Spangler, Nathan, (lumber)
Seaman, Samuel, (paid)
Grant, J. F., (paid)
Beene, Samuel, (surveying)

Estate Record Name
Dutton, David (Cont.)
Sales of Inventory:
Clayton, Daniel, (cow & mule)
Clayton, Sampson, (cow & mule)
Dutton, Frances (items listed)
Cunningham, Jesse
Dutton, Wm., (pigs, filley,tools)
Tyner, Steve J., (hogs)
Crow, Michael K., (gray horse)
Crow, G. W., (wagon)
Sale of Negroes
Beene, Samuel, (commissioner)
Ryan, William, (witness)
Frazier, John, (witness)
Reece, M., (note)
Williams, Jas., (note)
Allen, Jack
Clayton, L. S. (purch.prop.)
Cunningham, Jesse, (purch prop.)
Dutton, Wm., (purch.prop.)
Tyner, Stephen I., (purch.prop.)
Clayton, Wm., (purch.prop.)
Crow, G. W., (purch.prop)
Williams, Elias, (paid)
Povvy & Parks, (paid)

Estate Record Name
Dutton, David (Cont.)
Lewis & Cothran, (paid)
Newkirk, Jas., (paid)
See File 52
Dutton, David
Box 4 File 52 1854
Names in File:
Crow, G. W., (adm.)
Dutton, Francis, (widow)
Estes, R. Judge
Dutton, Malissa
Spangler, Martha
Spangler, Isaac
Dutton, Lavica
Crow, Michael K.
Crow, Matilda
Crow, Geo. W., (adm.)
Crow, Amanda, (w/o Geo.)
Dutton, William
Dutton, Thomas
Winston, J. G.
See File 51 (Total File)
Microfilm Roll 66 continued

Estate Record Name	**Estate Record Name**

E

Estate Record Name
Earp, Wesley
Box 4 File 53 1890-1895
Names in file:
Earp, Theodore W., (Estate)
Earp, Robert S., (minor)
Earp, William G. (S.), (minor)
Rockholt, Letitia A., (guardian)
Rockholt, Letitia A., (aunt)
Fuller, W. J., (guar.ad.litem)
Phillips, P. D., (bond)
Morgan, S. D., (bond)
Cook, W. C. D., Judge
Nicholson, E. P.
Payne & Gardner Mdse.
Rockholt, Tom
Payne, M. F.
Rockholt, L. A., Mrs., (guar.)
Edwards, D. L.
Box 4 File 54 1908
Names in file:
Edwards, Rose, (widow)
Edwards, Clarence, (minor)
Edwards, Clessie, (minor)
Jacobs, J. A., (father-in-law)
Jacobs, J. A., (adm.)
Edwards, L. P., (adm.bond)
Howard & Hunt, (attys.)
Croley, J. A., Judge
Edwards, H. N.
Box 4 File 55 1908
Names in file:
Edwards, L. P., (bro., adm.)
Edwards, A. E., (mother)
Edwards, S. C., (heir)
Edwards, Dessie, (heir)
Edwards, Georgia, (heir)
Edwards, Minnie, (heir)
Jacobs, J. A., (adm.bond)

Estate Record Name
Edwards, H. N. (Cont.)
Croley, Jas. A., Judge
Edwards, Henry (Colored)
Box 4 File 56
Names in file:
Sawyer, Chas., (adm.,friend)
Edwards, Cora, (wife)
Edwards, Ross, (minor)
Edwards, Babe, (minor)
Edwards, Vick, (minor)
Edwards, Joicy, (minor)
Edwards, Chick, (minor)
Kerby, Joicy Edwards
Presley, I. M., (guar.ad litem)
U. S. Fidelity & Guar. (bond)
Ft. Payne Water Co., (paid)
Croley, Jas. A., Judge
Edwards, John E.
Box 4 File 57 1905-1906
Names in file:
Edwards, W. S.,(guardian)
Edwards, J. F., (guardian)
Copeland, A. C., (guar.ad litem)
Land, 445 acres
Appleton, John E., Juror
Davis, John A., (atty.)
Croley, Jas. A., Judge
Robinson, Audy, (blacksmith pd)
Jones Bros. Store, (paid)
Oliver Hall Co., (roofing, pd.)
Killian, B., Store, (paid)
Oliver Hall Co.,(burial exp.)
Appleton, T. H., (med.)
Cagle, J. A., (juror)
Newman, F. P., (juror)
Sanders, W. T., (juror)
Matthews, J. H., (juror)
Appleton, W. N., (juror)

Estate Record Name

Edwards, John E. (Cont.)
- Frost, W. H., (juror)
- Smith, B. N., (juror)
- Appleton, Jas. G., (juror)
- Templeton, John L., (juror)
- Smith, H. F., (juror)
- Norwood, R. N., (juror)
- Mosteller, W. E., (Adv.)
- Clinks, (auctioneer)
- **Receipts:**
- Norwood, R. M., (rent)
- Coker, J. W., (rent)
- Sarton, W. T., (rent)
- Ward, N. W.
- Edwards, W. S., (cash)
- Edwards, W. S. & N. J., (cash)
- Kerby, Turner, (cash)
- Parker, W. J., (cash)
- Jones, G. M., (cash)
- Gilbreath, M. N., (adm.ad litem)
- Newman, Frank
- Appleton, W. R.
- Appleton, James
- Appleton, Jack
- Sanders, Thos.
- Norwood, Rufus
- Smith, Baswell
- Frost, Hale
- Cagle, Jack
- Smith, Huston
- Mathews, John
- Templeton, J. A.
- Chitwood, W. J., (sheriff)
- Chitwood, Green, (deputy)
- Edwards, W. S., (guar.bond)
- Edwards, John, (guar.bond)
- Smith, C. W., (guardian bond)
- Sinard, J. T., (guardian bond)
- Appleton, T. H., (Dr.)
- Cain, Wall, (tax coll. 1905)
- Oliver Hall Co., (burial case)

Estate Record Name

Edwards, John E. (Cont.)
- Jones Bros., (coat & vest)
- Coker, Hannah, (care of father)
- Farmers Merchant Bank
- Crump, R. M.
- Contintal Gin Co.
- Smith, A. W., Treas.
- Mosteller, W. E., (editor)
- *Collinsville Courier*, (adv)
- Reeves, Geo. W.
- Croley, Jas. A., Judge
- **Sale of Personal Property:**
- Smith, James, (cultivator)
- Barksdale, William, (sythe cradle)
- Petty, W. D., (disk harrow)
- Coker, J. W., (disk plow)
- Dobbs, R. D., (hoe & tools)
- Coker, L. R., (fork & shovel)
- Edwards, J. F., (plow & tools)
- Jones, J. E., (screw plate & auger)
- Dobbs, R. D. (plane & hand saw)
- Edwards, J. F., (2-hoes)
- Coker, J. W., (2-turning plows)
- Dobbs, R. D., (cultivator)
- Appleton, (ox yoke)
- Barksdale, J. H.,(scrap iron,shears)
- Ellis, Wm., (turning plow)
- Coker, J. W., (shears,wool mower)
- Mattox, J. H. (hole digger)
- Jones, Ben, (well pump)
- Dobbs, R. F., (chains, saw, plow)
- Frost, Hale, (turning plow)
- Kilgore, John, (buggy & hames)
- Appleton,J. E.,(churn,tub,kettle)
- Jones, William, (4-jugs)
- Jones, N. B., (jugs & jars)
- McGee, Berry, (meat cutter)
- Coker, T. A., (jars)
- Robert, Chas., (jars)
- Smith, J. S., (jug)
- Jones, Joe, (jars)

Estate Record Name
Edwards, John E. (Cont.)
Swindell, Wm.,(jars)
Petty, W. D., (check lines)
Baker, Geo., (saddle & scrap iron)
Griffin, J. M., (2-horse wagon)
Fortenberry, Berry, (hog)
Stephens, E. T., (2-hogs)
Petty, W. B., (hog)
Roberts, Chas., (hog)
Graves, Josh
Ellis, Wm., (3-pigs)
Appleton, John, (sow & pigs)
Kelley, Sol, (sow & pigs)
Kilgore, J. M., (sow)
Barksdale, J. H. (shop tools)
Appleton, John, (disk harrow)
Pardon, Bob, (wheat)
Frost, Hale, (syrup)
Smith, J. S., (syrup)
Barksdale, Wm.,(mower & rake)
Barksdale, Wm., (road scrape,etc.)
Edwards, J. F., (wheat drill)
Jones, W. P., (Jigs)
Coker, J. W., (cow & calf)
Jones, Ben, (machinery)
Edwards, J. F. (mare,mule,cow)
Graves, John, (hay)
Appleton, John, (hay)
See File 58
Edwards, John E.
Box 4 File 58 1906-1907
Names in file:
Edwards, W. S., (son, adm.)
Roden, Louisa J.
Gilbreath, Margaret J.
Ellis, C. P.
Ellis, W. P., (h/o C. P.)
Coker, Tera A.
Coker, T. D., (h/o Tera A.)
Coker, Hannah I.
Coker, J. W., (h/o Hannah)

Estate Record Name
Edwards, John E. (Cont.)
Edwards, John F.
Reeves, Berry, Mrs. (dec'd)
Reeves, Charles A.
McBroom, Nancy M.
McBroom, P., (h/o Nancy)
Williams, Ruth E. (w/o Earnest)
Williams, Earnest
Reeves, George
Green, Lily Bell, (w/o J. A.)
Green, J. A.
Walden, O. P., (w/o N. L.)
Walden, N. L.
Daniels, Lizzie, (minor)
Edwards, J. F.
Reeves, G. W.
McBroom, N. M.
Reeves, N. M.
Norwood, S. B., (atty.)
Garrison, M. F., (NP)
Walden, Pearl, Mrs.
Pate, Rosa/Rosey
McBroom, Nancy M.
Reeves, C. A.
Williams, Ruth E.
Reeves, Geo. W.
Green, Lillie Belle, (minor)
Williams, P.
Walden, O. P., (minor)
Copeland, A. C., (guar.ad litem)
Collinsville Courier
Roden, L. J.
Chitwood, W. J., (sheriff)
Davis, John A., (NP)
Ellis, W. P. (purchased land)
Ellis, C. P., (purchased land)
Coker, J. D., (purchased land)
Coker, T. A., (purch.land)
Coker, J. W., (purch.land)
Coker, H. I., (purch.land)
Edwards, J. F., (purch.land)

Estate Record Name
Edwards, John E. (Cont.)
U S Fidelity & Guaranty
Sawyers, Charles M. T.
Templeton, J. L., (appraiser)
Jones, W. P., (appraiser)
Smith, C. W., (appraiser)
Edwards, E. A., (asst.surveyor)
Graves, J. S., (clerk)
Swindell, Wm., (auctioneer)
Dobbs, Frank, (clerk)
Nicholson, L. S., (survey)
Ward, N. W., (selling land)
Smith, Thos. H., (adv.)
Cain, Wall, (tax coll. 1905-6)
Appleton, W. N., (aid surveyor)
Sawyer, Chas M.
Davis, John A., (fees)
Grave Monument $55.00
Mosteler, W. E., (adv.)
Mosteler, W. E., Mrs. (NP)
Edwards, John E., (monument)
Smith, C. W., (witness)
Newman, J. W., (witness)
Wall, Fred, (commissioner)
Daniel, L. J., (guardian)
Roden, Louise Jane
Green, L. B., Mrs.
Gilbreath, Marcus N.
Roden, L. J.
Hale, P. C., (clerk)
Mosteller, W. E., (adv.)
The Collinsville Courier
Fort Payne Journal
Smith, T. H., (editor, adv.)
Ward, W. W., (selling land)
Daniel, Lizzie D.
Ellis, Catherine P.
Coker, Walter, (h/o Hannah)
Receipts:
Norwood, R. M., (cotton rent)
Fortenberry, W. C., (cotton rent)

Estate Record Name
Edwards, John E. (Cont.)
Box 4 File 58 1906-1907
Sarton, W. T., (cotton rent)
Coker, J. W., (cotton rent)
Edwards, J. F., (cotton rent)
Edwards, J. F., (hay)
Coker, J. W. (hay)
Wright, Jas., (acct. due)
Coker, J. W., (rent)
Edwards, W. S. (note)
Edwards, W. S, & N. J., (note)
Parker, W. J., (note)
Jones, G. M., (note)
Roberts, F. M., (note)
Sale of Personal Property:
Jones, E. B., (corn)
Ashman, W, A., (corn)
Kirby, B. F., (corn)
Kearby, J, P., (corn)
Sizemore, J. S., (corn)
Swindell, W., (corn)
Ward, M. B., (corn)
Edwards, John, (dishes)
Coker, Walter, (dishes)
Forten, Tip, (butter dish)
Roden, L. J., (pitcher)
Jones, Joe, (forks & knives)
Coker, L. J., (sugar bowls)
Ashmen, W. A., (sugar bowl)
Ward, Mrs.
Barksdale, W. M, (knives)
Jones, W. P., (clock)
Coker, T. A., (frame)
Edwards, John, (clock)
Jones, W. P., (trunk)
Kilgo, W. M., (gun)
Gilbreath, M. J., (cotton)
Ellis, W. P., (gun)
Edwards, John, (gun)
Coker, T. A., (wool rolls)
Roden, L. J., (wool rolls)

Estate Record Name
Edwards, John E. (Cont.)
Sarton, Mrs., (wool rolls)
Edwards, W. S., (wool rolls)
Coker, Walt, (bedstead)
Mattox, Arthur, (bedstead)
Sizemore, Mrs., (kitchen safe)
Edwards, Earnest, (razor)
Barksdale, W. M., (umbrella)
Barksdale, J. H., (bed springs)
Barksdale, W. M., (saw set)
Barksdale, W. M., (razor)
Ashmen, W. A., (bed springs)
Stevenson, O. B., (bedstead)
Jones, Joe, (3-chairs)
Coker, Walter, (3-chairs)
Maddox, Arthur, (3-chairs)
Swindell, W. M., (4-chairs)
Cagle, Amos, (3-chairs)
Coker, Walter, (wardrobe, lamps)
Madox, Arthur, (table)
Roden, L. J., (sewing machine)
Smith, James, (jars)
Freem?, T. M., (jars)
Tidmore, W. J., (basket)
Jones, Melt, (pinchers)
Jones, Joe, (bucket)
Roden, L. J., (stove)
Norwood, Mrs., (safe)
Barksdale, J. F., (saddle)
Tidmore, J. H., (safe)
Kilgore, Mrs., (gun)
Jones, George, (bedstead)
Ellis, W. P., (bowls)
Gilbreath, M. M., (pots)
Gilbreath, O. D., (bits & bell)
Appleton, Jas., (bell)
Kirby, B. F., (jug)
Killian, Bill, (wheel spin)
Edwards, Mrs., (wheel spin)
Sizemore, J. S., (syrup)
Mayfield, W. A., (syrup)

Estate Record Name
Edwards, John E. (Cont.)
Freeman, F.M., (syrup)
Matox, John, (barrel)
Barksdale, W. M.,(fruit jars)
Matox, Arthur, (cupboard)
Barksdale, J. H., (barrel)
Smith, James, (and. Irons)
Coker, Hannah, (bedding)
Coker, Paul, (corn sheller)
Nicholson, Lem, (wagon bed)
Cunningham, (corn)
Killian, W. E., (cotton seed)
Chandler, Arthur, (cotton seed)
Jones, W. P., (corn)
Nicholson, L. S., (corn)
Jones, W. B., (hay)
Cunningham, Messer, (fodder)
Meeks, H. E., (fodder)
See File 57
Ellis, Charles T.
Box 4 File 59 1908-1929
Names in file:
Ellis, Pallie, M., (widow, adm.)
Ellis, Nelda, (dau.)
Ellis, Albert, (son)
Ellis, Robert H., (son)
Croley, Jas. A. Judge
White, J. M., (adm.bond)
Maxwell, A., (adm.bond)
White, W. C., (adm.bond)
White, John L.,(adm bond)
Presley, Isbell, (atty)
Culberson, C. Y., (notary pub.)
Malone, G. L., Judge
Ellis, P. M., (widow)
Ellis, Gladys Charles
Notes Due:
Dean, Allen, (note)
Riddle, W. R., (note)
Crane, W. H. (note)
Ellis, J. S., (note)

Estate Record Name
Ellis, Charles T. (Cont.)
Crane, Jack, (note)
Palmer, F. M., (note)
Raley, J. C., (note)
Price, Bass, (note)
Lea, Dock, (note)
Shelton, J. W., (note)
Shelton, M. T., (note)
Dean, W. T., (note)
Browder, B. D., (note)
Durham, J. M., (note)
Smith, J. M., (note)
Crow, J. M., (note
Palmer, Geo., (note)
Smith, Sherman, (note)
Raley, J. C., (note)
Ellis, Edgar, (note)
Warren, James, (note)
Accounts Due:
Highfield, G. W., (acct.due)
Harris, Gean, (acct. due)
Hammons, Mead, (acct.due)
Hamrick, G. W., (acct. due)
Roden, T. C., (acct. due)
Roden, Nip, (acct. due)
Reynolds, W. W., (acct. due)
Raley, W. H., (acct. due)
Reynolds, R. H., (acct. due)
Taylor, A. B., (acct. due)
Bray, J. W., (acct. due)
Berry, John, (acct. due)
Goss, R. G., (acct.due)
Gifford, Geo., (acct. due)
Dean, Frank, (acct. due)
Day, C. E., (acct. due)
Dean, E. B., (acct. due)
Lyons, D. D., (acct. due)
Chadwick, B. F. (acct. due)
Palmer, F. M., (acct. due)
Pruitt, J. W., (acct. due)
Keith, William, (acct. due)

Estate Record Name
Ellis, Charles T. (Cont.)
Keith, C. G., Mrs., (acct. due)
Kerby, J. C., (acct. due)
Harwood, Will, (acct. due)
Hardinger, Richard, **(acct.due)**
Hicks, J. D., (acct. due)
Henegar, M. O., (acct. due)
Ellis, M. E., Mrs., (acct.due)
Ezzelle, J. E., (acct. due)
Henegar, G. T., (acct. due)
Wade, L. H., (acct. due)
Warren, James, (acct. due)
Triplett, J. F., (acct. due)
Templeton, S. C., (acct. due)
Chambers, Barry, (acct. due)
Stalvey, G. W., (acct. due)
Walraven, Andy, (acct. due)
Williams, J. L., (acct. due)
Wright, Edgar, (acct. due)
Mickens, Vergil, (acct. due)
McClimore, John, (acct. due)
Keane, W. P., (acct. due)
Cordell, Hattie, (acct. due)
Cuzzort, M. B., (acct. due)
Cordell, H. F., (acct. due)
Davenport, J. H., (acct. due)
Jones, J. W., (acct. due)
Byrd, T. C., (acct. due)
Keith, Joseph, (acct. due)
Keith, C. D., (acct. due)
Keith, D. L., (acct. due)
Hollman, Earnest, (acct.due)
Haney, H., Jr., (acct. due)
Howell, J. M., (acct. due)
Carmichael, Frannie, (acct.)
Underwood, Tom, (acct.)
Wade, T. L., (acct. due)
Wade, J. T., (acct. due)
Wright, Wallace, acct. due)
Wright, J. N., (acct due)
Reece, Henry, (acct. due)

Estate Record Name

Ellis, Charles T. (Cont.)
- Riddle, W. R., (acct. due)
- Haigwood, W. E., (acct.due)
- Carrell, William J., (acct.)
- Riddle, R. R., (acct. due)
- Lyons, Bule, (acct. due)
- Fuller, Wit. (acct. due)

Ellis, Margaret E.
- Box 4 File 60 1914
- Names in file:
- Sale of Land for Division
- Ellis, J. C., (son, adm.)
- Ellis, Anna
- Ellis, Alfred
- Moore, Dessie, (w/o John)
- Moore, John W.
- Hall, Mary, (w/o Eugene)
- Hall, Eugene
- Keith, Margaret, (w/o C. H.)
- Keith, C. H.
- Ellis, Julia
- Shankles, Alice, (w/o Shankles)
- Shankles, John?
- Ellis, Jason
- Hall, Mary, (adm.bond)
- Ellis, Julia, (adm.bond)
- Moore, D. D., (adm.bond)
- Keith, Margaret, (adm.bond)
- Shankles, Alice, (adm.bond)

Ellis, Nancy
- Box 4 File 61 1889-1900
- Names in file:
- Ellis, William, (son, guardian)
- Nicholson, E. P., (doctor)
- Howard, M. W., (atty)
- Cook, W. C. D.
- Ellis, William, (guardian)
- Pope, W. E., (guar.ad litem)
- Wood, J. Y., (Simmons/adm)
- Wilder, J. T., (US Pension Agt.)
- York, F. J., (guardian bond)

Estate Record Name

Ellis, Nancy (Cont.)
- Crow, W. F., (guardian bond)
- Hawkins, W. J., (attest)
- Frazier, P. M., (sheriff)
- Campbell, A. L., (jury forman)
- Coley, John
- Durham, J. M.
- Clark, W. C.
- Frazier, P. B.
- Dobbs, James M.
- Burt, Thomas
- Baxter, James
- Campbell, H. B.
- Thompson, A. W.
- McCartney, A. P.
- Little, N. B.
- Baker, James R.
- York, F. M., (witness)
- Gifford, Thos. V., (witness)

Elrod, M. E.,
- Box 4 File 62 1900
- Names in file:
- Martin, John R., (exec.,nephew)
- Martin, C. S.
- Johnson, C. A.
- Cook, Ida C.
- Clundy, John F.
- Allen, Emily
- Fleming, Fannie
- Turner, Susan
- Bryant, Almer
- Hughes, Ann
- Hanby, Mary, (dec'd.sister)
- Bryant, Sarah, (decd.sister)
- Martin, J. R., (adm.)
- Cook, J. W., (appraiser)
- King, C. W., (appraiser)
- Lowry, D. R., (appraiser)
- Tinnons, Levi, (estate)
- Warren, S. D., (note)
- Sizemore, F. J., (note)

Estate Record Name

Elrod, M. E., (Cont.)
- Alexander, Lee, (note)
- Martin, C. S., (note)
- Johnson, W. R., (adm.bond)
- Cook, W. R., (adm.bond)
- Martin, C. S., (adm.bond)
- Elrod, M. E., Mrs.
- Cook, W. C. D., Judge
- Black, E. W., (JP)
- Holiday, A. L., (paid)
- Shannon, James R., (med.ser)
- Chastain, J. B., (tombstone)
- Cochran, L. L., (atty)
- Chitwood, W. J., (sheriff)
- *Fort Payne Journal*
- Smith, Thos. H., (editor)

Elrod, Nelson
- Box 4 File 63 1887-1889
- Names in file:
- Elrod, Martha M., (widow)
- Nichols, Julia A, (w/o Wm. H.)
- Nichols, William H., (adm)
- Rucks, Mary Frances
- Rucks, E. P., (h/o Frances)
- Gallaway/Galaway
- Galaway, Jerisha B.
- Gallaway, Perry C., (h/o Jerisha)
- Elrod, Jacob O., (son)
- Elrod, Sarah V.
- Rucks, Elisha P.
- Rucks, M.F.
- Bethune, Adeline Viola
- Bethune, Wm., (h/o Viola)
- Norton, Estelle, (w/o Eugene)
- Norton, Eugene
- Elrod, Amelia
- Elrod, Ida E., (minor)
- Spencer, Ida E.
- Spence, Martin V.
- Martin, J. C.
- Norton, E. H.

Estate Record Name

Elrod, Nelson (Cont.)
- Norton, D. E.
- Bethune, W. J.
- Bethune, A. V.
- Gallaway, P. C.
- Gallaway, J. D.
- South, W. T., (bid on land)
- Nichols, W. H., (purch.land)
- Rucks, E. P., (JP)
- *Fort Payne Journal*
- Smith, Thomas H., (editor)
- Nichols, W. H., (exec.bond)
- Rucks, Elisha P. (exec.bond)
- Houston, Thomas T., (bond)
- Nichols, J. G., (exec.bond)
- Elrod, J. G., (exec.bond)
- Cochran, L. L., Judge
- Johnson, Daniel, (deposition)
- Spencer, Henry T., (deposition)
- Houston, Thos.T.,(comm)
- Sale of Land for Division
- Houston, T. T.
- Fuller, W. T., (guar.ad litem)
- Elrod, Ida, (minor)
- Martin, J. C., (bought corn)
- Nichols, W. H., (bought oats)
- Steel, W. A., (tax coll. 1888)

Elrod, P. W.
- Box 4 File 64 1908
- Names in file:
- Sale of Land for Division
- Elrod, Narsis, (widow)
- Elrod, C. C., (minor)
- Pope, Jesse D., (guar.ad litem)
- Elrod, Narsisus/Nansissus
- Smith, Andrew J., (appraiser)
- Porter, O. C., (appraiser)
- Norton, E. H., (JP)
- Hamrie, J. R., (purch.land)
- Hamrie, J. E., (purch.land)
- Cook, T. J., (deposition)

Estate Record Name

Elrod, P. W. (Cont.)
- Hale, P. C., (commissioner)
- Croley, Jas. A., Judge

Elrod, Richard M.
- Box 4 File 65 1893
- Names in file:
- Widow's Exemption
- Elrod, Nancy E. E., (widow)
- Elrod, Millican
- Elrod, Sussannia
- Elrod, Velmer
- Elrod, Lethia
- Elron, Palmyra
- Elrod, Julia
- Elrod, William
- Mitchell, E. A., (appraiser)
- Bailey, J. S., (appraiser)
- Fountain, W. W., (JP)
- Cook, W. C. D., Judge

Elrod, Samuel T.
- Box 4 File 66 1890-1905
- Names in file:
- Homestead Exemption
- Elrod, Susan, (widow)
- Elrod, Wm. H., (adm.bond)
- Cook, T. J., (adm.bond)
- Haralson, J. B., (adm.bond)
- Croley, J. A., Judge
- Cochran, L. L., Judge
- Fountain, W. W., (JP)
- Elrod, George, (brother)
- Elrod, David D., (brother)
- Farmer?, Elizabeth A., (sister)
- Elrod, Nelson, (brother, dec'd.)
- Elrod, Wm. H., (nephew, adm.)
- Cook & Presley, (attys.)

Elrod, Thomas
- Box 4 File 67 1899-1900
- Names in file:
- Elrod, James W., (minor)
- Elrod, Andrew, (minor)

Estate Record Name

Elrod, Thomas (Cont.)
- Elrod, Josephine, (minor)
- Elrod, George, (minor)
- Elrod, Mary, (minor)
- Elrod, Elina, (minor)
- Ferguson, J. B., (guar.ad litem)
- Sargent, Roberta
- Elrod, Artie, (minor)
- Elrod, Alice, (minor)
- Elrod, Robert
- Cook, W. C. D., Judge
- Frazier, R. W., (guardian)
- Frazier, R. W., (sheriff)
- DeShields, J. G.
- Elrod, George G., (witness)
- Phillips, J. H., (witness)
- Scott, D. M., (carpentry work)
- Nichols, Charles
- Nichols, C. L., (house repair)
- Elrod, Eula (Lula)
- Barrett, J. H., (appraiser)
- Graves, H. L. (tax coll 1900)
- Isbell, John B., (deposition)
- Frazier, R. W., (deposition)
- Payne, John L., (take depos.)
- Davis & Haralson, (atty.)
- Stott, Middleton, (appraiser)
- Smith, James, (appraiser)
- Sargent, Artie
- Elrod, William
- Masters, Josephine Elrod
- Sargent, Roberta Elrod
- Burnes, J. D., (JP)
- *The DeKalb Times*
- Mills, J. Walter, (editor)
- Pope, W. E., (guar.ad litem)
- Reed, W. D., (tax coll. 1899)
- *The Fort Payne Journal*
- Elrod, J. N., (house repairs)
- Ma?, F. H., (purch.land)
- Hall, F. B., (witness)

Estate Record Name
Elrod, Thomas (Cont.)
Phillips, P. G., (witness)
Stott, A. C., (witness)
Engle, Jacob
Box 4 File 68 1850-1857
Names in file:
Engle, Daniel, (adm.)
Cox, Thomas G., (guar.bond)
Stowers, Charles, (guar.bond)
Estes, Reubin, Judge
Allen, H. T., (JP)
White, George, (witness)
Rees, D. V.
Rees, J. C.
White, S. M.
Ramsey, A. C.
Burgess, T. J., (selling prop.)
Ward & Penn
Ward, L. P.
Morgan, Wm. C. (JP)
Penn, James
Stowers, Charles, (appraiser)
Favors, Joel, (appraiser)
Cox, T. A.
Burgess & Stowers, (note)
Ramsey, R. H. & A. C., (note)
Burgess, Alexander
Rees, John, (note)
Rice, T. S.
Rice, D. W.
Stowers, Chas., (note)
Ramsey, A. C., (note)
Sale of Personal Property:
Sanson, Owen, (tools, razor)
Sauls, D. W., (piggin)
Engle, Mary, (1-chest)
Hammett, James, Sr. (Utensils)
Burgess, F. J., (1-lot gearing)
Young, R. M., (2-chains)
Lankford, Andrew, (chain)
Ramy, B., (curry comb)

Estate Record Name
Engle, Jacob (Cont.)
Sanson, Owen, (saddle, bell)
Sauls, D. W., (log chain)
Cox, T. G., (1-bell)
Keener, J. M., (horse collar)
Shrum, David, (gun barrel)
Johnson, Hoyt, (plow stock)
Gray, John M., (plow stock)
Favor, Joel, (fodder)
Engle, Mary, (2-hogs)
Engle, Simeon, (5-hogs)
Keener, J. M., (chair)
Sauls, D. W., (black heifer)
Sauls, D. W., (red heifer)
Ward, L. P., (cow)
Ellis, Labom, (black mare)
Hamett, Perry, (sorrel mare)
Stowers, Charles, (colt)
Engle, Alfred, (bridle)
Estes, Bethelhem
Box 4 File 69 1866-1878
Dobbs, Stephen E. (adm.)
Chavies, William E., (bond)
Chavies, Manervia, (bond)
Pendergraph, William P., (bond)
Pendergraft, Sarah C., (bond)
Dobbs, W. W., (adm.bond)
Brandon, P. A., Judge
Dobbs, S. E., (adm.)
Dobbs, L. A., (atty.)
McCampbell, John, (adm.of)
Estes, James R. P., (estate)
Franklin, J. N., Judge
Griffin, W. R., (sheriff)
Estes, James K. T. (P.)
Box 4 File 70 1861
Names in file:
Campbell, John, (adm.bond)
Campbell, J. E. A., (adm bond)
Estes, W. N., (adm.bond)
Estes, Reuben, Judge

Estate Record Name

Estes, James K. T. (P.) (Cont.)
  Estes, James K. P. Estate
  Estes, James

Euloe, Grace
  Box 4 File 71 1908
  Names in file:
  Enlow/Euloe
  Euloe, Grace, (hearing)
  Euloe, Edwin H.
  Croley, Jas. A., Judge
  Downs, T. L., (sheriff)
  Baxter, J. W., (dep.sheriff)
  end of roll 66

Evatt, Ola, et al
  Box 4 File 72 1908-1909
  Names in file:
  Sale of Land for Division
  Evatt, Ola, (minor)
  Amos, Ollie, (minor)
  Milwee, J. A., (guardian, friend)
  Amos, B. T.
  Slone, S. B., (guardian as litem)
  Berry, Minnie, (take deposition)
  Davis, Reuben, (bond)
  Davis, W. C., (bond)
  Daniel, R. T., (bond)
  Davis, R. E., (Justice Peace)
  Croley, Jas. A., (Judge)
  Isbell & Presley, Atty.
  Isbell, John B., (Atty)
  Hunt, Howard
  Howard & Hunt, (Atty)
  Telitha Waldrop Estate
  Waldrop, Telitha, (Estate)
  Waldrop Property
  Gilbreath, W. B., (witness)
  Copeland, A. C., (witness)
  Weatherton, John T. (purch.land)
  Milwee, James A., (Commissioner)
  Roden, J. M., (paid)
  Stone/Slone, T.? (paid)

Estate Record Name

Evett, Thompson
  Box 4 File 73 1871-1872
  Names in file:
  Evett/Evatt
  Evett, James W., (adm)
  Evett, W. J., (adm. Bond)
  Kirkland, B. J., (adm.bond)
  Kirkland, G. K., (adm.bond)
  Guest, G. B., (adm.bond)
  Day, Wiley, (witness)
  Summerour, Ezekial, (witness)
  Heirs:
  Evett, H. V., (Mississipi)
  Evett, Hamilton
  Evett, J. Vann
  Evett, Samuel
  Evett, James
  Armstrong, Lucy
  Armstrong, Wm., (h/o Lucy)
  Mullin, Jensey, (Kentucky)
  Mullin, Thomas, (h/o Jensey)
  Evett, Palestine, (minor)
  Evett, Catherine T., (minor)
  Evett, G., (minor)
  Evett, John J., (minor)
  Beck, Louisa Ann
  Beck, Wm., (h/o Louisa)
  Evett, W. T., heirs
  Evett, Thompson, (minor)
  Evett, George J. (minor)
  Evett, Elizabeth, (minor)
  Evett, I. Vann, (minor)
  Mullin, Matilda, (Floyd Co.GA)
  Mullin, William, (h/o Matilda)
  Mullin, Augustus, (minor)
  Mullin, John, (minor)
  Mullin, Alphonso, (minor)
  __, Jackson
  __, Vicy, w/o Jackson
  Booth, Elizabeth
  Booth, Jeptha, (h/o Elizabeth)

Estate Record Name
Evett, Thompson (Cont.)
Evett, Hunley V., (Mississippi)
Evett, Hamilton L., (DeKalb Co.)
Evett, Sam G., (DeKalb Co.
Evett, I. Vann, (DeKalb Co.)
Evett, Palestine, (DeKalb Co.)
Evett, James, (DeKalb Co.)
Armstong, Lucy, (Jackson Co.)
Evett, Texas Co., (minor)
Evett, John N., (minor)
Beck, Lidia A., (DeKalb Co.)
Beck, William, (h/o Lidia)
Evett, W. J., (adm)
Sale of Goods & Chattels:
Armstrong, W., (cow & calf)
Armstrong, Wm.,(book & kettle)
Evett, Sousana A, (wash pot)
Evett, Sousana (smoothing iron)
Armstrong, Louisa K. (spinning wheel, bedsted, & 30#?)
Kirkland, G. H., (saddle, chest)
Kirkland, G, H. (table, bedsted, loom and jar)
Evatt, W. J., (purch. land)
King, James W., (JP)
Kirkland, B. J., (Appraiser)
Payne, A. F., (taking testimony)
Chitwood, R. (guardian ad litem)
Kirkland, W. J., (paid)
Horton, Preston, (appraiser)
Rains, Robert, (appraiser)
Kirkland, J. D., (paid)
Tucker, R., (paid)
Evett, J. L., (paid)
Smith, Henry, (paid)
Horton, A. J., Judge
McCurdy, J. A. M.
Chitwood, R. C., (notice)
Griffin, Wm.
Dunlay, R. H., (atty.)
Dunlay & Jacoway, (atty)

Estate Record Name
Everett, Andrew
Box 4 File 74 1910
Names in file:
Everett, W. L. (adm.)
Everett, W. L., (oldest bro.)
Everett, Mittie, (sister)
Mullins, Melvesta (sister)
Mullins, Melvesta Everett
Everett, Annie, (sister)
Everett, Thursey, (sister)
Everett, Elma, (sister)
Everett, S. C., (father)
Everett, Annie, (mother)
Everett, W. R.
Everett, Thomas
Mullins, Malvinda
Mullins, James, (h/o Malvinda)
Everett, Thomas W., (note)
Durham, John J. (adm.bond)
Durham, W. A., (adm.bond)
Dawson, J. C., (appraiser)
Dickson, H. F., (appraiser)
Tumlin, J. Noah, (appraiser)
Ayers, J. W., (JP)
Newman, G. Y., (burial exp.)
Isbell, John B., (atty)
Hunt, M. W.,, (agent, atty.)
Everett, Thomas W. (note)
Brock, W. M., (note)
Smith, L. M.
Everett, F. W.
Everett, S. C., (note)
Everett, T. W., (note)
Killian, W. E., (note)
Everett, Andrew, (note)
Cain, Wall, (witness)
Sales of Property:
Dunlap, W. E., (mule)
Everett, W. L., (cultivator)
Smith, M. (plow)
Thurman, W. J., (plow stock and harrow)

F

Estate Record Name
Fields, James
Box 4 File 75 1851-1852
Names in file:
Bynum, William, (adm)
Fields, Millican, (minor)
Fields, Disey Ann, (adm)
Fields, Vienne, (minor)
Fields, Mary E., (minor)
Estes, Reuben, Judge
Sale of Property:
McCampbell, Soloman, (mule)
McCurdy, James, (colt)
Chitwood, Wm., (mare)
Lawson, William, (cow & calf)
Bryan, William, (cow)
Dobbs, David, (cow)
Whitman, Blanton
Minnix, James, (cow)
Murphey, N., (yearlings)
Mays, S., (sows and pigs(
Fields, B., (sows and pigs)
Rutledge, David, (rifle)
Bynam, Jessie, (yoke oxen & wagon)
Lusk, Robert C., (appraiser)
Poe, James C., (appraiser)
Murphey, N., (appraiser)
Hoge, John R.
Malone & Hoge
Jack, Thom. J., (blacksmith pd.)
Walden, W. B.
Winston & Hoge, (paid)
George, C. D.
Jett, Joseph M.
Major, Samuel
Jett, B. T.
Jett, Bailess
Jett, Joseph M.
Fields, James

Estate Record Name
Fields, James (Cont.)
George, H. P.
Cunningham, Jesse, (JP)
Winston & George
Hoge, John J.
Fields, James
Box 4 File 76 1860-1862
Names in file:
Fields, William
Fields, Dicy/Disy Ann (minor)
Fields, Vina/Vianna, (minor)
Fields, Mary Ellen, (minor)
Fields, Elizabeth
Luttrell, Elizabeth Fields
Fields, William, (guardian)
Bynum, William, (bond)
Fields, William
Box 4 File 77 1861-1864
Names in file:
Bynum, William, (adm)
Fields, Vianna, (minor)
Fields, Mary E., (minor)
Fields, Disy A., (minor)
Hulgan, S. P., (appraiser)
Gregg, C., (appraiser)
Osburn, Jackson, (appraiser)
Findley, John B., (JP)
Fields, John B., (JP)
Franklin, John N., Judge
Estes, R., (bond)
Hoge, J. K., (bond)
McPherson, Joseph
McPherson, George
Grant, J. F., (pd- printers)
Murphrey, M. (pd-clothing)
Hulgan, Thomas, (note to Fields)
Jett, Daniel, (note)
Anderson, James, (note)

Estate Record Name
Fields, James (Cont.)
Bynum, Wm., (note)
Winston, John G., (acct paid)
Majors, Alexander, (paid)
Majors, W. W.
Grant, J. F.
Fishel & Brothers
Box 4 File 78 1879-1880
Names in file:
Division of Land
Brandon, Phillip A., Judge
Nicholson, O. P., (joint owner)
Nicholson, Oling P.
Nicholson, Mary B., (heir)
Pendergrass, Sinda, (heir)
Cantrell, John, (heir)
Carr, Peter, (heir)
Fishel, Morris, (merchant)
Fishel, Julius, (merchant)
Fishel & Brothers
Polk, W. D. (appraiser)
Coker, W. D. (appraiser)
Smith, Charles W., (appraiser)
Watts, L. B., (appraiser)
Ward, Jas. S,, (appraiser)
Donegan, W. H., (jury forman)
Maps of Property
McCullough, A. W. (ct.clerk)
McNutt, R. C., (sheriff)
McSpadden & Carden, (atty)
Carden, Hugh W., (atty)
McSpadden, S. K., (atty)
Franklin, J. N., Judge
Wood, Wm. B.,(Judge Cir.Ct.)
Fletcher, William S.
Box 4 File 79 1857-1864
Names in file:
Box, P. D., (adm)
McCampbell, John, (bond)
Hoge, Joseph, (bond)
Jones, Henry, (bond)

Estate Record Name
Fletcher, William S. (Cont.)
Fletcher, J. C., (dec'd)
Fletcher, Sarah, (minor)
Fletcher, Margaret, (minor)
Fletcher, Harriet, (minor)
Fletcher, John F., (minor)
Fletcher, Elizabeth H.
Law, Louisa
Law, J. C.
Fletcher, J. F.
Fletcher, Joseph W.
Fletcher, A.
Fletcher, William F., (minor)
Fletcher, F. W., (minor)
Fletcher, Charles, (minor)
Fletcher, F. S. , (minor)
Horton, A. J., Judge
Fletcher, M. S.
Fletcher, Marthey A.
Fletcher, Wm. S., (guardian)
Franklin, John N., Judge
Crump, Bethel, (bond)
Griffin, William, (sheriff)
Morgan, J. T., (dep.sheriff)
Law, J. C., (note)
Rus, John, (note, acct)
Sale of Property:
Pursell, John, (sundries)
Baird, E. B., (buggy & hog skins)
Box, P. D., (cross cut saw)
Crump, J. T., (wheel barrow)
Fletcher, Elizabeth, (barrels)
Fletcher, Elizabeth, (mare & horse)
Fletcher, M. J., (yearling)
Ward, A. J., (pd. 1861 taxes)
Folsom, Charles R.
Box 4 File 80 1900-1905
Names in file:
Folsom, Wm. F., (adm)
Folsom, Herbert A., (son) (R.I.)
Folsom, Wm. F.., (brother)

Estate Record Name

Folsom, Charles R. (Cont.)
- Folsom, Herbert Arthur, (heir)
- Chickamauga Undertaking Co.
- Harris, T. G., (attested will)
- Miller, C. B., (attested will)
- Love, S. D., (attested will)
- Croley, Jas. A., Judge
- White, E., (agent, Western Union)
- The DeKalb Co. Hotel
- Rainey, S. L., (hotel damages)
- Anderson, R. E., (juror)
- Little, N. B., (juror)
- Green, P. M., (juror)
- Guest, J. H. E., (juror)
- Howard, S. B., (juror)
- McCartney, A. P., (juror)
- Faulkner, J. N. B., (juror)
- Tinn, W. E., Dr., (juror)
- Houston, A. W., (Comm.)
- Campbell, H. B., (appraiser)
- Minot, Wm. H., (appraiser)
- DeShields, J. G., (appraiser)
- Berry, W. E., (NP)
- Clark, Louis V. & Co., (bond)
- Clark, Louis V., (bond)
- Sawyer, C. M., (atty)
- Cook, W. D. C., Judge
- Attwoods, J. L., (Boston)
- Tasker, C. E., (burial exp.)
- Dell, John L., (Boston)
- Burial at Boston, Mass.
- Presley, C. M., (services)
- *The Fort Payne Journal*
- Haynes, E. J., (1900 tax)
- Rogers, B. A.
- List of Investments
- Haynes, Edward W., (1901 tax)
- Warner-Smiley Co., (casket)
- Wade, H. E., (paid)
- Orr, Perry, (paid)
- Williams, Tom, (paid)

Estate Record Name

Folsom, Charles R. (Cont.)
- Coleman, Green, (paid)
- Jackson, Ben, (paid)
- Jones, W. C., (paid)
- Orr, Oscar, (paid)
- Lane, Alex, (paid)
- Rogers & Son, (paid)
- Rodgers, F. R., (services)
- Sanford & Farnum (Granite Memorial -Boston)

Force, S. F.
- Box 4 File 81 1877
- Names in file:
- O'Rear, Francis M., (adm)
- O'Rear, Charlotte J., (w/o F. M.)
- Blake, John B.
- Blake, Margaret, (w/o John B.)
- Force, Benjamin
- Cole, A. F.
- Cole, Georgia A., (w/o A. F.)
- Cole, Sally May
- O'Rear, Samuel
- O'Rear, R. M.
- May, Sarah E.
- Force, Ben, (Texas)
- Force, S. F., (Valdosta, Ga)
- O'Rear, George, (Rome, Ga.)
- O'Rear, Sarah, (w/o George)
- Force, L. M.
- O'Rear, F. M.
- Blake, Sally May
- Force, Catherine
- Crow, Clark, (deposition)
- Casey, W. H., (deposition)
- Paine, Benj. F. (took deposition)
- McCurdy, J. A.
- Ferguson, W. S. (tax coll-1876)
- Brandon, P. A., Judge
- O'Rear, F. M., (purch.land)

Fountain, W. W.
- Box 4 File 82 1906

Estate Record Name
Fountain, W. W., (Cont.)
Sale of Land for Division
Fountain, Mollie, Mrs.
Fountian, Oma, (minor)
Fountain, Arty, (minor)
Fountain, Grady, (minor)
Copeland, A. C., (guar.ad litem)
Guest, N. C., (witness)
Hall, T. H., (witness)
Hall, Burris, (witness)
Reeves, D. B., (purch.land)
Cook & Presley, (atty)
Burel, L. H.
McCord, W. H., (JP)
Presley, I. M., (Comm.)
Fountain, W. W.
Box 4 File 83 1906
Names in file:
Exemption before Adm.
Fountain, Mollie, (widow)
Fountain, Oma, (minor)
Fountain, Arty, (minor)
Fountian, Grady, (minor)
Guest, Newton C.
Morgan, J. M.
Croley, J. A., Judge
Fant/Fout, Hettie
Box 4 File 84 1902
Names in file:
Fout/Fant
Fant, James, Mrs., Estate
Fant, James, (guardian)
Fant, James, (father of minors)
Fant, William, (deceased)
Fant, Hattie, (minor)
Fant, Tomie, (minor)
Fant, Herman, (minor)
Fant, Bertha, (minor)
Croley, J. A., (bond)
Rucks, E. P.
Fowler, Owen/Oren H.

Estate Record Name
Fowler, Owen/Oren H.
Box 4 File 85 1896-1898
Names in File:
Killian, E. S., (1st adm.)
Fowler, Alfred E., (2nd.adm)
Fowler, Alfred E., (father)
McCartney, John, (bond)
Moore, Lance, (bond)
Killian, E. S., (bond)
McCartney, C. H.
Cook, W. C. D., Judge
Francis, Jeremiah
Box 4 File 86 1866
Names in File:
Blevins, Richard M., (bond)
Blevins, Gains, Sr., (bond)
Adkins, Washington, (bond)
Francis, Nancy Jane, (minor)
Blevins, Richard M., (guardian)
Estes, Reuben
Franklin, J. H.
Box 4 File 87 1909
Names in File:
Homestead Exemption
Franklin, Mary Allen, (widow)
Franklin, Jesse B., (minor)
Franklin, Wallace A., (minor)
Franklin, Earl R., (minor)
Franklin, John H., (minor)
Meadows, John M. (comm.)
Hughes, Wm. R., (comm.)
Franklin, Allen
Croley, Jas. A., Judge
Franklin, John N.
Box 4 File 88 1893-1931
Names in File:
Franklin, J. R., (bond)
Morgan, S. J., (bond)
Horton, G. R., (bond)
Cook, W. C. D., Judge
Franklin, James B., (son,adm)

Estate Record Name
Franklin, John N. (Cont.)
Ferguson, Nancy, (widow)
Blake, Fannie
Blake, S. T., (h/o Fannie)
Franklin, Thomas B.
Franklin, W. M.
Killian, Lucinda, (w/o A. C.)
Killian, A. C.,
Franklin, Benjamin
Dean, Martha, (w/o Henry)
Dean, Henry
Campbell, John F.
Campbell, Roxie, (minor)
Campbell, Lewis, (minor)
Franklin, Bradshaw (minor)
Franklin, Sallie
Franklin, J. P.
Franklin, A. G.
Franklin, J. B., (adm.)
Bell, Mary, (w/o D. W.)
Bell, D. W.
Franklin, Ben
Franklin, Thomas
Killian, L. C.
Franklin, J. P.
DeShields, J. G., (guar.ad litem)
Bush, Martha, Mrs.
Bush, O. P., (h/o Martha)
Scott, Roxie, (w/o Charles)
Scott, Charles
Campbell, Isaac
Campbell, Lewis, (s/o Isaac)
Shankles, Sally
Stinson, Mary
Blake, Melvina
Davis, John D., (NP)
Killian, Thomas
Franklin, Green
Killian, Mary
Kean, Susie
Guartney, Gene

Estate Record Name
Franklin, John N. (Cont.)
Franklin, Earl
Shankles, Sallie
Davis & Haralson, (atty)
Hawkins, N. T.(J.)
Wolfes, C. A., (Spec.Judge)
Blake, B. P.
Blake, I. C.
Blake, M.
Lyons, Bula, Mrs.
Campbell, J. W. (N.)
Bell, E. L.
English, Annie
Lewis, Eva
Marrtin?, C. J.
Burgis, A. M., (Avandale, Al.)
Thompson, J. L., (dep.sheriff)
Bell, M. E., (adm)
Bell, Tom E., Estate
Guest, J. H. E. (deposition)
Chitwood, W. J., (deposition)
Presley, I. M., (took deposition)
Petition to Sell Land
Fort Payne Journal, (adv.)
Davis & Haralson, (atty)
Ferguson, Thomas
Dean, Sudie
Guartney, Genie
Franklin, Janie
Franklin, Wallace
Franklin, Bradshaw
Blake, Dayamin?
Black, Isaac
Lyon, Brelde?
Blake, I.
Lewis, William, Mrs.
Faulkner, Fannie, Mrs., (heir)
Franklin, Jesse
Campbell, Lewis
Hawkins, Jas. F., (sheriff)
Woods, Ed, (dep.sheriff)

Estate Record Name

Franklin, John N. (Cont.)
Frost, S. T., (witness)
McSpadden, Maggie Frost, (wit.)
Frost, Hardy, (witness)
Frost, Griff, (witness)
Tate, John Ike, (witness)
Tate, Wallace, (witness)
Hunter, Cleo Tate, (witness)
Ingle, Thenie, (witness)
Burnett, Louie Tate, (witness)
Lesley, Bonnie Tate, (witness)
Lesley, Geaner Tate, (witness)
Lesley, M. H. Tate, (witness)
Haas, Myrtle Scott, (witness)
Ferguson, George, (witness)
Notes due Franklin Estate:
Hicks, H., (note)
Franklin, Thomas & W.M.,(note)
Franklin, Thomas, (note)
Hicks, O. L., (note)
Franklin, J. B. (note)
Killian, A. C., (note)
West, Jas., (note)
Franklin, Ben, (exp. paid)
Bell, Mary, (paid)
Franklin, J. S., (witness)
Walthall, S. L., (coffin)
Bush, G. V., Dr. (medical ser.)
Collins, J. H., (JP)
Quin, W. E. & Co., (medicine)
Killian & Son,(burial materials)
Bell, D. W., (various expense)
Green, Bill, Dr., (medical)
Killian, E. S., (aid)
Russell, W. W., (paid)
Hunt, Luke P., (NP)
Property Sold:
Bell, Mary, (cow & calf)
Horton, D. D., (cow & calf)
Horton, J. P., (plow & buggy)
Horton, G. R., (book desk)

Estate Record Name

Franklin, John N. (Cont.)
Bell, Mary, (dining safe)
Johnson, G. W., (table)
Bell, Mary, (cook table)
Coleman, G. M., (half bedsted)
Blake, Fannie, (hymn book)
Franklin, W. M., (testament)
Horton, D. D., (history book)
Franklin, Thomas, (Bible)
Franklin, W. M.,(1-lot books)
Killian, Mrs., (center table)
Killian, Mrs., (wash stand)
Horton, D. D., (bed blanket)
Franklin, Thos., (bed blanket)
Franklin, W. M., (coverlet)
Bell, Mary, (quilt, bedsted)
Coleman, G. M., (quilt)
Horton, G. R., (quilts)
Horton, D. D., (quilts)
Blake, Fannie, (bed springs)
Franklin, Thomas, (wrench)
Chitwood, W. J., (purch.land)
Hartline, C. H., (purch. land)
Hunt, C. H., (purch.land)
Croley, Jas. A., Judge
Horton, G. R., (bond release)
Morgan, S. J., (bond release)
Malone, G. L., Judge
Franklin, Martha, Mrs.
Box 4 File 89 1899-1901
Names in File:
Franklin, John N., (husband)
Franklin, John N., (adm)
Franklin, James B., (son,adm)
Guest, J. H. E., (adm.bond)
Isbell, John B., (adm bond)
Pendergrass, P. G., (adm.bond)
Pruett, L. J., (adm.bond)
Horton, G. R., (adm.bond)
Heirs:
Franklin, John N.

Estate Record Name
Franklin, Martha, Mrs. (Cont.)
Franklin, John B.
Ferguson, Nancy, Mrs.
Blake, Fannie, Mrs.
Franklin, A. G.
Franklin, Thomas
Franklin, W. M.
Killian, Lucinda, Mrs.
Bell, Mary, Mrs.
Bush, Martha, Mrs.
Franklin, Jno. P.
Franklin, Benjamin
Campbell, Roxie, (minor)
Campbell, Lewis, (minor)
Campbell, Jane & Ike's children
Franklin, Bradshaw
Franklin, Samuel's son
Pope, W. E., (guar.ad litem)
Dean, Martha
Blake, Leabon
Killian, A. C.
Bush, O. P
Dean, Henry
Bell, D. W.
Campbell, Sallie
Campbell, John
Campbell, Jane, (dau.of dec'd.)
Howard & Isbell, (atty)
Quin & Co., (paid)
Killina, H. E., Dr., (services)
Green, W. M., MD, (medical)
Wills, J. Walter, (paid)
The DeKalb Times
Yeuell, Claris, editor
Davis, John A., (note)
Franklin, William H. F.
Box 4 File 90 1849-1858
Names in File:
Franklin, LaFayette, (minor)
Franklin, Benjamin, (minor)
Franklin, Elizabeth A.

Estate Record Name
Franklin, William H. F. (Cont.)
Malone, Elizabeth A.
Lankford, John M., (guardian)
Clayton, Sampson, (guardian)
Davidson, Joseph, (bond)
Lyons, John, (bond)
Taylor, Green B., (guardian, bond)
George, Charles D., (bond)
Gibson, Jacob W., (bond)
Humphries, John J., (bond)
Franklin, John N., (bond)
Walden, J. B., (Judge-1849)
Notes due Estate:
Bruce, John M., (note)
Roberts, R., (note)
Clayton, D., (note)
Taylor, Bruce, (note)
George, C. D., (note)
Humphries, John T., (note)
Haralsen & Clayton, (atty).)
Boarding School (pd. for minors)
Malone, E. A.
Freeman, Robert K., (paid)
Watson, John, (JP)
Williams, __, (paid)
Estes, R., Judge (1855)
Franklin, D. L., (paid)
Franklin, M. D. L., (paid)
Hollingsworth, (clothing/minors)
Phillips, Ross, Judge, (1854)
Hollingsworth,(clothing/LaFayette)
Reeds School, (Tuition paid)
Boarding School, (tuitions paid)
Majors, A. W., (paid)
Clayton, Sampson, (final acct.)
Frazer, Dorcas
Box 4 File 91 1851-1858
Names in File:
Frazier/Frazer
Frazer, John B., (adm)
Frazier, Robert, (son)

Estate Record Name
Frazer, Dorcas (Cont.)
Frazier, John. B., (son)
Frazier, Patrick, (son)
Baxter, Sarah Frazier, (dau)
Baxter, Willis, (h/o Sarah)
Lankford, Susan Frazier, (dau.)
Lankford, Robert E., (h/o Susan)
Dobbs, Eliza Frazier, (dau.)
Dobbs, James G., (h/o Eliza)
Backster/Baxter, Gary
Backster/Baxter, Willis
Sale of Property:
Dobbs, (table, cow and calf)
Jett, David, (chairs)
Lankford, Susana, (racks & oven)
Baxter, Sary, (coffee pot)
Frazer, Robert, (cow and bell)
Backster, Welles,(shoats)
McCampbell, Saleanar, (pr.stelards)
Martin, James B., (atty. paid)
Morgan, John T., (atty.paid)
Frazer, John, (adm) VS
Turner, Alfred, (Chennault estate)
Chennault, John, Estate
Hayden, Thomas
Chennault, W. J.,
Turner, J.
Martin, W. B.
Dill, John
Sookey, Negro Woman
Cunningham, John, (witness)
Malone, George W., (witness)
Hoge, John K., (guar. bond)
May, Wm. H., (guar.bond)
McCampbell, Saleman, (guar.bond)
Majors, Samuel, (appraiser)
Baker, James, (appraiser)
Snodgrass, (paid)
Ragland, (attest)
Cunningham, Jesse, (JP)
Cunningham, N, L., (paid)

Estate Record Name
Frazer, Dorcas (Cont.)
Pope, B., (atty)
Nicholsen, D. L., (note)
Rogers, Reece, (note)
Waldon, J. B., (note)
Baxter, Willis, (note)
Lankford, R. E., (note)
Frazier, R., (note)
McCampbell, John, (prop.line)
Walden, John B., (purch.land)
Walden, George, Sr.(surety)
Winston, John G., (surety)
Frazier, P. B. (Polland B.)
Box 4 File 92 1889-1896
Names in File:
Exemption to Minors
Frazier, Ida C.. (minor)
Frazier, Jackson S., (minor)
Frazier, Byron M., (minor)
Frazier, Charles N., (minor)
Frazier, Robert L., (guardian)
(brother of minors)
Baxter, R. M., (guar.bond)
Poe, W. R., (guar.ad litem)
Green, Ida C,
Green, P. M.
McSpadden, Allen, (appraiser)
McSpadden, H. A.
Key, Joshua, (appraiser)
Campbell, Isaac, (appraiser)
Frazier, Polland B. (died 3/1889)
No widow
Russell, J. E.
Cochran, L. L., Judge
Busan, J. J. (tuition)
Rorex, W. D.,(tuition for Charlie)
Rorex, W. L., (board)
James West Gen. Mdse.
Frazier, R. L.
Johnson, Dr., (Bryon acct.)
Baxter, J. R., (pd. school exp.)

Estate Record Name
Frazier, P. B. (Polland B.) (Cont.)
Accounts:
Dobbs, James
Jones, M. A., Mrs., (loan)
Wilborn, Thomas, (cash)
Green, Mat, (cash)
Collins, (tuition)
McBroom, (order)
Frazier, Jack, (cash)
McBroom, A. M., (mdse.)
Frazier, Chas.& Bryan, (books)
Horton, (books)
Slone, (books)
Annet, (tuition, cash)
Johnson, Dr., (medical, cash)
Frazier, Byron , (cash)
Frazier, Bob, (cash)
Frazier, Pat, (cash)
Frazier, C. N.,
Jones, M. A., (Byron's board)
Marshall, H. G.
Freeman, Elisha
Box 5 File 1 1858
Freeman, Ann, (guardian)
Freeman, David C., , (minor)
Freeman, Moses, (minor)
Freeman, William, (minor)
Freeman, Martha Ann, (minor)
Freeman, Zachariah, (minor)
Freeman, James, (minor)
Freeman, Francis, (minor)
Freeman, Ann, (bond)
Clayton, Daniel, (bond)
Estes, William N., (bond)
Cunningham, Jesse, (clerk C.Ct.)
Frizzell, James
Box 5 File 2 1902
Sale of Land for Division
Frizzell, Louis R., Trustee
Nixon, G. W., Trustee
Frizzell, James, (deceased)

Estate Record Name
Frizzell, James (Cont.)
Frizzell, Al, (deceased)
Nixon, G. W., VS: Frizzell, L.R.,et al
Earp, Jacob W., (joint owner)
Earp, Phillip W., (joint owner)
Earp, Robert S., (joint owner)
Sharop, Katt B., (joint owner)
Earp, William G., (joint owner)
Frizzell, Fannie, (joint owner)
Rogers, R. C., (witness)
Young, W. H., (witness)
Frizzell, L. R., et al, (joint owners)
Ragan/Rogan, J. C., (witness)
Campbell, H. B.
Chitwood, W. J.
Hawkins, W. J., (Comm.)
Davis, John A., (NP)
Presley, I. M., (guar.ad litem)
Pegler, D. C., (purch.land)
Davis & Haralson, (atty)
Chitwood, (sheriff)
Chitwood, Joel, (dep.sheriff)
Furr, Georgia, et al
Box 5 File 3 1882-1883
Names in File:
Starnes. B. R., (estate)
Furr, Georgie Ann, (minor)
Furr, Rosa, (minor)
Furr, Mary M., (minor)
Furr, W. D., (guardian)
Furr, Daniel
Furr, D. A.
Furr, Walter,
Starnes, Basis & Rachel
Starnes, Basil, (deceased)
Starnes, Rachel, (deceased)
Roberts, G. W., (school acct.)
Stewart, S. W., (tuition paid)
Cobb, T. J., (tuition paid)
Cobb, L. J., (schooling)
Wood, J. H., (schooling paid)

Estate Record Name **Estate Record Name**

G

Estate Record Name

Gallaway, John R.

Box 5 File 4 1895-1903

Names in file:

Gallaway, John T., (minor, son)
Gallaway, John R., (father)
Gallaway, Thomas P., (guardian)
Gallaway, T. P., (grandfather)
Gallaway, W. H., (bond)
Rogers, T. J., (bond)
Nicholson, B. H., (bond)
Gallaway, T. P., (bond)
Gallaway, M. L., (bond exec.)
Elrod, J. T., (bond, exec.)
Rogers, Joel C., (bond exec.)
DeShields, J. G., (sheriff)
Workman, S. J., (deputy)
Kogers/Rogers
Cook, W. C. D., Judge
Davis & Haralson, (atty)
DeShields, J. G., (guar.ad litem)
Gallaway, D. P., (bid on land)
Howard, J. M., (JP)
Smith, J. C., (purchased land)
The Fort Payne Journal
Smith, Thomas H., (publisher)
Smith, James C., (witness)
Smith, Samuel, (witness)
Hendrix, M. M., (comm.)
Fuller, W. T., (guar.ad litem)
Rogers, J. W., (JP)
Howard, J. M., (tax coll. 1893-95)

Garrison, Anderson J.

Box 5 File 5 1915

Names in file:

Garrison, J. B.
Garrison, H. D., (son, petitioner)
Garrison, T. J.
Garrison, Kate B.

Estate Record Name

Garrison, Anderson J. (Cont.)

Garrison, John
Smith, S. E., Jr., (minor)
Smith, S. E., (father of minor)
Garrison, H. D., (adm.bond)
Bohling, J. W., (adm.bond)
Haralson, J. B., (adm.bond)
Croley, Jas. A. Judge

Garrett, T. R. (G. R.)

Box 5 File 6 1909

Names in file:

Homestead Exemption
Garrett, Mary, (widow)
No minor children
Burt, Henry, Sr., (comm.)
Majors, S. N., (comm.)
Carral, R., (JP)
Croley, Jas. A. Judge

Garmany, John

Box 5 File 7 1890-1906

Names in file: File 1 of 2

Garmany, Margaret E., (dau)
Kenemore, Margaret Garmany
Garmany, Franklin B. (son)
Rose, Sarah R. (dau)
Ragesdales, Mary A., (dau)
Garmany, John, Jr., (son)
Garmany, Fleming E. (son)
Kenemore, Mary Casider
Garmany, George W., (son)
Barbor, Henry
Barbor, Mary A., (dau.)
Kenemore, Americus I., (dau)
Kenemore, Grif, (son of Americus)
Pruett, S. L. (guar.ad litem)
Garmany, Flem, (non compus mentis)
Brown, Ada, (g-dau.)
Reeves, O. A., (witness to will)

Estate Record Name
Garmany, John (Cont.)
Culver, N. S., (witness to will)
Workman, S. D., (JP)
Barber, William H., (grandson)
Will entered and contested
Kenemore, Grif, (minor)
Rose, Fannie Garmany
Garmany, Mary
Garmany, Anna
Garmany, Samuel
Pope, T. W., (JP)
Culver, LaFayette, (paid)
Hicks, John, (paid)
Culver Johnithon, (paid)
Padgett, J. T., (paid)
Pruitt, S. L., (paid)
Cook & Presley
Workman, S. D., (paid)
Croley, J. A., Judge
Garmany, John
Box 5 File 8 1906-1907
Names in file: File 2 of 2
Sale of Land for Division
Garmany, Bart
Kenemore, Margaret E.
Garmany, John, Jr.
Garmany, Franklin B.
Rose, Fannie
Garmany, Flem
Kenemore, Griff
Brown, Ada A.
Garmany, Samuel
Garmany, Mary A.
Garmany, Amsia S.
Barbour, Henry
Barbor/Barbour
Garmany, George
DeShields, J. G., (testimony)
Traylor, G. R., (testimony)
Copeland, A. C., (guardian)
Kenemore, Grif, (minor)

Estate Record Name
Garmany, John
Brown, Ada A., (minor)
Garmany, Flem, (non-comp.)
Presley & Cook, (atty)
Stone, B. C., (sp.dep.sheriff)
Chitwood, W. J., (sheriff)
Garmany, Bart, VS:
Kenemore, Margaret E., et al
Pope, F, M., (JP)
Cook & Presley, (atty)
Kenemore, M. J.
The DeKalb Record, (notices)
Yeuell, Claris, (editor)
Garmany, Martha
Garmany, S. M.,
Garmany, Mannery
Garmany, Annie S.
Pruett, L. C., (guardian)
Haralson, P. B.
Chitwood, W. J., (sheriff)
Stone, B. C., (sp.dep.sheriff)
McSpadden, H. A.,(took test.)
Croley, J. A., Judge
Garmany, Sam. M.
Garmany, Bart, (purchased land)
Presley, I. M., (comm.)
Garmany, J. H.
Garrett, H.W. B.
Box 5 File 9 1894
Names in File:
Garrett, Thomas R., (son)
Rogers, Mary A., (dau)
Jackson, Desalemona, (dau)
Jackson, James E., (h/o Des.)
Garrett, Mary W., (minor)
Garrett, Wallace, (son, Dec'd.)
Campbell, H. B., (guar.ad litem)
Garrett, W. S., (son)
Lankford, Ellen E.
Lankford, Jeff D., (h/o Ellen)
Walker, Susan E.

Estate Record Name

Garrett, H.W. B. (Cont.)
- Walker, J. N., (h/o Susan)
- Walker, S. E.
- Cook, W. C.
- DeShields, J. G.
- Rogers, Elijah
- Jackson, John E.
- Rogers, Mary A., (petitioner)
- Garrett, William S.
- Lankford, J. D.
- Howard, M. W.
- Garrett, T. R.
- Jackson, D. A.
- Stewart, T. G., (witness)

Garrett, Malichi B., et al
- Box 5 File 10 1854-1881
- Names in File:
- Son of Thomas Garrett, deceased
- Garrett, Malichi B., (minor)
- Garrett, Sarah, (guardian)
- Webb, Garrett W. (minor)
- Webb, Sarah Jane, (minor)
- Webb, Brunston W.
- Webb, Lavice Garrett, (dec'd.) (mother of Webb minors)
- Garrett. Sarah, (guar.bond)
- Lyons, John, (guar.bond)
- Beesan, Jesse G. (guar.bond)
- Green, Anthony, B., (guar.bond)
- Green, A. B., (adm.) (Thomas Garrett Estate)
- Walden, Geo. S., (witness)
- Haralson, W. J. & H. C.,(attys)
- Parker, J. M., (Justice of peace)
- Garrett. M. B. Appeal, (bond)
- Dobbs, L. S., (bond)
- Cravens, James R., (bond)
- Webb, G. W., (bond)
- Dobbs, L. A., (atty)
- Walden, J. B., (atty)
- Stewart, J. J., (pd. for mule)

Estate Record Name

Garrett, Malichi B., et al
- Final Settlement -
- Burrett College, TN
- Burrett Gen -
- Board Paid for Minors
- Franklin, J. N., Judge
- Wills Valley Railroad (claim)
- Garrett, M. B., 1881 (File for final settlement)
- Frazier, P. M., (sheriff)
- Williams, Jas., (JP)
- Phillips, H.
- Brock, Andrew, (JP)
- Estes, R., Judge
- Phillips & Roberts
- Blackwell, J. M., (tuition/minors)
- Blackwell, James M., (tuition)
- Fortune, W., (paid)
- Hudson, L. W., (JP)
- Phillips, P. D.
- Phillips, H & Co., (paid)
- Fletcher, A. J., (paid)
- Dodson, C. C., (tuition/minors)
- Trusler, Hammack Thomas (Commerce School)

Garrett, Thomas
- Box 5 File 11 1849-1859
- Names in File: File 1 of 2
- Garrett, Sarah, (widow)
- Garrett, Henry W. B.
- Garrett, Thomas J.
- Stewart, Nancy
- Stewart, John J., (h/o Nancy)
- Rook, Lilia A.
- Rook, John T., (h/o Silia/Lilia)
- Garrett, Matilda B.
- Phillips, Matilda Garrett
- Phillips, P., (h/o Matilda)
- Webb, Garrett W.
- Webb, Jane
- Webb, Lovica Garrett

Estate Record Name
Garrett, Thomas (Cont.)
Webb, E. B., (h/o Lovica)
Garrett, H. W. B.
Stewart, John
Parker, James
Walden & McSpadden, (atty)
Stewart, John J., (Sp. adm.)
Roberts, Richard, (adm.bond)
Lyon, William, (adm.bond)
Garrett, H. W., (adm.bond)
Bogle, J. C., (adm.bond)
Haralson, W. J., (adm.bond)
Green, A. B., (adm)
Williams, James, (purchas. land)
Secured by Lankford, John M.
Secured by Phillips, P. D.
Estes, R., Judge
Parker, James, (JP)
Stewart, J. J., (note)
Davis, Thomas, (note)
Garrett, H. W., (note)
Webb, E. W., (note)
Garrett, Jesse, (note)
Lyon, Thomas, (note)
Smed?, Thomas D., (note)
Crouse, John, (note)
Crawford & Anderson, (note)
Evans, Isaac, (note)
Dutton, Samuel, (note)
Garrett, Wesley M., (note)
French, Samuel B., (note)
Horton, Elizabeth, (note)
Mathews?, James, (note)
Garrett, H. W. B., (note)
Crisman, James, (note)
Reese, Anderson, (note)
Lankford, R. E., (note)
Garrett, J. B., (note)
Jones, Drury, (note)
Cooper, William, (note)
Harison, George, (note)

Estate Record Name
Garrett, Thomas (Cont.)
Wheeler, Drury C., (note)
Pritt?, J. C. (note)
Sample, W. M., (note)
Griffith, Elizabeth, (note)
Harrison, H. C., (note)
Bryant, W, (note)
Hibbs, Jeremiah, (note)
Smith, J. W. L., (note)
Hammack, W., (note)
Fortune, W., (note)
Patterson, S. L., (note)
Clayton, Daniel., (note)
Collins, R. M., (clerk)
Lankford, R. E., (JP)
Brock, Andrew, (paid)
Hammack, W., (paid)
Burnett, S. E., (paid)
Davidson, Joseph, (board/Jesse)
Clayton, Daniel, (JP)
Rook, Silvey/Lilia
Stewart, J. J., (son-in-law)
Garrett, Melinda
Garrett, Jesse A.
Garrett, Valeria V. (minor)
Garrett, Malachi B.
Little, Thomas, (witness/will)
Parker, James, (witness/will)
Negro Man, Alfred
Negro Man, Long
Negro Woman, Sarah
Tate, Mabin
Garrett, Thomas T., (guardian)
Winston, Wm. O.
Wills Valley RR, ($800 claim)
Oliver, J. H.
Haralson, J. R.
Garrett, Sarah, (guardian)
Belsher, Joseph, (paid)
Hammack, Thomas, (paid)
Collins, R. M., (clerk)

Estate Record Name

Garrett, Thomas (Cont.)
- Thornberry, William, (sued)
- Baldwin, James C., (tax 1855)
- Patterson, L. D.
- Rice, Joseph
- Rice, Joe
- Mills, W.
- Parson,
- Davis,
- Crouse, Jos.
- Ivins/Evans, Isaac
- Crawford & Anderson
- Dutton, Samuel
- Crismas, James
- Reece, Andrew
- Harison, George
- Wheler, Drurye C.
- Harbin, James
- Rowden, J. C.
- Harrison, H. C.
- Briant, Wm.
- Hibs, Jeremiah
- Ham, Wm.
- Frazier, Patrict, (sp.coroner)
- Lankford, R. E., (adm) Gatlin
- Frazier, John B., (Gatlin File)
- Hawkins, Raleigh, (Gatlin File)
- Gatlin, Eliza (See Gatlin File)
- Chitwood, R.., (JP)
- Hulgan, S. P. Witness
- Baxter, G. W.
- Hasturn, Hannah
- Higins, W.
- Gaskins, James
- Pankey, Edwards
- Beck, Daniel
- Cooper, William, (note)
- George & Harrison, (note)
- Wheeler, (note)
- Pivett, J. C., (note)
- Samples, W. M., (note)

Estate Record Name

Garrett, Thomas (Cont.)
- Swader, Thomas, (note)
- King, Richard, (note)
- Willoughby, J. H.
- Carden, J. W.
- McBrayer, H. P., (teacher)
- Sheppards, Anderson W.
- Roberts, W. J.
- Brock, Anderson, (JP)
- Reece, Andrew
- Thagog, R.
- Gask, Jos.
- Mason, Peter
- Estes, R., Judge
- Brandon, H. H., (acct.)
- Killian, Daniel, (acct.)
- Roberts, Phillip R.
- Garrett, Valeria
- Winston, Edward
- Hammack, Willoughby, (JP)
- Garrett, M. B.
- Garrett, J. G.
- Stewart, Eliza
- Stiff, Joseph Edward
- McCampbell, Solloman
- Thomas Garrett Will

Garrett, Thomas
- Box 5 File 12 1854-1856
- Names in File: File 2 of 2
- Garrett, Jesse, (minor)
- Garrett, Valesia V., (minor)
- Garrett, Matilda, (minor)
- Garrett, Sarah , (widow)
- Henderson, Hiram, (acct.)
- Harrison, George
- Slicgog?, Richard, (note)
- Martin, James
- Samole, W. M.
- Webb, E. B.
- Landford, John
- Lankford, William

Estate Record Name
Garrett, Thomas (Cont.)
Hibbs, Jeremiah
Jones, Drury
(assign debt of P.D.Phillips)
Walker, W. J.
Newkirk, James, (note)
Jones, Bert
McCloud, William M.
Cooper, Wm.
Norton, Samuel
French, Samuel H.
Cooper, John C.
Garret, J. R.
Davis, Houstin H.
Garrett, Sarah, (relinquish dowry)
Stewart, John J., (adm)
Phillips, Matilda C.
Sarrett, W. B., (witness)
Fortune, William
Estes, R., Judge
Rooks, J.
Green, A. B., (adm)
Phillips, P. D., (purchased land)
Ward, T. G., (JP)
Macky, A. A., (acct.)
Negro, Charles, (paid)
Fike, Mrs., (services)
Negro Woman, Lil, (paid)
Willis, Mark, (paid)
Negro Woman, Emily, (paid)
Parker, James, (JP)
Fortune, William
Swader, Francis, (paid
for services for widow Garrett)
Brock, A., (JP)
Winston & George, (paid)
Findley, John B., (paid)
McBrayer, H. P., (JP)
McSpadden, T. K. Belle, (paid)
Brock, Andrew, (JP)
Williams, James, (JP)

Estate Record Name
Garrett, Thomas (Cont.)
Phillips, Pleasant D.
Killian, Daniel, (paid)
Warren, S. D.
Moore, Alexndria
Brock, Daniel Anderson, (JP)
Snider, C.
Rogers, Reece, (cotton seeds)
Evans, Isaac, (paid)
Beesen & Phillips
Parker, James, (paid)
Lyon, John, (paid)
Mooney, M. P.
Patterson, John, (paid)
Little, Thomas, (paid)
Figures, W. B. (subscription)
Huntsville Southern Advocate
Wilson, R. D., (JP)
Beck, Daniel, (paid)
Pankey, Edward, (paid)
Lankford, R. P.
Rook, Sylvia A.,(w/o John)
Rook, Silvey/Sylvia/Lilia
Evans, Isaac, (paid)
Cunningham & Linton
Cunningham, C. T., (JP)
Cox, W. P.
Willoughby, J. F.
Rinehart, M., (JP)
Hammack, A. J.
Phillips, P. D., (notes assigned)
Privett, Paines C.
Rowlins, John
Webb, E. B.
Young, James F.
Wallace, William
Wheeler, Drury
Blake, John Ben
Webb, Garrett W., (g-son)
Webb, Jane, (g-dau.)
Webb, Lavica Garrett, (dau.)

Estate Record Name

Garrett, Thomas (Cont.)
- Negro Man, Ilias
- Negro Man, Guy
- Negro Man, William
- Negro Man, Jacob
- Negro Man, Frank
- Negro Man, Ephrian
- Negro Man, Alfred
- Negro Man, Israel
- Hawkins, B. F.
- Sloan & Hawkins
- Holloway, Jesse
- Carter, A. W.
- Davenport, Lilbourn H.
- Hoge, J. M.
- Hoge, J. R.
- Cunningham, N. L. (pd)
- Porter & Haralson
- Garrett, H. W. B. (purchas. land)
- Phillips, P. J., (surety)
- Parker, James, (surety)
- Griffity, Elizabeth
- Haralson, Wm. J.
- Cooper & Nicholsen, (atty)
- Garrett, Sylvia A.
- Phillips, Matilda, (w/o P. D.)
- Garrett, Sarah
- Garrett, Thos. J.
- Stewart, John J.
- Stewart, Nancy
- Rook, John J.
- Rook, Sylvia
- Phillips, P. D.
- Phillips, Matilda
- Stewart, John J.
- Stewart, Nancy
- Rook, John J.
- Rook, Sylvian

Property Sold:
- Patterson, L. D., (mule)
- McCampbell, Solomon, (mule)

Estate Record Name

Garrett, Thomas (Cont.)
- Hammack, Wm., (mule)
- Warren, Samuel, (hogs)
- Swader, Francis, (hogs)
- Hulgan, S. P., (hogs)
- Lyons, P. M., (hogs)
- Lyons, P. M., (sow & pigs)
- Hammock, (hogs)
- Scott, Thos., (cow & calf)
- McNutt, R. C., (cow)
- Pendergrass, J. W.
- Cunningham, John, (cow)
- Gipson, John, (cow & calf)
- Harris, John, (hogs)
- Green, A. B., (adm)
- Rook, S. A.
- May, W. H.
- Bunsan, T. G.
- Cunningham, Jesse
- Rogers, Reece
- Hughes, A., (paid)
- Stiff, L. M., (paid)
- Davenport, R. R.
- Black & Cobb
- Black, Geo. S.
- Lackey, G. G.
- Tucker, James
- Baxter, James
- Rook, Silva/Sylvia
- Pankey, Edw'd., (paid)
- Beck, Dan'l., (paid)
- Parker, James, (paid)
- Little, Israel, (paid)
- Figures, W. B., (paid)
- Belcher, Joseph, (paid)
- Beason & Phillips, (paid)
- Davenport, R. R., (paid)
- Paterson, L. J., (paid)
- Evans, Israel, (paid)
- Reese & Rogers, (paid)
- Malone, G. W., (paid)

Estate Record Name

Garrett, Thomas (Cont.)

Little, Thos., (paid)
Hulgan, F., (paid)
Hulgan, P. (paid)
Ryan, Wm., (paid)
Williams, Jas., (paid)
Estes, R., (paid)
Brock, Andrew, (appraiser)
Parker, James, (appraiser)
Rogers, Reese, (appraiser)
Swader, Francis, (appraiser)
Roberts, W. I., (witness)
Brock, Andrew, (JP)
Beeson & Phillips
May, Wm. H.
Estes & May
Sloan & Hawkins
Hawkins, B. F.
Cunningham, Jesse, (paid)
Halloway, Jesse H.
(coffin for servant, Charles)
Chitwood, Richard, (JP)
Carter, A. W., (medical)
Davenport, Lilbourne, (medical)
Tatum, Samuel, (JP)
Little, Thomas
Hughes, A. A., (sheriff)
Rice, Joseph, (dep.sheriff)
Phillips, Pleasant D., (purch.land)
Hammack, Thos., (surety)
Hammack, W. N., (surety)
Williams, James, (purch.land)
Hammack, W. N., (surety)
Rogers, Reese, (surety)
Killian, Elias
Garrett, H. W. B., (purch land)
Phillips, P. J., (surety)
Parker, James, (surety)
Griffith, Elizabeth
Cooper & Nicholsen, (atty)
Garrett, Sylvia A.

Estate Record Name

Garrett, Thomas (Cont.)

Phillips, Matilda
Phillips, P. D.
Garrett, Saray
Garrett, Thos. J.
Stewart, John J., (note)
Rallings, J. (note)
Privitt, (note)
Webb, E. B.
King, James, (note)
Jones, Isaac, (note)
Hammack, (note)
Wallace, Wm., (note)
Wheeler, Drura, (acct.)
Henderson, Hiram, (acct.)
Sampley, Wm.
Lankford, John
Hibbs, Jeremiah
Briant, Wm., (acct.)
Jones, Drura, (acct.)
Davis, H. K. (acct.)
Crouse, Jno., (acct.)
French, Samuel B.
Means, A. M.
Newkirk, James
McCloud, Wm.
Sampley, Wm., (acct.)
Gask, James, (acct.)
Mooney, Wm. H., (note)
Carden, J. W.?, (acct)
Briant, Polly, (insolvent)
Howell, Jno., (insolvent)
Bryant, Wm., (acct.)
Garrett, Blount, (acct.)
Carter, F. W., (acct.)
Sutten, Samuel, (acct.)
Killian, Elias, (acct.)
Ward, John, (insolvent)
Lyons, Wiley, (insolvent)
Lyons, H., (insolvent)
Griffith, Elizabeth, (insolvent)

Estate Record Name
Garrett, Thomas (Cont.)
Griffith, Jessie, (insolvent)
Baxter, F. W., (insolvent)
Hartrum, H., (insolvent)
Alfred, Henry (insolvent)
Higgins, (acct.)
Baxter, Wills, (acct.)
Willoughby, Hammack, (acct.)
Hammack, Willoughby, (acct.)
Tatum, Sam'l., (paid)
Phillips, P. J., (paid)
French, J. C., (paid)
Beason & Phillips, (paid)
Fletcher, J. A., (paid)
Rice, James, (paid)
Fortune, Wm., (paid)
Hammock, Thos., (paid)
Garrett, T. J., (paid)
Hammack, Wm. N., (paid)
Baxter, James, (paid)
Parsons, James, (paid)
Mackey, A. M., (paid)
Fortune, Wm., (paid)
Phillips, P. D., (paid)
Beason, J. G., (paid)
Nicholson, J. E., (paid)
Swader, F., (paid)
Winston, J. G., (paid)
McSpadden, T. K. B., (paid)
Brock, A., (paid)
Lankford, R. P., (paid)
Belcher, J. B., (paid)
Stuart/Stewart
Collins, R. M., (guar.ad litem)
Baker, Asa
Morgan, D. C.
May, Wm. H. (guar.ad litem)
McSpadden, T. K., (atty)
Collins, Robert M., (guar.ad litem)
Green, A. B., (adm)
Cooper & Nicholsen, (atty)

Estate Record Name
Garrett, Thomas (Cont.)
Williams, James, (JP)
Garret, Thomas J. (guardian)
Garrett, Valeria V. (minor)
Garrett, Jessey A., (minor)
Winston, William, (atty)
Garrett, Sarah
Garrett, Henry H. B.
Garrett, Thomas J.
Stuart, John J.
Stuart, Nancy
Stuart/Stewart
Garrett, Lavicey
Webb, Lavicey Garrett
Webb, Elias B.
Webb, Sarah Jane
Webb, Garrett W.
Garrett, Malichi B. (minor)
Garrett, Sylvia Ann
Rook, John
Garrett, Matilda, (of age)
Garrett, John A.
Garrett, Valenia V., (minor)
Garrett, Henry, (representative)
Edwards, Joseph, (sheriff)
Collins, R. M., (guar.ad litem)
Garrett, Sarah, (widow)
Baker, Asa
Morgan, D. C.
May, Wm. H., (guar.ad litem)
McSpadden, T. K. (atty)
Collins, Robert M., (guar.ad litem)
End or Roll 67
Garrett, Thomas R.
Box 5 File 13 1894-1897
Names in File:
Sales of Land for Division
Garrett, W. S., et al
Garrett, Thomas
Garrett, Willis
Garrett, Emily C., (Estate)

Estate Record Name
Garrett, Thomas R.
Garrett, Emily C., (w/o H.W.B..)
Garrett, H. W. B., (deceased)
Walker, Susan
Walker, J. N., (h/o Susan)
Lankford, Ellen
Lankford, Jeff D., (h/o Ellen)
Rogers, Mary A.
Rogers, Elijah, (h/o Mary)
Jackson, Desdemona
Jackson, James E., (h/o Desdemona)
Garrett, Mary A., (minor)
Poe, W. R., (guardian ad litem)
Cook, W. C. D., Judge
Cochran & Haralson
Cochran, Earl
The Fort Payne Journal
Roberts, F. M., (witness)
Heard, Solon E., (witness)
Cochran, L, L., (atty)
Ward, N. W., (commissioner)
Roberts, George R.,Sr. (pur.land)
Roberts, J. M., (commissioner)
Nicholson, L. S., (JP)
DeShields, J. G., (sheriff)
Gatlin, Eliza Jane
Box 5 File 14 1869
Names in File:
Gatlin, Harrison
Gatlin, George, (minor)
Gatlin, Louisa J., (minor)
Gatlin, James, (deceased)
Lankford, Robert E., (adm)
Harris, Gaines A., (appraiser)
Bouldin, Elijah, (appraiser)
Painter, Hardy, (appraiser)
Warren, R. J., (JP)
See Box 5, File 11
Dunlap & Dobbs
Hoge, J. K.
Sale of Personal Property:

Estate Record Name
Gatlin, Eliza Jane
Gatlin, H., (churn)
Hawkins, H., (saddle, bed, etc.)
Hawkins, Alex., (chair & pigs)
Lankford, R., (corn)
Painter, H., (sow and pigs)
Ferguson, W., (sow & pigs)
Hawkins, G., (sow and pigs)
Painter, James, (sow & pigs)
Shadwick, J.,(hog)
Lankford, P. G., (hog)
Franklin, J. N., Judge
Gatlin, Eliza Jane
Box 5 File 15 1881
Lankford, R. E., (adm)
Brandon, P. A., (comm.)
Gatlin, Harrison, (adm.)
Lankford, Robert E., (prior adm)
Sale of 40-acres land
Turnery & Beeson, (atty)
Gazaway, Jesse
Box 5 File 16 1852-1853
Names in File:
Gazaway, Ellender, (widow)
Gazaway, Henry H., (son, adm)
Gazaway, John, (son)
Gazaway, Caleb G., (son, minor)
Gazaway, William, (deceased)
Carr, Rosa, (widow of William)
Gazaway, Nancy Ann
Gazaway, Jane
Barnes, Martha A.
Barnes, Davidson, (h/o Martha)
Lankford, John M., (bond)
Lankford, R. B.
Lankford,, John, (guar.ad litem)
Ward, Obadiah W., (bond)
Newman, Moses C. (bond)
Ward, O. W., (bond)
Lea, Allen, (surveyor)
Lee, Allen, (surveyor)

Estate Record Name
Gazaway, Jesse
Thomasen, J. F., (appraiser)
Welborn, John F. (appraiser)
Gilbreath, A. R., (appraiser)
Benge, V. C., (appraiser)
Featherstone, Jesse (citation)
Beeson, Jesse G., (bond & appraiser)
Brock, Andrew, (appraiser)
Gilbreath, Asa, (appraiser)
Collins, Louis M., (appraiser)
Benge, Clinton , (appraiser)
Stewart, Robert, (appraiser)
Venable, J., (appraiser)
Gazaway, John, (bought land)
Estes, R., (JP)
Hughes, Abner H., (sheriff)
Hughes, A. A., (sheriff)
Porter & Haralson
Beesan & Phillips
Brock, Andrew, (JP)
McClain/McClane, Daniel
Haralson, W. J.
Cagle, L. H., (paid)
Parsons, James, (paid)
Beeson, J. F., (paid)
Lindley, J. B., (paid)
Green, Anthony B., (paid)
Walden, J. B., (paid)
Wilborn, J. L., (paid)
Sale of Personal Property:
Gazaway, H. H., (33# tobacco)
Lyon, Nathaniel, (Bedstead)
Gazaway, John, (clock)
Gazaway, E., (trunk)
Gazaway, John, (table)
Stoner, A., (hand saw)
Stone, A., (2-kegs & sythe)
Stewart, Robert, (reap hook)
Bryant, Henry, (wheat)
Venable, Isaac, (oats)
Bryant, Henry, (sorrel horse)

Estate Record Name
Gazaway, Jesse (Cont.)
Gazaway, Caleb, (colt)
Gennett, Elizabeth
Box 5 File 17 1909-1911
Names in File:
Shepherd, Anna E., (daughter)
Shepherd, G. W. J., (adm)
Shepherd, G,W.J., (h/o Anna)
Howard, M. H., (bond)
Hunt, Luke P., (bond)
Howard & Hunt, (atty)
Maston, O. C., MD, (acct)
Sheppard, W.D.J., Dr.
Wright, Dr.
Quinn & Wright
Smith, T. H., (printing)
Cross, F. M.,(trip to Cincinnati)
Shepherd, Anna, (res.Illinois)
Wales, C. F. M., (claim)
Isbell, John B.
Campbell, H. B.
George, Charles D.
Box 5 File 18 1838-1873
Names in File: File 1 of 3
George, H. P.
Collins, Alfred, (claim)
Hall, Aaron, (claim)
George, John K.
Dilbeck, A. W., (JP)
Collins, A., (Exec.1869)
Turnley, M. J., (atty)
Petty, Wiley D. (adm)
Reed, W. D., (bond)
Collins, N. S., (bond)
Collins, J. H., (bond)
Nicholson, T. J., (bond)
Brandon, P. A., Judge
Hoge, John K., (guar.ad litem)
Bridges, Sarah, (minor)
Tiner, Caroline
George, Charles, (minor)

Estate Record Name
George, Charles D. (Cont.)
George, Mary, (minor)
George, Thomas, (minor)
Strickland, Barbara
George, Thomas H.
George, Ellen, (c/o Thos. H.)
George, James, (c/o Thos. H.)
George, Mary, (c/o Thos. H.)
George, Thomas, (c/o Thos. H.)
Notes Due Estate:
Cook, B. F.
Clayton, W. P.
Driskill, W. A.
Driskill, W. L.
Estes, W. N.
Gregory, R.
Hughes, A. A.
Hoge, P. G.
Hoge, Jas.
James, J.
Morris, H.
May, W. H.
Smith, S. J.
Gilbert, H.
Tiner, G. J.
Walden, J. B.
Word, J. D.
Nichlson, D. L.
Nicholson, J.
Findley, J. B.
Winston, J. J.
Hays, W. J.
Cunningham, Jesse
Hoge, Jas.
Harris, H.
Davidson, Sol
Morris, H.
Adams, B. S.
Casey, W. P.
DeKalb Lodge
McCampbell, Sol

Estate Record Name
George, Charles D. (Cont.)
Franklin, J. N.
Bankston, J. P.
Malone, G. W.
Estes, R.
Hoge, J. K.
May, W. H.
Luck, Thomas
Davidson, Sol
Nicholson, D. L.
Collins, A.
Clayton, Daniel
Hulgan, R. M.
Reese, John
Tiner, S. J.
Ward, O. M.,
Collins, Alford/Alfred, (exec)
McCampbell, Sol, (land)
Estes, W. N., (security)
Estes, R., (security)
Baxter, F. M.
Baxter, S. W.
Horton, A. J., Judge
Ferguson, W. L., (tax 1877)
Estes, William N., (sale of land)
Hammock, Thomas, (security)
Bon__?, John T., (security)
Collins, A., (sale of land)
Estes, W. N., (security)
Estes, R., (security)
Brogan, Steven, (security)
Hoge, John K., (security)
Warren, L. D., (security)
Major, A. W., (security)
Barnard, J. L., (security)
Promissory Notes:
Cox, A.
Major, A. W.
Walden, J. B.
Ward, J. D.
Nicholson, D. L.

Estate Record Name
George, Charles D. (Cont.)
Findley, J. B.
Hays, W. J.
Hoge, James
Hoge, J. R.
Morris, J.
Adams, B. J.
Cassey, W. P.
DeKalb Lodge
May, L. G.
McCampbell, Sol
Nicholson, D. L.
Tiner, J. J.
Barnard, J. L.
McNewman, R.
Cunningham, J.
Cunningham, L. D.
Bankston, J. F.
Malone, G. W.
Johnson, J. R.
Estes, P.
Hoge, J. R.
May, W. H.
Turk, Thomas
Nicholson, D. L.
Collins, A.
Clayton, Danl.
Hulgan, R. M.
Hays, W. G.
Walker, _ J.
Hoge, James
Brannon, J. L.
Hammock, Thomas
Cunningham, A. L.
Weaver, D.
Majors, A. W.
Brannard, J. L.
Burgess, Thos. J.
Reese, John
Tiner, F? J.
Ward, O. W.

Estate Record Name
George, Charles D. (Cont.)
Jenks/Jinks, Ephrain
Jett, Bailess A.
Jackson, Daniel
Turk, Robert M., (witness)
Johnson, Joseph B.
Jones, W. B.
Jack, Thomas M.
Johnson, Hamilton
Isbell, William
Hail, Lindsey
Harper, Jesse
House, Thomas
Welch, Thomas, (witness)
Hayes, A. K.
Howard, John H.
Hagler, W. T.
Hill, Thomas
Hoyl, Andrew F.
Hoyl, A. F.
Heard, M. J.
Heard, Martin T.
Hall, Elijah
Harrison, William
Hibbs, Newton
Clayton, Sam
Bryson, John, (witness)
Hoge, Samuel
Hopkins, C. Frank
Hall, Aaron
Dibbeck, A. W. (JP)
Hickson, J. P.
Beesen, W. B. (witness)
Higgins, R. W.
Houston, William
Harrel, Enoch
See Files 19, 20 and 21
Harold, Enoch
Harold/Harrel
Glazner, John
Gibbs, Thomas W.

Estate Record Name

George, Charles D. (Cont.)
- Graddy, Lewis
- Grady, Lewis
- Garden, James
- Jolson, John
- Golson/Jolson
- Graham, Thomas
- Majors, A. W. (witness)
- Grady, James O.
- O'Grady, James
- Newkirk, James
- Norton, Roswell
- Nicholson, Wm. J.
- Driskill, W. L. (JP)
- Mitchell, James D.
- Mitchell, Robert
- Malone, James
- Mitchell, H. B.
- Martin, A.
- McNair, Price
- Hulgan, Robert
- Martin, Martin
- McCrow,
- Matheny, Green B.
- MacLeod, L. J.
- McClain, W. G.
- McKelvey Wm.
- McFay, Henry H.
- Meadows, William
- Adams, B. S., (JP)
- ___, Alexander
- Dobbs, Solomon
- Michell, A. J.
- McPherson, George
- McDaniel, William
- James, William L.
- Livingston, L.
- Lamar, Thos. F.
- Lovorn, John
- Loving/Lovorn, John
- Long, N. P.

Estate Record Name

George, Charles D. (Cont.)
- Lovein, Thomas
- Lewis, B.
- Lewis, Bunnal
- Lamar, James
- Smith, S. C.
- Kelly, Lewis
- Foster, J. R.
- King, Loomis
- King, S. H.
- King, Soll
- King, G. W.
- King, James M.
- King, D. P.
- Killian, John
- Killian, Daniel
- King, James F.

George, Charles D.
- Box 5 File 19 1839
- Names in File:
- Strickland, Barbara
- Roberts, William J., (guar.ad litem)
- Bridges, Sarah, (minor)
- George, Ellen, (minor)
- George, Mary, (minor)
- George, Thomas, (minor)
- Infant of Caroline Tiner
- Tiner, Caroline
- Franklin, J. N., Sheriff
- Brock, Andrew
- Hardin, Mary D.
- Ramey, C. C., (JP)
- Price, G. W., (KY)
- Gray, Allen
- Box, C. O., (JP)
- Edwards, Jeptha
- White, S. M., (JP)
- Malone, G. W.
- Graves?, Jason
- McCampbell, John M.
- Sibert, John W.

Estate Record Name
George, Charles D.
Box 5 File 19 1839
Briston, E. T.
Briston, W.
Briant, Joseph
George, H. P.
Findley, I. B., Judge
Rees, John
Malone, Nathaniel
Hulgan, R. M.
Majors, Samuel, (JP)
Banks, Hugh R.
Hull, Sam J.
Banks, Wiley
Gregory, Robert
Collins, A., (adm)
McCampbell, Sol
Findley, John B.
McCurdy, N. W.
McCurdy, Warren
Ward, John D.
Carden, C. C., (JP)
Strickland, Barbara
Clayton, Solomon
Kennedy, Wm. E., (TN)
Bradley, E. H., (ARK)
Starnes, B. R.
Winston, W. O.
Nicholson, Mary B. R.
Nicholson, L. M.
Watts, W. J.
Wiggins, R. W.
Nicholson, D. L.
Smith, Jackson, (JP)
Estes, R., Judge
Adams, B. L.S.
Roberts, R., (witness)
Collins, A.
Roberts, Richard
Watts, W. J.
Cannon, J. K.

Estate Record Name
George, Charles D. (Cont.)
Rees, John
Bratton, Alexander
George, Robert
Owens, Wesley, (JP)
Colyer, D. G., (clerk)
Thurman, B. R., (JP)
Cogin, Wesley
Nicholson, W. L.
Douglas, Joseph
Findley, George
Cranford, George
Barclay, Thomas C., (JP)
Gilbreath, M.
Rees, John
Carter, A. W.
MacNewman, R.
McNarian, Richard
Burgess, G. F.
George, C. D.
Winston & Finley
White, S. M., (JP)
Edwards, N. I. J.
Griffin, James M.
Strickland, Burrel
Dobbs, J. J., (F. F.)
Edwards, Warren
George, Charles D.
Box 5 File 20 1840-1878
Names in File: File 2 of 3
Frazier, P. M., (sheriff)
Turnley, M. J., (atty)
Hoge, James
Walker, P. J.
George, Charles D. (Land Grant)
Taylor, Zachary, President
Petty, Wesley D.
Collins, Mahala E,, (paid)
Collins, James H., (paid)
Barnard, J. T., (paid)
Hammock, Thos., (paid)

Estate Record Name

George, Charles D. (Cont.)

Box 5 File 20 1840-1878

Hoge, Joseph, (paid)
Vann, A. G.
Yarbrough, J. W.
Petty, W. J.
Edwards, John
Edwards, Nettie
Malone, E. T.
Malone, R. J.
Winston, John N.
See files 18, 20, and 21
Luck, Thomas
Turk/Luck/Tuck
Tyner, Stephen J. (paid)
Higgins, J. W., (attest)
Starnes, B. R.
McBroom, Thos.
Phillips, B. G.
Barnard, J., (paid)
Hoge, John K., (paid)
Morris, J. T.
Stiff, L. M., (paid)
Clayton, Daniel, (paid)
Smith, J. L. F.
Newman, M. C.
Sibert, Henry
Franklin, J. N., (sheriff)
Walden, J. B.
Gilbreath, Samuel
Dobbs, Silas P.
Stiff, Lellie, (paid)

Notes Due Estate:

Cox. T. G. A.
Cook, B. F.
Clayton, Wm. P
Driskil, W. T.
Driskil, W. A.
Estes, W. H.
Gregory, Robert
Hughes, A. A.

Estate Record Name

George, Charles D. (Cont.)

Hoge, J. K.
Hoge, Jas.
James, J.
Morris, H.
Majors, A. W.
May, W. H.
Smith, S. J.
Sibert, H.
Tyner, S. J.
Walden, J. D.
Ward, J. D.
Nicholson, D.L.
Nicholson, J. F.
Finley, J. B.
Cunningham, Jesse
Hoge, Jas.
Hoge, J. R.
Morris, H.
Davidson, Sol
Adams, B. S.
Casey, W. P.
DeKalb Lodge
May, P. G.
McCampbell, Sol
Franklin, J. N.
Tiner, G. J.
Barnard, P.? T.?
McMahan, R.
Bankston, G. S.
Malone, G. W.
Johnson, J. R.
Cunningham, E.
Hoge, J. K.
Turk, Thos.
Davidson, Sol
Franklin, J. N.
Nicholson, D. L.
Collins, A.
Clutey?, Paul?
Hulgan, R. M.

Estate Record Name
George, Charles D. (Cont.)
McCampbell, Sol
Estes, W. N.
Estes, R.
Collins, A,
Hays, W.. J.
Walker, Peter J.
Hammock, Thos.
Cunningham, N. T.
Warren, Samuel D.
Majors, A. W.
Barnard, J. L.
Burgess, Thos. J.
Reese, John
Tiner, S. J.
Ward, O. W.
Word/Ward
Collins, Alfred
Cunningham, N. T.
Hoyl, Joseph
Barnard, J. D.
Tiner, Charles George
Tiner, Caroline
Strickland, Barbary
George, Ellen, (minor)
George, James, (minor)
George, Mary, (minor)
George, Thomas, (minor)
Children of Thomas H. George
Turnley, M. J., (atty)
Reese, Thomas S., (affidavit)
Reese, John
Brandon, P. A., Judge
Bridges, Sarah, (minor)
Horton, A. J., Judge
Collins, Alfred
Higgins, Robert W., (witness to will)
Morris, Jonathan T., (witness to will)
Estes, R., Judge
Unborn child of Caroline Tyner
Nicholson & Higgins (atty)

Estate Record Name
George, Charles D. (Cont.)
Petty, W. D.
Gilbreath, Samuel, (purch.land)
Canther, J. Y. (land joining)
Warren, N. M., (land joining)
Walden, J. B., (surety)
Warren, N. M., (surety)
Lot adj. Cunningham, N. L.
Lot adj. Majors, A. W.
Walden, J. B., (purch.lot)
Ward, A. J., (surety)
Gilbreath, S. C., (surety)
Dobbs, Silas P., (purch.land)
Haralson, W. J., (surety)
Hoge, Joseph, (surety)
Turney, M. J., (paid)
Frazier, Pat M., (sheriff)
Moore, And.
Barclay, Thos. C., (JP)
Gilbreath, J. M., (Judge,Marshall)
Malone, G. W.
Horton, A. J., Judge
Haralson, W. G.
George, Charles D., (signature)
Sales of Personal Property:
Ward, John D., (saddle)
Nicholson, David L., (book)
Findley, John B., (books)
Williams, W. N., (book)
Davis, John, (pistol)
Hays, W. J., (book)
Davidson, J. D.
Hays, W. O., (book)
Johnson, J. R., (book)
McBroom, S., (books)
Jack, Allen, (books)
May, (surgery book)
Johnson, J. R., (surgery book)
Bankston, J. G. (Poison book)
Hoge, W. O., (books)
Bankston, J. S., (dictionary)

Estate Record Name
George, Charles D. (Cont.)
Williams, W, W,(books)
Vann, A. J., (midwife book)
Bankston, (medical books)
Hanks, J. S., (book)
Hoge, W. A., (medical book)
Nicholson, D. L., (med.book)
Williams, W. N., (anatomy book)
Walden, J. B., (table)
Williams, W. H., (dictionary)
Ward, A. J., (book)
Hoge, N. J., (book)
Bankston, J. S., (books)
Bankston, J. L., (latin book)
Cunningham, Jesse, (bible & books)
Lankford, R. P., (book)
Franklin, J., (book)
Davidson, J. A.
Davidson, Joseph
Tuck, T., (books)
Appleton, J., (book)
Ward, J. D., (book)
Glazner, G. T., (book)
Nicholson, D. L., (gold watch)
Griffin, Wm.
Appleton, J.
Bankston, J. S., (battery)
Hoge, W., (surgical case)
Estes, R., (rule)
McBroom,
Cunningham, T. (tooth drawer)
Ward, J. G., (fish hooks)
Hoge, J. K., (looking glass)
Collins, A., (box of junk)
Ligins, T. H. Lynn
Hulgan, M., (fiddle)
Hoge, J. K., (trunk & contents)
Watts, Benj., (M scale)
Collins, A., (travel truck)
Williams, W.W.,(fancy snuff box)
Vann, A. J., (snuff box)

Estate Record Name
George, Charles D. (Cont.)
Ramey, John, (bracelet & rings)
Jack, Arch, (silver pencils)
Franklin, J., (spining scales)
Bankston, J. S., (instruments)
Swader, Washington
Ramey, John, (chain)
Porter, C. C. (picture)
Lyons, S. O., (plates)
Watts. Benj., (candle sticks)
Hulgan, A., (cup & plate)
Tyner, S. J., (plates)
Findley, J. B. (glass salt set)
Williams, W. W., (musical box)
Franklin, J., (bible)
Newman, R. C., (books)
McBroom, S., (pocket knife)
McBroom, S., (pocket book)
Davis, John, (soap)
Scott, N., (brush)
Williams, W. W., (money belts)
Watts, Benj., (powder horn)
Cunningham, L. C., (trunk)
Simpson, J.
Yancy, W., (buggy whip)
Johnson, J. R..(med.equipment)
Ward, J. G., (med.instruments)
Johnson, J. R., (bottle Colemel)
Ward, J. G., (niter)
Newman, R. C., (calamill)
Vann, A. M., (sp.lance)
Cunningham, Jesse, (arsenic)
Findley, J. B., (arrow root)
Watts, Benj., (pulverized ginger)
Sims, Wm., (cobalt)
Williams, W. W. N., (iodine)
May, P. G., (iron carbonate)
Cunningham, T., (sulfur & spice)
May, P. G., (saddle bags)
Collins, A., (asfoedila)
Hays, W. O., (sundries)

Estate Record Name
George, Charles D. (Cont.)
May, P. G., (box vials)
Hays, W. O., (quinine)
Vann, A. J., (quinine)
Bankston, J. S., (quinine)
McBroom, Jeff
Davidson, Sol, (horse collar)
DeKalb Lodge
McBroom, Stephen, (scissors)
Hayes, Dr., (stethoscope)
McNaran, Richard, (pitcher)
Franklin, J. N., (table)
McCampbell, Sol, (Lantern)
Hill, Jas., (candles)
Nicholson, D. L., (lamp)
Adkins, John, (iodine)
Sims, W. O.
Ward, J. G., (salts)
Findley, J. B., (jars)
Collins, G., (camphor)
Tyner, Stephen J., (curtains)
Morris, Henry
Phillips, Ben, (jug and bottles)
Jack, Thomas, (buggy crop)
Findley, Jno. B., (basket)
Hoge, Joseph, (curtains)
Estes, R. (tongs & curtains)
Davidson, Joseph, (pr.tongs)
Davidson, Jas., (musical box)
Hoge, James, Sr. (spinning wheel)
Findley, J. P., (spinning wheel)
Davidson, Joseph, (lamp)
Calloway, M. C., (pr.steelards)
Bates, Benj., (box)
Pates/Bates
Nicholson, T. E. (dr. bags)
Nicholson, D. L., (canteen)
Tyner, Stephen J. (hames & chairs)
Collins, Alf., (gin.pand?)
Hays/Hoge
Davidson, J., (candles)

Estate Record Name
George, Charles D. (Cont.)
Ryan, Amos, (pitcher)
Porter, C. C., (picture)
McBroom, Stephen, (skillet)
Hayes, Dr., (thermometer)
Phillips, Ben, (drawing knife)
Warren, Edward, (skillet)
Dobbs, Jaby, (oven & lid)
Calloway, Martin, (?)
Newman, (lamp)
Davidson, Joseph, (corn)
Davidson, Jno., (corn)
Hoge, Jas., (corn)
Hill, Berry, (oats)
McNirnan, Richard, (wheat)
Estes, R., (cotton gin)
Estes, R., (thrasher, fan, & gear)
Adams, B. S., (16 bu.corn)
Luck, Thomas, (corn)
Tuck/Luck/Turk
Collins, Alfred, (corn)
Morris, Wesley, (oats)
Morris, J. T., (parcel)
Harris/Morris
Hagler, Columbus, (box)
Morris, J. T., (table & cloth)
Calloway, M. C., (crane)
Finley, Jno., (cup board)
Roberts, Isham, (table)
Hoge, J., (plow)
Davidson, J., (grindstone)
Jack, Thomas, (old irons)
Porter, C. C., (quilting frame)
Jones, Thomas, (coffee mill)
McCampbell, Sol, (cart)
Morris, J. T., (sundries)
Roberts, Isham, (harrow)
Small, Baxter, (1-hd cattle)
Davidson, J., (plows)
Estes, R., (double tree)
Tyner, Stephen J., (scythe)

Estate Record Name
George, Charles D. (Cont.)
Roberts, Isham, (wheat)
Jack, Thomas, (wheat)
Hayes, Dr., (corn)
Warren, Samuel, ((corn)
Green?, R. G., (corn)
Value of Notes:
Johnson, James R., (note)
Jack, Allen, Jr., (note)
Bankston, John V., (note)
Walden, John B., (note)
Davis, John, (note)
Ward, Isaac G., (note)
Ward, A. J., (note)
Lankford, R. F., (note)
Griffin, Wm., (note)
Appleton, John, (note)
Tuck, Thomas, (note)
Glazner, L., (note)
Hoge, John K., (note)
Simon, T., (note)
Hulgan, Alfred, (note)
Watts, Berry, (note)
Ramey, John, (note)
Jack, Arch, (note)
Nicholson, Isaac E., (note)
Swader, G. W., (note)
Brandon, W. C., (note)
Russell, C. A., (note)
Porter, C. C., (note)
Scott, Newton, (note)
Yancy, William A., (note)
Siniard, James, (note)
Tyner, Stephen J., (note)
Freeman, R. C., (note)
Malone, G. W., (note)
Majors, A. W., (note)
McCampbell, Sol, (note)
Sims, W. J., (note)
May, J. G., (note)
Adkinson, John, (note)

Estate Record Name
George, Charles D. (Cont.)
Majors, Sam, (note)
DeKalb Lodge, (note)
McNaren, Rich, (note)
Hill, James, (note)
Hill, Berry, (note)
Ryan, Amos, (note)
Philips, Ben, (note)
Warren, Edward, (note)
Dobbs, Jabze?, (note)
Calloway, M. C., (note)
Morris, J. G., (note)
Roberts, Isham, (note)
Warren, Sam, (note)
Adams, B. S., (note)
Jack, G. M., (note)
Hoge, Joseph, (note)
Davidson, James, (note)
Bates, Ben, (note)
Davidson, John, (note)
Driskill, F. A., (note)
Hagler, C., (note)
Jones, Thomas, (note)
Statement A - Accts. Due Estate
Armstrong, James
Adams, Thomas
Adair, W. F.
Allen, Lerry
Adkinson, John
Arthur, Charles
Appleton, Joseph
Adams, Silas
Alexander, Thomas
Adair, John K.
Adair, Sarah
Brandon, Calvin
Blancit, George
Beck, J. D.
Bridges, Luke
Burney, John M.
Bolen, W. H.

Estate Record Name
George, Charles D. (Cont.)
Burges, Z. J.
Blackburn, Jackson
Berry, Jackson
Burney, John B.
Brock, David
Brackens, Tinsley
Brock, Hiram
Brock, Stanford
Bradley, E. H.
Brock, Eliz.
Blackburn, Jaby
Brock, M.
Bryant, C. C.
Berry, Jess
Burk, Wil
Bryant, Preston
Baxter, Willis
Blanton, Whit
Bratton, Alex.
Bryant, Wm.
Brown, Wm.
Brown, Wm.(at Van Buren)
Bates, Ben F.
Brice, James
Brooks, Isaac
Barkley, Andrew L.
Brock, Nicey
Busby, Dunnell
Baxter, Wash
Busby, John
Baxter, James, Sr.
Baxter, James J.
Brinsfield, Simson
Buster, Sam
Bridges, Robt.
Bridges, Frank J.
Bowen, Ebenezer
Bruce, John M.
Beavers, Allen
Bridges, Thos.

Estate Record Name
George, Charles D. (Cont.)
Barksdale, George
Botsfield, Mr.
Bryant, Wm.
Bryant, Wm.
Barksdale, Sherod
Brock, James
Burt, Grover
Brock, Isaiah
Blackburn, John
Blackburn, Elijah
Bryant, Rial
Beeson, Jesse G.
Barkley, Saml. M.
Brock, Mary
Brock, Elina
Brock, Wilborn
Brandon, Hugh H.
Berry, John
Berry, Caroline
Baker, James
Bolen, Rueben
Brice, John P.
Brown, A.
Bishop, Jackson
Brock, Henry
Bartel, Fredrick
Blackwell, A. L.
Busby, Seaborn
Brock, Josiah
Brock, Harris
Blackburn, Rebecca
Busby, James A.
Brindley, A. R.
Busby, James A.
Bryson, John P.
Boswell, George
Brandon, P.
Bearden, Diannah
Bearden, M. S.
Brooks, James

Estate Record Name
George, Charles D. (Cont.)
Accts. Due Estate (Cont.)
Buster, W. & C.
Burnett, J. W.
Brock, Larkin
Barr, M. A.
Barnes, Geo. A.
Brinkley, R. T.
Bean, R. F.
Baxter, Jesse, Jr.
Bynum, Jesse G.
Brown, R. H.
Clayton, W. H.
Carr, H.
Carden, C. C.
Carden, N. H.
Chitwood, John
Chasteen, Jacob
Clayton, Sol
Clayton, Daniel, Sr.
Chaney, Wm.
Chasteen, Ramey
Couch, Jackson
Crow, Wash.
Carney, D. K.
Cooper, John
Clark, Oliver
Chick, M.
Crow, Robt.
Carder, Sarah
Crisman, James
Chasteen, J. B.
Clayton, Perry
Comer?, John
Carter, Glover
Collins, R. M.
Chaney, Jackson
Cunningham, John
Calaway, M.
Clayton, S.
Coggin, Wesley

Estate Record Name
George, Charles D. (Cont.)
Casey, O. P.
Cane, James
Cave/Cane/Care
Casey, Frank
Casey, W. P.
Clark, Saml.
Carter, John J.
Carter, Mary
Carter, Angelina
Cannady, M.
Carter, Hugh
Camp, John M.
Carter, C.
Carr, Joseph
Christain, Mr.
Chitwood, E.
Cox, Thos. A.
Carroll, Peter
Chitwood, Richard
Cannon, John K.
Capshaw, Thos.
Cole, Ben
Campbell, Henry
Cunningham, N. L.
Cunningham, Lafayette
Cawley, James
Clarkson, Lucy
Clayton, Danl., Jr.
Carter. G. W.
Collins, A. Y.
Collins, O. D.
Cook, B. F.
Childers, John
Carter, Aaron
Cooker, H.
Chasteen, J. C.
Copley. J. S.
Chaney & Hendrick
Clayton, Wm. P.
Cowen, David

Estate Record Name

George, Charles D. (Cont.)

Driskill, W. L.
Driskill, Wm.
Davidson, Jas.
Dutton, Francis
Driskill, Wm., Jr.
Dobbs, Elijah
Dutton, John
Dobbs, Jaby
Drain, John
Denham, Jas.
Davidson, Wm.
Driskill, T. A.
Davidson, Sol.
Driskill, Joseph
Driskill, Eliz.
Dobbs, James G.
Davidson, John
Dilbeck, Noah
Depriest, John O.
Denham, Susan
Davis, Riley
Davis, E., Mrs.
Denham, Wm.
Durting, Saml.
Drake, John
Dutton, Saml.
Driskill, W. L.
Driskill, W. A
Echols, W. B.
Estell, S. H.
Everett, Wm.
Estes, W. N.
Engle, E. H.
Estes, Robt.
Estes, Rueben
Edwards, Joseph
Fletcher, Hugh
Fortune & Watts
Fowler, Richard
Frazer, John B.

Estate Record Name

George, Charles D. (Cont.)

Findley, John B.
Frazer, Dorcas
Fullerwider, David
Frazer, Robt.
Fields, Gilbert
Fields, Elizabeth
Fields, James
Fike, Harlon
Flowers, John
Fletcher, Jackson
Findley, W. W.
Favors, John A.
Freeman, Elisha
Floyd, James
Fitzgerald, T. M.
Funderburk, James
Flowers, Strother
Funderburk, George W.
Funderburk, C. C.
Fielder, N. W.
Fielder, N. W.
Fields & Co.
Fisher, C. P. C.
Furrow, Saml.
Farmer, Rueben
Garrett, Tatum
Gray, A. L.
Glazener, Giles
Garner, Geo. W.
Gravett, Melvina
Graves, John, Sr.
Graves, Hiram
Gasque, John M.
Gazaway, Mrs.
Goggin, E. T.
Gregory, Robt.
Griffin, Nancy
Graves, Ira
Gerard, Richard
Gentry, Eliza

Estate Record Name
George, Charles D. (Cont.)
Graves, Arthy Ann
Glazener, Jesse
George, Thomas H.
Griffin, Wm.
Graham, Gideon
Garrett, Thos., Sr.
Gorum, Marion
Garrett, James, Jr.
Graves, John
George, Mary E.
Gains, Robt.
George, H. P.
Graddy, James O.
Graham, Thos.
Gholston, John
Gardner, James
Graddy, Lewis
Gibbs, Thos. W.
Hammock, W.
Harris, Nancy A.
Humphreys, John J.
Hibbs, Dempsey T.
Hollins, Hugh
Hall, John
Hendricks, Madison
Hickson, Jere
Hall, Aaron
Hughes, A. A.
Henderson, N. W.
Hoge, Levi
Houston, Edley
Harrison, J. E. T.
Hibbs, Newton
Hendricks, Mrs.
Hill, Berry
Hendricks, Mr.
Hibbs, Sarah
Harrell, Enoch
Holcomb, Wm. H.
Hudson, Thos.

Estate Record Name
George, Charles D. (Cont.)
Hopkins, C. Frank
Hill, James
Hoge, Joseph
Reeves, Hugh
Hendrix, Joab
Hendricks, James
Henderson, John
Harrison, Agness
House, J. G.
Hayes, James H.
Hagles, Columbus C.
Hulgan, S. P.
Holcomb, John P.
Hawkins, F. M.
Hayes, Oliver
Hurd, Rachael
Houston, Wm.
Hall, Levi
Hayes, Virgil
Houston, Wm., Jr.
Hurd, Lucinda
Harkins, James M.
Hastens, Stephen
Hughes, David D.
Hoge, John K.
Hoge, Jas.
Higgins, R. W.
Bradford, J. T.
Harrison, Wm.
Hall, Elijah
Heard, M. T.
Hoyl, A. F.
Hill, Thos.
Howard, John L.
Hagler, Wm. T.
House, Thos.
Hayes, A. K.
Harper, Jesse
Hale, Lindsay
Isaac, J. C.

Estate Record Name
George, Charles D. (Cont.)
Isbell, Wm.
Johnson, Hezekiah
Johnson, C. A.
Johnson, Hamilton
Johnson, Elizabeth
Jack, Allen
Jones, Susan
Jones, W. L.
Jones, Thos.
Jones, Jane
Jett, J. M.
Jordan, George W.
Jack, Thos.
Jones, Nancy
Jones, Joseph
Jones, W. B.
Johnson, Joseph B.
Jackson, Daniel
Jenkins, Rueben
Jett, Bayless
James, J. Ashley
Jenks, E.
King, Adelia
King, James
Kirkland, Miss
Killian, John
Killian, John A.
Killian, Elias
Killian, Daniel
King, Wm.
King, Lewis P.
King, Geo. W.
King, Sol. H.
King, Lunas
Kelley, Lewis
Loving, L. B.
Long, Marion
Lamar, James
Lewis, Burrell
Lackey, Wm., Sr.

Estate Record Name
George, Charles D. (Cont.)
Lord, Charles
Lovern, Thos.
Lovern, John
Lawrence, Joseph
Lowry, James
Lackey, Wm.
Loving, Eliz.
Loyd, James
Light, Meredith
Lankford, J. L.
Long, W. P.
Lamar, T. F.
Livingston, L.
Lackey, Saml.
Matheny, Winny
McCampbell, John
Malone, George W.
Mullins, Wm.
Malone, Eliz.
McDaniel, Wm.
Martin, Martha
Moody, J. J.
McPherson, George
Mitchell, Abner
Matheny, Jack
Merrell, Haley
Mays, Stephen
McBroom, Stephen
McSpadden, Moses
Mullins, Dick
Murphy,
McPherson, E.
Morgan, Jere
Morrow, George
McCurry, Mr.
Meadow, John
Mitchell, James
Morris, Henry
Michell, Alex. T.
Mitchell, Alex.

Estate Record Name
George, Charles D. (Cont.)
Accts. Due Estate (Cont.)
Dobbs, Sol.
Merrett, James
Miller, John
Majors, A. W.
Malone, David A.
Morgan, Nathan
McKelvey, George
McCampbell, Sol.
Malone, Levy/Lerry
Mynatt, Wm. C.
Mitchell, M.
Mays, Henry
Meadows, Wm.
Martin, Jane
Morgan, J. B.
Maddra, James T.
Mulwee, George
McCracken, George
Moseley, Canady
May, W. H.
Morris, J. T.
McCoy, H. H.
Mckelvey, Wm.
Mauldin, W. G.
McLoud, L. J.
Matheny, G. R.
McCrow, James
Martin, Robt.
McNair, Prince
Martin, D. S.
Mound, A.
Mitchell, H. B.
Malone, James
Mitchell, Robt. & James
Mitchell, Robt. & James
McNearon, Rich.
McLeroy, A.
McKey, Alex.
Matheny, Jane

Estate Record Name
George, Charles D. (Cont.)
McPherson, Mary
Nicholson, W. J.
Newman, Simpson
Newkirk, John
Norton, Roswell
Newkirk, Henry
Newkirk, H. H..
Newkirk, Hiram
Nicholson, W. D.
Nicholson, Thos.
Nicholson, Mary
Newman, M. C.
Nicholson, Mary
Newkirk, James
Nicholson, M.
Nichols, J. B.
Norrell, Nancy
Nichols, James
Nichols, J. G.
Nave, Warren
Nicholson, John
Norton, James
Norton, Mrs.
Nicholson, Wm.
Owens, Newton
Owens, Wm.
Odom, Mr.
Owens, Hugh
Owens, Gilford
Osborn, W. C.
Owens, Raymond
Owens, John T.
Owens, Thos.
Oliver, James H.
Pendleton, Eliza
Porter, B. F.
Porter, C. C.
Patterson, L. D.
Pratt, Jonathan
Pate, Aaron

Estate Record Name
George, Charles D. (Cont.)
Phillips, Ben
Price, Lewis
Parker, Russell
Previn, Elizabeth
Poe, Wash.
Penn, James
Porter, James
Porter, Richard
Padgett, Jacob
Pinkerton, Thos.
Privett, James
Porter, Silas
Patrick, Austin
Patton, Geo. E.
Peak, Richard
Pervin, M.
Poe, James C.
Pace, Burrell
Peak, Judy
Painter, Lewis
Paty, W. P.
Perry, Hanibal
Poe, W. T.
Ryan, Wm.
Rudy, Jacob
Reed, Nancy
Read, Marion
Roden, Z. T.
Raburn, Rebecca
Richards, C. H.
Roberts, Isham
Raines, Buck
Reed, Amy
Roberts, C.
Ravlin, Albert
Rice, Miller
Robertson, Lindsey
Rucks, G. W.
Robinson, John
Rhodes, Wm.

Estate Record Name
George, Charles D. (Cont.)
Roberts, Rich'd.
Rees, John
Rodgers, Wright
Raines, Saml.
Ray, Middleton
Reed, James, Sen.
Ryan, Amos
Reeves, Redding
Rice, Jos.
Ross, John
Reed, George
Reed, Susan
Ramsey, Rich'd.
Rice, J.
Roden, Calvin
Ryan, Marshall
Reed, Ben
Russell, R. M.
Reeve, Jas. A.
Rook, Wiley W.
Riddlespunger, Eliz. Ann
Riddlespunger, Old Lady
Ramsey, John
Rucks, Celphia
Roden, Wm.
Reeves, J. H.
Riggs, Wm.
Reeves, Eliz.
Reynolds, Wm.
Ryan, Peter
Roberts, John A.
Riddle, Tyre
Rowan, Saml.
Rich, Elijah
Reeve, Seme O.
Richards, John
Smith, John
Sammons, Nelson
Smith, Sarah Jane
Simpson, James

Estate Record Name

George, Charles D. (Cont.)

Smith, Saml.
Smith, J. W. L.
Standfield, Geo. R.
Smith, Maria
Sedberry, S. H.
Smith, Joel
Smith, Eliza R.
Stapler, Amos
Spangler, Nath.
Spangler, Gid
Stiff, L. M.
Sims, E., Mrs.
Slayton, S. C.
Smith, Jas. Wm.
Saterfield, Jesse
Smith, Nancy
Smith, Jane
Smith, Thomas
Slayton, Eliz.
Smith, Elisha
Smith, Joseph
Smith, James M.
Smith, Felix
Smith, Eliz., Mrs.
Smith, James
Smith, Henry E.
Sibert, Wm.
Smith, Sarah, Miss
Smith, Wm.
Sims, W. J.
Shook, O S.
Sims, James R.
Stuart, John J.
Smedley, J. R.
Snider, Delila
Sanders, Harrison
Sibert, Henry
Southerland, James
Strickland, A. B.
Smith, Ed

Estate Record Name

George, Charles D. (Cont.)

Starling, Mrs.
Tyner, S. J.
Tickett, Ezekiel
Taylor, G.
Tidwell, Wm.
Thomas, Wm. A.
Tobert, Wesley
Thompson, Joshua
Teague, Isaac
Taylor, Sol
Taylor, John
Taylor, Skelton
Tackett, John
Thompson, John L.
Tims, Mrs.
Tims, Harrison
Trafensted, Mary
Tuck, Thomas
Tate, Mayben
Tufton, Mary E.
Tyner, Wm.
Taylor, Stephen
Tidwell, Elenor
Trout, J. G.
Tate, J. H.
Clayton, Henry
Watts, W. J.
Wilson, J. M.
Williams, James
Wilder, Malina
Whatley, William
Walden, John B.
Withrow, Martha
Wilson, R. F.
Ward, O. W.
Winply, J. N.
Ward, Isaac
Warren, Saml., Jr.
Watts, S. T.
Withrow, Mary

Estate Record Name

George, Charles D. (Cont.)

Works, Wm.
Winston, Wm. O.
Ward, Mary
Wilkenson, E. R.
Whitt, W. P.
Whitt, Shade
Wright, Geo.
Wright, James C.
Horton, Jesse B.
Walls, Wm.
Walls, Burd
Wood, B. F.
Wilks, Minor
Ward, Malinda
Walker, Wm.
Watkins, John A.
Williams, Henry
Walker, John
Ward, A. J.
Wesson, Mr.
Winston, John G.
Watts & Fisher
Whitten, Inman
Waddell, W. C.
White, George
Wards, John D.
Watts, Thos. B.
Wilks, Wash.
Wright, J. F.
Wilson, Elijah
Witt, Abner
Wilder, Jesse
Watson, James
Wiggs, Henry
Webb, E. B.
Wilks, H. J.
Washburn, J. B.
Willis, W. F.
Young, John
Yancey, Wm.

Estate Record Name

George, Charles D. (Cont.)

Young, Lewis
Vandergriff, Thos.
Vann, A. J.
Tickets, Jury
Adams, B. ?
Cash on Hand at death
Sale of Personal Property
Sales of Real Estate

End of Statement A

Statement C - Claims Against Estate

Whatley, Wm., (a/c)
Phillips, Ben, (a/c)
Winston, Wm. O., (notes)
V.R.R., (subscription)
Wiley, Banks & Co. (SC), (note)
Findley, John B.. (a/c)
Harden, Mary B., (KY)(note)
Jones, Netty J., (notes)
Walden, J. B., (claim)
Winston & Son, (a/c)
Winston & Poe, (a/c)
Winston J. G., (notes)
Burnes, J. B., (a/c)
Lamar, James, (note)
Baxter, James, (a/c)
Mackey, L. A. H., (note)
Ward, John B., (note)
Barkley, Saml., (a/c)
Sibert, Henry, (a/c)
May, W. H., (a/c)
Hoge, John R., (a/c)
Fielder, N. W., (a/c)
Mitchell, James, (note)
Ward, A. J., (note)
Estes & May, (note)
Wilder, M. (a/c)
Sibert, J. W., (notes)
Killian, A., (a/c)
McPherson, George, (a/c)
Hunter, J. P., (a/c)

Estate Record Name

George, Charles D. (Cont.)

Statement C - Claims Against Estate

Ramey, S., (note)
Forney, W. H., (note)
Beeson, J. G., (a/c)
Adams, B. S., (a/c)
Rhodes, Wm., (a/c)
Watts, W. J., (a/c)
Smith, S. J., (a/c)
Blackburn, E., (a/c)
Ward, Malinda, (a/c)
Ward, O. W., (note)
Hagler, Wm. T., (a/c)
Dobbs, Elijah, (a/c)
Crisman, James, (a/c)
Banskston, J. S., (note)
Winston, W. O., (atty) (note)
Strickland, B., (a/c)
Long, Wm. P., (a/c)
Sibert, John W., (a/c)
Yancy, Wm. A., (note)
Holcomb, Wm., (a/c)
Lewis, Burrell, (a/c)
Lamar, James, (a/c)
Estes, R., (a/c)
Davidson, James, (a/c)
Sansom, F. M., (note)
Rees, John, (note)
Cannon, J. K., (a/c)
Clayton, Sol, (a.c)
Eskin, Z. W. & Co., (note)(TN)
McCampbell, Sol, (a/c)
Morris, Smith & Harrison, (a/c)
Rees, John, (a/c)
Nicholson, W. J. (a/c)
Cunningham, N. L. S., (a/c)
Douglass, Jos., (a/c)
Weatherford, J. G., (a/c)
McCurdy, N. W., (a.c)
Kennedy, W. E., (a/c) (TN)
Gregory, Robt., (a/c)

Estate Record Name

George, Charles D. (Cont.)

Anibles & Whitaker, (note)(SC)
Nicholson, Mary B.,(a/c)
Carter, A. W., (a/c)
Driskill, W. L., (a/c)
Malone, Nath'l, (note)
Jones, Nettie J., (note)
Higgins, R. W., (a/c)
End of Schedule C-Claims
Newman, Moses C., (bought land)
Newman, W. M., (security)
Siniard, J. D., (security)
McCampell, Sol, (bought lot)
Estes, W. N., (security)
Estes, R. (security on note)
Hays, W. J., (bought lot)
Nicholson, D. L., (security)
Franklin, J. N., (security)
Canthers, J. Y., (bought lot)
Nicholson, D. L., (security)
Nicholson, Isaac, (security)
Newkirk, Hiram, (Estate)
Strickland, Barbara, (claim)
Carden, C. C., (JP)
Edwards, Joseph, (sheriff)
Edwards, Nettie J.vs:Collins,(adm)
Lankford, R. P., (clerk)
Edwards, John, (h/o Nettie)
Findley, J. B., (JP)
Sims, Wm. J.
Beeson, W. B., (JP)
Buson/Beeson
Bridges, Louisa/Lewis
(parent of Sarah Bridges)
Chitwood, Ezekiel, (note)
Clark, O. P., (note)
Crow, G. M.
Roberts, R., (JP)
Petty, W. D., (adm. 1880)

George, Thomas H. - Estate
filed with Charles D. George

Estate Record Name
George, Thomas H. - Estate
filed with Charles D. George
George, Charles D., (adm)
George, Mary G. (widow of T. H.)
Statement A - Accounts Due Estate
Adkins, John
Adams, Ben
Adams, Ambrose
Blanton, Richard
Burt, Grover
Bridges, F. J.
Burgess, J. B.
Briant, Thomas
Blanton, Whit
Bishop, Wm.
Bynum, Jesse
Baxter, Wash
Burgess, Jesse
Burt, James
Briant, R.
Busbee, James
Baker, A.
Bryant, Wm.
Clayton, Daniel, Jr.
Cooper, Eli
Clayton, Sol, Jr.
Collins, Young
Carter, Hugh
Clayton, Craig
Coggin, Wesley
Clayton, Sol
Clayton, S.
Chapman, John
Chitwood, Richard
Clayton, Dan
Collins, R. M.
Chitwood, Wm.
Chitwood, Andy
Clark, K.
Collins, Mrs.
Cunningham, John

Estate Record Name
George, Thomas H. - Estate (Cont.)
filed with Charles D. George
Dobbs, Stephen
Dobbs, Jabey
Davis, William
Davis, W. G.
Dobbs, S. P.
Davidson, Sol
Davidson, John
Davidson, William
Drake, John
Davis, Abe
Davis, Geo.
Estes, Wm.
Estes, Rueben
Epperson, Robt.
Estes, James
Farmer, Rueben
Farmer, Jonathan
Findley, W. W.
Frazer, Mrs.
Findley, J. B.
Fortner, A.
Frazer, John
Franklin, John
Frazer, Robert
Frazer, Brown
Gubbs, Wm.
George, C. D.
Garrett, Tatum
Green, A. B.
Garrett, Jason
Garrett, Thomas, Sr.
Garrett, Thos., Jr.
Graham, G.
Garrett, H. W. B.
Hagler, W. T.
Higgins, R. W.
Hartrum, Hannah
Hughes, A.
Hartrum, Chloe

Estate Record Name

George, Thomas H. - Estate (Cont.)
filed with Charles D. George
Haynes, C.
Haralson, J. S.
Hulgan, Robt., Sr.
Hulgan, R. M.
Hulgan, Alfred
Haralson, W. J.
Hunter, J. P.
Hoge, J. K.
Headerly, A. R.
Isbell, John
Jett, Bayless
Jack, Thomas
Johnson, D.
Lankford, John
Lowry, W. T.
Lute, Isaac
Little, Jas. R.
Mullins, Wm.
McCampbell, Frank
McCampbell, John
Malone, G. W.
McCampbell
Majors, A. W.
May, W. H.
McCurdy, McLin
McPherson, Geo,
McPherson, Isaac
McFarland, Byron
McCampbell, Alex.
Poe, W. T.
Porter, John R.
Porter, B. F.
Phillips, A.
Ryan, A. L.
Reece, Jos., Sr.
Reece, Robt.
Roberts, W. J.
Rogers, Rees
Rook, John

Estate Record Name

George, Thomas H. - Estate (Cont.)
filed with Charles D. George
Richard, John
Rector, Elijah
Reece, G. W.
Sims, Wm. J.
Sims, W. J.
Stanfield, Geo.
Strickland, Barby
Swaffer, M.
Shook, O.
Strickland, Burrell
State Claims
Tackett,
Tyner, Jack
Thomason, D.
Toins, Harvey
Loins/Toins
Walden, J. B.
Walden, Jos.
Wilch, Jas.
Williams, James
Watts, Jesse
Walker, P. J.
Ward, J. G.
Ward, Andy
Walker, John
Winston, J. N.

Statement B - Accounts Due Estate

Adams, B. S.
Adams, William
Adams, Ambrose
Bryant, Preston
Bankston, D.
Busbee, Jas.
Baxter, Jesse
Baxter, Wash
Baker, Asa
Bryant, Thos.
Bird, John
Bridges, Frank

Estate Record Name
George, Thomas H. - Estate (Cont.)
filed with Charles D. George
Bates, Ben
Bryant, William
Cunningham, John
Collins, A. Y.
Clayton, Wm.
Caldwell, D.
Collins, R. M.
Chitwood, Rich
Chitwood, Joel
Coggins, Wesley
Clayton,
Counts,
Davis, Wm.
Dobbs, Stephen
Estes, Wm.
Estes, R.
Epperson, Robert
Estes, Jas.
Frazer, J. B.
Frazer, Robt.
Fiseman, Brock
Findley, J. B.
Hall & Nicholson
Horton, Preston
Hoge, J. K.
Haralson, W. J.
Hoge, Jas.
Holloway,
Gilbreath, Frank
George, C. D.
Jack, Jeff
Jett, J.
Lewis, B.
Lankford, Robert
Lackey, Saml.
Lackey, Isam
Little, James
McCampbell, Sol
McPherson, Hand

Estate Record Name
George, Thomas H. - Estate (Cont.)
McNutt, Robert
McBrayer, H. P.
McCurdy, Frosty
McDaniel,
McCurdy,
Nicholson, D. L.
Norton, Mr.
Patterson, Saml.
Price, Henderson
Paden, John
Rogers, Reese
Rogers, John
Rook, Job
Small, Baxter
Slayton, Stephen
Swaffer, M.
Strickland, B.
Sims, W.
Taylor, John
Tenis, Harper
Thurman,
Tyner, Jack
Statement B - Accounts Due Estate
Walker, Peter J.
Walker, Ben
Wright, J. T.
Williams, Morgan
Statement C - Notes Due Estate
Garrett, Thomas B.
Hulgan, R. M.
Baxter, J.
Jett, J. M.
Martin, Robert
Coggin, Wesley
McBrayer, H. P.
Chitwood, Rich
McCampbell, Sol
Frazer, Robt.
Rogers, Reese

Estate Record Name

George, Thomas H. - Estate (Cont.)
filed with Charles D. George

Statement D - Exp.- Widow of T.H.

Fields, E., Mrs.
Calloway, M. C.
Chitwood, P. C.
Collins, Jane
McPherson, G. W.
Chitwood, M.
Winston, J. G.
F?, Jesse B.

Statement E - Claims against T. H.

Morrison, W. A.
Tyner, L. J.
Poe, J. C.
Baker, Asa
Haralson, J. W.
Malone, G. W.
Jett, J. M.
Baxter, Willis
Hoge, J. K.
Collins, R. M.
Morrison, Wm.
George, T. H.
Estes & May
Dobbs, Stephen
Weatherford, J. G.
Morrison, W. A.
Ward, Isaac Y.
Edwards, J.

Statement F - Notes Collected

Wimpee, J. A.
Chitwood, Wm.
Garrett, H. W. B.
Chitwood, Andy
Lankford, J. M.
Franklin, J. N.
Walker, John
McPherson, George
Slayton, Stephen
Chitwood, Joel

Estate Record Name

George, Thomas H. - Estate (Cont.)
Horton, Preston
McPherson, Geo.
Garrett, Thos. J.
Baker, Asa
Nicholson, D. L.
McCurdy, McLen
End of Thomas H. George

George, Charles D.
Box 5 File 21 1861-1880
Names in File: File 3 of 3
See Files 18, 19, and 20
Accounts Due Estate:
Wilks, H. J.
Martin, W.
Reeves, Simeon O.
Mackey, Henry H.
Rowen, Samuel
Rich, Elijah
Norton, James
Nicholson, Wm. J.
Majors, Elijah
Newkirk, James
Newkirk, H. H.
King, G. W.
Lovin, John
Kelly, Lewis
Levin, Thomas
Killiam, John
Lamar, Thomas F.
King, Solomon
King, D. P.
Lewis, B.
King, James J.
Livingston, L.
Lackey, Samuel L.
McPherson, George
Moore, A.
Mitchell, Alex
Dobbs, Sol
McGraw, James

Estate Record Name
George, Charles D. (Cont.)
Box 5 File 21 1861-1880
McNair, Price
Mitchell, A. S.
Morris, J. T.
Mitchell, Robert
Brown, R.
Malone, James
Matheney, Green B.
MacLeod, L. J.
Mitchell, W. B.
McKelvey, Wm.
Nicholson, John
Patterson, L. D.
Jett, B. A.
Jones, Wm. B.
Smith, Edward
Baxter, Jesse
McJenkins, Rueben
Wall, William
Johnson, Joseph B.
Porter, C. C.
Hoyle, A. F.
Isbell, Wm.
Sibert, Henry
Jackson, Daniel
Hill, Thomas
Harl, Enoch
Hoge, Thomas
Howard, John H.
Hail, Lindsey
Wilder, Jesse
Gibbs, Thos. H.
Gains, Robert
Graddy, James O.
Graham, Gideon
Gibbs, Thos. W.
George, H. P.
Golston, John
Frazer, Robt.
Graddy, Lewis

Estate Record Name
George, Charles D. (Cont.)
Furrer, Samuel
Frazer, John B.
Farmer, Rueben
Saunders, Harrison
Snider, Sehlar
Gardner, James
Sims, William
Rains, Wm. H.
Rich, Elijah
Spangler, Nathan
Sims, J. R.
Riddle, Tyre
Ryan, Peter
Roberts, Calvin
Robertson, John
Smedley, John R.
Perry, Hanibal
Poe, Wm. T.
Pinkerton, Thos. B.
Carter, Aaron
Drake, John
Coggins, Wesley
Cox, T. C.
Childess, John
Cowen, Davis
Clark, O. P.
Coker, H.
Dobbs, J. G.
Crisman, James
Chitwood, E.
Collins, Edward
Heard, Marlin
Crossley, J. S.
Carter, A. W.
Chitwood, John
Chastain, Joseph
Chaney & Hendricks
Cannon, J. K.
Echols, Wm. B.
Estell, S. H.

Estate Record Name
George, Charles D. (Cont.)
Cook, B. F.
Davidson, James
Clayton, Daniel
Chastain, J. C.
Armstrong, James
Higgins, R. W.
James, Ivashly?
Richards, John
Southerland, James
Simes, James R.
Driskill, W. L.
Driskill, W. A
Driskill, T. S.
Durting, Saml.
Davidson, James
Brandon, C. F.
Brisen, John P.
Bryan, Columbus
Bosewell, George
Barkley, S. W.
Brison, John
Brock, James
Brock, Isaac
Brock, Thomas H.
Brandon, Hugh H.
Beam, R. F.
Walden, John B.
Bynum, Jesse G.
Baxter, James
Watley, Wm.
Buzby, James
Brandon, Phillip
Brindlee, R. T.
Webb, E. B.
Wilkerson, E. R.
Robertson, Lindsay
Wright, James
Witt, A.
Bearden, Martins
Bryant, Wm.

Estate Record Name
George, Charles D. (Cont.)
Burt, Graves
Brock, Henry
Watson, James
Wilson, Eliza
Higgins, R. W.
Harl, Enoch
Brock, James
Burk, Amos
Barnes, George A.
Blanton, Whit
Hale, Lindsay
Taylor, Solomon
Tate, S. H.
Ward, T. G.
Brock, Larkin
Witt, A.
Wright, J. F.
Wright, George
Vandergriff, T. M.
Wilder, Jesse
Findley, J. B.
Harper, Jesse
Heard, Marline
Harl, Enoch
House, Thomas
Hall, Elijah
Hand, M. T.
Thompson, Henry
Hale, Lindsay
Hages, A. K.
Hopkins, C. Frank
Graham, Gideon
Higgins, R. W.
Buster, W. A.
Buster, C. K.
Cave, James
Mauldin, W. G.
Brock, Harris
Bearden, Dianah
Malone, James

Estate Record Name
George, Charles D. (Cont.)
Shook, O, S.
Gregory, Robt.
Adams, Silas
Watts, S. T.
Cunningham, J.
Burnett, S. W.
Trout, J.
Davidson, Joseph
Jack, Allen, Sen.
Harrison, Wm.
Johnson, Hamelton
Coggin, Wesley
Baxter, C. W.
Crisman, James
McCampell, S.
McCambell, John
Buzby, James R.
Adams, B., (medical)
Appleton, R. C., (mdse)
Alexander, Thos., (medical)
Adair, Thos. K. (mdse)
Adair, Sarah, (mdse)
Beck, J. D., (mdse)
Bridges, Lewis, (mdse)
Burnger?, John M.
Bowlin, Wm. H.
Burgess, Jesse
Blackburn, Jackson
Berry, Jackson, (mdse)
Burnes, J. B., Dr. (mdse)
Brock, David, (mdse & med.)
Bruckin, Tinsley, (mdse)
Brock, Hiram
Adams, B, S.
Tacker, Ezekiel
Lamar, James
Yancey, Wm. A.
Ward, J. W.
Newkirk, H. H.
Brandon, Calvin

Estate Record Name
George, Charles D. (Cont.)
Clayton, Wm. H., (boots)
Blanchet, George
Wood, Benj. F.
Adams, Thomas
Adair, W. F.
Allen, Leroy
Adkinson, John
Arthur, Charles
Appleton, Joseph
Jinks, Ephram
Fisher, C. P. C.
Norton, Roswell
Barr, M. A.
Nosham, J. D.
Collins, A. Y.
Newman, Simpson
Barksdale, Sherod
Rhudy, Jacob
Hagler, Wm. T.
King, Sol F.
Bratten, Alex
Tiner, S. J.
Strickland, A. B.
Clayton, Dan
Clayton, Solomon
Branden, H. H.
Vann, A. J.
Clayton, Wm. P.
Hibbs, N. J.
Whatley, Wm.
Brock, Stanford
Bradley, E. H.
Brock, Elizabeth
Blackburn, Jabus
Brock, Meridith
Bryan, Columbus
Berry, Jeptha
Burk, Wilburn
Bryan, Preston
Baxter, Willis

Estate Record Name

George, Charles D. (Cont.)
- Blanton, Whitman
- Bratton, Alex
- Braseal, William
- Brown, William
- Bates, Benj.
- Brice, James
- Bartles, Frederick
- Blackwell, A. L.
- Bugley, Seborn
- Carr, Hannah
- Carden, Columbus
- Crisman, James
- Corbin, N. H.
- Chitwood, John
- Chastain, Jacob
- Clayton, Solomon
- Clayton, Daniel
- Chaney, William
- Chastain, Raney
- Couch, Jackson
- Crow, Washington
- Carnes, D. R.
- Cooper, John
- Clark, Oliver
- Cheek, Maniel L.
- Crow, Robert
- Burt, Graves
- Brock, Isaac
- Blackburn, John
- Blackburn, Elijah
- Bryan, Ryan
- Beeson, Jesse G.
- Barkley, S. M.
- Brock, Mary, Miss
- Brock, Eliziah, Miss
- Brock, Wellborn
- Brandon, Hugh
- Berry, John
- Berry, Carlin
- Baker, James

Estate Record Name

George, Charles D. (Cont.)
- Bouldin, Rueben
- Brice, John P.
- Brown, Alfred
- Brock, Elizabeth, Miss
- Bushof, Jack
- Brock, Henry
- Brock, Nicey
- Buzby, Derrell
- Baxter, Washington
- Buzby, John
- Baxter, James
- Brunsfield, Simpson
- Butler, Samuel
- Bridges, Robert
- Bridges, F. J.
- Bruce, John M.
- Beavers, Allen
- Bridges, Thomas
- Botsfield, Wm.
- Bryan, Wm.
- Barksdale, Sherod
- Brock, James
- Carter, Sarah
- Crisman, James
- Chastain, A. B.
- Clayton, Perry
- Conner, James
- Carter, Glover
- Collins, Robt.
- Chaney, Jackson
- Cunningham, John
- Calaway, Martin
- Clayton, Sampson
- Dobbs, Jabus
- Drain, John
- Denham, James
- Davidson, Wm.
- Driskill, Tollapher
- Davidson, Solomon
- Davidson, Joseph

Estate Record Name

George, Charles D. (Cont.)
- Driskill, Elizabeth, (medical)
- Davidson, James
- Dobbs, James B.
- Dibbeck, Noah
- Dilbeck/Dibbeck
- Depriest, John O.
- Denham, Susan
- Davis, Riley
- Davis, Elizabeth, Mrs.
- Everett, Wm.
- Estes, Wm.
- Carroll, Peter
- Chitwood, Richard
- Cannon, J. K.
- Capshaw, Thomas
- Cole, Benj.
- Campbell, Henry
- Cunningham, N. L.
- Cunningham, Lafayette
- Corby, James
- Bankston, Lucy, Miss
- Driskill, W. L.
- Driskill, Wm. & W. A.
- Davidson, James
- Driskill, Wm., Sen.
- Dobbs, Elijah
- Duton, John
- Coggin, Wesley
- Casey, O. P
- Cave, James
- Casey, Franklin
- Clark, Samuel
- Carter, John A.
- Carter, Mary, Miss
- Carter, Angelin, Miss
- Kennedy, Mavina
- Carter, Hugh, Dr.
- Camp, James M.
- Carr, Joseph
- Chastain, Wm.

Estate Record Name

George, Charles D. (Cont.)
- Chitwood, Ezekiel
- Cox, Thos. G. A.
- Engle, E. W.
- Estes, Robert
- Fletcher, Hugh
- Watts, Fortune
- Fowler, Richard
- Estes, Rueben
- Edwards, Joseph
- Frazer, John
- Findley, John B.
- Frazer, Darcus
- Frazer, Robert
- Fullenwider, David
- Fields, Gilbert
- Fike, Harland
- Humphreys, John J.
- Hibbs, Dempsey L.
- Hughs & Collins
- Hall, John
- Hendricks, Madison
- Hall, Adam
- Hickson, Jeremiah
- Hughes, A. A.
- Henderson, A. W.
- Hoge, Lemuel
- Houston, E.
- Harrison, J. E. F.
- Hammack, Thos.
- Hibbs, Newton J.
- Hendricks, Mrs.
- Casaway, Mrs.
- Coggins, E. T.
- Buzby, Robert
- Groves, Ira, (mdse)
- Garard, Richard
- Gentry, Eliza
- Graves, ? Ann, Miss
- Glazener, Jesse
- George, Thos. H., (mdse)

Estate Record Name
George, Charles D. (Cont.)
Griffin, Wm., (mdse)
Graham, Gideon
George, H. P., (mdse)
Garrett, Thomas, (mdse)
Garrett, James, Jr.
Graves, John, Jr.
Hammack, John
Hammock/Hammack
Harrison, Nancy Ann, Miss
Fields, James, (medical)
Fields, Elizabeth, (medical)
Flowers, John, (medical)
Fletcher, Jackson, (medical)
Findley, Wm., (medical)
Favors, John, (medical)
Freeman, Elisha, (medical)
Floyd, James, (mdse)
Fitzgerald, T. N., (mdse)
Funderburk, James C., (med.)
Flowers, Strodder, (mdse)
Funderburk, Geo. W., (mdse)
Fielder, H. W., (mdse)
Fielder & Co., (mdse)
Fisher, C. P.
Garret, Tatum, (mdse)
Gray, A. L., (mdse)
Glazener, Giles, (mdse)
Garner, C. W., (mdse)
Gravit, Malvina, Mrs.
Graves, John, Sr.
Graves, Hiram
Gasque, John M.
Hill, Berry/Benny, (mdse)
Hendricks, Mc_,(medical)
Hibbs, Sarah, Miss
Hamel, Enoch, (medical)
Holcomb, Mc_
Hudson, Thos.
Hudson, Thos., Mr.
Hopkins, C. F., (medical)

Estate Record Name
George, Charles D. (Cont.)
Hill, James
Hoge, Joseph
Reeve, Hugh,(freeman of color)
Hickson, Jerry
Hendricks, Joab, (mdse)
Hendricks, James
Henderson, John
Harrison, Agnesia, (mdse)
House, J. G., (mdse)
Hoge, James H., (mdse)
Hagler, Columbus, (mdse)
Holcomb, John P.
Hawkins, F. M.
Hayes, Oliver P.
Heard, Rachel, (mdse)
Houston, Wm. F. (mdse)
Hall, Levi, (mdse)
Hayes, Virgil, (mdse)
Houston, Wm., (medical)
Hood, Lucinda, (medical)
Hulgan, Stephen R., (medical)
Hawkins, James M., (medical)
Hastings, Stephen, (medical)
Hughes, David F., (medical)
King, Adelia, (medical)
King, James, (mdse)
Kirklan, Miss, (medical)
Killian, John A., (medical)
Killian, Elias, (medical)
Killian, Daniel, (medical)
King, Wm., (medical)
Isaac, J. C.
Johnson, Hezekiah
Brindle Asa, (medical)
Johnson, C. A.
Johnson, Hamilton, (mdse)
Johnson, Elijah H.
Jack, Allen
Jones, Sugar
Jones, Wm. L.

Estate Record Name
George, Charles D. (Cont.)
Jones, Thomas
Jones, Jane
Jett, J. M.
Jordan, George W.
Jack, Thos.
Jones, Nancy
Lovens, L. B.
Long, Marion
Lamar, James
Lewis, Burwell
Lackey, Wm. Sr.
Love, Charles
Loven, Thomas
Loven, John
Lawrence, Joseph
Lowry, James
Lackey, Wm.
Lovell, Elizabeth
Loyd, James
Light, Meredith
Lankford, L.
Matheny, Wilmoth
McCampbell, John
Malone, George W.
Mullins, William
Malone, Elizabeth
McDaniel, William
Martin, Martha, Miss
Moody, J. J.
McPherson, Geo., (medical)
Mitchell, Abner, (medical)
Matheny, Jack, (medical)
Merrell, Rily T.
Hoge, Stephen
McSpadden, Moses
Morris, Henry
Miller, John
Majors, A. W.
Malone, David A.
Morgan, Nathan

Estate Record Name
George, Charles D. (Cont.)
Accounts Due Estate: (Cont.)
McKelvey, George
McCampbell, Solomon
Malone, Leroy
Mynatt, Wm. C.
Mitchell, Manerva
Mayes, Henry
Meadow, William
Martin, Jane, Miss
Morgan, John B.
Maderly, James T.
Mulwee, George W.
McCrackin, George
Mosely, Canada
McCampbell, John
May, Wm.
Morris, J. T.
McNearn, Richmond
Moore, Abraham
McElroy, Andrew
Mackey, Alexander
Morris & George
Nicholson, Wm.
Nicholson, Wm. R.
Newman, Simpson
Newkirk, John
Horton, Roswell
Newkirk, Henry
Newkirk, Hiram
Nicholson, W. D.
Nicholson, Thos.
Nicholson, Mary, Miss
Newman, M. C.
Nicholson, L. M.
Newkirk, James
Nicholson, Mercer
Nichols, John B.
Norrel, Nancy
Nichols, James
Nichols, J. G.

Estate Record Name
George, Charles D. (Cont.)
- Owens, Newton
- Owens, William
- Odem, Mr.
- Owens, Hugh
- Owens, Gilford
- Oashburn, Wm. C.
- Owens, Raymond
- Owens, John T.
- Owens, Thomas
- Oliver, T. H.
- Pendleton, Eliza
- Porter, Berry
- Porter, C. C.
- Patterson, L. D.
- Pratt, J. J.
- Pate, Aaron
- Philips, Benj.
- Price, Lewis
- Parker, Russell
- Pervin, Elizabeth
- Poe, Washington
- Poe, Sarah
- Penn, James
- Porter, James
- Padget, Jacob
- Porter, Richardson
- Pinkerton, Thos.
- Pivit, James
- Potter, Silas
- Patrick, Austin
- Peak, Richard
- Pervin, L. S.
- Poe, James
- Pace, Burwell
- Peck, Judah
- Painter, L. Lewis
- Patey, Wm. P.
- Patton, George
- Roden, Taskon
- Rayburn, Rebecca

Estate Record Name
George, Charles D. (Cont.)
- Richards, C.
- Roberts, Isham
- Raines, Buck
- Reed, Amy, Mrs.
- Roberts, Calvin
- Reeve, Hugh
- Rankin, Albert
- Rice, Miller
- Robertson, Lindsey
- Rucks, G. W.
- Robertson, John
- Smith, Rhody
- Richard, Robert
- Reece, John
- Rogers, Wright
- Rains, Samuel
- Ray, Huddleton
- Reed, James, Sr.
- Ryan, Amos
- Redden, Reeve
- Rice, Joseph
- Ross, John
- Reed, George
- Reed, Susan, Mrs.
- Ramsey, Richard
- Rice, Ayonah
- Roden, Calvin
- Ryan, Samuel M.
- Reed, Berry
- Smith, Sarah
- Smith, William
- Sims, Wm.
- Shook, O. S.
- Sims, James R.
- Stewart, John J.
- Tiner, Stephen J.
- Tacket, Ezekiel
- Taylor, Manah
- Tidwell, William
- Thomas, W. A.

Estate Record Name
George, Charles D. (Cont.)
Box 5 File 21 1861-1880
Tolbert, Wesley
Smith, Mariah
Se_berry, S. C.
Smith, Jack
Smith, Eliza R., Miss
Stapler, Amos
Spangler, Nathan
Spangler, Old Man
Stiff, L. M.
Sims, Elizabeth, Miss
Slayton, Stephen
Smith, James
Satterfield, Jesse
Smith, Nancy, Miss
Smith, Jane, Miss
Smith, Thomas
Slaton, Elizabeth
Smith, Elisha
Smith, Joseph
Crisman, Baby
Smith, J. M.
Smith, Felix
Smith, Elizabeth, Mrs.
Smith, James
Smith, Henry E.
Sibert, Wm.
Thompson, Joshua
Teage, Isaac
Taylor, Solomon
Taylor, John
Taylor, Skelton
Tacket, John
Thompson, John L.
Tims, M. C.
Tims, Harrison
Traffanstedt, Joseph
Tuck, Thomas
Tate, Mayben
Tutton, Mary E., Mrs.

Estate Record Name
George, Charles D. (Cont.)
Tiner, William
Taylor, Stephen
Tidwell, Ellenor
Watts, W. J.
Wilson, J. M.
Williams, James
Wilder, Malissa
Ward, O. W.
Wimpey, John H.
Ward, Isaac
Watt,
Wilburn, Mary, Mrs.
Ward, Mary
Whit,
Wright, George
Whorton, Jesse
Wells, William
Wells, Bird
Wood, B. F.
Wilkes, Minor
Ward, Malinda, Mrs.
Walker, William
Watkins, Strong
Williams, Henry
Walker, John
Ward, A. J.
Wesson, Mrs.
Winston, John G.
Fischer, Watts V.
Whitten, Jurene
Waddle, Wm. C.
White, George, Dr.
Wern?, John
Watts, Thos. B.
Wilkes, Washington
Young, John
Williams, Yancy
Yancy, Williams
Yancey, Lewis
Brock, Harris

Estate Record Name

George, Charles D. (Cont.)
- Barksdale, Sherod
- Blackburn, Rebecca
- Carroll, Peter
- Chitwood, Richard
- Cunningham, John
- Coggin, Wesley
- Stesophy, Isaac
- Clayton, Solomon
- Collins, R. M.
- Crisman, James
- Davidson, James
- Dobbs, Elijah
- Denham, William
- Findley, John B.
- Coggin, E. T.
- Hoge, John K.
- Morrison, J. Thomas
- Mullins, Dick
- Matheny, Jane
- Malone, Leroy H.
- Morris, Henry
- McPherson, Mary, Mrs.
- Nave, Warren
- Nicholson, Wm.
- Nicholson, L. M.
- Starling, Old Man
- Reynolds, Wm.
- Crisman, James
- Appleton, T. N.
- Bryant, Wm.
- Long, W. P.
- Ticket for Jury
- Blevins, Richard
- Wheeler, Benj.
- Gains, Robert
- Porter, C. C.
- Adams, B. S.
- Reed, Berry
- Smith, Sarah J.
- Smith, Joseph J., Mrs.

Estate Record Name

George, Charles D. (Cont.)
- Small, Matthew
- George, Mary E.
- Nicholson, Wm. J.
- Clayton, Daniel
- Wilkes, Minor
- Buzby, J. R.
- Morris, Thomas
- Dobbs, Jabus
- Norton, W.
- Driskill, W.
- Morris, Henry
- Ticket, Jury

Gibson, George
- Box 5 File 22 1886-1892
- Names in File:
- Gibson, F. P., (adm)
- Wilborn, James S.
- Wilborn, T. A., (bond)
- Warren, Lot, (bond)
- Warren, C. W., (bond)
- Green, P. M., (bond)
- West, James, (bond)
- Cochran, L. L., Judge
- Franklin, A. G., (sheriff)
- Gibson, F. P., (heir)
- Gibson, Geo. F., (heir)
- Gibson, Alvin C., (heir)
- Blevins, Mary C. (heir)
- Blevins, John L., (h/o Mary)
- Slaughter, Virginia, (heir)
- Slaughter, W. R., (h/o Virginia)
- Slaughter, Malinda, (heir)
- Slaughter, Perry R., (h/o Malinda)
- Gibson, Nancy J., (heir)
- Slaughter, V. H., (dau.)
- Dobbs, L. A., (atty)
- Blevins, R. M.
- Frazier, P. M., (sheriff)
- Gibson, Nancy Jane
- Brewer, John, (summons)

Estate Record Name
Gibson, George (Cont.)
Box 5 File 22 1886-1892
Dean, James, (summons)
Blevins, Eve, (summons)
Adkins, Judy, (summons)
Young, Ben, (summons)
Tinker, Cobb, (summons)
Payne, Thomas, (summons)
Austin, Lafayette, (summons)
Austin, James, (summons)
Steele, Wyatt, (summons)
Smith, Wm. O., (summons)
Blevins, James, Sr., (summons)
Adkins, H. H., (sp. deputy)
Adkins, Benj., (summons)
Blevins, Richard, (summons)
Adkins, Smith, (witness)
Smith, Loney, (summons)
Smith, James, (summons)
Appleton, W. H., (dep.sheriff)
Adkins, Andy, (summons)
Davis & Haralson
Oyler, Geo. W., (paid)
Blevins, R. M., (paid)
Howard, J. M., (tax 1889 pd)
Gibson, N. J., (paid)
Steel, W. A., (paid)
Smith, W. O., (paid)
Austin, M., (paid)
Adkins, B. F., (paid)
Young, Ben, (paid)
Fricks, A. T. (paid)
Howard, J. M.
Adkins, A. J.
Slaughter, William R.
Appleton, W., (sheriff)
Jurors:
Mitchell, H. C., (farmer)
Lyon, A. J., (farmer)
Culberson, Charles, (farmer)
Slaton, J. M., (farmer)

Estate Record Name
Gibson, George (Cont.)
Weaver, J. R., (livery stable)
Johnson, Joseph, (farmer)
Humble, D. T., (farmer)
Edmondson, W. E., (farmer)
Culpepper, J. B., (farmer)
Williams, W. B., (farmer)
West, James, (merchant)
Polse, T. J., (farmer)
Larmore, T. J., (farmer)
Dean, Wm., (farmer)
Stewart, D. B., (farmer)
Collins, J. H., (jury foreman)
Special Jury 1887:
Furr, W. D
Lyons, J. L.
Parish, R. M.
Sisemore, Wofford
Killian, Henry
Lowry, S. C.
Wells, J. F.
Marsh, J. B.
Baker, J. M.
Morgan, J. T.
Collins, J. H.
Gillaspe, W. Y.
Davenport, J.
Smith, M. V.
Hulgan, F. M.
Kean, Solomon R.
Petit Jurors - 1889:
Warren, C. W.
Newman, J. N.
Frazier, P. J.
Howard, F. M.
Burt, E.
Freeman, F. M.
Hatfield, W. H.
Lewis, John M.
Lackey, G. W.
Keef, Thomas

Estate Record Name
Gibson, George (Cont.)
Box 5 File 22 1886-1892
Morgan, James P.
Johnson, J. S.
Pitts, John
Patrick, Josua
Davis, H. S.
See File 23
Gibson, George
Box 5 File 23 1887-1891
Names in File:
Gibson, F. P., (adm.)
Blevins, Mary
Blevins, John L., (h/o Mary)
Slaughter, Virginia
Slaughter, W. R., (h/o Virginia)
Gibson, F. P.
Gibson, Nancy
Slaughter, Malinda
Slaughter, Pleasant R., (Malinda)
Gibson, George F.
Gibson, A. C.
Austin, James F., (appraiser)
Payne, Thomas, (appraiser)
Steel, Wyatt, (appraiser)
Cochran, L. L., Judge
Haralson & Son
Dobbs & Howard, (atty)
Slaughter, Pleas, (rented land)
Blevins, Henry, (rented land)
Franklin, A. G., (sheriff)
Frazier, P. M., (sheriff)
Dean, James, (citation)
Adkins, Andy, (deposition)
Blevins, R. M., (deposition)
Fuller, W. T., (clerk, c.court)
Mitchell, H. C., (juror)
Igou, A. J., (juror)
Culberson, Charles, (juror)
Slaton, J. M., (juror)
Weaver, J. R., (juror)

Estate Record Name
Gibson, George (Cont.)
Johnson, Joseph, (juror)
Humble, D. T., (juror)
Edmondson, W. E., (juror)
Culpeper, J. B., (juror)
Williams, W. B., (juror)
West, James, (juror)
Pope, T. J., (juror)
Laramore, T. J., (juror)
Dean, William, (juror)
Stewart, D. B., (juror)
Jury for validity of Will
Lea, William, (commissioner)
Thomason, T., (commissioner)
Baxter, F. M., (commissioner)
Fricks Brothers, (acct paid)
Fort Payne Journal
Smith, Thos. H.
Fricks, Dr., (services)
Austin, Lafayette, (witness)
Austin, James, (witness)
Adkins, Benjamin, (witness)
Blevins, Richard, (witness)
Steel, Wyatt, (witness)
Smith, William O., (witness)
Blevins, James, Sr., (witness)
Smith, Loney, (witness)
Payne, Thomas, (witness)
Davis & Haralson, (atty)
Adkins, Emily, (witness)
Blevins, E. M., (witness)
Brewer, John, (witness)
Dean, James, (witness)
Young, Ben, (witness)
Tinker, Cobb, (witness)
Smith, James, (witness)
Fricks, A. T., (purchased land)
Sale of Personal Property:
Franklin, A. G., (auctioneer)
Cureton, G. W., (cow & mule)
Austin, W., (cow)

Estate Record Name
Gibson, George (Cont.)
Allison, W., (cow)
Smith, A., (bull)
Lusk, W. D., (sow & pigs)
Slaughter, W., (wagon)
Blevins, J. A., (blacksmith tools)
Slaughter, M., (fruit dryer)
Blevins, E., (bee hive)
Byrd, W. A., (gun)
Simpson, R., (clock)
Poluma, (chairs)
Norwood, (chairs)
Simpson, J., (chairs)
Blansit, B., (saddle)
Blevins, G., (1-pr glasses)
Franklin, (pillows)
Slaughter, (quilt & bed)
Blevins, G., (bed clothes)
Adkins, J., (bed clothes)
Slaughter, W., (bed clothes)
Weldon, (sheets)
Slaughter, V., (bed & plate)
Simpson, J., (bedstead, dishes)
Weldon, (stove, table, plates)
Blevins, C. G., (dish pan)
Gardner, J., (glassware)
Cureton, (churn & piggins)
Gibson, N., (jars)
Blevins, Jeff, (wheel gears)
Adkins, Bill, (sugar barrel)
Smith, A., (sorghum pitcher)
Simpson, R., (cups & saucers)
Blevins, M., (knives, forks)
Slaughter, V., (cupboard, shovel)
Simpson, J., (wash tub)
Oyler, (andiron)
Gibson, P., (saddle)
Blevins, C., (plow)
Weldon, (rul/reel)
Harris, W., (shovel)
Blevins, Jeff, (barrels)

Estate Record Name
Gibson, George (Cont.)
Dean, (boards)
Gibson, P., (candle molds)
Weldon, (keg)
Lusk, (sow & pigs)
Stovall, (sow & pigs)
Gibson, Jacob W.
Box 5 File 24 1862-1873
Names in File:
Beck, Thomas, (adm)
Brock, Andrew, (appraiser)
Carson, John T., (appraiser)
Nicholson, T. J., (sheriff)
Franklin, John N., (appraiser)
Beck, Thomas, (bond)
Tate, Robert, (bond)
Gibson, Emily, (bond, adm.)
Gibson, J. C., (bond, adm)
Lankford, R., (bond)
Venable, Isaac, (bond)
Tate, Aaron, (bond)
Clayton, C. P., (JP)
Carson, John C. T.
Gibson, Jacob W.
Findley, R. B.
Hoge, John K.
Horton, A. J., Judge
Dobbs, W. F., (dep. sheriff)
Lankford, David, (receipts)
Bynam, Jesse, (receipts)
Hastings, Stephen, (receipts)
Dean, Aaron, (receipts)
Lankford, Robert, (receipts)
Gilbert, Addison D.
Box 5 File 25 1902
Names in File:
Gilbert, Agnes Lavon, (widow)
Gilbert, Agnes Lavon, (exec.)
Will in Boston, MA, 1902
Curry, James J., (witness to will)
Follemsbee, Geo. I., (witnessl)

Estate Record Name
Gilbert, Addison D. (Cont.)
Sweeney, Edmond, (witness)
True, J. L., (JP, Florida)
Graham, F. C., (NP, Florida)
Sawyer, Charles M. T., (atty)
Real Property in DeKalb Co.
Croley, Jas. A., Judge
Gilbert, G. B.
Box 5 File 26 1902
Names in File:
Gilbert, N. C., (widow)
Gilbert, Merrida/Mindy, (minor)
Gilbert, Marcus L., (minor)
Gilbert, Gordon L., (minor)
Gilbert, Florence, (minor)
Gilbert, Ovie/Avie, (minor)
Gilbert, W.H., (adm., brother)
Little, Marion, (JP)
Gilbert, W. H., (bond)
Norris, H. N., (bond)
Pophern, A. J., (bond)
Popham/Pophern
DeShields, J. G., (guar.ad litem)
Clements, J. H., (appraiser)
Norris, Z. T., (appraiser)
Marbut, J. M., (appraiser)
Notes due Estate:
Pendergrass, J. A. & D. A., (note)
Orr, R. D., (note)
Fountain, J. M. & E., (note)
Downs, G. C., (note)
Rutleely?, S & Berry, (note)
Brown, J. W. & T. W., (note)
Johnson, W. C., (note)
Upton, D., (note)
Gilbert, J. A., (note)
Clements, J. H., (note)
Gilbert, Samuel L.
Box 5 File 27 1915-1921
Names in File:
Gilbert, S. W., (adm, g-son)

Estate Record Name
Gilbert, Samuel L. (Cont.)
Johnson, J. E., (bond)
Yarbrough, W. R., (bond)
Croley, Jas. A., Judge
Gilbert, J. A.
Hallmark, M. E., Mrs.
Hallmark, John, (h/o M. E.)
Gilbert, J. D.
Gilbert, D. L.
Gilbert, P. P.
Gilbert, B. F.
Gilbert, S. W.
Gilbert, T. B.
Gilbert, J. I.
Frascett, Amedia
Frascett, A. H., (h/o Amedia)
Raines, Mollie
Raines, (h/o Mollie)
Gilbreath, J. E.
Box 5 File 28 1883
Names in File:
Gilbreath, Noble, (adm)
Wallace, John, (bond)
Wallace, James P., (bond)
Haralson & Haralson
Guardian Bond
Gilbreath, J. S. & Mollie J.
Box 5 File 29 1915-1916
Names in File:
Exemption before Admin.
Gilbreath, Mollie J., (widow)
Gilbreath, Sim T., (minor)
Prince, Joe S., (adm., petitioner)
Prince, Joseph S., (friend)
Williams, Irvin, (appraiser)
Yarbrough, J. L., Sr., (appraiser)
Cagle, Wm.
Smith, Elizabeth
Bogle,
Nicholson, L. S., (NP)
Campbell, H. B., (clerk C.Court)

Estate Record Name
Gilbreath, J. S. & Mollie J. (Cont.)
Croley, Jas. A., Judge
Gilbreath, M. H.
Box 5 File 30 1911-1912
Names in File:
Gilbreath, Sallie, (widow)
Gilbreath, S. A., Mrs., (widow)
Gilbreath, J. V.,(adm., son)
Gilbreath, W. T.
Gilbreath, G. O.
Meeks, S. T.(Tressie)
Ivie, M. A., Mrs., (Mattie)
Yarbrough, J. L., (bond)
Gilbreath, O. G., (bond)
Black, Jno. W., (appraiser)
Gains, James T., (bond)
Dunlap, R, L., (appraiser)
Chastain, John B., NP)
Osborne, Ernest, (minor)
Howard, H. B.
Jones, E. B.
Norwood, H. P., (wood)
Marbut, J. M., (medicine)
Howard & Hunt
Hunt, Hunt & Wolfes
Robertson, A. P., (paid)
Robertson, E. L., (paid)
Wright, W. J., Dr., (services)
Collinsville Savings Bank
Oliver Hall Co.
Chastain, J. B., (pd. making deed)
Railroad Fare
MacWhorter, H. P., Dr.
Smith, S. P., Dr.
Black, J. W., (paid for corn)
Warren, F. M., (paid taxes)
Justice, J. W., (mdse.)
KDS Hardware Co
Plunkett, B. L., (blacksmith)
Griffin, H. F., (blacksmith)
Griffin, T. H., (blacksmith)

Estate Record Name
Gilbreath, M. H. (Cont.)
Chastain, J. B., (monument $125.)
Jones, W. B.
Jones, R.
Fort Payne Journal (notices)
Hubbard, B. T., (dep.sheriff)
Howard, M. W.
Notes Due Estate:
Ragan, Bonnie, (note)
Hodges, T. E. & I. M., (note)
Chandler, M. D., (note)
Chandler, J. M., (note)
O'Shields, D. O., (note)
Burgess, J. A., (mules)
Brown, Ben, (note for mules)
Word, J. J. & O. B., (note)
Gravitt, L,, (syrup mill)
Gilbreath, J. & A. C., (note)
Meeks, S. E. & S. T., (note)
Gilbreath, W. T. & N. O., (note)
Robertson, A. P. (corn & hogs)
Robertson, E. L., (corn & hogs)
Smith, James, (corn & mule)
Hearn, J. D. , (receipts)
Carnes, J. H., (rec. for mule)
Gilbreath, G. O., (rec.for mule)
Gilbreath, Peter M.
Box 5 File 31 1860
Names in File:
Gilbreath, Nancy E., (adm)
Armstrong, James N., (bond)
Cox, James A., (bond)
Gilbreath, Nancy Elizabeth
Estes, R., Judge
Gilbreath, Thomas
Box 5 File 32 1853
Names in File:
Lowry, Levi, (pd. for nursing
& services during sickness)
Chitwood, Richard, (JP)
Gilbreath, Wm. B.

Estate Record Name

Gilbreath, Wm. B.
Box 5 File 33 1887
Names in File:
Gilbreath, Mary A., (widow)
Widow's Exemption
No minor children
Gilbreath, J. S., (PJ)
Smith, W. A., (appraiser)
Yarbrough, J. C., (appraiser)
Cochran, L. L., Judge

Gilchrist, W. D.
Box 5 File 34 1914
Names in File:
Gilchrist, Ruth C., Mrs., (widow)
Exemption before Administration
Vann, L. S.,Mrs., (mortgage deed)
Lee, R. E., (second mortgage)
Westbrooks, Wiley H., (appraiser)
Stephenson, Willard, (appraiser)
Stevensen/Stephenson, Willard
Marshall, P. G., (Acting Judge)

Giles, E. W.
Box 5 File 35 1883
Names in File:
Giles, E. W., (minor)
Giles, W. J., (guardian)
Youngblood, M., (Estate)
Brock, George, (bond)
Hall, O. L., (bond)
Franklin, John N., Judge

Gilliland, Grace
Box 5 File 36 1911-1912
Names in File:
Gilliland, Grace Iola, (minor)
Gilliland, Beulah, (mother)
Gilliland, Pink M., (father)
Smith, Beulah Gilliland,(guar.)
Jones, W. P., (bond)
Jones, J. O., (bond)
Gilliland, M. E., (citation)
Chandler, Wm., (sheriff, Atalla)

Estate Record Name

Gilliland, Grace (Cont.)
Croley, Jas. A., Judge
Gilliland, M. E., (receipts of note)
Gilliland, Mary J., (receipts of note)
Gilliland, M. E., (grandmother)
Smith, Beulah, (guardian)
Horn, W. C., (purchased lot)

Gilliland, Pink M.
Box 5 File 37 1910
Names in File:
Gilliland, Beulah I., (widow)
Gilliland, Grace Iola, (minor)
Jones, W. P., (bond)
Edwards, W. S., (bond)
Curtis, J. Valdor, (guar.ad litem)
Gilliland, H. F., (MD), Dr.
(services and casket)
McConnell, (paid)
Boaz Marble Works, (paid)
The Currier (notices)

Gipson, John C.
Box 5 File 38 1905
Names in File:
Gipson, Alpha A., (widow)
Gipson, Lemuel, (minor)
Gipson, Manuel, (minor)
Gipson, Maude, (minor)
Gipson, Maggie, (minor)
Gipson, Henry G., (minor)
Gipson, John, (minor)
Gipson, James, (minor)
Gipson, Gracie, (minor)
Gipson, Hershell, (minor)
Thomas, George, (appraiser)
Meadows, Pinkney, (appraiser)
Little, Marion, (JP)

Gipson, Lemuel, et al
Box 5 File 39 1905
Names in File:
Gipson, A. A., Mrs., (mother)
Copeland, A. C., (guar.ad litem)

Estate Record Name

Gipson, Lemuel, et al (Cont.)
  Treadway, Arrie E.,
   (sister of minors & guardian)
  Gipson, Lemuel, (minor)
  Gipson, Manuel, (minor)
  Gipson, Maude, (minor)
  Gipson, Maggie, (minor)
  Gipson, Henry G., (minor)
  Gipson, John, (minor)
  Gipson, James, (minor)
  Gipson, Grace, (minor)
  Gipson, Hershell, (minor)
  Smith, A. T., (bond)
  Hulgan, J. W., (bond)
  Hulgan, S. N., (bond)
  Little, Marion, (bond) (JP)
  Gipson, W. M., (testimony)
  Little, Marion, (testimony)

Glaspy, W. J.
  Box 5 File 40 1915
  Names in File:
  Glaspy, L. F., Mrs., (widow)
  Exemption before Admin.
  Smith, E. M., (appraiser)
  Lawson, G. W., (appraiser)
  Graves, William V., (NP)
  Croley, Jas. A., Judge

McGlohon, Gordon
  Box 5 File 41 1906-1909
  Names in File:
  McGlobon/McGlohan
  McGlohon, Dora, (widow)
  McGlohon, James H., (minor)
  McGlohon, Stella, (minor)
  McGlohon, Margaret, (minor)
  Downer, T. J., (sheriff)

Gober, G. W.
  Box 5 File 42 1862
  Names in File:
  York, John G., (bond & adm)
  Estes, R., (bond)

Estate Record Name

Gober, G. W. (Cont.)
  Malone, G. W., (bond)
  Franklin, John, Judge

Godfrey, J. H.
  Box 5 File 43 1890
  Names in File:
  Powers, O. S., (adm.)
  Buell, C. Y., (bond)
  Fisher, C. W., (bond)
  Godfrey, J. H., (unmarried)
  Godfrey, (brother in GA.)
  Goade, W. J., (acquaintance)
  Nix & Campbell, (casket)
  McNichols
  Howard & Blake
  Goade, W. J., (burial expense)
  Haralson, Sidney, (boarding)
  Blake, Howard, (boarding)
  Hairlston, Charley
  Haralston/Hairlston
  Green, A. B., Dr. (services)
  Cochran, L. L., Judge
  Fowlks, F. V., (MD), (services)
  Franklin, J. M., (taxes)
  Ft. Payne Bldg. Co., (pd)
  Johnson, H., (Bldg. Co.)
  Fort Payne Journal

Goins, John
  Box 5 File 44 1904
  Names in File:
  Goins, L. B., (adm, son)
  Howard, G. M., (attested will)
  Goins, Ameila, (widow)
  Beaty, Rhody C.
  Beaty, J. E., (h/o Rhody)
  Howard, Fannie T.
  Howard, W. S., (h/o Fannie)
  Goins, Jas. W.
  Goins, John
  Goins, Joseph W.
  Howard, C. H., (attested will)

Estate Record Name
Goins, John (Cont.)
Justice, George W., (bond)
Smith, S. P., (bond)
Jones, E. B., (bond)
Chitwood, W. J., (sheriff)
Nichols, W. N., (dep.sheriff)
Cook, W. C. D., Judge
Graham, Thomas
Box 5 File 45 1907-1908
Names in File:
Graham, Thomas, (estate)
Graham, M. A., Mrs. (guardian)
(mother of minors)
Graham, W. A., (minor)
Graham, Emma, (minor)
Graham, Vann, (minor)
Graham, Edgar, (minor)
Graham, Melvin, (minor)
Graham, Mary Lou, (minor)
Rucks, J. T., (bond)
Rucks, W. A., (bond)
Copeland, A. C., (guar.ad litem)
Sale of Land for Division
Rucks, Joel T., (witness)
Pharr, G. W., (witness)
Berry, Minnie (take depositions)
Presley, I. M. (commissioner)
Gilbert, A. W., (purch. Land $735)
Croley, Jas. A., Judge
Isbell and Presley, (atty)
Grant, William
Box 5 File 46 No Date
Names in File:
Minor Heirs of William Grant
Davenport, Wm., (minor)
Davenport, J. H., (minor)
Davenport, C. C., (minor)
Davenport, Erskin, (minor)
Davenport, Adalaid, (minor)
Davenport, O. J.,(guardian)

Estate Record Name
Gravitt, Lodwick
Box 5 File 47 1892
Names in File:
Gravill, Lodwick, (minor)
Roden, Anna E., (minor)
Hendrick, Melvina, (guardian)
Dunlap & Dobbs
Horton, A. J., Judge
Graves, Alice
Box 5 File 48 1889
Names in File:
Graves, James, (father, guar.)
Graves, Alice, (minor)
Williams, D. C., (bond)
Roberts, Geo. W., (bond)
Fuller, W. T., (guar.ad litem)
Cochran, L. L, Judge
Graves, Nancy
Box 5 File 49 1899-1911
Names in File:
Ellenburg, H. T., (guardian)
Hairel, John, (bond)
Graves, H. B., (bond)
Graves, Joshua, (bond)
Graves, Henry, (bond)
Groves, A., (attest)
Roden, C. F., (attest)
Gilbreth, S. W. (work on well)
Hale, P. C.
Cain, Wall, (tax coll. 1905-8)
Dobbs, W. J.
Smith, E. J.
Templeton, J. L.,(care of Nancy)
Graves, W. V.
Copeland, A. C.
Oliver Hall Co.
Graves, H. L., (tax coll. 1904)
Campbell, H. B., (guar.ad litem)
McWhorter, H. P.,(paid)
Warren, F. M., (tax coll. 1911)
Warren, H. L., (tax coll. 1909)

Estate Record Name

Graves, Nancy (Cont.)

Smith, R. M., (labor on farm)
Smith, A. T., (labor on farm)
Smith, W. A., (labor on farm)
Rutledge, E., J., (work on farm)
Amos, T. A., (work on farm)
More, L. O., (work on farm)
Graves, H. T., (material/house)
Reed, W. D., (tax coll.1899)
Graves, James L., (building house)
Smith, Elizabeth, (paid)
Lackey, L. B. (pd. lumber)
Hall, O. L., (paid)
Graves, J. S., (labor on house)
Thomson, W. M., (work on farm)
Gilbreath, Stant, (work on chimney)
Donley, R., (pd.work on well)

Receipts, Income Received:

Graham, R. E., (rents)
Smith, A. T. (rents)
Smith, W. A., (corn)
Smith, W. A., (rents)
Smith, R. M., (rent)
Smith, J. D., (corn)
Strong, Geo., (corn)
Graves, R. A., (interest)
Thompson, J. F., (corn)
Smith, W. A., (corn)
Graham, E. L., (rent)
Graham, E., (rent)
Dobbs, J. W., (rent)
Smith, R. M., (rent)
Wallace, E. L., (corn)
Gray, David, (corn)
Graves, H. L., (interest)
Graves, J. J., (corn)
Green, W. J., (corn)
Nalor, S. J., (corn)
Winsor, H. H., (corn)
Roden, W. W., (corn)
Young, Rueben, (syrup)

Estate Record Name

Graves, Nancy (Cont.)

Williams, S. A., (timber)
Gadsden Mill Co., (wheat)
Dickson, W. W., (rent)
Dobbs, J. W., (rents)
Roden, Geo, (rents)
Smith, J. B., (corn)
Smith, R. M., (cotton)
Dickson, W. W., (cotton)
Graves, Dan, (cotton)
Graves, (cotton rent)
Johnson, J. S., (corn rent)
Graves, Josuah, (cotton seeds)
Wesson, W. A., (corn rent)
Marsh, J. B., (hay rent)
Gadsden Distrib. (corn rent)
Dobbs, W. J., (cotton rent)
Graham, E. L., (rent)
Graves, Alex., (cotton rent)
Wall, Barksdale, (corn rent)
Gilbreath, B. N., (corn rent)
Stephens, Bob, (corn rent)
Morgan, W. G., (corn rent)
Killian, B., (cotton seeds)
Graves, J. A., (cotton seeds)
Marony, Jas., (hay)
Cook, W. H., (hay)
Dobbs, J. B., (cotton rent)
Dobbs, R. D. , (cotton rent)
Roden, W. L., (interest)
Roden, V. J. M., (interest)
Waldrop, R. L., (corn)
Spencer, H. L., (cotton seeds)
Graves, H. T., (adm, nephew)

Brothers and sisters of Nancy:

Graves, Joshia
Graves, Henry
Wilson, Martha, Mrs.
Ellenburg, Jane
Templeton, Agatha Ann
Ellenburg, H. T., (guar. 1900)

Estate Record Name

Graves, Nancy (Cont.)

DeShields, J. G., (guar.ad litem)
Gilbreath, (note)
Graves, H. B. & W. V., (note)
Roden, J. M., (note)
Graves, J. S., (note)
Graves, A., (note)
Roberts, J. W., (tax coll.)
McWhorter, H. F., (med.bill)
Bartlett, John T., (casket & ser.)
Oliver Hall Co., (burial expense)

Receipts, Rents & Farm Sales:

Smith, J. H., (cotton rent)
Smith, J. H., (hay)
Morgan, Frank, (cotton rent)
Richardson, John, (corn & hay)
Burk, C. C. (corn and hay)
Graves, R. A., (corn)
Bates, L. F., (corn)
Allen, John, (rent)
Tidmore, J. A., (corn)
Morgan, Frank, (rent)
Harris, J. W., (corn)
Cunningham, W.H.
Hairrel, Mose, (corn)
Hairrel, Dick, (corn)
Smith, J. W., (corn)
Smith, J. P., (corn)
Graves, J. S.
Dobbs, J. W., (corn)
Nales, C. C., (corn)
Smith, W. S., (hay)
Renfro, T. H., (note)
Dobbs, Joe, (interest)
Ellenburg,, H. T., (interest)

Paid:

Smith, E. J., (labor)
Templeton, J. L., (Nancy's board)
Bartlett, John, (guino note)
Kirby, A. C., (burial exp.)

Cash receipts 1898:

Estate Record Name

Graves, Nancy (Cont.)

Graves, H. B.
Lipscomb, J. D.
Smith, W. A.
Frost, Hale
Templeton, J. L.
Graves, James M.
Black, John
Graves, James L.
Absher, J. S.
Watson, John
Rutsey, E. J.
Jones, G. W.
Bell, James
Johnson, Col.
Roden, James
Kemp, Sol
Smith, B. N.
Dixon, W. W.
Dobbs, R. D.
Gilbreath, Stant
Hall, O. L.
Dooly, R., (work on well)
Graves, J. S., (work on house)
Moore, Oliver, (paid)
Rutsey, E. J., (paid)
Reed, W. D., (tax paid)
Smith, Elizabeth, (paid)
Graves, James L, (paid)

Cash Receipts, 1900-02

Graves, James
Amos, Tobe, (sorghum rent)
Amos, Tobe, (cotton rent)
Smith, W. A., (cotton rent)
Rutsey, E. J., (rent)
Rutsey, E. J., (wheat rent)
Amos, Tobe, (corn)
Nicholson, B. H., (note)
Bone, W. B., (corn)
Johnson, C. C., (corn)
Bone, John, (corn)

Estate Record Name
Graves, Nancy (Cont.)
Box 5 File 49 1899-1911
Dobbs, R. D., (cotton seeds)
Thompson, Jno., (corn)
Thomas, Mont, (corn)
Green, W. J., (corn)
Henry, Edie, (corn)
Dempsey, Harvey. (corn)
Cagle, Mack, (corn)
Smith, David, (corn)
Morony, Jos., (corn)
Dempsey, W. H., (corn)
Kemp, S. A., (corn)
Smith, W. A., (interest)
Thompson, J. F., (cotton rent)
Graham,
Graves, W. H., (corn)
Graves, W. H., (wheat)
Smith, Dave, (corn)
Karue, Mrs., (corn)
Barksdale, Wm., (corn)
Blansit, Mr., (corn)
Cash Receipts, 1900-02 Cont.
Harp, W. M., (corn)
Downs, Bob, (corn)
Smith, W. A., (oats)
Smith, B. N., (sorghum)
Smith, R. M., (cotton rent)
Beavers Farm
Graham, L. E., (rent)
Notes & Accts. Due:
Peak, S. B., (note)
Eason, B. G., (note)
Nicholson, W. C., (note)
Price, J., (acct.)
Rucks, W., (acct.)
Nicholson, M. M., (acct.)
Brock, Angeline
Jolley, Leanda, (acct,)
Talley, H. P. (acct,)
Brown, John, Col., (acct)

Estate Record Name
Graves, Nancy (Cont.)
Munro, (acct.)
Wesson, J. W., (acct.)
Petty, Art, (acct.)
Carden, Rebeca, (acct.)
Vann, S. J., (acct.)
Casey, W. L., (acct.)
Pinkerton, R. A., (acct.)
Hardwick, W. C., (acct.)
Johnson, Pagley, (acct.)
Mataken, Wade, (acct.)
Receipts, Rents & Sales:
Tidwell, (cotton rent)
Fletcher, George, (corn)
Harpe, Jess, (corn)
Allen, John R., (rent)
Croley, J. A., (rent)
Brooks, John, (corn)
Jack, James, (corn)
Bradley, M. J., (corn)
Bush, J. W., (corn)
Roden, Alex, (corn)
Chumby, W. J., (corn)
Gilbreath, (hay)
Dobbs, W. J., (cotton rent)
Ward, J. S., (hay)
Sims, J. A., (corn)
Chumley, P. M., (corn)
Burns, L. D., (corn)
Bartlett, Geo., (corn)
Roden, Geo., (corn)
Nicholson, L. S., (corn)
Yancy, R. J., (corn)
McClain & Co., (timber)
Winston, H. H., (corn)
Black, S. D., (corn)
Smith, J. H., (hay)
Hill, J. S., (cotton seed)
Cash, J. N., (corn)
Hall, J. W., (cotton rent)
Green, W. J., (corn)

Estate Record Name
Graves, Nancy (Cont.)
Chumley, J. P., (corn)
Nailer, C. C., (corn)
Dobbs, John, (cotton rent)
Teague, Albert, (corn)
West, Tom (corn)
Bradley, Ellis, (corn)
Rogers, John, (corn)
Penn, Geo., (corn)
Mosley, Jas., (corn)
Flavis?, Jno., (corn)
Mashburn, Jesse, (corn)
Bearden, J. W., (corn)
Fletcher, John, (corn)
King, W. D., (corn)
White, Jno, (corn)
Cain, Paul, (corn)
Smith, J. G., (cotton rent)
Norwood, B. H., (cotton rent)
Dobbs, J. W., (cotton rent)
Peter White & Co., (seeds)
Smith, J. H., (cotton rent)
Martin, (rent)
Burns, L. D., (corn)
Receipts, Rents & Sales:
Collins, Kirby, (cotton seeds)
Bates, Lee, (corn)
Hale, Jno., (hay)
Graves, H. L., interest
Fletcher, Toby, (corn)
Graves, H. B., (interest)
Carley, J. A., (interest)
Ellenburg, H. J., (corn)
Tidwell, D., (cotton rent)
Burris, J. D., (corn)
Walden, J. V.,
Fletcher, George, (corn)
Green, Tom, (rent)
Harpe, Jesse, (corn)
Smith, E. L., (rent)
Konen, Tom, (rent)

Estate Record Name
Graves, Nancy (Cont.)
Smith, D. S., (corn)
Smith , R. M., (corn)
Lipscomb, Thos.
Lipscomb, T. H.
Roden, John
Bunn, J. T.
Pall, D. C.
Bowen, H. N.
Traffanstedt, Jas., (corn)
Traffanstedt, J. G., (corn)
Harp, Jesse, (corn)
Swan, J. G.
Swain, G. W.
Halbrooks, J. G.
Barksdale, J. A.
Roberts, J. C .
Stephens, B. A.
Sale of Personal Property:
Wesson, J. W., (wheel head)
Nicholson, B. H., (tin pan & jar)
Ward, J. R., (sack corn)
Word/Ward
Small, Harriet, (turpentine)
Waldorf, Dalas, (pr.hames)
Chumler, Z. P., (pr.hames)
Coker, W. D., (oven & lid)
Small, W. A., (glass panes)
Smith, Charlie, (box glass)
Nicholson, B. H., (sack flour)
Small, W. A., (bar iron)
Tidmore, Jere, (mattock & tub)
Beavers, Wood, (hoes)
Adams, D. W., (1-mattock)
Coker, W. D., (rake and hoe)
Small, Henry, (spade)
Smith, Wm., (pr.shoes)
Hall, J. W., (pr.shoes)
Coker, W. D., (shoes)
Smith, Allen, (shoes)
Small, W. A., (shoes & boots)

Estate Record Name
Graves, Nancy (Cont.)
Box 5 File 49 1899-1911
Horton, W. P., (shoes)
Wesson, J. W., (boots)
Petty, Wiley, (1-axe)
Doyle, E. C., (oil can)
Tidmore, M. M., (1 inch auger)
Wesson, J. W., (2 inch auger)
Waldrop, W. D., (2 inch auger)
Fur, Daniel, (1 inch auger)
Nicholson, B. H., (tin bucket)
Siniard, J. W., (tin bucket)
Williams, D. C., (2 lb. Spice)
Nicholson, B. H., (cake pan)
Petty, W. D., (cake pans)
Hall, J. W., (night glass)
Nicholson, L. S., (1-lot tin)
Tidmore, H. J., (cross cut file)
Nicholson, B. H., (sifter)
Wood, John, (sifter)
Davis, J. M., (2-dippers)
Small, Henry, (sole leather)
Cantrill, Jesse, (side leather)
Clayton, S. H., (1-dipper)
Beavers, Wood, (dipper)
Hall, J. M., (dipper)
Martin, D. C., (tin bucket)
Chaney, Dasey, (tin bucket)
Wesson, J. W., (tin bucket)
Heard, Strode, (bucket & lid)
Tidmore, J. H., (bucket & lid)
Small, W. A., (funnel)
Collins, N. S., (funnel)
Tidmore, J. H., (grindstone)
Wesson, J. W., (dipper strainer)
Reed, James, (tin bucket)
Smith, William, (oil can)
Reed, James, (oil can)
Small, W. H., (night glass)
Smith, William, (shot gun)
Petty, W. D., (sausage grinder)

Estate Record Name
Graves, Nancy (Cont.)
Tidmore, A. B., (boiler)
Tidmore, A. B., (piece casting)
Kirby, Wm., (oven)
Tidmore, H., (stretchers)
Appleton, J. N., (box/bottles)
Johnson, Paley, (coffee mill)
Tidmore, J. C., (1-clevis)
Adams, D. W., (broad axe)
Mills, W. K., (bucket & iron)
Croft, W. J., (1-chisel)
Hall, J. W., (cradle & contents)
Beavers, A. W., (set planes)
Adams, D. W., (hand saw)
Beavers, A. W., (1-wood ?)
Clayton, S. J., (1-foot ad?)
Small, W. A., (1-wood clamp)
Nicholson, B. H., (1-boot tree)
Small, W. A., (clevis & cutter)
Adams, D. W., (chisel & keg)
Small, Henry, (1-axe)
Tidmore, M. M., (box/copper)
Gray, William B. (Cont.)
Box 5 File 50 1859-1866
Names in File:
Gray, Allen, (adm)
Gray, Joseph
Gray, Jacob
Gray, Asa
Gray, George
Gray, Thomas
Burgess, Elizabeth
Burgess, Richard, (h/o Elizabeth)
Gray, David
Gray, William
Gray, John
Gray, J. B.
Gray, G. W.
Gray, J. M.
Young, Lafayette F., (witness)
Gilliland, W. B., (witness)

Estate Record Name
Gray, William B. (Cont.)
Box 5 File 50 1859-1866
King, Benjamin, (comm.)
Box, P. D., (JP)
O. P. Hill & Co.
McBrayer, H. P.
Franklin, J. N.
Griffin, Wm., (sheriff)
Morgan, J. T., (dep.sheriff)
Stiff, L. W., (notices)
Estes, R.
King, B. F., (paid)
White, George, (note)
Garner, F. M.
Lankford, John
Jenkins, William
James, S.
Giland, W. B.
Porter, James D.
Hill, O. P. (paid)
Birens, Joseph
Strother, James
Mihollen, J. T.
Rees, John
Jenkins, W. M., (purch.land-$246)
Green, Grief S.
Box 5 File 51 1877-1883
Names in File:
Green, Fannie S, (widow, exec)
Green, Sarah J., (minor)
Green, Philmon M., (minor)
Green, Jesse B.,(minor)
Green, John Foster, (minor)
Green, Anthony B., (minor)
Chitwood, R., (guardian/minors)
Green, F. S., (exec.)
Chitwood, William, (wit.to will)
Benge, D. C., (wit.to will)
Haralson, W. J., (wit.to will)
Frazier, P. M., (sheriff)
Hawkins, B. H. (dep.sheriff)

Estate Record Name
Green, Grief S. (Cont.)
Haralson, William J.
Chitwood, William C.
Benge, DeWitt C.
Brandon, P. A., Judge
Green, Elizabeth, (holds note)
Green, William P.
Box 5 File 52 1879
Names in File:
Petition to sell land
McNutt, Robert C., (adm.)
Rea, Sallie, (widow)
Rea, E. W.
Green, Sallie E.
Ray, Sallie E. Green
Ray/Rea
Ray, Charles W., (h/o Sallie)
McNutt, R. C.
Haralson, Henry C., (witness)
Payne, A. F., (witness)
Poe, W. R., (commissioner)
Dobbs, L. A., (atty)
Hailey, Samuel R., (claim)
Dobbs, L. A., (purch.land)
Griffin, Paralee
Box 5 File 53 1876
Names in File:
Branden, P. A., Judge
Jack, Thos. M., (appraiser)
McCurdy, Nathaniel W., (appraiser)
Hudson, Thomas W., (appraiser)
Chaney, John, (bond)
Collins, Alfred, (bond)
Griffin, William P., (adm)
Sale of Personal Property:
Brice, G. T., (Mare)
Griffin, Wm., (colt)
Griffin, Wm., (bedstead)
Griffin, Wm., (wardrobe)
Griffin, James, (pigs)
Brice, G. T., (geese & side saddle)

Estate Record Name
Griffin, Travis
Box 5 File 54 1901-1908
Names in File:
Griffin, Travis, (minor)
(heir of Wilborn Siniard)
Griffin, N. G., (guardian)
Griffin, N. W.
Griffin, Nolin/Nolen/Nolan
Chaney, J. M., (bond)
Wesson, W. J., (bond)
Bates, J. P., (bond)
Siniard, W. D., (bond)
Griffin, Nolin G.
Chitwood, W. J., (sheriff)
Croley, J. A., Judge
DeShields, J. G., (guar.ad litem)
Austin, D., (sheriff-Jackson Co)
Siniard, Wilborn, (purch.land)
Griswold, Edward P.
Box 5 File 55 1896-1899
Names in File:
Griswold, Mary Catherine B.
(adm.and widow)
Griswold, Edward Browning
(adm.and son)
Griswold, Mary Maude, (dau.)
Griswold, Grace, (dau.)
Griswold, Harold T., (son)
Cook Co., Il. (will filed)
Follansber, G. W., (wit. to will)
Irwin, Harry S., (wit.to will)
McIlvaine, Alan C.,(wit.to will)
Kohlsact & Christian
Reddick, James, (Ill. Clerk)
Smith, Willis D.
Davenport, Patrick, (appraiser)
Anderson, Henry C., (appraiser)
Farnum, Frank C., (appraiser)
Guest, Green
Box 5 File 56 1907
Names in File:

Estate Record Name
Guest, Green (Cont.)
Guest. T. H. E., (adm, son)
Thurman, J. L. (bond)
Horton, G. R., (bond)
Downer, J. H., (bond)
Faulkner, J. H., (bond)
Parker, M. D., (attest)
Guest, J. W.
Gilbreath, Elizabeth
Jones, M. E.
Guest, J. M.
Guest, S. P.
Guest, J.
Guest, W. C.
Smith, Ida
Horton, Dellie
Guest, J. G.
Guest, J. A.
Roden, J. M., (paid)
Gilbreath, P. H., (paid)
Callahan, G. R., (paid)
Ryan, Albert, (paid)
Ryan, Thomas, (paid)
Gilbert, Tobe, (paid)
Brandon, P. A., (paid)
Berry, Wm., (paid)
Southerland, Ralon, (paid)
Light, A. L., (paid)
Railroad Fare (paid)
Guest, Olaber
Box 5 File 57 1867
Names in File:
Application to sell property
Masters, B. F., (adm.)
Franklin, J. N., Judge

Estate Record Name	Estate Record Name

H

Estate Record Name
Hairel, Deliah
Box 5 File 58 1907-1909
Names in File:
Hairel, John, (husband)
Smith, Elizabeth
Graves, Joshua
Graves, Henry
Roden, Mary, (w/o Geo.)
Roden, George
Graves, Alexander
Ellenburg, F. J., Mrs., (w/o H. T.)
Ellenburg, H. T.
Templeton, Ortha, (w/o John)
Templeton, John
Garrett, H. B.
Massie, Alice
Massie, Louis
Morris, Sarah A.
Graves, Pink
Graves, H. L., (adm)
Graves, Nancy
Wilson, Martha
Graves, H. B.
Wilson, John
Wilson, Hattie, (sister)
Wilson, William
Wilson, Alex
Wilson, Hiram
Abbot, Judie, Mrs.
Cavatt, Sallie
Wilson, Henry
Graves, Alex
Graves, H. B., (nephew)
Graves, John
Wilson, Joshua
Davis, T. G., (sheriff)
Baxter, J. W., (dep.sheriff)
Graves, James G., (dec'd.)

Estate Record Name
Hairel, Deliah (Cont.)
Graves, L. K.
Smith, W. C., (note)
Barkley, G. W., (note)
Smith, Tom, (printer)
Cook & Presley, (atty)
Howard & Hunt, (atty)
Guest, R. H. E., (tombstone)
Downs, (appraiser)
Nations, (appraiser)
Graves, N. L., (witness)
Graves, James L.
Graves, H. J., (father of Deliah)
Heard, John
Graves, E. L.
Graves, H. L., (bond)
Graves, H. B., (bond)
Ellenburg, H. T., (bond)
Graves, Henry, (bond)
Graves, Alex., (bond)
Isbell & Presley
Croley, J. A., Judge
Copeland, A. C., (guar.ad litem)
Graves, Nancy, (unsound mind)
Templeton, Ortha/Martha
Wilson, Hattie/Hettie
Hall, Bryan
Box 5 File 59 1886
Names in File:
Hall, Indiana M., (widow)
Heard, Solon E., (appraiser)
Masters, J. M., (appraiser)
Dunlap, R.A.D., (atty)
Homestead Exemption
Hall, J. A., Sr.
Box 5 File 60 1911-1912
Names in File:
Hall, Josie C., (widow)

Estate Record Name
Hall, J. A., Sr. (Cont.)
Hall, James A., Jr., (son, adm.)
Hall, Charles W., (son, adm)
Hall, Willard Otis Wayne
Hall, Victor W.
Small, Emma E. (w/o Henry)
Small, Henry
Hall, Oliver L.
Hall, Wayne O. W.
Hall, Charles A. (guardian)
Harbour, Maude, Mrs.
Harbour, C. C., (h/o Maude)
Hall, Oliver G.
Nicholson, M. G., (witness)
Brindley, Carl, (witness)
Hall, James B.
Box 5 File 61 1874-1875
Names in File:
Nicholson, O. P., (adm)
Sibert, Henry, (appraiser)
Williams, D. C., (appraiser)
Collins, A., (appraiser)
Frazier, Patrick M., (adm)
Mills, J. P.
Clayton, Solomon H., (note)
Dobbs, L. A., (atty)
Nicholson, T. J.,(sp.adm 1874)
Norton, A. J., Judge
Vann, A. J., (med.services)
Wesson, W. J., (note)
Small, W. A., (bond)
Nowlin, D. S., (bond)
Peak, S. B., (note)
Eason, B. J., (note)
Nicholson, C. W., (note)
Personal Property Sold:
Mills, (19-penholders)
Small, H., (1-pr suspenders)
Appleton, (suspenders)
Beavers, (suspenders)
McNearon, (suspenders)

Estate Record Name
Hall, James B. (Cont.)
Lackey, (suspenders)
Long, (suspenders & shirt)
Clayton, (2-shirts)
Small, Wm., (shirt)
Anderson, C., (vest)
Tidmore, A., (vest)
Hall, Josie, (3-linen collars)
Peak, Marion, (hat)
Tidmore, (hat)
Hall, Josie, (3-yds.lace)
Barkdale, (lace)
Adrian, James, (2-hats)
Clayton, Sol. H., (hat)
Wesson, J. W., (hat)
Tidmore, A., (shirt)
Tidmore, Wm., (hat)
Anderson, C., (2-hats)
Hall, Josie, (cotton floss)
Small, W. A., (hat)
Peek, M., (hat)
Wesson, J. W., (bolt of lace)
Tidmon, Jere, (knitting needles)
Hall, J. B., (1-doz.spools thread)
Siniard, J. W., (spools of thread)
Shirley, John, (spools of thread)
Hall, J. G., (thread)
Tidmore, D. H., (thread)
Clayton, M. A., (thread)
Kearly, Alf, (thread)
Tidmore, Wm., (thread)
Tidmore, J. H., (knitting needles)
Small, W., (knitting needles)
Collins, Tone, (knitting needles)
Copeland, Sam, (knitting needles)
Small, W. A., (spool thread)
Nicholson, E. P., (spool thread)
Small, W. A., (16-thimbles)
Tidmore, J. H., (1-doz silk thread)
Hall, Josie, (1-doz silk thread)
Nicholson, O. P., (5-finger rings)

Estate Record Name

Hall, James B. (Cont.)
- Wesson, J. W., (spool silk twist)
- Siniard, Mrs., (2-breast pins)
- Nave, Polk, (breast pin)
- Hall, J. C. (2-breast pins)
- Hall, J. M., (breast pin)
- Copeland, Sam, (4-boxes hair pins)
- Shirley, John, (comb)
- Tidmore, J. H., (pr.spectacles)
- Hall, J. C., (bolt of lace)
- Copeland, Sam, (shoe knife)
- Heard, Solon, (shoe knife)
- Edwards, John, (shoe knife)
- Hall, J. M., (shoe knife)
- Adrian, James, (shoe knife)
- Talley, M., (shoe knife)
- Edwards, Wm., (shoe knife)
- Clayton, Sol, (shoe knife)
- Tidmon, A. B., (steelyards)
- Sibert, Henry, (steelyards)
- Tidmore, Jere, (steelyards)
- Small, Eddy, (2-clothe brushes)
- Stancil, (clothe brush)
- Wesson, J. W., (5-clothe brushes)
- Hall, J. C., (hair brushes)
- Siniard, Mrs., (2-hats)
- Tidmore, Wm., (hat)
- Wesson, J. W., (ladies hats)
- Nicholson, Scott, (lady's hat)
- Small, Eddy, (box slate pencils)
- Hall, Bryant, (ground pepper)
- Hall, Josie, (box of ground pepper)
- Adrian, James, (pen points)
- Wesson, J. W., (20 yds linen)
- Adrian, James, (1-roll leather)
- Massey, Lewis, (1-roll leather)
- Siniard, J. W., (1-roll leather)
- Wesson, J. W., (2-rolls leather)
- Black, Oliver,
- Nicholson, O. P., (4-shirts)
- Siniard, Mrs., (shirt)

Estate Record Name

Hall, James B. (Cont.)
- Heard, Solon, (3-shirt)
- Adrian, James, (shirt)
- Siniard, J. W., (2-coats & thread)
- Tidmore, A. B., (24 skn.thread)
- Wesson, J. W., (62 skn.thread)
- Appleton, J. B., (knives & forks)
- Hall, J. M., (knives & forks)
- Nicholson, M., (ladies gloves)
- Hall, Josie, (gloves)
- Wesson, J. W., (20 prs.gloves)
- Tidmore, Wm., (ladies gloves)
- Reed, James, (necktie)
- Nicholson, O. P., (32-ties)
- Wesson, J. W., (glass screws)
- Hall, J. M., (10-yds poplin)
- Nicholson, O. P., (poplin)
- Siniard, J. W., (13-yds poplin)
- Nave, (piece worsted)
- Siniard, J. W., (2-pr gloves)
- Coker, D. W., (bed casters)
- Siniard, J. W., (bed casters)
- Hall, Jacob, (bed casters)
- Wesson, J. W., (shoes & boots)
- Siniard, J. W., (boots)
- Jolley, J. B., (boots)
- Hall, J. M., (boots & suspenders)
- Clayton, S. H., (boots & shoes)
- Small, Henry,(Linsey & worsted)
- Small, W. A., (suspenders)
- Brock, (shoes)
- Tidmore, J.H., (shoes)
- Kirby, Dock, (pr.shoes)
- Small, W. A., (shoes)
- Brock, G., (shoes)
- Coker, W. D., (shoes)
- Anderson, C., (shoes)
- Smith, Charlie, (clock)
- Freeman, C., (pr.suspenders)
- Nicholson, L. S., (suspenders)
- Adrian, D. W., (suspenders)

Estate Record Name
Hall, James B. (Cont.)
Gilbreath, E., (10-yds.Linsey)
Small, Harriett, (6-pr suspenders)
Small, W. A., (churn & buttons)
Watts, L. B., ((suspenders)
Appleton, Newton, (hat)
Tidmore, M. M., (hat)
Brock, G., (hat)
Griffin, Nolan, (hat)
Hall, J. M., (hat)
Adrian, James, (hat & gloves)
Clayton, S. H., (hat)
Collins, N. S., (collar)
Nicholson, B. H.,(coat)
Hayes, G., (1-pr pants)
Nicholson, L. S., (coat)
Nicholson, B. H., (ladies hose)
Nicholson, B. H., (pearl buttons)
Martin, J. C., (1-card buttons)
Lock, J. W., (1-card buttons)
Beavers, J. W., (1-card buttons)
Small, H. C., (buttons)
Tidmore, A. B., (buttons & gloves)
Small, H., (gloves)
Frazier, Pat, (gloves)
Stewart, M. R., (gloves)
Bogle, Mat, (gloves)
Brock, G., (gloves)
Smith, Wm., (comb)
Siniard, Wm., (comb)
Tidmore, J. M., (comb)
Toliver, L. M., (comb)
Watts, L. B., (comb)
Tidmore, H., (comb)
Meadows, Wm., (comb)
Siniard, Tom, (comb)
Adams, D. W.,(comb)
Nicholson, L. S. (comb)
Brandon, P. A. (5-pr.hose)
Brock, J. E. (3-pr.hose)
Mills, W. K., (3-pr hose)

Estate Record Name
Hall, James B. (Cont.)
Small, W. A., (hose & combs)
Nicholson, B. H., (2-pr.hose)
Black, Oliver, (1-card buttons)
Chaney, Hosey, (1-card buttons)
Anderson, Scipis?,(1-card buttons)
Hall, J. M., (satchel)
Black, C. H., (satchel)
Smith, G. W., (1-box tacks)
Brandon, P. A., (4-yds checks)
Tidmore, J. H., (14-yds Jeans)
Small, H., (ribbon)
Wesson, J. W., (ribbon)
Brock, G., (2-pr.hose)
Small, H. C., (ribbon)
Nicholson, Josie, (ribbon)
Small, M. A., (ribbon)
Nicholson, L. S., (table)
Tidmore, (book)
Nicholson, Josie, (bracelets)
Tidmore, H. J. (combs)
Cheyney, Hosey. (comb)
Tidmore, Casey, (comb)
Tidmore, Hence, (5-combs)
Heard, Strode, (6-combs)
Appleton, T. N., ((3-pr.hose)
Smith, W., (1-pass book)
Watts, L. B., (1-pass book)
Small, M. A., (3-combs)
Davis, J. P., (3-bot.turpentine)
Small, W. A., (3-bot.turpentine)
Lock, J. W., (butter disk)
Wesson, J. W., (glass dishes)
Coker, W. D., (molasses ?)
Hall, J. M., (molasses ?)
Barksdale, Wm., (molasses ?)
Small, H., (table)
Hall, J. M., (shot gun)
Reed, James, (1-molasses ?)
Wesson, J. W., (1-molasses ?)
Tidmore, Hence, (salt stand)

Estate Record Name
Hall, James B. (Cont.)
Chaney, Posey, (2-whit stones)
Lock, J. W., (salt ?)
Heard, Strode, (bowl)
Barksdale, White, (pocket knife)
Nicholson, B. H., (pocket knife)
Hall, J. M., (pocket knife)
Tidmore, A. B., (1-plow stock)
Small, W. A., (Irons)
Nicholson, E. P. (6-lamp ?)
Mills, (curry brush)
Nicholson, O. P., (bridles & bits)
Hall, Jacob, (bridles & bits)
Wesson, J. W., (3-locks & belts)
Hall, Jim, (leather belts)
Lynch, Newton, (leather belts)
Anderson, C., (2-leather belts)
Small, W. A., (shoe punch)
Mills, (pitcher)
McNesson, Thom., (pitcher)
Hall, Josie,(4-pitchers &E120 needles)
Coker, D. W., (pitcher)
Small, W. A.,(needles)
Small, W. A., (needles)
Jones, Wm., (needles)
Hall, Josie, (needles & pins)
Teets, Mrs., (needles)
Tidmore, Wm., (needles)
Small, Henry, (needles)
Wesson, J. W., (needles & pins)
Lynch, Newton, (pins)
Lynch, Newton, (shaving cream)
Teets, (shaving cream)
Coker, D., (shaving cream)
Wesson, J. W., (sh.cream)
Small, Eddie, (knife)
Kerley, A., (knife)
Wesson, J. W., (box gun tubes)
Hall, J., (knife)
Horton, (vinegar stands)
Wesson, J. W., ((butter dish)

Estate Record Name
Hall, James B. (Cont.)
Hall, Josie, (box soda)
Beavers, (shoes)
Appleton, (shoes)
Nicholson, E. P., (shoes)
Teets, (shoes)
Anderson, C., (shoes)
Shirley, (shoes)
Hall, Jacob, (23 yds cottonade)
Lock, John, (pc. cottonade)
Wesson, J., (ginghams & linen)
Hall, Josie, (blch.domestic)
Nave, (pc. Masailles)
Wesson, J. W., (Birdseye diaper)
Nave, (Marsailles)
Coker, D. W., (20-yds cottonade)
Coker, D. W., (jeans)
Nicholson, E. P., (cassimer)
Hall, Jacob, (49-yds.calico)
Tidmore, A., (pc.goods)
Mills, 10-yds.lawn p.k.)
Coker, D. W.,(8-yds lawn)
Tidmore, A., (pc.p.k.)
Sinard, W. E., (P. K.)
Wesson, J. W., (P.K. & boots)
Hall, Josie, (12-yds veiling)
Siniard, (hat)
Hall, Jacob, (hat)
Adrian, James, (2-hats & shoes)
Kelly, Turner, (2-hats)
Kelly, Doc., (2-pr gloves)
Nicholson, M., (1-pr shoes)
Hall, Josie, (7 oz. Aniline)
Copeland, Sam, (1-pr shoes)
Collins, Tone, (1-pr shoes)
Sloan, James, (1-pr shoes)
Nicholson, O. P., (gent's hose)
Hall, Josie, (10-bottles cinnamon)
Hall, J. G., (shoes&4-rubber combs)
Hall, J. C., (bolt of ribbon, comb)
Wesson, J. W., (ribbon & combs)

Estate Record Name
Hall, James B. (Cont.)
Siniard, Mrs., (bolt of ribbon)
Collins, Tone, (rubber comb)
Nicholson, E. P., (2-bot. ?)
Hall, J. M., (3-fine combs)
Hall, J. G., (coat)
Small, W. A., (2-coats, 3-pants)
Edwards, Wm., (1-Balmoral)
Hall, J. C., (1-Balmoral & vest)
Edwards, Wm., (2-boxes collars)
Hall, J. C., (3-boxes collars)
Nicholson, E. P., (vest)
Hall, J. C., (8-bot.peppermint)
Kelly, Turner, (1-box collars)
Wesson, J. W., (6-boxes collars)
Smith, Wm., (1-doz braid)
Adrian, James, (bunch of braids)
Hall, J. M., (2-bot. vermifuge)
Small, W. A., (2-bot. Vermifuge)
Nicholson, E. P., (1-bot.vermifuge)
Hall, J. G., (sheep shears)
Small, W. A., (sheep shears)
Adrian, James, (bunch of ruffles)
Wesson, J. W., (ruffles & lace)
Tidmore, A. B., (bunch of ruffles)
Siniard, J. W., (ruffles)
Hall, J. C., (bunch of ruffles & lace)
Adrian, J., (lace)
Sibert, Henry, (1-pc. worsted)
Hall, J. C., (bunch of cuffs)
Wesson, J. W.,(box coffin screws)
Collins, Tone, (1-jar camphor)
Small, W. A., (1-jar salt peter)
Wesson, J. W., (1-jar salts)
Tidmore, Jere, (1-jar alum)
Hall, J. M., (empty jar)
Nicholson, E. P., (disentery med.)
Wesson, J. W., (nerve & bone linim.)
Copeland, Sam, (1-bot liniment)
Small, Wm., (2-bot castor oil)
Adrian, James, (1/2 gross buttons)

Estate Record Name
Hall, James B. (Cont.)
Nicholson, E. P., (buttons)
Adrian, J., (1/2 gross buttons)
Hall, J. G., (1-gross buttons)
Edwards, John, (1-gross buttons)
Kerly, James, (buttons)
Clayton, Sol, (1-bot liniment)
Russell, Charlie, (5-bot liniment)
Wesson, J. W., (3-bot.liniment)
Kerly, Alf, (1-box buttons)
Tidmore, J. H., (1-box buttons)
Tidmore, Henry, (1-box buttons)
Wesson, J. W., (pad lock)
Wesson, J. W., (7 bunches braid)
Nicholson, E. P., (bunch braid)
Siniard, Mrs., (15-yds P. K.)
Roberts, (1-bot. Turpentine)
Wesson, J. W., (4-bot.terpentine)
Roberts, George, (pr suspenders)
Shirley, John, (3-pr.suspenders)
Nicholson, E. P., (2-pr.hose)
Wesson, J. W., (11-pr.hose)
Small, W. A., (vest)
Tidmore, Jere, (1-set Triggers)
Russel, Chas., (straw hat)
Sibert, Henry, (2-straw hats)
Small, W. A., (2-straw hats)
Sibert, Henry, (shirt)
Shirley, John, (buttons)
Wesson, J. W., (spoons)
Edwards, John, (spoons)
Beavers, Wm., (top bucket)
Roberts, George, (1-pr hose)
Hall, J. C., (snuff box)
Wesson, J. W., (elastic cord)
Nicholson, E. P., (silk netts)
Wesson, J. W., (silk netts)
Hall, J. C., (cod liver oil)
Wesson, J. W., (cherry pectoral)
Nicholson, E. P., (cough med.)
Wesson, J. W.,(candy vermifuge)

Estate Record Name

Hall, James B. (Cont.)
Box 5 File 61 1874-1875
Wesson, J. W. (eye wash)
Sibert, Henry, (2-boxes pills)
Tidmore, Jere, (7-boxes pills)
Nicholson, E.P.,(7-bot.Demoville)
Copeland, Sam, (8-boxes Roxin)
Wesson, J. W., (2-bot.med.)
Sibert, Henry, (Iodine-potassium)
Nicholson, E. P., (calomil)
Wesson, J. W. (liniment)
Edwards, John, (7-combs)
Nicholson,Scott,(lamp chimneys)
Beavers, Wm., (lamp burner)
Edwards, John, (6-lamp burners)
White, M. P., (hair pins)
Wesson, J. W., (11-watch keys)
Nicholson, M. M., (1-box screws)
Edwards, John, (1-box brads)
Nicholson, Scot, (lock)
Wesson, J. W., (sand paper)
Edwards, John, (2-doz.buckles)
Hall, J. M., (10-yd pants linen)
Boyd, (2-1/2 yds Jeans)
Wesson, J. W., (fish hooks)
White, M. P., (8-plow moles)
Jones, E. P., (plow wing)
Wesson, (1-lot screws)
Nicholson, E. P., (19-yds linen)
White, M. P., (2-pr hose)
Nicholson, M. M.,(5-pr hose)
White, M. P., (2-belts)
Wesson, J. W., (11-yds.bobinett)
Wesson, J. W., (Lot coffin trimming)
Wesson, J. W., (wrapping paper)
Wesson, J. W.,(guano strower)
Tidmore, A. B., (3-chairs)
Nicholson, Scott, (sack flour)
Wesson, J. W.,(2-bx.moss oil)
Hall, J. M., (basket, jug & pitcher)
Nicholson, S. S.,(shotgun)

Estate Record Name

Hall, James B. (Cont.)
Nicholson, B. H., (rifle)
Johnson, N. G.,(measure)
Tidmore, M. M. (measure)
Nicholson, O. P., Adm., signed
Brandon, P. A., Judge, signed
Hall, J. M.
Box 5 File 62 1867
Names in File:
Hall, Amy, (adm)
Taxes paid 1867
Hall, M. B. .
Box 5 File 63 1912
Names in File:
Hall, N. J., Mrs., (widow)
Exemption before administration
No minor children
Cochran, John J., (appraiser)
Glover, W. J., (appraiser)
Lackey, L. B., (JP)
Croley, Jas. A., Judge
Hall, Oliver
Box 5 File 64 1909
Names in File:
Sale of Land for Division
Hall, O. L.
Harrell, Burl
Harrell, William
Osborne, J. L.
Newman, Osborn
Osborn, J. H.
Osborn, J. E.
Osborn, James F.
Osborn, John
Glass, Kate, (w/o William)
Glass, William
Swain, Mary J.
Mills, Sarah, (w/o A. B.)
Mills, A. B.
Osborn, Chas.
Swain, W. N., (h/o Mary Jane)

Estate Record Name

Hall, Oliver
- Osborn, Newman
- Pope, J. D., (commissioner)
- Copeland, A. C., (deposition)
- Mitchell, W. J., (deposition)
- Pope, Davis
- Hale, P. C., (commissioner)
- Davis & Pope, (atty)
- Osborn, J. L., (minor)
- Osborn, Charles, (minor)
- Presley, I. M., (guar.ad litem)
- Hairel, Burt
- Hariel, Wm.
- Osborn, J. R.
- Hall, O. H., (bought land)

Hammock, Aaron G.
- Box 5 File 65 1866-1871
- Names in File:
- Hammack/Hammock
- Lewis, Mary Ann Hammock
  (only heir at law)
- Lewis, Benjamin F., (dec.'d)
- Hammock, Thomas, (adm 1869)
- Lewis, Fannie, (minor)
- Lewis, Samuel, (minor)
- Lewis, Mary, (minor)
- Lewis, Benjamin, (minor)
- Hammock, Aaron G., (will)
- Hammock, Clancy Ann, (wife)
- Hammock, Mary Ann, (dau.)
- Hammock, Wm. H., (bond)
- Campbell, Lewis, (bond)
- Jack, Thos. J., (bond)
- Parker, James, (appraiser)
- Frazer, John B., (appraiser)
- Hawkins, James, (appraiser)
- Hammock, William N.
- Hammock, Aaron G.
  Polk Co. Ga. Estate
- Union Newspaper, Gadsden
- Smith, P. J.,(editor)

Estate Record Name

Hammock, Aaron G.
- *Republican Union*
- Horton, A. J., Judge
- *Herald*
- Snodgrass, A., (editor)
- Dunlap, Dobbs & Jacoway
- Dobbs, L. A., (atty)
- Lewis, M.A., vs: Hammock, Thos.
- Hoge, James M., (Jackson Co)
- Malone, G. W., (witness)
- Hoge, James M., (witness)
- Luckes, Joseph
- Normance, W. W.
- Cuperton, Adam,(bought lot)
- **Claims Against Estate:**
- Dobbs, J. M.
- Baxter, James
- Dutton, A.
- Cunningham, James
- Clinch, John
- Davis,
- Count, Isaac
- Swader, Francis
- Ervins, Isaac
- Henderson, Viard
- Hunter, J. T.
- Fike, David C.
- Swafford, J. M.
- Brandon, C. F.
- Campbell, Harris
- Fike, Robert
- Hickson, Jeremiah
- Patterson, Hammock
- Sotherland, B. R.
- McPherson, Wm.
- McKenney, L. W.
- Dutton, M. J.
- Sutherland, Wm.
- McPherson, T. J.
- Reese, Samuel
- Hughes, Green

Estate Record Name

Hammock, Aaron G.
- Reese, Wiley
- Livingston, C. M.
- Malone, G. W., (note)
- Cunningham, John, (acct.)
- Carethers, J. Y., (acct.)
- House, Wm. J., (note)
- Stron, Hortman Holfin & Co.
- Phillips, H. & Co., (note)
- Wimpsy, T. W., (Polk Co. Ga)
- Young, A. (note)
- Lewis, Mary A., (interest)
- Payne, A. F., (JP)
- Sotherlin, Wm. H., (note)
- Phillips, P. D., (attest)
- Dunlap, R.A.D.
- Horton, A. J., Judge, 1869
- Smith, T. J., (adv.)
- Collins, T. B., (agent)
- Walden, J. B., (legal services)
- Matthal, L. H., (burial expense)
- Smith & Meeks, (pub.notices)

Paid:
- Nicholson & Collins, (legal serv.)
- Lewis, Mary Ann
- Hess, J. A., (tax coll. 1869)
- Turnley, M. J., (prof.services)
- Jacoway, J. G., (services)
- Wimpee, F. M., (coffin)
- Nicholson & Collins, (legal serv.)

Notes Due Estate:
- Jacoway, J. C., (notes)
- Southerland, W. R., (note)
- Hand, J. W., (note)

Hammock, Marion
- Box 5 File 66 1908
- Names in File:
- Hammock, Charlott, (widow)
- Springs, Henry, (minor)
- Springs, Jordan, (g-f of Henry)
- Isbell & Presley, (atty)

Estate Record Name

Hammock, Marion (Cont.)
- Hammock, Claracy/Clarsy
- Sale of Land for Division
- Hammock, George
- Hammock, Will
- Teague, Polly Hammock
- Copeland, A. C., (guar.ad litem)
- Horton, G. R., (deposition)
- Chitwood, W. J., (deposition)
- Berry, Minnie, (commissioner)
- Presley, I. M., (commissioner)
- Croley, J. A., Judge
- Downs, T. L., (sheriff)
- Kerley, C.
- Jones, T. A.
- Hammock, C. Lasey
- Davenport, Sam
- *The DeKalb Record*
- Hammock, Charley
- Parish, S. L., (bought land)

Hammock, W.
- Box 5 File 67 1889
- Sale of Land for Division
- Hammock, J. J., (l/6 interest)
- Hammock, Wallace, (l/6 interest)
- Griffith, E. E., (1/6 interest)
- Webb, W. G., (l/6 interest)
- Garrett, Thomas, (1/6 interest)
- Thomason, Mary E., (l/6 interest)
- Thomason, John F.,(h/o Mary)
- Howard, M. W.
- Howard, Sallie A.
- Thomason, Mary Elizabeth
- Griffith, E., Mrs.
- Campbell, Isaac, (deposition)
- Dobbs, S. E., (deposition)
- Campbell, Isaac, (commissioner)
- Frazier, P. M., (sheriff)
- Frazier, Brown, (dep.sheriff)
- Cochran, L. L., Judge
- Dobbs & Howard

Estate Record Name

Hammock, W.
  Dobbs, W. M.
  Davis, C. C.
  Hammock, Willoughby (place)
  Lyons, W. S. A.
  Lankford, J. D.
Hammon, Elizabeth
  Box 5 File 68 1892
  Names in File:
  Hammon, William P.,(minor)
  Hammon, Rufus A., (minor)
  Hammon, Geo. Houston., (minor)
  Hammon, Elizabeth, (mother)
  Hammon, W. W., (father)
  Hammon, W. W., (guardian)
  Lankford, Elizabeth
  Lankford, J. M., Estate
  Lankford, W. A.
  Fort Payne Journal
  Fuller, W. T., (guar.ad litem)
  Campbell, Isaac, (bond)
  Howard, M. W., (bond)
  Killian, E. S., (bond)
  DeShields, J. G., (sheriff)
  Workman, S. D.,(dep.sheriff)
Hammond, C. B.
  Box 5 File 69 1918
  Names in File:
  Hammond, Nina, (minor)
  Hammond, C. B., (guardian)
  Hammond, W. J., (g-f of minor)
  Hicks, R. H., (g-f of minor)
  Hicks, R. H., (custody of minor)
  Cochran, Earl, (bond)
  Campbell, J. N., (bond)
  Anderson, W. B.,(bought land)
  Johnson, J. A.,(guar.ad litem)
  Croley, Jas. A., Judge
Hammond, William C.
  Box 5 File 70 1884
  Names in File:

Estate Record Name

Hammond, William C. (Cont.)
  Hammon/Hamman/Hammond
  Price, James M.,(adm)
  Davenport, F. M.,(bond)
  Price, R. S., (bond)
  Price, M. M., (bond)
  Campbell, Henry, (witness)
  Dobbs, Stephen E., (witness)
  Webb, Garrett W., (comm.)
  Franklin, J. N., Judge
  Dobbs & Howard, (atty)
  Hammon, B. H.
  Hammon, W. W.
  Price, Cornelia E., (w/o J. M.)
  Price, J. M.
  Davenport, Ellen, (w/o F. M.)
  Davenport, F. M.
  Hammons, D. F.
  Hammons, N. A.
  Jett, A. J., (w/o Joseph)
  Jett, Joseph
  Crabtree, Minerva, (w/o Wm.)
  Crabtree, William
  Thompson, Darthula, (w/o Frank)
  Thompson, Frank
  Hammon, J. V., (residing in TX)
  Sizemore, A. G., (bought land)
  Crabtree, M. E.
  Smith, T. H.
  Thompson, D. J.
  Hammon, William
  Jett, J. A.
  Hammon, Jas.
  Hammon, B. G.
  Franklin, A. G.
  Campbell, H. B.
  Frazier, J. M., (sheriff)
  Dobbs, S. E.
  Campbell, I., (guard.ad litem)
  Franklin, A. G., (sheriff)
Hansell, Robert

Estate Record Name
Hansell, Robert
Box 5 File 71 1917
Names in File:
Sale of Land for Division
Hansell, Willie, (minor)
Hansell, Georgia, (minor)
Hansel, Robert, (guardian, brother)
Father deceased
Pope, John L., (bond)
Bryant, D. E., (bond)
Hansell, Maude, (heir)
Scott, Chas. J., (atty)
Pope, John L., (purchased land)
Croley, Jas. A., Judge
Haralson, Henry C.
Box 5 File 72 1884-1888
Names in File:
Haralson, Ella V., (widow, adm)
Haralson, Peter Bennett, (minor)
Haralson, William L., (minor)
Haralson, Walter U., (minor)
Haralston, Helen, (minor)
Haralson, Minnie L., (minor)
Stanaffer, William H., (bond)
Stanaffer, Lemuel J., (bond)
Haralson, W. J. (bond)
Haralson, W. W., (guar.bond)
Haralson, C. J., (guar.bond)
West, James, (guar.bond)
Durham, John,(guar.bond)
Durham, J. M., (guar.bond)
Johnson, C. P., (guar.ad litem)
Russell, J. E., (witness)
Haralson, W. W., (witness)
Fuller, W. T., (commissioner)
Christensen, L. M., (witness)
Davis, John A., (commissioner)
Disque, Augusta, (witness)
Young, C. H., (witness)
Kennedy, F. H., (JP)
Isbell, John B., (witness)

Estate Record Name
Haralson, Henry C. (Cont.)
Everett, James
Fort Payne Investment Co.
(purchased land for $11,000)
Hardman, Ella J.
Box 5 File 73 1908
Names in File:
Hardman, Nettie, (minor)
Hardman, Effie, (minor)
Hardman, Ervin, (minor)
Hardman, Estell, (minor)
Hardman, Lola, (minor)
Hardman, G. W., (guardian)
Hardman, G. W., (father)
Hardman, John J., (bond)
Hardman, N. L., (bond)
Hare, Major
Box 5 File 74 1915
Names in File:
Ala.Gr.Sou. RR Co. Claim
US Fidelity & Guaranty Co.
Moore, E., (representative)
Hare, A. G., (father)
Hare, S. E., (mother)
Haygood, W. M.,(JP) Blount, Al.
Kay, James, (friend, adm)
Harp, M. T.
Box 5 File 75 1912
Names in File:
Harp, W. T./ M. T.
Harp, N. E., Mrs., (widow)
Exemption before admin.
Powell, D. W., (appraiser)
Bishop, G. J.,(appraiser)
Harper, Ida
Box 5 File 76 1902-1906
Names in File:
Harper, J. D., (adm)
Harper, S. D., (bond)
Wright, C. W., (bond)
Tucker, G. W., (bond)

Estate Record Name

Harper, Ida (Cont.)
- Berry, P. B., (bond)
- Wright, O. W., (appraiser)
- Tucker, G. W., (appraiser)
- Wilson, M. M., (appraiser)
- Johnson, Tolitha, (w/o Wm.)
- Johnson, William
- Harper, T. W.
- Harper, N. S.
- Allen, Margaret, (w/o J.D.)
- Allen, J. D.
- Harper, Tara/Tera/Terah
- Watson, Missouri, (w/o J.)
- Watson, Junken
- Harper, Albert
- Allen, Edmond
- Clayton, Nancy
- Clayton, Ida
- Allen, James
- Bearden, Alonzo
- Bearden, Oscar
- Bearden, Charles
- Bearden, Oma
- Drain, Parilee
- Drain, Alice, (minor)
- Drain, Lou, (minor)
- Drain, Ida,(minor)
- Drain, Mack, (minor)
- Drain, Oliver, (minor)
- Drain, William, (minor)
- Harper, William
- Harper, Y. S.
- DeShields, J. G., (guar.ad litem)
- Berry, Preston, (witness)
- Richey, Lumpkin, (witness)
- Bethune, D. L., (comm.)
- Morgan, S. T.
- Harper, Wm. P.
- Clayton, Nannie
- Clayton, H. M.
- Clayton, Ida

Estate Record Name

Harper, Ida (Cont.)
- Allen, James
- Allen, Ed
- Harper, Terah
- Harper, W. L.
- Harper, S. N.
- Harper, Albert
- Allen, Mary, (deceased)
- Allen, Nancy
- Allen, Ida
- Allen, James
- Bearden, Elizabeth, (deceased)
- The Fort Payne Journal
- Smith, Thos. H., (notices)
- Davis & Haralson
- Davis, John A., (paid)
- Cain, Wall, (tax coll. 1905)
- Wright, C. W., MD, (medical)
- Morgan, T. S.
- Graves, H. L. (tax coll. 1902-4)
- Wright, Kittie, (medicine, paid)
- Mayes, Joe, (purchased land)
- Morgan, W. C.,(surety for Mayes)
- Morgan, T. S., (surety for Mayes)
- Allen, J. D., (note due estate)
- Austin, D. O., (sheriff, Etowah Co.)
- Harper, T. W.
- Chandler, Wm.,(sheriff-Etowah)
- Adams, G. Z., (sheriff)
- Coleman, A. B., (dep.sheriff)
- Gibson, J. C., (JP)

Harper, John P.
- Box 5 File 77 1862
- Names in File:
- Neely, John M., (minor)
- Neely, Mahala H.,(minor)
- Neely, Charles M., (minor)
- Nealy/Neely
- Neely, James A., (guardian)
- Roberts, Richard, (bond)
- Berry, A. J., (bond)

Estate Record Name

Harper, John P.
    Harper, John D., Estate
    Franklin, J. N., Judge
Harris, E. L.
    Box 5 File 78 1926
    Names in File:
    Sale of Land for Division
    Harris, E. L., Mrs., (deceased)
    Harris, Mildred, (minor)
    Harris, Doris, (minor)
    Harris, Mattie Janie, (minor)
    Johnson, J. A., (guardian)
    Pharr, G. W., (deposition)
    McCartney, C. H., (deposition)
    Presley, I. M., (commissioner)
    Malone, G. L., Judge
    Harris, E. L., (purchased land)
    Smith, Thos. H.,(notices)
Harris, R. C.
    Box 5 File 79 1904
    Names in File:
    Harris, Thomas A., (minor)
    Harris, James O., (minor)
    Harris, R. C., (guardian)
    Smith, A. T., (bond)
    Croley, J. A., (bond)
    DeShields, J. G., (guar.ad litem)
    Harris, R. C., (guar.bond)
    Sale of Land
Harris, Robert C.
    Box 5 File 80 1898
    Names in File:
    Harris, Narcis, (widow)
    Harris, Belvin, (minor)
    Harris, Elijah, (minor)
    Harris, Elisha, (minor)
    Harris, Walter, (minor)
    Harris, Jesse, (minor)
    Harris, Hester, (minor)
    Harris, Vesten, (minor)
    Harris, Della, (minor)

Estate Record Name

Harris, Robert C. (Cont.)
    Allen, A. A., (appraiser)
    Henley, William L.,(appraiser)
    Pharr, G. W., (JP)
Hartline, B. P.
    Box 5 File 81 1902-1921
    Names in File:
    Hartline, Mary A., (minor)
    Hartling, Lizzie, (minor)
    Cordell, Sarah, (m/o minors)
    Hartline, J. A., (guardian)
    Hartline, J. A., (uncle of minors)
    Payne, M. A., (bond)
    Blansit, A. D., Jr., (bond)
    Steele, W. A., (bond)
    Long, David, (bond)
    Copeland, A. C., (guar.ad litem)
    Hartline, John C.
    Personal Property Sold:
    Grarfy, J. M., (mules)
    Hartline, J. A., (cow & calf)
    Cureton, W. H., (harrow)
    Ellis, William, (horse collar)
    Durham, B. D., (pitch fork)
    Cureton, W. C., (mattock)
    Chadwick, W. H., (saw)
    Schooling for minors paid
    Cook & Presley, (atty) paid
    Middleton, D. L., Dr., paid
    Green, P. B., Dr., paid
    Hartline, Mary, (died)
    Clark, Lizzie Hartline
Harvey, Henry B.
    Box 5 File 82 1909
    Names in File:
    Harvey, Florence P., (widow)
    Harvey, Harry
    Harvey, Roy C., (minor)
    Harvey, Catherine, (minor)
    Harvey, Florence P., (adm.)
    Campbell, H. B., (bond)

Estate Record Name

Hawkins, Adam L.
Box 5 File 83 1879-1880
Names in File:
Hawkins, Drucilla C., (widow)
Hawkins, Drucilla C., (adm)
Hawkins, Robert H.
Hawkins, Susan K.
Hawkins, Benjamin H.
Hawkins, James P.
Hawkins, Rutha L.
Hawkins, D. A.
Hawkins, Louisa R.
Hawkins, Drucilla N.
Reece, Wm. S., (adm.bond)
Reece, Andrew, (adm.bond)
Brock, Wilborn, (appraiser)
Blackwell, B. H., (appraiser)
Frazier, B. P.
Privett, F. F., (witness)
Poe, W. R., (witness)
Privett, Frank, (witness)
Hawkins, J. J., (adm bond)
Hawkins, D. A., (adm.bond)
Brandon, P. A., Judge
Dobbs, L. A., (atty)
Cooper, Thos. T., (land joins)
Green, A. B.
Riley, J. C., Estate
Killian, A. C., (prop.line)
Cooper, Thos., (prop.line)
McCurdy, John A., (prop.line)
Haralson, H. C.,(prop.line)
Haralson, A. C., (bought land)
Campbell, A. L., (witness)
Poe, W. R., (commissioner)
Payne, A. F., (guar.ad litem)
NcNutt, R. C., (sheriff)
Killian, A. C., (bought land)
Cunningham, J. M., (bought land)
Cooper, Thos. B., (bought land)
Davis, Jno. A., (guar.ad litem)

Estate Record Name

Hawkins, Adam L. (Cont.)
Jackson, W. A., (note)
Jackson, James A., (trustee)
Poe, William A.
Hammack, Thos., (witness)
Hammack, H. I., (witness)
Paid:
Green, A. B.
Poe, R., (NP) (JP)
Nichols, A. M.
Smith, Thos, H., (notices)
Duff, S. W., (burial outfit)
Sayers, Frances, (loan paid)
McWhorter, A. M., (medical)
McWhorter, H. P., (medical)
Hill, J. A.
Russell, S. L.
Ferguson, W. L., (tax coll 1875-8)
Brock & Son
Malone, G. W., (note paid)
Killian, C.
Bennett, A. A.
Sampley, J. C.
Leath, E. L.
Lloyd, John E., (surveying)
Fischer, Gustavis
Hawkins, Ben
Box 5 File 84 1902
Names in File:
Phillips, P. D., (claim paid)
Hawkins, B. F.
Box 5 File 85 1876
Names in File:
Hawkins, Mary A., (petitioner)
Hawkins, Mary A., (adm)
Davenport & Long
Brandon, P. A., Judge
Hawkins, Emery
Box 5 File 86 1877
Names in File:
Hawkins, Sarah C., (adm)

Estate Record Name
Hawkins, Emery (Cont.)
Frazier, P. M., (sheriff)
Brandon, P. A., Judge
Hawkins, George W.
Box 5 File 87 1899-1906
Names in File:
Hawkins, George W., (minor)
Hanna, J. A., (guardian)
Duncan, F. F., (bond)
Prestwood. P. B., (bond)
Whited, Jas. P., (bond)
Hawkins, James, Estate
Hawkins, R., Estate
Cook, W. C. D., Judge
Driskill & Cordell
The Dekalb Record
Driskill, E. H.
Glover, G. S. (NP)
Hawkins, James
Box 5 File 88 1883
Names in File:
Hawkins, Alexander, (minor)
Hawkins, Nealey, (minor)
Hawkins, M. E., (minor)
Hawkins, James T.,(minor)
Hawkins, H. E., (minor)
Hawkins, Melba J., (minor)
Hawkins, Pauline Beene
(mother or minors)
Beene, Jacob, Estate
(grandfather of minors)
Hawkins, James, Sr., (guardian)
Frazier, P. M., (bond)
Hawkins, James T.
Box 5 File 89 1889-1895
Names in File:
Sale of Land for Division
Hawkins, Mollie J.
Hawkins, Mahilda
Myers, Hattie
Hawkins, Hulda J.

Estate Record Name
Hawkins, James T. (Cont.)
Hawkins, Geo. W.,(minor)
(son of second wife)
Hawkins, James T.,(minor)
Hawkins, Hattie D., (minor)
Hawkins, Hulda J., (minor)
Hawkins, James
Phillips, P. D., (guardian)
McGuffey, W. C. H., (bond)
Beene, T. J., (bond)
Myers, Hattie Hawkins
Phillips, Pleasant D.
Reed, W. D., (tax coll. 1897)
Cochran, Earl, (notices)
Hawkins, Jessie (minor)
Box 5 File 90 1897-1904
Names in File:
Hawkins, Preston, Estate
Hawkins, Preston, (father)
Hawkins, Martha, (mother)
Hawkins, Jessie, (minor)
Crabtree, Robert, (guardian)
Lowry, Geo., M.D., (deposition)
Davenport, E. L.,(deposition)
Davenport, Erskin T., (deposition)
Culberson, Cy., (commissioner)
Hawkins, Jessie, living w/mother
Payne, John L., (guar.ad litem)
Davis & Haralson, (atty)
DeShields, J. G., (guar.ad litem)
Hawkins, John
Box 5 File 91 1859-1867
Names in File:
Hawkins, James, (adm.)
Hawkins, Elizabeth
Hawkins, Alexander
Welch, Mary A., (w/o Geo.)
Welch, George
Lowry, Elizabeth, (w/o James)
Lowry, James
Hawkins, Raleigh

Estate Record Name

Hawkins, John (Cont.)
Hawkins, John
Hawkins, Alex
Hawkins, Wm. C.
Chadwick, Blanch Emiline
Chadwick, George
Hawkins, Raleigh, Jr.
Hawkins, Preston
Hawkins, Benjamin
Cooper, Lucinda, (w/o James)
Cooper, James
Hawkins, Mary Ann
Street, Francis M.
Street, Malinda Hawkins
Hawkins, Mahulda/Malinda
Hawkins, J. John
Phillips, Abner
Welch, Geo. W.
Austin, Jonathan
Nicholson, D. L., (atty)
Estes, R., Judge
Walker, W. A., (paid)
Ashburn, Robert T., (paid)
Clayton, Sol S., (paid)
Walden, J. B.
Smith, P. J., (notices)
Horton, A. J., Judge
Nicholson, B. N. & D. L.
Bynum, W.
Stuart, Samuel, Estate
Stuart, Jane, (minor of Samuel)
Hawkins, James, (guardian)
Rankin, J., (bond)
Rogers, J. A., (bond)
Bouldin, E., (JP)
Hawkins, James, (bond)
Beene, Jacob, (bond)
Blansit, A. D., (bond)
Bouldin, Wm., (appraiser)
Candler, (appraiser)
Walker, Wm., (appraiser)

Estate Record Name

Hawkins, John (Cont.)
Phillips, Abner, (appraiser)
Sale of Personal Property:
Hawkins, Mary Ann, (bedstead)
Hawkins, Elizabeth, (bedstead)
Hawkins, Blanche, (bed & table)
Hawkins, Elizabeth, (bed)
Hawkins, Mary A.,(loom, harness)
Hawkins, W., (skillet & lid)
Hawkins, Mary Ann, (cow & yearling, 2 ovens & lids, pots & hooks, dishes, pitcher, forks, jars, jars, 60# cotton & 6-chairs)
Hawkins, Elizabeth, (Breadtray, wheels & cards)
Cooper, James, (60#salted meat)
Hawkins, Wm., (3-chairs, hames and collars)
Cooper, James, (18 hogs)
Hawkins, Elizabeth, (cow & calf)
Hawkins, Blanch, (cow & calf)
Hawkins, Preston, (2-calves)
Welch, Geo. W., (cow)
Austin, Jonathan, (mare)
Hawkins, James, (box)
Hawkins, Mary Ann, (table)
Hawkins, Elizabeth (24-geese)
Steel, John, (bedstead)
Morgan, Wm. L.
Durham, T. C.
Cooper, James

Hawkins, Miles W.
Box 5 File 92 1911-1912
Names in File:
Hawkins, Mattie A., (widow)
Hawkins, M. Hope, (minor, son)
Carlisle, L. A.
Carlisle, Ida Hawkins
Carlisle, Daniel, (h/o Ida)
Hawkins, Luna
Hawkins, Millard, (g-child)

Estate Record Name

Hawkins, Miles W. (Cont.)
Hawkins, Walter, (g-child)
Hawkins, Elmer, (g-child)
Hawkins, Lewis
Hawkins, James, (deceased)
Hawkins, Echols
Hawkins, Louisa
Hawkins, James
Harris, Thos. G., (adm)
Hicks, G. L.
Hawkins, M. W.
Harris, T. G., (sheriff)
Widow's Exemption
Breland, J. E., (appraiser)
Rice, J. A., (appraiser)
Hicks, Robert H., (appraiser)
Harris, G. L., (sheriff)
Notes Due Estate:
Fossett, A. H.
Dempsey, W. H.
Hicks, G. L., (NP)
Farr, W. B.
Weaver, F. A.
Mitchell, A. U.
Fossett, A. H & Amelia
Davis & Pope, (atty)
Taylor, John D., (atty)

Hawkins, Raleigh
Box 5 File 93 1883-1893
Names in File:
Harris, Lemuel A., (Exec.)
Fuller, W. T. (adm bond)
Campbell, I., (bond)
Blackwell, B. H., (adm bond)

Hawkins, Rebecca E.
Box 5 File 94 1887-1897
Names in File:
Sale of Land for Division
Hawkins, James T., Estate
Hawkins, Rebecca E., (widow)
Chadwick, A. J.

Estate Record Name

Hawkins, Rebecca E. (Cont.)
Joint owners of land
Hawkins, James T.
Hawkins, Hattie O.
Hawkins, Hulda J.
Hawkins, Alexander
Blake, Margaret E.
Blake, Thomas
Hawkins, Geo. W.,(son of Rebecca)
Hawkins, Sarah C.
Morgan, Sarah Hawkins
Hawkins, Cornelia
Blake, M. E.
Hawkins, A. L.
Myers, Hattie O.
Hawkins, Mahula J.
Hicks, George, (appraiser)
York, John,(appraiser)
Hicks, J. W., (purchased land)
Phillips, P. D., (surety on note)
York, John, (surety on note)
Ragon, J. C., (witness)
York, F. M., (note)
Collins, O. H., (comm.)
DeShields, J. G., (sheriff)
Davis & Haralson, (atty)
Chadwick, Rebecca Hawkins
Chadwick, A. J.
Fuller, W. T., (guar.ad litem)

Hawkins, William C.
Box 5 File 95 1874
Names in File:
Hawkins, Mary A., (adm)
Beene, Jacob, (bond)
Beene, W. J., (bond)

Hawes, James
Box 5 File 96 1855-1857
Names in File:
Hawes, Jeff, (guardian)
Hawes, Jefferson
Hawes, James, (minor)

Estate Record Name

Hawes, James (Cont.)
- Hawes, Sampson, Estate
- Estes, Reuben, Judge
- Haws/Hawes

Hays, Hugh A.
- Box 5 File 97 1861
- Names in File:
- Hayes/Hays
- Sale of Land for Division
- Hayes, Amanda A.
- Hayes, Harrate
- Hayes, Elizabeth
- Hayes, William G.
- Hayes, James L. (H.)
- Hayes, George B.
- Hayes, Mary M.
- Hayes, Martha A.
- Berry, Elvanie E., (w/o John)
- Berry, John
- Reed, Sarah M. (w/o B. A.)
- Reed/Reece, B. A.
- Sibert, Henry, (adm)
- Sibert, Henry, (adm.bond)
- Edwards, Joseph, (bond)
- Lackey, William , (bond)
- Estes, Reuben, Judge
- Petty, W. D., (appraiser)
- Mitchell, James, (appraiser)
- Beavers, Allen, (appraiser)
- Beavers, Allen, (witness)
- Petty, Thomas, (witness)
- Hammons, James, (comm)

Hays, James H.
- Box 5 File 98 1861
- Names in File:
- Hayes/Hays
- Hays, Mary J., (widow)
- Hays, Mary J., (guardian)
- Hayes, Charles, (minor)
- Hayes, Henry, (minor)
- Hayes, Emily, (minor)

Estate Record Name

Hays, James H. (Cont.)
- Hayes, Mary, (minor)
- Petty, Thomas, (adm)
- Walden, W. B., (atty)
- Higgins, R. W., (atty)
- Paid in Confederate Money
- Walden J. B., (Higgins Estate)
- Hoge, John K., (guar.ad litem)
- Horton, A. J., Judge

Head, Cornelison, et al
- Box 6 File 1 1911-1918
- Names in File:
- Head, J. C., (father, guardian)
- Head, Cornelison, (minor)
- Head, Alma, (minor)
- Head, Nancy C., (minor)
- Head, Ella, (minor)
- Head, Mary, (mother, dec'd.)
- Croft, W. Y., Estate, (g-father)
- Bradley, W. A., (guar.bond)
- Fant, J. F., (bond)
- Elrod, A. W., (guardian bond)
- Murphy, Alma Head
- Croley, Jas. A., Judge

Heald, Harmon G.
- Box 6 File 2 1859-1865
- Names in File:
- Edwards, J. E., (adm)
- Edwards, Joe, (confederacy bond)
- Cunningham, J. L. (Centre, Al)
- Horton, A. J., Judge
- Heald, Samuel
- Crump, Amanda Heald
- Glass, Joseph A.
- Heald, William G.
- Heald, H. P.
- Heald, William Gregg
- Heald, Samuel G. (Lewis)
- Heald, Andrew Jackson
- Heald, James Ferdinan
- Heald, Henry Patrick

Estate Record Name
Heald, Harmon G. (Cont.)
Glass, Mary Ann Elizabeth
Glass, Joseph, (h/o Mary)
Crump, Amanda, (w/o John)
Crump, John
Heald, Joseph, (minor)
Heald, Joseph D.
Hoge, John K, (guar.ad litem)
Malone, George W., (adm.bond)
Hoge, Joseph, (adm.bond)
Edwards, Joseph, (adm,bond)
Edwards, Jesse, (adm.bond)
Bynum, Williams
King, Elisha, (appraiser)
Humphries, John T., (appraiser)
Crump, R. C., (appraiser)
Franklin, John N., Judge, (1862)
Wesson, King J.
Johnson, M. M.
Box, P. D., (juror)
Houston, Abram B., (juror)
Walker, Jeremiah, (juror)
Berry, A. J., (juror)
Scot, W. P., (juror)
Crump, _. C., (juror)
Heald, Harmon Gregg, (will)
No wife or children
Brothers & Sisters Heirs
Edwards, Joseph E., (adm)
Land, 240 acres, $3500.
Sales of Land for Division
Holcomb, E. J., (pur. Land)
Gibbs, John, (surety note)
Heald, Henry, (surety note)
Cox, G. A., (surety note)
Crump, John W.
Heald, Joseph Delaware
Crump,
Crump, Amanda Heald
Glass, Mary A. Heald
Crump, C. J.

Estate Record Name
Heald, Harmon G. (Cont.)
Notes Due Estate:
Huff, Valentine
Rhea, Lewis
Chaney, John
Sanson, M. & R. H.
Harnett, Jesse & James
Glass, Joseph A.
White, S. M., (JP)
Sale of Personal Property:
Sisk, Luiza, (corn)
Bouldin, Elizabeth, (corn)
Johnson, Martha, (corn)
Hammett, Nancy, (corn)
Lafoy, Mrs., (corn)
Homan, Mrs., (corn)
Tailor, Matilda, (corn)
Phillips, Rebecca, (corn)
Campbell, Ann, (corn)
Gilbreath, Mrs. & Sims, (corn)
Harelson, W. J., (corn)
Cox, T. G. A., (barrell
Crump, R. C., (barrel)
Wauldin, J. B.
Trump, Mandy, (tray)
Glass, Joseph, (shovel & ax)
McKing, P. (set dog-irons)
Hamett, Vincy, (tea kettle)
Crump, R. C., (pot & dishes)
Edwards, Margaret, (sifter)
Heald, H. P., (pails)
Thomas, John, (jars)
Heald, H. P., (oven & skillet)
Hammett, James, (iron)
Battles, J., (tea cups)
Hammett, James,(bowl & pitcher)
McKiney, P. (water bucket)
Powel, Charity, (safe & saddle)
Powel, C., (bed & bedstead)
Engle, Philly, (bed clothes)
Britt, J. B., (bed & bedstead)

Estate Record Name
Heald, Harmon G. (Cont.)
Carter, C. L., (looking glass)
Heald, H. P., (clock)
Glass, J. A., (6-chairs)
Glass, J. A., (sythe & cradle)
Crump, R. C., (lumber)
Heald, H. P., (wheel for gin)
Heald, H. P., (boards)
Burgess, T. J., (wheat box)
Sanson, Mary, (10 bu. Oats)
Humphry, John
Burgess, James, (corn)
Stowers, John, (corn)
Battles, J.
Burgess, T. G., (box)
Crump, Mandy, (chest)
Crump, R. C., (fodder)
Sale Sept. 26, 1862
Franklin, J. N., Judge
Hammett, James, (hoes)
Gray, Allen, (scrap iron)
Heald, W. P., (tools)
Glass, J. A., (plows)
McDaniel, Wm., (plows)
Shuffield, Isham, (plow gears)
Glass, J. A., (saw)
Heald, W. J. (screw auger)
Heald, H. P., (carriage tree)
McDaniel, Wm.,(buggy tire)
McKing, Peter, (plow stock)
Crump, R. C., (lathe & tools)
Shuffield, Isham, (grind rock)
Crump, R. C., (carpenter tools)
Powell, Charity, (feather bed)
McDaniel, Wm., (table)
Crump, R. C., (coffee mill)
Crump, R. C., (jars & pitcher)
Thrasher, Elias, (ox wagon)
Baxter, J. P., (brown bay horse)
Yearan, Newton, (gray horse)
Green, John, (bay horse)

Estate Record Name
Heald, Harmon G. (Cont.)
Glass, J. A., (thrash)
Wesson, J. M., (saddle)
Glass, J. A., (books)
Vinson, E. R., (book)
Wagon, C., (books)
Estes, J. W., (books)
Crump, Manda, (2-cows)
McClendon, J., (corn)
Burgess, James, (corn)
McKing, Peter, (corn)
Maulden, J. B., (corn)
Thompson, J. L., (corn)
Stafford, M., (corn)
Maulden, J. B. (corn)
McDaniel, Wm., (corn)
Morton, Wm. H., (corn)
Nailor, Jerry, (corn)
Britt, J., (corn)
Notes Due Estate:
Thompson, J. L., (note)
Maulden, J. B., (note)
McDaniel, Wm., (note)
Rhea, Lewis
Sansom, Owe M.
Keener, Mark
Rothwell, George
Chany, John
McKing, Peter
Lankford, Simeon
Sansom, Lemuel
King, Elisha
Hammett, Jesse
Glass, Joseph A.
Benett, A.
Hundley, W. L.
Blare, L. C.
Paid:
Stiff, L. M., (adv.)
Standifer, Lemuel J., (witness)
Walden, J. B.,(services)

Estate Record Name

Heald, Harmon G. (Cont.)
Box 6 File 2 1859-1865
Crump, Roland, (witness)
Mckinley, Peter, (witness)
Whitton, S. M.

Heald, Harmon G. (Cont.)
Box 6 File 3 1862
Names in File:
Edwards, Joseph, (adm)
Heald, H. G., (deceased)
McKinney, Peter
Crump, R. C.
Heald, William G.
Heald, Samuel L.
Heald, Andrew J.
Heald, Thomas T.
Glass, Mary A.
Heald, Mary A.
Glass, Joseph A.
Crump, Amanda
Crump, John W,
Carter, C. T., (JP)
Heald, James F.
Heald, Henry

Heard, E. Solen
Box 6 File 4 1922
Names in File:
Heard, John W., (nephew, adm)
Heard, Wallace, (nephew)
Clayton, Mary Ann, (niece)
Robinson, Evaline, (niece)
Dobbs, Leola, (deceased)
Dobbs, Sidney
Dobbs, Erskin
Dobbs, Hoyt
Presley, I. M., (guar.ad litem)
Braswell, Mary, (deceased)
Heard, I. A.,(newphew)
Heard, F. J., (nephew)
Heard, S. E., (nephew)
Heard, Marvin

Estate Record Name

Heard, E. Solen (Cont.)
Heard, Oscar
Heard, C. W.
Heard, G. W.
Nowlin, B. A., (witness)
Wilbanks, W. A., (witness)
Heard, J. W., (adm)
Croley, J. A., Judge

Hearn, John D.
Box 6 File 5 1916
Names in File:
Hearn, M. F., (widow, adm)
Hearn, Mary F., (widow)
Hearn, J. A.
Hearn, J. D.
Hearn, J. O.
Hearn, Lillie
Hearn, J. C.
Hearn, Olin
Hearn, A. W.
Baker, John Martin
Baker, Raymon E.
Baker, Lora, (w/o John H.)
Baker, John H.
Martin, J. R., (bond)
Curtis, J. Valor (bond)
Croley, Jas. A., Judge
McWhorter, Lamar, Dr., (paid)
Oliver Hall Co., (paid)
Baker, Lora, (share paid)
Weathington, J. T., (note pd.)
Justice, G. M., (note paid)
Gaines, J. T., (mortg. paid)
Jones, E. B., (note paid)
Emmet, H. O., (funeral exp.)
Emmett, H. P., (burial exp.)
Griffin, L. H., (acct. paid)

Hemmingway, Josiah
Box 6 File 6 1831-1850
Names in File:
Beeson, Jesse G., (adm)

Estate Record Name
Hemmingway, Josiah (Cont.)
Box 6 File 6 1831-1850
Names in File:
Hemmingway, Wm.
Walden, J. B.
McFarlane, Lettie E.
McFarlane, Wilburn/Milburn
McSpadden, John, (oath)
Swader, Thomas, (witness)
Freeman, D. S.
Merrell, Wm.
Reece, Andrew, (oath)
Beeson, J. G., (JP)
Grant, J. P.
Walden, J. B., (JP)
Mitchell, G. W.
Garrett, H. B.
Freeman, D. T., (land rent)
Mills, W. F., (JP)
Notes Due Estate:
Beeson, Jesse G.
Hilton, F. C.
Thomas, James
McFarlane, L. E.
Wilburn, L. D.
Bryant, Thomas
Brabbin, H. S.
Paid:
Mitchell, Geo. W.
Figures, W. B.
Beeson,
Gravit, J. F.
McSpadden, John
Reece, Andrew
Gibson, J. W.
Swader, Thomas
Walker, W. C.
McFarlane, L. E.
Edwards, Joseph
Freeman, D. C.
Champion, Dr.

Estate Record Name
Hemmingway, Josiah (Cont.)
Majors, G. W.
Estes, R.
Walden, W.
North, Oliver, (agent)
Insolvent Notes Due Estate:
Thomas, James
Hilton, F. C.
Bobbin/Brabbin, H. S.
Bryant, Thos.
Sale of Personal Property:
Beck, Thomas, (plow)
Beck, Daniel, (shaving glass)
Cunningham, Sarah, (skillet, bed)
Davenport, R., (hat & clothing)
Freeman, D. T., (corn & fodder)
Holleman, Wm. K., (cotton shirts)
Hammack, Thos.,(clevis, hat, bed, furniture & other)
Kean, John P., (shovel, plow, etc.)
Crow, Wm., (overcoat & bible)
Clayton, Daniel, Sr., (11-cattle)
Mynatt, Wm., (waist coats)
Reece, Andrew, (coat & other)
Swader, Francis, (saddle, ax, trunk)
Swader, Thos., (plows & table)
Bryant, Allen
Hannah, T., (frame print)
Cain, (box & contents)
Swader, F., (trunk)
Cunningham, (furniture)
Cain, John, (clock & plow)
Reece, Andrew, (hoes)
Swader, Wm., (table)
Cain, John, (grindstone,saddle bags, clevis, plow, & iron wedge)
Cunningham, J., (hat)
Crow, Wm., (oven)
Rawlings & Hooke
Hibbs, Gerome
Box 6 File 7 1851

Estate Record Name

Hibbs, Gerome (Cont.)
Names in File:
Gerime/Geraine/Gerome
Hibbs, Jane, (adm)
Patterson, L. D., (adm)
Lankford, J. M., (bond)
Williams, James, (bond)
Lackey, Samuel, (bond)

Hicks, Acel R.
Box 6 File 8 1898
Names in File:
Hicks, Acel R., (will)
Hicks, Mary J., (wife, exec)
Hicks, A. R. & wife
Hicks, J. L. & Jos. J.
Day, W. D., (witness will)
Hicks, George L., (son)
Hicks, James J., (son)

Hickson, E. P.
Box 6 File 9 1898
Names in File:
Hickson, Frank
Nicholson, E. P., Dr.,(services)
DeShields, (sheriff)

Higgins, Robert W.
Box 6 File 10 1862-1872
Names in File:
Walden, John B., (adm)
Winston, Ed, (bond)
Winston, Edward, (appraiser)
Lankford, R. P., (appraiser)
Estes, R., Judge
Notes Due Estate:
Mays, James F.
Taylor, E. N.
Wade, C. C.
George, C. D.
Brown, William
Higgins & Porter
Blevins, James
Nicholson & Higgins

Estate Record Name

Higgins, Robert W. (Cont.)
Petty, Thomas
Smith, Jane
Pemberton, R.
Smith, Sarah Jane
Morgan, John
Otwell, W. H.
Armstrong, James
Williams, John E.
Higgins, J. W.
Sivone, J. W.
Bennett, A. G.
Poe, J. C.
Findley vs: Morgan
Malone vs: Haralson
Edwards, J.
Chaney, J.
Riggs, W. M.
Malone, G. W.
Ryan, Wm.
Burris, Samuel
Thomson, J. L.
Bibb, J. M.
Berry, Simon
Baldwin, J.
Walker, P. J.
Winston, J. G.

Hill, E. J., et al
Box 6 File 11 1905-1909
Names in File:
Sales of Land for Division
Hill, E. J.
Hill, Henry H.
Hill, James T.
Hill, Lucinda
Taffanstedt, Isabelle
Hill, E. J. vs: Shelley, Talley, et al
Shelley, Talley
Wright, Mary
Shelley, Georgia L.
Shelley, Frank

Estate Record Name

Hill, E. J., et al (Cont.)
- Shelley, Isabelle
- Shelley, Mattie J.
- Shelley, Robert
- Simpson, S. B., (deposition)
- Pendergrass, A. R., (deposition)
- Collins, O. H.,(took deposition)
- Davis, John A., (atty)
- Traffanstedt, W. J., (bought land)
- Hill, Henry H.,(guardian)
- Hill, James T., (minor)
- Shelley, W. T.
- Shelley, Georgia Lue

Hill, Jesse
- Box 6 File 12 1844
- Names in File:
- Hill, Jesse, Mrs., (wife)
- Hawkins, Elijah, (oath)
- Beeson & Phillips
- Banks vs: Hill, (paid)
- Kelley, Lewis, (paid)
- Bell, S. F., (paid)
- Murphy, Robert, (paid)
- Cunningham, Jesse, (JP)
- Naylor, Polydore, (paid)
- Bynum, William, (paid)
- Kelly, Isaac M.
- Mitchell, G. W., (JP)
- Winston, John G., (acct.paid)
- Reese, Martin, (witness)
- Bouldin, Elijah, (JP)
- George, C. D., (medicine)
- Monroe, W.
- Carter, A. W., (medicine)
- Buntor, Willis, (witness)

Hill, John R.
- Box 6 File 13 1855
- Names in File:
- Hill, John R., (physician)
- Snodgrass, Alex, (adm)
- Snodgrass, Alex, (guardian)

Estate Record Name

Hill, John R. (Cont.)
- Snodgrass, Susan Jane, (minor)
- Hill, Susan Jane
- Hill, Camelia, (minor)
- Snodgrass, Alexander, guar.)
- Cunningham, John, (bond)
- Poe, James C., (bond)
- Higgins, R. W., (atty)
- Laramore, V. C., (bond)
- Hammack, Thomas, (bond)
- **Debts Due Hill & Nicholson:**
- Blanton, Whit
- Jett, Daniel
- Chitwood, Mithias
- Winston, John G.
- Ryan, Samuel M.
- Chitwood, Richard
- Edmondson, Thomas
- Lewis, John
- Hulgan, J.
- George, Thos. H.
- Foster, John
- Dobbs, Elijah
- Jack, Jefferson
- Shook, A. J.
- McFarlane, Bryan
- Wilkes, R. W.
- McPherson, George
- Poe, James C.
- Hoge, John K.
- Roberts, Isam
- Jett, Joseph
- Lusk, Robert M.
- Findley, William
- Busby, James
- Baxter, Marion
- Hawkins, Henry
- Thomas, E. B.
- Horton, Dicy
- Frazer, Robert
- Bogle, J. C.

Estate Record Name
Hill, John R. (Cont.)
Chitwood, William
Harris, Larkin
Adkinson, John
Haralson, A. J.
Haralson, W. J.
McPherson, Isaac
Cowart,
Nelson, Mrs., (s-i-l)
Stewart, John
Phillips, Jesse
Tucker, James
Cochran, Pinkney
Norton, James
Nelson, William
McCraw, Jesse
Favor, John
Swafford, Moses
Hammonds, Wm. H.
Jack, Allen
Wilson, William
Clayton, Thomas
Templeton, Levi
Shelton, John
Hamlin, John
Starnes, John
Edwards, Joseph
Garrett, Jesse
Warren, Henry
Ford, Wm.
King, Edelia
Walden, Jno. B.
Ward, Andrew
Bennett, Wm. H.
May, W. H.
Crossly, Scot
Fandren, Miss
Isbell, William
McCurdy, M.
Williams,
Easley, Solomon

Estate Record Name
Hill, John R. (Cont.)
Easley, Jesse
Nelson, Martha
Clayton, John
Hamilton, Alfred
Beasley, Wm.
Blackburn, John
Coggins, Wesley
Brock, Hiram
Ward, John D.
Roberts, James
Murphy, Mardis
Fisher, C.P.S.
Funderburk, C. C.
Pressly, H. M.
Graves, James
Patterson, L. D.
Baxter, James, Sr.
Clayton, Sampson
Collins, Robt.
Burten, Francis
Smith, Eliza
Gasaway, Robert
Sims, W. J.
Hill, James
Reeves, Hugh
Callahan, John
Burk,
Bryant, C. C.
Clark, Perry
Fricks, Harrison
McGraw, Jesse
Newton, Elijah
Mays, Henry
Majors, Samuel
Phillips, Benj.
Dutton, Mrs.
Privett, Frank
Malone, George M.
Nicholson, James A.
Brice, John M.

Estate Record Name
Hill, John R. (Cont.)
Nicholson, Wm. R.
Collins, Jane
Notes Due Estate:
Swaffer, Moses
Chasteen, Alex
Light, Wiley
Baxter, Marion
Withrow, Rich, Jr.
Withrow, Rich, Sr.
McPherson, Isaac
Rogers, Rees
Baker, James R.
Baxter, J. W.
Stone, Joel
Clayton, Wm. H.
Bryant, Preston
Collins, Charles
Norton, Roswell
Hoges, Joseph
Thurman, S.
Cunningham, Lafayette
Burt, Elijah
Bruce, J. M.
McPherson, Geo.
McCurdy, Sam
Hulgan, R. M.
Blanton, White
Poe, James C.
Busbee, James
Hays, John
Baxter, James, Sr.
Baxter, Jesse, Sr.
Campbell, J. W.
Baxter, Jesse, Jr.
Baxter, Marion
Stafford, Wm. R.
Fields, Elizabeth
Busbee, Durrell
Patterson, John
Accounts Due Estate:

Estate Record Name
Hill, John R. (Cont.)
Cagle, Valentine
Mackey, John
Sample, Jesse
Chastain, Jesse
Findley, John B.
Walden, John B.
Musgrove, James
Chastain, John
Collins, John L.
McPherson, James
McPherson, Mary E.
Bogle, Joseph C.
Frazer, Dorcas
Callahan, Wm. H.
Haws, Jeff
Haws, James
Estes, Wm. N.
Mays, James F.
Baker, James
Chitwood, Wm.
Hill, James
Lewis, Burrell
Carroll, Peter
Rogers, Reece
Little, Thomas
Norton, Gares
Davis, Thomas
Walker, Peter J.
Grady, A. E.
Tucker, James
Hill, John R., (practicing physician)
Clayton, Sampson
Bryant, Wm.
Seamone, Saml.
McCurdy, Saml. R.,
Burkeat, Mr.
Bryant, Columbus
Busbee, John
Burk, James
Clark, Perry

Estate Record Name
Hill, John R. (Cont.)
Account Due Estate:
Dobbs, Silas
Fields, Harrison
Mays, Stephen
Worthington, Mr.
Brown, Edward H.
Talley, H. H.
Hamby, E. H.
Little, John
Isbell, John
Walls, Bundy
Jack, Pleasant
Rice, Joseph
Lackey, Isaac
Coggin, Wesley
Porter, C. C.
Privett, Frank
Jett, Railess
McPherson, Richard
May, W. H.
Hill, James
McCampbell, John
Reaves, Hugh
Dobbs, David
Chitwood, Matilda
Winston, John G.
Bacon, Washington
Estes, R.
Callahan, John
Collections:
Clayton, W. H.
Norton,
Cunningham, E. L.
Burt, Elijah
Hays, James
Baxter, James
Baxter, Willis
Baxter, Marion
Field, E. L.
Patterson, John

Estate Record Name
Hill, John R. (Cont.)
Cagle, V.
Withrow, Jane
Musgrove, Jason
McPherson, Mary E.
Bogle, Jos. C.
Haws, Jeff
Estes, W. N.
Mays, Jas. F.
Chitwood, Wm.
Carroll, Pete
Rogers, Rees
Davis, Thos.
Walker, P. J.
Stone, Joel
Tucker, Jas.
Hamby, P.
Light, Wiley
Chitwood, M.
Winston, J. G.
Little, Thos.
Bacon, W.
Burt, James
Accounts & Notes:
Etters, H. R.
Nelson, Hill
Jack, Thos. J.
Baker, Asa
Wilks, R. W.
Baptist Church
Baxter, Jas.
Stone, J. B.
Stephens, Slayton
Baxter, Willis
Beeson & Phillips
Hoge, J. K. & J. M.
Nicholson, J. E.
Majors, A. W. & Son
Haralson, W. J.
Malone, G. W.
Pendergrass, Alex

Estate Record Name
Hill, John R. (Cont.)
Box 6 File 13 1855
May, W. H.
Estes, Mary/May
Hays, J. H.
Nicholson, J. W.
Hill & Nicholson Accts:
Jett, David
Newkirk, Henry
Thomas, E. B.
Horton, Dicy
Harris, Larkin
Dobbs, E.
Poe, J. C.
McFarland, Byron
Murphy, Mardy
Easley, Sol
Hamilton, Al
Hill, Joseph
Box 6 File 14 1910
Names in File:
Hill. C. A., Mrs., (widow)
Exemption before Admin.
No Minor Children
Durham, W. O.
Love, G. W.
Russell, H. C., (JP)
Fossett, Seaborn
Hill, William J.
Box 6 File 15 1903-1905
Names in File:
Sale of Land for Division
Hill, E. J., (adm)
Hill, Josie, (minor)
Tribble, David, (minor)
Tribble, Wm., (minor)
Tribble, Alma, (minor)
Hill, Luther
Trible, W. W.
Presley, I. M, (guar.ad litem)
Denton, Jennie, (w/o M. J.)

Estate Record Name
Hill, William J. (Cont.)
Denton, M J.
Pruett, Hattie, (w/o J. R.)
Pruett, J. R.
Crane, Fannie, (w/o Dock)
Crane, Dock W.
Wolf, Alice, (w/o Aloy)
Wolf, S. A., (Aloy)
Campbell, H. B., (guar.ad litem)
McCallan, J. M., (bond)
Simpson, S. B., (bond)
Bush, G. V., (bond)
Davis & Haralson
Davis, John A.
Hill, E. J., (purchased land)
Brown, Thos. B., (deposition)
Williams, G. B., (deposition)
Pruett, H. A.
Prewitt/Pruett
Wolf, Alice M.
Hill, J. A.
Crane, Fannie A.
Crane, D. W.
Fort Payne Journal, (notices)
Smith, Thomas H., (editor)
Graves, H. L., (tax coll.1901-4)
Sale of Personal Property:
Swader, Francis, (saddle & ax)
Cunningham, John, (ax, handsaw)
Reece, Andrew, (ax & hoe)
Cunningham, Sarah, (bucket)
Cain, John, (shovel & bucket)
Davenport, R., (hat)
Swader, T., (set of gears)
Cain, John, (carpenter tools)
Beck, T., (plow)
Swader, Wm., (table)
Mynatt, Wm.
Cain, John, (grindstone)
Crow, Wm., (overcoat & Bible)
Beck, D., (shaving glass)

Estate Record Name
Hill, William J. (Cont.)
Sale of Mule $50. & Land $500.
Rent from Farm 1901-1904
Hixon, James
Box 6 File 16 1893-1895
Names in File: File 1 of 2
Hixon, Nancy E., (widow)
Hixon, N. E.,
Hixon, Oscar, (heir)
Hixon, Ada/Ider, (minor)
Hixon, Eugene, (minor)
Hixon, Lula, (minor)
Hixon, Stella, (minor)
Hixon, Emanuel, (minor)
Hixon, Minnie, (minor)
Hixon, Franklin, (minor)
Hixon, Venice, (minor)
Hixon, Oscar, (guardian)
Fuller, W. T., (guar.ad litem)
DeShields, J. G., (guar.ad litem)
Culberson, C. Y., (adm)
Hixon, N. E., Mrs., Estate
Hixon, N.E. vs:Wells, Myron H.
Value for Use of Property
Davis & Harrison, (atty)
Wells, Myron H.
DeShields, J. G., (sheriff)
Nicholson, E. P., (M. D.)
Pension Check
Winston, J. W., (atty)
Acct. Due Estate:
Parish, R. W., (mortgage)
Drake, J. C., (mortgage)
Wells, Marion/Myron, (claim)
Bell, C. N., (appraiser)
Lamar, C. T., (appraiser)
Culberson, Chas., (JP)
Paid:
Howard, J. M. (tax coll. 1896)
Nicholson, E. P., (med ser.)
Dean, A. C., (burial expense)

Estate Record Name
Hixon, James (Cont.)
Moore, Lake, (legal ser.)
Burkhart, J. B., (paid)
Hixon, Nancy, (house-Valley Head)
Jennings, H. C., (attest)
Hixon, Oscar, (board/minors)
School Books for minors
Garrett, W. W., (attest)
Young, W. H., (receipts)
Holleman, Ben, (attest)
Davenport, E. C. & Co.
Bray, C.,(summons)
Hixson, James
Box 6 File 17 1897-1899
Names in File: File 2 of 2
Hixon/Hixson
Hixon, Ada, (minor)
Hixon, Eugene, (minor)
Hixon, Lula, (minor)
Hixon, Stella, (minor)
Hixon, Emmanual, (minor)
Hixon, Minnie, (minor)
Hixon, Franklin, (minor)
Hixon, Venice, (minor)
Hixon, Oscar
Payne, John L., (guar.ad litem)
DeShields, J. G., (guar.ad litem)
Hixon, Oscar, (board/minors)
Hixon, Oscar vs: Minors
Frazier, Robert W., (sheriff)
Hixson, James, (US soldier)
(Co. A, 10th Tn. Vol. Cav.)
Russell, W. W., Gen. Mdse.
The Fort Payne Journal
Smith, Thom. H, (notices)
Smith & Rogers Gen. Mdse.
Chadwick, Lula
Chadwick, D. P.
Reed, W. D., (tax coll.1896-9)
Davis & Haralson
Nicholson, E. P., (affidavit)

Estate Record Name

Hixson, James (Cont.)
- Davenport, E. C., (paid)
- Winston, J. N.
- Waddle, B. B.
- Hixon, Ader
- Hixon, George
- Jennings, H. C., (NP)
- Cochran, Earl, (editor)
- Fort Payne Bank
- McKowan, James
- Wright, J. W.
- Wells, M. H.
- Goldston, W. H., (witness)
- Webb, D. H. , (witness)
- Bell, C. M., (witness)
- Jennings, H. C., (witness)
- Parish, R. W.
- Parish, M. L.
- Howell, W. N., (witness)
- Guest, R. J., (paid)
- Killian, E. S., (paid)
- Baxter, L. C., Mrs. (2-hats, paid)
- Grossean, Ernest
- Alexander, Judith, Miss, (paid)
- Hixon, Oscar, (support of minors)
- Lankford, Wm. C., (land rent)
- Frazier, R. W., (guardian)
- Hixon, N. E. (receipts)
- Hixon, Venice, (expenses)
- Baxter, Lula C.
- Dobbs, S. R.
- Blackwell, Mrs.
- DeShields, J. F.
- Davenport & Co. E. G.?

Hixson, Nancy E., (N. E.)
- Box 6 File 18 1898
- Names in File:
- Hixon, N. E., (widow of James)
- Hixon, James, (deceased)
- Hixon, Minnie
- Hixon, Frank

Estate Record Name

Hixson, Nancy E., (N. E.) (Cont.)
- Hixon, Venice
- Hixon, Emanuel
- Hixon, Oscar
- Hixon, John D.
- Hixon, Ada
- Chadwick, Lula
- Chadwick, Adolphus
- Howell, Martha L., (w/o N.)
- Howell, Nell
- Hixon, Alanzo
- Walton, Janice/Jennie
- Walton, Raymond, (h/o J.)
- Hixon, Eugene
- Hixon, Stella
- Hixon, N. E.
- Culberson, C. Y., (adm)
- Davenport, E. T., (bond)
- McKown, J. H., (bond)
- Price, R. S., (JP)
- Wright, J. W., (JP)
- Lowry, G., (commissioner)
- Campbell, H. B., (guar.ad litem)
- Wright, J. W., (deposition)
- Price, R. S., (deposition)
- Hixon, Oscar, (citation)
- Frazier, R. W., (sheriff)
- Davis & Haralson, (atty)
- Cook, W. C. D., Judge
- Turner, John T., (purch.land)

Hixson, Oscar
- Box 6 File 19 1897-1898
- Names in File:
- Sale of Land for Division
- Hixon, Alanzo
- Hixon, James, Estate
- Hixon, N. E., Estate
- Hixon, John D.
- Hixon, Ada
- Chadwick, Lula
- Chadwick, Adolphus

Estate Record Name
Hixson, Oscar (Cont.)
Howell, Martha
Howell, Nell
Hixon, Eugene
Hixon, Stella
Hixon, Minnie
Hixon, Frank
Hixon, Venice
Hixon, Emanuel
Hixon, Oscar vs: Hixon heirs
Frazier, R. W., (sheriff)
Lankford, W. C.
Davenport, J. G., (witness)
Lowry, Newt, (witness)
Larmore, C. T., (witness)
Campbell, A. L., (witness)
Barnard, Frank, (witness)
Fuller, W. T.
Campbell, Isaac, (witness)
Carroll, T. T., (witness)
Hixon Land, 240 acres,
Carmichal, G. P., (witness)
Carroll, T. T., (bid on land)
(243 acres,Wills Creek-$675)
McGuffey, James M.
(purchased land-$810.)
Carroll, Taylor, (land joins)
Nix, Ella G.,Mrs., (purch.land)
Cochran, Earl, (commissioner)
Cochran, L. L. (atty)
Blake & Taylor Lot
Wells, Myron, (land & lot)
Winston, J. N., Dr., (land)
Hodge, Jennie Peek
Box 6 File 20 1888
Names in File:
Peck/Peek
Peek, Jennie, (minor)
Peek, James H., (father)
Peek, James H., (guardian)
Wilson, Benj., Estate

Estate Record Name
Hodge, Jennie Peek (Cont.)
Hodge, Jennie Peek
Pope, T. J., (guar.bond)
Mitchell, H. C.,(guar.bond)
Petty, W. D.,(attest)
Denton, S. D., (witness)
Cochran, L. L., Judge
Hodgens, J. P. (Hodges)
Box 6 File 21 1909
Names in File:
Hodges/Hodgens
Hodgens, J. P., Estate
Hodges, Nora Mae, (minor)
Hodges, Jasper C., (minor)
Hodges, Campbell I., (minor)
Hodgens, T. V.,(father/guardian)
Hodgens, T. V., (guar.bond)
Abney, W. H., (bond)
Mann, T. L., (bond)
Croley, Jas. A., Judge
Hodges, Thomas
Hodges, L. J., Mrs.
Box 6 File 22 1908-1916
Names in File:
Sale of Land for Division
Hodges, L. M., Mrs. (petition)
Hodges, Henry,(minor)
Hodges, Robert, (minor)
Morgan, Eula, (minor)
Morgan, Wesley, (h/o Eula)
Slone, S. B., (guardian ad litem)
Isbell & Scott, (atty)
Hodges vs: Brannon & Mosley
Campbell, H. B., (clerk)
Isbell & Presley, (atty)
DeShields, J. G., (deposition)
Downs, T. L, (deposition)
Berry, Minnie, (took deposition)
Mosley, Walter
Brannon, J. A., (bought land)
Holcomb, Jeremiah

Estate Record Name

Holcomb, Jeremiah
Box 6 File 23 1852-1874
Names in File:
Holcomb, Emily, (widow, adm)
Box, P. D., (adm)
Box, Sarah, (w/o P. D.)
Horton, Ann E, (w/o P. J.)
Horton, Perrin J.
Taylor, Tabitha M, (w/o D.G.C.)
Taylor, Duncan G. C.
Yeagin, Mary Holcomb, (w/o J.)
Yeagin, Jasper
Horton, Clarissa, (w/o G. C.)
Horton, Gilbert C.
Holcomb, John
Holcomb, John, (minor)
Moore, (guardian)
Taylor, Jeremiah
Horton, Betsy
Horton, P.
Box, Patrick, A., (bond)
Holcombe, Jeremiah, (bond)
Edwards, Jesse, (bond)
Box, Patrick A., (JP)
Crump, Bethel, (bond)
Horton, A. J., Judge
Holcomb, Emily, (bond)
Box, P. D., (bond, $8000.)
Patterson, John M., (bond)
Taylor, D. G. C., (bond)
Walker, Jeremiah, (bond)
Estes, Reuben, Judge
Delk, David, Petitioner
Horton, A. J., Judge
Chitwood, R., (Register)
Mosley, M.
Griffin, Wm.,(sheriff)
Thompson, J. T., (dep.sheriff)
Yeargen/Yeargin
Crump, Bethel, (witness)
Edwards, Jesse, (witness)

Estate Record Name

Holcomb, Jeremiah (Cont.)
McBryer, H. P., (comm)
Edwards, Jeptha, (witness)
Walden, J. B., (atty/plaintiff)
Paid:
Morgan, Thomas
Edwards, Jeptha
Yeargin, Jasper
McBryar, H. P.
Box, P. D.
Hill & Co., O. P.
Williams, Thomas R.
Cain & Edwards
Hollingsworth, H. W. P
Walden, J. B.
Box, R. D.
Snider, C.
Reece, John
Penn, N. L.
Franklin, J. N.
Wilson, James
Parsons, J.
Smith, J. S. D.
Barnes, M.
Yeargin, Joseph
Horton, P. J.
Lankford, Silas
Barnes, Pleasant
Horton, A. J., (court cost)
Bennett, John
Barnes, T. J.
Crump,
Burgess, T. J.
Crump, B.
Receipts:
Stout, J.
Southerland, W.
Sampley, W.
Gasgan, James
Moony, W. H.
Clayton, C., Sr.

Estate Record Name
Holcomb, Jeremiah (Cont.)
Carden, J. W.
Mason, Peter
Moore, M.
Roberts, R.
Burt, James
Davis, W. G.
Rogers, R.
Rawlings, John
King, J. H.
Rawlings, W.
Jones, Isaac
Bryant, Polly
Hunter, Casper
Howell,
Bryant, W.
Garrett, Blont
Griffin, Anna
Estes, R.
Mathona, Wm.
Carter, A.
Rogers, Reece
Dutton, Sam'l.
Hammack, Willoughby
Bilsher, John
Moore, Jas.
Garrett, Isher
Killian, O.
Beeson, J. G.
Buson/Beeson
Killian, Elias
Brandon, H. H.
King, Richard
Hammack, W. N.
Busbee, Jas.
Ward, John
Tate, M. (W.)
Stout, J. J.
Little, W.
Little, L.
Garrett, H. W. B.

Estate Record Name
Holcomb, Jeremiah (Cont.)
Garrett, Thomas, Estate
Green, A. B. (adm. Garrett Estate)
Accounts Due Estate:
Wilson, Joseph
Tabor, John
Edwards, Jesse
Sitz, John
Henry, J. B.
White, Wm.
Byers, A.
Woodward, E. L.
Horton, A. B.
Wilson, Jesse
Horton, P. Z.
Rucks, J. F.
White, John C.
Crump, Bethel
Penn, N. S.
Hill, O. R.
Stiff, L. M.
Williams, R. D. R.
Williams, Thomas R.
Lucy, W. E.
Gilbreath, G.
Walker, J. W.
Morgan, T. J.
Wilson, James
Penn, James
Rees, James
Cobb, P. G.
Yeargin, J. B.
Walker, Jeremiah
Flecher, W. S.
Patterson, D. U.
Setze, James
Peak, Anna
Peak, Rhoda
Box, P. D., (adm)
Cooper, Ann
Franklin, J. N.,(sheriff)

Estate Record Name
Holcomb, Jeremiah (Cont.)
Alex, Slave
Alcy, Slave
Paid:
Woodward, E. L.
Wilson, Joseph
Taylor, Allen
Williams, R.
Williams, Thomas R.
Morgan, Thos. J,
Penn, James,(medicine)
Cobb, P. G.
Walker, Jeremiah
Lucy, W. E. & Co.
Silbert, H. & Co.
Penn, N. S.
Beeson, W. B., (JP)
Rees, John (paid)
Lity, John, (paid)
Tabor, John, (paid)
Vicent, W. A., (paid)
Rink, John F., (paid)
Delk, David vs: Adm & Heirs
Dunlap, R. A., (atty)
Lay, William
Bradford, Tipten
Horton, A. J.
Clayton, Sol S., (register)
Notes & Accounts:
Garrett & Stewart Accts.
Small, H. W.
Stewart, John
Webb, E. B.
Small, Jesse
Smiley, Wm. D.
Crawford & Anderson Accts.
Avans, Isaac
Dutton, Sam'l.
Webb, E. B.
Garrett, Hub
Reece, Andrew

Estate Record Name
Holcomb, Jeremiah (Cont.)
Box 6 File 23 1852-1874
Garrett, Jesse
Lankford, R. E.
Notes:
Hanson, Geo.
Harben, James
Privett, James C.
Samply, W. N.
Griffin, Elizabeth
Hamison, H. C.
Bryant, W.
Hubbs, Jeremiah
Smith, W. L.
Lyon, Sol. Thos.
Stout, Z.
Southerland, W.
Sampley, W.
Gasgen, James
Hammock, Thos.
Paid:
Gray, Allen
Rees, Thomas
White, William
Cannon, L. W.
Watson, A. W.
Burgess, T. J.,(note)
Lankford, J. M. (witness)
Avery, Allen, (note)
Lankford, John M., (note)
Burgess, T. J., (claim)
Horton, Ann E., (w/o P. J.)
Lay, William, (note)
Rook, John, (note)
Lay, Chas. W., (witness)
Cooper, Elim, (witness)
Walker, Jeremiah, (JP)
Estes, R., Judge
Yeargin, Jasper, (bought land)
Horton, P. J., (bought Alcy)
Sibert, John, (bought wagon)

Estate Record Name

Holdridge, George M.
Box 6 File 24 1910-1925
Names in File:
Homestead Exemption
Holdridge, Martha J., (widow)
Holdridge, R. W., (son)
Holdridge, J. C., (son)
Holdridge, Mildred, (minor)
Holdridge, Neva, (minor)
Minor children of J. C.
Holdridge, J. C., Mrs.
Kimsey, G. W., (appraiser)
Pruett, P. D., (appraiser)
Kidd, Louis W.
Hayes, W. C., (JP)
Bailey & Curtis, (atty)
Malone, G. L., Judge

Holland, Hugh
Box 6 File 25 1854-1859
Names in File:
Blevins, Jonathan, (adm.)
Sutton, LeRoy, (JP)
Dade County, GA.
Holland, Daniel, (son)
Holland, Eliza
Cuzzort, Eliza Holland
Holland, Sarah Jane
Stephens, Sarah Jane Holland
Stephens, James, (h/o Sarah)
Holland, Nancy
Holland, Ruth
Holland, Ephraim
Holland, James
Cuzzort, David, (h/o Elizabeth)
Cuzzort, Elizabeth
Lindsay, H., Dr.
Higgins, R. W.
Adkins, Moris
Tinker, Benjamin, (witness)
Countess, Newnan
West, Isaac G.

Estate Record Name

Holland, Hugh (Cont.)
O'Neal, James
Blevins, Gaines, (witness)
Holland, Ephraim, (bought land)
40 acres - $312.
Tinker, Benj., (surety on note)
Sale of Personal Property:
Holland, Daniel, (2-calves)
Blevins, James, (yoke of steers)
Adkins, Washington
Blevins, David
Cuzzant, David
Stephens, Sarah
Holland, James
Thomas, Alex
West, J. L.
Steel, John
O'Neal, Cicero
Cuzzort,
Cuzzort, Eliza
Brock, W. E.
Highfield, John

Holland, John
Box 6 File 26 1852-1853
Names in File:
Holland, W. F., (adm)
Holland, William F., (bond)
Crow, John, (bond)
Crow, Isaac, (bond)
Beene, Jacob, (JP)
Hamman, John V., (appraiser)
Smith, Benjamin, (appraiser)
McCandless, Wm., (appraiser)
Estes, R., Judge
Sale of Personal Property:
Crow, Mary, (sorrell horse)
Crow, Mary, (sorrell mare)
Crow, Mary, (corn)
Crow, James, (corn)
Henagar, Z. W., (yoke/steers)
Hamman, John, (yearling)

Estate Record Name
Holland, John (Cont.)
Johnson, Richmond,(sow & pigs)
McCandless, Wm., (cart)
Crow, Mary, (furniture, etc.)
Holloway, W. M.
Box 6 File 27 1898-1899
Names in File:
Holloway, Florence, (widow)
Widow's Exemption
Holloway, Wesley, (minor)
Holloway, Ollie, (minor)
Holloway, Ethel, (minor)
Holloway, Florence, (mother)
Davis, Joe L., (appraiser)
Davis, Peter P., (appraiser)
Davis, John A., (NP)
Chitwood, Richard, (JP)
Holmes, Owen T.
Box 6 File 28 1904
Names in File:
Hall, Margaret Holmes, (adm)
Hall, Margaret H., (sole heir)
Hall, Oliver L. (bond)
Cox, J. C., (NP)
Ala. Coal & Iron Stock, Par $100.
(19,992 sh., val. $250.)
Horton, Herbert H.
Box 6 File 29 1914
Names in File:
Horton, A. C., (adm, bond)
Horton, Della
Isbell, John B., (bond)
Scott, Chas. J., (bond)
Horton, William P., Estate
Horton, J. B., Administrator
Box 6 File 30 1879-1882
Names in File:
Horton, Malinda, (widow)
Horton, Jesse B., (adm)
Horton, Jennie B. (I.), (minor)
Horton, Thomas B., (minor)

Estate Record Name
Horton, William P., Estate (Cont.)
Horton, Richard Amanda,(minor)
Horton, Emanuel
Payne, A. L., (guar.ad litem)
Campbell, A. L., (witness)
Payne, A. L., (witness)
Haralson, H. C., (deposition)
Brandon, P. A., (deposition)
Webb, G. W., (comm.)
Hughes, David D., (bond)
Malone, R. J., (bond)
Hoge, J. K., (appraiser)
Estes, John R., (appraiser)
Majors, Sam'l., (appraiser)
Horton, J. B., (father of W.P.)
Smith, Thos. H., (purch.land)
Petty, W., (land borders)
Ward, Sam, (land borders)
Horton, Richard, Estate
Haralson, H. C., (witness)
Brandon, P. A., (witness)
Phillips, A., (witness)
Dobbs, L. A., (atty)
Horton, W. P., Estate
Huff, George M., (purch.land)
Patrick, J. M., (purch.land)
Attway, S. K., (comm.)
Cochran, L. L., Judge
Pope, W. E., (guar.ad litem)
Horton, Malinda I. C.
Petty, Jesse W.
Franklin, J. N., Judge
Chitwood, Jennie Horton
Chitwood, Reuben
Campbell, H. B., (guar.ad litem)
Hill, George, (rented land)
Notes & Accounts Due Estate:
Huff, G. M.
Lyons, J. H.
Hibbs, C. G.
Moore, T.

Estate Record Name

Horton, William P., Estate (Cont.)
Kuykendall, John
Oliver, Henry
Crump, Elbert
Haralson, H. C.
Mills, W. K.
Roberts, L. F.
McClenon, C. P.
Huff, G. M. & Petty, J. M.
Stafford, J. A.
Simpson, John
Hoge, John K.
Chitwood, Richard
County Claims
Keener, P.
Taylor, J. F.
Kendall, John
Carr, Joe
Dobbs, Elijah
McNann, Jesse
McNutt, Millard
McNann, William
Norton, J.
Payne, Warren
Petty, J. M.
Roberts, William
Robertson, David
Russell, Andy
Simpson, James
Slone, Bill
Tyner, S. J.
Taylor, H. S.
Williams, Charley
Hooper, S.
Fite, B. B.
Paid:
Petty, T. W., (work on farm)
Wesson, J. W., (paid)
Smith, Thos. S., (paid)
Davis, John A., (guar.ad litem)
Tate, A. S., (paid)

Estate Record Name

Horton, William P. Estate (Cont.)
Horton, J. B., Administrator
Box 6 File 30 1879-1882
Dobbs, A. L., (paid)
Steel, W. A., (tax coll 1888)
Davis, R. C., (tax coll. 1887)
Patrick, J. W., (tax 1880)
Cunningham, George, (paid)
Stewart, S. W., (paid)
Johnson, J. R., (witness)
Sale of Personal Property:
Watts, Moses, (corn)
Roden, John, (corn)
Walker, Wm., (corn)
Oliver, Henry, (corn)
Hawkins, Jacob, (corn)
Davis, H. G., (cow,calf & bull)
Thomas, M., (sything cradle)
Horton, John, (shears)
Horton, J., (drawing knife, axe)
Davis, A.G., double shovel plow)
Jett, D. P., (mule)
Hammack, Ranson
Payne, Asa, (2 shoats)
Isbell, Matt, (2-shoats)
Beeson, J., (plow, clevis)
Pendergrss, Jas., (2-shoats)
Stafford, W. P., (2-shoats)
Isbell, Floyd, (2-shoats)
Horton, J. B., (wagon)
Horton, J. B., (harness)
Beeson, Floyd, (shoat)
Baxter, F. M., (clerk)
Walden, J. D., (clerk)
Sale, May 13, 1879
Horton, Malinda, (adm)
Horton, Jesse B.
Box 6 File 31 1910
Names in File:
Horton, Eliza J., (widow)
Wife & Children named in will

Estate Record Name
Horton, Jesse B. (Cont.)
Horton, Andrew C.,(son)
Davis, Mary J.
Stafford, Rosa S.
Baxter, Napper S.
Chitwood, Jennie Bell, (g-c)
Horton, Thomas B., (g-child)
McGullion, Richard Amanda
Chitwood, Lillie, (g-child)
Bott, Eliza J, (g-child)
Horton, Andrew B., (adm)
Collins, J. M., (witness/will)
Ryan, L. E., (witness)
Collins, O. H., (witness)
Collins, J. W., (J. M.)
Debts Due Estate:
Mitchell, W. J.
Sparks, Butler
Chitwood, Green & Lillie
Cook, L. E.
Chitwood, R. H.
McGullion, E. L.
Durham, J. M.
Miller, E. W., & J. W.
Miller, W. G.
Horton, D. D.
Frazier, P. J.
Horton, H . H.
Estes, John, (appraiser)
Killian, John, (appraiser)
Ryan, Luther, (appraiser)
Slone, Jesse, (land borders)
Malone, Benj.,(land borders)
Majors, Widow, (land borders)
Horton, Malinda J. C.
Box 6 File 32 1881-1882
Names in File:
Horton, Jennie J., (minor)
Chitwood, Jennie Horton
Horton, Thomas B., (minor)
Horton, Richard A., (minor)

Estate Record Name
Horton, Malinda J. C. (Cont.)
Pope, W. W., (guar.ad litem)
Horton, Jesse B., (adm)
Brandon, Phillip A., (witness)
Haralson, Henry C., (witness)
Dobbs, L. A., (atty)
Payne, A. F., (guar.ad litem)
Howard, Milford W., (comm)
Petty, J. M., (adm.)
(brother of Malinda)
Williams, D. C., (appraiser)
Collins, N. S., (appraiser)
Jacoway, Thomas R., (appraiser)
Tiner, J. C., (JP)
Williams, Daniel L., (pur.land)
DeShields, J. G., (sheriff)
Workman, G. D., (dep.sheriff)
Paid:
Vann, A. J., (medical ser.)
Tiner, Jas. C., (JP)
Huff, G. M., (fence repair on farm)
Petty, W. D., (JP)
Petty, James M.
Howard, M. W.
Campbell, A. L.
Stephenson, J. M., (made coffin)
Tiner, J. C., (JP)
Jacoway, Thomas R., (note)
Gilbert, R. F.
Erwin, Sam, (wheat)
Watts, L. B., (JP)
Baxter, J. R., (attest)
McCurdy, John A.
Attaway, S. K.
Watson, G. M., (blacksmith)
Johnson, J. R., (JP)
Camp, Grover & Co.,(note)
Allman, Z., (agent)
Majors, Saml., (appraiser)
Malone, R. J., (adm.)
Malone, Geo. W., Estate

Estate Record Name

Horton, Malinda J. C. (Cont.)

Busbee, A. J.
Dobbs, L. W.
Clayton, R. R.
Bennett, A. G., (JP)
Kean, S. K.
Killian, Geo. W., (JP)
Collins, James H.
Bennett, G. G., (med.services)
Poe, W. R., (NP)
Ferguson, W. L.,(tax coll 1879)
Busby, S. J.
Dutton, M. M.
Ingrin, W. A., (note)
Vann, A. G.
Black, W. L.
Smith, Thomas H.
Collins, N. S.
McWhorter, H. P., (medical)
Hall, Mackey & Co.
Johnson, J. R., MD., (medical)
Nicholson, T. J.
Teague, Frank B., (medical)
Cowan, S. W., (JP)
Cain, R. W., (medical acct.)

Horton, Paron J.

Box 6 File 33 1865-1874
Names in File:
Horton, Elizabeth, (widow)
Whitt, Shade M., (adm)
White/Whitt
Horton, A. B.
Gilbreath, Eliza Horton
Gilbreath, Geo., (h/o Eliza)
Whitt, Caroline Horton
Horton, J. S.
Horton, C. B.
Horton, G. G.
Horton, W. C. (H. C.)
Horton, May J., (w/o S.N.)
Horton, Simpson N.

Estate Record Name

Horton, Paron J. (Cont.)

Horton, Sarah, (minor)
Horton, Ellen, (minor)
Penn, Lucy Norton
Penn, Lucy , (widow of N.S.)
Penn, N. S.
Penn, Mary
Penn, Stephen
Horton, Harvey J., (brother)
Horton, James S.
Horton, Gilbert G.
Horton, J. Simpson
Whitt, Caroline, (w/o S. M.)
Horton, Jeptha
Horton, Harvey
Leath, Parlee Horton
Leath, W. J., (h/o Parlee)
McClendon, Nelly Horton
McClendon, Burl, (h/o Nelly)
Horton, Archie
Scott, Martin F., (appraiser)
Amos, James, (appraiser)
Madderra, J. T., (appraiser)
White, S. M., (JP)
Hoge, John K., Judge
Dobbs, L. A., (atty)
Edwards, J. E. (paid)
Payne, A. F., (guar.ad litem)
Burgess, T. J.
White, S. M., (adm)
Jacoway, G. W., (paid)

Notes & Accounts Due Estate:

Lester, J. H.
Cummings, Hiram
Taylor, William
Horton, J. S.
Edwards, Jeptha
Low, John
Campbell, Chilnessee
Jones, Mary E.
Murdock, R. M.

Estate Record Name

Horton, Paron J. (Cont.)

Box 6 File 33 1865-1874

Murdock, Thomas
Wilburn, Seburn
Stockstill, James
Payne, Andrew
McCormack, David
Payne, John
Pollard, Frank
Griffin, Henry
Gilbreath, A. A.
Davidson, Azzle
Pollard, Grandy
Semore, Wm.
Thompson, John L.
Leeth, Isaac

Sale of Personal Property:

Gilbreath, M. A., (bedstead)
Gilbreath, Perry, (book)
Gilbreath, A. R., (gridstone)
Stowers, John, (desk)
McMahan, W. P., (file)
Penn, Stephen, (sundries)
Watts, H., (old iron)
Whitt, S. M., (spade)
Ward, L. P., (wagon & iron)
Yarbry, James, (steelyards)
Whitt, S. M., (heel sweep)
Horton, A. B., (trunk)
Penn, S.,(log chain)
Green, John, (blacksmith tools)
Banister, John, (screw plate)
Davidson, A. S., (buggy)
Graves, J., (mare & colt)
Ward, L.P. (wagon)
Cain, W. S., (JP)
Dunlap, R. A. D.

Horton, Preston B.

Box 6 File 34 1902-1915

Names in File:

Chitwood, Wm. J.,(adm)

Estate Record Name

Horton, Preston B. (Cont.)

Guest, Griffin, (minor)
Berry, John, (minor)
Berry, Douglas,(minor)
DeShields, J. G., (guar.ad litem)
Horton, John P.
Jack, Georgia Ann
Sellers, Martha
Johnson, Juskin
Jones, Pollie
Collins, Alabama
Downer, Fannie
Reynolds, Mary
Horton, D. D.
Horton, J. P.
Horton, G. R.
Smith, Ider
Guest, Nicie
Chitwood, Martha
Guest, G. P.
Guest, Ruben J.
Durham, Ida
Thurman, Mary
Guest, Griffin
Berry, Sarah
Isabell, Zona
Waldrop, Dovie
Berry, Preston
Berry, Mindy
Collins, Pollie
Coleman, Douglas
More, W. E., (appraiser)
Boggs, Wm. (appraiser)
Hamilton, H. G. (Note due)
Hamilton, Henry & Fannie, (note)
Hunt, Luke E., (atty)
Horton, John
Croley, J. A.

Horton, W. P.

Box 6 File 35 1879-1892

Names in File:

Estate Record Name
Horton, W. P. (Cont.)
Horton, Malinda C., (widow)
Horton, James B., (adm)
Horton, Jennie I. B., (minor)
Horton, Thos. B., (minor)
Horton, Richard A., (minor)
Hoge, John K., (appraiser)
Estes, John R., (appraiser)
Majors, Samuel, (appraiser)
Frazier, P. M., (bought land)
Horton, J. B.
Brandon, P. A., Judge
Notes & Accts. Due Estate:
Petty & Huff, (note)
Petty, J. M., (note)
Stafford, J. A., (note)
Simpson, John, (note)
Hoge, John K., (note)
Chitwood, Rick, (note)
County claims
Keener, P., (note)
Banner, J. M.
Galbreath, Joseph
Kennon, P., (note)
Benge, George C.
Kirkland, Taylor R., (note)
Phillips, A. P., (note)
Nicholson, T. J., (note)
Hendley, W.
Kuykendall, John, (note)
Carter, V., (acct.)
Barr, Jas., (acct.)
Dobbs, Eliza, (acct.)
Fight, B. R., (acct.)
McKenmore, Jessie, (acct)
McClenond, Pollie, (acct)
McNutt, Millard, (acct.)
McNarwell, William, (acct.)
Norton, James, (acct.)
Payne, Nannie, (acct)
Petty, J. M., (acct)

Estate Record Name
Horton, W. P. (Cont.)
Roberts, William, (acct)
Roberts, G. W., (acct)
Ryan, A. A., (acct.)
Roberson, David
Russell, Andy
Riddle, Lewis, (acct)
Simpson, James, (acct)
Sanford, James, Jr. (acct)
Stone, Bill, (acct)
Stewart, Sam, (acct)
Gynan, S. J., (acct)
Taylor, John, (acct)
Taylor, H. S., (acct)
Tate, Aron, (acct)
Williams, Charley, (acct)
Paid:
Busby, A. J.
Smith, Thos. H.
Kean, S. R.
Collins, J. H.
Downer, S. K.
Black, W. L.
Johnson, L. R.
Ingram, W. A.
Bennett, A. G.
Majors, Sam
Irvins, Sam
Davis, A. G.
Smith, L. H.
Busbee,
Wesson, J. W.
Davis, H. G.
Fortner, A. H.
Davis, John A.
Steward, S. W.
Thomas, Jack
Receipts:
Petty, J. N., (rents)
Frazier, P. M., (rents)
Petty, James, (rents)

Estate Record Name
Horton, W. P. (Cont.)
Dobbs, L. A., (rents)
Dobbs, L. W., (wheat)
Notes Compromised:
Dutton, M. M.
Dobbs, R. D.
Huff, G. M.
Lyons, G. H.
Hibbs, J. G.
Crump, Albert
Collins, J. H.
Roberts, L. F.
McClendon, C. P.
Petty, John
Stafford, J. A.
Simpson, John
Hoge, J. K.
Chitwood, Rich
Nicholson, T. J.
Taylor J. F.
Phillips, F.
Bennett, Isiah
Kirkendall, John
Carter, V.
Barr, Jas.
Dobbs, Elijah
Fight, B. R.
McNarian, Jessie
McClendon, Pollie
McNutt, Millard
McNarian, William
Norton, James
Payne, Warren
Roberts, William
Roberts, G. W.
Robertson, David
Russell, Andy
Riddle, Lewis
Sanford, James
Slone, Bill
Stewart, Sam

Estate Record Name
Horton, W. P. (Cont.)
Box 6 File 35 1879-1892
Tiner, S. J.
Taylor, John
Taylor, H. S.
Williams, Charles
Houghton, Samuel
Box 6 File 35 1893-1897
Middlesex, Mass. Will
Names in File:
Houghton, Mary, (widow)
Houghton, Mary, (exec.)
Houghton, Edward M.
Dutton, Alice M., (dau)
Dutton, Harry, (h/o Alice)
Dutton, Marion, (g-dau)
Dutton, Mary, (g-dau)
Clark, Mary E., (sister)
Blackstone, Louisa, (g-dau)
Clark, Samuel S., (g-son)
Clark, John E., (g-son)
Eaton, Pamelia Ann, (sister)
Sargent, Maria A.
Converse, Marquis M.
Pearson, Edward
Shaw, Wm. F.
Cooledge, Charles H.
Houghton, Alanson, (bro.dec'd.)
Houghton, Ida, (dau of Alan)
Vannevar, Hattie M.
Cole, Susie M.,(employee)
White, M. J., Mrs.,(employee)
Riley, John, (employee)
Quimby, David
Massachusetts Estate
Sawyers, Chas., (local atty)
Land in DeKalb Co.
House, Della
Box 6 File 37 1916
Names in File:
Sale of Land for Division

Estate Record Name

House, Della (Cont.)
- House, Della, Mrs.
- Bramlett, Effie, (minor)
- Bramlett, J. R., (h/o Effie)
- Satterfield, Pearl, (minor)
- Satterfield, Grover, (h/o Pearl)
- Hicks, Sherman, (minor)
- Presley, I. M., (guar.ad litem)
- Bruce, Walter, (testimony)
- Satterfield, G. C.
- Orr, Thomas A., (commissioner)
- Satterfield, Grover & Pearl (purchased land)

Houston, William
- Box 6 File 38 1896-1897
- Names in File:
- Sale of Land for Division
- Houston, E. M. vs: Heirs
- Houston, E. M.
- May, Jane
- Houston, Mary Jane
- Hood, Mary
- Porter, A. C.
- Davis, John A.
- Frazier, R. W.
- Houston, Pollie
- Houston, Ealley
- Houston, Samuel
- Houston, James
- Reid, Lucy
- Houston, William M.
- Frazier, Lucy
- Houston, A. W.
- Swinner, Moses
- Swinne, Labon
- Houston, C. M.
- Frazier, R. W., (sheriff)
- Porter, O. C., (witness)
- Wyatt, J. J., (witness)
- Isbell, John B., (comm.)
- Mullins, John, (dep.sheriff)

Estate Record Name

Houston, William (Cont.)
- Ward, C. G., (bought land)
- Darby, W. F.
- Isbell, J. B., (witness)
- May, M. J., Mrs.
- Davis & Haralson, (atty)
- Davis, John A.
- Frazier, Nancy
- Swinner, W. J.
- Monroe, Harrie
- Monroe, Martha

Hughes, Green
- Box 6 File 39 1860-1869
- Names in File:
- Hughes, Rufina
- Cook, Rufina Hughes, (w/o L.A.)
- Cook, L. A.
- Parsons, Elvira Hughes
- Parsons, Labon, (h/o Elvira)
- Hughes, James, (minor)
- Crabtree, Sarah Hughes
- Crabtree, (h/o Sarah)
- Davis, Nancy Hughes
- Davis, (h/o Nancy)
- Hughes, William, (minor)
- Hughes, Missouri, (minor)
- Hughes, Alsey/Aelsey, (widow)
- Blancit, A. D., (adm)
- Davenport, R. R., (bond)
- Rogers, W. C., (bond)
- Hoge, John K., Judge
- Harris, Gains A., (appraiser)
- Beene, Sarah, (appraiser)
- Bouldin, Elijah, (appraiser)
- Harry, James A., (appraiser)
- Beason, M. G., (appraiser)
- Hawkins, James, (appraiser)
- Beene, Jacob, (appraiser)
- Brown, J. G., (appraiser)
- Dower, set off - 1/3 estate
- Griffin, Wm., (sheriff)

Estate Record Name
Hughes, Green
Petition to Sell Land
Austin, S. B., (JP)
Blancitt, Archibald D., (adm)
Cook, R. C.
Cook Lemuel A.
Parsons, Mary E., (w/o Layburn)
Parsons, Layburn
Davis, Nancy Catherine
Crabtree, Sarah E.
Dunlap, R. A. D., (comm.)
Paid:
Hannah, A. B., (note)
Morgan, J. T.
Ashburn, R. T.
Smith, P. J.
Harris, J. A.
Masters, J. M.
Blansit, A. D.
Blevins, A. J.
Nicholson, D. L.
Nicholson & Collins
Hawkins, James
Beene, Jacob
Ashburn, Robert
Austin, S. B.
McGuffey, Buford
Countiss, Neman
Humble, G. W.
McGuffey, W. C.
Hunter, Casper
Box 6 File 40 1881-1882
Names in File:
Emsley, George, (adm)
Hunter, Richard F., (bond)
Payne, A. F., (bond)
Webb, G. W., (bond)
Jackson, J. (bond)
Graves, Jas. R., (bond)
Jack, Julia, (w/o John)
Jack, John

Estate Record Name
Hunter, Casper (Cont.)
Hunter, James P.
Hutchings, Matilda, (w/o D.A.)
Hutchings, David A.
Emsley, Kate, (w/o George)
Emsley, George
Lyons, Allison
Lyons, Thomas G.
Southerlen, Nancy, (w/o C.)
Southerlen, Caswell
Southerland/Southerlen
Emsley, R. C., (dau)
Frazer, P. B., (witness)
Hyde, Harmon
Box 6 File 41 1906
Names in File:
Hyde, Licy P., (widow, adm)
Hyde, Tedle, (minor)
Hyde, Dessie May, (minor)
Hyde, Homer, (minor)
Goodhue, Amos E., (bond)
Sawyer, M. T., (bond)
Allen, G. E., (NP)
End of Roll 70

J

Estate Record Name
Jack, Adeline
Box 6 File 42 1896
Names in File:
Jack, Adeline, (unmarried)
Jack, Thomas M., (adm,brother)
Jack, Wallace
Beavers, Lucy
Ward, Kate
Warren, James
Freeman, Callie
Warren, Clayton
Williams, Jennie
Clayton, Sampson
Clayton, Scott
Jack, John P., (deceased)
Davis & Haralson, (atty)
Cook, W. C. D., Judge
Jack, Thomas M., (adm.bond)
Sutherland, C. D., (adm bond)
Thomas, J. W., (adm bond)
Jack, Allen
Box 6 File 43 1868-1871
Names in File:
Sales of land for division
Hammack, Harriet Jack
Hammack, Thomas, (h/o Harriet)
Isaacs, Mary J. Jack
Isaacs, Josiah C., (h/o Mary)
Jack, Thomas J., (adm)
Jack, John M.
Jack, William
Cunningham, Nancy Jack
Cunningam, George
Jack, Allen G.
Jack, Daniel B.
Clayton, Martha Ann Jack
Clayton, W. H.
Jack, George (W. M.)

Estate Record Name
Jack, Allen (Cont.)
Jack, James H.
Horton, A. J., Judge
Jack, Thomas J.
Nicholsen, T. J., (sheriff)
Chitwood, Mathias, (witness)
Chitwood, Mat
Cunningham, Jesse, (witness)
Nicholson, T. J., (dep.sheriff)
Brandon, P. A., (took testimony)
Brandon, P. A., (clerk)
Land-East Side Big Wills Creek
Dunlap & Dobbs, (atty)
Griffin, Wm., (sheriff)
Dunlap, RAD
Jack, Thomas J., (purch.land)
Davis, William G., (purch.land)
Mitchel, Wm., (bid on land)
Baxter, F. M., (purch.land)
Little, Isaac, (bought land)
Haralson, W. J. (note receipts)
Stuart, J. J., (note receipts)
Franklin, John M., (note rec.)
Carithers, J. Y., (paid)
Malone, G. W., (paid)
Winston, J. G., (paid)
Figures, W. B., (paid)
Horton, A. J., (paid)
Brandon, P. A., (paid)
Osborne, Isham, (paid)
Rogers, H. C., (paid)
Frazier, P. B., (paid)
Cunningham, Isaac, (paid)
Guest, G. B., (paid)
Osborne & Couch
Sloan, Delilah, (paid)
Estes, David, (paid)
Parker, James, (paid)

Estate Record Name
Jack, Allen (Cont.)
Grant, J. F., (paid)
Hoge, Y. K., Judge
Carithers, J. F., (med.acct.)
McCurdy, J. A., (tax 1866)
Figures, W. B., (notices)
Huntsville Advocate
Smith, P. J., (notices)
Guest, G. B., (repairs to farm)
Winston, J. S., (paid)
Brock, George, (JP)
Caristers, James G., (medical)
Caristers, Mary, (paid)
Copy-Oath of Allegiance
Estes, R.
Asbur, J. S., (work on farm)
Cash, James, (work on farm)
Couch, W., (work on farm)
Grant, J. F., (paid)
Confederate Money $372.00
Notes due Estate:
McCampbell, John, (note)
Harleston, J. W., (note)
Jack, James H. (note)
McNutt, R. C., (note)
Jack, W. M., (note)
Franklin, J. N., (note)
Cunningham, Jesse, (note)
Davis, A., (note)
Clayton, Wm. H., (note)
Haralson, W. J., (note)
Jack, Thos. J., (note)
Hammack, Thos., (note)
Cunningham, John, (note)
Stewart, John J., (note)
Jacoway, J. A., (note)
Johnson, J. R., (note)
Grant, J. H., (printer)
Personal Property Sold:
Couch, Willis, (wheat)
Osborne, Isham, (wheat)

Estate Record Name
Jack, Allen (Cont.)
Russell, Dr., (wheat)
Chitwood, Joel, (molasses)
Clayton, W. H., (cotton)
Russell, Dr., (oats)
Hammack, Thos., (side leather)
Baxter, Marion, (corn, leather)
Clayton, W. H., (corn)
Killian, D. S., (corn)
Baxter, F. M., (corn)
Jack, Jas., (corn)
Hammack, Thos., (wheat)
Clayton, W. H., (cotton)
Baxter, F. M., (cotton)
Hagler, W. I., (corn)
Malone, G. W., (cotton)
Lawson, W., (corn)
Hudson, T., (oats and corn)
Baxter, M., (corn)
Allen, A., (corn)
Hartimans, J. M., (corn)
Nicholson, B., (wheat)
Andrews, Silas, (wheat)
Collins, J. B., (5-gal sorghum)
Jack, Allen, Jr.
Box 6 File 44 1858-1868
Names in File:
Jack, J. M., (adm)
Majors, A. W., (bond)
Roberts, W. J., (bond)
Jack, James
Jack, Allen, Jr.
Winston, J. G. & Co., (mdse)
Estes, R., Judge
Franklin, J. N., Judge
Jack, Jeremiah M., (adm)
Jack, Thomas J., (adm)
Jacks, Nancy, (estate)
Sale of Personal Property:
Ward, Caroline, (table, cupboard & ware, looking glass, & chest)

Estate Record Name
Jack, Allen, Jr. (Cont.)
Jacks, James M., (yoke ox, buggy, furniture, blacksmith tools, chain, hogs, and clock)
Jack, Marthy, (bed & furniture)
Jack, Adlin, (trunk)
Hammack, Thos., (corn)
Inghram, W. N., (corn)
Clayton, S. S., (corn)
Andrews, S., (cotton)
Cunningham, John, (flax wheel)
Killian, D. S., (meal seive, bucket)
Little, Thos. J., (smoothing irons)
Baxter, G. W., (pitcher)
Allen, Hiram, (jar)
Dobbs, J. F., (piggins)
Harleston, W. J. (ax)
Baxter, James, (saw, etc.)
Franklin, John N., (molasses & bridle)
McNutt, R. C., (3-chairs)
Osborne, L. A., (shotgun)
Rogers, Reece, (barrel & wine jar)
Brandon, J. L., (barrel)
Johnson, J. R., (kettle)
Hammack, Thos., (oven & lid, tea kettle, dishes, silver spoons leaf table, etc.)
Philips, P. L., (oven & pitch fork)
Cunningham, G. W., (dinner pot)
Clayton, W. H., table, cupboard & brass kettle)
Baxter, J. P., (skillet & lid, fire shovel and tongs)
Jack, John M., (hoes, shovel, dog irons, bed & furniture)
Davis, Abraham, (cup & saucers, bureau, cow, yearling, sythe and spoons)
Jacaway, J. G., (pitchfork, teaspoons & cutting knife)
Hawkins, James, (hammer,

Estate Record Name
Jack, Allen, Jr. (Cont.)
dishes, molasses, heifer, 5-sheep, candle stick & candle mold)
Jack, Jeff, (books)
Jack, Mont, (books, trunk, saddle, wagon, horse & gear, plow)
Hagler, C. C., (books)
Jack, Thomas, (Webst. Dictionary)
Ward, A. F., (Davis Arithmetic)
Jacks, Thomas J., (silver spoons, loom, grindstone, other items)
Chitwood, Mathias, (appraiser)
Grafton, D. R., (appraiser)
Cunningham, John, (appraiser)
Jacks, James
Sibert, J. W.
Hunt, James
Carithers, J. Y.
Minster, J. G.
McNutt, R. C., (note)

Jack, Elizabeth
Box 6 File 45 1884-1896
Names in File:
Ward, Malinda, (heir)
Ward, Noah W., (Exec)
Smith, P. H., (witness to will)
Newman, G. Y., (witness/will)
Newman, M. E., (witness/will)
Jack, Thomas M.
Jack, Adeline
Ward, Malinda, (w/o N. W.)
Ward, N. W.
Beavers, Lucy, (w/o M. M.)
Beavers, M. M.
Freeman, Callie, (w/o James)
Freeman, James
Warren, James
Williams, Jennie, (w/o Henry)
Williams, Henry B.
Campbell, H. B., (guar.ad litem)
Clayton, Warren, (minor)

Estate Record Name
Jack, Elizabeth (Cont.)
 Jack, Wallace
 Clayton, Sampson
 Clayton, George S.
 Jack, Geo. M.
 Jack, Allen
 Jack, Moses
 Jack, Isabella
 Jack, Nancy
 Johnson, Susan, Mrs.
 Nicholson, L. S., (JP)
Jack, J. M.
 Box 6 File 46 1886
 Names in File:
 Jack, Adeline, (sister)
 Jack, Elizabeth, (sister)
 Jack, Martha J., (adm)
 Smith, Thos. H., (guar.ad litem)
 Jack, Wallace, (minor)
 Jack, Lucy, (minor)
 Bruce, William F., (appraiser)
 McBroom, D. P., (appraiser)
 Heard, Strade, (appraiser)
 Jacoway, Henry J., (appraiser)
 Majors, Samuel N., (appraiser)
 Franklin, A. G., (sheriff)
 Franklin, John N., Judge
 Webb, G. M., (witness)
 Brandon, P. A., (witness)
 Campbell, Isaac, (comm)
 Davis, John A., (atty)
 Haralson & Son, (atty)
Jack, Jeremiah M.
 Box 6 File 47 1884-1885
 Names in File:
 Jack, Martha J., (adm)
 Jack, W. J.
 Sells, Jno. T., (bond)
 Brandon, H. H., (bond)
 Killian, Ellias, (bond)
 Killian, Henry E., (bond)

Estate Record Name
Jack, Jeremiah M. (Cont.)
 Jack, Elizabeth
 Jack, Thomas J., (bond)
 Jack, Wallace, (witness)
 Jones, William P., (decd.)
 Edwards, N. J.
 Edwards, John
 Edwards, W. S.
 Edwards, Nancy, (w/o Wm.P.)
 Jones, G. M.
 Jones, Wm. P.
 Jacoway, H. J., (appraiser)
 McBroom, D. P., (appraiser)
 Heard, G. S. V., (appraiser)
 Bruce, W. F., (appraiser)
 Majors, S. N., (appraiser)
 Masters, J. K., (appraiser)
 Garrett, H. W. B., (JP)
 Jack, Wallace E.
 Jack, Lucy E.
 Jacks, Martha J., (adm)
 Accounts Due Estate:
 Arthur, House
 Howard, John
 Arthur, Polk
 King, John
 Garrett, Henry, (colored)
 McFarlane, James
 Daniel, Joseph
 Killian, D. S.
 Killian, John
 Whatley, Burrel
 Drake, Berry
 Berry, Thomas
 Nowlin, Beverly
 Bandon, H. H.
 Baxter, John
 Harlson, Winkett
 Hulgan, L. P.
 Burt, Wm.
 Ward, James B.

Estate Record Name

Jack, Jeremiah M. (Cont.)

Burt, John
Parker, Cicero
Fell, Brown
Killian, Daniel
Killian, Elias
Baxter, Thos.
Arther, Joseph
Ward, C. P.
Burt, James
Edwards, Lucy
Burt, George
McPherson, Jefferson
Lewis, Benjamin
Bogle, John, (colored)
Shaw, Hogan
Heard, Strode
Cronin, Hiram

Notes Due Estate:

Horn, Thos. J.
Hagler, J. W.
Killian, Henry
Morgan, A. S.
Frazier, Robt.
Killian, W. N.
Edmondson, W. E.
Dutton, Abe
Burt, Thos.
Burt, Marion
Carroll, Robert C.
Bryant, Grase
Adair, R. J.
Madden, A. A.
Robinson, D. G.
Jarnagin, A.
Thompson, B. C.
Killian, J. S.
Crowder, T. O.
O'Shields, John
Drake, Berry
Pits, J. N.

Estate Record Name

Jack, Jeremiah M. (Cont.)

Bagley, N. F.
Cobb, Thos.
Copeland, John
Davenport, J. G.
McNutt, M. W.
Newkirk, Lane
Shaw, R. H.
Jolly, J. V.
Hefner, Wm.
McCallie, Andrew
Thomas, E. B.
Hunt, John
McCartney, Alexander
Parker, Robert
Whaley, W. W.
Fike, D. C.
Newkirk, James
Killian, Henry E., (appraiser)
Killian, Elias, (appraiser)
Jack, Thos. J., (appraiser)
Franklin, A. G., (sheriff)

Jack, Nancy

Box 6 File 48 1857-1879
Names in File:
Jack, Nancy,(widow of James Jack)
To set off dower
Jack, J. M., (adm)
Haralson & Son, (atty)
Hammack, Thomas, (bond)
Winston, Ed, (bond)
Jack, J. M., (adm. Bond)
Ward, Caroline
Jack, Thomas M.
Jack, Adaline
Jack, Elizabeth
Jack, John P.
Jack, James
Goggins, Martha, (w/o E. T.)
Goggins, E. T.
Greenfield, Martha J.

Estate Record Name

Jack, Nancy (Cont.)
- Greenfield, J.
- Ward, Kate, (w/o N. W.)
- Ward, Noah W.
- Clayton, Mary E.
- Clayton, W. H., (guardian)
- Hughes, A. A., (sheriff)
- Clayton, Sampson, (appraiser)
- Ward, Andrew J., (appraiser)
- Goggins, E. T., (appraiser)
- McCampbell, John, (appraiser)
- McBroom, Stephen, (appraiser)
- Estes, R., Judge
- Killian, Henry, (testimony)
- Ward, Andrew J., (testimony)
- Lankford, R. J. (comm.)
- Killian, Elias, (appraiser)
- McCallie, A., (appraiser)
- Williams, Neviah, (appraiser)
- Estes, R., (note)
- Jack, J. M. (brother of James)
- Edwards, N. J., (exec.)
- Jones, W. L.

Jackson, John
- Box 6 File 49 1897
- Names in File:
- Jackson, Margaret, (widow)
- Exemption to Widow
- Jackson, Simion, (minor)
- Elrod, W. H., (witness)
- Hicks, J. T., (witness)
- Shelley, R. J., (JP)
- Cook, W. C. D., Judge

Jackson, Maude
- Box 6 File 50 1911-1912
- Names in File:
- Jackson, Maudie, (minor)
- Jackson, R. H., (guardian, husband of Maudie)
- Wells, W. L., (guar.bond)
- Hawkins, W. A., (guar.bond)

Estate Record Name

Jackson, Maude (Cont.)
- Pace, Isaac, (g-father's estate)
- Wells, W. L., (father of minor)
- Croley, Jas. A., Judge

Jackson, William
- Box 6 File 51 1911-1912
- Names in File:
- Crabtree, Martin, (adm)
- Crabtree, Louisa, (w/o Martin)
- Jackson, Rebecca, (widow)
- Jackson, Warren
- Jackson, Harvey
- Jackson, Irvin
- Jackson, John A.
- Jackson, Paralee, (w/o James)
- McDaniel, James
- McDaniel, Paralee Jackson
- Jackson, Albert
- Jackson, Caroline, (w/o Samuel)
- Pinkerton, Caroline Jackson
- Pinkerton, Samuel
- Jackson, Albert, (minor)
- Stewart, Sarah, (deceased)
- Stewart, Benajah, (w/o John B.)
- Wilkerson, John B.
- Steward/Stewart
- Crabtree, Louisa Jackson
- Crabtree, Wm. C.
- Wilkerson, Elizabeth, (dau)
- Wilkerson, John, (minor)
- Wilkerson, James, (minor)
- Wilkerson, Lewis, (minor)
- Wilkerson, Elizabeth, (minor)
- Wilkerson, Benjakin, (minor)
- Wilkerson, Kathy, (minor)
- Wilkinson, Malinda, (w/o John)
- Wilkerson, John
- Jett, Joseph, (testimony)
- Thornburg, William, (testimony)
- Hammond, William, (testimony)
- Thomason, John, (comm.)

Estate Record Name

Jackson, William (Cont.)
- Estes, R. Judge
- Walden, J. B., (atty)
- Snider, C., (tax 1857-58)
- Davenport, R. R. Jr.
- Hamman, G. B., (JP)
- Davenport & Blackwell
- Crabtree, G. W., (rent corn and wheat)
- Butt, D. L. R.
- Triffe, W. H.
- Jackson, Albert, (minor)
- Sales of Land for Division
- Crabtree, Martin, (purch.land)

Jacoway, Henry J.
- Box 6 File 52 1899-1900
- Names in File:
- Jacoway, Lillie, (widow)
- Jacoway, Robert, (minor)
- Jacoway, Jennie, (minor)
- Jacoway, John, (minor)
- Jacoway, Samuel, (minor)
- Jacoway, Lou, (minor)
- Jacoway, Sue, (minor)
- Jacoway, Peggie, (minor)
- Jacoway, Henry, (minor)
- Jacoway, Mary, (minor)
- Jacoway, Dodge?, (minor)
- Jacoway, Fred M., (over 21)
- Jacoway, Fred M., (filed will)
- Jacoway, Benj. J. (proof of will)
- Jacoway, J. P., (proof of will)
- Cunningham, John, (note pd)

Jacoway, W. V.
- Box 6 File 53 1904
- Names in File:
- Sale of Land for Division
- Jacoway, W. V., (joint owner)
- Martin, Jeff, (joint owner)
- Hughes, D. B., (joint owner)
- Jacoway, Fred M., (witness)

Estate Record Name

Jacoway, W. V. (Cont.)
- Blevins, Polk P., (witness)
- Cook, John M., (comm.)
- Presley, I. M., (atty)
- Smith, Thos. H., (newspaper ads)
- Chitwood, W. J., (sheriff)
- Faulkner, J. W., (JP)
- Jacoway, W. V., (purchased land)

Johnson, A. J.
- Box 6 File 54 1912
- Names in File:
- Exemption before Adm.
- Johnson, Easter E., (widow)
- No minor children
- Homestead, 159 acres
- Mayes, Jinks, (appraiser)
- Dowdy, W. T., (appraiser)
- Mauer, T. L., (JP)

Johnson, James D.
- Box 6 File 55 1858-1867
- Names in File:
- Johnson, Reuben, (adm)
- Sibert, John W., (bond)
- Ward, O. W., (bond)
- Reeves, James H., (guardian)
- Reeves, Mary Elisa, (minor)
- Reeves, Ezekial B., (minor)
- Reeves, James P., (minor)
- Reeves, Sarah A., (minor)
- Reeves, Hannah J., (minor)
- Reeves, Reuben J., (minor)
- Reeves, A. J.
- Johnson, R. C., (adm)
- Reeves, E. B.
- Walden, W. B., (magistrate)
- Griffin, William, (sheriff)
- **Accounts Due Estate 1856:**
- Hit, Henry
- Hester, O.
- Hooper, C.
- Puvin, C.

Estate Record Name

Johnson, James D. (Cont.)
- Capart, C.
- Penn, Stevin
- Teague, Mary
- Right, Hannah
- Paget, Alford
- Carethers, J. Y.
- Reeves, James A., (note)
- Hall, S. M., (note)
- Hall, Yancy, (note)
- Reeve, N. W., (note)
- Sibert, J. W, (note)
- Johnson, R. C., (note)
- Smith, H. B., (note)
- Lovens, L. D., (note)
- Roden, B. H., (note)
- Davis, J. J., (note)
- Coats, J. T., (note)
- Pace, Burel, (note)
- Waldrop, S., (note)
- Norman, Henry, (note)
- Penn, William, (note)
- Thomas, Berry J., (note)
- Patrick, Thomas A., (note)
- Sibert, J. W., (note)
- Ward, B. J., (note)
- Right, John, (note)
- Milwee, G. W., (note)
- Hendricks, Joab, (note)
- Chaney, P., (note)

Johnson, Joseph
- Box 6 File 56 1855-1867
- Names in File:
- Johnson, Nancy, (widow, adm)
- Wilson, Joseph, (adm)
- Yeargan, Memory N., (adm)
- Yeargen/Yeargin/Yeargan
- Johnson, Amanda
- Gaines, Wm. A., (bond)
- Gaines, Mary Ann, (w/o Wm.)
- Yeargan, Harriett, (w/o M.N.)

Estate Record Name

Johnson, Joseph (Cont.)
- Johnson, Larry
- Lea, Allen
- Henry, I. B.
- Johnson, James B., (minor)
- Johnson, Charlotte N., (minor)
- Johnson, Erastus V., (minor)
- Johnson, Sarah Elizabeth, (minor)
- Wilson, John
- Lucy, W. E.
- Willson, Joseph
- Willson, Andrew
- Willson/Wilson
- Yeargan, John B., (bond)
- Williams, J. M., (bond)
- Johnson, Nancy, (bond)
- Yeargan, M. N., (bond)
- Walker, Jeremiah, (JP)
- Ramsey, G. W., (bond)
- Cobb, P. G., Dr. (med.services)
- Gilliland, Charlotte Johnson
- Gilliland, John E., (h/o Charlotte)
- Johnson, James E., (deceased)
- Walker, J. C. (sold land to Nancy)
- Walker, Betsy, (w/o J. C.)
- Johnson, Henry
- Dean & Edwards, (paid)
- Sale of Real Prop. - $2815
- Lucy, W. E., (receipts)
- Fuller, Sidney, (rent, R.E.)
- Vincent, Henry, (receipts)
- Currey, Benj. E., (receipts)
- Higgins, R. W., (paid)
- Lee, Allen, (surveyor, pd)
- King, James R., (JP)
- Igou, A. J., (appraiser)
- Venable, J., (appraiser)
- Henry, J. B., (mdse, paid)
- Johnson, Hugh, (guardian)
- Johnson, Amanda G.
- Gaines, Wm. A., (purch.land)

Estate Record Name
Johnson, Joseph (Cont.)
Johnson, Amanda S.,(purch.land)
Johnson, Nancy, (purch.land)
Yeargin, M. N., (purch.land)
Wilson, Joseph, (secured loan)
Clain, Wm. L, (legal services)
Ross, George
McBryar, H. P., (JP)
Collins, R. M., (clerk)
Jones, Wm.
Griffin, Wm., (sheriff)
Porter, J. D.
Higgins, R. W., (atty)
Johnson, Hannah Jane
Gilliland, John E., (guardian)
Johnson, H. M.
Gilliand, D. M.
Dower to Nancy Johnson
Burgess, T. J., (appraiser)
Penn, James, (appraiser)
Stowers, Charles, (appraiser)
McBrayer, J. T., (appraiser)
Chaney, John, (appraiser)
Edwards, Joseph, (sheriff)
Ramsey, G. W., (appraiser)
Sheppard, A. W., (appraiser)
Gilliand, D. M., (p.e. appraiser)
Box, P. J., (JP)
Hamman, B. G., (JP)
Sale of Personal Property:
Shrum, David, (sythe & cradle)
Young, Fayette, (spade)
Gilliand, D. M., (lot of iron)
Young, Robert, (tools)
Wilson, Joseph, (wedge)
Gileran, D. N., (mattock)
Shrum, David, (collars)
Johnson, Nancy, (side saddle)
Sitrye, William, (saddle)
Shrum, James N., (1-lot gear)
Christopher, Wm.,(saw,drawing knife)

Estate Record Name
Johnson, Joseph (Cont.)
Ramsey, G. W., (barrels)
Yeargan, M. N., (oven & pan)
Shrum, J. N., (pot)
Wilson, Joseph, (pr. steers)
Ward, J. G., (double barrel gun)
Hammitt, James, (bell)
Marinna, John, (2-cows & calf)
Sansum, M., (cow)
Vinson, W. A., (1-steer)
Yeargen, M. N., (cow)
Sansum, M., (yearling)
Hollingsworth, Thomas, (10-hogs)
Rolls, A. P., (5-best hogs)
Ralls/Rolls
Widow, (chairs)
Thomson, John C.,(4-horse wagon)
Beane, E., (sorrel mare)
Rolls, A. P., (gray mule)
Yeargan, Joseph, (bay mule)
Coots, Henry, (mare mule)
Coots/Coats
Bolin, Nobel, (mule)
Yeargen, M. N., (corn)
Turinten, D. C., (corn)
Bennett, A. D., (corn)
Widow, (oats, thrash, 6-sheep, and 8-pigs)
Paid from Estate:
Lucy, W. E.
Henry, J. B., (cloth, ribbon,etc.)
Rees, John, (mdse)
Young & Hughes
Wilson, Andrew
Curry, B. E.
McWhorter, James M.
Snider, C., (tax 1857)
Hill, O. P.
Taylor, G. B.
Cain, W. L.
Land, A. J.

Estate Record Name
Johnson, Joseph (Cont.)
Gilliland, D. M.
Wilson, John
Carithers, J. Y.
Curtain, O. W.
King & Edwards
Edwards, Jeptha
Higgins & Porter
Rees, T. G.
Rees, D. V.
Allen, H. T., (JP)
Blevins, (medical)
Pickens, H. W., (JP)
Ralls, Jno.
Willson, Joseph
Willson/Wilson
Rees, T. L.
W. E. Lucy Co.(nails,bridle, etc.)
Curry, Benjamin E.
Young, Wm. C.
Willson, Andrew
Nicholson & Higgins
Gilliand, John E., (Charlotte exp.)
Johnson, M. J., Mrs.
Box 6 File 57 1910
Names in File:
Will Destroyed
Johnson, D. H., (husband)
Stephens, E. C., Mrs., (sister)
Sister named as heir in will
Johnson, Cecil, (step-son)
Johnson, Norman, (step-son)
Stephens, E. G. H., (h/o E.C.)
Young, Rebecca, (witness)
Dees, John, (witness)
Johnson, M. B., (witness)
Branden, Jim, (witness)
Johnson, D. H., (witness)
Johnson, Cecil, (witness)
Johnson, Norman, (witness)
Stephens, E. C., Mrs., (adm)

Estate Record Name
Johnson, M. J., Mrs. (Cont.)
Copeland, A. C., (attest will)
Copeland, Stella, (attest will)
Sargent, Julia, (summons)
Arrington, Rebecca, (summons)
Yering, Rebeca, (summons)
Isbell, John B., (atty for D. H.)
Stephens, E. C., (plaintiff)
Jury Trial in favor of plaintiff
Downs, T. L., (sheriff)
Jurors:
Killian, R. L.
Tate, D. M.
Price, B. N., (jury foremen)
Stephen, Bob
Milton, Asberry
Majors, Charley
Price, Benjamin
Gifford, Thomas
Chitwood, P. Rufus
Gaines, O. Joe
Hodges, Jib B,
Gilbert, Wiley W.
Harris, D. C.
Jack, David A.
Myers, Frank B.
Corbin, W. Thomas
Monroe, John D.
Bell, Larkin H.
Crow, Geo. W.
Holden, Robert L.
Hammonds, A. Lee
Hope, Joe H.
Jenkins, W. H.
Davenport, Thos. B.
Isbell, W. Sherman
Milner, F. A.
Howard & Hunt, (atty)
DeShields, J. G., (clerk cir.court)
Brandon, James, (summons)
Jackson, M. B., Mrs., (summons)

Estate Record Name

Johnson, M. J., Mrs. (Cont.)
- Deas, Joe
- Deas, Etta
- Stephens, Maud
- Stephens, Jas.

Johnson, Rachel C., Mrs.
- Box 6 File 58 1915-1916
- Names in File:
- Smith, M. V., (brother, adm)
- Hixson, J. E., (attest will)
- Isbell, John B., (attest will)
- Smith, Joseph, (brother, deceased)
- Smith, Jesse
- Smith, Caroline
- Smith, Henry
- Smith, Martha
- Wright, Mary Smith, (sister, decd.)
- Wright, Hannah
- Wright, Lucy
- Wright, Rebecca
- Wright, Haseltine
- Wright, Hallatine
- Wright, Joseph
- Smith, J. B., (bond)
- Todd, J. W., (bond)
- Isbell, John, (bond)
- Johnson, R. C., (Rachel)
- Presley, I. M., (guar.ad litem)

Johnson, Reuben C.
- Box 6 File 59 1862-1872
- Names in File:
- Johnson, Mariah W., (widow, adm)
- Johnson, James S.
- Yancy, Margaret Johnson
- Yancy, A. W., (h/o Margaret)
- Johnson, Mary M., (minor)
- Johnson, Reuben J. D., (minor)
- Yancy, M. E., (bond)
- Yancy, A. W., (bond)
- Johnson, James S., (bond)
- Johnson, R. Jefferson D.

Estate Record Name

Johnson, Reuben C. (Cont.)
- Mays, Mary M., (w/o Martin)
- Mays, Martin
- Yancy, Margaret
- Yancy, Andrew W.
- Chumley, W. Y., (testimony)
- Norman, Henry, (testimony)
- Walden, J. B., (atty)
- Brandon, P. A., (guar.ad litem)
- Nicholson & Collins, (atty)
- Burgess, T. J., (sheriff)
- Ward, A. W., (bond)
- Dalrymple, J. D., (note)
- Confederate Money $460.25
- Higgins, R. W., (note)
- Moody, J. J., (note)
- Mullins, Wm., (note)
- Walton, J. B., (note)
- Pruett, W. W., (note)
- Chumney, L. P., (note)
- McDaniel, Wm., (note)
- Davis, J. J., (note)
- Horton, A. J., Judge
- Johnson, M. W., (bond)
- Ervin, B. F., (bond)
- Tabor, F. M., (bond)
- Mays, Mary Johnson, (minor)
- Mays, Martin, (h/o Mary)
- Hoge, John K., (guar.ad litem)
- Norman, Wiley M. (appraiser)
- Ward, O. W., (appraiser)
- Estes, R., (bond)
- Newman, W. M., (bond)
- Hoge, John K., Judge
- Johnson, Mariah W., (dower)
- Widow of Johnson, Reubin C.
- Hamlin, L. E., (paid)
- Griffin, Henry, (paid)
- Garmany, G. G., (paid)
- Vann, A. J., (medical services)
- Milwee, G. W., (paid)

Estate Record Name

Johnson, Reuben C. (Cont.)
- Johnson, Mariah, (purch.land)
- Hills, Gabrill, (blacksmith, pd)
- Milwee, G. W., (JP)
- Norman, Henry, (paid)
- Griffith, Wm., (paid)
- Chumley, Wm. Y., (paid)
- Newman, M. N., (note)
- Ward, L. P., (note)
- **Sale of Personal Property:**
- Johnson, M. W., (buggy, horse, plow, gears, yoke oxen)
- Chumble, Wm., (yoke oxen)
- Johnson, M. W., (heifer)
- Horton, Jas. M., (sow & pigs)
- Smith, A. B., (sow and pigs)
- Ward, L. P., (corn)
- Witt, Robt., (corn)
- Farris, D. C., (corn)
- Payne, Mrs., (corn)
- Hanset, James, (corn)
- Farris, T. C., (corn)
- Chumley, Mrs., (corn)
- Cisk, Louisa, (corn)
- Newman, Wiley, (corn)
- Harrison, Caroline, (corn)
- Harrison, Cathrine, (corn)
- Estes, R., (dep. clerk)

Johnson, Richmond
- Box 6 File 60 1875
- Names in File:
- Johnson, Lucretia C., (widow)
- Smith, Henry H., (bond)
- Ramsey, John W., (atty)
- Ellison, Mr.
- Johnson, Ales.
- Brandon, P. A., Judge

Johnson, Samuel
- Box 6 File 61 1925-1926
- Names in File:
- Johnson, Jane, (widow)

Estate Record Name

Johnson, Samuel (Cont.)
- King, Jewel, (adm, g-daughter)
- King, J. D., (bond)
- Floyd, M. T., (bond)
- Holleman, Ernest J.,(heir)
- Davenport, E. T., (appraiser)
- White, J. M., (appraiser)
- Dean, George W., (appraiser)
- Johnson, Mary Jane
- Bailey, H. T.
- King, W. H.
- Malone, G. L., Judge
- AGSRR Co
- Bailey & Curtis, (legal services)
- Hansard, E. L., (gasoline)
- King, W. A., (repairs on house)
- Smith, Thos. H., (notices)
- *Fort Payne Journal*
- Shop, AGS
- Edwards, D. N., (paid)
- Hansard, E. L.
- Valley Head Mercantile, (paid)
- Johnson, Mary Jane, Mrs. (paid)
- Edwards, D. N., (note)
- Alexander, John, (note)
- King, W. A., (note)
- Holleman, T. W., (acct.)
- Holleman, Jake, (acct.)
- Johnson, Samuel
- Johnson, Jefferson
- Johnson, Nancy
- Johnson, Wm.
- Johnson, George
- Johnson, Jesse
- Johnson, Newton
- Johnson, John
- Johnson, Martha, (minor)
- Johnson, Mary, (minor)
- Johnson, Lewis, (minor)

Jones, Abram W.
- Box 6 File 62 1855-1858

Estate Record Name

Jones, Abram W. (Cont.)
Names in File:
Jones, Mary E., (exec.,widow)
Gilbreath, George, (exec.)
Jones, Dicy Ann
Gilbreath, Dicy Ann
Gilbreath, R. A., (h/o Dicy)
Jones, William Coner
Jones, Fanny Jane
Jones, George W.
Jones, Sarah Mariah
Jones, Elvana
Jones, Thomas J.
Gilbreath, G. E., (attest will)
Jones, G. W., (attest will)
Gilbreath, J. E.
Gilbreath, A. P., (JP)
Notes Due Estate
Hitt, Henry
Burnes, Samuel
Thompson, Jeremiah J. F.
Holmon, Isaac
Denham, James
Nalor, Jeremiah
Madriah, James T.
Gilbreath, A. P., (JP)
Griffin, Wm.
Griffin, Henry
Seymore, G. W.
Seymore, J. F.
George, S. B.
Thompson, John L.
Denham, William
Wright, John
Beeson, W. B., (JP)
Penn, N. S., (appraiser)
Sibert & Co.
Sibert, John W., (JP)
Parr, A. A., (tuition paid)
Davis, J. J., (paid for hog)
Carithers, J. G., Dr., (medical)

Estate Record Name

Jones, Abram W. (Cont.)
Ward & Edwards, (burial exp.)
Sibert, J. W., (paid)
Gilbert, John, (JP)
Edwards, Jeptha
Edwards, Jep, (paid)
Dilbeck, A. W., (JP)
Smith Acct, (paid)
Gilbreath, John M.
Horton, A. B., (appraiser)
Scott, (appraiser)
Burnes, Samuel, (appraiser)
Horton, A. B., (appraiser)
White, S. M.
Penn, James
Walden, J. B.
Jones, George W.
Box 6 File 63 1858-1863
Names in File:
Jones, Mary E., (widow)
Gilbreath, George
Jones, Allen, (adm)
Dobbs, S. E., (bond)
Lankford, R. B., (bond)
Jones, Jane, (adm)
Gilbreath, George, (appraisal)
Griffin, Henry, (appraisal)
Chumley, W. Y., (appraisal)
Milwee, G. W., (JP)
Jones, Janes, (adm-G.W.Jones)
Edwards, J., (sheriff)
Estes, R., Judge
Hoge, J. K., (JP)
Gilbreath, Ellison
Accounts Due Estate-1863
Burns, Thos.
Jones, Mary
Fortune, William
Milwee, John
Norrell, C. P.
Chrismon, James

Estate Record Name
Jones, George W. (Cont.)
Reeves, Noah
Brown, Alfred
Walker, John
Reed, George
Ward, O. W.
Barksdale,
Padgett, Jacob
Burns, John
Beeson, W. B.
Mays, A. B.
Mays, H. C.
Accounts Due Estate-1862
Justice
Hays, Thomas
Roden, W. B.
Lynch, L. W.
Ramsy, David
Bookout,
Vann, Dr.
Thompson, J. J. F.
Mays, J. F.
Burns, Sam
Isbel, J.
Owens, William
Roden, J. B.
Davis, J. J.
Redmond, Nathan
Pace, Burrel
Fortune, William
Carightey, J. T.
Milwee, J. A.
Mays, Henry
Carns, D. R.
Jones, Mary
Ward, C. W.
McNair, D.
Watson, Jesse
Griffin, Wm., (acct)
Padget, F. M., (acct)
Campbell, Benson

Estate Record Name
Jones, George W. (Cont.)
Nation, James
Roden, Jeremiah
Griffin, Marborn
Burny, John
Walker, John
Owen, John T.
Welborn, D. R.
Ward, S. T.
Boldin, Noble
Davidson, William
Davis, Gabe
Whitty, N. M.
Knove
Newman, M. C.
Yarberry, Jas.
Green, John
Boldin, R.
Roden, W. W.
Welborn,
Roden, B. H.
Owens, Wm.
Farris, Dr.
Hays, Thomas
Hendricks, M.
Yarberry, Jas.
Carns, D. R.
Roden, Jeremiah
Braszeal, Wm.
Thompson, J. J., Jr.
Owens, A.
Yancy, Wm. A.
Brown, Thos, (note)
Burnes, Thos.
Reeves, Noah
Roden, Zeolum
Dilbect, A. M., (note)
Freeman, M. C., (note)
Burns, Jeremiah, (note)
Braszeal, J. J. F., (note)
Roden, Zealious, (note)

Estate Record Name

Jones, George W. (Cont.)

Boldin, Noble, (note)
Nations, James, (note)
Lipscomb, J. D., (note)
Payne, John H., (note)
Wilson, J. M., (note)
Padget, M., (note)
George, Henry, (note)
Wilson, Thos., (acct.)
Payne, A. P., (acct.)
Carns, D. R. (acct)
Mays, J. F., (acct.)
Roden, Z., (acct.)
Ramsey, D. C., (acct.)
Roden, John, (note)
Roden, B. H., (acct.)
Campbell, Robt., (acct.)
Roden, W. B.
Burns, Gam
Stowey, J.
Hays, T. W.
Carns,
Boldin, R.
Burns, John
Mays, J. F., (acct.)
Green, John
Pace, Burrel
Lynch, L. W.
Witt, A.
Vann, A. J.
Isbell, Jas.
Harrison, Eddey
Harrison, Wm.
Dilbeck, Noah
Witt, R.
Groves, H.
Pollard, P.
Nicholson, Mary B., (acct.)
Whitty, M., (acct)
Watson, Jesse, (acct)
Gordon, H. M., (acct.)

Estate Record Name

Jones, George W. (Cont.)

Jones & Carythers - 1861
Owens, Wm., (acct)
Owens, A., (acct)
Reed, George
Paterson, W. J.
Upton, Henry
Milwee, John
Page, Burrel
Smith, John
Lipscomb, J. D., (acct.)
Braszeal, John
Roden, John
Roden, William
Braszeal, Wm.
White, George, (acct)
Jones, G. W., (acct)
Carythers, J., (acct)
Smith, William
Watson, Jesse, (acct)
Hays, Vergil
Hays, Thomas
Fortune, Wm.
Roden, G. F.
Bookout,
Reeves, E.
Chitwood, R.
Payne, F.
Laythom, J. C.
Freeman, H.
Freeman, M., (acct)
Owens, Raymon
Vann, A. J.
Burns, John
Payne, A. P.
Bryant, Wm.
Coffee, Joel
Adams, Wm.
Brown, Mrs.
Redmond, Nathan
Padgett, L., (acct)

Estate Record Name
Jones, George W. (Cont.)
Box 6 File 63 1858-1863
Mays, H. C.
Mays, A. B., (acct)
Russell, D. C., (acct)
Roden, James, (acct)
Graves, A., (acct)
Ramsy, D. C., (acct)
McNair, D., (acct)
Nathan, James, (acct)
Griffin, Maborn
Lumpkin, Robt., (acct)
Jones, John
Box 6 File 64 1891-1896
Names in File:
Jones, Charles, (minor)
Jones, Lucy, (minor)
Jones, Stanton, (minor)
Jones, Cora, (minor)
Jones, Clinton, (minor)
Jones, Horace, (minor)
Jones, Thomas, (guardian)
Jones, Thomas, (bond)
Jones, W. T., (bond)
Kerby, L. B., (bond)
O'Rear, Samuel A., (bond)
Jennings, Henry C., (JP)
Cochran, L. L., Judge
DeShields, J. G., (sheriff)
Fuller, W. T., (guar.ad litem)
Smith, H. H., (bond)
Davenport, E. T., (paid)
Davenport, N. S. Co., (paid)
Campbell, H. B. (guar.ad litem)
Davis & Haralson, (atty)
Gray, John, (work on farm)
Taylor, T. A.
Blalock, D. S., (for Jones Children)
Lowry, W. A.
Tayler, T.N.F., (schooling)
Hardwick, Wm.

Estate Record Name
Jones, John (Cont.)
Winston, J. N., MD, (medical)
Stanton, Thomas L., (tuition)
Stanton, Almed L., (tuition)
Howard, J. M., (tax 1891-95)
Davis, Agnew
Jones, John
Crow, N. H., (pd for Cora)
Kirby/Kerby
Kirby, Jesse, (paid)
Cochran, Earl, (editor)
Fort Payne Journal, (notices)
Neal, Dora J., (tuition for Cora)
Crow, Clark
Reece, J. J., (note)
Strickland, Frank
Blackwall, D. S.
Crow, W. H.
Jones, John B.
Box 6 File 65 1893-1896
Names in File:
Sales of Land for Division
Clayton, John J., (adm)
Clayton, Mary C.,(w/o J. J.)
Clayton, Mollie C.
Clayton, John Jones
Jones, T. Z.
Jones, John E.
Jones, Barnie C.
Harper, E. D., (w/o M.A.)
Harper, M. A.
Crawford, Vada, (minor)
Crawford, Mattie, (minor)
Crawford, Nannie, (minor)
Crawford, Appie, (minor)
Crawford, Bessie, (minor)
Crawford, Martha, (deceased)
Crawford, James, (h/o Martha)
Price, Roxie, (deceased)
Price, Jack
Price, Lewis, (minor)

Estate Record Name
Jones, John B. (Cont.)
Price, Riley, (minor)
Price, Quinn, (minor)
Davis, Reubin C., (bond)
Sherman, J. R., (bond)
Poe, W. R., (guar.ad litem)
Copeland, Alexander C.
Gravitt, L. L., (JP)
Norwood, J. C., (notices)
Collinsville Clipper
Jones, Margaret, (repairs to house)
Gravitt, L, (JP)
Harper, M. A., (purch.land)
Jones, J. E., (purchased land)
Jones, B. C., (purchased land)
Jones, T. Z., (purchased land)
Howard, J. M., (tax 1895)
Harding, Sam., (witness)
Harding, Sam, Mrs., (witness)
Harding, Old, Mrs., (witness)
Campbell, C. A., (witness)
Little, N. B., (witness)
Robinson, Sylvester, (witness)
Holleman, E. J., (witness)
Mayes, Mrs., (witness)
Howard, Mrs., (witness)
Justice, W. L., (witness)
Gravitt, J. L., (comm)
Price, J. L., (Price minors)
Coffey, P. H., (attest)
Smith, S. P., MD, (paid)
Copeland, A. C., (appraiser)
Howard, J. M., (tax 1894)
Morris, John D., (coffin)
Crump, I. J., (gen.mdse)
Jones & Grady
Nicholson, L. S., (legal fees)
Sherman, J. R., MD, (med.)
Jones, Margaret, (w/o John E.)
Sale of Personal Property:
Jones, C. B., (yearling)

Estate Record Name
Jones, John B. (Cont.)
Bell, A., (yearling)
Brazel, T. J., (yearling)
Clayton, J. J., (cutting knife)
Gaines, R. A., (cutting knife)
Brazel, T. J., (loom)
Justis, W. J., (?)
Clayton, Molie, (sewing mach., wardrobe and clock)
Clayton, J. J., (table)
Harper, M. A., (feather bed)
Gains, R. A., (pilllows)
Harper, E. D., (mattress)
Davis, C. W., (bedstead)
Clayton, Mollie, (rocking chair)
Jones, Tildy, (3-chairs)
Clayton, Mollie,(chest& bookcase)
Jones, B. C., (jugs)
Jones, T. Z., (Lot of ware)
Clayton, J. J., (hoe)
Harper, M. A., (safe)
Davis, R. C., (wagon irons & saw)
Jones, T. Z., (spinning wheel cook stove, & hand saw)
Gravet, T., (coffee mill)
Jordin, A. B., (wash pot)
Gravet, W. G., (log chain)
Moris, J. W., (auger)
Dilbeck, W. J., (sythe & cradle)
Bell, A., (jack plane)
Davis, R. C., (ax)
Jones, B. C., (square)
Gravet, T., (buggy)
Black, J. E., (2-augers)
Hearn, J. J., (iron)
Clayton, J. J., (apple pealer)
Jones, J. E., (plow)
Jones, B. C.,(grindstone, pitchfork)
Harper, E. J., (chest)
Jones, B. C., (syrup mill)
Jones, T. Z., (2-bedsteads)

Estate Record Name

Jones, John B. (Cont.)
Gravitt, L. L., (JP)
Paid Out:
Howard, J. C.
Crump, J. S.
Hensley, J.
Morris, James W.
Nomond, J. C.
Hennon, J. R.

Jones, John R.
Box 6 File 66 1913-1914
Names in File:
Brock, Florence, (exec.)
Brock, Florence E., (dau.)
Bass, Fannie R. (w/o F. C.)
Bass, Frank C.
Sims, Alice F. (Allie)
Sims, A. L., (h/o Alice)
Jones, Hugh E.
Jones, Richard T. (Richmond)
Dunson, Ralph, (minor)
Dunson, Richmond T., (minor)
Dunson, Dorotha, (minor)
Dunson, Marcus M., (guardian)
Dunson, Lillie, (deceased)
Jones, E. D.
Brock, Eula
Gibson, J. E., (witness)
Nicholson, M. G., (witness)
Wilbanks, W. A., (comm.)
Baker, E. M., (guar.ad litem)
Smith, M. W., (testimony)
Black, W. R., (attest will)
Smith, N. C., Mrs., (attest will)
Bartlett, J. T., (Undertaker)
Wright, W. T., Dr., (medical)
Cochran & Russell
Dobb, W. J.
White, W. T., (blacksmith)
Smith, H. H., (notices)
Broom, G. W., (auctioneer)

Estate Record Name

Jones, John R. (Cont.)
Brindley, V. M., (JP)
Hulsey, H. W., (stock)
Coker, J. W., (road time)
Roberts, W. J., (tax)
Smith, M. W., (witness)
Simons, Lee
Bean, S. W., (blacksmithing)
Chastain, J. B., (monument)
Coker, Walter, (monument exp)
Nicholson, M. H., (acct.)
McWhorter, H. P., Dr., (med.)
Smith, R. H., (atty)
Wilson, D. W., MD, (medical)
Taylor, A. J.
Fricks, G. E., (witness)
Bradford, W. R., (atty)
Graves & Son, (burial outfit)
Davis & Pope
Kirby, A. C.
Sales of Land for Division
Tidmore, E. C., (purchased land)
Wilbanks, (commissioner)
Notes Due Estate:
Marbut, J. M.
Morgan, C. L.
Siniard, Ewie
Siniard, Mattie
Brindley, M., (JP)
Sale of Personal Property:
Simpson, C. L., (cook stove)
Lambert, J. R., (oil can & bucket)
Leak, A. S., (2-pans & plow)
Williams, (table)
Simpson, W. W., (table)
Taylor, B. G., (safe)
Simpson, Claude, (sausage mill)
Simpson, Will, (pitcher, lantern, coffee pot, double plow stock guanno distributor & corn sheller)
Mattox, Arthur, (6-chairs)

Estate Record Name

Jones, John R. (Cont.)
Jones, J. E., (keg)
Smith, M. D., (1-last)
Tidmore, J. M., (pr.and.irons)
Tidmore, W. J., (pr. and.irons)
Simpson, C. L., (bedstead)
Appleton, John, (145 bundles fodder)
Tayler, B. G., (bedstead & springs)
Livingston, C. H., (bedstead, mattress)
Taylor, B. H., (mattress)
Livingston, C. M., (dresser)
Taylor, B. G. (old dresser)
Renfro, Tom, (harrow & plow stock)
Wood, J. W., (mail box)
Lambert, J. R., (pitchfork)
Black, J. T., (junior cultivator)
Brock, Eula, (top buggy)
Wood, J. W., (one horse wagon)
Tidmore, W. J., (old buggy)
Tidmore, W. J., (buggy)
Tidmore, C. B., (mare)
Watson, Luther, (hames & traces)
Livingston, O. H., (monkey wrench)
Edwards, W. S., (milk cow)

Jones, Joseph
Box 6 File 67 1861
Names in File:
Edwards, Joseph, (adm)
Coleman, Lewis
Notes Due Estate:
Igo, S. E.
Igo, A. J.
Igou/Igo
McCormack, Thos.
Green, A. B.
Venable, Isaac
Craven, Dr., (acct.)
Sampley, Mr., (acct)
Sales of Personal Property:
McCormack, (1-mare)
Hartman, E., (1-colt)

Estate Record Name

Jones, Joseph (Cont.)
Igo, S. E., (cow & calf)
Estes, Reuben, Judge

Jones, Mahulda Ann
Box 6 File 68 1901-1904
Names in File:
Jones, George H., (son, adm)
Jones, Noah S.
Jones, M. S.
Farris, M. E., (w/o M. D.)
Farris M. D.
Izell, R. S., (w/o Jesse)
Izell, Jesse
Robinson, Charlotte, (w/o Luff)
Robinson, Luff
Jones, William
Jones, Leila
Jones, Eddie, (minor)
Jones, Lizzie, (minor)
Jones, Louisa, (minor)
Jones, Loula, (minor)
Jones , Aloryo, (minor)
Jones, Valolia, (minor)
Jones, Groves, (minor)
Jones, John H., (minor)
Jones, Lucinda, (minor)
Baker, Nettie, (minor)
Baker, Ida, (minor)
Robinson, William, (minor)
Robinson, Noah, (minor)
Robinson, Ada, (minor)
Robinson, Rosa, (minor)
Jones, G. H., (adm)
Culver, Viola
Culver, Oscar
Williams, James
Williams, Cora
Cain, Wall, (dep.sheriff)
Chitwood, W. J., (sheriff)
Causey, Bailey
Causey, Homer

Estate Record Name
Jones, Mahulda Ann (Cont.)
Causey, Elbert
Causey, Albert
Causey, Elizabeth
Baker, Lula
Baker, Willis
Baker, Loula
Baker, Mittie
Howard & Isbell, (atty)
Smith, Thos. H., (publisher)
Fort Payne Journal
Jones, G. H., (claim)
Faulkner, J. N., (JP)
Bailey, A. H., Dr., (witness)
Stewart, Samuel, (witness)
Jones, Fannie, (purchased land)
Jones, N. S.
Jones, W. S.
Jones, Willis
DeShields, J. G., (guar.ad litem)
Jones, M. S.
Jones, M. E.
Izell, J. T.
120 acres land
Howard & Isbell, (atty)
Jones, G. H., (adm bond)
Izell, R. S.
Durham, J. M., (bond)
Jones, M. S., (bond)
Bailey, A. H. (bond)
Izell, J. T., (bond)
Baker, Howard
Baker, Nettie
Baker, Ida
Jones, Thomas A.
Box 6 File 69 1911
Names in File:
Exemption before Adm.
Jones, Elizabeth, (widow)
No minor children
Mauldin, W. M., (commissioner)

Estate Record Name
Jones, Thomas A. (Cont.)
Bishop, W. W. (commissioner)
Major, P. M., (JP)
Croley, Jas. A., Judge
Jones, William L.
Box 6 File 70 1853-1877
Names in File:
Jones, Netty Jane, (N. J.), widow of William L. Jones
Edwards, Netty Jane Jones
Edwards, John, (h/o Netty)
Jones, George Melton, (minor)
Jones, Nancy Jane, (minor)
Jones, William Pinkey, (minor)
May, William H., (guar.ad litem)
Lea, Allen, (atty)
Edwards, N. J., (exec.)
House, Jacob G., (exec.)
Malone, Geo. W., (guar.ad litem)
Estes, R., Judge
Appleton, Thomas N., (witness)
Starnes, Basil R., (witness)
Appleton, G., (witness)
Morgan, John B., (witness)
Crisman, Jas., (witness)
Edwards, Joseph, (sheriff)
Driskill, Warner, (witness)
Nicholson, Lemuel M.
George, Chas. D.
Dunlap & Dobbs, (atty)
Edwards, Nancy J.
Edwards, Wm. S., (h/o Nancy)
Jones, Wm. P.
Jones, George M.
Newman, M. C., (appraiser)
Starnes, B. R., (appraiser)
Small, R. B., (appraiser)
Appleton, T. N., (appraiser)
Nicholson, J. J., (sheriff)
Pentecastle, Cochran
Gilliland, Wm. H.

Estate Record Name | **Estate Record Name**

Jones, William L. (Cont.)
- Edwards, John, (purchased land)
- Cox, Thos. G. A., (security)
- Edwards, Nete J. (bond)
- Edwards, John, (bond)
- Cox, T. G. A., (bond)
- Mullins, Wm., (bond)
- Edwards, Nete J., (guardian)
- Cunningham, Jesse, (clerk)
- Dunlap, Dobbs & Jacoway
- Appleton, J. M., (witness)
- Franklin, J. N., (sheriff)
- Reeve, James L., (paid note)
- Jones, N. J., (widow)
- Garrett & Edwards, (note)
- Reeve, N. V., (note)
- Newman, M. C., (paid)
- Higgins, R. W., (paid)
- Small, I. B., (tuition for children)
- Stewart, N. C., (paid)
- Walden & McSpadden, (fees)
- Small, J. B., (schooling)
- Walden, J. B., (paid)
- Vann, A. J., (paid)
- Reeves. J. A., (paid)
- Porter, B. H., (paid)
- Confederate Money $2500.00
- George, Charles D.
- Cunningham, John
- Harralson, Wm. S.
- Jones & Reeves
- Stanfield, G. R.
- Murphy, R.
- Crisman, James

Aamus, M., 6
Abbitt, A. B., 14
Abbot, Allen, 11
Abbot, Judie, Mrs., 199
Abbott, Huts? (Cuts?), 14
Abbott, Tobias, 10
Abbott, William, 14
Abercrombie, John, 1
Abercrombie, Erb, 1
Abercrombie, J. M., 1
Abercrombie, John, 1, 101
Abercrombie, Jonnie, 1
Abercrombie, Martha J., 1
Abercrombie, Mary Jane, 1
Abercrombie, Mary Susan, 1
Abercrombie, Ohpelia, 1
Abercrombie, Ruthie, 1
Abercrombie, Ruthy, 1
Abercrombie, W. S., 1
Abernathy, M. J., 110
Abney, W. H., 229
Abraham & Co., 14
Absher, J. S., 192
Adair, A. P., 84
Adair, John K., 158
Adair, R. J., 247
Adair, Sarah, 158, 175
Adair, Thos. K., 175
Adair, W. F., 158, 175
Adams Willie, 1
Adams, ?, 1
Adams, A. H., 1, 2
Adams, Ambrose, 22, 169, 170
Adams, B, S., 175
Adams, B. ?, 167
Adams, B. J., 151
Adams, B. L.S., 153
Adams, B. S., 150, 152, 154, 157, 158, 168, 170, 182
Adams, B., 175
Adams, Ben, 169
Adams, D. W., 194, 195, 202
Adams, Eunica, 1
Adams, G. Z., 210
Adams, George W., 74
Adams, Marie, 2
Adams, Mary, 1
Adams, Molly, 50
Adams, S. B. (S. D.), 17
Adams, Sallie, 74
Adams, Silas, 158, 158
Adams, Thomas, 158, 175
Adams, W. A., 74, 76
Adams, W. H., 1, 31
Adams, William, 170
Adams, Wm., 257
Adkins, A. J., 4, 15, 183
Adkins, Alvin, 3, 16
Adkins, Andy, 183, 184
Adkins, B. F., 16, 47, 183
Adkins, Ben, 4
Adkins, Benj., 183
Adkins, Benjamin F., (B. F.), 2
Adkins, Benjamin F., 2, 3
Adkins, Benjamin, 184
Adkins, Bill, 185
Adkins, Calvin, 16
Adkins, Charlotte W., 4
Adkins, Charlotte, 4
Adkins, D. L. G., 2, 3, 47
Adkins, D. L., 4
Adkins, Dock, 2, 4
Adkins, E. B., 2
Adkins, Emily, 184
Adkins, Enoch B., 3
Adkins, G. M., 4
Adkins, G. W., 3. 4
Adkins, Gaines, 16
Adkins, Geo. (Leo), 2
Adkins, George W., 2
Adkins, H. G., 4
Adkins, H. H., 183
Adkins, J. C., 2, 3, 4, 35, 36
Adkins, J. D., 4
Adkins, J. F. C., 3
Adkins, J. F., 3
Adkins, J. G., 2
Adkins, J., 4, 185
Adkins, James C., 4
Adkins, Jess, 3
Adkins, Jesse, 16
Adkins, John F., 4
Adkins, John, 157, 169
Adkins, Judy, 183
Adkins, Lottie, 4
Adkins, M. E., 4
Adkins, M. E., Mrs., 5
Adkins, M. V., 2
Adkins, Madison, 11
Adkins, Mary, 2, 3
Adkins, Moris, 233
Adkins, Morris, 2, 3, 34
Adkins, Nancy, 2
Adkins, Olie, 4
Adkins, S. G., 4, 5
Adkins, Samuel, 4
Adkins, Smith, 2, 3, 183
Adkins, W. B., 3
Adkins, W. H., 4
Adkins, Washington, 35, 132, 233
Adkins, William, 11
Adkinson, John, 23, 158, 175, 233
Adrian, D. W., 201
Adrian, J., 204
Adrian, James, 200, 201, 202, 203, 204
Age-Herald, 108
AGSRR Co, 254
Aiken, James, 82
Akins, John W., 5
Akins, Joseph, 11
Ala. Coal & Iron Stock, 234
Ala. Great So RR Co., 57
Ala. Great Sou. Railroad, 103
Ala. State Treas., 109
Ala.Gr.Sou. RR Co., 209
Alby, 64
Alcy, Slave, 232
Aldrich, Anna M., 60
Aldrich, Herbert, 61
Aldrich, J. H. (T. H.), 60
Alex, Slave, 232
Alexander, John, 254
Alexander, Judith, Miss, 228
Alexander, Lee, 124
Alexander, P. M., 67
Alexander, Thomas, 158
Alexander, Thos., 175
Alford, William, 35
Alfred, Henry, 147
Alfred, William, 16, 32
Allen, A. A., 5, 211
Allen, A., 244
Allen, B. L., 73
Allen, Ben, 6
Allen, Benjamin, 5
Allen, Berry J., 6
Allen, Crosby, 5
Allen, Douglass, 70
Allen, E. F., 6
Allen, E. L., 41
Allen, Ed, 210
Allen, Edmond, 210
Allen, Edward F., 5
Allen, Emily, 123
Allen, G. E., 242
Allen, H. R., 6
Allen, H. T., 126, 252
Allen, Hiram A., 6
Allen, Hiram, 5, 245
Allen, Ida, 210
Allen, J. D., 210
Allen, J.A.Q., 6
Allen, Jack, 115
Allen, James, 210
Allen, Jefferson D., 5
Allen, Joe, 6
Allen, John R., 193
Allen, John V., 6
Allen, John W., 5
Allen, John, 11, 192
Allen, Joseph A., 5
Allen, L. B., 54
Allen, Leroy, 175
Allen, Lerry, 158
Allen, M. A., 20
Allen, M. J., Mrs., 5
Allen, Margaret, 210
Allen, Mary, 210
Allen, Minor, 5
Allen, N. T., 6
Allen, Nancy, 210
Allen, Nancy, 5
Allen, Rubie, 5
Allen, Ruth, 5
Allen, S. A., 6
Allen, Sally, 6
Allen, Sarah A., 5
Allen, Sarah, 6
Allen, W. F., 6
Allen, W. T., 5
Allen, William F., 5, 6
Allison, A. B., 6
Allison, H. R., 15
Allison, Robert, 35
Allison, W. M., 6
Allison, W., 185
Allison, Joseph, 78
Allman, Z., 236
Alsman, Lena, 105
Alsman, W. H., 105
American Carriage Co.,89
Aminer, July (Julia), Amos, 6
Amos (Amus) Julia , 6
Amos (Amus)(Aamus), M., 6
Amos (Amus)(AaMus), M., 6
Amos (Minor Children), 6
Amos, B. T., 127
Amos, J. F., 102
Amos, James, 237
Amos, James, 56
Amos, John F., 6
Amos, John, 6
Amos, M., 6
Amos, Madason, 6
Amos, Milton Hames, 6
Amos, Ollie, 127
Amos, Ollie, Mrs., 62
Amos, R. L., 106
Amos, S. D., 98, 100
Amos, T. A., 191
Amos, Tobe, 192
Amus, John, 6
Amus, M., 6
Anderson, Biddie, 59
Anderson, C., 200, 201, 203
Anderson, Catherine, 59

Anderson, Edward, 6
Anderson, Henry C., 197
Anderson, Ida M., 6
Anderson, James, 129
Anderson, John C., 62
Anderson, Joseph, 11, 13
Anderson, Lora, 6
Anderson, R. E., 6, 131
Anderson, R. Y., 107
Anderson, Reulla, 6
Anderson, Scipis?, 202
Anderson, W. B., 208
Anderson, W. N., 58
Andrew, Ennis (Emmir), 63
Andrew, Matthew V., 27
Andrews, James, 63
Andrews, S., 245
Andrews, Silas, 244
Anibles & Whitaker, 168
Annet, 137
Ansley (Ausley), 6
Ansley (Ausley), James A., 6, 7
Ansley, Edward J., 6
Ansley, Heulet L., 6
Ansley, Mattie J., 6
Ansley, W. J., 6, 7
Ansley,James M., 6
Appleton, 118, 200, 203
Appleton, Alf & Harriet, 88
Appleton, C. C., 29
Appleton, G., 262
Appleton, Hariett, 56
Appleton, J. B., 201
Appleton, J. E., 118
Appleton, J. M., 263
Appleton, J. N., 195
Appleton, J., 156
Appleton, Jack, 118
Appleton, James, 118
Appleton, Jas. G., 118
Appleton, Jas., 121
Appleton, John E., 117
Appleton, John, 119
Appleton, John, 158, 261
Appleton, Joseph, 158, 175
Appleton, Newton, 202
Appleton, R. C., 175
Appleton, T. H., 66, 117, 118
Appleton, T. N., 182, 202, 262
Appleton, Thomas N., 262
Appleton, W. H., 24, 183
Appleton, W. N., 117, 120
Appleton, W. R., 118
Appleton, W., 183
Applewhite, J. T., 7, 8
Archer, F. N., 98
Argo, J. H., 30
Arledge, Eli, 26
Armstong, Lucy, 128
Armstrong, James C., 8
Armstrong, James H., 8, 9
Armstrong, James N., 187
Armstrong, James, 158, 174, 221
Armstrong, John H., 8
Armstrong, John, 8
Armstrong, L. D., 8
Armstrong, Louisa K., 128
Armstrong, Lucy, 127
Armstrong, Mary A., 8
Armstrong, Mary Ann, 8
Armstrong, Sarah, 8
Armstrong, W., 128
Armstrong, William, 8
Armstrong, Wm., 127, 128
Arrington, Rebecca, 252
Arther, Joseph, 247
Arthur, Charles, 158, 175
Arthur, House, 246
Arthur, Polk, 111
Arthur, Polk, 246
Arthur, Ruth J., 111
Arthur, W. H., 44
Asbur, J. S., 244
Ashberry, A. B., 9
Ashberry, A. H., 15, 78
Ashberry, Eliza, 9
Ashberry, Jane, 9
Ashberry, Joseph Andrew, 9
Ashberry, Joseph, 9
Ashberry, Julian, 9
Ashberry, Loucinda, 9
Ashberry, Rufus, 9
Ashberry, William, 9
Ashburn, ?, 9
Ashburn, Bob, 9
Ashburn, Franklin, 12
Ashburn, Isaac, 9
Ashburn, Martin , 9, 10, 11, 12, 13, 32
Ashburn, R. T., 9, 242
Ashburn, Robert T., 9, 12, 214
Ashburn, Robert, 242
Ashburn, S. B., 9
Ashburn, Susan,10
Ashburn, William L.,10
Ashbury, Mary, 12
Ashman, W, A., 120, 121
Atkins (Adkins), 16
Atkins, A. W., 84
Atkins, Alvin, 15
Atkins, B. F., 14
Atkins, Ben, 14
Atkins, Calon, 15
Atkins, Calvin, 14
Atkins, Charlotte, 14
Atkins, Ezekiel, 15
Atkins, Gaines W., 15
Atkins, George, 14
Atkins, J. C., 15
Atkins, Jesse, 15
Atkins, Jessey, 15
Atkins, Morris, 14, 15, 16
Atkins, Samuel, 15
Atkins, W. W., 11, 13
Attaway, S. K., 236
Attway, S. K., 234
Attwoods, J. L., 131
Ausley (Ansley), 7
Ausley, Mattie J., 7
Ausley, Wm. J., 7
Austin, Belle, 47
Austin, D. O., 47, 210
Austin, D., 197
Austin, Daniel, 16
Austin, David, 16
Austin, Fannie, 47
Austin, George, 47
Austin, H. D., 2, 3
Austin, J. A., 11, 35, 44
Austin, J. C., 3, 47
Austin, J. F., 4
Austin, J. L., 4
Austin, James F., 184
Austin, James, 15, 183, 184
Austin, Jamima, 16
Austin, Jasper, 47
Austin, Jno D., 16
Austin, John A., 16
Austin, Jonathan, 12, 214
Austin, Lafayette, 183, 184
Austin, M. L., 2, 3
Austin, M., 183
Austin, Margaret, 47
Austin, Rebecca, 47
Austin, Robert, 12
Austin, S. B., 9, 10, 12, 242
Austin, Stephen B., 9
Austin, W. B., 2, 3
Austin, W. L., 2, 3, 47
Austin, W. M., 4
Austin, W., 184
Austin, William, 47
Austin, Willie, 47
Avans, Isaac, 232
Avery, Allen, 232
Ayers, A. K., 16
Ayers, Ada, 16
Ayers, Albert K., 16
Ayers, Alda, 16
Ayers, Ida, 16
Ayers, J. G., 16
Ayers, J. W., 128
Ayers, John G., 16
Ayers, W. G., 60
Babb, C. C., 90
Babbs, 90
Babo, 90
Back, Catherine, 59
Back, G. C., 59
Backster,Welles, 136
Backster/Baxter, Gary, 136
Backster/Baxter, Willis, 136
Bacon, W., 225
Bacon, Washington, 225
Baden (Paden), 79
Bagle (Bogle), 17
Bagle, Alice E., 17
Bagle, Ethel P., 17
Bagle, H. C., 17
Bagle, Joseph H., 17
Bagley, N. F., 247
Bagley, N., 26
Bailey & Curtis, 233, 254
Bailey & Weaver, 39
Bailey, A. H., 262
Bailey, A. K., 17
Bailey, Aaron, 90
Bailey, Annie A., 17
Bailey, Eliza J., 17
Bailey, G. P., 75
Bailey, H. T., 30, 254
Bailey, J. A., 17
Bailey, J. H. T., 31
Bailey, J. S., 125
Bailey, J. T., 1
Bailey, M. A., Mrs., 17
Bailey, W. H., 74, 76
Bailey, William P., 17
Bailey, William W., 17
Bailor, W. H., 113
Bain, Ethel, 40
Baird, E. B., 130
Baits, L. A., 99
Baits, L. H., 99
Baker & Baker, 105
Baker, A., 169
Baker, Asa, 147, 170, 172, 225
Baker, E. M., 260
Baker, Ellen, 17
Baker, Frances, 17
Baker, Geo., 119
Baker, Howard, 262
Baker, Ida, 261, 262
Baker, J. F., 17
Baker, J. H., 5

Baker, J. M., 183
Baker, James R., 17, 123, 224
Baker, James, 136, 159, 176, 224
Baker, John H., 219
Baker, John Martin, 219
Baker, Lee S., 105
Baker, Lora, 219
Baker, Loula, 262
Baker, Lula, 262
Baker, M. M., 97, 99
Baker, M. M., Mrs., 100, 101
Baker, M. W., 74, 76
Baker, Mittie, 262
Baker, Nettie, 261, 262
Baker, Raymon E., 219
Baker, Willis, 262
Baker, Woodrow Wilson, 17
Baldwin, J., 221
Baldwin, James C., 143
Baley, J. S., 76
Ballard, G. F., 17
Ballard, James A., 17
Ballard, Mirah, 17, 18
Ballenger, Pheba, 14
Ballenger, William, 14
Ballentine, E. F., Mrs., 106
Ballentine, Elizabeth, 105
Ballentine, Elmer, 105
Ballentine, Martin Luther, 105
Balletine, Elizabeth F., 105
Bandon, H. H., 246
Banister, John, 238
Banister, Thomas, 55
Bank of Valley Head, 85
Banks, 222
Banks, Hugh R., 153
Banks, Wiley, 153
Bankston, 156
Bankston, D., 170
Bankston, G. S., 154
Bankston, J. F., 151
Bankston, J. G., 155
Bankston, J. L., 156
Bankston, J. P., 150
Bankston, J. S., 155, 156, 157
Bankston, John V., 158
Bankston, Lucy, Miss, 177
Banner, J. M., 239
Banning, H. M., 73
Banskston, J. S., 168
Banter, M., 26
Baptist Church, 225
Barber, W. H., 44
Barber, William H., 140
Barbor, Henry, 139
Barbor, Mary A., 139
Barbor/Barbour, 140
Barbour, Henry, 140
Barbour, Margarett, 21
Barbour, William, 21
Barclay, G. T., 102
Barclay, Thomas C., 153
Barclay, Thos. C., 155
Barkdale, 200
Barkley, Andrew L., 159
Barkley, G. W., 199
Barkley, S. M., 176
Barkley, S. W., 174
Barkley, Saml. M., 159, 167
Barkley, Wm., 22
Barksdale, 256
Barksdale, E. J., 18
Barksdale, George, 159
Barksdale, J. A., 101, 194
Barksdale, J. F., 121
Barksdale, J. H., 100
Barksdale, J. H., 118, 119, 121
Barksdale, John W., 102
Barksdale, S. W., 18, 100
Barksdale, Sherod, 159, 175, 176, 182
Barksdale, W. J., 102, 103
Barksdale, W. M, 120, 121
Barksdale, W. S., 99, 101, 103
Barksdale, Walt, 102
Barksdale, White, 203
Barksdale, William, 118
Barksdale, Wm. 119, 193, 202
Barnard, Ethel, 18
Barnard, F. C., 52
Barnard, Frank, 52, 229
Barnard, J. D., 155
Barnard, J. L., 19, 150, 151, 155
Barnard, J. T., 153
Barnard, J., 154
Barnard, John, 27
Barnard, Lou W., 18
Barnard, Lucy, 18
Barnard, P.? T.?, 154
Barnes, Abner, 19
Barnes, Davidson, 148
Barnes, Edgar, 15
Barnes, Elizabeth, 18
Barnes, G. W., 18, 19
Barnes, Geo. A., 160
Barnes, George A., 174
Barnes, J. E., 108
Barnes, James, 19
Barnes, John, 18, 19
Barnes, M., 230
Barnes, Martha A., 148
Barnes, Pleasant, 230
Barnes, T. J., 230
Barnes, W. G., 19
Barnes, W. H., 35
Barnett, J. P., 91
Barr, Jas., 239, 240
Barr, M. A., 160, 175
Barrett, H. J., 101
Barrett, J. D., 88
Barrett, J. H., 125
Barsoms?, James, 114
Bartel, Fredrick, 159
Bartles, Frederick, 176
Bartlett, Geo., 193
Bartlett, J. T., 260
Bartlett, John F., 106
Bartlett, John T., 66, 190
Bartlett, John, 192
Bass, Fannie R. 260
Bass, Frank C., 260
Bass, Jesse, 19
Bata, William, 14
Batella, Alabama, 41
Bates, A. W., 112
Bates, Alabama, 97
Bates, Alvis, 20
Bates, Belle, 63
Bates, Ben F., 159
Bates, Ben, 158, 171
Bates, Benj., 157, 176
Bates, Esther, 20
Bates, F. M., 97
Bates, G. W., 92
Bates, Geo., 67
Bates, I.R., 20
Bates, Ida Ayers, 16
Bates, Irby, 20
Bates, J. D., 16
Bates, J. P., 197
Bates, Jesse, 19, 20
Bates, L. F., 88, 192
Bates, Lee, 194
Bates, Ollie, 63
Bates, Pink, 19, 20
Bates, Willie, 20
Batson, J. B., 89
Battles, J. N., 101
Battles, J., 217, 218
Bauerlee, I. Victoria, 46
Bauldin, Gidean, 20
Bauldin, Giden, 20
Bauldin, Hilley, 20
Bauldin, Noble, 20
Baxter, Angie, 50
Baxter, C. W., 175
Baxter, Dollie, 20, 21
Baxter, E. D. M., 21
Baxter, E. D., 21
Baxter, Eliza, 51
Baxter, Erskine, 20, 21
Baxter, F. M., 7, 44, 95, 107,150, 184, 235, 243, 244, 58
Baxter, F. W., 147
Baxter, Francis Marion, 20
Baxter, G. W., 143, 245
Baxter, Geo., 51
Baxter, George, 21, 51
Baxter, Houston, 50
Baxter, J. B., 20
Baxter, J. J., 20
Baxter, J. P., 218, 245
Baxter, J. R & F. M., 107
Baxter, J. R., 20, 136, 236
Baxter, J. W. (Willis), 20, 21
Baxter, J. W., 76, 127, 199, 224
Baxter, J. Willis, 51
Baxter, J., 171
Baxter, James J., 159
Baxter, James, 21, 22, 112, 123, 145, 147, 167, 174, 176, 206, 225, 245
Baxter, James, Jr., 23
Baxter, James, Sr., 159, 223, 224
Baxter, Jas., 225
Baxter, Jesse, 22, 41, 94, 170, 173
Baxter, Jesse, Jr., 160, 224
Baxter, Jesse, Sr., 224
Baxter, John, 246
Baxter, Julia, 20
Baxter, L. C., Mrs., 228
Baxter, Lena, 20, 21
Baxter, Lonie, 20
Baxter, Lonnie, 21
Baxter, Lucy, 21, 51
Baxter, Lula C., 228
Baxter, M., 244
Baxter, Marion, 222, 24, 225, 244
Baxter, Martin, 20
Baxter, May, 20, 21
Baxter, Napper S. 236
Baxter, O. B., 20
Baxter, Oscar, 21, 50, 94
Baxter, Pat, 26
Baxter, R. M., 136
Baxter, S. J., Mrs., 20
Baxter, S. W., 150
Baxter, Sarah Frazier, 136
Baxter, Sary, 136

Baxter, Susan A., 20
Baxter, T. C., 20, 21, 49
Baxter, T. J., 44
Baxter, Thomas C., 51
Baxter, Thomas, 20, 51
Baxter, Thos., 247
Baxter, Wash, 159, 169, 170
Baxter, Washington, 176
Baxter, Willis, 21, 22, 51, 136, 159, 172, 175, 225
Baxter, Wills, 147
Beam. R. F., 174
Bean, J. G., 80
Bean, R. F., 160
Bean, S. M., 81
Bean, S. W., 260
Bean, Samina, 80
Bean, Samira C., 81
Bean, Samira Crabtree, 79
Bean, Tol, 80
Bean, William, 60
Beane, E., 251
Beane, J. T., 80
Beane, T. J., 38
Beard, A. J., 97
Beard, Rusel. 98
Bearden, A. J., 103
Bearden, Alice, 39
Bearden, Alma, 23
Bearden, Alonzo, 210
Bearden, Charles, 210
Bearden, Dianah, 174
Bearden, Diannah, 159
Bearden, Elizabeth, 210
Bearden, F. M., 100
Bearden, Frances, 21, 23
Bearden, J. M., 99, 103
Bearden, J. W., 194
Bearden, James, 38
Bearden, M. S., 159
Bearden, Martins, 174
Bearden, O. J., 23
Bearden, Oscar, 210
Bearden, Sherman, 23
Bearden, Willie, 23
Bearden,Oma, 210
Beasley, Samuel B., 77
Beasley, Wm., 223
Beason & Phillips, 145, 147
Beason, J. G., 147
Beason, M. G., 241
Beaty, J. E., 189
Beaty, Rhody C., 189
Beavers Farm, 193
Beavers, 200, 203
Beavers, A. W., 195
Beavers, Allen, 159, 176, 216
Beavers, J. W., 202
Beavers, Lucy, 243, 245
Beavers, M. M., 245
Beavers, R. C., 98, 100
Beavers, Wm., 204, 205
Beavers, Wood, 194, 195
Beck, D., 226
Beck, Daniel, 143, 144, 220
Beck, Dan'l., 145
Beck, E. H., 75
Beck, Ester, 26
Beck, J. D., 158, 175
Beck, Lidia A., 128
Beck, Louisa Ann, 127
Beck, Lucinda, 24
Beck, Lusinda, Miss., 24
Beck, T. J., 102, 103
Beck, T., 226
Beck, Thomas, 23, 24, 185, 220
Beck, W. W., 24
Beck, William, 24, 128
Beck, Wm., 127
Beckom, George, 11
Becom, James, 10
Becom, Medow, 10
Becown (Becom), Louisa, 10
Been, Smiry, 81
Beene, Jacob, 24, 25
Beene, Geo T., 38
Beene, J. T., 38
Beene, Jacob T., 25
Beene, Jacob, 30, 32, 33, 213, 214, 215, 233, 241, 242
Beene, John P., 25
Beene, Nancy, 25, 31
Beene, Samuel, 25, 114, 115
Beene, Sarah, 241
Beene, T. J., 213
Beene, W. J., 25, 215
Beene, Wm., 25
Beesan & Phillips, 114, 149
Beesan, Jesse G., 141
Beesen & Phillips, 144
Beesen, W. B., 151
Beeson & Phillips, 146, 222, 225
Beeson, 220
Beeson, Belle, 113
Beeson, Eula L., 26
Beeson, Fannie S., 27
Beeson, Floyd, 235
Beeson, H. C., 26
Beeson, Henry C., 25
Beeson, J. F., 149
Beeson, J. G., 5, 168, 220, 231
Beeson, J., 235
Beeson, Jepe (Jesse), 26
Beeson, Jesse B., 25
Beeson, Jesse G., 25, 26, 27, 114, 219, 220, 149, 176
Beeson, Lula, 26
Beeson, V. Bell, 26
Beeson, W. B., 168, 232, 255, 256
Belcher, J. B., 26, 147
Belcher, Joseph, 27, 147
Belcher, W. T., 102
Beldin, Cason B., 60
Bell Telephone Co., 109
Bell, A. M., 27
Bell, A., 259
Bell, C. M., 39, 112, 228
Bell, C. N., 52, 227
Bell, Charles, 27
Bell, Charley, 27
Bell, D. W., 133, 134, 135
Bell, E. L., 133
Bell, J. R., 27
Bell, James W., 27
Bell, James, 192
Bell, L. D., 101
Bell, Larkin H., 252
Bell, Lillie, 27
Bell, M. E., 133
Bell, Mary, 133, 134
Bell, Mary, Mrs., 135
Bell, Maudie, 27
Bell, R. W., 27, 28
Bell, R. W., Mrs., 28
Bell, S. F., 222
Bell, Tom E., 133
Bell, W. J., 28
Bell, Wm., 29
Belsher, J. B., 96
Belsher, Joseph, 142
Belshire, J. B., 39
Benefield, J. R., 97
Benett, A., 218
Benge, Clinton, 149
Benge, D. C., 196
Benge, DeWitt C., 196
Benge, George C., 239
Benge, V. C., 149
Benjen, 85
Bennett, A. A., 212
Bennett, A. D., 251
Bennett, A. G., 221, 237, 239
Bennett, G. G., 237
Bennett, Isiah, 240
Bennett, John, 230
Bennett, Mitchell, 13
Bennett, Samford, 19
Bennett, Wm. H., 223
Benson, John, 31
Bentley, S. H., 90
Berry, ?, 28
Berry, A. I., 43
Berry, A. J., 28, 43, 210, 217
Berry, A. J., Sr., 28
Berry, Andrew Jackson, 28
Berry, Carlin, 176
Berry, Caroline, 159
Berry, Coleman Frances, 28
Berry, Douglas, 238
Berry, Eliza, 28
Berry, Elizabeth, 28
Berry, Elvanie E., 216
Berry, F. M., 28
Berry, H., 97
Berry, Hugh, 28
Berry, J. A., 95
Berry, Jackson, 159, 175
Berry, James Washington, 28
Berry, James, 23, 28
Berry, Jeptha, 28, 175
Berry, Jess, 159
Berry, John W., 28
Berry, John Wesley, 28
Berry, John, 122, 159, 176, 216, 238
Berry, Major, 28
Berry, Mary (Erwin), 28
Berry, Mindy, 238
Berry, Minnie, 1, 20, 39, 51, 53, 55, 73, 88, 127, 129, 190, 209, 229
Berry, Minnie, Miss, 49
Berry, Nancy Adeline, 28
Berry, P. B., 210
Berry, Preston, 210, 238
Berry, Robert Wilson, 28
Berry, Sarah, 28, 238
Berry, Simon, 221
Berry, Thomas, 246
Berry, W. E., 131
Berry, William, 28
Berry, Winnie, 28
Berry, Winnifred, 28
Berry, Wm., 197
Berryhill, L. C., 53
Berryhill, L. C., Mrs., 53
Betcher, Jno., 26
Bethune, A. V., 124
Bethune, Adeline V., 29
Bethune, Adeline Viola, 124
Bethune, C. L., Mrs., 28, 29

Bethune, Carrie L., 29
Bethune, Clara, 28
Bethune, Clarra L., 29
Bethune, D. L., 28, 210
Bethune, Effie L., 29
Bethune, Elmer, 28
Bethune, Elmer, et al, 28
Bethune, John E., 29
Bethune, John T., 29
Bethune, Maude V., 29
Bethune, O. L., 28
Bethune, Vennie L., 29
Bethune, Vinnie, 28
Bethune, W. J., 124
Bethune, W. T., 29
Bethune, William A., 29
Bethune, Wm., 124
Bibb, J. M., 221
Bibb, James M., 93
Bibbs, James M., 21
Biddle (Riddle), 18
Biddle, John V., 48
Biddle, John, 18, 19
Biddle, R. R., 80
Biddle, T. J., 78
Biddle, T. W., 48
Biddle, W. R., 2, 31
Biddle, William R., 18
Bidle, James, 27
Bidwell, S. W., 68
Big Wills Creek, 243
Bileups, John A., 77
Bilsher, John, 231
Bird, John, 170
Bird, S. M., 60
Bird, Wm. G, 60
Birens, Joseph, 196
Birk (Burk), M. O., 29
Birk (Burk), Yancy, 29
Birmingham Fertilizer Co., 52
Bishof, W.W., 5
Bishop, G. J., 209
Bishop, G. W., 99
Bishop, J. H., 91
Bishop, Jackson, 159
Bishop, Minnie, 48, 49
Bishop, R. S., 68
Bishop, W. W., 262
Bishop, Wm., 169
Black & Cobb, 145
Black Diamond Roofing, 49
Black, C. H., 202
Black, E. W., 65, 77, 124
Black, Geo. S., 145
Black, Geo. W., 65
Black, Isaac, 133
Black, J. E., 72, 83, 259
Black, J. H., 1, 97, 102
Black, J. H., Dr., 97
Black, J. P., 60
Black, J. T., 261
Black, J. W., 187
Black, Jno. W., 187
Black, John E., 83
Black, John H., Dr., 23
Black, John, 87, 192
Black, Oliver, 201, 202
Black, S. D., 193
Black, S. M., 90
Black, Sam, 100
Black, W. L., 237, 239
Black, W. R., 89, 90, 260
Blackburn, E., 168
Blackburn, Elijah, 21, 159, 176
Blackburn, Jabus, 175
Blackburn, Jaby, 159
Blackburn, Jackson, 159, 175
Blackburn, John, 159, 176, 223
Blackburn, Rebecca, 159, 182
Blackburn, W. F., 110
Blackstone, Louisa, 240
Blackwall, D. S., 258
Blackwell, A. L., 159, 176
Blackwell, B. H., 29, 212, 215
Blackwell, Bagley H., 29
Blackwell, H. L., 91
Blackwell, J. M., 141
Blackwell, James M., 141
Blackwell, John G., 29
Blackwell, John H., 29
Blackwell, Mrs., 228
Blackwell, Nancy S., 29
Blackwell, R. F., 76
Blackwell, Sallie, 29
Blackwell, Sallie, Mrs., 29
Blackwell, T. H., 75
Blackwell, T. J., 29
Blackwell, T. Y., 37
Blackwell, Thomas, 29
Blackwell, Walter, 29
Blake, 229
Blake, B. P., 29, 43, 133
Blake, Dayamin?, 133
Blake, Fannie B., 29
Blake, Fannie, 133, 134
Blake, Fannie, Mrs., 135
Blake, Fanny, 29
Blake, Howard, 189
Blake, I. C., 133
Blake, I., 133
Blake, Isaac, 29
Blake, J. B., 29, 30
Blake, J. G., 32
Blake, Jane, 40
Blake, John B., 131
Blake, John Ben, 144
Blake, L. M., 29
Blake, Leabon, 135
Blake, M. E., 215
Blake, M., 133
Blake, Margaret E., 215
Blake, Margaret N., 30
Blake, Margaret, 131
Blake, Melvina, 133
Blake, S. T., 133
Blake, Sally May, 131
Blake, T. B., 61
Blake, Thomas, 215
Blakemon, John T., 108
Blalock, D. S., 258
Blalock, David S., 30
Blalock, Joseph D., 30
Blalock, Lula, 30
Blalock, Nannie H., 30
Blalock, Taylor E., 30
Blanchet, George, 175
Blancit, A. D., 12, 14, 15, 31, 32, 38, 241
Blancit, C. C., 31
Blancit, Elizabeth, 31, 32
Blancit, G. H., 31
Blancit, George H., 31
Blancit, George, 158
Blancit, J. N., 31
Blancit, James P., 31
Blancit, John C., 31
Blancit, Leanah J., 31
Blancit, M. M., 31
Blancit, R. L., 71
Blancit, William, 31, 32
Blancitt, America L., 30
Blancitt, Archibald D., 242
Blancitt, C. C., 30, 32
Blancitt, Clement C., 30
Blancitt, Eliza J., 30
Blancitt, Elizabeth, 32
Blancitt, George, 32
Blancitt, J. C., 33
Blancitt, J. N., 33
Blancitt, James N., 30
Blancitt, John C., 30, 32
Blancitt, John J., 33
Blancitt, John, 32
Blancitt, Leanah, 33
Blancitt, Missianah, 32
Blancitt, N. D., 32
Blancitt, R. L., 36
Blancitt, William A., 30
Blancitt, Wm. A., 30
Blanset, A. D., Jr., 71
Blansett (Blansit), 30)
Blansett, Georgia, 30
Blansett, John, 30
Blansett, Kate, 30
Blansett, Nellie, 30
Blansett, Oscar, 30
Blansett, Tom, 30
Blansit (Blansitt) (Blansett), 30
Blansit, ?, 10
Blansit, A. D., 214, 242
Blansit, A. D., Jr., 211
Blansit, B., 185
Blansit, Chester A., 30
Blansit, D. M., 31
Blansit, Elizabeth, 31
Blansit, James N., 30, 31, 37
Blansit, Joseph P., 31
Blansit, Leona, 31
Blansit, Lillie M., 31
Blansit, Mr., 193
Blansit, Nancy A., 30
Blansit, Nancy J., 31
Blansit, Nonnie, Mrs., 31
Blansit, R. L., 4, 35
Blansit, Robert L., 31
Blansit, Widow, 14
Blansit, Wm., 31
Blansitt (Blancit), William, 31
Blansitt, Archibald, 32
Blansitt, B., 32
Blansitt, Jasper H., 32
Blansitt, Jim, 30
Blansitt, Leann, 32
Blansitt, Missiniah, 32
Blansitt, Ned, 31
Blanton, J. W., 94
Blanton, Richard, 169
Blanton, Whit, 159, 169, 174
Blanton, Whit, 22, 222
Blanton, White, 224
Blanton, Whitman, 96, 114, 176
Blare, L. C., 218
Blaylock, William, 18, 19
Blevins, 252
Blevins, A. D., 34
Blevins, A. J., 242
Blevins, A. L., 34
Blevins, Amilla, 34
Blevins, Ammilla, 34
Blevins, Amos (Amon), 33
Blevins, Bonnie, 34
Blevins, C. G., 185
Blevins, C., 185
Blevins, Calvin, 12, 15, 33, 34, 35
Blevins, David, 233
Blevins, E. B., 33
Blevins, E. M., 184

Blevins, E., 185
Blevins, Embeeson, 35
Blevins, Emily, 33, 35
Blevins, Emily, Mrs., 33
Blevins, Eve, 183
Blevins, F. M., 2, 3, 47
Blevins, G. J., 3, 4, 34
Blevins, G., 185
Blevins, Gaines, 33, 34, 36, 233
Blevins, Gains, 34
Blevins, Gains, Jr., 35
Blevins, Gains, Sr., 132
Blevins, H. E., 3
Blevins, H. T., 33, 34
Blevins, H. W., 2, 3, 33
Blevins, Hardie, 33
Blevins, Hardy W., 34
Blevins, Harry, 36
Blevins, Henry, 34, 36 184
Blevins, Ida May, 35
Blevins, J. A., 33, 185
Blevins, J. E., 34
Blevins, J. F., 35
Blevins, J. L., 33, 34
Blevins, J. M., 35, 36
Blevins, J. R., 35, 36
Blevins, J. T., 15, 81
Blevins, J. W., 36
Blevins, Jack W., 36
Blevins, Jackson, 11
Blevins, James, 10, 12, 33, 34, 35, 36, 221, 233
Blevins, James, Sr., 183, 184
Blevins, Jas., 11
Blevins, Jeff, 185
Blevins, Jesse R., 36
Blevins, Jesse, 35
Blevins, Jessie B., 11
Blevins, Jessie, 11
Blevins, Joe, 35
Blevins, John L., 13, 33, 34, 182, 184
Blevins, John, 11, 33, 34
Blevins, Jonathan, 233
Blevins, Jonathan, 9, 34, 233
Blevins, L. E., 3, 4
Blevins, Launa, 2
Blevins, Laura (Launa) E. , 2
Blevins, Laura, 3
Blevins, Lennie, 2
Blevins, Lorene, 2
Blevins, M. V., 35, 36
Blevins, M., 185
Blevins, Malinda, 36
Blevins, Manilla Ann, 34
Blevins, Marg. L., 10
Blevins, Marion, 47
Blevins, Martha Ann, 34
Blevins, Martin, 33
Blevins, Mary C., 182
Blevins, Mary, 184
Blevins, Melia, 34, 35
Blevins, Melvina V., 35, 36
Blevins, Millie, 35
Blevins, Milly, 35
Blevins, Minnie, 34
Blevins, Nancy, 33
Blevins, Norris, 13
Blevins, O. D., 34
Blevins, O. M., 33
Blevins, Oscar, 4
Blevins, Polk P., 249
Blevins, R. M., 182, 183, 184
Blevins, R. M., 4, 14, 33, 47, 58
Blevins, Rebecca, 33
Blevins, Richard M., 33, 132
Blevins, Richard, 11, 13, 36, 182, 183, 184
Blevins, Robert,10
Blevins, Rufinna, 12
Blevins, Rufus, 35
Blevins, Sarah, 34
Blevins, Stephens, 13
Blevins, Tenie, 3
Blevins, Teny, 3, 4
Blevins, V. B., 36
Blevins, V. M., 34
Blevins, V., 34
Blevins, Virgil, 35, 36
Blevins, W. H., 33
Blevins, W., 11
Blevins, William J., 35
Blevins, William, 14
Blevins, Wm., Jr., 35
Bloodworth, H. F., 99
Bloom, Ellen, 80
Boaz Marble Works, 188
Bobbin/Brabbin, H. S., 220
Bobo, C. C., 88, 89, 92
Bobo, Janey, 1
Bobo, Johnnie G. C., 20
Boggs, Anderson, 63
Boggs, William, 63
Boggs, Wm., 238
Bogle, 186
Bogle, J. C., 25, 96, 113, 142, 222
Bogle, John, 247
Bogle, Jos. C., 225
Bogle, Joseph R., 36
Bogle, Joseph C., 224
Bogle, Mat, 202
Bogles, Joseph C., 113
Bohanan, J. B., 17
Bohannon, Daily, 51
Bohannon, Daisy, 50
Bohanon, Lucinda, 49
Bohling, Henry, 36
Bohling, J. G., 7
Bohling, J. W., 139
Bohling, John, 36
Bolden, L. B., 98
Boldin, Noble, 256, 257
Boldin, R., 256, 257
Bolen, Rueben, 159
Bolen, W. H., 158
Bolin, E., 32
Bolin, Mattie, 61
Bolin, Nobel, 251
Boling, Henry, 36
Bolton, Bertie, 36
Bolton, Carl, 36
Bolton, J. M., 36
Bolton, Johnnie, 36
Bolton, Nora, 36
Bolton, Willie, 36
Bon__?, John T., 150
Bone, James H., 8
Bone, John, 192
Bone, W. B., 192
Bookout, 256, 257
Bookout, W. L., 46
Booth, Elizabeth, 127
Booth, Jeptha, 127
Boozer, C. C., 36, 37
Boozer, Carter, 37
Boozer, Christopher, 37
Boozer, Daniel, 37
Boozer, Elijah, 36
Boozer, George W. (H.), 36
Boozer, Henry, 37
Boozer, John W., 36
Boozer, P., 36
Boozer, Peter, 37
Boozer, Taylor, 37
Boozer, Wesley, 37
Boozer, Z. T., 37
Bosewell, George, 174
Boswell, George, 159
Botsfield, Mr., 159
Botsfield, Wm., 176
Bott, Eliza J, 236
Bouldin, Abe L., 37
Bouldin, Abraham L., 37
Bouldin, E. J., 38
Bouldin, E. L., 100, 102
Bouldin, E., 10, 12, 30, 214
Bouldin, Elijah Jackson, 37
Bouldin, Elijah, 12, 13, 33, 37, 38, 82,148, 222, 241
Bouldin, Elizabeth, 217
Bouldin, George W., 13
Bouldin, John F., 38
Bouldin, John Franklin, 37
Bouldin, Mariah, 37
Bouldin, Richard Grant, 37
Bouldin, Rueben, 176
Bouldin, Sarah Jane,
Bouldin, Thos., 42
Bouldin, Virgil, 104
Bouldin, William J., 37
Bouldin, Wm. G, 38
Bouldin, Wm. Grant, 37
Bouldin, Wm., 214
Bouth, T. J., 84
Bowen, Archie, 38, 39
Bowen, Ebenezer, 159
Bowen, H. N., 194
Bowen, J. L., 39
Bowen, John L., 39
Bowen, John T., 39
Bowen, M. C., 39
Bowen, M. E., 39
Bowen, Madison C., 39
Bowen, Marcus E., 39
Bowen, Slety A., 39
Bowen, Thomas L., 39
Bowen/Bowers, Sallie, 104
Bowens, J. B., 57
Bowens, Sallie, 39
Bowerman, Gratia E., 64
Bowker, J. A., 60
Bowlin, Wm. H., 175
Bowling, C. E., 106
Bowling, C. E., Mrs., 106
Bowling, Ida C., 106
Bowman, A. R., 54
Box, C. O., 152
Box, P. D., 130, 196, 217, 230, 231
Box, P. J., 251
Box, Patrick A., 230
Box, R. D., 230
Box, Sarah, 230
Boyd, 205
Boyd, Belzona, 39
Boyd, E. D., 42
Boyd, J. G., 53
Boyd, James, 43
Boyd, John H., 39
Boyd, John W., 69
Boyd, Robert, 39,
Boyd, S. C., 39
Boydston, A. C., 33
Boyston, Jane Blevins, 33

Boyston, Judie, 33
Brabbin, H. S., 220
Brackens, Tinsley, 159
Brackett, Francis V., 40
Brackett, Laura A. & Francis V., 40
Brackett, Laura A., 40
Bradford, 46
Bradford, J. T., 162
Bradford, Tipten, 232
Bradford, W. R., 260
Bradford, Wm., 75
Bradley, 112
Bradley, E. H., 153, 159, 175
Bradley, Ellis, 194
Bradley, Frank, 97
Bradley, M. J., 193
Bradley, Mary P., 65
Bradley, W. A., 216
Bradley, W. S., 65
Bradley, William A., 85
Bradon, P. A., 25
Brainerd, Addison, 32
Bramlett, Effie, 241
Bramlett, J. R., 241
Branam, Jacob, 12
Branden, H. H., 175
Branden, J. M., 97
Branden, Jim, 252
Branden, P. A., 5, 8, 12, 15, 30, 46, 196
Branden, T. A., 55
Brandon Bros., 74
Brandon, 114
Brandon, C. F., 114, 174, 206
Brandon, Calvin, 158, 175
Brandon, D. A., 40, 41
Brandon, Dave, 41
Brandon, David, 40
Brandon, H. H., 27, 49, 78, 114, 143, 231, 246
Brandon, H. H., Mrs., 49
Brandon, Hugh H., 159, 174
Brandon, Hugh T. 2
Brandon, Hugh T., et al, 40
Brandon, Hugh, 176
Brandon, J. A., 97
Brandon, J. L., 55, 56, 58, 65, 68, 78, 83, 85, 245
Brandon, James, 252
Brandon, John W., 40, 41
Brandon, Johnie Lou, 40
Brandon, Johnnie L. 41
Brandon, Jonnie Lou, 41
Brandon, Lela, 40, 41
Brandon, Margaret, 114
Brandon, P. A., 10, 18, 24, 25, 26, 28, 36, 40, 41, 87, 95, 126, 131, 148, 149, 155, 196, 197, 202, 205, 212, 213, 234, 239, 243, 246, 253, 254
Brandon, P., 159
Brandon, Phillip A., 68, 92, 130, 236
Brandon, Phillip, 174
Brandon, W. C., 158
Brandon, Wm., 23
Brannard, J. L., 151
Brannon & Mosley, 229
Brannon, Daniel, 41
Brannon, Ella, 41
Brannon, J. A., 103, 229
Brannon, J. L., 151
Branom, Richard, 14
Braseal, William, 176
Brassell, Josie Brock, 42
Braswell, Mary, 219
Braszeal, J. J. F., 256
Braszeal, John, 257
Braszeal, Wm., 256, 257
Bratten, Alex, 175
Bratton, Alex., 159, 176
Bratton, Alexander, 153
Bray, C., 227
Bray, D. H., 42
Bray, Houston, 42
Bray, Houston, et al, 41, 42
Bray, J. B., 42
Bray, J. W., 122
Bray, M. E., Mrs., 42
Bray, Shadrack, 8
Bray, William C., 48
Bray, William, 42
Brazel, T. J., 259
Breland, A. F. & Co., 80
Breland, A. F., 81
Breland, J. E., 215
Brewer, John, 182, 184
Briant, Joseph, 153
Briant, Polly, 146
Briant, R., 169
Briant, Thomas, 169
Briant, Wm., 143, 146
Brice, G. T., 196
Brice, James, 159, 176
Brice, John M., 223
Brice, John P., 159, 176
Bridges, F. J., 169, 176
Bridges, Frank J., 159
Bridges, Frank, 170
Bridges, Lewis, 175
Bridges, Louisa/Lewis, 168
Bridges, Luke, 158
Bridges, Robert, 176
Bridges, Robt., 159
Bridges, Sarah, 149, 152, 155, 168
Bridges, Thomas, 176
Bridges, Thos., 159
Bright, R. M., 102
Brindle Asa, 178
Brindlee, R. T., 174
Brindley, A. R., 159
Brindley, Carl, 200
Brindley, M., 260
Brindley, V. M., 75, 260
Brinkley, R. T., 160
Brinkley, V. M., 93
Brinsfield, Simson, 159
Brisen, John P., 174
Brisendine, E., 53
Brison, John, 174
Bristoe, Elizabeth T., 42
Bristoe, Elizabeth, 42
Bristoe, Samuel I., 42
Bristoe, Warrick, 42
Bristoe/Bristow/Bristo, 42
Briston, E. T., 153
Briston, W., 153
Bristow, E. T., 42
Bristow, Elisha, 42
Bristow, Sarah M., 42
Bristow, Warrick, 42
Britt, Henry, 75
Britt, J. B., 217
Britt, J., 218
Britte, H. L., 75
Broadwell, Annie, 39
Brock & Son, 212
Brock, 201
Brock, A. S., 44
Brock, A., 144, 147
Brock, Ala, 44
Brock, Alabama S, 44
Brock, Albert F., 42
Brock, Anderson, 143
Brock, Andrew, 5, 25, 29, 114, 141, 142, 144, 146, 149, 152, 185
Brock, Angeline, 193
Brock, Daniel Anderson, 144
Brock, David, 159, 175
Brock, Elina, 159
Brock, Eliz., 159
Brock, Elizabeth, 175
Brock, Elizabeth, Miss, 176
Brock, Eliziah, Miss, 176
Brock, Eula, 260, 261
Brock, Florence E., 260
Brock, Florence, 260
Brock, G., 201, 202
Brock, George, 188, 244
Brock, H. B., 20, 29, 53, 55, 73, 74 110
Brock, Harris, 22, 159, 174, 181
Brock, Henry, 109, 159, 174, 176
Brock, Hiram, 159, 175, 223
Brock, I. H., 42
Brock, Isaac, 174, 176
Brock, Isaiah H., 42
Brock, Isaiah, 159
Brock, J. E., 202
Brock, James, 159, 174, 176
Brock, Josiah, 159
Brock, Josie, 42
Brock, Larkin, 160, 174
Brock, M., 159
Brock, Mary, 159
Brock, Mary, Miss, 176
Brock, Meridith, 175
Brock, Nicey, 159, 176
Brock, R. H., 44
Brock, Rufus H., 44
Brock, S. Allie, 44
Brock, Stanford, 159
Brock, Stanford, 175
Brock, Thomas H., 174
Brock, W. E., 233
Brock, W. M., 128
Brock, Wellborn, 176
Brock, Wilborn, 5, 25, 159, 212
Brock, Wilburn, 5, 71
Brock, William H., 42
Brock, William, 29
Brogan, Steven, 150
Brombelow, 106
Brooks, Aaron, 43
Brooks, Benj., 113
Brooks, Elizabeth, 43
Brooks, Isaac, 159
Brooks, James, 159
Brooks, John, 43, 193
Brooks, Sarah, 43
Brooks, Susan, 43
Brooks, Will, 75
Brooks?, Elizabeth, 43
Brooks?, James, 43
Broom, G. W., 260
Brothers, N. W., 46
Brothers, W. W., 46
Browder, Albert, 24
Browder, B. D., 122
Browder, E. J., 43
Browder, J. T., 21
Browder, P. H., 27
Browder, T. E., 43
Brown, A., 159
Brown, Abby, 44

Brown, Able, 44
Brown, Abraham R., 43
Brown, Ada A., 140
Brown, Ada, 139
Brown, Affa E., 43
Brown, Alfred, 176, 256
Brown, Andrew J., 43
Brown, Annie John, 35
Brown, Ben, 187
Brown, C. C., 43
Brown, C. H., 60
Brown, C. J., 6
Brown, C. R., 43
Brown, Charles R., 44
Brown, Early, 102
Brown, Edith R., 35
Brown, Edward H., 225
Brown, Evie Ruth, 43
Brown, F. M., 102
Brown, Frank W., 44
Brown, Gilman A., 44
Brown, Golston, 9
Brown, J. A., 62
Brown, J. G., 241
Brown, J. W. & T. W., 186
Brown, James, 11
Brown, Jas. G., 11
Brown, Jeff, 101
Brown, Jimmie M., 43
Brown, Jimmie, 43
Brown, Joe, 75
Brown, John, Col., 193
Brown, Joseph C., 39
Brown, Josiah, 75
Brown, L. R., 35, 36
Brown, M. S., 9, 13, 15
Brown, Mary Maude, 43
Brown, Maude, 43
Brown, Mrs., 257
Brown, R. H., 160
Brown, R., 173
Brown, Rufus , 43, 44
Brown, S. E., Mrs., 43
Brown, S. W, 35
Brown, Steve, 35
Brown, T. J., 100, 101
Brown, T. W., 32
Brown, Thos, 256
Brown, Thos. B., 226
Brown, W. E., 13
Brown, W. R., 7
Brown, William, 18, 176, 221
Brown, Willie, 43
Brown, Willis, 43
Brown, Wm., 159
Brown's Academy, 44
Bruce, B. F., 44
Bruce, Bailey, 44, 45
Bruce, Benjamin F., 44
Bruce, Bertha A., 45
Bruce, Bolus, 73
Bruce, D. B., 102
Bruce, H. G., 44
Bruce, Harris, 45
Bruce, J. B., 44
Bruce, J. D., 44
Bruce, J. H., 45
Bruce, J. M., 224
Bruce, John B., 44, 45
Bruce, John M., 135, 159, 176
Bruce, John M., 22
Bruce, Mary A., 45
Bruce, Mary, 45
Bruce, Rufus, 45
Bruce, T. D., 44
Bruce, Thomas D., 45
Bruce, Thomas, 44
Bruce, W. A., 100
Bruce, W. F. 6, 44, 45, 246
Bruce, W. M., 100
Bruce, Walter, 241
Bruce, William F., 44, 246
Bruce, William, 44, 45
Bruckin, Tinsley, 175
Brumbeloe, J. H., 57, 106
Brumbeloe, J. S., 57
Brunsfield, Simpson, 176
Bryan, C. A., 61
Bryan, Charles M., 25, 45
Bryan, Columbus, 174, 175
Bryan, Effie M., 25, 45
Bryan, James J., 45
Bryan, James M., 25, 25
Bryan, James S., 25
Bryan, Marion, 25, 45
Bryan, Nancy L., 76
Bryan, Nancy, 78
Bryan, Preston175
Bryan, Ryan, 176
Bryan, T. M., 92
Bryan, Tabitha, 25, 45
Bryan, Wilbourne N., 25
Bryan, William E., 45
Bryan, William, 129
Bryan, Winbourne N., 45
Bryan, Wm. E., 25
Bryan, Wm., 176
Bryant, Allen, 220
Bryant, Almer, 123
Bryant, C. C., 159, 223
Bryant, Columbus, 224
Bryant, D. E., 209
Bryant, Daily, 50
Bryant, Daily, Mrs., 49
Bryant, Des, Mrs., 49
Bryant, E. Z., 50
Bryant, Elijah, 14
Bryant, Eliza, 9
Bryant, Ella M., 76
Bryant, Emley, 59
Bryant, George, 59
Bryant, Grase, 247
Bryant, Harriet A., 76
Bryant, Henry, 13, 149
Bryant, J. F., 76, 77
Bryant, J. W., 76
Bryant, James R., 14
Bryant, James, 14
Bryant, Joe, 11
Bryant, John, 59
Bryant, Nancy L., 77
Bryant, Polly, 231
Bryant, Preston, 159, 170, 224
Bryant, Rial, 159
Bryant, Sarah, 59, 123
Bryant, Thomas, 220
Bryant, Thos., 170, 220
Bryant, Vesten(Westen), 22
Bryant, W, 142
Bryant, W. E., 48
Bryant, W., 231, 232
Bryant, William, 171
Bryant, Wm., 9, 146, 159, 169, 174, 182, 224, 257
Bryce, James, 45
Bryce, Sarah F., 45
Bryce, William, 45
Bryson, John P., 159
Bryson, John, 151
Bryson, N. M., 45
Bryson, Nelson M., 45
Bryson, Ruth K., 45
Bryston, N. W., 27
Bucks, J. T., 1
Buddie, W. H., 94
Buell, C. Y., 189
Bugley, Seborn, 176
Bunden, James B., 46
Bunden, James, 46
Bunden, John W., 46
Bundren, James B., 46
Bundren, Napolian, 46
Bunn, J. T., 194
Bunsan, T. G., 145
Bunt, R. A., 109
Buntern, L. W., 114
Buntor, Willis, 222
Burel, L. H., 132
Burges, Z. J., 159
Burgess & Stowers, 126
Burgess, Alexander, 126
Burgess, Alice Gerturde, 46
Burgess, Elizabeth, 195
Burgess, F. J., 126
Burgess, G. F., 153
Burgess, Henry Richard, 46
Burgess, J. A., 21, 187
Burgess, J. B., 169
Burgess, James, 218
Burgess, Jesse, 169, 175
Burgess, Lilly May, 46
Burgess, Mollie Amella, 46
Burgess, Mollie, 46
Burgess, Richard, 195
Burgess, T. G., 218
Burgess, T. J., 56, 126, 218, 230, 232, 237, 251, 253
Burgess, T. P., 55
Burgess, Thomas B., 46
Burgess, Thomas Ed, 46
Burgess, Thos. J., 151, 155
Burgis, A. M., 133
Burgiss, G. A., 43
Burk (Birk), 29
Burk, 223
Burk, Amos, 174
Burk, C. C., 192
Burk, James, 224
Burk, M. D., 46
Burk, Wil, 159
Burk, Wilburn, 175
Burk, Yancy, 46
Burke, O. T., 29
Burkeat, Mr., 224
Burkhalter, Alex, 47
Burkhalter, Andrew, 47
Burkhalter, B. K., 47
Burkhalter, D. B., 33, 34, 46, 47
Burkhalter, D. C., 47
Burkhalter, Daniel B., 46
Burkhalter, Daniel, 47
Burkhalter, David B., 47
Burkhalter, E. M., 47
Burkhalter, F. B., 34
Burkhalter, G. H., 47
Burkhalter, G. W., 47
Burkhalter, George, 47
Burkhalter, I.N.F., 47
Burkhalter, J. D., 47
Burkhalter, James Polk, 47
Burkhalter, James, 47
Burkhalter, John, 47
Burkhalter, N. J., 47
Burkhalter, N. L., 47
Burkhalter, N. S., 47
Burkhalter, Nancy Ann, 47
Burkhalter, T. E., 47
Burkhart, J. B., 227

Burnes, J. B., 167, 175
Burnes, J. D., 125
Burnes, Samuel, 255
Burnes, Thos., 256
Burnett, J. B., 79
Burnett, J. W., 160
Burnett, John, 46
Burnett, Lizzie, 78
Burnett, Louie Tate, 134
Burnett, S. E., 142
Burnett, S. W., 175
Burnette, W. T., 69
Burney, John B., 159
Burney, John M., 158
Burnger?, John M., 175
Burns, Gam, 257
Burns, George, 47
Burns, J. B., 21
Burns, Jeremiah, 256
Burns, Jerry, 47
Burns, John B., 21
Burns, John, 60, 256, 257
Burns, L. D., 193, 194
Burns, S. M., Mrs., 47, 98
Burns, Sallie, 102
Burns, Sam, 256
Burns, Samuel, 84
Burns, Susan, 98
Burns, T. C., 47
Burns, Thos., 255
Burns, Zeal, 47, 99, 100
Burns, Zealos & Sallie, 102
Burns, Zealos, 102
Burnside, D., 48
Burnside, Delos, 47, 48
Burnside, DeWitt C., 48
Burnside, Ella , 48
Burnside, Franklin, 48
Burnside, J. D., 48
Burnside, Jessie J., 48
Burnside, Levie L., Mrs., 48
Burnside, Lyllis, 48
Burny, John, 256
Burrett College, TN, 141
Burrett Gen, 141
Burris, J. D., 194
Burris, Samuel, 221
Burshire, James, 22
Burt, Bain, 49, 50, 51
Burt, Bessie, 48, 49, 51
Burt, Billy, 50
Burt, Calvin, 50
Burt, Carl, 51
Burt, E., 183
Burt, Elijah, 22, 51, 95, 224, 225
Burt, Elisha, 50, 51
Burt, Fred, 51
Burt, Gain, 49
Burt, Geo., 49
Burt, George, 49, 247
Burt, Graves, 174, 176
Burt, Grover, 159, 169
Burt, H., 51
Burt, Henry, 50, 51
Burt, Henry, Sr., 139
Burt, J. T., 49
Burt, J. W., 51, 94
Burt, James, 48, 49, 50, 169, 225, 231, 247
Burt, Joe, 49, 50, 51
Burt, John T., 51
Burt, John Tom, 50
Burt, John, 50, 51, 247
Burt, Jos., 49
Burt, M., 49, 50, 51
Burt, Mack, 51
Burt, Margaret, 50
Burt, Marion, 49, 50, 51, 247
Burt, Mary, 49
Burt, Mary, et al, 49, 50
Burt, Palley, 51
Burt, Pallie, 51
Burt, Pally (Polly), 51
Burt, Polley, 51
Burt, Polly, 51
Burt, R. A., 41, 49, 53, 85
Burt, Reuben, 50, 51
Burt, Robert, 50, 51
Burt, Rube, 49
Burt, Ryal, 22
Burt, Thomas, 123
Burt, Thos., 247
Burt, Tom, 50
Burt, W. C., 53, 54, 93, 94
Burt, Wm., 246
Burten, Francis, 223
Burton, E., 34
Busan, J. J. 136
Busbee, 239
Busbee, A. J., 237
Busbee, Durrell, 224
Busbee, James, 169, 224
Busbee, Jas., 170, 231
Busbee, John Burns, 50
Busbee, John, 51, 224
Busbee, Nancy, 50
Busby, A. J., 239
Busby, Dunnell, 159
Busby, James A., 159
Busby, James, 222
Busby, John, 159
Busby, S. J., 237
Busby, Samuel, 95
Busby, Seaborn, 159
Bush, Alley, 10
Bush, G. V., 226
Bush, G. V., Dr. 134
Bush, G. V., MD, 49
Bush, J. W., 193
Bush, Martha, Mrs., 133, 135
Bush, O. P., 133, 135
Bush, Olive, 12
Bushof, Jack, 176
Buson/Beeson, 168, 231
Buster, C. K., 174
Buster, Sam, 159
Buster, W. & C., 160
Buster, W. A., 174, 174
Butler, J. S., 108
Butler, S. G., 94
Butler, Samuel, 176
Butram, Ephraim, 34
Butram, Laurahamy, 34
Butrum, Ferby (Fanby), 15
Butt, D. L. R., 249
Buttram, Ferby, 15
Buttrum, Jonathan, 15
Buzby, Derrell, 176
Buzby, J. R., 182
Buzby, James R., 175
Buzby, James, 174
Buzby, John, 176
Buzby, Robert, 177
Byars, T. J., 102
Byars, T. L., 100, 101
Byers, A., 231
Bynam, Jesse, 185
Bynam, Jessie, 129
Bynum, B. C., 106
Bynum, Jesse G., 160, 174
Bynum, Jesse, 169
Bynum, John W., 51, 52
Bynum, Mr., 106
Bynum, R. H,, 5
Bynum, Rachel, 51
Bynum, Sam, 63
Bynum, W., 214
Bynum, William, 129, 222
Bynum, Williams, 217
Bynum, Wm., 96, 130
Byrd, Alma C., 52
Byrd, C. B., 52
Byrd, J. B., 52
Byrd, J. M., 52
Byrd, James (J. M.), 52
Byrd, Maud (Maude), 52
Byrd, Maude S., 52
Byrd, T. C., 122
Byrd, Thomas C., 52
Byrd, W. A., 185
Byrd, W. F., 52
Byrd, Weaver R., 52
Byrd, Webb, 52
C. S. Williams & Co., 7
Cagle, A. L., 53
Cagle, Amos, 121
Cagle, Charles, 10, 34
Cagle, Della, 53
Cagle, Dora, 53
Cagle, Eliza J., 33
Cagle, Ellen, Mrs., 53
Cagle, Geo. M., 10
Cagle, J. A., 117
Cagle, J. L., 53
Cagle, J. R., 53
Cagle, Jack, 118
Cagle, Jasper L., 53
Cagle, John R., 53
Cagle, John, 53
Cagle, L. H., 149
Cagle, Laura, 53, 54
Cagle, Luke, 53
Cagle, Luke, 94
Cagle, Mack, 193
Cagle, Malinda, 10, 12
Cagle, Melvina, 33
Cagle, Robert L., 10
Cagle, S. A., Mrs., 53
Cagle, Stephen J., 10
Cagle, V., 225
Cagle, Valentine, 224
Cagle, Vasti, 53
Cagle, Vastie, 53
Cagle, Wm. J., 10
Cagle, Wm., 186
Cain & Edwards, 230
Cain, 220
Cain, John, 220, 226
Cain, Paul, 194
Cain, R. W., 42, 68, 237
Cain, W. C., 27
Cain, W. L., 251
Cain, W. S., 238
Cain, Wall, 37, 49, 53, 54, 66, 73, 74, 83, 94, 97, 110, 118, 120, 128, 190, 210, 261
Calaway, M., 160
Calaway, Martin, 176
Caldwell, C. A., 77
Caldwell, D., 171
Callah, J. H., 80
Callaham, J. F., 81
Callaham, Wm., 23
Callahan, G. R., 197
Callahan, John, 223, 225
Callahan, Wm. H., 224
Callan & Hoge, 92
Callan J. B., 54
Callan, Annie, 54
Callan, H. H., 54
Callan, James A., 54
Callan, Lizzie, 54
Callan, N. J., 54

Callan, S. E. (Sallie), 54
Callan, S. F., 54
Callan, Sallie E., Mrs., 54
Callan, Salllie E., 54
Callan, W. J., 92
Callins, Alfred, 64
Calloway, M. C., 157, 158, 172
Calloway, Martin, 157
Cambell, Bethel, 42
Camp, Grover & Co., 236
Camp, James M., 177
Camp, John M., 160
Camp, S. M., 16
Campbell & Killian, 112
Campbell & Lankford, 74
Campbell, A. L., 52, 54, 82, 112, 123, 212, 229, 234, 236
Campbell, Amanda, 50
Campbell, Ambe (Amby), 54
Campbell, Amos, 54
Campbell, Ann, 217
Campbell, B. P., 55
Campbell, Benson, 256
Campbell, C. A., 259
Campbell, Chilnessee, 237
Campbell, G. H., 54, 100
Campbell, George, 54
Campbell, H. B., 1, 5, 7, 16, 17, 20, 31, 40, 42, 44, 49, 54, 73, 82, 89, 92, 93, 94,106-110, 123, 131, 137, 140, 149, 186, 190,208, 211, 226, 228, 229, 234, 245, 258
Campbell, H. M., 47
Campbell, Harris, 206
Campbell, Henry B.107
Campbell, Henry, 160, 177, 208
Campbell, I., 81, 103, 208, 215
Campbell, Ike, 111, 135
Campbell, Isaac, 24, 38, 39, 54, 55, 82, 87, 112, 133, 136, 207, 208, 229, 246
Campbell, J. E. A., 126
Campbell, J. M. 54,
Campbell, J. N., 54, 208
Campbell, J. W. (N.), 133
Campbell, J. W., 224
Campbell, J., 7
Campbell, Jane & Ike, 135
Campbell, Jane, 42, 135
Campbell, John F., 133
Campbell, John H., 55
Campbell, John N., 54
Campbell, John, 55, 126, 135
Campbell, Killian & Russell, 112
Campbell, Laura, 54
Campbell, Lewis, 6, 25, 54, 55, 133, 135, 206
Campbell, Louis, 54
Campbell, Louise, 50
Campbell, Luther, 54
Campbell, Manassa, 55
Campbell, Manassy, 55
Campbell, Martha A., 74
Campbell, Martha, 54
Campbell, Martha, Mrs., 54
Campbell, Mary, 54
Campbell, Paul, 54
Campbell, Rebecca, 56
Campbell, Robt., 257
Campbell, Roxie, 133, 135
Campbell, Rufus, 54
Campbell, Sallie, 135
Campbell, W. H., 112
Campbell, Walter, 54
Candler, 214
Candler, J. M., 98
Cane, James, 160
Cannady, M., 160
Cannon, G. L., 76
Cannon, J. K., 153, 168, 173, 177
Cannon, J. L., 76
Cannon, John K., 160
Cannon, L. W., 232
Canoyer, Capt., 60
Cant, R. L., 20
Canther, J. Y., 155
Canthers, J. Y., 168
Cantrell, John, 130
Cantrell, N. L., 106
Cantrill, Jesse, 195
Capart, C., 250
Caperton, Wm., 35
Capshaw, Benjamin, 56
Capshaw, Elizabeth, 56
Capshaw, Thomas, 56, 177
Capshaw, Thos., 160
Capshaw, William, 56
Cardan, H. W., 8
Cardan, Hugh W., 8
Carden, C. C., 153, 160, 168
Carden, Christopher C., 56
Carden, Columbus, 176
Carden, Hugh W., 130
Carden, Hugh, 56
Carden, J. W., 114
Carden, J. W., 143, 231
Carden, J. W.?, 146
Carden, Laura, 56
Carden, N. H., 160
Carden, Rebecca, 56, 193
Carden, Sally, 56
Carder, Sarah, 160
Carethers, J. Y., 207, 250
Cargile, J. M., 78
Cargile, M. V., 78
Cargile, R. E., 78
Cargile, R. L., 78
Cargile, Russell, 78
Carightey, J. T., 256
Caristers, James G., 244
Caristers, Mary, 244
Carithers, J. F., 244
Carithers, J. G., 255
Carithers, J. Y., 243, 245, 252
Carithers, James G., 96
Carley, J. A., 194
Carlisle, Daniel, 214
Carlisle, Ida Hawkins, 214
Carlisle, L. A., 214
Carmichael, Frannie, 122
Carmichael, G. J., 63
Carmichal, G. P., 229
Carnes, D. R., 56, 176
Carnes, David R., 56
Carnes, J. H., 187
Carnes, James, 1
Carnes, Martha, 56
Carney, D. K., 160
Carns, D. R., 256, 257
Carns, 257
Carpenter, Docia, 56
Carpenter, Eldridge, 56
Carpenter, Frankie, 56
Carpenter, John F., 56
Carpenter, Margie, 56
Carpenter, Willie B., 56
Carpenter, Y., 56, 57
Carr, E. W., 57
Carr, Geo. H., 57
Carr, H., 160
Carr, Hannah, 176
Carr, Joe, 235
Carr, John, 57
Carr, Joseph, 160, 177
Carr, Martha, 57
Carr, Peter, 68, 130
Carr, Rosa, 148
Carral, R., 139
Carrell, William J., 123
Carriage & Mill, 112
Carrie, Peter, 22
Carrol, R. M., 49
Carroll, A., 109
Carroll, Pete, 225
Carroll, Peter, 160, 177, 182, 224
Carroll, R. M., 49
Carroll, R., 109
Carroll, Robert C., 247
Carroll, T. T., 229
Carroll, Taylor, 229
Carson, J. L., 75
Carson, John C. T., 185
Carson, John T., 185
Carson, Wm., 71
Carter, A. U., 61
Carter, A. W., 114, 145, 146, 153, 168, 173, 222
Carter, A., 231
Carter, Aaron, 160, 173
Carter, Andrew W., 96
Carter, Angelin, Miss, 177
Carter, Angelina, 160
Carter, C. L., 57, 218
Carter, C. T., 83, 84, 219
Carter, C., 160
Carter, F. W., 146
Carter, Glover, 160, 176
Carter, H. J. 57,
Carter, H., 39, 57
Carter, Hugh, 160, 169, 177
Carter, J. L., 57
Carter, J. S., 57
Carter, John A., 177
Carter, John J., 160
Carter, Mary A. 57,
Carter, Mary, 160
Carter, Mary, Miss, 177
Carter, O. D., 92
Carter, R. G., 57
Carter, Sarah, 57, 176
Carter, T. J., 85
Carter, Thoms J., 85
Carter, V., 239, 240
Carter, W. T., 57
Carter. G. W., 160
Caryle, J. J., 1
Caryle, L. L., 1
Carythers, J., 257
Casaway, Mrs., 177
Case, D. C., Mrs., 58
Case, Davy C., 57
Case, H. R., 3
Case, J. R., 3
Case, James R., 2
Case, James, 58
Case, John W., 58
Case, Joseph L., 58
Case, Josie, 57
Case, Josie, Mrs., 57
Case, Lora D., 58

Case, Mary Jane, 58
Case, Mrs., 15
Case, Oscar V., 58
Casey, Amanda E., 40
Casey, Andrew M., 40
Casey, Frank, 160
Casey, Franklin, 177
Casey, J. L., 58
Casey, Joel, 58
Casey, O. P, 177, 160
Casey, W. H., 131
Casey, W. L., 58, 193
Casey, W. P., 150, 154, 160
Cash, Alfred E., 58
Cash, C. C., 100
Cash, Decie, 97
Cash, Della O., 58
Cash, Ellis, 80
Cash, Emaline, 97
Cash, J. M., 98, 103
Cash, J. N., 193
Cash, James M., 23
Cash, James, 1, 244
Cash, Jesse, 58
Cash, Josie, 58
Cash, L, 58, 102
Cash, Nan, 103
Cash, R. A., 99
Cash, Reuben, 58
Cash, Stella E., 58
Cash, Van, 102
Cash, W. C., 102
Cassey, W. P., 151
Caster, A. W., 96
Castleton?, N. F., 27
Cauntis, John, 15
Causey, Albert, 262
Causey, Bailey, 261
Causey, Elbert, 262
Causey, Elizabeth, 262
Causey, Homer, 261
Cavatt, Sallie, 199
Cave, James, 114, 174, 177
Cave/Cane/Care, 160
Caverly, Charles M., 58
Cawley, James, 160
Caythers, J. T., 96
Cazort, Benjamin, 15
Cazort, Catherine, 15
Chadwick & Crow, 62
Chadwick, A. J., 38, 61, 215
Chadwick, A. M., 58, 59, 60
Chadwick, Adolphus, 228
Chadwick, Agnatha, 34
Chadwick, Andrew J., 61
Chadwick, Annie, 60
Chadwick, B. F., 60, 122
Chadwick, Benjamin, 59
Chadwick, Blanch Emiline, 214
Chadwick, C. W., 61
Chadwick, Charles W., 61
Chadwick, D. P., 227
Chadwick, Geo. R., 61
Chadwick, George, 214
Chadwick, H. D., 60
Chadwick, Harman, 59
Chadwick, Hellen, 60
Chadwick, Isaac, 59
Chadwick, J. B., 61
Chadwick, J. W., 59
Chadwick, James, 59, 61
Chadwick, John B.,61
Chadwick, Lafayette, 59
Chadwick, Lula, 227, 228
Chadwick, Mauda, 59
Chadwick, R. D., 60
Chadwick, Rebecca Hawkins, 215
Chadwick, Samuel M., 61
Chadwick, Samuel, 61
Chadwick, T. J., 61
Chadwick, Thomas J., 61
Chadwick, Thomas, 61
Chadwick, W. A., 61
Chadwick, W. H., 211
Chadwick, William A., 61
Chadwick, William, 59, 61
Chadwick, Wm. A., 61
Chadwick, Wm. R., 61
Chadwick, Wm., 59, 61
Chambers, A. B., 48
Chambers, Barry, 122
Chambers, C. W., 102
Chambers, John, 14
Champion, Dr., 220
Chandler, Arthur, 121
Chandler, Ellen L., 62
Chandler, J. M., 97, 187
Chandler, James M., 62
Chandler, Jesse, 109
Chandler, M. D., 187
Chandler, Minnie, 62
Chandler, Wm., 27, 188, 210
Chaney & Hendrick, 160, 173
Chaney, A. G., 68
Chaney, Dasey, 195
Chaney, Hosey, 202
Chaney, J. M., 197
Chaney, J., 221
Chaney, Jackson, 160, 176
Chaney, John, 68, 196, 217, 251
Chaney, P., 250
Chaney, Posey, 203
Chaney, William, 176
Chaney, Wm., 160
Chany, John, 218
Chapman, A. E., 61
Chapman, Harry E., Dr., 61
Chapman, John, 169
Chappell, George, 62
Chappell, H. B., 62
Chappell, James, 62
Chappell, John, 62
Chappell, Mary A., 62
Chappell, Robert, 62
Chappell, W. T., 62
Charles, Servant, 146
Chase, Amos C., 44
Chastain, A. B., 176
Chastain, Beadie, 62
Chastain, George W., 62
Chastain, George W., et al, 62
Chastain, J. B., 62, 85, 124, 187, 260
Chastain, J. C., 174
Chastain, Jacob, 176
Chastain, Jesse, 22, 224
Chastain, John B., 77, 187
Chastain, John, 224
Chastain, Joseph, 173
Chastain, Raney, 176
Chastain, Wm., 177
Chastain, Zanie, 62
Chasteen (Chastain), 62
Chasteen, Alex, 224
Chasteen, J. B., 160
Chasteen, J. C., 160
Chasteen, Jacob, 160
Chasteen, Ramey, 160
Chatman, A. A., 43
Chavies, Manervia, 126
Chavies, William E., 126
Cheek, Maniel L., 176
Chennault, 136
Chennault, John, 136
Chennault, W. J.,136
Cheyney, Hosey, 202
Chick, M., 160
Chickamauga Undertaking Co., 131
Chihester&Yancy, 107
Childers, John, 160
Childess, John, 173
Childs, Charles Frederick, 62
Childs, George Arthur, 62
Childs, Walter H., 62, 63
Chitwood, 137
Chitwood, A. G., 105
Chitwood, Andrew C., 95
Chitwood, Andrew, 23
Chitwood, Andy, 169, 172
Chitwood, C. C., 66, 95, 96
Chitwood, Clement C., 95
Chitwood, Clement, 22
Chitwood, D.C., 94
Chitwood, E., 160, 173
Chitwood, Elizabeth, 63
Chitwood, Emma, 49, 50, 51
Chitwood, Ezekiel, 168, 177
Chitwood, Green, 118, 236
Chitwood, Henry B., 63
Chitwood, Henry Bradford, 63
Chitwood, I. Y. & S. J., 94
Chitwood, J. C., 79
Chitwood, James N., 63
Chitwood, Jennie Bell, 236
Chitwood, Jennie Horton, 234, 236
Chitwood, Joel, 4, 70, 79, 94-96, 137, 171, 172, 244
Chitwood, John, 160, 173, 176
Chitwood, Lillie, 236
Chitwood, M. A., 63
Chitwood, M. J., 96
Chitwood, M., 172, 255
Chitwood, Martha, 238
Chitwood, Mary C., 49, 51
Chitwood, Mary J., 95
Chitwood, Mary Jane, 96
Chitwood, Mary, 50
Chitwood, Mat, 96, 243
Chitwood, Mathias, 96, 243, 245
Chitwood, Matilda, 225
Chitwood, Mattias, 96
Chitwood, Mithias, 222
Chitwood, P. C., 172
Chitwood, P. Rufus, 252
Chitwood, Pleasant, 63
Chitwood, R. C., 128
Chitwood, R. H., 63, 236
Chitwood, R. J., 63, 79
Chitwood, R. O., 112
Chitwood, R., 10, 27, 42, 68, 69, 86, 95, 128, 143, 196, 230, 257
Chitwood, Rebecca J., 64
Chitwood, Rebecca, 56
Chitwood, Reuben & William, 63

Chitwood, Reuben, 63, 234
Chitwood, Rich, 171, 240
Chitwood, Richard, 23, 46, 56, 86, 146, 160, 169, 177, 182, 187, 222, 234, 235
Chitwood, Rick, 239
Chitwood, Sarah, 95
Chitwood, W. J., 37, 49, 51, 52, 82, 83, 90, 103, 107, 109, 112, 118, 119, 124, 133, 134, 140, 190, 197, 207, 249, 261
Chitwood, W. P., 64
Chitwood, W. W., 63
Chitwood, Walter S., 63
Chitwood, William C., 196
Chitwood, William P., 63
Chitwood, William, 196, 223
Chitwood, Wm. J., 238
Chitwood, Wm., 25, 26, 129, 169, 172, 224, 225
Chitwood, Zoe, 78
Choate, Austin, 63
Choate, John, 108
Cholson, James, 22
Chote/Choat/Choate, 64
Chrismon, James, 255
Christain, Mr., 160
Christensen, L. M., 209
Christian, T. S. Jr., 60
Christopher, Wm., 251
Chumble, Wm., 254
Chumby, W. J., 193
Chumler, Z. P., 194
Chumley, J. P., 194
Chumley, Mrs., 254
Chumley, P. M., 193
Chumley, W. Y., 253, 255
Chumley, Wm. Y., 254
Chumney, L. P., 253
Cisk, Louisa, 254
City Drug Store, 108
Claiborne, Tate & Cowan, 89
Clain, Wm. L, 251
Clardy, Norman S., 72
Clark, Alfa, 19
Clark, Alpha, 18
Clark, E. F., 48
Clark, E. J., 4
Clark, J. B., 82
Clark, John E., 240
Clark, John, 10
Clark, K., 169
Clark, Lizzie Hartline, 211
Clark, Louis V. & Co., 131
Clark, Louis V., 131
Clark, Mary E., 240
Clark, O. P., 168, 173
Clark, Oliver, 160, 176
Clark, Perry, 223, 224
Clark, Saml., 160
Clark, Samuel S., 240
Clark, Samuel, 177
Clark, Shade, 13
Clark, W. C., 123
Clarkson, D. J., 64
Clarkson, Lucy, 64, 160
Clarkson, Sarah, 64
Clarkson, Susan, 64
Clary, David A., 64
Clary, David Gordon Hull, 64
Clary, Gordon McKay, 64
Clary, Kate L., 64
Clay, J. W., 90, 91, 92
Clay, J. W., et al, 92
Clayton, 171
Clayton, 200
Clayton, A. L., 65
Clayton, A. L., Dr., 102
Clayton, Arlie Jay, 65
Clayton, B. M., 65
Clayton, Baxter L., 65
Clayton, C. C., 16, 77
Clayton, C. P., 6, 25, 185
Clayton, C., Sr., 230
Clayton, Carl, 64
Clayton, Cash M., 65
Clayton, Clifford, 64
Clayton, Craig, 169
Clayton, D., 135
Clayton, Dan, 169, 175
Clayton, Daniel, 22, 114, 115, 137, 142, 150, 154, 174, 176, 182,
Clayton, Daniel, Jr., 169
Clayton, Daniel, Sr., 160, 220
Clayton, Danl., 151
Clayton, Danl., Jr., 160
Clayton, David, Sr., 22
Clayton, Dow (L. D.), 75
Clayton, Fannie, 64
Clayton, Floriene, 65
Clayton, George S., 246
Clayton, H. M., 210
Clayton, Henry, 166
Clayton, Hoss, 64
Clayton, Ida, 210
Clayton, J. J., 259
Clayton, James, 64
Clayton, Jesse, 65
Clayton, John J., 85, 258
Clayton, John Jones, 258
Clayton, John, 223
Clayton, L. J., 45
Clayton, L. S., 115
Clayton, L. S., Miss, 65
Clayton, M. A., 64, 69, 200
Clayton, M. B., (Mollie), 65
Clayton, M. L., 64, 65
Clayton, Martha Ann Jack, 243
Clayton, Martha, 49, 65
Clayton, Mary Ann, 219
Clayton, Mary C., 258
Clayton, Mary E., 248
Clayton, Mary O., 65
Clayton, Molie, 259
Clayton, Mollie B., 64, 65
Clayton, Mollie C., 258
Clayton, Mollie, 259
Clayton, Monah L., 65
Clayton, Mrs., 75
Clayton, Nancy, 210
Clayton, Nannie, 64, 210
Clayton, O. W., 65
Clayton, Ona L., 64
Clayton, Perry, 114, 160, 176
Clayton, R. B., 65
Clayton, R. R., 237
Clayton, Robert B., 65
Clayton, S. H., 195, 201, 202
Clayton, S. J., 195
Clayton, S. S., 245
Clayton, S. W., 88
Clayton, S., 22, 160, 169
Clayton, Sam, 151
Clayton, Sampson, 16, 23, 64, 115, 135, 176, 223, 224, 243, 246, 248
Clayton, Scott, 243
Clayton, Sherman W., 94
Clayton, Sol S., 214, 232
Clayton, Sol, 26, 160, 168, 169, 201, 204
Clayton, Sol, Jr., 169
Clayton, Sol. H., 200
Clayton, Solmon, 114
Clayton, Solomon H., 200
Clayton, Solomon, 153, 175, 176, 182
Clayton, Solomon, Sr., 22
Clayton, Stephen C., 64
Clayton, Thomas, 223
Clayton, Tom, 6
Clayton, W. C., 65
Clayton, W. H., 23, 160, 225, 243-245, 248
Clayton, W. P., 150
Clayton, W. W., 65
Clayton, Warren, 245
Clayton, William, 65
Clayton, Wm. B., 65
Clayton, Wm. C., 65
Clayton, Wm. H., 175, 224, 244
Clayton, Wm. P., 154, 160, 175
Clayton, Wm., 115, 171
Clements, J. H., 186
Cleveland, G. H., 41
Clinch, John, 206
Clinks, (auctioneer), 118
Clundy, John F., 123
Clutey?, Paul?, 154
Coats, Henry, 87, 88
Coats, J. T., 250
Cobb, L. J., 137
Cobb, P. G., 231, 232
Cobb, P. G., Dr., 250
Cobb, T. J., 137
Cobb, Thos., 247
Cobie, T. N., 90
Cochran & Haralson, 148
Cochran & Russell, 260
Cochran, 90
Cochran, Earl, 49, 54, 65, 72, 106, 110, 148, 208, 213, 228, 229, 258
Cochran, J. J., 88, 89, 106, 113
Cochran, John J., 89, 205
Cochran, L. L., 6, 15-18, 24, 27, 33, 38, 40, 43-45, 54, 56, 58, 64-66, 71, 77-79, 92, 104, 108, 111, 112, 124, 125, 136, 148, 182, 184, 188, 189, 190, 207, 229, 234, 258
Cochran, Lela F., 89
Cochran, Lela, 88
Cochran, Lucian, Jr., 66
Cochran, M. M., 66
Cochran, Maggie M., 65
Cochran, Pinkney, 223
Cochran, R. L., 71
Cochran, T. F., 66
Cochran, W. W., 65, 77
Coe (Cox), 88
Coe (Cox), W. A., 88
Coe, W. A., 113
Coffee, Joel, 257
Coffey, P. H., 259
Coffie, Lucinda S., 65
Coffie, W. H., 65
Coggin, E. T., 182

Coggin, Wesley, 160, 169, 171, 175, 177, 182, 225
Coggins, E. T., 177
Coggins, Vestly, 23
Coggins, Wesley, 171, 173, 223
Cogin, Wesley, 153
Cohen, J. J., 114
Coker, D. W., 201, 203
Coker, D., 203
Coker, E. D., 104
Coker, H. I., 119
Coker, H. P., 66
Coker, H., 173
Coker, Hannah I., 119
Coker, Hannah, 118, 121
Coker, J. C., 66
Coker, J. D., 66, 119
Coker, J. W., 66, 69, 118-120, 260
Coker, Jessie, 66
Coker, L. J., 120
Coker, L. R., 67, 104, 118
Coker, Lee R., 66
Coker, Lee, 66
Coker, Margaret, 66
Coker, O. D., 66
Coker, Paul, 66, 121
Coker, T. A., 118, 119, 120
Coker, T. D., 119
Coker, T. H., 77
Coker, Tera A., 119
Coker, W. D., 72, 77, 130, 194, 201, 202
Coker, W. D., Jr., 66
Coker, Walt, 121
Coker, Walter, 66, 67, 120, 121, 260
Coker, William D., Sr., 66
Colbert, __, 22
Cole, A. F., 131
Cole, Ben, 160
Cole, Benj., 177
Cole, Georgia A., 131
Cole, Sally May, 131
Cole, Susie M., 240
Coleman, A. B., 210
Coleman, Douglas, 238
Coleman, Elizabeth H., 67
Coleman, Elizabeth, 50
Coleman, Eva Frances, 67
Coleman, Fannie, 79
Coleman, Francis, 28
Coleman, G. H., 67
Coleman, G. M., 134
Coleman, George, 50
Coleman, Green, 131
Coleman, J. C., 67
Coleman, James G., 67
Coleman, James W., 67
Coleman, John, 67
Coleman, Lewis, 261
Coleman, Minervie, 50
Coleman, R. T., 67
Coleman, Robert, 50
Coleman, Sara J., 67
Coleman, Sarah Ann, 67
Coleman, Thomas A., 67
Coleman, W. L., 50, 74, 76
Coleman, Walter G., 67
Coley, John, 123
Collett, Angeline, 111, 112
Collett, Green C., 44
Collier, T. T., 99
Collins, 137
Collins, 168
Collins, A. Y., 160, 171, 175
Collins, A., 149, 150, 151, 153-156
Collins, A., 200
Collins, Alabama, 238
Collins, Alf., 157
Collins, Alford/Alfred, 150
Collins, Alfred, 67, 68, 69, 149, 155, 157, 196
Collins, Charles, 224
Collins, Della A., 70
Collins, Edward, 173
Collins, Eliza M., 110
Collins, F. C., 68, 69, 70
Collins, Frank C., 70
Collins, G., 157
Collins, J. Alfred, 70
Collins, J. B., 8, 244
Collins, J. H., 67, 68, 69, 70, 134,149, 183, 239, 240
Collins, J. M., 236
Collins, J. P., 63
Collins, J. W., 68, 236
Collins, James H., 67, 69, 153, 237
Collins, Jane, 172, 224
Collins, John L., 224
Collins, John W., 68, 69
Collins, Kirby, 194
Collins, Liza, 111
Collins, Louis M., 149
Collins, M. A., 70
Collins, Mahala E., 67, 68, 69, 153
Collins, Mahala, 67, 68
Collins, Mary, 70
Collins, Mollie, 69
Collins, Mrs., 169
Collins, N. S., 67, 68, 69, 149, 195, 202, 236, 237
Collins, Nina, 112
Collins, O. D., 160
Collins, O. H., 7, 79, 82, 108, 112, 215, 222, 236
Collins, Pollie, 238
Collins, R. M., 142, 147, 160, 169, 171, 172, 182, 251
Collins, Robert M., 147
Collins, Robt., 176, 223
Collins, S. W., 69
Collins, T. B., 8, 9, 12, 33, 69, 207
Collins, Tipton B., (T. B.), 69
Collins, Tipton B., 67, 68
Collins, Tone, 200, 203, 204
Collins, W. S., 68, 70
Collins, Wallin, 111
Collins, Willie, 70
Collins, Young, 169
Collinsville Clipper, 259
Collinsville Courier, 118, 119
Collinsville Savings Bank, 187
Colwick, Louis N, 106
Colyer, D. G., 153
Comer, A. F., 114
Comer?, John, 160
Compton, John, 60
Conaway, Elizabeth, 70
Conaway, James, 70
Conaway, John W., 70, 71
Conaway, John, 70
Conaway, Joshua, 70
Conaway, Margaret, 70
Conaway, R. P., 70
Conaway, Rachel, 70
Conaway, Sarah, 70
Conaway, Wm., 70
Conda, Emma, 71
Condra, George, 71
Condra, B. C., 71
Condra, Benj. C., 71
Condra, Charley & George, 71
Condra, Charley, 71
Condra, Emma M., 71
Condra, Emma, 71
Condra, George E., 71
Condra, George, 71
Condra, Lula E., 71
Condra, Nancy J. Francis, 33
Condra, W. H., 33
Conner, James, 176
Contintal Gin Co., 118
Converse, Marquis M., 240
Conway (Conaway), 70
Conway Joshua, 71
Conway, J. A., 57
Conway, Joshia, 71
Conway, R. P., 71
Conway, Sarah, 71
Conway, W. F., Mrs., 56
Cook & Presley, 3, 73, 83, 125, 132, 140, 199, 211
Cook Lemuel A., 242
Cook, Alta, 73, 74
Cook, Alta, Mrs., 72, 73
Cook, B. F., 9, 12, 33, 150, 154, 160, 174
Cook, B. H., 73
Cook, Benjamin F., 71
Cook, Clarra G., 73
Cook, H. S., 104
Cook, Ida C., 71, 72, 123
Cook, J. M., 73
Cook, J. W., 10, 65, 72, 76, 123
Cook, James , 10
Cook, James W., 10
Cook, Jas. W., 73
Cook, Joe W., 73
Cook, John M., 79, 89, 106, 249
Cook, John, 10
Cook, Joshua W., 72
Cook, L. A., 71, 241
Cook, L. E., 236
Cook, Lemuel A., 71
Cook, Lemuel, 13
Cook, Len D., 73
Cook, Maggie, 73
Cook, P. A., 10
Cook, Pearl, 39, 104
Cook, R. C., 242
Cook, Robert M., 10
Cook, Rufina Hughes, 241
Cook, Ruth G., 73
Cook, S. A., 72
Cook, Sarah A., 72, 76
Cook, Sarah G., 73
Cook, Spurgeon, 39
Cook, T. C., 66, 72
Cook, T. J., 39, 72, 73, 75, 88-90, 124, 125
Cook, W. C. D., 2, 4, 6, 16, 17, 21, 29, 31, 42, 45-47, 52, 70-73, 84, 89, 106, 109, 112, 117, 123-125, 139, 148, 190, 213, 228, 243, 248

Cook, W. C., 71, 141
Cook, W. D. C., 131, 132
Cook, W. H., 191
Cook, W. R., 124
Cook, William B., 73
Cooke, B. F., 13
Cooke, James, 13
Cooker, H., 160
Cooledge, Charles H., 240
Cooper & Baines, 113
Cooper & Nicholsen, 33, 145, 146, 147
Cooper, Ann, 231
Cooper, Armiza, 58
Cooper, Dolf, 46
Cooper, E. C., Mrs., 74, 75
Cooper, Eli, 169
Cooper, Elim, 232
Cooper, Frances, 75
Cooper, G. W., 68
Cooper, Gaines, 10
Cooper, Hammon, 14
Cooper, Jackson, 10, 12, 35
Cooper, James H., 74
Cooper, James, 13, 46, 214
Cooper, John C., 144
Cooper, John, 160, 176
Cooper, Joseph, 75
Cooper, Julius B, 75
Cooper, Julius, 76
Cooper, L. E., Mrs., 40
Cooper, Lillie Mae, 46
Cooper, Lucinda, 214
Cooper, Manora, 12
Cooper, Mary, 46
Cooper, Morris, 15
Cooper, Nancy E., 46
Cooper, Nicholson, 31
Cooper, Polly Ann, 14
Cooper, Sallie C., 74
Cooper, T. G., 46
Cooper, T. T., 40
Cooper, Thos. B., 212
Cooper, Thos. T., 212
Cooper, Thos., 212
Cooper, W. K., 75
Cooper, William, 75, 76, 142, 143
Cooper, Wm., 144
Coots, Henry, 251
Coots/Coats, 251
Copeland, A. B., 73
Copeland, A. C., 1, 5, 20, 21, 45, 53, 72, 73, 76, 77, 84, 85, 88, 89, 117, 119, 127, 132, 140, 188-190, 199, 206, 207, 211, 252, 259
Copeland, Alex C., 38
Copeland, Alexander A., 76
Copeland, Alexander C., 77, 259
Copeland, C. C., 20
Copeland, et al, 110
Copeland, Florence E., 42
Copeland, H. C., 88, 90
Copeland, J. B., 73
Copeland, J. C., 77
Copeland, J. R., 94
Copeland, Jack, 109
Copeland, James A., 76, 77
Copeland, James H., 77
Copeland, James, 77
Copeland, John T., 76
Copeland, John, 247
Copeland, M. W., 72
Copeland, Mack, 88, 90
Copeland, Nancy, 76
Copeland, Pinkney, 77
Copeland, S. H., 66
Copeland, Sam, 200, 201, 03, 204, 205
Copeland, Samuel H., 76
Copeland, Stella, 252
Copeland, W. L., 76
Copeland, William L., 76
Copeland, Wm. L., 77
Copley, J. S., 160
Corbin, Bonnie, 79
Corbin, Davis, 80, 81
Corbin, Dexter, 79
Corbin, N. H., 176
Corbin, Perlina Crabtree, 80
Corbin, Permelia C., 81
Corbin, W. Thomas, 252
Corby, James, 177
Cordell, Charlsie A., 78
Cordell, Charlsie, 78
Cordell, Ella, 61
Cordell, H. F., 122
Cordell, Hattie, 122
Cordell, Isaac, 78
Cordell, J. E., 78
Cordell, J. E., et al, 78
Cordell, Jospeh Edwin, 78
Cordell, Kimsey, 78
Cordell, Lizzie, 78
Cordell, Mary C., 78
Cordell, Nancy, 78
Cordell, Sarah, 211
Cordell, Susan E., 78
Corvin, H. Sebird, 32
Costello, Frank, 25, 26, 27
Cotnam, Fannie, 78
Couch, Eli, 79
Couch, Jackson, 160, 176
Couch, Pattie, 50
Couch, W. G., 20
Couch, W., 244
Couch, Willis, 244
Count, Isaac, 206
Count, J. P., 114
Countess, Newnan, 233
Countiss, John B., Sr., 4
Countiss, Neman, 242
Counts, 171
Counts, Isaac, 22
Cowan, S. W., 237
Cowart, 223
Cowen, David, 160
Cowen, Davis, 173
Cox & Crannell, 14
Cox (Coe), 88
Cox, A., 150
Cox, E. C., 79
Cox, G. A., 217
Cox, Ida M., 79
Cox, Ida, 79
Cox, J. C., 234
Cox, James A., 187
Cox, James, 8, 14
Cox, L. M., 79
Cox, Lela, 79
Cox, Lelah, 79
Cox, T. A., 126
Cox, T. C., 173
Cox, T. G. A., 5, 154, 217, 263
Cox, T. G., 126
Cox, Thomas G. A., 5
Cox, Thomas G., 126
Cox, Thos. A., 160
Cox, Thos. G. A., 177, 263
Cox, W. A., 88
Cox, W. P., 144
Cox, Willie, 79
Cox, Wm. H., 79
Crabtree, 80, 241
Crabtree, A. J., 81
Crabtree, Alf, 79, 81
Crabtree, Alfred W., 81
Crabtree, Alphi, 79
Crabtree, Andrew, 79, 81
Crabtree, B. F., 81
Crabtree, Ben, 79, 81
Crabtree, C. H., 80, 81
Crabtree, Charley, 80, 81
Crabtree, Charlie, 79
Crabtree, Ellen, 79
Crabtree, Elmire, 79
Crabtree, Emily, 80
Crabtree, Emily/Emmie, 81
Crabtree, Eula, 79
Crabtree, F. M., 79, 80, 81
Crabtree, G. W., 48, 79, 80, 81, 249
Crabtree, G. W., Jr., 80
Crabtree, Henry, 79, 81
Crabtree, J. W., 8
Crabtree, James A., 81
Crabtree, James, 80
Crabtree, Jas. A., 79
Crabtree, Louisa Jackson, 248
Crabtree, Louisa, 248
Crabtree, Lucy, 80
Crabtree, M. E., 208
Crabtree, Martin, 79, 81, 248, 249
Crabtree, Minerva, 208
Crabtree, Permelia, 79
Crabtree, R. A., 80
Crabtree, Robert, 213
Crabtree, Rufus, 79, 81
Crabtree, Russell, 13
Crabtree, Samuel A., 79
Crabtree, Sarah E., 242
Crabtree, Sarah Hughes, 241
Crabtree, Susan, 79
Crabtree, Thomas, 79
Crabtree, Velma, 79, 81
Crabtree, Vina, 81
Crabtree, Warren, 108
Crabtree, William, 208
Crabtree, Wm. C., 248
Crae, Isaac, 10
Crae, J. C., 10
Crane, D. W., 226
Crane, Dock, W., 226
Crane, Fannie, 226
Crane, J. E., 81, 82
Crane, J. F., 27
Crane, J. J., 27
Crane, J. J., 78
Crane, Jack, 122
Crane, W. H. 121
Cranford, George, 153
Craven, Dr., 261
Cravens, James R., 141
Crawford & Anderson, 142, 143, 232
Crawford, Appie, 258
Crawford, Bessie, 258
Crawford, James, 258
Crawford, Martha, 258
Crawford, Mattie, 258
Crawford, Nannie, 258
Crawford, Vada, 258
Craze, America, 37

Craze, Daniel, 82
Craze, Daniel, Jr., 82
Craze, Dewey, 82
Craze, Eva, 82
Craze, G. W., 38
Craze, George W., 37
Craze, James, 32
Craze, Martha, 82
Craze, Meta, 82
Craze, Rosa Belle, 82
Craze, U. A., 38
Craze, Union America, 37
Creole Marble Co., 51
Crisman, Baby, 181
Crisman, James, 142, 160, 168, 173, 175, 176, 182, 263
Crisman, Jas., 262
Crismas, James, 143
Croak, Mikel, 60
Croft, F. W., 77
Croft, J. H., 76
Croft, J. I., 91
Croft, Joseph H., 77
Croft, Lucinda, 77
Croft, T. W., 72
Croft, W. B., 72
Croft, W. J., 195
Croft, W. Y., 216
Croley, J. A., 1, 2, 5, 17, 20, 27, 29, 45, 47
Croley, J. A., 1, 7, 53, 55, 66, 72, 117, 125, 132, 140, 193, 197, 199, 207, 211, 219, 238
Croley, James A., l, 2, 5, 17, 18, 20, 23, 29, 31, 35, 40-43, 45, 47, 48, 49, 54, 56-58, 60, 62, 63, 66, 85, 97, 103, 104-106, 113, 117, 118, 121, 125, 127, 131, 134, 139, 186-190, 205, 208, 209, 216, 219, 229, 248, 262
Croley, N. E., 72
Croley, Nancy E., 72
Croley, W. C., 72
Croley, W. O., 72, 101
Cronin, Hiram, 247
Crosley, E., 84
Cross, Andrew, 10
Cross, F. M., 149
Cross, F. W., 109
Crossley, J. S., 173
Crossly, Scot, 223
Crouch, W. H., 91
Crouse, Jno., 146
Crouse, John, 142
Crouse, Jos., 143
Crow, Amanda, 113, 115
Crow, Belia A., 83
Crow, Bill, 83
Crow, C. M., 82
Crow, Calvin M., 38, 82
Crow, Calvin, 37, 82
Crow, Chesley M., 82
Crow, Clark, 131, 258
Crow, Dyse B., 83
Crow, E. D., 18
Crow, Elijah B., 82
Crow, Elijah, 37
Crow, Ella O., 83
Crow, G. B., 30
Crow, G. M., 168
Crow, G. W., 55, 78, 114, 115
Crow, Geo. W., 113, 115, 252
Crow, George G., 82
Crow, George W., 113
Crow, Green, 30
Crow, Ida M., 82
Crow, Isaac, 10, 12, 82, 233
Crow, J. M., 82, 83, 122
Crow, J. S. O., 82
Crow, James E., 82
Crow, James M., 37
Crow, James, 30, 233
Crow, John L., 82
Crow, John M., 82
Crow, John, 37, 233
Crow, M. K., 113
Crow, Malina, 113
Crow, Margaret, 82
Crow, Mary Ann, 25, 83
Crow, Mary, 82, 233, 234
Crow, Matilda, 115
Crow, Michael K., 113, 115
Crow, N. D., 83
Crow, N. H., 258
Crow, Ollie Isbell, 82
Crow, Ollie, 37
Crow, Prudence D., 82
Crow, Robert, 176
Crow, Robt., 160
Crow, Roma R., 82
Crow, Sam, 83
Crow, Sarah Jane Bouldin, 82
Crow, Sarah Jane, 82
Crow, Sarah, 37
Crow, Thomas J., 48
Crow, Thomas, 82, 83
Crow, W. A., 82
Crow, W. D., 82
Crow, W. F., 123
Crow, W. H., 258
Crow, W. J., 82
Crow, Wash., 160
Crow, Washington, 113, 176
Crow, Wm. F., 82
Crow, Wm. F., Jr., 82
Crow, Wm., 220, 226
Crowder, E. S., 112
Crowder, T. O., 247
Crumbley & Son, 72
Crumley, A. C., 76, 83
Crumley, Charlsie, 83
Crumley, Elizabeth, Mrs., 83
Crumley, George W., 83
Crumley, J. C., 77
Crumley, Lizzie, 83
Crumley, M. E, 77
Crumley, Margaret E., 76
Crumley, T. J., 77
Crumly, J. C., 77
Crumly, Jane, 77
Crumly, M. J., 73
Crumly, T. J., 77
Crump, _. C., 217
Crump, 217, 230
Crump, Albert, 240
Crump, Allie, 85
Crump, Amanda Heald, 216, 217
Crump, Amanda, 83, 217, 219
Crump, Anna, 85
Crump, B., 230
Crump, Bethel, 84, 130, 230, 231
Crump, C. J., 64, 91, 217
Crump, Charity, 84
Crump, Charles, 83
Crump, Elbert, 235
Crump, G. Anna, 85
Crump, Harriet, 84
Crump, Henry T., 84
Crump, I. J., 97, 259
Crump, Ira J., 84
Crump, J. C., 64, 84
Crump, J. F., 83
Crump, J. S., 260
Crump, J. T., 130
Crump, J. W., 55
Crump, James T., 55
Crump, John W., 83, 84, 217, 219
Crump, John, 217
Crump, M. J., Mrs., 83
Crump, M. W., 55, 83
Crump, Manda, 218
Crump, Mandy, 218
Crump, Marcus, 85
Crump, Martha, 84
Crump, Minnie, 83
Crump, Nora Elizabeth, 83
Crump, R. C. (Rolin C.), 84, 85
Crump, R. C., 83, 84, 217, 218, 219
Crump, R. M., 83, 118
Crump, Rhoda E., 85
Crump, Robert H., 83
Crump, Robert, 85
Crump, Roland, 219
Crump, Rolin C., 85
Crump, T. J., 84
Crump, W. B., 84
Crump, William, 84
Culberson, 30
Culberson, A. B., 85
Culberson, Alonzo B, 85
Culberson, C. Y, 30, 60, 78, 85, 121, 227, 228
Culberson, Charles, 183, 184
Culberson, Chas., 227
Culberson, Cy., 213
Culberson, J. N., 31
Culberson, Mary A., 85
Culberson, Vernon V., 85
Culpeper, J. B., 184
Culpepper, J. B., 183
Culver Johnithon, 140
Culver, LaFayette, 140
Culver, N. L., 1, 2, 31
Culver, N. S., 140
Culver, Oscar, 261
Culver, Viola, 261
Cummings, Hiram, 237
Cuningham, Jonathan, 108
Cunningam, George, 243
Cunningham & Linton, 144
Cunningham, 51, 107, 121, 220
Cunningham, A. L., 151
Cunningham, Blankin & Jno., 96
Cunningham, C. T., 144
Cunningham, E. L., 225
Cunningham, E., 154
Cunningham, F. M., 110
Cunningham, G. W., 245
Cunningham, George, 235
Cunningham, Isaac, 243
Cunningham, J. D., 30
Cunningham, J. L., 216
Cunningham, J. M., 212
Cunningham, J. W., 60
Cunningham, J., 74, 151, 175, 220
Cunningham, James, 206
Cunningham, Jesse, 129, 136, 137

Cunningham, Jesse, 23, 96, 114, 115, 145, 146, 150, 154, 156, 222, 243, 244, 263
Cunningham, John, 22, 23, 27, 42, 70, 85, 96, 113, 136, 145, 160, 169, 171, 176, 182, 207, 222, 226, 244, 245, 249, 263
Cunningham, L. C., 156
Cunningham, L. D., 151
Cunningham, L., 95
Cunningham, Lafayette, 160, 177, 224
Cunningham, M. E. V., 86
Cunningham, Mary E., 86
Cunningham, Mary, 21, 51
Cunningham, Messer, 121
Cunningham, N. I., 23
Cunningham, N. L., 86, 136, 145, 155, 160, 177
Cunningham, N. T., 155
Cunningham, Nancy Jack, 243
Cunningham, Sarah, 220, 226
Cunningham, T., 156
Cunningham, W.H., 192
Cunton, W. C., 2, 3
Cuperton, Adam, 206
Cureton, 185
Cureton, G. W., 184
Cureton, W. C., 4, 211
Cureton, W. H., 211
Currey, Benj. E., 250
Curry, B. E., 251
Curry, Benjamin E., 252
Curry, James J., 185
Curry, M. F.(H), 31
Curtain, O. W., 252
Curtis, J. Valdor, 188, 219
Curtis, N., 60
Curtis, W. B., 74, 76
Cushen, J. W. E., 24
Cutting, Elizabeth Swanton, 67
Cutting, Fannie Coleman, 67
Cutting, Harper, 67
Cutting, Henry, 67
Cutting, Herbert, 67
Cutting, Ida May, 67
Cuzzant, David, 233
Cuzzort, 233
Cuzzort, Benjamin, 15
Cuzzort, Catherine, 15
Cuzzort, David, 233
Cuzzort, Eliza Holland, 233
Cuzzort, Eliza, 233
Cuzzort, Elizabeth, 233
Cuzzort, M. B., 122
D. B. Loverman & Co., 7
Daley, P. C., 68
Dallas, Sam, 57
Dalrumple, J. B., 72
Dalrymlple, Henry H., 87
Dalrymple, Annie, 87
Dalrymple, Carrie, 87
Dalrymple, Elizabeth, 87
Dalrymple, H. B., 87
Dalrymple, H. H., 87, 88
Dalrymple, I. B., 87, 88
Dalrymple, J. B., 74, 76
Dalrymple, J. D., 55, 253
Dalrymple, James, 87
Dalrymple, John B., 87
Dalrymple, John W., 87
Dalrymple, L. J., 87
Dalrymple, Lindy/Leuda, 87
Dalrymple, Lizzie, 87
Dalrymple, Luda, 87
Dalrymple, Ludy, 87
Dalrymple, M. J., 87
Dalrymple, Minnie, 87
Dalrymple, Nancy, 87, 88
Dalrymple, Naomi J., 87
Dalrymple, P. B. (I. B.), 88
Dalrymple, Richard, 87
Dalrymple, Sarah A. C., 87
Dalrymple, Stephen, 88
Dalrymple, Thomas, 87
Dalryrmple, Linda/Lida, 87
Dalyrmple, I. B., 87
Dalyrmple, Sallie, 87
Dalyrymple, N. J., 87
Daniel, Joseph, 246
Daniel, L. J., 120
Daniel, Lizzie D., 120
Daniel, May, 97
Daniel, R. G., 60
Daniel, R. I., 98
Daniel, R. T., 127
Daniels, Lizzie, 119
Darby, Della, 89
Darby, Edgar W., 88, 89, 90
Darby, Emma E., 90
Darby, Ernest F., 88, 89, 90
Darby, Eunice E., 88
Darby, Idella J., 88, 90
Darby, Leila G., 90
Darby, Lela, 88
Darby, Lula V., 88, 90
Darby, Lula, 88
Darby, W. F., 88, 89, 90, 91, 92, 241
Darby, Willie, 88, 89
Darting, Wm., 23
Dary, William P., 96
Daugette, Palmer P., 17
Daughtry, J. M., 72
Davenport & Blackwell, 249
Davenport & Co. E. G.?, 228
Davenport & Co., 43, 52
Davenport & Crabtree, 52
Davenport & Long, 212
Davenport & McKowan, 80
Davenport, Adalaid, 190
Davenport, B. C., 17
Davenport, Bles, 17
Davenport, C. C., 190
Davenport, Casius, 92
Davenport, Cicero, 92
Davenport, D. B., 92
Davenport, David B, 92
Davenport, David B, et al, 92
Davenport, E. C. & Co., 227
Davenport, E. C., 228
Davenport, E. J., 85
Davenport, E. L., 213
Davenport, E. T., 30, 78, 92, 228, 254, 258
Davenport, Elizabeth, 92
Davenport, Ellen, 208
Davenport, Erskin T., 213
Davenport, Erskin, 190
Davenport, Erskine T., 92
Davenport, F. M., 92, 208
Davenport, Frank, 6
Davenport, G. W., 61
Davenport, George G., 61
Davenport, Henry D., 93
Davenport, Ida M., 92
Davenport, Ida, 92
Davenport, J. G., 17, 58, 92, 229, 247
Davenport, J. H., 122, 190
Davenport, J., 183
Davenport, Joe H., 92
Davenport, John H., 92
Davenport, Joseph G., 93
Davenport, Joseph H., 92
Davenport, Lilbourn H., 145
Davenport, Lilbourne, 146
Davenport, Lizzie, 93
Davenport, M. C., Mrs., 93
Davenport, N. A., 93
Davenport, N. S. Co., 258
Davenport, N. S., 5, 52, 92
Davenport, Nicholas S., 92
Davenport, Nick S., 55
Davenport, O. J., 92, 93, 190
Davenport, Orville J., 92
Davenport, Paine & Lowery, 38
Davenport, Patrick, 197
Davenport, R. B., 92
Davenport, R. R. Jr., 249
Davenport, R. R., 26, 55, 92, 145, 241
Davenport, R., 220, 226
Davenport, Radolphus R., 55
Davenport, Rodolphus B., 92
Davenport, Rodolphus R., 92
Davenport, Sam, 207
Davenport, Seaborn, 93
Davenport, Taylor, 92
Davenport, Thos. B., 252
Davenport, W. O., 92
Davenport, W. S., 6
Davenport, Wheeler, 93
Davenport, Wm., 190
Daveport, Ida, 93
David, Benj., 59
David, Matilda, 59
Davidson, A. B., 84
Davidson, A. S., 238
Davidson, Allen, 93
Davidson, Azzle, 238
Davidson, Frances, 93
Davidson, Henry, 93
Davidson, J. A., 156
Davidson, J. B., Mrs., 93
Davidson, J. D., 155
Davidson, J. M., 93
Davidson, J., 157
Davidson, James, 158, 168, 174, 177, 182
Davidson, Jas., 157, 161
Davidson, Jno., 157
Davidson, John, 93, 158, 161, 169
Davidson, Joseph, 93, 135, 142, 156, 157, 175, 176
Davidson, Lucinda, 93
Davidson, Mary, 93
Davidson, Matilda, 93
Davidson, Permelia, 93

Davidson, Sol, 150, 154, 157, 161, 169
Davidson, Solomon, 23, 176
Davidson, William, 169, 256
Davidson, Wm., 93, 161, 176
Davis & Haralson, 7, 16, 24, 45, 84, 103, 108, 110, 125, 133, 137, 139, 183, 184, 210, 213, 215, 226-228, 241, 243, 258
Davis & Harrison, 227
Davis & Pope, 30, 40, 63, 81, 206, 215, 260
Davis, 143, 206, 241
Davis, A. G., 235, 239
Davis, A. T., 93, 94, 95
Davis, A., 95, 99, 244
Davis, Abe, 44, 169
Davis, Abraham, 93, 95, 245
Davis, Agnew, 258
Davis, B. F., 100
Davis, C. C., 44, 45, 93, 94, 95, 100, 109, 208
Davis, C. L., 60
Davis, C. W., 259
Davis, Cary, 95
Davis, Charlsie G., 93
Davis, Christopher C., 93
Davis, E., Mrs., 161
Davis, Elizabeth, 93, 95
Davis, Elizabeth, Mrs., 177
Davis, G. W., 92, 98, 101
Davis, G., 95
Davis, Gabe, 256
Davis, Geo., 169
Davis, George H., Jr., 7
Davis, George, 93, 95, 96, 97
Davis, Green, 96
Davis, H. G., 235, 239
Davis, H. K., 146
Davis, H. S., 184
Davis, Houstin H., 144
Davis, J. D., 98, 99
Davis, J. H., 24
Davis, J. J., 250, 253, 255, 256
Davis, J. L., 95
Davis, J. M., 195
Davis, J. P., 202
Davis, J. R., 45
Davis, J. R., 99
Davis, James W., 93
Davis, James, 95, 96
Davis, Jno. A., 15, 212
Davis, Joe L., 234
Davis, Joel, 96
Davis, John A., 31, 40, 45, 47, 48, 51-53, 81, 82, 89, 93, 110, 117, 119, 120, 135, 137, 209, 210, 222, 226, 234, 235, 239, 241, 246
Davis, John C., 93
Davis, John D., 133
Davis, John, 95, 155, 156, 158
Davis, K. D., Dr., 61
Davis, K. D., MD. 61
Davis, Leila S., 93
Davis, Mary J., 236
Davis, N. E., Mrs., 97
Davis, N. G., 97
Davis, Nancy Catherine, 242
Davis, Nancy Hughes, 241
Davis, Nancy, 96
Davis, P. H., 97
Davis, P. I. (J.), 100
Davis, P. J., 101
Davis, P. P., 95
Davis, Peter P., 234
Davis, Polly Ann, 24
Davis, R. B., 92
Davis, R. C., 16, 38, 41, 44, 68, 77, 85, 92, 96-103, 235, 259
Davis, R. E., 97, 100, 127
Davis, Rastes, 99
Davis, Reuben C., 48, 77
Davis, Reuben, 1, 127
Davis, Reubin C., 16, 38, 259
Davis, Riley, 161, 177
Davis, Ruben E., 97
Davis, Rueben E., 45
Davis, Rueben, 40
Davis, S. L., 91
Davis, Sallie M., 96
Davis, Sarah, 96
Davis, T. G., 199
Davis, Tennessee/Tennie/A.T., 93
Davis, Tennie, 93
Davis, Thomas, 142, 224
Davis, Thos., 225
Davis, U. G., 102
Davis, W. C., 127
Davis, W. G., 169, 231
Davis, W. H., 101
Davis, W. J., 96
Davis, W. N., 101
Davis, W. W., 101
Davis, William C., 93
Davis, William G., 243
Davis, William, 95, 96, 169
Davis, William, W. P., 96
Davis, Wm., 95, 171
Dawson, A. F., 28, 29
Dawson, Alverice (Alverine) F., 28
Dawson, J. C., 128
Dawson, Mary, 44
Day, C. E., 122
Day, W. D., 221
Day, W. J., 80, 81
Day, Wiley, 127
De Shields, J. G., 7
Dean & Edwards, 250
Dean, 185
Dean, A. C., 227
Dean, Aaron, 185
Dean, Allen, 103, 121
Dean, B. P., 103
Dean, Berry, 103
Dean, Charles P., 103
Dean, Charles, 103
Dean, E. B., 122
Dean, Ed, 103
Dean, Elisa J. Blancitt, 30
Dean, Frank, 122
Dean, George W., 254
Dean, Henry, 103, 133, 135
Dean, J. E., 2
Dean, James, 183, 184
Dean, Jesse M., 103
Dean, Leander, 30
Dean, M. E., 103
Dean, Margaret E., 103
Dean, Martha Campbell, 54
Dean, Martha, 133, 135
Dean, N. S., 103
Dean, Nich, 103
Dean, Sudie, 133
Dean, Thomas S, 79, 103
Dean, Thomas, 79
Dean, W. E., 103
Dean, W. T., 82, 122
Dean, William, 18, 19, 103, 184
Dean, Wm., 183
Dearman, Fletcher, 104
Dearman, M. A., Mrs., 103, 104
Dearman, Martha, Mrs., 140
Dearman, Mary Lou, 104
Dearman, Robert, 104
Dearman, Sallie, 103
Dearman, Sophia, 104
Dearman, V. S., 104
Dearman, Wiley, 104
Deas, Etta, 253
Deas, Joe, 253
Deathridge, G. R., 10
Deaton, Henry, 104
Deaton, Joseph, 104
Deaton, L. F., 91
Deaton, S. H., 92
Deaton, William, 104
DeBerry, J. A., 75
Deckerson, J. C., 92
Deerman, Fletcher, 39
Deerman, J. D., 104
Deerman, M. A., Mrs., 39
Deerman, Martha, 39
Deerman, Mary Lou, 39
Deerman, Robert, 39
Deerman, Safa, 39
Deerman, Scott, 39
Deerman, Wyley, 39
Dees, John, 252
DeKalb Co. Bank, 7, 74, 89, 94
DeKalb Livery & Stable, 112
DeKalb Lodge, 150, 151, 154, 157, 158
DeKalb Record, 106
DeKalb Record, Newspaper, 97
Delk, David, 230, 232
Dell, John L., 131
Dempsey, Harvey, 193
Dempsey, W. H., 193, 215
Denham, James, 176, 255
Denham, Jas., 161
Denham, Susan, 161, 177
Denham, William, 182, 255
Denham, Wm., 161
Dennis, E. A., 24, 104
Dennis, Elijah A., 104
Dennis, James L., 104
Dennis, Joel T., 104
Dennis, Joel, 24
Dennis, Julia R., 104
Dennis, Margaret J., 104
Dennis, O. A., 24
Dennis, Texas A., 104
Dennis, Tina W., 104
Dennis, William F., 104
Denson, Bogue, 104
Denson, Geo. W., 104
Denson, George Erskin, 104
Denson, Mrs. Geo. W., 104
Denton, B. F., 72, 104
Denton, Dora, 104, 105
Denton, G. R., 105
Denton, George R., 105

Denton, J. H., 104
Denton, J. L., 105
Denton, James G., 104, 105
Denton, Jennie, 226
Denton, Luke, 105
Denton, S. D., 105, 229
Denton, Sam, 105
Depriest, John O., 161, 177
DeShields, 66, 221
DeShields, J. A., 31
DeShields, J. F., 228
DeShields, J. G., 28, 31, 41, 44, 46, 47-48, 51-52, 58, 64, 72-73,78, 82, 83, 89, 110 125, 131, 133, 139, 140-141, 148, 186, 192, 197, 208, 210-211, 213, 215, 227, 229, 236, 238, 252, 258, 262
DeShields, J. S., 56
DeShields, John G., 16, 64
DeShields, Lee, 1
DeShields, W. L., 31
Deuton, Isaac, 90
Deuton, S. R., 91
Dibbeck, A. W., 151
Dibbeck, Noah, 177
Dickerson, J. N., 74
Dickson, H. F., 128
Dickson, J. A. W., 100
Dickson, James, 99
Dickson, W. W., 191
Dilbeck, A. W., 149, 255
Dilbeck, Noah, 161, 257
Dilbeck, W. J., 259
Dilbeck/Dibbeck, 177
Dilbect, A. M., 256
Dill, John, 136
Dillashaw, John, 91
Disque, Augusta, 209
Dixon, J. G., 52
Dixon, James, 49
Dixon, W. W., 192
Dobb, Elijah, 22
Dobb, J. G., 114
Dobb, James G., 114
Dobb, R. F., 66
Dobb, Stephen E., 56
Dobb, W. J., 260
Dobbins, Alf M., 106
Dobbins, Alf, Mrs., 106
Dobbins, C. A., 106
Dobbins, Charles A., 105
Dobbins, Jesse A., 105, 106
Dobbins, Manervia, 106
Dobbs & Ewing, 58
Dobbs & Howard, 7, 15, 38, 58, 71, 184, 207, 208
Dobbs, 136
Dobbs, Alice, 107, 108, 109
Dobbs, Alma, 111
Dobbs, Angeline Collett, 111
Dobbs, Ara, 111
Dobbs, C. L., 109, 111
Dobbs, Cicero, 107
Dobbs, Cordia, 89
Dobbs, Cordie, 31, 40, 107, 111
Dobbs, Cornelia, 51
Dobbs, D. P., 111
Dobbs, David, 129, 225
Dobbs, Dora, 50
Dobbs, Dorcus C., 111
Dobbs, Dorcus, 112
Dobbs, Dorcus/Darius, 111
Dobbs, Dunlap, 9
Dobbs, E., 226
Dobbs, Earl, 106, 107, 109
Dobbs, Edna, 107, 109
Dobbs, Elijah, 22, 161, 168, 177, 182, 222, 235, 240
Dobbs, Eliza Frazier, 136
Dobbs, Eliza M., 111
Dobbs, Eliza, 239
Dobbs, Ella, 107, 111
Dobbs, Emma, 74
Dobbs, Erskin, 219
Dobbs, Eugene, 106, 107
Dobbs, Eugenia Ruth, 106
Dobbs, Eugenia, 107
Dobbs, Eula, 109
Dobbs, Frank, 31, 66, 67, 89, 111, 120
Dobbs, Frankie, 107, 111
Dobbs, Franklin, 111
Dobbs, Hardy, 40
Dobbs, Hoyt, 219
Dobbs, Ira F, 111
Dobbs, Ira R.(F), 111
Dobbs, Isa F., 112
Dobbs, J. B., 191
Dobbs, J. F., 245
Dobbs, J. G., 173
Dobbs, J. J., (F. F.), 153
Dobbs, J. M., 206
Dobbs, J. W., 191, 192, 194
Dobbs, J., 23, 48
Dobbs, Jabey, 169
Dobbs, Jabus, 176, 182
Dobbs, Jaby, 157, 161
Dobbs, Jabze?, 158
Dobbs, James B., 177
Dobbs, James D., 110
Dobbs, James G., 107, 111, 136, 161
Dobbs, James M., 111, 123
Dobbs, James, 111, 137
Dobbs, Jas. S., 111
Dobbs, Jeanie, 109
Dobbs, Jeannie, 108
Dobbs, Jennie, 66, 109
Dobbs, Joe, 192
Dobbs, John, 107, 111, 194
Dobbs, L. A., 5, 8, 9, 10, 12, 26, 28, 33, 42, 49, 68, 70, 84, 87, 96, 107, 108, 111, 126, 141, 182, 196, 200, 206, 212, 234, 236, 237, 240
Dobbs, L. F., 12
Dobbs, L. S., 141
Dobbs, L. W., 237, 240
Dobbs, Laura A., 74
Dobbs, Laura G., 106, 110
Dobbs, Laura, 107, 108, 111
Dobbs, Leola, 219
Dobbs, Lillian Earl, 106, 108, 109
Dobbs, Lucinda C., 112
Dobbs, Lucinda, 111
Dobbs, Lucy, 108, 109, 110
Dobbs, Mary, 111
Dobbs, Mittie, 107
Dobbs, Nannie M., 107, 111
Dobbs, Nannie, 111
Dobbs, Neely, 51
Dobbs, Nina, 107, 111
Dobbs, Olena, 107, 111
Dobbs, Ora, 107
Dobbs, Otto, 40
Dobbs, Pauline Collett, 111
Dobbs, R. D., 118, 191, 192, 193, 240
Dobbs, R. F., 66, 118
Dobbs, R. L., 52, 107, 111
Dobbs, Robert L., 111
Dobbs, Robert, 40
Dobbs, S. A., 49
Dobbs, S. E., 78, 106, 111, 126, 207, 208, 255
Dobbs, S. H., 107, 109
Dobbs, S. L., 111
Dobbs, S. P., 169
Dobbs, S. R., 106, 108, 109, 228
Dobbs, S.L., 112
Dobbs, Sam R., 110
Dobbs, Samuel R., 110
Dobbs, Sarah Alice, 110
Dobbs, Sarah H., 111
Dobbs, Sidney, 219
Dobbs, Silas P., 112, 154, 155
Dobbs, Silas T., 93
Dobbs, Silas, 225
Dobbs, Sol, 164, 172
Dobbs, Solomon, 152
Dobbs, Stephen E., 108, 109, 110, 126, 208
Dobbs, Stephen, 169, 171, 172
Dobbs, Stephen, 40
Dobbs, Thomas, 107, 111
Dobbs, W. F., 185
Dobbs, W. H., 55
Dobbs, W. J., 190, 191, 193
Dobbs, W. L., 108, 111
Dobbs, W. M., 107, 108, 208
Dobbs, W. N., 55
Dobbs, W. W., 1, 18, 36, 55, 107, 109, 110, 111, 112, 126
Dodd, B. W., 4
Dodd, L. A., 69
Dodd, M. H., 99, 101
Dodd, Missouri, 97
Dodd, Neal, 15
Dodd, O. L., 97
Dodd, Oliver, 102
Dodd, W. R., 99
Dodds, Charley, 40
Dodds, Cordia, 40
Dodds, L. A., 18, 41, 77
Dodds, Otto, 40
Dodds, Stephen, 40
Dodson, C. C., 141
Doe & Erwin, 108
Dollar, J. C., 72
Dollar, Jno. C., 102
Donegan, W. H., 130
Donley, R., 191
Dooley, J. G., 21
Dooly, Isaih, 71
Dooly, R., 192
Dorsey, A. J., 10
Dorsey, J. R., 10
Douglas, Joseph, 153
Douglas, S. S., 90
Douglass, Jos., 168
Dowdy, W. T., 249

Down, T. T., 20
Downer, Addie, 63
Downer, Charles, 63
Downer, Charles, Etherly, Cora, 63
Downer, Charley, 63
Downer, Elmer, 63
Downer, Ethel, 63
Downer, Fannie, 238
Downer, Horace, 63
Downer, J. H., 197
Downer, Lillie, 63
Downer, Luther, 63
Downer, Ollie, 63
Downer, S. K., 239
Downer, T. J., 189
Downer, W. C., 63
Downs, 199
Downs, Bob, 193
Downs, G. C., 186
Downs, T. L., 7, 20, 49, 73, 75, 127, 207, 209, 252
Doyle, C. C., 10
Doyle, E. C., 195
Drain, Alice, 210
Drain, Geo. D., 112
Drain, Ida, 210
Drain, J. D., 58
Drain, John, 112, 161, 176
Drain, Lou, 210
Drain, Mack, 210
Drain, Oliver, 210
Drain, Parilee, 210
Drain, William, 210
Drake, Berry, 246, 247
Drake, J. C., 227
Drake, John, 161, 169, 173
Driscill, Tobia, 22
Driskell, A. Jackson (A.J.), 112, 113
Driskell, Glen, 105
Driskell, Warner L., 93
Driskell/Driskell, 112
Driskil, W. A., 154
Driskil, W. T., 154
Driskill & Cordell, 213
Driskill, Andrew, 112
Driskill, Charles, 62
Driskill, E. H., 213
Driskill, Eliz., 161
Driskill, Elizabeth, 177
Driskill, F. A., 158
Driskill, J. W., 106
Driskill, Jess, 106
Driskill, Joseph, 161
Driskill, Maggie, 71
Driskill, Mary, 112
Driskill, S. C., 71
Driskill, Sanford, 71
Driskill, T. A., 161
Driskill, T. S., 174
Driskill, Tollapher, 176
Driskill, W. A., 150, 161, 174
Driskill, W. L., 9, 33, 114, 150, 152, 161, 168, 174, 177
Driskill, W., 182
Driskill, Warner, 262
Driskill, Wm. & W. A., 177
Driskill, Wm., 58, 161
Driskill, Wm., Jr., 161
Driskill, Wm., Sen., 177
Duff & Quin, 49
Duff, S. W., 212
Duff, W. S., MD, 49
Dugan House & Land, 89
Duggan, J. H., 59
Duggan, Julius, 59
Dugger, J. L., 59
Dumbach, Charles, 82
Dumbach, John, 82
Dumbach, Lawrence, 82
Dumbach, Rosa, 81
Dumbach, William, 81
Dunagin, W. H., 15
Duncan, Arlevia (Arlene), 39
Duncan, F. F., 213
Duncan, F. P., 113
Duncan, J. W., 77
Duncan, John W., 113
Duncan, Matilda, 113
Duncan, Nancy K., 113
Duncan, Nancy, 113
Duncan, R. D., 25, 71, 113
Duncan, R. D., Mrs., 77
Duncan, Robert H., 113
Dunlap & Dodds, 70, 95, 148, 190, 243, 262
unlap, Dobbs & Jacoway, 9, 42, 95, 206, 263
Dunlap, James, 26
Dunlap, R, L., 187
Dunlap, R. A., 9, 26, 232
Dunlap, R.A.D., 12, 26, 113, 199, 207, 238, 242
Dunlap, RAD, 243
Dunlap, W. E., 128
Dunlay & Jacoway, 128
Dunlay, R. H., 128
Dunson, Charles Richard, 113
Dunson, Dorotha, 260
Dunson, Dortha E., 113
Dunson, Lillie, 260
Dunson, M. M., 113
Dunson, Marcus M., 260
Dunson, R. E., 113
Dunson, Ralph, 260
Dunson, Richmond T., 260
Durham, 24
Durham, B. D., 211
Durham, Benj. D., 71
Durham, Ida, 238
Durham, J. J., 24, 58, 108
Durham, J. M., 45, 48, 85, 108, 112, 122, 123, 209, 236, 262
Durham, James M., 7
Durham, John J., 24, 31, 45, 128
Durham, John, 209
Durham, Madison, 10
Durham, Nora L., 85
Durham, Philip, 14
Durham, Polly Ann, 24
Durham, Rosa, 85
Durham, T. C., 214
Durham, W. A., 128
Durham, W. O., 226
Durham, William, 85
Durting, Saml., 161, 174
Duton, John, 177
Dutton Thomas, 113
Dutton, A., 206
Dutton, Abe, 45, 247
Dutton, Alice M., 240
Dutton, David, 113, 114, 115
Dutton, Francis, 113, 114, 115, 161
Dutton, Harry, 240
Dutton, James William, 113
Dutton, John, 161
Dutton, Lavica, 113, 115
Dutton, Lavice, 113
Dutton, Louisa, 113
Dutton, Luettean, 113
Dutton, M. I., 44
Dutton, M. J., 206
Dutton, M. M., 237, 240
Dutton, Malinda Dutton, 113
Dutton, Malissa, 115
Dutton, Mallissa, 113
Dutton, Marion, 240
Dutton, Martha, 113
Dutton, Mary, 240
Dutton, Melissa/Malissen, 113
Dutton, Michael, 113
Dutton, Mrs., 223
Dutton, S. L., 53, 54
Dutton, Saml., 161
Dutton, Sam'l., 231, 232
Dutton, Samuel, 114, 142, 143
Dutton, Sara, 113
Dutton, Thomas, 113, 115
Dutton, William, 113, 115
Dutton, Wm., 115
Dwyer, John J., 29
Dye, James, 27
Earp, Jacob W., 137
Earp, Phillip W., 137
Earp, Robert S., 117, 137
Earp, Theodore W., 117
Earp, Thos., 10
Earp, Wesley, 117
Earp, William G. (S.), 117
Earp, William G., 137
Easley, Benjamin, 14
Easley, Charles, 14
Easley, Dick, 14
Easley, Jack, 13
Easley, Jesse, 223
Easley, Sol, 226
Easley, Solomon, 52, 223

Eason, B. G., 193
Eason, B. J., 200
Eason, O. B., 75
Eaton, Pamelia Ann, 240
Eaves, W. T., 57
Echols, W. B., 161
Echols, Wm. B., 173
Edmondson, G. H., 100
Edmondson, J. B., 100, 101
Edmondson, John R., 94
Edmondson, S. J., 21
Edmondson, Sarah J., 51
Edmondson, Sarah Jane, 21, 51
Edmondson, Thomas, 222
Edmondson, W. E., 17, 21, 37, 49, 94, 183, 184, 247
Edwards, A. E., 117
Edwards, Babe, 117
Edwards, Chick, 117
Edwards, Clarence, 117
Edwards, Clessie, 117
Edwards, Cora, 117
Edwards, D. L., 117
Edwards, D. N., 254
Edwards, Dessie, 117
Edwards, E. A., 120
Edwards, Earnest, 121
Edwards, Georgia, 117
Edwards, H. N., 117
Edwards, Henry, 117
Edwards, J. E., 216, 237
Edwards, J. F., 117, 118, 119, 120

Edwards, J., 19, 84, 85, 172, 221, 255
Edwards, Jep, 255
Edwards, Jeptha, 55, 152, 230, 237, 84, 85
Edwards, Jesse, 46, 217, 230, 231
Edwards, Joe, 216
Edwards, John E., 117, 118, 119, 120, 121
Edwards, John F., 119
Edwards, John, 70, 118, 120, 154, 168, 201, 204, 205, 246, 262, 263
Edwards, Joicy, 117
Edwards, Joseph E., 217
Edwards, Joseph, 22, 83, 147, 161, 168, 177, 216, 217, 219, 220, 223, 251, 261, 262
Edwards, L. P., 117
Edwards, Lucy, 247
Edwards, Margaret, 84, 217
Edwards, Minnie, 117
Edwards, Mrs., 121
Edwards, N. I. J., 153
Edwards, N. J., 246, 248, 262
Edwards, Nancy J., 262
Edwards, Nancy, 246
Edwards, Nete J., 263
Edwards, Nettie J., 168
Edwards, Nettie, 70, 154
Edwards, Netty Jane Jones, 262
Edwards, Rose, 117
Edwards, Ross, 117
Edwards, S. C., 117
Edwards, Vick, 117
Edwards, W. F., 57
Edwards, W. S. & N. J., 118, 120
Edwards, W. S., 117, 118, 119, 120, 121, 188, 246, 261
Edwards, Warren, 153
Edwards, Wm. S., 262
Edwards, Wm., 201, 204
Eidson, R. W., 21
Eidson, Robert, 21
Eldridge, Wm. H., 63
Elis, James, 32
Eliza, 9
Ellenburg, F. J., Mrs., 199
Ellenburg, H. J., 194
Ellenburg, H. T., 190, 191, 192, 199
Ellenburg, Jane, 191
Ellis, A. J., 7, 38
Ellis, Abner J., 38
Ellis, Alfred, 123
Ellis, Anna, 123
Ellis, C. P., 119
Ellis, C. T., 27, 78
Ellis, Catherine P., 120
Ellis, Charles T., 78, 121, 122, 123
Ellis, Edgar, 122
Ellis, Ginty, 4
Ellis, Gladys Charles, 121
Ellis, J. C., 78, 123
Ellis, J. S., 121
Ellis, Jason, 123
Ellis, John, 59
Ellis, Julia, 123
Ellis, Labom, 126
Ellis, Laura A., 78
Ellis, M. E., Mrs., 122
Ellis, Margaret E., 123
Ellis, Mary E., 78
Ellis, Minnie E., 78
Ellis, Minnie, 4
Ellis, Nancy, 123
Ellis, Nelda, 121
Ellis, Ora May, 78
Ellis, P. M., 121
Ellis, Pallie, M., 121
Ellis, Robert H., 121
Ellis, W. P., 119, 120, 121
Ellis, William, 123, 211
Ellis, Wm., 38, 118, 119
Ellison, 60
Ellison, Mr., 254
Elrod, A. W., 83, 216
Elrod, Alice, 125
Elrod, Amelia, 124
Elrod, Andrew, 125
Elrod, Artie, 125
Elrod, C. C., 124
Elrod, David D., 125
Elrod, Elina, 125
Elrod, Eula (Lula), 125
Elrod, George G., 125
Elrod, George, 125
Elrod, Grif, Dr., 98
Elrod, H. W., 72
Elrod, Ida E., 124
Elrod, Ida, 124
Elrod, J. G., 42, 83, 97, 98, 124
Elrod, J. N., 125
Elrod, J. T., 103, 139
Elrod, Jacob O., 124
Elrod, James W., 125
Elrod, Josephine, 125
Elrod, Julia, 125
Elrod, Lethia, 125
Elrod, M. E., 123, 24
Elrod, M. E., Mrs., 124
Elrod, Martha M., 124
Elrod, Mary, 125
Elrod, Millican, 125
Elrod, Nancy E. E., 125
Elrod, Narsis, 124
Elrod, Narsisus/Nansissus, 124
Elrod, Nelson, 124, 125
Elrod, P. W., 124, 125
Elrod, Richard M., 125
Elrod, Robert, 125
Elrod, S. M., 83
Elrod, Samuel T., 125
Elrod, Sarah V., 124
Elrod, Susan, 125
Elrod, Sussannia, 125
Elrod, Thomas, 125, 126
Elrod, Velmer, 125
Elrod, W. A., 62, 65
Elrod, W. H., 248
Elrod, W. J., 100
Elrod, W. T., 101
Elrod, William, 125
Elrod, Wm. H., 125
Elron, Palmyra, 125
Emerson, T. H., 92
Emmet, H. O., 219
Emmett, H. P., 219
Emmett, R. N., 36
Emmett, R. W., 35
Emsley, George, 242
Emsley, Kate, 242
Emsley, R. C., 242
England, M. V., 16
England, M. W., 16
Engle, Alford, 84
Engle, Alfred, 126
Engle, Daniel, 126
Engle, E. H., 161
Engle, E. W., 177
Engle, Jacob, 126
Engle, Mary, 126
Engle, Philly, 217
Engle, Simeon, 126
English, Annie, 133
Enlow/Euloe, 127
Epperson, Robert, 171
Epperson, Robt., 169
Ervin, B. F., 253
Ervins, Isaac, 206
Erwin, Adalia, 84
Erwin, John A., 28
Erwin, L. F., 72, 90
Erwin, L. H., Dr., 88
Erwin, M. B., 84
Erwin, Marcus B., 84, 85
Erwin, Sam, 236
Eskin, Z. W. & Co., 168
Estell, S. H., 161, 173
Estes & May, 146, 167, 172
Estes, Bethelhem, 126
Estes, Burham, 9
Estes, David, 243
Estes, J. N., 37
Estes, J. W., 218
Estes, James K. P., 127
Estes, James K. T. (P.), 126, 127
Estes, James R. P., 126
Estes, James, 127, 169
Estes, Jas., 171
Estes, Jno. R., 85
Estes, John R., 79, 234, 239
Estes, John W., 42
Estes, John, 44, 63, 236
Estes, Lutitia M., 37
Estes, Mary C., 79
Estes, Mary, 42
Estes, Mary/May, 226
Estes, P., 151
Estes, R., 19, 20, 22, 26, 34, 42, 52, 55, 79, 93, 96, 115, 129, 135, 141-144, 146, 149, 150, 153, 155-157, 168, 171, 187, 189, 196, 214, 220, 221, 225, 231-233, 244, 248, 249, 253-255, 262,
Estes, Reuben, 9, 16, 56, 68, 87, 112, 113, 126, 129, 132, 216, 230, 261
Estes, Reubin, 104
Estes, Robert, 177
Estes, Robt., 161
Estes, Ruben, 96
Estes, Rueben, 29, 31, 161, 169, 177
Estes, T. N., 37
Estes, W. H., 154
Estes, W. N., 95, 96, 126, 150, 155, 161, 168, 225
Estes, W., 22
Estes, William N., 137, 150
Estes, Wm. N., 224
Estes, Wm., 23, 171, 169, 177
Etters, H. R., 225
Euloe, Edwin H., 127
Euloe, Grace, 127
Eustins, Geo., 108
Evans, Calvin, 112
Evans, Elizabeth J., 40
Evans, G. H., 3
Evans, Isaac, 142, 144
Evans, Israel, 145
Evans, J. H., 2, 3
Evans, J. M., 45
Evans, Pattie, 107

Evans, R. M., 40
Evans, Vina, 19
Evans, W. D., 75
Evans, Wilt, 20
Evatt, Ola, 127
Evatt, Ola, et al, 127
Evatt, W. J., 128
Evatt, W. L., 104
Everett, Andrew, 128
Everett, Annie, 128
Everett, Elizabeth, 70
Everett, Elma, 128
Everett, F. W., 128
Everett, G. A., 91
Everett, James, 209
Everett, Mittie, 128
Everett, S. C., 128
Everett, T. W., 128
Everett, Thomas W., 128
Everett, Thomas, 128
Everett, Thursey, 128
Everett, W. L., 128
Everett, W. R., 128
Everett, Wm., 71, 161, 177
Everitt, G. A., 91
Evett (Everett), 70
Evett, Catherine T., 127
Evett, E., 70
Evett, Elizabeth, 127
Evett, G., 127
Evett, George J., 127
Evett, H. V., 127
Evett, Hamilton L., 128
Evett, Hamilton, 127
Evett, Hunley V., 128
Evett, I. Vann, 127, 128
Evett, J. L., 128
Evett, J. Vann, 127
Evett, James W., 127
Evett, James, 26, 127, 128
Evett, John J., 127
Evett, John N., 128
Evett, Palestine, 127, 128
Evett, Sam G., 128
Evett, Samuel, 127
Evett, Sousana A, 128
Evett, Sousana, 128
Evett, Texas Co., 128
Evett, Thompson, 127, 128
Evett, W. H., 70
Evett, W. J., 127, 128
Evett, W. T., 127
Evett/Evatt, 127
Ezzelle, J. E., 122
F?, Jesse B., 172
Fairview Church, 89
Fandren, Miss, 223
Fant, Bertha, 132
Fant, Hattie, 132
Fant, Herman, 132
Fant, J. F., 216
Fant, James, 132
Fant, James, Mrs., 132
Fant, Tomie, 132
Fant, William, 132
Fant/Fout, Hettie, 132
Farmer & Citizen Bank, GA, 57
Farmer, __, 12
Farmer, Jonathan, 169
Farmer, Rueben, 161, 169, 173
Farmer, T. F., 37
Farmer, Wm., 96
Farmer?, Elizabeth A., 125
Farmers & Merchants Bank Boaz, 97
Farmers Merchant Bank, 118
Farnum, Frank C., 197
Farr, W. B., 215
Farrar, Sarah E., 110
Farrar, Sarah, 110
Farris M. D., 261
Farris, D. C., 254
Farris, Dr., 256
Farris, M. D., 2
Farris, M. E., 261
Farris, R. M., 107
Farris, T. C., 254
Faulkner, Fannie, Mrs., 133
Faulkner, J. H., 197
Faulkner, J. N. B., 78, 131
Faulkner, J. N., 262
Faulkner, J. W., 249
Faust, John Emory, 61
Favor, Joel, 126
Favor, John, 223
Favors, Joel, 126
Favors, John A., 161
Favors, John, 178
Featherstone, Jesse, 149
Fell, Brown, 247
Fellers, A. A., 60
Fenney?, J. E., 68
Ferguson, George, 134
Ferguson, J. B., 110, 125
Ferguson, James B., 52
Ferguson, Nancy, 133
Ferguson, Nancy, Mrs., 135
Ferguson, Thomas, 133
Ferguson, W. D., 18
Ferguson, W. L., 39, 46, 68, 92, 150, 212, 237
Ferguson, W. S., 18, 131
Ferguson, W., 148
Field, E. L., 225
Fielder & Co., 178
Fielder, George W., 70
Fielder, H. W., 178
Fielder, N. W., 68, 161, 167
Fielders, John, 100, 102
Fields & Co., 161
Fields, B., 129
Fields, Dicy/Disy Ann, 129
Fields, Disey Ann, 129
Fields, Disy A., 129
Fields, E., Mrs., 172
Fields, Elizabeth, 129, 161, 178, 224
Fields, Gilbert, 161, 177
Fields, Harrison, 225
Fields, James, 129, 130, 161, 178
Fields, John B., 129
Fields, Mary E., 129
Fields, Mary Ellen, 129
Fields, Millican, 129
Fields, Vianna, 129
Fields, Vienne, 129
Fields, Vina/Vianna, 129
Fields, William 129
Fight, B. R., 239, 240
Figures, W. B. 144, 145, 220, 243, 244
Fike, D. C., 247
Fike, David C., 206
Fike, David, 109, 110
Fike, Harland, 177
Fike, Harlon, 161
Fike, Mrs., 23, 144
Fike, Robert, 206
Finch, J. H., 98
Fincher, A. J., 91
Findley, 221
Findley, George, 153
Findley, I. B., 96, 153
Findley, J. B., 114, 150, 151, 156, 157, 168, 169, 171, 174
Findley, J. P., 157
Findley, Jno. B., 157
Findley, John B., 114, 129, 144, 153, 155, 161, 167, 177, 182, 224
Findley, R. B., 185
Findley, W. W., 161, 169
Findley, William, 222
Findley, Wm., 178
Finley, J. B., 154
Finley, Jno., 157
First National Bank, B'ham., 76
Fischer & Bros., 68
Fischer, D. S., 5
Fischer, Gustavis, 212
Fischer, Watts V., 181
Fiseman, Brock, 171
Fishel & Bros., 69
Fishel & Brothers, 130
Fishel, Julius, 130
Fishel, Morris, 130
Fisher, C. P. C., 161, 175
Fisher, C. P., 178
Fisher, C. W., 189
Fisher, C.P.S., 223
Fisher, G. A., 2, 3
Fisher, Geo., 27
Fisher, Wm., 73
Fite, B. B., 235
Fitzgerald, T. M., 161
Fitzgerald, T. N., 178
Fitzpatrick, H. A., 15
Flarity, J. T., 53
Flavis?, Jno., 194
Flecher, W. S., 231
Fleming, Fannie, 123
Fletcher, A. J., 141
Fletcher, A., 130
Fletcher, Charles, 130
Fletcher, Elizabeth H., 130
Fletcher, Elizabeth, 130
Fletcher, F. S., 130
Fletcher, F. W., 130
Fletcher, George, 193, 194
Fletcher, Harriet, 130
Fletcher, Hugh, 161, 177
Fletcher, J. A., 147
Fletcher, J. C., 130
Fletcher, J. F., 130
Fletcher, J. H., 97, 98
Fletcher, J. H., Boaz, 97
Fletcher, Jackson, 161, 178
Fletcher, James, 11
Fletcher, John F., 130
Fletcher, John, 194
Fletcher, Joseph W., 130
Fletcher, M. J., 130
Fletcher, M. M., 98, 101
Fletcher, M. S., 130
Fletcher, Margaret, 130
Fletcher, Marthey A., 130
Fletcher, Sarah, 130
Fletcher, Toby, 194
Fletcher, W. S., 46
Fletcher, William F., 130
Fletcher, William S., 130
Fletcher, Wm. S., 130
Floid, M. I., Dr., 80
Flowers, John, 161, 178
Flowers, Strodder, 178
Flowers, Strother, 161
Floyd, James, 161, 178

Floyd, M. T., 254
Follansber, G. W., 197
Follemsbee, Geo. I., 185
Follett, John A., Dr., 44
Follett, Martha E., 43
Folsom, Charles R., 130, 131
Folsom, Herbert A., 130
Folsom, Herbert Arthur, 131
Folsom, Wm. F., 130
Force, Ben, 131
Force, Benjamin, 131
Force, Catherine, 131
Force, L. M., 131
Force, S. F., 131
Ford, J. L., 70
Ford, Wm., 223
Forester, Joshua, 47
Forester, Peter, 10
Forester, Rebecca, 14
Forister, Elisha, 13
Forney, W. H., 168
Forrester, J. J., 38
Forrester, James, 16
Fort Payne Bank, 228
Fort Payne Bldg. Co., 107
Fort Payne Herald, 7
Fort Payne Investment Co., 209
Fort Payne Journal, 18, 21, 24, 38, 40, 41, 48, 58, 60, 61, 64, 70, 75, 76,106, 110, 120, 124, 133, 184, 187, 189, 208, 226, 254, 258, 262
Fort Payne Water Co., 74
Forten, Tip, 120
Fortenberry, Berry, 119
Fortenberry, W. C., 120
Fortner, A. H., 108, 239
Fortner, A., 169
Fortner, Arch, 108
Fortner, Archibald, 107
Fortune & Watts, 161
Fortune, W., 141, 142
Fortune, William, 144, 255, 256
Fortune, Wm., 147, 257
Fossatt, G. B., 75
Fossett, A. H & Amelia, 215
Fossett, A. H., 215
Fossett, Addie, 51
Fossett, Amelia, 215
Fossett, G. B., 76
Fossett, Jackson, 24
Fossett, Seaborn, 226
Fossitt, Addie, 49
Fossitt, Jackson, 24
Foster, J. R., 152
Foster, John, 8, 222
Foster, W. H., 2
Foster?, C. C., 41
Fountain, Arty, 132
Fountain, Grady, 132
Fountain, J. M. & E., 186
Fountain, Mollie, 132
Fountain, Mollie, Mrs., 132
Fountain, Oma, 132
Fountain, W. W., 125, 131, 132
Fountian, Grady, 132
Fountian, Oma, 132
Foust, A. L., 62
Fout/Fant, 132
Fowler, Alfred E., 132
Fowler, John A., 105
Fowler, Owen/Oren H., 132
Fowler, Richard, 161, 177
Fowlks, F. V., (MD), 189
Fox, Salethy, 40
Foys, Melia, Mrs. 53,
Frances, Hugh, 28
Frances, Malvina, 28
Francis, Coleman, 28
Francis, J. B., 108
Francis, J. M., 35
Francis, Jeremiah, 132
Francis, Josiah, 11
Francis, Nancy Jane, 132
Francis, Polly Ann Blevins, 33
Franklin Lumber Co., 108
Franklin, 185
Franklin, A. G., 24, 38, 41, 76, 77, 87, 133, 135, 182, 184, 208, 246, 247
Franklin, Allen, 132
Franklin, Ben, 133, 134
Franklin, Benjamin, 133, 135
Franklin, Bradshaw, 133, 135
Franklin, D. L., 135
Franklin, Earl R., 132
Franklin, Earl, 133
Franklin, Elizabeth A., 135
Franklin, Green, 133
Franklin, J. B., 133, 134
Franklin, J. H., 58, 132
Franklin, J. M., 189
Franklin, J. N., 6, 8, 10, 34, 41, 46, 87, 92, 107, 112, 113, 126, 130, 141, 148, 150, 152, 154, 157, 168, 172, 196, 197, 208, 211, 218, 230, 231, 234, 244, 263
Franklin, J. P., 133
Franklin, J. R., 132
Franklin, J. S., 134
Franklin, J. W., 9
Franklin, J., 29, 156
Franklin, Jackson, 24
Franklin, James B., 132, 134
Franklin, James R., 112
Franklin, Janie, 133
Franklin, Jas., 24
Franklin, Jesse B., 132
Franklin, Jesse, 133
Franklin, Jno. N., 6, 15
Franklin, Jno. P., 135
Franklin, Joe S., 53
Franklin, John B., 135
Franklin, John H., 132
Franklin, John M., 4, 243
Franklin, John N., 5, 6, 7, 8, 12, 29, 37, 38, 45, 56, 68, 82, 87, 96, 129, 130, 132, 133-135, 185, 188, 217, 245, 246
Franklin, John, 5, 9, 26, 27, 70, 169, 189
Franklin, LaFayette, 135
Franklin, M. D. L., 135
Franklin, Martha, Mrs., 134, 135
Franklin, Mary Allen, 132
Franklin, Sallie, 133
Franklin, Samuel, 135
Franklin, Thomas & W.M., 134
Franklin, Thomas B., 133
Franklin, Thomas, 133, 134, 135
Franklin, Thos., 134
Franklin, W. M., 133, 134, 135
Franklin, Wallace A., 132
Franklin, Wallace, 133
Franklin, William H. F., 135
Franklin,Thos., 109
Frascett, A. H., 186
Frascett, Amedia, 186
Frazer, Brown, 169
Frazer, Darcus, 177
Frazer, Dorcas, 23, 135, 136, 161, 224,
Frazer, J. B., 171
Frazer, John B., 135, 161, 173, 206
Frazer, John, 23, 136, 169, 177
Frazer, Mrs., 169
Frazer, P. B., 242
Frazer, Robert, 23, 136, 169, 177, 222
Frazer, Robt., 161, 171, 173
Frazier, B. P., 212
Frazier, Bob, 137
Frazier, Brown, 207
Frazier, Byron M., 136
Frazier, Byron, 137
Frazier, C. N., 137
Frazier, Charles N., 136
Frazier, John, 25
Frazier, Chas.& Bryan, 137
Frazier, Dorcas, 23
Frazier, Ida C., 136
Frazier, Ida, 48, 49, 50, 51
Frazier, J. A., 92
Frazier, J. M., 208
Frazier, Jack, 137
Frazier, Jackson S., 136
Frazier, Jennie, 48, 49, 50, 51
Frazier, John B., 23, 143
Frazier, John, 114, 115
Frazier, John. B., 136
Frazier, Lela, 48, 49, 50
Frazier, Levi, 65
Frazier, Lucinda, 50
Frazier, Lucy, 241
Frazier, Nancy, 241
Frazier, P. B. (Polland B.), 136, 137
Frazier, P. B., 5, 63, 123, 243
Frazier, P. J., 183, 236
Frazier, P. M., 40, 41, 58, 69, 71, 77, 86, 87, 96, 107-109, 112, 123, 141, 153, 182, 184, 196, 207, 213, 239
Frazier, Pat M., 155
Frazier, Pat, 137, 202
Frazier, Patrick M., 200
Frazier, Patrick, 136, 143
Frazier, Polland B., 71, 136
Frazier, R. L., 15, 136
Frazier, R. W., 21, 52, 110, 125, 228, 229, 241
Frazier, R., 136
Frazier, Robert L., 136
Frazier, Robert W., 104, 227
Frazier, Robert, 22, 135
Frazier, Robt., 247
Frazier, Walter, 48, 49, 50, 51
Frazier, Wyatt, 48, 49, 51
Frazier, Wyeth, 50

Frazier/Frazer, 135
Frederick, George, 12
Freem?, T. M., 121
Freeman, Ann, 137
Freeman, C., 201
Freeman, Callie, 243, 245
Freeman, D. C., 220
Freeman, D. S., 220
Freeman, D. T., 220
Freeman, David C., 137
Freeman, Elisha, 137, 161, 178
Freeman, F.M., 121, 183
Freeman, Francis, 137
Freeman, H., 257
Freeman, James, 137, 245
Freeman, M. C., 256
Freeman, M., 257
Freeman, Martha Ann, 137
Freeman, Moses, 137
Freeman, R. C., 158
Freeman, R. F., 95
Freeman, Robert K., 135
Freeman, William, 137
Freeman, Zachariah, 137
French, J. C., 147
French, Samuel B., 142, 146
French, Samuel H., 144
Fricks Bros., 77
Fricks Brothers, 184
Fricks, A. T., 61, 183, 184
Fricks, Dr., 184
Fricks, G. E., 260
Fricks, Harrison, 223
Fricks, Y. A., 8
Friendship Church, 89
Frizell, Carlton, 11
Frizell, Widow, 14
Frizzell, Al, 137
Frizzell, Fannie, 137
Frizzell, James, 137
Frizzell, L. R., et al, 137
Frizzell, Louis R., 137
Frost, Griff, 134
Frost, Hale, 118, 119, 192
Frost, Hardy, 134
Frost, Henry, 10, 12
Frost, John, 13, 112
Frost, Mary, 29
Frost, Pat, 29
Frost, S. T., 134
Frost, W. H., 118
Fry, Hestor Ann, 46
Fry, Joe, 10
Ft. Payne Bldg. Co., 189
Ft. Payne C & I, 112
Ft. Payne Coal & Iron, 112
Ft. Payne CT Mill, 112
Ft. Payne Hdwe & Mining, 112
Ft. Payne Hdwe., 112
Ft. Payne Journal, 112
Ft. Payne Plumbing, 112
Ft. Payne Water Co., 117
Fullenwider, David, 177
Fuller, B. B., 57, 90
Fuller, J. B., 91
Fuller, P. N., 73, 94
Fuller, Sidney, 250
Fuller, W. F., 52, 58
Fuller, W. J., 117
Fuller, W. L., 57
Fuller, W. R., 72
Fuller, W. T. 15, 16, 38, 41, 45, 52, 71, 83, 86, 108, 111, 112, 124, 139, 184, 190, 208, 209, 215, 227, 229. 258
Fuller, Wit., 123
Fullerton, T. C., 8
Fullerwider, David, 161
Funderburk, C. C., 161, 223
Funderburk, Geo. W., 178
Funderburk, George W., 161
Funderburk, James C., 178
Funderburk, James, 161
Fur, Daniel, 195
Furr, D. A., 137
Furr, Daniel, 137
Furr, Georgia, et al, 137
Furr, Georgie Ann, 137
Furr, Mary M., 137
Furr, Rosa, 137
Furr, W. D., 137, 183
Furr, Walter, 137
Furrer, Samuel, 173
Furrow, Saml., 161
GA.Agriculture Works, 97
Gadsden Distrib., 191
Gadsden Marble & Stone Co., 62
Gadsden Mill Co., 191
Gadsden Natl. Bank, 97
Gadsden Times, 69
Gaines Marble Co., 110
Gaines, J. T., 219
Gaines, J. T., Dr., 105
Gaines, Mary Ann, 250
Gaines, O. Joe, 252
Gaines, R. A., 72, 259
Gaines, Wm. A., 250
Gains, James T., 187
Gains, R. A., 259
Gains, Robert, 173, 182
Gains, Robt., 162
Gains, Tom, Dr., 105
Galaway, Jerisha B., 124
Galbreath, Joseph, 239
Gale, Dr., 108
Gallaway, D. P., 139
Gallaway, J. D., 124
Gallaway, John R., 139
Gallaway, John T., 139
Gallaway, M. L., 139
Gallaway, P. C., 124
Gallaway, Perry C., 124
Gallaway, T. P., 139
Gallaway, Thomas P., 139
Gallaway, W. H., 139
Gallaway/Galaway, 124
Gann, J. M. W., 99, 100
Gannett, Thomas, 7
Garard, Richard, 177
Garden, James, 152
Gardener, J. G., 15
Gardener, Mary, 46
Gardner, J., 185
Gardner, James, 162, 173
Gardner, Marion 32
Garmany, Amsia S., 140
Garmany, Anna, 140
Garmany, Annie S., 140
Garmany, Bart, 140
Garmany, Flem, 139, 140
Garmany, Fleming E., 139
Garmany, Franklin B., 139, 140
Garmany, G. G., 253
Garmany, George W., 139
Garmany, George, 140
Garmany, J. H., 140
Garmany, John, 139, 140
Garmany, John, Jr., 139, 140
Garmany, Mannery, 140
Garmany, Margaret E., 139
Garmany, Martha, 140
Garmany, Mary A., 140
Garmany, Mary, 140
Garmany, S. M., 140
Garmany, Sam. M., 140
Garmany, Samuel, 140
Garner, C. W., 178
Garner, F. M., 196
Garner, Geo. W., 161
Garrard (Gerard), 85
Garrard, A., 98, 101
Garrard, Cornelia, 85
Garrard, Melia, 85
Garrard, W. F., 98
Garrard, William, 85
Garret, J. R., 144
Garret, Sarah, 112
Garret, Tatum, 178
Garret, Thomas J., 147
Garrett & Edwards, 263
Garrett & Stewart, 232
Garrett Estate, 107
Garrett, Blont, 231
Garrett, Blount, 146
Garrett, Emily C., 147, 148
Garrett, H. B., 199, 220
Garrett, H. W. B., 140-142, 145, 146, 148, 169, 172, 231, 246
Garrett, H. W., 142
Garrett, H., 26
Garrett, Henry H. B., 147
Garrett, Henry W. B., 141
Garrett, Henry, 147, 246
Garrett, Hub, 232
Garrett, Isher, 231
Garrett, J. B., 142
Garrett, J. G., 143
Garrett, J. R. & W. R., 89
Garrett, J. R., 88, 89
Garrett, J., 100, 102
Garrett, James, Jr., 162, 178
Garrett, Jason, 169
Garrett, Jesse A., 142
Garrett, Jesse, 142, 143, 223, 232
Garrett, Jessey A., 147
Garrett, John A., 147
Garrett, Lavicey, 147
Garrett, M. B., 141, 143
Garrett, Malachi B., 142
Garrett, Malichi B., 141, 147
Garrett, Malichi B., et al, 141
Garrett, Mary A., 148
Garrett, Mary W., 140
Garrett, Mary, 139
Garrett, Matilda B., 141
Garrett, Matilda, 143, 147
Garrett, Melinda, 142
Garrett, Sarah, 141, 142, 143, 144, 145, 147
Garrett, Saray, 146
Garrett, Sylvia A., 145, 146
Garrett, Sylvia Ann, 147
Garrett, T. J., 147
Garrett, T. R. (G. R.), 139
Garrett, T. R., 141
Garrett, Tatum, 161, 169
Garrett, Thomas B., 171
Garrett, Thomas J., 141, 147

Garrett, Thomas R., 140, 147, 148
Garrett, Thomas T., 142
Garrett, Thomas, 27, 114, 141-147, 178, 207, 231
Garrett, Thomas, Sr., 169
Garrett, Thos. J., 145, 146, 172
Garrett, Thos., Jr., 169
Garrett, Thos., Sr., 162
Garrett, Tina (Nina), 111
Garrett, Valenia V., 147
Garrett, Valeria V., 142, 147
Garrett, Valeria, 143
Garrett, Valesia V., 143
Garrett, W. R., 89, 114
Garrett, W. S., 140
Garrett, W. S., et al, 147
Garrett, W. W., 79, 227
Garrett, Wallace, 140
Garrett, Wesley M., 142
Garrett, William S., 111, 141
Garrett, Willis, 147
Garrington, Harry A., 67
Garrison, Anderson J., 139
Garrison, H. D., 139
Garrison, John, 139
Garrison, Kate B., 139
Garrison, M. F., 119
Garrison, T. J., 139
Garron, Geo., 2
Gary, Wm. H., 75
Gasaway, Robert, 223
Gasgan, James, 230
Gasgen, James, 232
Gask, James, 146
Gask, Jos., 143
Gaskin, J. W., 100
Gaskins, James, 143
Gasque, John M., 70, 161, 178
Gasque, Martha, 70
Gasque, Milton, 70
Gasque, William, 70
Gatlin, Eliza Jane, 148
Gatlin, Eliza, 143
Gatlin, George, 148
Gatlin, H., 148
Gatlin, Harrison, 148
Gatlin, James, 148
Gatlin, Jane, 12
Gatlin, Louisa J., 148
Gatlin, Wm., 10
Gatling, B. T., 60
Gaudin Undertaking Co., 75
Gaudin, Jas. T., 75
Gazaway, Caleb G., 148
Gazaway, Caleb, 149
Gazaway, E., 149
Gazaway, Ellender, 148
Gazaway, H. H., 149
Gazaway, Henry H., 148
Gazaway, Jane, 148
Gazaway, Jesse, 148, 149
Gazaway, John, 148, 149
Gazaway, Mrs., 161
Gazaway, Nancy Ann, 148
Gazaway, William, 148
Gearrin, G. W., 3
Gennett, Elizabeth, 149
Gentry, Eliza, 161, 177
Gentry, J. L., 27
George & Harrison, 143
George, C. D., 22, 68, 129, 135, 153, 169, 171, 221, 222
George, Charles D., 135, 149-182, 263
George, Charles, 149
George, Chas. D., 262
George, Ellen, 69, 150, 152, 155
George, H. P., 129, 149, 153, 162, 173, 178
George, Henry, 257
George, James, 69, 150, 155
George, John K., 149
George, Mary E., 162, 182
George, Mary G., 169
George, Mary, 69, 150, 152, 153
George, Robert, 70, 153
George, S. B., 255
George, T. H., 169, 172
George, Thomas H., 150, 155, 162, 168-172
George, Thomas, 150, 152, 155
George, Thos. H., 23, 177, 222
Gerard, Cornelia, 85
Gerard, Richard, 161
Gerard, Will, 85
Gerime/Geraine/Gerome, 221
Geruthaur, Cosinna J., 26
Gholston, John, 162
Gibbs, J. M., 72
Gibbs, John, 217
Gibbs, Sallie, 55
Gibbs, Sally, 54
Gibbs, Thomas W., 151
Gibbs, Thos. H., 173
Gibbs, Thos. W., 162, 173
Gibbs, W. E., 83
Gibert, J. W., 114
Gibson, A. C., 184
Gibson, Alvin C., 182
Gibson, B. F., 15, 107
Gibson, Emily, 185
Gibson, F. P., 33, 182, 184
Gibson, Geo. F., 182
Gibson, George F., 184
Gibson, George, 15, 182, 183, 184, 185, 194
Gibson, J. C., 94, 104, 185, 210
Gibson, J. E., 260
Gibson, J. P., 97, 101
Gibson, J. R., 103
Gibson, J. W., 9, 220
Gibson, Jacob W., 135, 185
Gibson, Jacob, 27, 70
Gibson, N. J., 183
Gibson, N., 185
Gibson, Nancy J., 182
Gibson, Nancy Jane, 182
Gibson, Nancy, 184
Gibson, P., 185
Gibson, Sarah Blevins, 33
Gifford, Geo., 122
Gifford, R., 13
Gifford, Thomas, 252
Gifford, Thos. V., 123
Giland, W. B., 196
Gilbert, A. J., 89
Gilbert, A. W., 190
Gilbert, Addison D., 185, 186
Gilbert, Agnes Lavon, 185
Gilbert, B. F., 20, 91, 186
Gilbert, Ben F., 20
Gilbert, C. N., 102
Gilbert, D. L., 186
Gilbert, E. N., 5
Gilbert, Florence, 186
Gilbert, G. B., 186
Gilbert, G. W., Mrs., 76
Gilbert, Gordon L., 186
Gilbert, H., 150
Gilbert, J. A., 186
Gilbert, J. B., 56
Gilbert, J. D., 186
Gilbert, J. G., 63
Gilbert, J. I., 186
Gilbert, John, 255
Gilbert, L. D., 88
Gilbert, Longs, 75
Gilbert, M. P., 20
Gilbert, Marcus L., 186
Gilbert, Merrida/Mindy, 186
Gilbert, N. C., 186
Gilbert, Ovie/Avie, 186
Gilbert, P. P., 186
Gilbert, R. F., 236
Gilbert, S. W., 106, 186
Gilbert, Samuel L., 186
Gilbert, T. B., 186
Gilbert, Tobe, 197
Gilbert, W. H., 186
Gilbert, W. P., 7
Gilbert, Wiley W., 252
Gilbreath, 192, 193
Gilbreath, A. A., 55, 238
Gilbreath, A. C., 187
Gilbreath, A. P., 255
Gilbreath, A. R., 149, 238
Gilbreath, Asa, 149
Gilbreath, B. N., 84, 191
Gilbreath, C. N., 97
Gilbreath, Dicy Ann, 255
Gilbreath, E., 202
Gilbreath, Eliza Horton, 237
Gilbreath, Elizabeth, 197
Gilbreath, Ellison, 255
Gilbreath, Frank, 171
Gilbreath, G. E., 255
Gilbreath, G. O., 187
Gilbreath, G., 231
Gilbreath, Geo., 237
Gilbreath, George, 255
Gilbreath, J. & A. C., 187
Gilbreath, J. A., 97
Gilbreath, J. E., 186, 255
Gilbreath, J. M., 155
Gilbreath, J. S. & Mollie J., 186
Gilbreath, J. S., 188
Gilbreath, J. V., 187
Gilbreath, John A., 103
Gilbreath, John M., 255
Gilbreath, M. A., 238
Gilbreath, M. H., 187
Gilbreath, M. J., 120
Gilbreath, M. M., 8, 9, 121
Gilbreath, M. N., 118
Gilbreath, M., 153
Gilbreath, Marcus N., 120
Gilbreath, Margaret J., 119
Gilbreath, Martha C., 103
Gilbreath, Mary A., 188
Gilbreath, Mollie J., 186
Gilbreath, Mrs. & Sims, 217
Gilbreath, N. O., 187
Gilbreath, Nancy E., 187
Gilbreath, Nancy Elizabeth, 187
Gilbreath, Noble, 186

Gilbreath, O. D., 121
Gilbreath, O. G., 187
Gilbreath, P. H., 197
Gilbreath, Perry, 238
Gilbreath, Peter M., 187
Gilbreath, R. A., 255
Gilbreath, S. A., Mrs., 187
Gilbreath, S. C., 155
Gilbreath, S. E., 8
Gilbreath, Sallie, 187
Gilbreath, Samuel, 154, 155
Gilbreath, Sim T., 186
Gilbreath, Stant, 63, 191, 192
Gilbreath, Thomas, 187
Gilbreath, V. J., 98, 102
Gilbreath, W. B., 102, 127
Gilbreath, W. J., 102
Gilbreath, W. T. & N. O., 187
Gilbreath, W. T., 187
Gilbreath, Wm. B., 187, 188
Gilbreth, M. N., 56
Gilbreth, Madison H., 56
Gilbreth, S. W., 190
Gilchrist, Ruth C., Mrs., 188
Gilchrist, W. D., 188
Gileran, D. N., 251
Giles, E. W., 188
Giles, W. J., 188
Gilespie & Smyne, 7
Gillaspe, W. Y., 183
Gillespie, M. L., 62
Gilliam, Wm., 14
Gilliand, D. M., 251
Gilliand, John E., 252
Gilliland, Beulah I., 188
Gilliland, Beulah, 188
Gilliland, Charlotte Johnson, 250
Gilliland, D. M., 46, 252
Gilliland, Grace Iola, 188
Gilliland, Grace, 188
Gilliland, H. F., (MD), 188
Gilliland, John E., 250, 251
Gilliland, M. E., 188
Gilliland, Mary J., 188
Gilliland, Pink M., 188
Gilliland, W. B., 46, 195
Gilliland, Wm. H., 262
Gillis, Sarah, 47
Gilreath, M. M., 8
Ginn, W. P., 15
Gipson, A. A., Mrs., 188
Gipson, Alpha A., 188
Gipson, Elizabeth, (Eliza), 37
Gipson, Grace, 189
Gipson, Gracie, 188
Gipson, Henry G., 188, 189
Gipson, Hershell, 188, 189
Gipson, I. C., 26
Gipson, J. P., 100
Gipson, James, 188, 189
Gipson, John C., 188
Gipson, John, 145, 188, 189
Gipson, Lemuel, 188, 189
Gipson, Lemuel, et al, 188, 189
Gipson, M. C., 20
Gipson, Maggie, 188, 189
Gipson, Manuel, 188, 189
Gipson, Maude, 188, 189
Gipson, Melton, 37
Gipson, W. M., 189
Gipson, William, 37
Girard (Gerard), 85
Glasby, J. A., 7
Glasby, J. L., 7
Glascon, J. T., 92
Glascue, 90
Glaspy, L. F., Mrs., 189
Glaspy, W. J., 189
Glass, J. A., 218
Glass, Joseph A., 216, 217, 218, 218
Glass, Kate, 205
Glass, Mary A. Heald, 217
Glass, Mary A., 219
Glass, Mary Ann Elizabeth, 217
Glass, William, 205
Glazener, Giles, 161, 178
Glazener, Jesse, 162 177
Glazner, G. T., 156
Glazner, John, 151
Glazner, L., 158
Gleason, Monroe, 64
Glover, G. S., 213
Glover, W. J., 205
Goade, W. J., 189
Gober, G. J., 97
Gober, G. W., 189
Godfrey, 107
Godfrey, 189
Godfrey, J. H., 189
Godwin, C. B., 76
Goen, A. B., 69
Goggin, E. T., 114, 161
Goggin, Edmond T., 113
Goggins, E. T., 247, 248
Goggins, Martha, 247
Goins, Ameila, 189
Goins, Jas. W., 189
Goins, John, 189, 190
Goins, Joseph W., 189
Goins, L. B., 189
Goldston, W. H., 228
Golson/Jolson, 152
Golston, John, 173
Gooch, W. T., 15
Goodhue, Amos E., 242
Gordon, H. M., 257
Gorham, Alma, 97
Gorum, Marion, 162
Goss, R. G., 122
Gossett, James, 60
Graddy, James O., 162, 173
Graddy, Lewis, 152, 162, 173
Grady, A. E., 23, 224
Grady, James O., 152
Grady, Lewis, 152
Grafton, D. R., 245
Graham Beat Tax, 114
Graham, 193
Graham, E. L., 191
Graham, E., 191
Graham, Edgar, 190
Graham, Emma, 190
Graham, F. C., 72, 186
Graham, G., 169
Graham, Gideon, 162, 173, 174, 178
Graham, H. M., 72
Graham, L. E., 193
Graham, M. A., Mrs., 190
Graham, Mary J., 76
Graham, Mary Lou, 190
Graham, Melvin, 190
Graham, R. E., 191
Graham, R. H., 77
Graham, T. D., 77
Graham, Thomas, 152, 190
Graham, Thos., 162
Graham, Vann, 190
Graham, W. A., 190
Graham, W. B., 76, 77, 78
Graham, W. S., 57, 91
Grant, J. F., 43, 114, 129, 130, 244
Grant, J. H., 244
Grant, J. P., 220
Grant, T. I., 43
Grant, William, 92, 190
Grantham, Corinne J., 27
Grantham, Thomas, 27
Granthaur, Thomas, 26
Grarfy, J. M., 211
Grave, H. L., 110
Graves & Son, 260
Graves, ? Ann, Miss, 177
Graves, 191
Graves, A., 192, 258
Graves, Alex, 191, 199
Graves, Alexander, 199
Graves, Alice, 190
Graves, Arthy Ann, 162
Graves, Dan, 191
Graves, E. L., 199
Graves, H. B. & W. V., 192
Graves, H. B., 190, 192, 194, 199
Graves, H. F., 103
Graves, H. J., 98, 199
Graves, H. L., 1, 61, 62, 89, 94, 125 190, 191, 194, 199, 210, 226
Graves, H. T., 97, 99, 103, 191
Graves, Henry, 190, 191
Graves, Henry, 199
Graves, Hiram, 161, 178
Graves, Ira, 161
Graves, J. A., 191
Graves, J. J., 191
Graves, J. S., 120, 191, 192
Graves, J., 238
Graves, James G., 199
Graves, James L., 191, 192, 192
Graves, James M., 192
Graves, James, 190, 192, 223
Graves, Jas. R., 242
Graves, John, 119, 162, 199
Graves, John, Jr., 178
Graves, John, Sr., 161, 178
Graves, Josh, 119
Graves, Joshia, 191
Graves, Joshua, 190, 191
Graves, Joshua, 199
Graves, L. K., 199
Graves, N. L., 52, 199
Graves, Nancy, 190, 191, 192, 193, 194, 195, 199
Graves, Nora, Mrs., 62
Graves, Pink, 199
Graves, R. A., 191, 192
Graves, T. T., 99
Graves, W. H., 193
Graves, W. L., 61, 66
Graves, W. V., 62, 190, 192
Graves, William V., 189
Graves?, Jason, 152

Gravet, T., 259
Gravet, W. G., 259
Gravett, Melvina, 161
Gravill, Lodwick, 190
Gravit, J. F., 220
Gravit, Malvina, Mrs., 178
Gravitt, Claris, 1
Gravitt, J. L., 259
Gravitt, L. L., 259, 260
Gravitt, L., 74, 76, 83, 187, 259
Gravitt, Lodwick, 190
Gravitt, W. J., 42, 62
Gray, A. L., 161, 178
Gray, Allen, 152, 195, 218, 232
Gray, Asa, 195
Gray, David, 191, 195
Gray, Flavie Blalock, 30
Gray, G. W., 195
Gray, George, 195
Gray, J. B., 195
Gray, J. B., 63, 195
Gray, Jacob, 46, 195
Gray, John M., 126
Gray, John, 12, 195, 258
Gray, Joseph, 195
Gray, Thomas, 195
Gray, William B., 195
Gray, William, 195
Grayson, Cyntha, 14
Grayson, Thomas, 32
Green, A. B., 7, 41, 69, 103, 141, 142, 144, 145, 147, 169, 212, 231, 261
Green, A. B., Dr., 37, 189
Green, Anthony B., 141, 149, 196
Green, Bill, Dr., 134
Green, Blev., 112
Green, Elizabeth, 196
Green, F. S., 26, 196
Green, Fannie S., 25, 26, 27, 196
Green, Frank, 85
Green, G. S., 26, 27, 70
Green, G. W., 46, 98, 99
Green, G.A., 25
Green, George, 95
Green, Grief F., 70
Green, Grief S., 25, 26, 196
Green, H. N., 100, 102
Green, Ida C, 136
Green, J. A., 119
Green, J. H., 98
Green, J. W., 100
Green, Jacob, 15
Green, Jesse B., 196
Green, John Foster, 196
Green, John, 55, 218, 238, 256, 257
Green, L. B., Mrs., 120
Green, Lillie Belle, 119
Green, Lillie, 236
Green, Lily Bell, 119
Green, Mat, 137
Green, P. B. (M.D.), 1
Green, P. B., 58
Green, P. B., Dr., 2, 211
Green, P. M., 52, 103, 131, 136, 182
Green, Philmon M., 196
Green, Sallie E., 196
Green, Sarah J., 196
Green, T. S., 26
Green, Tom, 194
Green, W. J., 191, 193
Green, W. L., 97
Green, W. M., MD, 135
Green, William P., 196
Green?, R. G., 158
Greenfield, J., 248
Greenfield, Martha J., 247
Greer, J. A., 102
Greer, L. J., 100
Gregg, C. W., 98
Gregg, C., 129
Gregory, R., 150
Gregory, Robert, 23, 153, 154
Gregory, Robt., 161, 168, 175
Greyton, George, 41
Greyton, Mary, 41
Grider, C., 9
Grider, W. M., 5
Griffin, 56
Griffin, Anna, 231
Griffin, Elizabeth, 232
Griffin, H. F., 187
Griffin, H. W., 100
Griffin, Henry, 238, 253, 255
Griffin, J. H., 89, 99, 101
Griffin, J. M., 119
Griffin, J. T., 89
Griffin, James M., 153
Griffin, James, 196
Griffin, L. H., 219
Griffin, Maborn, 258
Griffin, Marborn, 256
Griffin, N. G., 197
Griffin, N. W., 197
Griffin, Nancy, 161
Griffin, Nolan, 202
Griffin, Nolin G., 197
Griffin, Nolin/Nolen/Nolan, 197
Griffin, Paralee, 196
Griffin, Perry, 42
Griffin, R., 63
Griffin, T. H., 187
Griffin, Travis, 197
Griffin, W. R., 95, 126
Griffin, W., 60
Griffin, William P., 196
Griffin, William, 42, 130, 249
Griffin, Wm., 12, 26, 33, 63, 70, 128, 156, 158, 162, 178, 196, 230, 241, 243, 251, 254, 255, 256, 257
Griffith, E. E., 207
Griffith, E., Mrs., 207
Griffith, Elizabeth, 142, 146
Griffith, Jessie, 147
Griffity, Elizabeth, 145
Griggle, G. W., 91
Grimes, Thomas, 14
Griswold, Edward Browning, 197
Griswold, Edward P., 197
Griswold, Grace, 197
Griswold, Harold T., 197
Griswold, Mary Catherine B., 197
Griswold, Mary Maude, 197
Grooms, Dan, 105
Grooms, M. J., 105
Gross, Adeline, 49
Grossean, Ernest, 228
Groves, A., 190
Groves, Bert, 14
Groves, H., 257
Groves, Ira, 177
Guartney, Gene, 133
Guartney, Genie, 133
Gubbs, Wm., 169
Gublett, J. G., 52
Guest, G. B., 8, 127, 243, 244
Guest, G. P., 238
Guest, Green, 197
Guest, Griffin, 238
Guest, J. A., 197
Guest, J. G., 197
Guest, J. H. E., 31, 103, 131, 133, 134
Guest, J. M., 197
Guest, J. W., 197
Guest, J., 31, 197
Guest, Mattie, Mrs., 62
Guest, N. C., 132
Guest, Newton C., 132
Guest, Nicie, 238
Guest, Olaber, 197
Guest, R. H. E., 199
Guest, R. J., 21, 228
Guest, Robert, 62
Guest, Ruben J., 238
Guest, S. P., 197
Guest, T. H. E., 197
Guest, W. C., 197
Guffey, Lillie M. Blansit, 31
Guice, Y. Y., 57
Guin (Quin), 41
Guin, G. A., 42
Gulledger, Jesse, 7
Gullegr, Jesse, Dr., 7
Gulon, James, 15
Gynan, S. J., 239
H. B. Brock Co., 110
Haas, Myrtle Scott, 134
Hackworth, J. B., 81
Hages, A. K., 174
Hagler, C. C., 245
Hagler, C. H., 26
Hagler, C. S., 26, 113
Hagler, C., 158
Hagler, Columbus, 157, 178
Hagler, J. W., 247
Hagler, W. I., 244
Hagler, W. T., 151, 169
Hagler, Wm. T., 162, 168, 175
Hagles, Columbus C., 162
Hagles/Hogles/ Hogler, 41
Haight, Jonathan, 64
Haigwood, W. E., 123
Hail, Lindsey, 151, 173
Hailey, Samuel R., 196
Hairel, Burt, 206
Hairel, Deliah, 199
Hairel, John, 190, 199
Hairell, John, 69, 94
Hairlston, Charley, 189
Hairrel, Dick, 192
Hairrel, Mose, 192
Hairston, Bell, 31
Haiston, R. M., 31
Halbrooks, J. G., 194
Hale, Jno., 194
Hale, Lindsay, 162, 174
Hale, P. C., 7, 45, 105, 120, 125, 190, 206
Hall & Nicholson, 171
Hall, 80
Hall, Aaron, 149, 151, 162
Hall, Adam, 177
Hall, Amy, 205
Hall, Bryan, 68, 199, 201
Hall, Burris, 132
Hall, Calvin, 14

Hall, Charles A., 200
Hall, Charles W., 200
Hall, Elijah, 151, 162, 174
Hall, Eugene, 123
Hall, F. B., 125
Hall, G. B., 102
Hall, H. M., 92
Hall, Indiana M., 199
Hall, Irby C., 75
Hall, J. A., 1, 29, 85, 94
Hall, J. A., Sr., 199, 200
Hall, J. B., 103, 200
Hall, J. C., 201, 203, 204
Hall, J. D., 1, 102
Hall, J. G., 200, 203, 204
Hall, J. H., 2, 99, 102
Hall, J. M., 195, 201-205, 68
Hall, J. O., 75
Hall, J. W., 76, 193, 194, 195
Hall, J., 203
Hall, Jacob, 201, 203
Hall, James A., Jr., 200
Hall, James B., 200, 201, 202, 203,204, 205
Hall, James H., 16
Hall, Jane D., Mrs., 98
Hall, Jim, 203
Hall, John, 162, 177
Hall, Josie C., 199
Hall, Josie, 200, 201, 203
Hall, Levi, 162, 178
Hall, M. B., 205
Hall, Mackey & Co., 69, 76, 237
Hall, Margaret H., 234
Hall, Margaret Holmes, 234
Hall, Mary, 123
Hall, N. J., Mrs., 205
Hall, Newton, 82
Hall, O. H., 206
Hall, O. L., 68, 69, 75, 188, 191, 192, 205
Hall, O. S., 69
Hall, Oliver G., 200
Hall, Oliver L., 200, 234
Hall, Oliver, 205, 206
Hall, P. C., 78, 83
Hall, Prescott, 107
Hall, R. C., 7
Hall, S. M., 250
Hall, T. H., 73, 90, 91, 132
Hall, Vann, 93
Hall, Victor W., 200
Hall, W. T., 102
Hall, Wayne O. W., 200
Hall, Willard Otis Wayne, 200
Hall, Yancy, 250
Hallmark, John, 186
Hallmark, M. E., Mrs., 186
Halloway, James, 12
Halloway, Jesse H., 146
Halls Dry Goods Co., 93
Halls, Dry Goods, 66
Ham, Wm., 143
Hamby, E. H., 225
Hamby, P., 225
Hamdey, W. D., 88
Hamel, Enoch, 178
Hames, Reba Cash Milton, 6
Hamett, Perry, 126
Hamett, Vincy, 217
Hamilton, Al, 226
Hamilton, Alfred, 223
Hamilton, H. G., 238
Hamilton, Henry & Fannie, 238
Hamison, H. C., 232
Hamlin, John, 223
Hamlin, L. E., 253
Hammack, 146
Hammack, A. J., 144
Hammack, H. I., 212
Hammack, Harriet Jack, 243
Hammack, John, 178
Hammack, Ranson, 235
Hammack, Thomas, 29, 114, 142, 222, 243, 247
Hammack, Thos., 26, 146, 177, 212, 220, 244, 245
Hammack, W. N., 146, 231
Hammack, W., 114, 142
Hammack, Willoughby, 143, 147, 231
Hammack, Wm. N., 147
Hammack, Wm., 145
Hammack/Hammock, 206
Hamman, B. G., 251
Hamman, G. B., 249
Hamman, Idella, 52
Hamman, John V., 233
Hamman, John, 233
Hamman, W. J., 52
Hammett, James, 84, 217, 218
Hammett, James, Sr., 126
Hammett, Jesse, 218
Hammett, Nancy, 217
Hammitt, James, 251
Hammock, 145
Hammock, Aaron G., 206, 207
Hammock, C. Lasey, 207
Hammock, Charley, 207
Hammock, Charlott, 207
Hammock, Clancy Ann, 206
Hammock, Claracy/Clarsy, 207
Hammock, George, 207
Hammock, J. J., 207
Hammock, Marion, 207
Hammock, Mary Ann, 206
Hammock, Mary S., 37
Hammock, Thomas, 114, 150, 151, 206
Hammock, Thos., 84, 147, 153, 155, 206, 232
Hammock, Vaney, 38
Hammock, W., 38, 162, 207, 208
Hammock, Wallace, 207
Hammock, Will, 207
Hammock, William N., 206
Hammock, Willoughby, 208
Hammock, Wm. H., 206
Hammock/Hammack, 178
Hammon, B. G., 19, 208
Hammon, B. H., 208
Hammon, Elizabeth, 208
Hammon, Geo. Houston, 208
Hammon, J. V., 208
Hammon, Jas., 208
Hammon, Rufus A., 208
Hammon, W. W., 208
Hammon, William P., 208
Hammon, William, 208
Hammon/Hamman/Hammond, 208
Hammond, C. B., 208
Hammond, Nina, 208
Hammond, W. J., 208
Hammond, William C., 208
Hammond, William, 38, 248
Hammonds, 52
Hammonds, A. Lee, 252
Hammonds, Wm. H., 223
Hammons, B. G., 18
Hammons, D. F., 208
Hammons, James, 216
Hammons, Mead, 122
Hammons, N. A., 208
Hamond, J. M., 45
Hamrick, G. W., 122
Hamrick, J. D., 29
Hamrick, W. X., 4
Hamrie, J. E., 124
Hamrie, J. R., 124
Hanby, Mary, 123
Hand, J. W., 207
Hand, M. T., 174
Handage, Elizabeth, 37
Hanes, S. H., 91
Haney, H., Jr., 122
Haney, Jefferson, 59
Haney, Myrtle, Mrs., 31
Haney, Nettie, Mrs., 30
Haney, Wm., 13
Hanks, J. S., 156
Hanna, A. B., 9, 92
Hanna, J. A., 213
Hannah, A. B., 242
Hannah, Josie, 49
Hannah, T., 220
Hannan, B. G., 8
Hansard, E. L., 254
Hansel, Robert, 209
Hansell, Georgia, 209
Hansell, Maude, 209
Hansell, Robert, 208, 209
Hansell, Willie, 209
Hanset, James, 254
Hanson, Geo., 232
Haralsen & Clayton, 135
Haralsen, W. J., 46
Haralson & Collins, 70
Haralson & Haralson, 18, 48, 186
Haralson & Son, 24, 44, 184, 246, 247
Haralson, 221
Haralson, A. C., 212
Haralson, A. J., 223
Haralson, C. J., 209
Haralson, Ella V., 25, 209
Haralson, H. C., 212, 234, 235
Haralson, Henry C., 25, 196, 209, 236
Haralson, J. B., 7, 66, 72, 95, 125, 139
Haralson, J. R., 142
Haralson, J. S., 22, 170
Haralson, J. W., 172
Haralson, Minnie L., 209
Haralson, P. B., 140
Haralson, Peter Bennett, 209
Haralson, Sidney, 189
Haralson, W. C., 40, 41
Haralson, W. G., 155
Haralson, W. H., 76
Haralson, W. I., 23
Haralson, W. J. & H. C., 141

Haralson, W. J., 8, 25, 27, 70, 142, 149, 155, 170, 171, 196, 209, 223, 225, 243, 244
Haralson, W. R., 1, 5
Haralson, W. W., 17, 20, 42, 44, 52, 54, 76, 95, 103, 107, 109, 209
Haralson, W., C., 41
Haralson, Walter U., 209
Haralson, William J., 196
Haralson, William L., 209
Haralson, Wm. J., 70, 145
Haralston & Haralston, 8, 38
Haralston, H. C., 38
Haralston, Helen, 209
Haralston, J. W., 38
Haralston, P. P., 75
Haralston, W. C., 41
Haralston, Wallace, 41
Haralston/Hairlston, 189
Harben, James , 232
Harbin, James, 143
Harbour, C. C., 200
Harbour, Maude, Mrs., 200
Harden, H. D., 42, 102
Harden, Mary B., 167
Hardin, Mary D., 152
Harding, Old, Mrs., 259
Harding, Sam, Mrs., 259
Harding, Sam., 259
Hardinger, Richard, 122
Hardman, Effie, 209
Hardman, Ella J., 209
Hardman, Ervin, 209
Hardman, Estell, 209
Hardman, G. W., 209
Hardman, John J., 209
Hardman, Lola, 209
Hardman, N. L., 209
Hardman, Nettie, 209
Hardwick, W. C., 193
Hardwick, Wm., 258
Hardy, Gaines A., 38
Hare, A. G., 209
Hare, Major, 209
Hare, S. E., 209
Harelson, W. J., 217
Hariel, Wm., 206
Harison, George, 142, 143
Harkins, James M., 162
Harl, Enoch, 173, 174
Harleston, J. W., 244
Harleston, W. J., 245
Harlow, Ella Elizabeth, Mrs., 67
Harlson, Winkett, 246
Harlson, Wm. J., 113
Harlston, Davis, 7
Harmett, James, 217
Harnett, Jesse & James, 217
Harold, Enoch, 151
Harold/Harrel, 151
Harp, Jesse, 194
Harp, M. T., 209
Harp, N. E., Mrs., 209
Harp, W. M., 193
Harp, W. T./ M. T., 209
Harpe, Jess, 193
Harpe, Jesse, 194
Harper, Albert, 210
Harper, E. D., 258, 259
Harper, E. J., 259
Harper, E. L., 91
Harper, Ida, 209, 210
Harper, J. D., 209
Harper, Jesse, 151, 162, 174
Harper, John D., 211
Harper, John P., 210, 211
Harper, M. A., 258, 259
Harper, N. S., 210
Harper, S. D., 209
Harper, S. N., 210
Harper, T. W., 210
Harper, Tara/Tera/Terah, 210
Harper, Terah, 210
Harper, W. L., 210
Harper, William, 210
Harper, Wm. P., 210
Harper, Y. S., 210
Harper, Zeke, 90
Harralson, W. W., 15
Harralson, Wm. S., 263
Harrel, Enoch, 151
Harrell, Burl, 205
Harrell, Enoch, 162
Harrell, William, 205
Harrelson, W. C., 41
Harriet, Negro Girl, 31
Harris, Belvin, 211
Harris, Ben, 37
Harris, D. C., 252
Harris, Delfry, 100
Harris, Della, 211
Harris, Doris, 211
Harris, E. A., 75
Harris, E. F., 102
Harris, E. L., 89, 211
Harris, E. L., Mrs., 211
Harris, Elijah, 211
Harris, G. L., 215
Harris, G. W., 61
Harris, Gaines A., 148
Harris, Gains A., 241
Harris, Gean, 122
Harris, H., 150
Harris, Hester, 211
Harris, J. A., 242
Harris, J. D., 110
Harris, J. W., 102, 192
Harris, James O., 211
Harris, James, 14
Harris, Jesse, 211
Harris, John, 145
Harris, Larkin, 22, 223, 226
Harris, Lemuel A., 215
Harris, M. H., 57
Harris, Mattie Janie, 211
Harris, Mildred, 211
Harris, Nancy A., 162
Harris, Narcis, 211
Harris, R. C., 211
Harris, Robert C., 211
Harris, S. A., 61
Harris, Samuel, 14
Harris, Sarah J., 61
Harris, Sarah, 61
Harris, T. G., 36, 45, 131, 215
Harris, T. N., 91
Harris, T., 17
Harris, Thomas A., 211
Harris, Thos. G., 215
Harris, Vesten, 211
Harris, W. A., 83
Harris, W. M., 5
Harris, W. R., 57
Harris, W. S., 81
Harris, W., 185
Harris, Walter, 211
Harris, William, 3, 4
Harris/Morris, 157
Harrison, Agnesia, 178
Harrison, Agness, 162
Harrison, Caroline, 254
Harrison, Cathrine, 254
Harrison, Eddey, 257
Harrison, George, 143
Harrison, H. C., 142, 143
Harrison, J. E. F., 177
Harrison, J. E. T., 162
Harrison, J. J., 72
Harrison, J. J., MD, 83
Harrison, Nancy Ann, Miss, 178
Harrison, W. J., 6
Harrison, William, 151
Harrison, Wm., 162, 175, 257
Harry, James A., 241
Hartimans, J. M., 244
Hartline, A., 12
Hartline, B. P., 211
Hartline, C. H., 134
Hartline, J. A., 13, 108, 211
Hartline, J. P., 108
Hartline, John C., 211
Hartline, Mary A., 211
Hartline, Mary, 211
Hartline, W. A., 11
Hartling, Lizzie, 211
Hartman, E., 261
Hartrum, Chloe, 169
Hartrum, H., 147
Hartrum, Hannah, 169
Harvey House & Land, 89
Harvey, Catherine, 211
Harvey, Charles, 108
Harvey, Florence P., 211
Harvey, Harry, 211
Harvey, Henry B., 211
Harvey, Jefferson, 59
Harvey, Lewis, 114
Harvey, R. B., 106
Harvey, Roy C., 211
Harvey, W. H., 91, 92
Harvey, W. O., 89, 91
Harvy, Benson, 106
Harwood, Will, 122
Hasley, G. R., 16
Hastens, Stephen, 162
Hastings, Stephen, 178, 185
Hasturn, Hannah, 143
Hatfield, W. H., 15, 183
Hatton, Thompson, 54
Hawes, James, 215, 216
Hawes, Jeff, 215
Hawes, Jefferson, 215
Hawes, Sampson, 216
Hawes, Samuel, 22
Hawk, James M., 78
Hawkins, A. E., 106
Hawkins, A. L., 215
Hawkins, Adam L., 212
Hawkins, Alex, 25, 148, 214
Hawkins, Alexander, 213, 215
Hawkins, Alice V., 25
Hawkins, B. F., 145, 146, 212
Hawkins, B. H., 196
Hawkins, Belle, 25
Hawkins, Ben, 212
Hawkins, Benjamin H., 212
Hawkins, Benjamin, 13, 214
Hawkins, Bettie, 61
Hawkins, Blanch, 214
Hawkins, Blanche, 214
Hawkins, Chas., 109, 110
Hawkins, Cornelia, 25, 215

Hawkins, D. A., 212
Hawkins, Drucilla C., 212
Hawkins, Drucilla N., 212
Hawkins, Echols, 215
Hawkins, Elijah, 222
Hawkins, Elizabeth, 213, 214
Hawkins, Elmer, 215
Hawkins, Emery, 212, 213
Hawkins, F. M., 162, 178
Hawkins, G., 148
Hawkins, Geo. W., 213, 215
Hawkins, George W., 213
Hawkins, H. A., 24
Hawkins, H. E., 213
Hawkins, H., 148
Hawkins, Hattie D., 213
Hawkins, Hattie O., 215
Hawkins, Hattie, 25
Hawkins, Henry, 222
Hawkins, Hulda J., 213, 215
Hawkins, Huldah, 25
Hawkins, J. J., 46, 212
Hawkins, J. John, 214
Hawkins, Jacob, 235
Hawkins, James C., 4
Hawkins, James M., 178
Hawkins, James P., 212
Hawkins, James T., 25, 213, 215
Hawkins, James, 6, 108, 206, 213-215, 241-245
Hawkins, James, Sr., 213
Hawkins, Jas. F., 133
Hawkins, Jas. M., 9
Hawkins, Jessie, 213
Hawkins, John N., 24, 38, 45
Hawkins, John, 13, 213, 214
Hawkins, John, Sr., 32
Hawkins, Lewis, 215
Hawkins, Louisa R., 212
Hawkins, Louisa, 215
Hawkins, Luna, 214
Hawkins, M. E., 213
Hawkins, M. Hope, 214
Hawkins, M. W., 215
Hawkins, Mahilda, 213
Hawkins, Mahula J., 215
Hawkins, Mahulda/Malinda, 214
Hawkins, Margaret, 25
Hawkins, Maria, 25
Hawkins, Martha, 213
Hawkins, Mary A., 212, 214, 215
Hawkins, Mary Ann, 13, 214
Hawkins, Mattie A., 214
Hawkins, Melba J., 213
Hawkins, Miles W., 214, 215
Hawkins, Millard, 214
Hawkins, Mollie J., 213
Hawkins, N. T.(J.), 133
Hawkins, N. T., 7
Hawkins, N., 7
Hawkins, Nealey, 213
Hawkins, Pauline Beene, 213
Hawkins, Preston, 9, 213, 214
Hawkins, R. H., 54
Hawkins, R., 213
Hawkins, Raleigh, 143, 213, 215
Hawkins, Raleigh, Jr., 214
Hawkins, Raugley, Jr.,10
Hawkins, Rebecca E., 215
Hawkins, Robert H., 212
Hawkins, Rutha L., 212
Hawkins, Sarah Ann, 31
Hawkins, Sarah C., 212, 215
Hawkins, Susan K., 212
Hawkins, W. A., 248
Hawkins, W. J., 123, 137
Hawkins, W., 214
Hawkins, Walter, 215
Hawkins, William C., 215
Hawkins, Wm. C., 214
Hawkins, Wm. J., 25
Hawkins, Wm., 214
Haws, James, 224
Haws, Jeff, 224, 225
Haws/Hawes, 216
Hayden, Thomas, 64, 136
Hayes, A. K., 151, 162
Hayes, Amanda A., 216
Hayes, Charles, 216
Hayes, Dr., 157, 158
Hayes, Elizabeth, 216
Hayes, Emily, 216
Hayes, G., 202
Hayes, George B., 216
Hayes, Harrate, 216
Hayes, Henry, 216
Hayes, J. M., 102
Hayes, James H., 162
Hayes, James L. (H.), 216
Hayes, Martha A., 216
Hayes, Mary M., 216
Hayes, Mary, 216
Hayes, Oliver P., 178
Hayes, Oliver, 162
Hayes, Virgil, 162, 178
Hayes, W. C., 233
Hayes, W. I., 96
Hayes, William G., 216
Hayes/Hays, 216
Hayes/Hays, 216
Haygood, J. B., 100
Haygood, Thomas C., 74
Haygood, W. M., 209
Haynes, C., 170
Haynes, E. J., 131
Haynes, Edward W., 131
Haynie, E. N., 72
Hays, Georgia, 77
Hays, Hugh A., 216
Hays, J. H., 77, 226
Hays, James H., 216
Hays, James, 225
Hays, John, 224
Hays, Mary J., 216
Hays, T. W., 257
Hays, Thomas, 256, 257
Hays, Vergil, 257
Hays, W. G., 151
Hays, W. J., 150, 151, 155, 168
Hays, W. O., 155, 156, 157
Hays/Hoge, 157
Hazel (Hazle), 85
Hazel, Nora, 85
Hazelett, Etta, 48
Hazelnut, George, 13
Hazle, Nora Crump, 84
Hazle, Nora, 84
Hazle, Oliver, 84
Hazle, Samuel, 84, 85
Head, Alma, 216
Head, Cornelison, 216
Head, Cornelison, et al., 216
Head, Ella, 216
Head, G. W., 42, 100
Head, J. C., 216
Head, J. W., 91
Head, Mary, 216
Head, Nancy C., 216
Headerly, A. R., 170
Heald, Andrew J., 219
Heald, Andrew Jackson, 216
Heald, H. G., 219
Heald, H. P., 216, 217, 218
Heald, Harmon G., 216, 217, 218, 218, 219
Heald, Harmon Gregg, 217
Heald, Henry Patrick, 216
Heald, Henry, 217, 219
Heald, James F., 219
Heald, James Ferdinan, 216
Heald, Joseph D., 217
Heald, Joseph Delaware, 217
Heald, Joseph, 217
Heald, Mary A., 219
Heald, Samuel G. (Lewis), 216
Heald, Samuel L., 219
Heald, Samuel, 216
Heald, Thomas T., 219
Heald, W. J., 218
Heald, W. P., 218
Heald, William G., 216, 219
Heald, William Gregg, 216
Heard, C. W., 219
Heard, E. Solen, 219
Heard, F. J., 219
Heard, G. S. V., 109, 246
Heard, G. W., 219
Heard, I. A., 219
Heard, J. T., 68
Heard, J. W., 219
Heard, John W., 219
Heard, John, 199
Heard, M. J., 151
Heard, M. T., 162
Heard, Marlin, 173
Heard, Marline, 174
Heard, Martin T., 151
Heard, Marvin, 219
Heard, Oscar, 219
Heard, Rachel, 178
Heard, S. E., 219
Heard, Salon E., 93, 148, 199
Heard, Solon E., 94, 201
Heard, Strade, 246
Heard, Strode, 195, 202, 203, 247
Heard, Wallace, 219
Hearn, A. W., 219
Hearn, J. A., 219
Hearn, J. C., 219
Hearn, J. D., 187, 219
Hearn, J. J., 259
Hearn, J. O., 219
Hearn, John D., 219
Hearn, John T., 8
Hearn, Lillie, 219
Hearn, M. F., 219
Hearn, Mary F., 219
Hearn, Olin, 219
Heatley, J. H. 97
Heaton, Jack, 94
Heaton, Louis, 88
Heaton, S. L., 1
Hefner, Wm., 247

Heftinstall, J. C., 90
Hemmingway, Josiah, 219, 220
Hemmingway, Wm., 220
Hemphill, J. P., 105
Hemphill, W. P. 54,
Henagar, Z. W., 233
Henderson, 90
Henderson, A. W., 177
Henderson, Hiram, 143, 146
Henderson, John, 162, 168
Henderson, N. W., 162
Henderson, Viard, 206
Hendley, W., 239
Hendrick, Melvina, 190
Hendricks, James, 162, 178
Hendricks, Joab, 178, 250
Hendricks, M., 256
Hendricks, Madison, 162, 177
Hendricks, Mc_, 178
Hendricks, Mr., 162
Hendricks, Mrs., 162, 177
Hendrix, Jas. M., 27
Hendrix, Joab, 162
Hendrix, M. M., 139
Henegar, G. T., 122
Henegar, George, 14
Henegar, Isam, 12
Henegar, M. O., 122
Henegar, Moses, 6
Henegar, Sham I., 10
Henley, William L., 211
Hennon, J. R., 260
Henry, A. G., 77
Henry, Edie, 193
Henry, G. W., 99
Henry, I. B., 250
Henry, J. B., 231, 250, 251
Henry, Nannie, 1
Henry, W. E., 99
Henry, W. H., 100, 102
Hensley, J., 260
Herald, 206
Herman, H. A., 43
Herme, F., 79
Hermes, Frank, 79
Herren Bros., 7
Herrin, James, 14
Hersey, H., 34
Herst, 41
Hess, I. A., 26
Hess, J. A., 207
Hess, Willis, 10
Hester, Frank, 21
Hester, O., 249
Hewitt, F. A., Jr., 17
Hewitt, R. G., 108
Hibbs, C. G., 234
Hibbs, Dempsey L., 177
Hibbs, Dempsey T., 162
Hibbs, Gerome, 220, 221
Hibbs, J. G., 240
Hibbs, Jane, 221
Hibbs, Jeremiah, 22, 142, 144, 146
Hibbs, N. J., 175
Hibbs, Newton J., 177
Hibbs, Newton, 151, 162
Hibbs, Sarah, 162
Hibbs, Sarah, Miss, 178
Hibs, Jeremiah, 143
Hicks, A. L., 107
Hicks, A. R. & wife, 221
Hicks, Acel R., 221
Hicks, Ann, 83
Hicks, Annie, 82
Hicks, G. L., 80, 81, 215
Hicks, George L., 221
Hicks, George, 215
Hicks, H., 134
Hicks, J. D., 122
Hicks, J. L. & Jos. J., 221
Hicks, J. T., 248
Hicks, J. W., 215
Hicks, James J., 221
Hicks, John, 140
Hicks, Mary J., 221
Hicks, O. L., 134
Hicks, P., Dr., 106
Hicks, R. H., 208
Hicks, Robert H., 215
Hicks, Sherman, 241
Hicks, T. E., 53
Hickson, E. P., 221
Hickson, Frank, 221
Hickson, J. P., 151
Hickson, Jere, 162
Hickson, Jeremiah, 177, 206
Hickson, Jerry, 178
Hickson, Lynday, Mrs., 30
Higdon, G. C., 2
Higgins & Porter, 221, 252
Higgins, 147
Higgins, J. W., 154, 221
Higgins, R. W., 151, 162, 168, 169, 174, 216, 222, 233, 250, 251, 253, 263
Higgins, Robert W., 42, 155, 221
Higgins, Robert, 52
Higgins, W. V., 51
Highfield, G. W., 122
Highfield, John, 233
Highfield, Jonathan, 13
Highfield, Malinda, 14
Higins, W., 143
Hill & Co., O. P., 230
Hill & Nicholson, 226
Hill, 222
Hill, Adeline, 49
Hill, Berry, 157,158, 162
Hill, Berry/Benny, 178
Hill, C. A., Mrs., 226
Hill, Camelia, 222
Hill, E. J., 221, 226
Hill, E. J., et al, 221, 222
Hill, Eli, 18, 19, 32
Hill, Eliza, 18
Hill, Ely, 19
Hill, George, 234
Hill, Henry H., 221, 222
Hill, J. A., 212, 226
Hill, J. S., 193
Hill, James T., 221, 222
Hill, James, 158, 162, 178, 223, 224, 225
Hill, Jas., 157
Hill, Jesse, 222
Hill, Jesse, Mrs., 222
Hill, John R., 222, 223, 224, 225, 226
Hill, John, 6
Hill, Joseph, 24, 226
Hill, Josie, 226
Hill, Lucinda, 221
Hill, Luther, 226
Hill, M. J., 91
Hill, Margaret, 5
Hill, Mose, 17
Hill, O. P., 196, 251
Hill, O. R., 231
Hill, R. L., 71, 91
Hill, Robert L., 18
Hill, Susan Jane, 222
Hill, Thomas, 151, 173
Hill, Thos., 162
Hill, William J., 226, 227
Hills, Gabrill, 254
Hilton, F. C., 220
Hilyer, John, 63
Hilyer, Johnie, 63
Hit, Henry, 249
Hitt, Henry, 255
Hixon, Ada, 227, 228
Hixon, Ada/Ider, 227
Hixon, Ader, 228
Hixon, Alanzo, 228
Hixon, Emanuel, 227, 228, 229
Hixon, Emmanual, 227
Hixon, Eugene, 227, 228, 229
Hixon, Frank, 228, 229
Hixon, Franklin, 227
Hixon, George, 228
Hixon, James, 227, 228
Hixon, John D., 228
Hixon, Linday (Linda), 30
Hixon, Lula, 227
Hixon, Minnie, 227, 228, 229
Hixon, N. E., 227, 228
Hixon, N. E., Mrs., 227
Hixon, Nancy E., 227
Hixon, Nancy, 227, 228
Hixon, Stella, 227, 228, 229
Hixon, Venice, 227, 228, 229
Hixon/Hixson, 227
Hixson, J. E., 253
Hixson, James, 227, 228
Hixson, Nancy E., (N. E.), 228
Hixson, Oscar, 228, 229
Hobbs & Howard, 44
Hodge, A. J., 36, 37
Hodge, Elizabeth, 36
Hodge, Jennie Peek, 229
Hodgens, J. P., 229
Hodgens, J. P., Estate, 229
Hodgens, T. V., 229
Hodges, 229
Hodges, B. E., 77
Hodges, Campbell I., 229
Hodges, Henry, 229
Hodges, I. M., 187
Hodges, J. W., 67
Hodges, Jasper C., 229
Hodges, Jib B, 252
Hodges, L. J., Mrs., 229
Hodges, L. M., Mrs. 229
Hodges, Nora Mae, 229
Hodges, Robert, 229
Hodges, T. E. & I. M., 187
Hodges, Thomas, 229
Hodges/Hodgens, 229
Hoge, D. S., 32
Hoge, J. K. & J. M., 225
Hoge, J. K., 8, 96, 129, 148, 150, 154, 156, 170-172, 234, 240, 255
Hoge, J. M., 109, 145, 225
Hoge, J. R., 145, 151, 154
Hoge, J., 157
Hoge, James H., 178
Hoge, James M., 206
Hoge, James, 151, 153
Hoge, James, Sr., 157
Hoge, Jas., 150, 154, 157, 162, 171

Hoge, John F., 30
Hoge, John J., 129
Hoge, John K., 8, 12, 25, 70, 88, 95, 96, 114, 136, 149, 150, 154, 158, 162, 182, 185, 216, 217, 222, 235, 237, 239, 241, 253
Hoge, John R., 59, 129, 167
Hoge, John, 19
Hoge, Joseph, 23, 130, 154, 155, 157, 158, 162, 178, 217, 224
Hoge, Lem, 109
Hoge, Lemuel, 177
Hoge, Lemuel?, 44
Hoge, Levi, 162
Hoge, N. J., 156
Hoge, P. G., 150
Hoge, Samuel, 151, 179
Hoge, Thomas, 96, 173
Hoge, W. A., 156
Hoge, W. O., 155
Hoge, W., 156
Hoge, Y. K., 244
Hogler, I. W., 41
Hogue, D. S., 114
Holbrook, W. L., 51
Holbrooks, 94
Holbrooks, G. W., 94
Holburra, Sarah, 71
Holcomb, E. J., 217
Holcomb, Emily, 230
Holcomb, Jeremiah, 229, 230, 231, 232
Holcomb, John P., 162, 178
Holcomb, John, 230
Holcomb, Mc_, 178
Holcomb, W. T., 90
Holcomb, Wm. H., 162
Holcomb, Wm., 93, 168
Holcombe, Jeremiah, 230
Holden, Robert L., 252
Holdridge, George M., 233
Holdridge, J. C., 233
Holdridge, J. C., Mrs., 233
Holdridge, Martha J., 233
Holdridge, Mildred, 233
Holdridge, Neva, 233
Holdridge, R. W., 233
Holiday, A. L., 124
Holland, Daniel, 233
Holland, Eliza, 233
Holland, Ephraim, 233
Holland, Hugh, 233
Holland, James, 233
Holland, Jesse, 4
Holland, John, 233, 234
Holland, Nancy, 233
Holland, Ruth, 233
Holland, Sarah Jane, 233
Holland, W. F., 233
Holland, William F., 233
Holleman, Ben, 227
Holleman, E. J., 18, 52, 259
Holleman, Ernest J., 254
Holleman, Jake, 254
Holleman, T. W., 254
Holleman, Wm. K., 220
Hollemon, F., 26
Hollerman, R. E., 43
Hollingsworth, 135
Hollingsworth, H. W. P., 230
Hollingsworth, Thomas, 251
Hollins, Hugh, 162
Hollman, Earnest, 122
Holloman, E. T., 38
Holloway, 171
Holloway, Ethel, 234
Holloway, Florence, 234
Holloway, Jackson, 13
Holloway, Jesse, 22, 145
Holloway, Newton, 13
Holloway, Ollie, 234
Holloway, W. M., 234
Holloway, Wesley, 234
Holmes, J. T., 61
Holmes, Owen T., 234
Holmes, T. C., 61
Holmes, Thomas W., 61
Holmes, William A., 36
Holmon, Isaac, 255
Holsomback, W. J., 84
Holsonback, J. N., 84
Holsonback, W. J., 85
Holtzclaw, Dr., 43
Homan, Mrs., 217
Honea, J. G., 106
Honea, J. T., 105
Honey, J. T., 106
Hood, Lucinda, 178
Hood, Mary, 241
Hooper, A. B., 23
Hooper, C., 249
Hooper, E. S., 23
Hooper, J. F., 97, 103
Hooper, S., 235
Hope, Joe H., 252
Hopkins, C. F., 22, 178
Hopkins, C. Frank, 151, 162, 174
Hopkins, M. E., 107
Horn, Thos. J., 247
Horn, Thos., 41
Horn, W. C., 188
Horton A. G., 33
Horton, 105, 137, 203
Horton, A. B., 55, 56, 231, 237, 238, 255
Horton, A. C., 234
Horton, A. J., 5, 8, 9, 17, 25, 29, 42, 52, 55, 56, 59, 63, 70, 87, 88, 93, 95, 113, 114, 128, 130, 150, 155, 185, 190, 206, 207, 214, 216, 230, 232, 243, 253
Horton, Andrew B., 236
Horton, Andrew C., 236
Horton, Ann E, 230, 232
Horton, Archie, 237
Horton, Betsy, 230
Horton, C. B., 237
Horton, Clarissa, 230
Horton, D. D., 134, 236, 238
Horton, Della, 234
Horton, Dellie, 197
Horton, Dicy, 222, 226
Horton, Eliza J., 235
Horton, Elizabeth, 142, 237
Horton, Ellen, 237
Horton, Emanuel, 234
Horton, Francis, 105
Horton, G. G., 237
Horton, G. R., 105, 132, 134, 197, 207, 238
Horton, Gilbert C., 230, 237
Horton, H. H., 236
Horton, Harry, 105
Horton, Harvey , 237
Horton, Harvey J., 237
Horton, Herbert H., 234
Horton, J. B., 79, 234, 235, 239, 238
Horton, J. P., 46, 134
Horton, J. S., 237
Horton, J. Simpson, 237
Horton, J., 235
Horton, James B., 239
Horton, James S., 237
Horton, Jas. M., 254
Horton, Jennie B. (I.), 234
Horton, Jennie I. B., 239
Horton, Jennie J., 236
Horton, Jeptha, 237
Horton, Jesse B., 167, 234, 235, 236
Horton, Jesse B., 52
Horton, John P., 238
Horton, John, 235, 238
Horton, Malinda C., 239
Horton, Malinda I. C., 234
Horton, Malinda J. C., 236, 237
Horton, Malinda, 234, 235
Horton, Mattie, 105
Horton, May J., 237
Horton, P. J., 55, 230, 232
Horton, P. T., 46
Horton, P. Z., 231
Horton, P., 230
Horton, Paron J., 237, 238
Horton, Perrin J., 230
Horton, Preston B., 238
Horton, Preston, 128, 171, 172
Horton, R. R., 109
Horton, Richard A., 236, 239
Horton, Richard Amanda, 234
Horton, Richard, 234
Horton, Roswell, 179
Horton, S. W., 55
Horton, Sarah, 237
Horton, Simpson N., 237
Horton, Thomas B., 234, 236
Horton, Thos. B., 239
Horton, W. A., 46
Horton, W. C. (H. C.), 237
Horton, W. P., 195, 234, 238, 239, 240
Horton, William P., 234, 235
Houghton, Alanson, 240
Houghton, Edward M., 240
Houghton, Ida, 240
Houghton, Mary, 240
Houghton, Samuel, 240
House, Della, 240, 241
House, Della, Mrs., 241
House, J. G., 162, 178
House, Jacob G., 262
House, Thomas, 151, 174
House, Thos., 162
House, Wm. J., 207
Houston, A. W., 72, 103, 110, 131, 141
Houston, Abram B., 217
Houston, Bill, 90
Houston, Billy, 110
Houston, C. M., 241
Houston, Caroline, 111
Houston, E. M., 111, 241
Houston, E., 177
Houston, Ealley, 241
Houston, Edley, 111, 162
Houston, Idene, 56
Houston, James, 56, 241

Houston, Jas. C., 56
Houston, Mary Jane, 241
Houston, Pollie, 241
Houston, Samuel, 241
Houston, T. C., Mrs., 111
Houston, T. T., 124
Houston, Thomas T., 124
Houston, Thos.T., 124
Houston, W. I., 92
Houston, William M., 241
Houston, William, 151, 241
Houston, Wm. F., 178
Houston, Wm., 162, 178
Houston, Wm., Jr., 162
Howard & Blake, 189
Howard & Hunt, 33, 49, 74, 80, 89, 106, 117, 127, 149, 187, 199, 252
Howard & Isbell, 29, 37, 79, 103, 135, 262
Howard, B. M., 33
Howard, Benj., 59
Howard, Benjamin, 59
Howard, C. G., 33
Howard, C. H., 189
Howard, Eliza J. Blancitt, 30
Howard, Emma, 59
Howard, Emmie, 59
Howard, F. M., 85, 183
Howard, Fannie T., 189
Howard, G. M., 189
Howard, H. B., 187
Howard, Henry, 30
Howard, J. C., 260
Howard, J. M., 7, 16, 106, 108, 112, 139, 183, 227, 258, 259
Howard, James M., 72
Howard, John Calvin, 33
Howard, John G., 59
Howard, John H., 151
Howard, John L., 162
Howard, John, 110, 246
Howard, Laura, 85
Howard, M. H., 149
Howard, M. W. C., 107
Howard, M. W., 33, 37, 75, 76, 78, 87, 103, 111, 112, 123, 141, 187, 207, 208, 236
Howard, M. W., Mrs., 75
Howard, M., 108
Howard, Martha, 59
Howard, Marthy, 59
Howard, Milford W., 236
Howard, Mrs., 259
Howard, Polly Ann Francis, 33
Howard, S. B., 131
Howard, S. M. J., 79
Howard, S. O., 112
Howard, Sallie A., 207
Howard, Sallie A., 37
Howard, Samuel, 79
Howard, W. L., 91
Howard, W. S., 189
Howell, 231
Howell, J. M., 122
Howell, Jno., 146
Howell, Martha L., 228
Howell, Martha, 229
Howell, Nell, 228, 229
Howell, W. N., 228
Hoyl, A. F., 151, 162
Hoyl, Andrew F., 151
Hoyl, Joseph, 155
Hoyle, A. F., 173
Hubbard, B. T., 187
Hubbs, Jeremiah, 232
Huckabee, Ester, 34
Huckaby, H. C., 24
Huckaby, John, 35
Huckaby, W. P., 29
Huckaby, W. T., 28
Huckely, John, 34
Huckley, Ester, 34
Hudson, L. W., 141
Hudson, T. W., 114
Hudson, T., 244
Hudson, Thomas W., 196
Hudson, Thos., 162, 178
Hudson, Thos., Mr., 178
Huff, C. D., 100
Huff, G. M., 234, 235, 236, 240
Huff, George M., 234
Huff, Valentine, 217
Hughes, A. A., 32, 146, 149, 150, 154, 162, 177, 248
Hughes, A. R., 32
Hughes, A., 145, 169
Hughes, Abner H., 149
Hughes, Alsey/Aelsey, 241
Hughes, Ann, 123
Hughes, Cash?, 13
Hughes, D. B., 249
Hughes, D. D., 44, 96
Hughes, David D., 162, 234
Hughes, David F., 178
Hughes, Green, 206, 241, 242
Hughes, J. B., 24
Hughes, J., 12
Hughes, James, 241
Hughes, Jim, 13
Hughes, Martha, 13
Hughes, Missouri, 241
Hughes, Rufina, 241
Hughes, William, 241
Hughes, Wm. R., 132
Hughs & Collins, 177
Hughs, D. B., 62
Hulgan, A., 156
Hulgan, Alfred, 158, 170
Hulgan, F. M., 183
Hulgan, F., 146
Hulgan, J. W., 189
Hulgan, J., 222
Hulgan, L. P., 246
Hulgan, M., 156
Hulgan, P., 146
Hulgan, R. M., 150, 151, 153, 154 170, 171, 224
Hulgan, Robert, 22, 152
Hulgan, Robt., Sr., 170
Hulgan, S. N., 46, 189
Hulgan, S. P., 129, 143, 143, 162
Hulgan, Stephen R., 178
Hulgan, Thomas, 129
Hull & Spencer, 32
Hull, Sam J., 153
Hulsey, H. W., 260
Hulsey, J. H. (F.), 60
Humble, B. H., 60
Humble, D. M., 30
Humble, D. T., 183, 184
Humble, G. W., 242
Humble, J. T., 38
Humphreys, John J., 162, 177
Humphries, Amanda Crump, 83
Humphries, Amanda, 83
Humphries, J. T., 83
Humphries, John J., 135
Humphries, John T., 22, 135, 217
Humphry, John, 218
Hundley, James, 15
Hundley, W. L., 218
Hunt & Tally, 5
Hunt & Wolfes, 35, 62, 106
Hunt, C. H., 134
Hunt, Howard, 127
Hunt, Hunt & Wolfes, 187
Hunt, James, 245
Hunt, John, 247
Hunt, Luke E., 238
Hunt, Luke P., 134
Hunt, Luke P., 78, 149
Hunt, Luther P., 33
Hunt, M. W, 128
Hunt, R. C., 104
Hunt, R. H., 81
Hunter, Casper, 231, 242
Hunter, Casper?, 26
Hunter, Cleo Tate, 134
Hunter, J. P., 96, 167, 170
Hunter, J. T., 206
Hunter, James P., 242
Hunter, Julius, 13
Hunter, Mary J., 104
Hunter, Mosley, 104
Hunter, Richard F., 242
Huntsville Advocate, 244
Huntsville Southern Advocate, 144
Hurd, Lucinda, 162
Hurd, Rachael, 162
Hurst, Caroline E., 41
Hurst, Caroline, 40
Hurst, J. I., 41
Hurst, J. S., 40, 41
Hurst, Jos., 41
Hurst, Joseph, 40, 41
Hurst, Lonie, 90
Hurt, W. E., 72
Hutchings, David A., 242
Hutchings, Matilda, 242
Hyde, Dessie May, 242
Hyde, Harmon, 242
Hyde, Homer, 242
Hyde, Licy P., 242
Hyde, Tedle, 242
Hyler, Wm. L., 22
Ide, D. M., 58
Igo, A. J., 261
Igo, George, 19
Igo, S. E., 261
Igou & Tatum, 80, 81
Igou, A. I. (A. J.), 11
Igou, A. J., 8, 184, 250
Igou, A. M., 80
Igou, G. A., 81
Igou, George, 80
Igou, J. N., 11
Igou, J. S. N., 14
Igou/Igo, 261
Inghram, W. N., 245
Ingle, Hugh A.J., 28
Ingle, Malachi C., 28
Ingle, Mary E., 28
Ingle, Mary Eliza, 28
Ingle, Peter M., 28
Ingle, Sarah Berry, 28
Ingle, Sarah E., 28
Ingle, Sarah Elizabeth Berry, 28
Ingle, Sarah, 28
Ingle, Thenie, 134
Ingle, William Alonza, 28
Ingle, William, 28
Ingle, Wilson A., 28
Ingram, Fannie, 21
Ingram, W. A., 239
Ingrin, W. A., 237

Irvins, Sam, 239
Irwin, Harry S., 197
Isaac, J. C., 162, 178
Isaacs, Josiah C., 243
Isaacs, Mary J. Jack, 243
Isabell, Zona, 238
Isbel, J., 256
Isbell & Presley, 31, 57, 73, 78, 88, 98, 127, 190, 199, 207, 229
Isbell & Scott, 88, 229
Isbell, Floyd, 235
Isbell, Howard, 29
Isbell, J. B., 29, 89, 241
Isbell, Jas., 257
Isbell, John B., 1, 20, 31, 37, 48, 51, 55, 79, 89, 103, 125, 127, 128, 134, 149, 209, 234, 241, 252, 253
Isbell, John, 104, 170, 225, 253
Isbell, Matt, 235
Isbell, W. Sherman, 252
Isbell, William, 151, 223
Isbell, Wm., 163, 173
Isbell, Zona M., 37
Isdel, Jem, 99
Isell, John, 22
Israel, J. M., 99, 101, 102
Israel, J. W., 98, 99
Israel, Jas. W., 102
Israel, L., 99, 102
Israell, J. M., 98
Ivey, N. T., 72
Ivie, M. A., Mrs., (Mattie), 187
Ivie, Mattie, 187
Ivins, Leonidas, 14
Ivins/Evans, Isaac, 143
Izell, J. T., 262
Izell, Jesse, 261
Izell, R. S., 261, 262
J. C. Crump & Co., 85
J. F. Hooper Bank, 97
J. W. Cavenger & Co., 89
Jacaway, J. G., 245
Jack, Adeline, 243, 243, 245, 246, 247
Jack, Adlin, 245
Jack, Allen G., 243
Jack, Allen, 114, 155, 163, 178, 223, 243-245
Jack, Allen, Jr., 158, 244, 245
Jack, Allen, Sen., 175
Jack, Arch, 156, 158
Jack, Betty, 26
Jack, Daniel B., 243
Jack, David A., 252
Jack, E. L., 25
Jack, Elizabeth L. Mickler, 25
Jack, Elizabeth L., 27
Jack, Elizabeth, 245, 246, 247
Jack, G. M., 158
Jack, Geo. M., 246
Jack, George (W. M.), 243
Jack, Georgia Ann, 238
Jack, Isabella, 246
Jack, J. M., 244, 246, 247, 248
Jack, J. N., 96
Jack, James H., 243, 244
Jack, James, 193, 244, 247
Jack, Jas., 244
Jack, Jeff, 171, 245
Jack, Jefferson, 222
Jack, Jeremiah M., 244, 246, 247
Jack, John M., 243, 245
Jack, John P., 243, 247
Jack, John, 242
Jack, Julia, 242
Jack, Lucy E., 246
Jack, Lucy, 246
Jack, Martha J., 246
Jack, Marthy, 245
Jack, Mont, 245
Jack, Moses, 246
Jack, Nancy, 246, 247, 248
Jack, Pleasant, 225
Jack, T. I., 96
Jack, Thom. J., 129
Jack, Thomas J., 96, 243, 244, 246
Jack, Thomas M., 25, 27, 151, 243, 244, 247
Jack, Thomas, 157, 158, 170, 245
Jack, Thos. J., 206, 225, 244, 247
Jack, Thos. M., 41, 196
Jack, Thos., 41, 163, 179
Jack, W. J., 246
Jack, W. M., 244
Jack, Wallace E., 246
Jack, Wallace, 243, 246
Jack, William, 243
Jackaway, Henry, 44
Jacks, James M., 245
Jacks, James, 245
Jacks, Martha J., 246
Jacks, Nancy, 244
Jacks, Thomas J., 245
Jackson, Albert, 248, 249
Jackson, Ben, 131
Jackson, C. B., 89
Jackson, C. P., 89
Jackson, Caroline, 248
Jackson, D. A., 141
Jackson, Daniel, 151, 163, 173
Jackson, Desalemona, 140
Jackson, Desdemona, 148
Jackson, G. H., 101
Jackson, Harvey, 248
Jackson, Irvin, 248
Jackson, J. 242
Jackson, J. H., 103
Jackson, James A., 212
Jackson, James E., 140, 148
Jackson, James, 64
Jackson, John A., 248
Jackson, John E., 141
Jackson, John, 248
Jackson, Luther, 63
Jackson, M. B., Mrs., 252
Jackson, Margaret, 248
Jackson, Martha J., 64
Jackson, Maude, 248
Jackson, Maudie, 248
Jackson, Neal, 90
Jackson, Nealy, 74
Jackson, Paralee, 248
Jackson, R. H., 248
Jackson, Rebecca, 248
Jackson, Simion, 248
Jackson, W. A., 212
Jackson, Warren, 248
Jackson, William, 248, 249
Jaco, Jasper, 74
Jaco, Martha, 50
Jaco, W. L., 76
Jacobs, J. A., 117
Jacobs, S. H., 99
Jacoups, S. H., 100, 101
Jacoway, 9
Jacoway, Alice, 20
Jacoway, Benj. J., 249
Jacoway, Benjamin J., 20
Jacoway, Bob, 63
Jacoway, Dodge?, 249
Jacoway, Fred M., 249
Jacoway, Fred, 73
Jacoway, G. W., 237
Jacoway, H. J., 41, 246
Jacoway, Henry J., 9, 246, 249
Jacoway, Henry, 249
Jacoway, J. A., 244
Jacoway, J. C., 26, 207
Jacoway, J. G., 6, 24, 93, 207
Jacoway, J. P., 24, 249
Jacoway, Jennie, 249
Jacoway, John G., 12
Jacoway, John, 249
Jacoway, Lillie, 249
Jacoway, Lou, 249
Jacoway, Mary Elizabeth, 20
Jacoway, Mary, 249
Jacoway, Peggie, 249
Jacoway, Robert, 249
Jacoway, Samuel, 249
Jacoway, Sue, 249
Jacoway, T. R., 49
Jacoway, Thomas R., 236
Jacoway, W. A., 114
Jacoway, W. V., 1, 20, 21, 49, 73, 74, 249
Jacoway, W. W., 2
Jacoway, William V., 106
Jacoway, Wm. & J. P., 24
Jacoway, Wm. V., 20
Jacoway, Wm., 24
James West Gen. Mdse., 136
James, Albert, 107
James, Ivashly?, 174
James, J. Ashley, 163
James, J., 150, 154
James, Luella, 50
James, M. J., Mrs., 57
James, S., 196
James, William L., 152
Jane, 9
Jane, Negro Girl, 33
Jarman (Jarmon), 74
Jarman, Lula, 75
Jarman, Lula, Mrs., 75
Jarman, W. T., 75
Jarmon, Alice, 74
Jarmon, Caloin, 74
Jarmon, Herman, 74
Jarmon, Lula, 74, 75
Jarmon, Lyman, 74
Jarmon, W. T., 74
Jarnagin, A., 247
Jay, Rubin, 60
Jeffins & Payne, 7
Jenkins, Bessie M., 2
Jenkins, G. W., 15
Jenkins, J. T., 103
Jenkins, Joe, 2, 3
Jenkins, John, 39, 60
Jenkins, Margaret, 2
Jenkins, R. R., 2
Jenkins, Rachael R., 103
Jenkins, Rachel, 104
Jenkins, Rachel, 39
Jenkins, Rueben, 163
Jenkins, W. H., 252
Jenkins, W. M., 196
Jenkins, W.J.N., 2
Jenkins, William, 196

Jenks, E., 163
Jenks/Jinks, Ephrain, 151
Jennings, H. C., 227, 228
Jennings, Henry C., 258
Jett, A. J., 208
Jett, B. A., 173
Jett, B. T., 129
Jett, Bailess A., 151
Jett, Bailess, 129
Jett, Bayless, 163, 170
Jett, D. P., 108, 235
Jett, Daniel, 129, 222
Jett, David, 136, 226
Jett, J. A., 208
Jett, J. M., 163, 171, 172, 179
Jett, J., 171
Jett, Joseph M., 22, 129
Jett, Joseph, 208, 222, 248
Jett, Railess, 225
Jett, Samuel, 95
Jinks, Ephram, 175
Johnson, A. J., 249
Johnson, Ales., 254
Johnson, Amanda G., 250
Johnson, Amanda S., 251
Johnson, Amanda, 250
Johnson, Ann, 18
Johnson, C. A., 123,163, 178
Johnson, C. C., 6, 192
Johnson, C. P., 25, 87, 209
Johnson, C. Pickney, 42
Johnson, Cecil, 252
Johnson, Charlotte N., 250
Johnson, Col., 192
Johnson, Cornelia A., 111
Johnson, D. H., 252
Johnson, D. J., 106
Johnson, D., 170
Johnson, Daniel, 87, 124
Johnson, David, 66
Johnson, Dr., 136, 137
Johnson, Easter E., 249
Johnson, Elijah H., 178
Johnson, Elizabeth, 163
Johnson, Erastus V., 250
Johnson, F. F., 99
Johnson, G. W., 134
Johnson, George, 254
Johnson, H. M., 251
Johnson, H., (Bldg. Co.), 189
Johnson, H., 58
Johnson, Hamelton, 175
Johnson, Hamilton, 151, 163, 178
Johnson, Hannah Jane, 251
Johnson, Henry, 250
Johnson, Hezekiah, 163, 178
Johnson, Hoyt, 126
Johnson, Hugh, 250
Johnson, J. A., 2, 85, 208, 211
Johnson, J. E., 20, 186
Johnson, J. R., 151, 154, 155, 156, 235, 236, 244, 245
Johnson, J. R., MD., 237
Johnson, J. S., 98, 184, 191
Johnson, J. Samuel, 52
Johnson, James B., 250
Johnson, James D, 249, 250
Johnson, James E., 250
Johnson, James R., 158
Johnson, James S., 253
Johnson, Jane, 254
Johnson, Jas. R., 86
Johnson, Jefferson, 30, 254
Johnson, Jesse, 254
Johnson, John, 254
Johnson, Joseph B., 151, 163, 173
Johnson, Joseph, 183, 184, 250, 251, 252
Johnson, Juskin, 238
Johnson, L. F., 90
Johnson, L. R., 239
Johnson, L. T., 92
Johnson, Larry, 250
Johnson, Len, 90
Johnson, Lewis, 254
Johnson, Lucretia C., 254
Johnson, M. B., 252
Johnson, M. J., Mrs., 252, 253
Johnson, M. M., 217
Johnson, M. W., 253, 254
Johnson, Mariah W., 253
Johnson, Mariah, 254
Johnson, Martha, 217, 254
Johnson, Mary Jane, 67, 254
Johnson, Mary Jane, Mrs., 254
Johnson, Mary M., 253
Johnson, Mary, 254
Johnson, N. G., 205
Johnson, Nancy, 250, 251, 254
Johnson, Newton, 254
Johnson, Norman, 252
Johnson, Nute, 18
Johnson, Pagley, 193
Johnson, Paley, 195
Johnson, R. B., 102
Johnson, R. C., (Rachel), 253
Johnson, R. C., 7, 249, 250
Johnson, R. Jefferson D., 253
Johnson, R., 7
Johnson, Rachel C., Mrs., 253
Johnson, Reuben C., 253, 254
Johnson, Reuben J. D., 253
Johnson, Reuben, 249
Johnson, Reubin C., 253
Johnson, Richmond, 234, 254
Johnson, Robert, 27
Johnson, Samuel, 67, 254
Johnson, Sarah Elizabeth, 250
Johnson, Susan, Mrs., 246
Johnson, Thomas, 111
Johnson, Tolitha, 210
Johnson, W. C., 186
Johnson, W. R., 88, 92, 124
Johnson, William, 12, 114, 210
Johnson, Wm., 10, 254
Johnston, W. S., 42
Jolley, J. B., 201
Jolley, L. M., 91
Jolley, Leanda, 193
Jolly, B. P., 39
Jolly, J. V., 247
Jolly, L. M., 66, 72
Jolson, John, 152
Jones & Carythers, 257
Jones & Grady, 259
Jones & Reeves, 263
Jones , Aloryo, 261
Jones Bros. Store, 117
Jones Bros., 118
Jones, 90
Jones, Abram W., 254, 255
Jones, Albert, 11
Jones, Allen, 255
Jones, Asa, 11, 14
Jones, B. C., 75, 76, 259
Jones, B. G., 7
Jones, B. G., Mrs., 7
Jones, Barnie C., 258
Jones, Ben, 118, 119
Jones, Bert, 144
Jones, Bertie, Mrs., 43
Jones, Bird, 7
Jones, C. B., 259
Jones, C. J., 80
Jones, Charles, 258
Jones, Charley, 80
Jones, Clinton, 258
Jones, Cora, 258
Jones, D. A., 43
Jones, D. L., 85
Jones, Dicy Ann, 255
Jones, Drura, 146
Jones, Drury, 142, 144
JJones, E. B., 62, 65, 76, 83, 101, 120, 187, 190, 219
Jones, E. D., 260
Jones, E. N., 60, 85
Jones, E. P., 205
Jones, Eddie, 261
Jones, Eliza, Mrs., 79
Jones, Elizabeth, 59, 262
Jones, Elvana, 255
Jones, Fannie, 262
Jones, Fanny Jane, 255
Jones, Fred, 43
Jones, G. H., 1, 261, 262
Jones, G. M., 118, 120, 246
Jones, G. R., 2
Jones, G. W., 59, 101, 192, 255, 257
Jones, Geo. W., 59
Jones, George H., 261
Jones, George M., 262
Jones, George Melton, 262
Jones, George W., 255, 256, 257, 258
Jones, George, 121
Jones, Groves, 261
Jones, Hardie, 43
Jones, Henry, 130
Jones, Horace, 258
Jones, Hugh E., 260
Jones, Isaac, 146, 231
Jones, J. A., 60
Jones, J. E., 118, 259, 261
Jones, J. O., 188
Jones, J. W., 99, 122
Jones, Jane, 163, 179, 255
Jones, Janes, 255
Jones, Jas. Wm., 11
Jones, Joe, 118, 120, 121,
Jones, John B., 258, 259, 260
Jones, John E., 258
Jones, John H., 261
Jones, John R., 260, 261
Jones, John, 258
Jones, Johnson, 15

Jones, Joseph, 11, 14, 163, 261
Jones, L. M., 92
Jones, Leila, 261
Jones, Lizzie, 261
Jones, Louisa, 261
Jones, Loula, 261
Jones, Lucinda, 261
Jones, Lucy, 258
Jones, M. A., 137
Jones, M. A., Mrs., 137
Jones, M. E., 197, 262
Jones, M. S., 261, 262
Jones, Mahulda Ann, 261, 262
Jones, Margaret, 259
Jones, Mary E., 237, 255
Jones, Mary, 255, 256
Jones, Melt, 121
Jones, Minnie, 7
Jones, N. B., 118
Jones, N. J., 263
Jones, N. S., 262
Jones, Nancy Jane, 262
Jones, Nancy, 163, 179
Jones, Nettie J., 168
Jones, Netty J., 167
Jones, Netty Jane, (N. J.), 262
Jones, Noah S., 261
Jones, Pollie, 238
Jones, R., 187
Jones, Richard T. (Richmond), 260
Jones, Sam, 109
Jones, Sarah Mariah, 255
Jones, Stanton, 258
Jones, Sugar, 178
Jones, Susan, 163
Jones, T. A., 207
Jones, T. Z., 258, 259
Jones, Thomas A., 262
Jones, Thomas J., 255
Jones, Thomas, 157, 158, 179, 258
Jones, Thos., 163
Jones, Tildy, 259
Jones, Valolia, 261
Jones, W. B., 121, 151, 163, 187
Jones, W. C., 131
Jones, W. L., 163, 248
Jones, W. P., 119, 120, 121, 188
Jones, W. S., 262
Jones, W. T., 258
Jones, William Coner, 255
Jones, William L., 262, 263
Jones, William P., 246
Jones, William Pinkey, 262
Jones, William, 118, 261
Jones, Willis, 262
Jones, Wm. B., 173
Jones, Wm. C., 13
Jones, Wm. L., 178
Jones, Wm. P., 246, 262
Jones, Wm., 203, 251
Jonnah, 64
Jordan, C. C., 93, 94
Jordan, George W., 163, 179, 190
Jordan, H. D., 68
Jordan, Henry R., 68
Jordan, J., 98, 99
Jordan, T. J., 101
Jorden, H. R., 68
Jordin, A. B., 259
Jose, Edwin H., 67
Joseph, 9
Joseph, M. V., 108
Judge Jackson County, 5
Julia, 9
Justice, 256
Justice, G. M., 219
Justice, G. W., 101, 106
Justice, J. H., 101
Justice, J. N., 101
Justice, J. W., 187
Justice, W. L., 98, 101, 102, 259
Justis, W. J., 259
Karue, Mrs., 193
Kay, James, 209
KDS Hardware Co., 187
Kean, Elcanay, 70
Kean, J. P., 38
Kean, Jane, 70
Kean, John P., 25, 220
Kean, S. K., 237
Kean, S. R., 239
Kean, Solomon R., 183
Kean, Susie, 133
Kean, W. C., 27
Keane, W. P., 122
Kearby, J, P., 120
Kearly, Alf, 200
Keath (Keith), 48
Keath, C. G., 48
Keath, Marteal, 18
Keath, Rufus, 10
Keath, William R., 48
Keef, John, 104
Keef, Thomas, 183
Keele, E. R., 107
Keener, Beuna, 85
Keener, Buena, 85
Keener, Geo. W., 94
Keener, J. M., 126
Keener, J. P., 85
Keener, John, 85
Keener, Mark, 218
Keener, Mary F., 85
Keener, Mary, 84
Keener, P., 68, 235, 239
Keith (Keath), 48
Keith, Ben, 80
Keith, C. D., 122
Keith, C. G., 47, 48, 82
Keith, C. G., Mrs., 122
Keith, C. H., 123
Keith, Colonel C., 47
Keith, D. L., 122
Keith, G. A., 80, 81
Keith, J. A., 81
Keith, John, 52
Keith, Joseph, 122
Keith, Josie, 17
Keith, M., 48
Keith, Margaret, 123
Keith, Marshall, 18
Keith, Thomas, 17
Keith, Tobe, 18, 19
Keith, W. R., 48
Keith, William R., 48
Keith, William, 122
Keith, Willie, 80
Kelley & Davenport, 112
Kelley, Joe, 75
Kelley, Lewis, 163, 222
Kelley, Sol, 119
Kelley, Thomas B., 94, 107
Kelly, Doc., 203
Kelly, Isaac M., 222
Kelly, J. T., 75, 76
Kelly, Lewis, 152, 172
Kelly, Turner, 203, 204
Kelsoe, Allison, 15
Kelton, Jno. F., 46
Kemp, S. A., 62, 193
Kemp, Sol, 192
Kendall, John, 235
Kenemore, Americus I., 139
Kenemore, Grif, 139, 140
Kenemore, M. J., 140
Kenemore, M. T., 31
Kenemore, Margaret E., 140
Kenemore, Margaret E., et al, 140
Kenemore, Margaret Garmany, 139
Kenemore, Mary Casider, 139
Kennedy, Alex, 64
Kennedy, D. L., 31
Kennedy, F. H., 58, 209
Kennedy, Mavina, 177
Kennedy, Sarah E., 7
Kennedy, W. E., 168
Kennedy, Wm. E., 153
Kenner, Buna C., 85
Kennon, P., 239
Keolin Clay Mfg., 108
Kerby (Kirby), 48
Kerby, H. H., 46
Kerby, Hugh H., 46
Kerby, J. C., 122
Kerby, J. N., 81
Kerby, J. S., 46
Kerby, John W., 46
Kerby, Joicy Edwards, 117
Kerby, L. B., 30, 258
Kerby, Louisa E., 46
Kerby, M. M., Mrs., 54
Kerby, Turner, 118
Kerley, A., 203
Kerley, C., 207
Kerley, James, 80
Kerly, Alf, 204
Kerly, James, 204
Kerr, Maggie, 67
Key & Richmond, 7
Key, America, Mrs., 30
Key, Joshua, 136
Kidd, E. G., 97
Kidd, E. H., 103
Kidd, J. J., 97
Kidd, Louis W., 233
Kidd, W. A., 100
Kilgo, W. M., 120
Kilgore, J. M., 119
Kilgore, James, 13, 104
Kilgore, John, 118
Kilgore, Mrs., 121
Killiam, John, 172
Killian & Co. 53,
Killian & Son, 134
Killian, A. C., 7, 133, 134, 134, 212
Killian, A. F. (T.), 58
Killian, A. F., 58
Killian, A., 167
Killian, B. B., 109
Killian, B., Store, 117
Killian, B., 93, 191
Killian, Bill, 121
Killian, C., 212
Killian, D. J., 41
Killian, D. S., 244, 245, 246
Killian, D. S., Mrs., 93
Killian, Dan, 26
Killian, Daniel, 143, 144, 152, 163, 178, 247
Killian, E. S., 6, 40, 71, 110, 132, 134, 208, 228
Killian, E., 41

Killian, Elias, 114, 146, 163, 178, 231, 247, 248
Killian, Ellias, 246
Killian, G. W., 40, 53
Killian, Geo. W., 237
Killian, H. E., 45, 53
Killian, H. H., 54
Killian, Henry E., 246, 247, 248
Killian, Henry, 183
Killian, Hugh, 53
Killian, Ida, 107, 107, 109
Killian, J. S., 247
Killian, Jeanie, 109
Killian, Jim, 107
Killian, Joe, 110
Killian, John A., 163, 178
Killian, John, 41, 152, 163, 236, 246
Killian, Josephine, 107, 109
Killian, L. C., 133
Killian, Lucinda, 133
Killian, Lucinda, Mrs., 135
Killian, M. H., 109
Killian, Mary A., 44
Killian, Mary, 133
Killian, Mollie, 44
Killian, Mrs., 134
Killian, O., 231
Killian, R. L., 252
Killian, S. A., 53
Killian, S. F., 63
Killian, Thomas, 133
Killian, W. E. & B., 110
Killian, W. E., 93, 121, 128
Killian, W. N., 247
Killian, W. S., 49
Killian, W. T., 41, 49
Killian, Wallace, 107, 109
Killian, William T., 95
Killian, Zoe, 107, 110
Killian, Zora, 109
Killian, Zorah, 109
Killin, Jeanie, 109
Killina, H. E., Dr., 135
Kilpatrick, J. A., 99
Kimsey, G. W., 105, 233
King & Edwards, 252
King, Adelia, 163, 178
King, B. F., 196
King, Benjamin, 196
King, C. W., 123
King, D. P., 152, 172
King, Edelia, 223
King, Elisha, 217, 218
King, G. W., 152, 172
King, Geo. W., 163
King, J. D., 254
King, J. H., 231
King, J. R., 8
King, James F., 152
King, James J., 172
King, James M., 152
King, James R., 250
King, James R., 70
King, James W., 128
King, James, 14, 146, 163, 178
King, Jewel, 254
King, Joe, 109
King, John, 246
King, Lewis P., 163
King, Loomis, 152
King, Lunas, 163
King, O. D., 106
King, R., 8
King, Richard, 143, 231
King, S. H., 152
King, Samuel, 75
King, Sol F., 175
King, Sol. H., 163
King, Soll, 152
King, Solomon, 172
King, Tom, 1, 2
King, W. A., 254
King, W. D., 194
King, W. F., 8
King, W. H., 8
King, Wm., 163, 178
Kirby (Kerby), 48
Kirby, A. C., 88, 106, 192, 260
Kirby, B. F., 120, 121
Kirby, Dock, 201
Kirby, Fannie, 70
Kirby, H. C., 105
Kirby, H. H., 48
Kirby, H. J. (I), 80
Kirby, J. N., 81
Kirby, James, 80
Kirby, Jesse, 258
Kirby, Julia E. Collins, 69
Kirby, Julia E., 67
Kirby, M. W., 68, 69
Kirby, Rockey, 39, 40
Kirby, S. W., 43
Kirby, Thomas, 80
Kirby, Tom, 80
Kirby, Wm., 195
Kirby/Kerby, 258
Kirk, W. P., 8
Kirkendal, T. A., 112
Kirkendall, John, 240
Kirklan, Miss, 178
Kirkland, B. J., 127, 128
Kirkland, G. H., 128
Kirkland, G. H., 8, 76
Kirkland, G. K., 127
Kirkland, J. D., 128
Kirkland, Miss, 163
Kirkland, R., 75
Kirkland, Reuben, 75
Kirkland, Taylor R., 239
Kirkland, W. J., 128
Knove, 256
Koalin Prop. Dekalb Co., 108
Koerner, 36
Koerner, Lilliam M., 36
Koerner, William, 36
Koerner, Wm. F., 36
Koerner, Wm. F., MD, 36
Koger, Charles, 37
Koger, Margaret, 37
Koger, Meary, 37
Koger, Nancy A., 37
Koger, R. H., 30
Koger, Robert, 37
Koger, Sarah, 37
Koger, Syntha, 37
Koger, William, 37, 38, 81, 82
Koger, Wm., 30, 37, 38
Kogers/Rogers, 139
Kohlsact & Christian, 197
Konen, Tom, 194
Kramer & Graves, 112
Kully?, James M., 46
Kuykendal, W. L., 106
Kuykendale, T. A., 67
Kuykendall, John, 235, 239
Kuykendall, Lesser, 105
Kuykendall, T. A., 91
Kyle, Nelsen, 5
L. A. Dodds & M. W. Howard, 108
L. J. Sharp & Co., 112
Lackey, 200
Lackey, G. G., 145
Lackey, G. W., 39, 183
Lackey, Isaac, 225
Lackey, Isam, 171
Lackey, J. W. 94
Lackey, J., 94
Lackey, L. B., 191, 205
Lackey, Saml., 163, 171
Lackey, Samuel L., 172
Lackey, Samuel, 221
Lackey, V. L., 90
Lackey, William , 216
Lackey, Wm., 163, 179
Lackey, Wm., Sr., 163, 179
Lacky, Levi, 67
Lacky, Rebecca Malinda, 67
Lacky, Victor L, 67
Lafoy, Mrs., 217
Lainbeath, Jesse, 114
Lamar, C. T., 227
Lamar, James, 64, 93, 152, 163, 167, 168, 175, 179
Lamar, T. F., 163
Lamar, Thomas F., 172
Lamar, Thos. F., 152
Lambert, J. R., 260, 261
Lambert, Thomas, 5
Lameri (Lamar), 64
Lan? Iron Mountain Co., 41
Land, A. J., 84, 251
Land, S. J., 2
Land, T. B., 68
Landers, T. F., 77
Landford, John, 143
Lane, Alex, 131
Lane, C. T., 83
Lane, Vadney Jane Dutton, 113
Lankford, A. E., 27
Lankford, Andrew, 126
Lankford, David, 185
Lankford, Elizabeth, 208
Lankford, Ellen E., 140
Lankford, Ellen, 148
Lankford, I. M., 96
Lankford, J. B., 26
Lankford, J. D., 94, 141, 208
Lankford, J. L., 163
Lankford, J. M., 172
Lankford, J. M., 27, 208, 221, 232
Lankford, J. N., 71
Lankford, Jeff D., 140, 148
Lankford, Jim, 27
Lankford, John M., 96, 135, 142, 148, 232
Lankford, John, 146, 148, 170, 196
Lankford, L., 179
Lankford, P. G., 71, 148
Lankford, P. H., 29, 96
Lankford, R. B., 148, 255
Lankford, R. E., 136, 142, 143, 148, 232
Lankford, R. F., 158
Lankford, R. J., 248
Lankford, R. P., 144, 147, 156, 168, 221
Lankford, R. T., 93
Lankford, R., 148, 185
Lankford, Robert E., 136, 148
Lankford, Robert, 171, 185
Lankford, Sallie, 29
Lankford, Silas, 230

Lankford, Simeon, 218
Lankford, Susan Frazier, 136
Lankford, Susana, 136
Lankford, T. R., 56
Lankford, W. A., 71, 208
Lankford, W. C., 229
Lankford, William, 143
Lankford, Wm. C., 228
Lankford, Y. M., 59
Lann, J. M., 44
Lantham, E. E., 75
Lanthom, Nettie, 7
Laramore, T. J.,184
Laramore, V. C., 6, 26, 27, 222
Larmore, C. T., 229
Larmore, G. J., 52
Larmore, T. J., 183
Lassater, W. J., 72
Law, C. J., 72
Law, J. C., 130
Law, Louisa, 130
Lawenthal, H., 108
Lawrence, Florence, Mrs., 73
Lawrence, J. P., 41
Lawrence, Jas. R., 110
Lawrence, Joseph, 163, 179
Lawrence, Lee, 15
Lawrence, Rebecca, 15
Lawson, A. J., 81
Lawson, G. W., 189
Lawson, W., 244
Lawson, William, 129
Lax, E. T., 50
Lax, Jas., 50
Lax, Lou, 50
Lax, Mary, 50, 51
Lax, Thomas, 50
Lay, Chas. W., 232
Lay, Nancy W., 74
Lay, William, 232
Laythom, J. C., 257
Lea, A. B., 18
Lea, Ab, 19
Lea, Abner, 80
Lea, Allen, 8, 18, 30, 37, 148, 250, 262
Lea, Dock, 122
Lea, G. W., 81
Lea, Geo., 19
Lea, George, 18, 80
Lea, J. B., 82
Lea, James, 8, 12
Lea, Mariah Bouldin, 37
Lea, Mary C, 81
Lea, Samantha C., 81
Lea, Samantha Crabtree, 79
Lea, Samanthy, 81
Lea, Samatha Crabtree, 80
Lea, Sarah, 19
Lea, W. A., 17
Lea, Walter, 18, 19, 48
Lea, William, 18, 19, 30, 184
Lea, Wm., 37
Leak, A. S., 260
Leak, M. A., 90
Leanard, Ora, 48
Leath, B. L., 100
Leath, B. T., 55
Leath, E. L., 212
Leath, Parlee Horton, 237
Leath, Susanah, 55
Leath, W. J., 237
Leath, Wm. J., 55
Leatherwood, Agnes F., 40
Leatherwood, R. L., 40
Lee, A. B., 74, 76, 88
Lee, Allen, 30, 32, 148, 250
Lee, John, 30
Lee, Mariah A., 38
Lee, R. E., 75, 188
Lee, William, 19, 38
Leeth, C. J., 100
Leeth, G. A., 101, 102
Leeth, Isaac, 238
Leeth, M. P., 101
Lelleman, E. F. , 27
Lesley, Bonnie Tate, 134
Lesley, Geaner Tate, 134
Lesley, M. H. Tate, 134
Lester, J. H., 237
Letin, 64
Lett, James, 60
Levin, Thomas, 172
Lewis & Cothran, 115
Lewis, __ , 19
Lewis, B., 152, 171, 172
Lewis, Ben, 96
Lewis, Benjamin F., 206
Lewis, Benjamin, 206, 247
Lewis, Bunnal, 152
Lewis, Burrell, 22, 163, 168, 224
Lewis, Burwell, 179
Lewis, Eva, 133
Lewis, Fannie, 206
Lewis, J. L., 113
Lewis, John M., 183
Lewis, John, 70, 90, 96, 222
Lewis, Jonathan, 14
Lewis, M. A., 206
Lewis, Mary A., 207
Lewis, Mary Ann Hammock, 206
Lewis, Mary Ann, 207
Lewis, Mary, 14, 206
Lewis, Samuel, 206
Lewis, W. E. 54,
Lewis, W. L., 113
Lewis, William, Mrs., 133
Light, A. L., 197
Light, L. L., 74, 76
Light, Meredith, 9, 163, 179
Light, Miley, 56
Light, Wiley, 56, 224, 225
Ligins, T. H. Lynn, 156
Lilas, Negro Boy, 33
Liles, L. A., 74
Lillie, T. J., 71
Lincoln, B. A., 81
Lindley, J. B., 149
Lindsay, H., 233
Lindsey, A. C., 7
Liner, James, 69
Lipscomb, J. D., 192, 257
Lipscomb, L. J., 99, 100
Lipscomb, T. H., 101, 103, 194
Lipscomb, Thos., 194
Lisscomb, L. J., 98
Litlejohn, Lillian, 82
Litsey, W. F., 72
Little, Belden, 21
Little, Dick, 21
Little, Isaac, 22, 243
Little, Israel, 145
Little, James, 171
Little, Jas. R., 170
Little, John, 225
Little, L., 231
Little, Marion, 17, 186, 188, 189
Little, N. B., 123, 131, 259
Little, Thomas, 142, 144, 146, 224
Little, Thos. J., 245
Little, Thos., 146, 225
Little, W., 231
Littlejohn, J. F., 82
Littlejohn, W. S., 83
Lity, John, 232
Lively, 58
Lively, Emery, 59
Lively, John, 59
Lively, M. C., 21, 94
Lively, W. C., 20, 110
Livingston, C. H., 261
Livingston, C. M., 207, 261
Livingston, E. F., 114
Livingston, L., 152, 163, 172
Livingston, O. H., 261
Lloyd, John E., 212
Lock, J. W., 202, 203
Lock, John, 203
Locks, J. H., 27
Loeb, Emil, 108
Logan, R. M., 100, 101
Logan, W. L., 102
Loins/Toins, 170
Lolis, Marshall, 14
Long, 200
Long, Charles, 77
Long, David, 211
Long, H. M., 102
Long, James, 6, 18, 25, 26, 55
Long, Jennie, 49
Long, Marion, 163, 179
Long, N. P., 152
Long, W. P., 163, 182
Long, W. R., 68
Long, Wm. P., 168
Longshore, Marietta, 42
Lord, Charles, 163
Lorene, Negro Woman, 33
Louins, W. H., 84
Louise, 64
Love, Charles, 179
Love, G. W., 226
Love, J. W., 2
Love, Mrs., 109
Love, S. D., 131
Lovein, Thomas, 152
Loveless, Green B., 67
Loveless, Mary Jane, 67
Lovell, Elizabeth, 179
Loveman, A. B., 108
Loveman, Joseph & Leo, 108
Loven, John, 179
Loven, Thomas, 179
Lovens, L. B., 179
Lovens, L. D., 250
Lovern, John, 22, 163
Lovern, Thos., 163
Lovewell, G. W., 94
Lovin, John, 172
Loving, Eliz., 163
Loving, L. B., 163
Loving/Lovorn, John, 152
Lovins, L. B., 42, 87
Lovins, Lemuel, 87
Lovorn, John, 152
Low, John, 237
Lowe, John E., 15
Lowery, Adams, 12, 21
Lowery, D. R., 72

Lowery, Hattie P., 72
Lowery, Lou, 72
Lowery, S. C., 38
Lowery, Samuel C., 38
Lowes, Adam,10
Lowndes Co., 58
Lowrence, G. A., 56
Lowrey, Alva, 77
Lowrey, J. A., 78
Lowrey, Ocie, 72
Lowrey, Orien, 72
Lowry, Adam, 9
Lowry, C. E., (Elizabeth), 61
Lowry, C. E., 61
Lowry, C. L., 54
Lowry, C. W., 67, 91
Lowry, Chevy Elizabeth, Mrs., 61
Lowry, D. R., 72, 123
Lowry, Elizabeth, 61, 213
Lowry, F. M., 71
Lowry, G., 228
Lowry, Geo. M., 38
Lowry, Geo., M.D., 92, 213
Lowry, J. M., 61
Lowry, James, 163, 179, 213
Lowry, Levi, 13, 187
Lowry, Lony (Lory), 12
Lowry, Manora A., 71
Lowry, Newt, 229
Lowry, S. C., 52, 183
Lowry, T. C., 67
Lowry, W. A., 258
Lowry, W. T., 170
Loyd, J. W., 88, 89
Loyd, James, 163, 179
Lucas, J., 58
Luck, Thomas, 150, 154, 157
Luckes, Joseph, 206
Lucy, W. E. & Co., 232
Lucy, W. E., 231, 250, 251
Lumpkin, Robt., 258
Lumpkin, T. J., 15
Lunsford, W. G. Co., 107
Lusk, 185
Lusk, J. M., 27
Lusk, Josiah, 12, 13
Lusk, Robert C., 129
Lusk, Robert M., 222
Lusk, T. B., 67
Lusk, W. D., 2, 3, 4, 185
Lute, Isaac, 170
Luth, B. T., 55
Luth, Emmon, 55
Luth, Inman, 55
Luther, T. B., 106
Lutterel, John, 95
Lutterell, B. G., 91
Luttrell, Elizabeth Fields, 129
Lybrand, G. W., 57
Lybrand, T. B., 105
Lybrand, Walter, 57
Lynch, L. W., 256, 257
Lynch, Newton, 68, 69, 203
Lyon, A. J., 183
Lyon, Brelde?, 133
Lyon, John, 144
Lyon, Nathaniel, 149
Lyon, Sol. Thos., 232
Lyon, Thomas, 142
Lyon, William, 142
Lyon, Wm., 96
Lyons, Allison, 242
Lyons, Bula, Mrs., 133
Lyons, Bule, 123
Lyons, D. D., 122
Lyons, Ellen, 21, 51
Lyons, G. H., 240
Lyons, H., 146
Lyons, J. H., 234
Lyons, J. L., 183
Lyons, John, 135, 141
Lyons, P. M., 145
Lyons, S. O., 15
Lyons, Thomas G., 242
Lyons, Thomas, 24, 26, 70, 71
Lyons, W. S. A., 208
Lyons, W. W., 52
Lyons, Wallace, 39, 43
Lyons, Wiley, 146
M___, C. J., 56
Ma?, F. H., 125
Machey, Alex, 22
Machinery: Grist Mill, 89
Mackey, A. H., 68, 114
Mackey, A. M., 147
Mackey, Alexander, 179
Mackey, Henry H., 172
Mackey, John, 224
Mackey, L. A. H., 167
Macky, A. A., 144
MacLeod, L. J., 152, 173
MacNewman, R., 153
MacWhorter, H. P., Dr., 187
Madden, A. A., 247
Madderra, J. T., 237
Maddox, Arthur, 121
Maddra, James T., 164
Maderly, James T., 179
Madox, Arthur, 121
Madriah, James T., 255
Maffett, J., 92
Mafield, W. A., 101
Magratt, Thomas, 60
Mahaffey, Richard, 11
Mahaffey, Wm., 11
Mahan, S.V., 6
Mahan, Susan, 6
Mahon, Archibald, 14
Major Brothers, 51
Major, A. W., 150, 151, 152, 154, 155, 158, 164, 170, 179
Major, P. M., 262
Major, S. N., 44
Major, Samuel, 129
Majors, A. W. & Son, 225
Majors, A. W., 23, 96, 113, 114, 135, 244
Majors, Alexander, 130
Majors, Charley, 252
Majors, Elijah, 172
Majors, Elisha, 22
Majors, F. E., 44
Majors, Fannie E., 44
Majors, Fannie, 44
Majors, G. W., 220
Majors, John, 108
Majors, N. S., 44
Majors, S. N., 45, 94, 139, 246
Majors, Sam, 44, 158, 239
Majors, Sam'l., 234, 236
Majors, Samuel N., 246
Majors, Samuel, 96, 114, 136, 153, 223, 239
Majors, W. W., 130
Majors, Widow, 236
Mallicott, L. A., Dr., 43
Malon, R. J., 69
Malone & Hoge, 129
Malone Gen.Store, 31
Malone, 221
Malone, Benj., 236
Malone, David A., 164, 179
Malone, E. A., 135
Malone, E. H., 69, 85
Malone, E. T., 154
Malone, Eliz., 163
Malone, Elizabeth A., 135
Malone, Elizabeth, 179
Malone, G. J., 35, 96
Malone, G. L., 21, 30, 31, 39, 51, 74, 121, 134, 211, 233, 254
Malone, G. W., 5, 78, 95, 96, 114, 145, 150-52, 154-155, 158, 170, 172, 189, 206, 207, 212, 221, 225, 243, 244
Malone, Geo.W., 85, 93, 236, 262
Malone, George L., 78
Malone, George M., 223
Malone, George W., 69, 70, 79, 96, 136, 163, 179, 217,
Malone, Henry, 23
Malone, J. A., 31
Malone, James, 110, 152, 154, 164, 174,
Malone, Jim, 58
Malone, John, 22
Malone, Leo W., 69
Malone, Leroy H., 182
Malone, Leroy, 179
Malone, Levy/Lerry, 164
Malone, Nathaniel, 153
Malone, Nath'l, 168
Malone, R. J., 68, 154, 234, 236
Malone, R. W., 86
Malone, S. J., 79
Malone, T. C., 98, 99, 100
Malone, T. P., 99
Malone, T. P., Mrs., 98
Malone, Wallace C., 78
Malone, Wm., 55
Manley, Vastie Cagle, 53
Mann, G. W., 47
Mann, T. L., 229
Marbut, J. M., 186, 187, 260
Marfit, John, 60
Marinna, John, 251
Marion Bros. Gen. Mdse, 98
Marks, C. C., 57
Marona, G. F., 36
Marona, J. F., 35
Marony, Jas., 191
Marrtin?, C. J., 133
Marsh, J. B., 54, 183, 191
Marsh, W. C., 94
Marshall, H. G., 137
Marshall, Hugh S., 24
Marshall, Hugh, 1
Marshall, Ida, Mrs., 91
Marshall, Lolis, 12, 14
Marshall, P. G., 17, 188
Marson, J. T., 101
Marson, M. R., 101
Martin, 194
Martin, A., 152
Martin, Amanda, 72
Martin, C. S., 83, 123, 124
Martin, D. C., 195
Martin, D. S., 164
Martin, J. C., 87, 124, 202

Martin, J. M., 99, 101
Martin, J. R., 123, 219
Martin, James B., 136
Martin, James C, 72
Martin, James, 143
Martin, Jane, 164
Martin, Jane, Miss, 179
Martin, Jeff, 249
Martin, John R., 123
Martin, Martha, 163
Martin, Martha, Miss, 179
Martin, Martin, 152
Martin, Robert, 171
Martin, Robt., 164
Martin, W. B., 136
Martin, W., 172
Mashburn, Jesse, 194
Mason, J. E. J., 12
Mason, James W., 10
Mason, Peter, 143, 231
Mason, Sarah A., 10
Massey, Lewis, 201
Massie, Alice, 199
Massie, Louis, 199
Masters, B. F., 87, 197
Masters, B. T., 87
Masters, Ben, 87
Masters, Ella, Mrs., 91
Masters, J. K., 246
Masters, J. M., 12, 33, 68, 94, 199, 242
Masters, Josephine Elrod, 125
Maston, O. C., MD, 149
Mataken, Wade, 193
Mathen, J. H. 77
Matheney, Green B., 173
Matheny, G. R., 164
Matheny, Green B., 152
Matheny, Jack, 163, 179
Matheny, Jane, 164, 182
Matheny, Wilmoth, 179
Matheny, Winny, 163
Mathes, Alex, 2
Mathews, John, 118
Mathews?, James, 142
Mathis, Alex, 3
Mathis, DeAnn, 84
Mathis, Samuel, 84
Mathona, Wm., 231
Maton, J. T., 1
Matox, Arthur, 121
Matox, John, 121
Matthal, L. H., 207
Matthews, J. H., 117
Matthews, W. M., 90
Mattox, Arthur, 121, 260
Mattox, Ethel, 20
Mattox, J. H., 118
Mauer, T. A., 73
Mauer, T. L., 249
Maulden, J. B., 218
Mauldin, W. G., 164, 174
Mauldin, W. M., 262
Maxwell & Jones, 43
Maxwell, A., 60, 121
Maxwell, L. O., 17
Maxwell, Louie O., 17
May, 155
May, Daniel, 56
May, J. B., 88
May, J. G., 158
May, Jane, 241
May, L. G., 151
May, M. J., Mrs., 241
May, P. G., 154, 156, 157
May, Robert, 56
May, Sarah E., 131
May, Stephen, 96
May, W. H., 21, 23, 26, 145, 150, 151, 154, 164, 167, 170, 223, 225, 226
May, William H., 262
May, William R., 25, 27
May, Wm. H., 52, 114, 136, 146, 147
May, Wm.,179
Mayes, Henry, 179
Mayes, J. H., 98
Mayes, Jinks, 249
Mayes, Joe, 210
Mayes, Mrs., 259
Mayfield, W. A., 121
Mays, A. B., 256, 258
Mays, Fletcher, 23
Mays, H. C., 256, 258
Mays, Henry, 164
Mays, Henry, 223, 256
Mays, J. F., 256, 257
Mays, James F., 221, 224
Mays, Jas. F., 225
Mays, Martin, 253
Mays, Mary Johnson, 253
Mays, Mary M., 253
Mays, S., 129
Mays, Stephen, 163, 225
Mc _____, J. M., 1
McAbee, T. A., 62

McArver, J. B., 107
McBee, Chessie L., 93
McBrayer, 76
McBrayer, H. P., 143, 144, 171, 196
McBrayer, J. T., 46, 251
McBroom & Malone, 20
McBroom, 137, 156
McBroom, A. M., 40, 94, 137
McBroom, D. P., 246
McBroom, Jeff, 157
McBroom, N. M., 119
McBroom, Nancy M., 119
McBroom, P., 119
McBroom, S., 155, 156
McBroom, Stephen, 23, 157, 163, 248
McBroom, Thos., 154
McBryar, H. P., 230, 251
McCallan, J. M., 226
McCallie, A., 248
McCallie, Andrew, 247
McCambell, John, 175
McCamby, Alex, 95
McCampbell, 170
McCampbell, Alex., 170
McCampbell, E. A., 96
McCampbell, Frank, 23, 170
McCampbell, John M., 152
McCampbell, John, 126, 130, 136, 163, 170, 179, 225, 244, 248
McCampbell, R., 11
McCampbell, Saleanar, 136
McCampbell, Saleman, 136
McCampbell, Sol, 150, 151, 153, 154, 155, 157, 158, 164, 168, 171
McCampbell, Solloman, 143, 145, 179
McCampbell, Soloman, 96, 129
McCampbell's House, 79
McCampell, S., 175
McCampell, Sol, 168
McCamy, J. A., 31
McCamy, J. N., 31
McCandless, Wm., 233, 234
McCartnery, A. P., 46
McCartney & Co, 74
McCartney, A. P., 123, 131
McCartney, Alexander, 247
McCartney, C. H. 36, 54, 66, 132, 211
McCartney, J. H., 93
McCartney, John H., 55, 73
McCartney, John, 132
McCartney, Maggie, Mrs., 66
McCartney, W. A., 109
McCarty, A. P., 54
McCawley, Alex, 96
McCenless, 32
McClain & Co., 193
McClain, 8
McClain, B. H., 54
McClain, Leona Blansit, 31
McClain, M. S., 77
McClain, W. G., 152
McClain/McClane, Daniel, 149
McCland, 71
McCland, Polly, 71
McCland/ McLeoad, Mary, 70
McClendon, Burl, 237
McClendon, C. P., 240
McClendon, J., 218
McClendon, James, 84
McClendon, Nelly Horton, 237
McClendon, Pollie, 240
McClenon, C. P., 235
McClenond, Pollie, 239
McClimore, John, 122
McClintock, Clarence, 48
McClintock, Ella, 48
McClintock, Walter, 48
McCloud, William M., 144
McCloud, Wm., 146
McClung, Mary E., 112
McCluskey, J. W., 2
McCollough, F. F., 99
McCommack, Albert , 8
McConnell, 188
McConnell, O. L., 98
McCord, Col., 106
McCord, E. O. M., 106
McCord, E. O., 97
McCord, W. H., 132
McCormac, O. L., 102
McCormack, 261
McCormack, David, 238
McCormack, Thos., 261
McCormick, J. P., 101
McCormick, J. V., 101
McCormick, O. L., 103
McCowan, James, 30
McCoy, H. H., 164
McCoy, Hughey, 14
McCracken, George, 164, 179
McCrary, R. C., 27
McCrasy, Robert, 27
McCraw, Jesse, 223
McCrow, 152
McCrow, James, 164
McCullough, A. W., 130
McCurdy, 171
McCurdy, 82
McCurdy, Frosty, 171
McCurdy, J. A. M., 128

McCurdy, J. A., 7, 26, 38, 39, 42, 96, 131, 244
McCurdy, James, 129
McCurdy, John A., 24, 212, 236
McCurdy, M., 223
McCurdy, Macklin, 52
McCurdy, McLen, 172
McCurdy, McLin, 170
McCurdy, N. W., 153, 168
McCurdy, Nathaniel W., 48, 196
McCurdy, Sam, 224
McCurdy, Saml. R., 224
McCurdy, W. A. & W. B., 24
McCurdy, Warren, 153
McCurry, Mr., 163
McDaniel, 171
McDaniel, 8
McDaniel, Alexander, 13
McDaniel, Elizabeth M., 14
McDaniel, J. T., 88
McDaniel, James, 248
McDaniel, Mary J., 46
McDaniel, Paralee Jackson, 248
McDaniel, W. S., 89
McDaniel, William, 152, 179
McDaniel, Wm. M., 84
McDaniel, Wm., 11, 55, 163, 218, 253
McDavid, J. M., 72
McDonough, R. N., 93, 94
McDonough, Wood, 61
McDowell, E. L., 98
McDowell, Julia, 50
McDowell, Martha, 50
McDowell, Mary, 50
McElroy, Andrew, 179
McElvay, 23
McFarland, Byron, 170, 226
McFarlane, Bryan, 222
McFarlane, James, 246
McFarlane, L. E., 220
McFarlane, Lettie E., 220
McFarlane, Wilburn/Milburn, 220
McFay, Henry H., 152
McGee, Berry, 118
McGee, E. C., 62
McGhee, Rosan, 74
McGill Hardware, 89
McGlobon/McGlohan, 189
McGlohon, Dora, 189
McGlohon, Gordon, 189
McGlohon, James H., 189
McGlohon, Margaret, 189
McGlohon, Stella, 189
McGlothling, John, 60
McGraw, James, 60, 172
McGraw, Jesse, 223
McGuffey, Buford, 242
McGuffey, James M., 229
McGuffey, W. C. H., 213
McGuffey, W. C., 242
McGuire, Geo. S., 81
McGullion, E. L., 236
McGullion, Richard Amanda, 236
McHaffey, Wm., 10
McHan, E. A., 24, 58
McIlvaine, Alan C., 197
McIntire, Charles F., 67
McJenkins, Rueben, 173
McKagg, Hugh, 12
McKelvey Wm., 152
McKelvey, George, 164, 179
Mckelvey, Wm., 164, 173
McKenmore, Jessie, 239
McKenney, L. W., 206
McKenzie, W., 66
McKey, Alex., 164
McKiney, P. 217
McKing, P., 217
McKing, Peter, 218
Mckinley, Peter, 219
McKinney, Peter, 219
McKinnon, A., 74
McKinzie, J. A., 60
McKowan, James, 228
McKown, J. H., 228
McKown, J. M., 30
McLeod, W. A., 100, 102
McLeod/ McCland, Mary, 70
McLeroy, A., 164
McLoud, L. J., 164
McMahan, C. B., 42
McMahan, J. W., 72, 91, 97
McMahan, R., 154
McMahan, S. W., 8
McMahan, W. P., 238
McMillon Elijah, 59
McNair, D., 256, 258
McNair, Price, 152, 173
McNair, Prince, 164
McNann, Jesse, 235
McNann, William, 235
McNaran, Abner, 23
McNaran, Richard, 157
McNaren, Rich, 158
McNarian, Jessie, 240
McNarian, Richard, 153
McNarian, William, 240
McNaron, 103
McNaron, Abner, 22
McNaron, Sarah, 63
McNaron, T. B., 97
McNaron, W. R., 63
McNaron, William C., 113
McNaron/McNearon, 112
McNarwell, William, 239
McNearn, Richmond, 179
McNearon, 200
McNearon, Rich., 164
McNearon, William, 112
McNesson, Thom., 203
McNewman, R., 151
McNichols, 189
McNirnan, Richard, 157
McNutt, J. I., 44, 68
McNutt, John W., 44
McNutt, M. W., 247
McNutt, Millard, 235, 239, 240
McNutt, R. C., 5, 18, 27, 36, 38, 58, 68, 130, 145, 196, 244, 245
McNutt, R. S., 26
McNutt, Robert C., 196
McNutt, Robert, 171
McPherson, Arch, 102
McPherson, E. E., 101, 103
McPherson, E., 163
McPherson, G. W., 172
McPherson, Geo, 170, 172, 179, 224
McPherson, George, 129, 152, 163, 167, 172, 222
McPherson, Hand, 171
McPherson, Isaac, 170, 223, 224
McPherson, J. L., 99, 102
McPherson, James, 224
McPherson, Jefferson, 247
McPherson, Joseph, 129
McPherson, Mary E., 224, 225
McPherson, Mary, 164
McPherson, Mary, Mrs., 182
McPherson, Richard, 225
McPherson, T. J., 206
McPherson, W. A., 100
McPherson, Wm., 206
McQuire, Geo. S., 80
McSpadden & Carden, 130
McSpadden, Allen, 27, 136
McSpadden, B. A., 17
McSpadden, B. J., 7
McSpadden, C. A., 5
McSpadden, H. A., 6, 21, 73, 89, 107, 110, 136, 140
McSpadden, Hiram A., 5, 71
McSpadden, John, 220
McSpadden, M. J., 6
McSpadden, Maggie Frost, 134
McSpadden, Mary, 6
McSpadden, Moses, 163, 179
McSpadden, S. D., 27
McSpadden, S. K., 130
McSpadden, T. K. B., 147
McSpadden, T. K. Belle, 144
McSpadden, T. K., 147
McWhorter, A. M., 212
McWhorter, Dr., 108
McWhorter, H. A., 18
McWhorter, H. F., 192
McWhorter, H. M., 110
McWhorter, H. P., 28, 94, 109, 190, 212, 237
McWhorter, H. P., Dr., 110, 260
McWhorter, James M., 251
McWhorter, Lamar, Dr., 219
Meader, A. L., 90
Meaders, A. L., 91
Meaders, R. C., 91
Meadow, John, 163
Meadow, William, 179
Meadows, John M., 132
Meadows, P. J., 17
Meadows, Pinkney, 188
Meadows, William, 152
Meadows, Wm., 164, 202
Means, A. M., 146
Mechler, Husten, 27
Medbury, Mary C., 44
Medlock, H. H., 91
Medlock, L. L., 82
Medlock, Lizzie, 83
Meeks, H. E., 121
Meeks, M. M., 69
Meeks, S. E. & S. T., 187
Meeks, S. T. (Tressie), 187
Meeks, S. T., 187
Meigs, J. H., 84
Melton, H. W., 11
Melton, John, 11
Melton, W. G., 110
Melton, Wm. P., 11

Mergan, 90
Merrell, Haley, 163
Merrell, Rily T., 179
Merrell, Wm., 220
Merrett, James, 164
Merrill, Brandman, 44
Merrill, Charles E., 44
Merrill, John B., 44
Michell, A. J., 152
Michell, Alex. T., 163
Michler, E. L., 26
Mickens, Vergil, 122
Mickler, Jacob, 25
Middlebrooks, J. T., 97, 101
Middlebrooks, T. J., 102
Middleton, D. L., Dr., 211
Mihollen, J. T., 196
Mikels, C. C., 63
Miler, Chamberlain, 26
Miler, Judy Chamberlain, 26
Milican, Levi, 32
Miligan, Levi, 32
Miller, C. B., 131
Miller, D. M., 53
Miller, E. W., 236
Miller, Ette, 50
Miller, Frank, 39
Miller, G. W., 7
Miller, J. B., 38, 106
Miller, J. F., 66
Miller, J. R., MD, 94
Miller, J. T., 66, 94
Miller, J. W., 236
Miller, John, 164, 179
Miller, Lucy, 50
Miller, Luella, 50
Miller, Nancy E., 25
Miller, S. W., 2
Miller, T. J., MD, 94
Miller, W. G., 236
Miller, William, 50
Miller, Zoe, 110
Millican, Andrew, 13, 14
Millican, Lory, 12
Millican, Wm., 13
Milligan, James, 11
Milligan, Lory, 11
Milligan, M., 11
Milligan, Wm., 11
Mills, 200, 203
Mills, A. B., 205
Mills, J. P., 200
Mills, J. W., 85
Mills, J. Walter, 125
Mills, Sarah, 205
Mills, W. F., 220
Mills, W. K., 77, 195, 202, 235
Mills, W., 143
Milner, F. A., 252
Milner, F. M., 98, 100
Milner, J. A., 99
Milton, Asberry, 252
Milwee, G. W., 88, 250, 253, 255
Milwee, George, 56
Milwee, H. H., 97, 99
Milwee, J. A., 99, 127, 256
Milwee, James A., 23, 40, 58, 97, 127
Milwee, Jas. A., 45
Milwee, John, 255, 257
Milwee, W. E., 101, 103
Milwee, W. T., 97
Minnix, James, 129
Minot, Harry, 107
Minot, Lucy, 107, 110
Minot, Wm. H., 131
Minott, W. H. H., 103
Minster, J. G., 245
Mires, Jacob, 60
Mitchel, Wm., 243
Mitchell, A. S., 173
Mitchell, A. U., 215
Mitchell, Abner, 163, 179
Mitchell, Alex, 163, 172
Mitchell, Alice, 50
Mitchell, E. A., 125
Mitchell, G. W., 220, 222
Mitchell, Geo. W., 220
Mitchell, H. B., 152, 164
Mitchell, H. C., 183, 184, 229
Mitchell, Hugh, 50
Mitchell, James D., 152
Mitchell, James, 163, 167, 216
Mitchell, M., 164
Mitchell, Manerva, 179
Mitchell, Robert, 152, 173
Mitchell, Robt. & James, 164
Mitchell, W. B., 173
Mitchell, W. J., 63, 206, 236
Mitchell, Wm., 22
Moman, Charles, 39
Moman, Zolly, 39
Momar, Zollie, 103
Monroe, Harrie, 241
Monroe, J. D., 54
Monroe, John D., 252
Monroe, Martha, 241
Monroe, S. D., 58
Monroe, T. F., 73
Monroe, T. L., 57
Monroe, W., 222
Moody, J. J., 163, 179, 253
Moody, J. T., 21
Moody, T. E., 2
Moon, A. W., 64
Mooney, M. P., 144
Mooney, Wm. H., 146
Moony, W. H., 230
Moore, 230
Moore, 60
Moore, A., 172
Moore, Abraham, 179
Moore, Alexndria, 144
Moore, Alvin, 73
Moore, And, 155
Moore, D. D., 123
Moore, Dessie, 123
Moore, E., 209
Moore, Ellen Crabtree, 80, 81
Moore, Ellen, 80, 81
Moore, Ellen, Mrs., 80
Moore, F. A., 48
Moore, Harris, 73
Moore, Ida, Mrs., 73
Moore, James, 18
Moore, Jas. H., 98
Moore, Jas., 231
Moore, John W., 123
Moore, L. O., 101
Moore, L. P., 56
Moore, Lake, 227
Moore, Lance, 79, 132
Moore, Lola, 73
Moore, M., 231
Moore, Mrs., 80
Moore, Oliver, 192
Moore, T., 234
Moore, Viola. 73
Moore, W. E., Dr., 49
Moore, W. J., 54
Moore, Willie, 73
Moragne, Eula, 25
Moragne, Eulale (Eulah), 27
Moragne, J. B., 27
Moragne, John, 25
More, John, 98
More, L. O., 99, 191
More, W. E., 238
Morgan, 221
Morgan, A. S., 247
Morgan, Amanda J., 25
Morgan, C. L., 260
Morgan, D. C., 147
Morgan, David, 23
Morgan, Eliza J. (Berry), 28
Morgan, Eula, 26, 229
Morgan, Frank, 192
Morgan, J. A., 66
Morgan, J. B., 164
Morgan, J. M., 132
Morgan, J. T., 130, 183, 196, 242
Morgan, James P., 184
Morgan, Jere, 163
Morgan, John B., 23, 179, 262
Morgan, John T., 136
Morgan, John, 28, 67, 221
Morgan, Maria S., 25
Morgan, Nathan, 164, 179
Morgan, S. D., 117
Morgan, S. J., 66, 132, 134
Morgan, S. T., 210
Morgan, Sarah Hawkins, 215
Morgan, T. J., 231
Morgan, T. S., 91, 210
Morgan, Thomas, 230
Morgan, Thos. J, 232
Morgan, W. A., 11
Morgan, W. C., 210
Morgan, W. G., 191
Morgan, W. H., 94
Morgan, Wesley, 229
Morgan, William D., 32
Morgan, Wm. C., 126
Morgan, Wm. L., 214
Morgan, Wm., 12
Moris, J. W., 259
Morony, Jos., 193
Morris & George, 179
Morris, A. R., 14
Morris, H., 150, 154
Morris, Henry, 157, 163, 179, 182
Morris, J. G., 158
Morris, J. T., 154, 157, 164, 173, 179
Morris, J. W., 65, 76
Morris, J., 151
Morris, James W., 260
Morris, John D., 259
Morris, Jonathan T., 155
Morris, Pierce, 110
Morris, Sarah A., 199
Morris, Smith & Harrison, 168
Morris, Thomas A., 11
Morris, Thomas, 23, 182
Morris, Wesley, 157
Morrison, A. R., 14
Morrison, J. T., 102
Morrison, J. Thomas, 182
Morrison, John, 29
Morrison, W. A., 172
Morrison, Wm., 172
Morrow, George, 163
Morton, J. M., 77

Morton, Wm. H., 218
Moseley, Canady, 164
Mosely, Canada, 179
Moses, 64
Mosley, J. N., 60
Mosley, Jas., 194
Mosley, M., 91, 230
Mosley, S. W., 57
Mosley, Walter, 229
Mosteler, W. E., 120
Mosteler, W. E., Mrs., 120
Mosteller, W. E., 118, 120
Moulton, Martha C., 44
Moulton, William P., 44
Mound, A., 164
Mulinax, Tine, 99
Mullin, Alphonso, 127
Mullin, Augustus, 127
Mullin, Jensey, 127
Mullin, John, 127
Mullin, Matilda, 127
Mullin, Thomas, 127
Mullin, William, 127
Mullinax, T. W., 99
Mullins, Dick, 163, 182
Mullins, James, 128
Mullins, John, 241
Mullins, Malvinda, 128
Mullins, Melvesta Everett, 128
Mullins, Melvesta, 128
Mullins, William, 179
Mullins, Wm., 163, 170, 253, 263
Mulwee, George W., 179
Mulwee, George, 164
Munro, 193
Murdock, A. O., 62, 106
Murdock, J. O., 76
Murdock, R. M., 237
Murdock, R. W., 98, 100
Murdock, T. H. 55,
Murdock, T. W., 55
Murdock, Thomas, 238
Murphey, Alice Ann, 44
Murphey, N., 129
Murphey, Patrick, 44
Murphrey, M., 129
Murphy, 163
Murphy, Alma Head, 216
Murphy, Mardis, 223
Murphy, Mardy, 226
Murphy, R., 263
Murphy, Robert, 23, 222
Murray, Telitha Deaton, 104
Murry, Lelitha, 104
Musgrove, James, 224
Musgrove, Jason, 225
Myers, Frank B., 252
Myers, Hattie Hawkins, 213
Myers, Hattie O., 215
Myers, Hattie, 213
Myers, T. F., 66
Mynatt, Wm. C., 164, 179
Mynatt, Wm., 220, 226
Myricks, R. G., 76
Myricks, Richard, 37
N. Phillips & Co., 114
Nailer, C. C., 194
Nailer, C.F., 98
Nailer, L. J., Mrs., 39
Nailer, M. H., 97
Nailer, Riller, 39
Nailor, Jerry, 218
Naler, C. C., 40, 97, 99
Naler, C. F., 100
Naler, G. J., 99, 100
Naler, J. N., 98
Naler, J. R., 100, 102
Naler, J. W., 100
Naler, L. J., 39
Naler, Nailor, Nalor, 39
Naler, S. J., 100, 102
Naler, W. A., 98
Nales, C. C., 192
Nales, C. F., 98
Nales, G. J., 98, 99
Nalor, Jeremiah, 255
Nalor, M. F., 103
Nalor, S. J., 191
Name Unknown, 41
Nance, James, 60
Nappier, T. S., 49
Nathan, James, 258
Nation, James, 256
National Marble Mills, 62
Nations, 199
Nations, James, 257
Nations, W. T., 52, 73
Natt, W. J., 23
Nave, 201, 203
Nave, J. P., 66
Nave, James P., 66
Nave, Lizzie, 66
Nave, Polk, 201
Nave, S. E., 66
Nave, Warren, 164, 182
Naylor, Poly, 43
Naylor, Polydore, 222
NcNutt, R. C., 212
Neal, Dora J., 258
Nealy/Neely, 210
Neely, Charles M., 210
Neely, James A., 210
Neely, John M., 210
Neely, Mahala H., 210
Negro Man, Alfred, 142, 146
Negro Man, Ephrian, 145
Negro Man, Frank, 145
Negro Man, Guy, 145
Negro Man, Ilias, 145
Negro Man, Israel, 145
Negro Man, Jacob, 145
Negro Man, Long, 142
Negro Man, William, 145
Negro Woman, Emily, 144
Negro Woman, Lil, 144
Negro Woman, Sarah, 142
Negro, Charles, 144
Nelson, C. J., 101
Nelson, C. L., 38
Nelson, F, W, & David, 89
Nelson, Geo., 89
Nelson, Hill, 225
Nelson, J. M., 52
Nelson, J. S., 48
Nelson, Joseph G., 44
Nelson, Martha, 223
Nelson, Mrs., 223
Nelson, P. J., 100
Nelson, Pleasant M., 52
Nelson, W. J., 97
Nelson, William, 223
New England Drug Store, 112
New, Luke L., 75
Newel, Emily, Mrs., 67
Newell, Emily, Mrs., 67
Newkirk, H. H., 164, 172, 175
Newkirk, Henry, 164, 179, 226
Newkirk, Hiram, 22, 164, 168, 179
Newkirk, J. F., 41
Newkirk, James F., 41
Newkirk, James, 58, 144, 152, 164, 172, 179, 247
Newkirk, Jas., 115
Newkirk, John, 164, 179
Newkirk, Lane, 247
Newman, 157
Newman, F. P., 117
Newman, Frank, 118
Newman, G. Y., 128, 245
Newman, J. N, 183
Newman, J. W., 95, 120
Newman, M. C., 154, 164, 179, 256, 262, 263
Newman, M. E., 245
Newman, M. N., 254
Newman, Moses C., 79, 148, 168
Newman, Osborn, 205
Newman, R. C., 156
Newman, Simpson, 164, 175, 179
Newman, W. M., 168, 253
Newman, Widow, 22
Newman, Wiley, 254
Newmans, C. S., 58
Newmin, M. C., 114
Newton, Elijah, 223
Nichelson, Doc, 18
Nichlson, D. L., 150
Nichols, A. M., 212
Nichols, C. F., 73
Nichols, C. L., 72, 73, 83, 100, 101, 125
Nichols, Callie, (Mrs. P. C.), 72
Nichols, Charles, 125
Nichols, D. L., 8
Nichols, H. H., 92
Nichols, H., 90
Nichols, J. B., 88, 164
Nichols, J. G., 124, 164, 179
Nichols, James, 164, 179
Nichols, John B., 179
Nichols, John, 79
Nichols, Julia A, 124
Nichols, M. C., Mrs., 91
Nichols, P. C., 72
Nichols, R. A., 39
Nichols, Thomas, 110
Nichols, W. H., 124
Nichols, W. N., 72, 190
Nichols, William H., 124
Nicholsen & Collins, 8
Nicholsen, D. L., 5, 56, 63, 136
Nicholsen, E. P., MD, 38
Nicholsen, L. S., 77
Nicholsen, T. J., 243
Nicholson & Collins, 207, 242, 253
Nicholson & Higgins, 34, 155, 221, 252
Nicholson & Howard, 76
Nicholson, B. H., 58, 69, 77, 139,192, 194, 195, 202, 203, 205
Nicholson, B. N. & D. L., 214
Nicholson, B., 244
Nicholson, C. R., 88, 89
Nicholson, C. W., 200
Nicholson, Charlie, 91
Nicholson, D. L., 5, 25, 84, 96, 150, 151, 153,154, 156, 157, 168, 171, 172, 214, 242
Nicholson, David L., 155

Nicholson, E. P., 117, 123, 200, 203, 204, 205, 227
Nicholson, E. P., Dr., 221
Nicholson, E. P., MD, 52
Nicholson, Isaac E., 158
Nicholson, Isaac, 168
Nicholson, J. A., 85
Nicholson, J. E., 147, 225
Nicholson, J. F., 154
Nicholson, J. J., 262
Nicholson, J. W., 226
Nicholson, J., 150
Nicholson, James A., 223
Nicholson, John, 164, 173
Nicholson, Josie, 202
Nicholson, L. M., 153, 179, 182
Nicholson, L. S., 94, 105, 120, 121, 148, 186, 193, 195, 201, 202, 246, 259
Nicholson, Lem, 121
Nicholson, Lemuel M., 262
Nicholson, Louise, 105
Nicholson, M. G., 200, 260
Nicholson, M. H., 26, 260
Nicholson, M. M., 76, 91, 193, 205
Nicholson, M., 164, 201, 203
Nicholson, Mary B., 130, 168, 257
Nicholson, Mary B. R., 153
Nicholson, Mary, 27, 164
Nicholson, Mary, Miss, 179
Nicholson, Mercer, 179
Nicholson, O. P., 130, 200, 201, 203, 205
Nicholson, Oling P., 130
Nicholson, S. S., 205
Nicholson, Scot, 205
Nicholson, Scott, 201, 205
Nicholson, T. E., 157
Nicholson, T. J., 149, 185, 200, 237, 239, 240, 243
Nicholson, Thos., 164, 179
Nicholson, W. C., 193
Nicholson, W. D., 69, 164, 179
Nicholson, W. J., 164, 168
Nicholson, W. L., 153
Nicholson, Warren D., 22
Nicholson, William, 22
Nicholson, Wm. J., 152, 172, 182
Nicholson, Wm. P., 43
Nicholson, Wm. R., 179, 224
Nicholson, Wm., 164, 179, 182
Nickelson, Doc, 19
Nicklson, D. L., 26
Nicklson, Doc., 19
Nickolson, Mary, 25
Nickson, Isaac, 92
Nix & Campbell, 108, 112, 189
Nix, A. J., 107
Nix, Ella G., 107
Nix, Ella G.,Mrs., 229
Nix, Ella, 107
Nix, Joe J., 24, 71, 107, 111
Nix, Joe, 107
Nix, L. E., 100,102
Nix, N. B., 107
Nix, Ruby, 107
Nix, Winter, 107
Nixon & Webster Co., 41
Nixon, G. W., 137
Noble, Samuel, 82
Nobles, William, 84
Nomond, J. C., 260
Norman, Henry, 87, 250, 253, 254
Norman, Wiley M., 253
Normance, W. W., 206
Norrel, Nancy, 179
Norrell, C. P., 255
Norrell, Nancy, 164
Norris, H. N., 186
Norris, Jack, 75
Norris, Z. T., 186
North, Oliver, 220
North, T. J., 97
Norton, 225
Norton, A. J., 200
Norton, D. E., 124
Norton, E. H., 92, 98, 101, 124
Norton, Estelle, 124
Norton, Eugene, 124
Norton, Gares, 224
Norton, J., 235
Norton, James, 164, 172, 223, 239, 240
Norton, Mr., 171
Norton, Mrs., 164
Norton, Roswell, 152, 164, 175, 224
Norton, Samuel, 144
Norton, W., 182
Norvel, W. C., 60
Norwood, 185
Norwood, B. H., 194
Norwood, H. P., 187
Norwood, J. C., 259
Norwood, Jno. C., 16
Norwood, Mrs., 121
Norwood, R. M., 118, 120
Norwood, R. N., 118
Norwood, Rufus, 118
Norwood, S. B., 119
Norwood, S. W., 107
Nosham, J. D., 175
Novelle, Fannetta, 94
Novelle, Jannette, 94
Nowlin, B. A., 109, 219
Nowlin, B. S. Co., 54
Nowlin, Beverly, 246
Nowlin, D. S., 200
Nunn, J. F., 91
Nunn, John F., 77
Nunn, John R., 77
O. P. Hill & Co., 196
Oashburn, Wm. C., 180
Odem, Mr., 180
Odom, Mr., 164
O'Grady, James, 152
Olds, C. P., Dr., 48
Oliver & Hunt Co., 75
Oliver Hall Co., 75, 117, 118, 187, 190, 192, 219
Oliver, Henry, 235
Oliver, J. H., 142
Oliver, James H., 23, 165
Oliver, T. H., 180
Olyer, Smith, 15
O'Neal, A. C., 12
O'Neal, Alfred, 12
O'Neal, Cicero, 233
O'Neal, Evaline, 59
O'Neal, H. A., 12
O'Neal, James, 12, 233
O'Neal, John W., 14
O'Neal, Zachariah, 14
O'Rear, Charlotte J., 131
O'Rear, F. M., 131
O'Rear, Francis M., 131
O'Rear, George, 131
O'Rear, R. M., 131
O'Rear, Samuel A., 258
O'Rear, Samuel, 6, 131
O'Rear, Sarah, 131
Orr, Oscar, 131
Orr, Perry, 131
Orr, R. D., 186
Orr, Thomas A., 241
Osborn, Charles, 206
Osborn, Chas., 205
Osborn, J. E., 205
Osborn, J. H., 205
Osborn, J. L., 206
Osborn, J. R., 206
Osborn, James F., 205
Osborn, John, 205
Osborn, Newman, 206
Osborn, W. C., 164
Osborne & Couch, 243
Osborne, Ernest, 187
Osborne, Isham, 243, 244
Osborne, J. L., 205
Osborne, L. A., 245
Osburn, Jackson, 129
O'Shieds, H. H., 95
O'Shield, H. H., 90
O'Shields, D. O., 187
O'Shields, Felix, 106
O'Shields, H. H., 5, 89, 91
O'Shields, J. G., 94, 106
O'Shields, John, 247
Otinger, L. F., 99
Otwell, W. H., 221
Owen, Billie, 39
Owen, John T., 256
Owen, M. T., 39
Owen, W. L., 91
Owens, 105
Owens, A., 256, 257
Owens, Albert, 105
Owens, Charley, 105
Owens, E. M., 65
Owens, G. W., 57
Owens, G., 57
Owens, Gilford, 164, 180
Owens, Hugh, 164, 180
Owens, John T., 38, 164, 180
Owens, Luther, 105
Owens, Newton, 164, 180
Owens, Raymon, 257
Owens, Raymond, 164, 180
Owens, Roy, 105
Owens, Sophia D., 105
Owens, Thomas, 180
Owens, Thos., 164
Owens, W. L., 90
Owens, Wesley, 153
Owens, William, 180, 256
Owens, Wm., 164, 256, 257
Oyler, 185
Oyler, A. J., 16
Oyler, Daniel, 13
Oyler, Elizabeth, 15
Oyler, Frederick, 13
Oyler, Geo. W., 183
Oyler, George, 13
Oyler, James, 15, 16
Oyler, Samuel, 15, 16
Oyler, Smith, 16
Pace, Burel, 250
Pace, Burrel, 256, 257

Pace, Burrell, 165
Pace, Burwell, 180
Pace, Isaac, 248
Pace, J. L., 77
Pack, G. C., 59
Pack, G. F., 101
Pack, G. M., 99
Pack, Johnson, 59
Paden, John, 79, 171
Paden, Robert, 23, 79
Padget, F. M., 256
Padget, Jacob, 180
Padget, M., 257
Padgett, J. T., 140
Padgett, Jacob, 165, 256
Padgett, L., 257
Page, Burrel, 257
Paget, Alford, 250
Pain, John, 55
Paine, B. F., Dr., 18
Paine, Ben F., 18
Paine, Benj. F., 131
Paine, Benjamin F., 48
Paine, Mearia L., 48
Painter, A. J., 71
Painter, Alexander, 12
Painter, H., 148
Painter, Hardy, 10, 12, 16, 37, 148
Painter, Jackson, 14
Painter, James, 32, 148
Painter, L. Lewis, 180
Painter, Lewis, 165
Painter, M. H., 38
Painter, Nancy Serena, 38
Painter, Nancy, 37
Pall, D. C., 194
Palmer, F. M., 122
Palmer, Geo., 122
Palmore, I. H., 11
Palmore, Widow, 14
Palner, F. V., 27
Pankey, Edward, 144
Pankey, Edwards, 143
Pankey, Edw'd., 145
Panther, Alex., 13
Panther, C., 11
Pardon, Bob, 119
Parish, M. L., 228
Parish, R. M., 183
Parish, R. W., 227, 228
Parish, S. L., 51, 207
Parker, Cicero, 17, 247
Parker, J. M., 141
Parker, James, 96, 114, 142, 144, 145, 146, 206, 243,
Parker, M. D., 197
Parker, Robert, 247
Parker, Russell, 165, 180
Parker, W. J., 118, 120
Parkes, William, 114
Parkes, Wm., 114
Parliwood, W. J., 17
Parr, A. A., 255
Parrish/Parish, 51
Parson, 143
Parsons, Elvira Hughes, 241
Parsons, J., 230
Parsons, James, 147, 149
Parsons, L. L., 74
Parsons, Labon, 241
Parsons, Layburn, 242
Parsons, Mary E., 242
Parsons, T. C., 114
Partwood, W. J., 74, 76
Pate, Aaron, 164, 180
Pate, Rosa/Rosey, 119
Paterson, L. J., 145
Paterson, W. J., 257
Pates/Bates, 157
Patey, Wm. P., 180
Patrick, Austin, 165, 180
Patrick, J. M., 84, 234
Patrick, J. W., 235
Patrick, Josua, 184
Patrick, Thomas A., 250
Patrick, Thos. A., 43
Patridge, Harvey W., 64
Patterson & Herrin, 7
Patterson, D. U., 231
Patterson, Hammock, 206
Patterson, John M., 230
Patterson, John, 144, 224, 225
Patterson, L. D., 143, 145, 164, 173, 180, 221, 223
Patterson, S. L., 142
Patterson, Saml., 171
Patterson, T. P., 89
Patton, Geo. E., 165
Patton, George, 180
Patty, R. J., 88
Patty, R. J., Dr., 91
Paty, W. P., 165
Paxton, John, 11
Pay, Fillip, 60
Payne & Gardner Mdse., 117
Payne & Payne, 61
Payne, A. F., 26, 42, 69, 111, 112, 128, 196, 207, 212, 236, 237, 242
Payne, A. H., 85
Payne, A. J., 61
Payne, A. L., 234
Payne, A. P., 257
Payne, Amanda J., 61
Payne, Amanda, 61
Payne, Amond J., 61
Payne, Andrew, 238
Payne, Asa, 235
Payne, Eliza J., 63
Payne, F. M., 63
Payne, F., 257
Payne, H. C., 80, 81
Payne, H. G., 6
Payne, H. P., 69
Payne, J. L., 110
Payne, John H., 257
Payne, John L, 109, 125, 213, 227
Payne, John, 238
Payne, M. A., 211
Payne, M. F., 117
Payne, Mrs., 254
Payne, Nannie, 239
Payne, S. F., 33
Payne, Thomas, 4, 9, 33, 58, 61, 183, 184
Payne, W. D. M., 110
Payne, W. H., Jr., 61
Payne, Warren, 235, 240
Peace, D. J., 72
Peacock, Henry, 5
Peak, Anna, 231
Peak, Isaac, 60
Peak, J. S., 20
Peak, Judy, 165
Peak, Marion, 200
Peak, Rhoda, 231
Peak, Richard, 165, 180
Peak, S. B., 163, 200
Pearson, Edward, 240
Pearson, W. K., 11
Peck, Judah, 180
Peck/Peek, 229
Peek, James H., 229
Peek, Jennie, 229
Peek, L. H., 74
Peek, Lavada, 46
Peek, M., 200
Peek, Oscar, 109
Pegler, D. C., 137
Pell, Jas., 73
Pellers, A. A., 60
Pemberton, R., 221
Penager, John C., 59
Pendergraft, Sarah C., 126
Pendergraph, William P., 126
Pendergrass, A. R., 222
Pendergrass, Alex, 225
Pendergrass, J. A. & D. A., 186
Pendergrass, J. W., 145
Pendergrass, Nora, 20
Pendergrass, P. G., 134
Pendergrass, Porter G., 103
Pendergrass, Sinda, 130
Pendergrss, Jas., 235
Pendleton, Eliza, 164, 180
Penn, Geo., 194
Penn, J. W., 110
Penn, James, 126, 165, 180, 231, 232, 251, 255
Penn, Lucy , 237
Penn, Lucy Norton, 237
Penn, Mary, 237
Penn, N. L., 230
Penn, N. S., 231, 232, 237, 255
Penn, S., 238
Penn, Stephen, 55, 237, 238
Penn, Stevin, 250
Penn, William, 250
Pentecastle, Cochran, 262
Peppers, A. L., 101
Peppers, D. L., 99, 101
Peppers, J. L., 106
Peppers, S. W., 99
Peraley, J., 91
Perkins, W. C., 85
Perry, Hanibal, 165, 173
Perry, R. M., 39
Perry?, Noah, 114
Pervin, Elizabeth, 180
Pervin, L. S., 180
Pervin, M., 165
Peter White & Co., 194
Pettitt, H., 60
Pettitt, W. P., 61
Petty & Huff, 239
Petty, Art, 193
Petty, J. M., 235, 236, 239
Petty, J. N., 239
Petty, James M., 236
Petty, James, 239
Petty, Jesse W., 234
Petty, John, 240
Petty, T. W., 235
Petty, Thomas, 28, 216, 221
Petty, W. B., 119
Petty, W. D., 68, 118, 119, 155, 168, 195, 216, 229, 236
Petty, W. J., 154
Petty, W. S., 68
Petty, W., 234
Petty, Wesley D., 153
Petty, Wiley D., 68, 149
Petty, Wiley, 195
Pharr, G. W., 39, 190, 211
Pharr, G. W., 88, 90, 104
Philips, Ben, 158
Philips, Benj., 180
Philips, P. L., 245

hillips & Roberts, 141
hillips, A. E., 90
hillips, A. J., 109
hillips, A. P., 91, 239
hillips, A., 170, 234
hillips, Abner, 25, 32, 214
hillips, B. G., 154
hillips, Ben, 157, 165, 167
hillips, Benj., 223
hillips, C. J., 25
hillips, Caleb, 23
hillips, Corinna J., 25
hillips, Elizabeth, 37
hillips, Ellis, 80, 81
hillips, F., 240
hillips, H & Co., 141, 207
hillips, H. M., 72
hillips, H. P., 96
hillips, H., 141
hillips, Hattie M., 72
hillips, Hattie P. 72
hillips, J. H., 125
hillips, J. W., 100
hillips, Jesse, 223
hillips, John, 37
hillips, M. E., 37, 81
hillips, Margaret C., 81
hillips, Margaret Crabtree, 79
hillips, Margaret, 81
hillips, Matilda C., 144
hillips, Matilda Garrett, 141
hillips, Matilda, 145, 146
hillips, P. D., 26, 108, 117, 141, 142, 144, 145, 146, 147, 207, 212, 213, 215
hillips, P. G., 126
hillips, P. J., 145, 146, 147
hillips, P. S., 26
hillips, P., 141
hillips, Paul Corbin, 79
hillips, Pleasant D., 83, 144, 146, 213
hillips, R. D., 114
hillips, Rebecca, 217
hillips, Ross, 135
hillips, Sam'l, 23
hillips, W. F., 72
ckens, A. M., 90
ckens, A. W., 72
ckens, D. F., 41
ckens, Frank, 90
ckens, H. W., 252
ckens, Henry W., 113
Pickens, J. F., 57
Pickens, J. M., 57, 63, 88, 89, 90
Pickens, J. M., Jr., 90
Pierce, John A., 8
Pinkerton, Caroline Jackson, 248
Pinkerton, R. A., 193
Pinkerton, Samuel, 248
Pinkerton, Thos. B., 173
Pinkerton, Thos., 165, 180
Pits, J. N., 247
Pitts, John, 184
Pivett, J. C., 143
Pivit, James, 180
Plunket, G. T., 98, 100, 101
Plunkett, B. L., 187
Poe, J. C., 172, 221, 226
Poe, James C., 114, 129, 165, 222, 224
Poe, James, 180
Poe, R., 212
Poe, Sarah, 180
Poe, W. R., 5, 7, 82, 107, 108, 136, 148, 196, 212, 237, 259
Poe, W. T., 165, 170
Poe, Wash., 165
Poe, Washington, 180
Poe, William A., 212
Poe, Wm. T., 173
Pointer, Joshua, 89
Polk, W. D., 130
Pollard, Frank, 238
Pollard, Grandy, 238
Pollard, P., 257
Polse, T. J., 183
Poluma, 185
Pope, B., 136
Pope, Davis, 206
Pope, F. M., 140
Pope, J. D., 40, 54, 65, 78, 206
Pope, J. E., 90, 91
Pope, Jesse D, 40, 105, 124
Pope, John L., 209
Pope, T. J., 184, 229
Pope, T. W., 140
Pope, W. E., 6, 70, 123, 125, 135, 234
Pope, W. W., 236
Popham/Pophern, 186
Pophern, A. J., 186
Porter & Haralson, 145, 149
Porter, A. C., 241
Porter, B. F., 22, 164, 170
Porter, B. H., 263
Porter, Benj. J., 52
Porter, Berry, 180
Porter, Brad, 11
Porter, C. C., 156, 157, 158, 164, 173, 180, 182, 225
Porter, J. D., 251
Porter, James D., 196
Porter, James, 21, 165, 180
Porter, Jane, 21
Porter, John R., 170
Porter, Nancy, 59
Porter, O. C., 124, 241
Porter, Richard, 165
Porter, Richardson, 180
Porter, Silas, 165, 180
Potter, Richard, 13
Povvy & Parks, 115
Powel, C., 217
Powel, Charity, 217
Powell, B. M., 102
Powell, Charity, 218
Powell, D. W., 209
Powell, J. C., 57
Powell, J. E., 102
Powell, J. S., 46
Powell, Jno. S., 46
Powell, R. M., 103
Powell, W. H., 89
Powers, O. S., 189
Pratt, J. J., 180
Pratt, John, 22
Pratt, Jonathan, 164
Prenell, Mary, 16
Presley & Cook, 140
Presley, C. M., 131, 132, 133, 137
Presley, I. M., 1, 35, 39, 40, 48, 54, 57, 60, 63, 66, 73, 78, 79, 81, 88, 94, 105, 106, 117, 140, 190, 206, 207, 211, 219, 226, 241, 249, 253
Presley, Isbell, 121
Presley, J. M., 8
Pressgrove, J. S., 108
Pressley & Isbell, 20
Pressley, I. M., 17
Pressly, H. M., 223
Presswood, Francis M., 13
Presswood, Will, 73
Prestwood. P. B., 213
Preswood, Sarah J., 46
Preswood, Wilson, 13
Previn, Elizabeth, 165
Previtt, Calvin, 22
Previtt, Henley, 50
Prewitt, Rebecca, 4
Prewitt/Pruett, 226
Price, B. N., 252
Price, Bass, 122
Price, Benjamin, 252
Price, Cornelia E., 208
Price, G. W., 152
Price, Henderson, 171
Price, J. L., 259
Price, J. M., 208
Price, J., 193
Price, Jack, 258
Price, James M., 92, 208
Price, Lewis, 165, 180
Price, Lewis, 180, 258
Price, M. M., 208
Price, Quinn, 259
Price, R. L., 31
Price, R. S., 93, 208, 228
Price, R., 32
Price, Riley, 259
Price, Roxie, 258
Prigmore, E. M., 61
Prince, Joe S., 186
Prince, Joseph S., 186
Pritt?, J. C., 142
Privett Heirs, 49, 50
Privett S. L., 51
Privett, Charles, 50
Privett, Elisha, 50
Privett, Eliza, 50
Privett, Ervin, 50
Privett, F. F., 212
Privett, Frank, 49, 212, 223, 225
Privett, Fred, 50
Privett, George, 49
Privett, Glenn, 50
Privett, James C., 232
Privett, James, 165
Privett, Jessie, 50
Privett, Joseph, 50
Privett, Lillian, 50
Privett, Napolean, 49
Privett, Paines C., 144
Privett, Pleasant, 50
Privett, Sally, 50
Privett, Thompson, 50
Privett, William, 50
Privitt, 146
Prouty, James L, Jr., 67
Pruett, A. S., Capt., 84
Pruett, H. A. 226
Pruett, Hattie, 226
Pruett, J. M., 72
Pruett, J. R., 226
Pruett, L. C., 140
Pruett, L. J., 134
Pruett, P. D., 105, 233
Pruett, S. L., 20, 72, 139
Pruett, W. W., 253
Pruitt, J. W., 122
Pruitt, S. L., 140

Puckett, Elizabeth, 34
Puckett, Silas, 34
Pugh, A., 100, 103
Purcell, Mary, 15
Pursell, John, 130
Puvin, C., 249
Pyron, W. C., 95
Quillen, Manervia, 59
Quillen, Manervy, 59
Quimby, David, 240
Quin & Co., 49, 135
Quin & Wright, 21
Quin, Jos. J., 36
Quin, Mary J., 107
Quin, W. E. & Co., 108, 134
Quin, W. E., 7, 18, 41, 55, 74, 103, 106, 110
Quin, W. E., Dr., 52
Quinn & Wright, 149
Raburn, Rebecca, 165
Rachel Conway, 70
Ragan, Bonnie, 187
Ragan, John C., 83
Ragan/Rogan, J. C., 137
Ragesdales, Mary A., 139
Ragland, 136
Ragland, Patrick, 23
Ragon, J. C., 215
Raines, 186
Raines, Buck, 165, 180
Raines, Mollie, 186
Raines, Saml., 165
Rainey, S. L., 131
Rains, J. P., 102
Rains, Robert, 90, 128
Rains, Samuel, 180
Rains, Wm. H., 173
Raley, J. C., 122
Raley, Matthias, 26
Raley, W. C., 27
Raley, W. H., 122
Rallings, J. 146
Ralls, Jno., 252
Ralls/Rolls, 251
Ramey, C. C., 152
Ramey, John, 156, 158
Ramey, S., 168
Ramsey, A. C., 126
Ramsey, D. C., 257
Ramsey, G. W., 250, 251
Ramsey, H. R., 98
Ramsey, H., 102
Ramsey, John W., 254
Ramsey, John, 103, 165
Ramsey, John, 97
Ramsey, R. H. & A. C., 126
Ramsey, Richard, 180
Ramsey, Rich'd., 165
Ramsy, D. C., 258
Ramsy, David, 256
Ramy, B., 126
Ramy, John, 55
Randall, John, 5
Randolph, 107
Randolph, Jennie, 107, 110
Rane/Rave, 89
Rankin, Albert, 180
Rankin, J., 214
Rape, W. M., 77
Raper, Sarah, 12
Rave, C. W., 89
Ravlin, Albert, 165
Rawlings & Hooke, 220
Rawlings, John, 231
Rawlings, W., 231
Rawlston, Alex, 12
Ray, Charles W., 196
Ray, Elizabeth, 59
Ray, Huddleton, 180
Ray, Middleton, 165
Ray, Sallie E. Green, 196
Ray/Rea, 196
Rayburn, Rebecca, 180
Raymond, Walter B., 36
Rea, E. W., 196
Rea, Sallie, 196
Read, Marion, 165
Reaves, Hugh, 225
Rector, Elijah, 170
Rector, J. A., 100
Redden, Reeve, 180
Reddick, James, 197
Redmond, Nathan, 256, 257
Reece, A. D., 109
Reece, Andrew, 143, 212, 220, 226, 232
Reece, Dovine, 64
Reece, G. W., 170
Reece, Henry, 122
Reece, I. (J.), 26
Reece, J. J., 258
Reece, John, 180, 230
Reece, Jos., Sr., 170
Reece, M., 115
Reece, Robt., 170
Reece, Wm. S., 212
Reed, Amy, 23, 165
Reed, Amy, Mrs., 180
Reed, Ben, 165
Reed, Berry, 180, 182
Reed, C. C., 68
Reed, Carrie, 69
Reed, Cornelia C., 68, 69
Reed, Emma L., 69
Reed, George, 165, 180, 256, 257
Reed, James P., 68
Reed, James, 22, 195, 201, 202
Reed, James, Sen., 165
Reed, James, Sr., 180
Reed, Julian, 95
Reed, Mary, 93
Reed, Nancy, 165
Reed, Sarah C., 70
Reed, Sarah M. 216
Reed, Susan, 165
Reed, Susan, Mrs., 180
Reed, W. D., 52, 61, 68, 69 108, 110, 125, 149, 191, 192, 213, 227,
Reed, Walter, 93
Reed, William D., 68
Reed/Reece, B. A., 216
Reeds School, 135
Rees, D. V., 126, 252
Rees, J. C., 126
Rees, James, 231
Rees, John, 126, 153, 165, 168, 196, 232, 251
Rees, T. G., 252
Rees, T. L., 252
Rees, Thomas, 232
Reese & Rogers, 145
Reese, Anderson, 142
Reese, Andrew, 25
Reese, John, 150, 151, 155
Reese, Martin, 222
Reese, Samuel, 206
Reese, Thomas S., 155
Reese, W. S., 26
Reese, Wiley, 207
Reese, William, 59
Reeve, Daniel M., 84
Reeve, Hester A., 84
Reeve, Hester, 84
Reeve, Hugh, 178, 180
Reeve, James A., 84
Reeve, James L., 263
Reeve, Jas. A., 165
Reeve, Julia A., 84
Reeve, N. V., 263
Reeve, N. W., 250
Reeve, Seme O., 165
Reeves, 21
Reeves, A. J., 249
Reeves, Berry, Mrs., 119
Reeves, C. A., 119
Reeves, C. C., 88
Reeves, Charles A., 119
Reeves, D. B., 132
Reeves, E (C). R., 55
Reeves, E. B., 249
Reeves, E., 257
Reeves, Eliz., 165
Reeves, Ezekial B., 249
Reeves, F. Hugh, 22
Reeves, G. W., 119
Reeves, Geo. W., 118, 119
Reeves, George, 119
Reeves, Hannah J., 249
Reeves, Hugh, 162, 223
Reeves, J. H., 165
Reeves, J. L., 94
Reeves, James A., 250
Reeves, James H., 249
Reeves, James P., 249
Reeves, Julia, 49
Reeves, Mary Elisa, 249
Reeves, N. M., 119
Reeves, Noah, 256
Reeves, O. A., 139
Reeves, Redding, 165
Reeves, Reuben J., 249
Reeves, Sarah A., 249
Reeves, Simeon O., 172
Reeves, Sintha, 59
Reeves, Smith, 59
Reeves, T. W., 55
Reeves. J. A., 263
Reid, Lucy, 241
Reister, John Edwards, 64
Relly, C., 84
Rena, Negro Woman, 31
Renfro, T. H., 192
Renfro, Tom, 261
Renfroe, Bob, 109
Republican Union Newspaper, 42
Republican Union, 206
Revel, E. R., 77
Rex?, J. D.. 24
Reynolds, Mary,
Reynolds, R. H., 122
Reynolds, W. W., 122
Reynolds, Wm., 165, 182
Rhea, Lewis, 217, 218
Rhodes, W., 22
Rhodes, Wm., 26, 165, 168
Rhudy, Jacob, 175
Rice, Ayonah, 180
Rice, C. M., 92
Rice, D. W., 126
Rice, J. A., 215
Rice, J., 165
Rice, James, 147
Rice, Joe, 143
Rice, John & Martha, 7
Rice, Jos., 165
Rice, Joseph, 143, 146, 180, 225
Rice, Miller, 165, 180
Rice, T. S., 126
Rice, Walter, 71
Rich, Elijah, 165, 172, 173

Rich, T. M., 94
Richard, John, 170
Richard, Robert, 180
Richards, C. H., 165
Richards, C., 180
Richards, John, 165, 174
Richards, Maggie, 113
Richards, Mary Lilly, 113
Richardson, John, 192
Richey, A. P., 89
Richey, Lumpkin, 210
Richey, Wm., 29
Richolson, ?,10
Riddle (Biddle), William H., 18
Riddle(Biddle), Minnerva, 18
Riddle, Lewis, 239, 240
Riddle, R. R., 123
Riddle, Thomas, 18
Riddle, Tyre, 165, 173
Riddle, W. R., 121, 123
Riddlespunger, Eliz. Ann, 165
Riddlespunger, Old Lady, 165
Rider, __, 109
Rider, F. M., 109
Riders, F. M., 17
Ridgeway W. P., 92
Ridgeway, W. M., 73
Ridway, W. F., 90
Riggs, W. M., 221
Riggs, Wm., 165
Right, Hannah, 250
Right, John, 250
Riley, J. C., 212
Riley, J. M., 46
Riley, John, 60, 240
Rinehart, M., 144
Rink, Jno. F., 9
Rink, John F., 232
Risk, John R., 9
Robbins, Walker, 63
Roberson, David, 239
Robert, Chas., 118, 119
Roberts, 204
Roberts, Bertha, 48
Roberts, C. Y., 39, 104
Roberts, C., 165
Roberts, Calvin, 29, 49, 173, 180
Roberts, Charles, 39, 93
Roberts, Chas., 66, 67
Roberts, Dallis, 48
Roberts, E. F., 39
Roberts, E. J., 104
Roberts, Emma, 39, 104
Roberts, Emma, Mrs., 104
Roberts, Eva, 36
Roberts, F. M., 36, 87, 120, 148
Roberts, G. W., 67, 69, 137, 239, 240
Roberts, G. W., Sr., 66
Roberts, Geo. W., 190
Roberts, George R.,Sr., 148
Roberts, George W., 69
Roberts, George, 204
Roberts, I. B., 95, 96
Roberts, Isam, 222
Roberts, Isham B., 23
Roberts, Isham, 95, 157, 158, 165, 180
Roberts, J. C., 194
Roberts, J. M., 148
Roberts, J. R., 36
Roberts, J. W., 29, 66, 68, 95, 192
Roberts, James, 223
Roberts, Joe G., 62
Roberts, John A., 165
Roberts, Kent, 48
Roberts, L. F., 235, 240
Roberts, M. J., 68
Roberts, Minervia, 36
Roberts, Nancy J., 93
Roberts, Nannie, 67
Roberts, Phillip R., 143
Roberts, R. M., 96
Roberts, R., 96, 135, 153, 168, 231
Roberts, Richard, 22, 113, 142, 153, 210
Roberts, Rich'd., 165
Roberts, S. E., (Sallie), 69
Roberts, Sallie E., 67, 68, 69
Roberts, Syntha, 38
Roberts, Thomas, 13
Roberts, W. G., 36
Roberts, W. I., 146
Roberts, W. J., 68, 143, 170, 244, 260
Roberts, W. P., 68
Roberts, W. R., 66, 67
Roberts, W. T., 68
Roberts, William J. 56, 152
Roberts, William, 235, 239, 240
Robertson, A. P., 187
Robertson, David, 235, 240
Robertson, E. L., 187
Robertson, J. A.. 1
Robertson, John, 173, 180
Robertson, Lindsay, 174
Robertson, Lindsey, 165, 180
Robinson, Ada, 261
Robinson, Andy, 69, 94
Robinson, Audy, 117
Robinson, Charlotte, 261
Robinson, D. G., 247
Robinson, Evaline, 219
Robinson, Hiram, 14
Robinson, J. T., 64
Robinson, John, 165
Robinson, Luff, 261
Robinson, Noah, 261
Robinson, Rosa, 261
Robinson, Sylvester, 259
Robinson, William, 261
Rockhall, H., 11
Rockholt, L. A., Mrs., 117
Rockholt, Letitia A., 117
Rockholt, Tom, 117
Rocter, Elijah, 23
Rode, G. W., 11
Roden, Alex, 193
Roden, Anna E., 190
Roden, B. H., 250, 256, 257
Roden, C. F., 190
Roden, Calvin, 165, 180
Roden, G. F., 257
Roden, G. W., 98
Roden, Geo., 99, 191, 193
Roden, George, 199
Roden, H. E., 98, 100, 101, 103
Roden, J. B., 256
Roden, J. E., 98
Roden, J. M., 81, 127, 192, 197
Roden, J. W., 100
Roden, James, 62, 192, 258
Roden, Jeremiah, 256
Roden, John, 194, 235, 257
Roden, L. J., 119, 120, 121
Roden, Louisa J., 119
Roden, Louise Jane, 120
Roden, Mary, 199
Roden, Nip, 122
Roden, R. B., 98
Roden, T. C., 122
Roden, Taskon, 180
Roden, V. J. M., 191
Roden, W. B., 256, 257
Roden, W. L., 99, 191
Roden, W. N., Dr., 99
Roden, W. V., 62, 97
Roden, W. W., 8, 191, 256
Roden, Walsie, 97
Roden, William, 257
Roden, Wm. G., 97
Roden, Wm., 165
Roden, Z. T., 165
Roden, Z., 257
Roden, Zealious, 256
Roden, Zeolum, 256
Rodgers, F. R., 131
Rodgers, R. S., 15
Rodgers, Wright, 165
Roe, J. B., 101
Roe, J. W., 101
Roe, John, 59
Roe, R. B., 45, 100
Roe, Robert, 45
Rogers & Son, 131
Rogers, A. M., 15
Rogers, A. W., 15
Rogers, America Crabtree, 80
Rogers, B. A., 131
Rogers, Elijah & Davis, 94
Rogers, Elijah, 141, 148
Rogers, H. C., 243
Rogers, J. A., 214
Rogers, J. W., 139
Rogers, Joel C., 139
Rogers, John, 171, 194
Rogers, Mary A., 140, 141, 148
Rogers, R. C., 137
Rogers, R., 231
Rogers, Reece, 108, 136, 144, 145, 224, 231, 245
Rogers, Rees, 170, 224, 225
Rogers, Reese, 146, 171
Rogers, T. J., 139
Rogers, W. C., 241
Rogers, Will, 109
Rogers, William E., 67
Rogers, Wm., 94
Rogers, Wright, 180
Rollins, J. C., 101
Rolls, A. P., 251
Rone, J. F., 89
Rook, Job, 171
Rook, John J., 145
Rook, John T., 141
Rook, John, 147, 170, 232
Rook, Lilia A., 141
Rook, S. A., 145
Rook, Silva/Sylvia, 145
Rook, Silvey/Lilia, 142
Rook, Silvey/Sylvia/Lilia, 144
Rook, Sylvia A., 144
Rook, Sylvia, 145
Rook, Sylvian, 145
Rook, Wiley W., 165
Rooks, J., 144

Rooney, J. D., 7
Rorex, W. D., 136
Rorex, W. L., 136
Rose, B. D., 1
Rose, Fannie Garmany, 140
Rose, Fannie, 140
Rose, R. F., 2
Rose, Sarah R., 139
Roseborough, S. B., 12
Ross, George, 251
Ross, J. W., 60
Ross, John, 60, 165, 180
Ross, Lem C., 36
Rothell, __, 110
Rothwell, George, 218
Rowan, Saml., 165
Rowden, J. C., 143
Rowe, Charles P., 67
Rowen, Samuel, 172
Rowlins, John, 144
Rubedont, Nanne, 101
Rucks, C. P., 87
Rucks, Celphia, 165
Rucks, E. P., 65, 72, 124, 132
Rucks, Elisha P., 124
Rucks, G. W., 165, 180
Rucks, J. F., 231
Rucks, J. T., 190
Rucks, J. W., 57
Rucks, Joel T., 190
Rucks, M. F., 124
Rucks, Mary Frances, 124
Rucks, W. A., 190
Rucks, W., 193
Rudy, Jacob, 165
Rupell, 114
Rus, John, 130
Rush, W. D., 98
Ruskin, J. T., Dr., 7
Russ, C. C., 16
Russ, Wm., 59
Russel, Chas., 204
Russell, A. G., 77, 90
Russell, Amelia, 107
Russell, Andy, 235, 239, 240
Russell, B. J., 78
Russell, B. Y., 78
Russell, C. A., 83, 158
Russell, C. H., 78
Russell, Charlie, 204
Russell, D. C., 258
Russell, Dr., 244
Russell, H. C., 78, 226
Russell, J. E., 7, 40, 136, 209
Russell, J. H., 78
Russell, James E., 6
Russell, Kate, 78
Russell, M. L., 78
Russell, Mathew, 13
Russell, Matilda J., 11
Russell, Miles R., 14
Russell, R. M., 78, 165
Russell, S. L. 212
Russell, Sam, 78
Russell, W. W., 1, 2, 52, 57, 63, 73, 74, 109, 112, 134
Russell, W. W., Gen. Mdse., 227
Russell, W., 110
Rutledge, David, 129
Rutledge, E., J., 191
Rutledge, M. J., 110
Rutledge, W., 60
Rutleely?, S & Berry, 186
Rutsey, E. J., 192
Ryan, A. A., 239
Ryan, A. L., 170
Ryan, Albert, 197
Ryan, Amos, 22, 23, 157, 158, 165, 180
Ryan, L. E., 236
Ryan, Luther, 236
Ryan, Marshall, 23, 165
Ryan, Peter, 165, 173
Ryan, R. M., 62
Ryan, Robert, 62
Ryan, S., 5
Ryan, Samuel M., 180, 222
Ryan, Seaman, 22
Ryan, Thomas, 197
Ryan, W. T., 74, 75
Ryan, William, 115
Ryan, Wm., 23, 96, 165, 221
Ryon, Thomas, 8
Ryon, W. C., 88, 94
Sadler, Keziah, 13
Saffolds, L. L., 57
Sammons, Nelson, 165
Samole, W. M., 143
Sample, Jesse, 224
Sample, W. M., 142
Samples, B., 8
Samples, W. M., 143
Sampley, B. H., 8
Sampley, Bradford, 8
Sampley, J. C., 212
Sampley, Jesse C., 104
Sampley, Mr., 261
Sampley, Nancy Ann, 8
Sampley, Oliver, 55
Sampley, Samuel, 55
Sampley, Theodore55,
Sampley, W., 230, 232
Sampley, Wm., 146
Samply, W. N., 232
Samuel Scroggins Place55,
Sanborn, Betsy Brown, 44
Sanborn, George W., 44
Sander, C., 39
Sanders, Harrison, 166
Sanders, Thos., 118
Sanders, W. T., 117
Sandy, 64
Sanford & Farnum, 131
Sanford, James, 240
Sanford, James, Jr., 239
Sanford, John A., 38
Sansom, F. M., 168
Sansom, Lemuel, 218
Sansom, Owe M., 218
Sanson, M. & R. H., 217
Sanson, Mary, 218
Sanson, Owen, 126
Sansum, M., 251
Sargent, Artie, 125
Sargent, G. D., 20
Sargent, Julia Baxter, 20
Sargent, Julia, 252
Sargent, Maria A., 240
Sargent, Roberta Elrod, 125
Sargent, Roberta, 125
Sargent, S. D., 63
Sarrett, W. B., 144
Sarton, Johnson, 45
Sarton, Mrs., 121
Sarton, W. T., 118, 120
Saterfield, Jesse, 166
Saterwhite, David, 11, 13
Satterfield, G. C., 241
Satterfield, Grover & Pearl, 241
Satterfield, Grover, 241
Satterfield, J. E., 89
Satterfield, Jesse, 181
Satterfield, Pearl, 241
Sauls, D. W., 126
Sauls, John, 98
Sauls, O. N., 97, 100
Saunders, Harrison, 173
Sawyer, C. M. T., 94, 106
Sawyer, C. M., 110, 131
Sawyer, Charles M. T., 186
Sawyer, Charles, 108
Sawyer, Chas M., 120
Sawyer, Chas. M. T., 93
Sawyer, Chas., 117
Sawyer, M. T., 242
Sawyers, Charles M. T., 120
Sawyers, Chas. M. T., 63, 67
Sawyers, Chas., 240
Saye, H. P.105
Saye, J. H., Mrs., 91
Saye, W. W., 105
Sayers, Frances, 212
Schwelz Bros., 52
Scot, W. P., 217
Scott, 255
Scott, Calvin, 77
Scott, Charles, 133
Scott, Chas. J., 209, 234
Scott, D. A., 98, 98
Scott, D. M., 125
Scott, D. O., 99
Scott, Dave, 98
Scott, G. B., 98
Scott, G. V., 74
Scott, G. W., 73
Scott, J. C., 104
Scott, J. H., 7
Scott, J. M., 99, 106
Scott, J.W.T., 4
Scott, John, 36
Scott, Martin F., 237
Scott, N., 156
Scott, Newton, 158
Scott, Roxie, 54, 133
Scott, Thomas, 26
Scott, Thos., 145
Scotts, Lizzie, 97
Scruggs, John, 11
Se_berry, S. C., 181
Seaman, Samuel, 114
Seamone, Saml., 224
Sears, J. M., 28
Sedberry, S. H., 166
Segmire, Sam'l., 22
Self, J. C., 77
Sellers, Martha, 238
Sells, A. A., 34
Sells, Jno. T., 246
Semore, Wm., 238
Setze, James, 231
Seymore, G. W., 255
Seymore, J. F., 255
Seymore, Saml., 22
Shadwick (Chadwick), 34
Shadwick, Agenetta, 34
Shadwick, J., 148
Shadwick, James, 34
Shaffer, Samuel, 30
Shankle, Jesa, 19
Shankle, Lesa, 18
Shankles, Alice, 123
Shankles, B. R., 24
Shankles, Elizabeth, 71
Shankles, G. W, 1
Shankles, Geo. W., 1
Shankles, George, 8
Shankles, Hannah, 24
Shankles, Hanner, 24
Shankles, Jesse, 24, 48

Shankles, Jno., 9
Shankles, John?, 123
Shankles, July, 9
Shankles, Nancy Ann, 8
Shankles, Robt., 9
Shankles, Sallie, 133
Shankles, Sally, 133
Shannon, James R., 124
Sharf, D. J. & Co., 43
Sharop, Katt B., 137
Shasteen , John, 9
Shasteen, Jno., 9
Shasteen, John, 9
Shaw, H. E., 61
Shaw, Hogan, 247
Shaw, R. H., 247
Shaw, Wm. F., 240
Sheffard, James M., 63
Shelley & Taffanstatt, 91
Shelley, Frank, 221
Shelley, Georgia L., 221
Shelley, Georgia Lue, 222
Shelley, Isabelle, 222
Shelley, Mattie J., 222
Shelley, R. J., 248
Shelley, Robert, 222
Shelley, Talley, 221
Shelley, Talley, et al, 221
Shelley, W. L., 91
Shelley, W. T., 222
Shelton, A. W., 8
Shelton, J. W., 122
Shelton, John, 223
Shelton, M. T., 122
Shelton, W. T., 59
Shepard, 58
Shepherd, Anna E., 149
Shepherd, Anna, 149
Shepherd, Dr., 108
Shepherd, G. W. J., 110, 149
Sheppard, A. W., 251
Sheppard, W.D.J., Dr., 149
Sheppards, Anderson W., 143
Sherherd, G. W. T., 110
Sherman, J. R., 259
Sherman, J. R., MD, 259
Sherman, James R., 85
Sherman, John, MD, 85
Shirley, 203
Shirley, John, 200, 201, 204
Shirly, M. L., 92
Shivers, Nettie. 7
Shocum, E. T., 64
Shook, A. J., 222
Shook, O S., 56, 175, 180
Shook, O., 170
Shop, AGS, 254
Shrader, Fenie, 46
Shrum, David, 126, 251
Shrum, J. N., 251
Shrum, James N., 251
Shuffield, Isham, 218
Shuffield, J., 83, 84
Sibert & Co., 255
Sibert, H., 154
Sibert, Henry, 154, 166, 167, 173
200, 201, 204, 205, 216
Sibert, J. W., 167, 250, 255
Sibert, Jadie/Josie, 94
Sibert, John W., 152, 168, 249, 255
Sibert, John, 42, 232
Sibert, Josie, Mrs., 94
Sibert, Wm., 166, 181
Silbert, H. & Co., 232
Simes, James R., 174
Simmons, H. P., 101
Simon, T., 158
Simons, Lee, 260
Simpson, C. L., 260, 261
Simpson, Claude, 260
Simpson, Cummings, 11, 34
Simpson, J., 156, 185
Simpson, James, 3, 4, 165, 239
Simpson, Jim, 2
Simpson, John, 235, 239, 240
Simpson, M. W., 98, 99, 100
Simpson, Mack, 109
Simpson, N. H., 49
Simpson, R., 185
Simpson, S. B., 222, 226
Simpson, W. A., 90
Simpson, W. H., 49
Simpson, W. W., 260
Simpson, Will, 260
Sims, A. L., 260
Sims, Alice F. (Allie), 260
Sims, E., Mrs., 166
Sims, Elizabeth, Miss, 181
Sims, J. A., 193
Sims, J. R., 173
Sims, James R., 166, 180
Sims, Jesse M., Jr., 94
Sims, Jesse, 94
Sims, W. J., 158, 166, 170, 233
Sims, W. N., 36
Sims, W. O., 157
Sims, W., 171
Sims, William, 173
Sims, Wm. J., 168, 170
Sims, Wm., 156, 180
Sinard, J. T., 118
Sinard, W. E., 203
Singer Mfg. Co., 40
Siniard, 203
Siniard, Ewie, 260
Siniard, J. D., 168
Siniard, J. W., 195, 200, 201, 204
Siniard, James, 158
Siniard, Mattie, 260
Siniard, Mattie, Mrs., 62
Siniard, Mrs., 201, 204
Siniard, Palistine, 64
Siniard, Tom, 202
Siniard, W. D., 197
Siniard, Wilborn, 197
Siniard, Wm., 202
Sisemore, A. G., 10
Sisemore, Richland, 10
Sisemore, Wofford, 183
Sisk, Luiza, 217
Sitrye, William, 251
Sitton, John, 13
Sitz, John, 231
Sivone, J. W., 221
Sizemore, A. G., 11, 35, 208
Sizemore, A. J., 11
Sizemore, Allen, 12
Sizemore, F. J., 123
Sizemore, I. H., 11
Sizemore, J. S., 120, 121
Sizemore, Mrs., 121
Sizemore, Richard, 11, 13
Sizemore, Tennessee Agnes, 46
Sizemore, W. H., 110
Slaten, J. F., 102
Slater, P. L., 87
Slaton, B. F., 18, 19
Slaton, C. G. (T.G.), 11
Slaton, Elisha, 70
Slaton, Elizabeth, 181
Slaton, J. F., 99
Slaton, J. M., 183, 184
Slaton, Jane, 18
Slaton, Polly Ann, 70
Slaton, Robert, 15
Slaton, Susan, 70
Slattan, Thomas, 12
Slatton, Carrison, 13
Slatton, E. A., 18
Slatton, John, 35
Slaughter, 185
Slaughter, M., 185
Slaughter, Malinda, 182, 184
Slaughter, Perry R., 182
Slaughter, Pleas, 184
Slaughter, Pleasant R., 184
Slaughter, V. H., 182
Slaughter, V., 185
Slaughter, Virginia, 182, 184
Slaughter, W. L, 2, 3
Slaughter, W. R., 182, 184
Slaughter, W., 185
Slaughter, William R., 183
Slay, J. M., 42
Slayton, E. A., 26
Slayton, Eliz., 166
Slayton, S. C., 166
Slayton, Stephen C., 64
Slayton, Stephen, 171, 172, 181
Slicgog?, Richard, 143
Sloan & Hawkins, 145, 146
Sloan, Delilah, 243
Sloan, James, 203
Slone & Hawkins, 113
Slone (Stone) Jesse, 8
Slone, 137
Slone, Bill, 235, 240
Slone, Jesse, 5, 63, 236
Slone, Lula Condra, 71
Slone, S. B., 36, 72, 80, 94, 127, 229
Slone, Sam C., 71
Slone, William, 113
Small, 114
Small, Baxter, 157, 171
Small, Eddie, 203
Small, Eddy, 201
Small, Emma E., 200
Small, H. C., 202
Small, H. W., 232
Small, H., 200, 202
Small, Harriet, 194, 202
Small, Henry, 66, 76, 194, 195, 200, 201, 203
Small, I. B., 263
Small, J. B., 263
Small, Jesse, 232
Small, M. A., 202
Small, M. L., 78
Small, Mathew, 30
Small, Matthew, 182
Small, R. B., 262
Small, W. A., 194, 195, 200, 201, 202, 203, 204
Small, W. A., 77
Small, W. H., 195
Small, W., 200
Small, Wm., 200, 204
Smalley, G. M., 73

Smed?, Thomas D., 142
Smedley, J. R., 166
Smedley, John R., 173
Smiley, Wm. D., 232
Smith & Malone, 110
Smith & Meeks, 207
Smith & Roberts, 68
Smith & Rogers Gen. Mdse., 227
Smith, R. M., 194
Smith, 255
Smith, A. B., 55, 254
Smith, A. P., 65
Smith, A. T., 189, 191, 211
Smith, A. W., Treas., 118
Smith, A., 185
Smith, Allen, 194
Smith, Andrew J., 124
Smith, B. F., 26
Smith, B. N., 118, 192, 193
Smith, B., 11
Smith, Baswell, 118
Smith, Benjamin, 233
Smith, Beulah Gilliland, 188
Smith, Beulah, 188
Smith, Bonnie M., 43
Smith, Bonnie, Mrs., 43
Smith, C. G., 11
Smith, C. W., 118, 120
Smith, Caroline, 253
Smith, Carroll, 11
Smith, Charles W., 65, 130
Smith, Charlie, 194, 201
Smith, Chas. W., 97
Smith, Chichester & Young, 108
Smith, D. M., 24
Smith, D. R., 80
Smith, D. S., 194
Smith, Daniel, 10
Smith, Dave, 193
Smith, David, 11, 24, 193
Smith, E. J., 190, 192
Smith, E. L., 194
Smith, E. M., 189
Smith, E. P., 80
Smith, Echols, Brunett Hdwe Co., 97
Smith, Ed, 166
Smith, Edward, 173
Smith, Elisha, 24, 166, 181
Smith, Eliz., Mrs., 166
Smith, Eliza R., 166
Smith, Eliza R., Miss, 181
Smith, Eliza, 223
Smith, Elizabeth, 186, 191, 192, 199
Smith, Elizabeth, Mrs., 181
Smith, Felix, 166, 181
Smith, Frank, 90
Smith, G. H., 8
Smith, G. W., 202
Smith, George S., 68
Smith, Grey, 11
Smith, H. B., 250
Smith, H. F., 118
Smith, H. H., 81, 258, 260
Smith, Hardy', (Place), 36
Smith, Hardy, 35
Smith, Henry E., 166, 181
Smith, Henry H., 38, 254
Smith, Henry, 9, 11, 13, 128, 253
Smith, Hiram, 10, 11, 13
Smith, Houston, 66
Smith, Huston, 118
Smith, Ida, 197
Smith, Ider, 238
Smith, J. B., 191, 253
Smith, J. C., 139
Smith, J. D., 191
Smith, J. G., 194
Smith, J. H., 192, 193, 194
Smith, J. L. F., 154
Smith, J. L., 24
Smith, J. M., 122, 181
Smith, J. P., 192
Smith, J. S. D., 230
Smith, J. S., 118, 119
Smith, J. W. L., 142, 166
Smith, J. W., 93, 192
Smith, J., 24
Smith, Jack, 181
Smith, Jackson, 11, 153
Smith, James C., 139
Smith, James M., 166
Smith, James, 34, 90, 118, 121, 125, 166, 181, 183, 184, 187
Smith, Jane, 18, 24, 166, 221
Smith, Jane, Miss, 181
Smith, Jas. Wm., 166
Smith, Jeptha, 24
Smith, Jesse, 49, 253
Smith, Jey, 11
Smith, Joel, 166
Smith, John F., 97
Smith, John T., 54
Smith, John, 14, 80, 165, 257
Smith, Joseph J., Mrs., 182
Smith, Joseph, 18, 166, 181, 253
Smith, Julia, 66
Smith, L. H., 239
Smith, L. M., 128
Smith, L., 8
Smith, Levosa, 35
Smith, Lomey, 33, 47
Smith, Loney, 3, 4, 15, 183, 184
Smith, Lucinda C., 10
Smith, M. D., 261
Smith, M. L., 65
Smith, M. V., 27, 80, 183, 253
Smith, M. W., 260
Smith, M., 128
Smith, Maria, 166
Smith, Mariah, 181
Smith, Marinda, 43
Smith, Martha, 253
Smith, Mary Amelia, 67
Smith, N. C., Mrs., 260
Smith, Nancy M., 65
Smith, Nancy, 166
Smith, Nancy, Miss, 181
Smith, P. C., 91
Smith, P. H., 245
Smith, P. J., 42, 206, 214, 242, 244
Smith, P. L., 80
Smith, Peter, 59
Smith, R. H., 66, 94, 260
Smith, R. M., 191, 193
Smith, Rhody, 180
Smith, Robert, 59
Smith, Rufina, 8
Smith, S. C., 152
Smith, S. E., 139
Smith, S. E., Jr., 139
Smith, S. J., 150, 154, 168
Smith, S. L., 24
Smith, S. M., 61
Smith, S. P., 84, 97, 190
Smith, S. P., Dr., 187
Smith, S. P., MD, 259
Smith, Salley, 70
Smith, Sally, 70
Smith, Sam P., Dr., 83
Smith, Saml., 166
Smith, Samuel, 139
Smith, Sarah J., 182
Smith, Sarah Jane, 165, 221
Smith, Sarah T., 24
Smith, Sarah, 180
Smith, Sarah, Miss, 166
Smith, Sherman, 122
Smith, T. H., 43, 57, 120, 149, 208
Smith, T. H., Mrs., 108, 110
Smith, T. J., 207
Smith, Thom. H, 227
Smith, Thomas A., 24
Smith, Thomas H., 5, 18, 21, 38, 46, 52, 61, 74, 84, 110, 124, 139, 226, 237
Smith, Thomas N., 7
Smith, Thomas S., 60, 106
Smith, Thomas, 53, 70, 85, 166, 181
Smith, Thos. H., 249, 254, 262
Smith, Thos. H., 41, 76, 88, 94, 120, 124, 184, 210-212, 234, 239, 246
Smith, Thos. S., 235
Smith, Tom, 199
Smith, W. A., 102, 191, 192, 193
Smith, W. C., 199
Smith, W. F., 61
Smith, W. H., 2, 3, 8
Smith, W. J., 43
Smith, W. L., 54, 232
Smith, W. O., 10, 183
Smith, W. S., 192
Smith, W., 202
Smith, Wilbur, 75
Smith, William O., 184
Smith, William, 8, 14, 19, 65, 180, 195, 257
Smith, Willis D., 197
Smith, Wm. O., 183
Smith, Wm., 10, 166, 194, 202, 204
Snider, C., 39, 112, 144, 230, 249, 251
Snider, Cornelius H., 112
Snider, Cornelius, 96
Snider, Delila, 166
Snider, Sehlar, 173
Snodgrass, 136
Snodgrass, A., 206
Snodgrass, Alex, 222
Snodgrass, Alexander, 23, 222
Snodgrass, Susan Jane, 222
So. Railroad Co., 54
Sookey, Negro Woman, 136
Sormond, J. M., 15
Sotherland, B. R., 206
Sotherlin, Wm. H., 207
Sou. Railway Co., 40
South, W. T., 124
Southerland, H. A., 76

Southerland, James, 166, 174
Southerland, M. E., 94, 95
Southerland, R. J. & R. B., 95
Southerland, Ralon, 197
Southerland, W. A., 74
Southerland, W. R., 207
Southerland, W., 230, 232
Southerland/Southerlen, 242
Southerlen, Caswell, 242
Southerlen, Nancy, 242
Southerlin, C. E., 47
Southerlin, Charley, 47
Souwell, G. W., 18
Span?, (Spear?) Emily, 28
Span?, (Spear?) William, 28
Spangler, A., 60
Spangler, Gid, 166
Spangler, Gidean, 23
Spangler, Isaac, 23, 113, 115
Spangler, Martha, 23, 113, 115
Spangler, Nath., 166
Spangler, Nathan, 114, 173, 181
Spangler, Old Man, 181
Sparks, Butler, 236
Sparks, Howell O., 97
Sparks, J. F., 92
Sparks, J., 72
Sparks, Manda, 102
Sparks, N. O., 47
Sparks, R., 77
Sparks, S., 103
Sparks, Samuel, 102
Sparks, W. A., 102
Spaulding, 58
Spaulding, J. S., 112
Spears, Mrs., 110
Spears, W. H., 109
Spears, W. L. & O. L., 92
Spears, W. T., 91
Spears, Will, 109
Spence, Hellen, 108
Spence, Martin V., 124
Spencer, G. M. D., 70
Spencer, H. L., 191
Spencer, Henry T., 124
Spencer, Ida E., 124
Spencer, J. C, 73
Spencer, W. A., 83
Spring, David, 5
Spring, I. W., 29
Springs, Henry, 207
Springs, Jordan, 207
Stackman/Stockman, R. L., 74
Staff, James, 91
Stafford, Anderson, 14
Stafford, Bessie, 50
Stafford, J. A., 235, 239, 240
Stafford, J. M., 104
Stafford, Jennie, 50, 51
Stafford, Jennie, Mrs., 49
Stafford, M., 218
Stafford, Mahlon, 9
Stafford, N. A., 11, 14
Stafford, Rosa S., 236
Stafford, W. P., 235
Stafford, Wm. R., 224
Stalvey, G. W., 80, 122
Stalvey, George, 79
Stalvey, Lizzie, 81
Stalvey, Lizzie, Mrs., 79
Stamps, E. R., 112
Stanaffer, Lemuel J., 209
Stanaffer, William H., 209
Stancil, 201
Stancil, J. M., 102
Standfield, Geo. R., 166
Standifer, Lemuel J., 218
Stanfield, G. R., 263
Stanfield, Geo., 170
Stanley, J. P., 107
Stanley, J. T., 45
Stanton, Almed L., 258
Stanton, Thomas L., 258
Stapler, Amos, 166, 181
Staples, John L., 39
Stapp, Eunice E., 89
Stapp, Eunice, 88
Stapp, Jno., 75
Starling, Mrs., 166
Starling, Old Man, 182
Starnes, B. R., 137, 153, 154, 262
Starnes, Basil R., 262
Starnes, Basil, 137
Starnes, Basis & Rachel, 137
Starnes, John, 223
Starnes, Rachel, 137
State of Alabama, 74
Staton, Elisha, 71
Staton, G. W., 8
Steavens, C. H., 45
Steel, Alexander, 34, 35
Steel, Amanda J., 4
Steel, Christopher, 11
Steel, Claude, 4
Steel, Isaac, 4, 14, 15
Steel, James, 2, 3, 15
Steel, John, 11, 33, 214, 233
Steel, Levi, 14
Steel, Malvina, 4
Steel, Maude, 4
Steel, Millie Blevins, 33
Steel, Ransom, 11
Steel, W. A., 2, 15, 77, 124, 183, 235
Steel, W. H., 3
Steel, Wyatt, 184
Steele, Daisy, Mrs., 30
Steele, John, 33
Steele, W. A., 34, 44, 45, 211
Steele, Wyatt, 183
Stelvey (Stalvey), 80
Stephen, Bob, 252
Stephens, B. A., 194
Stephens, Bob, 191
Stephens, E. C., 252
Stephens, E. C., Mrs., 252
Stephens, E. G. H., 110, 252
Stephens, E. T., 119
Stephens, J. M., 73
Stephens, J. R. T., 16
Stephens, J. R., 100
Stephens, James, 233
Stephens, Jas., 253
Stephens, Mary, 13
Stephens, Maud, 253
Stephens, Sarah Jane Holland, 233
Stephens, Sarah, 233
Stephens, Slayton, 225
Stephens, W. C., 91
Stephens, Walter, 94
Stephens, Willis, 13
Stephenson, J. M., 236
Stephenson, Willard, 188
Stesophy, Isaac, 182
Stevens, J. W., 73
Stevens, Levi, 55,
Stevensen/Stephenson, Willard, 188
Stevenson, J. M. & S. A., 90
Stevenson, O. B., 121
Steward, S. W., 239
Steward/Stewart, 248
Stewart, Benajah, 248
Stewart, D. B., 183, 184
Stewart, Eliza, 143
Stewart, J. I., 96
Stewart, J. J., 141, 142
Stewart, J. L., 96
Stewart, John J., 96, 141, 142, 144, 145, 146, 180, 244
Stewart, John, 142, 223, 232
Stewart, M. R., 202
Stewart, Margaret, 9
Stewart, N. C., 263
Stewart, Nancy, 141, 145
Stewart, R. A. 110
Stewart, Robert, 14, 149
Stewart, S. W., 137, 235
Stewart, Sam, 239, 240
Stewart, Samuel, 9, 262
Stewart, Sarah, 248
Stewart, T. G., 141
Stewart, Thomas G., 7, 24, 38, 44, 64, 78
Stewart, Thomas, 108
Stewart, Thos. G., 24, 38, 64
Stiff, Edward, 22
Stiff, Joseph Edward, 143
Stiff, L. M., 145, 154, 166, 181, 218, 231
Stiff, L. W., 196
Stiff, Lellie, 154
Stinson, __, 109
Stinson, J. F., 52
Stinson, Mary, 133
Stinson, S. M., 52
Stintson, Robert, 60
Stockman, R. L., 76
Stockstill, James, 238
Stone, A., 149
Stone, B. C., 1, 140
Stone, B. W., 91
Stone, Bill, 239
Stone, J. B., 225
Stone, Joel, 224, 225
Stone, O. D., 91
Stone, Virgil, 42
Stone, W. B., 90
Stone, W. F., 10
Stone, W. J., 9
Stone/Slone, T.?, 127
Stoner, A., 149
Stoner, Caldean, 13
Stoner, Randolph, 12
Stoner, W. C., 104
Stoner, W. E., 30
Stonicher, T. W., 101
Stott, A. C., 126
Stott, D. M., 87
Stott, Drayton E., 87
Stott, Drayton M., 87
Stott, Drayton, 87
Stott, L. M., Jr., 87
Stott, Middleton, 125
Stott, W. M., 98, 99, 101
Stout, J. J., 231
Stout, J., 230
Stout, R., 31
Stout, Z., 232
Stout, Zeno, 24
Stovall, 185
Stovall, Eugene, 67

Stovall, Martha Victory, 67
Stovall, R. E., 67
Stowers, Charles, 126, 251
Stowers, Chas., 126
Stowers, John, 218, 238
Stowey, J., 257
Strawn, R. S., 99
Street, A. M., 61
Street, A., 9
Street, Alfred, 13
Street, E. O., 12
Street, Francis M., 214
Street, Malinda Hawkins, 214
Streets, Martha, 13
Strickland, A. B., 166, 175
Strickland, B. J, 75
Strickland, B., 168, 171
Strickland, Barbara, 69, 150, 152, 153, 168
Strickland, Barbary, 155
Strickland, Barby, 170
Strickland, Burrel, 153, 170
Strickland, Frank, 258
Strickland, L. M., 75
Stron, Hortman Holfin & Co., 207
Strong, Geo., 191
Strother, James, 9, 196
Strowd, J. D., 101
Stuart, B. S., 27
Stuart, J. J., 243
Stuart, Jane, 214
Stuart, John J., 147, 166
Stuart, John, 18, 68, 92
Stuart, Nancy, 147
Stuart, Samuel, 214
Stuart/Stewart, 147
Stubblefield, Melvinia, 59
Stubblefield, Melviry, 59
Sullivan, F. J., 114
Sullivan, Francis J., 114
Summerour, Ezekial, 127
Summerville, 105
Summerville, George, 105
Summerville, Glen, 105
Summerville, James, 105
Summerville, Josie D., 105
Summerville, S. L., 57
Summerville, Watson, 105
Sutherland, C. D., 243
Sutherland, Wm., 206
Sutten, Samuel, 146
Sutton, LeRoy, 233
Swader, A. J., 9
Swader, F., 147, 220
Swader, Francis, 144, 145, 146, 206, 220, 226
Swader, G. W., 158
Swader, Margaret, 9
Swader, T., 226
Swader, Thomas, 143, 220
Swader, Thos., 220
Swader, Washington, 156
Swader, Wm., 220, 226
Swaffer, M., 170, 171
Swaffer, Moses, 224
Swafford, J. M., 206
Swafford, John, 12
Swafford, Moses, 223
Swain, G. W., 194
Swain, Mary J., 205
Swain, W. N., 205
Swan, J. G., 194
Swan, W. B., 100
Swann, John, 77
Swann, W. B., 97, 101, 103
Sweeney, Edmond, 186
Sweet, Jane, 13
Swindell, W. M., 121
Swindell, W., 120
Swindell, Wm., 119, 120
Swinne, Labon, 241
Swinner, Moses, 241
Swinner, W. J., 241
Swofer, M., 22
Tabor, F. M., 42, 253
Tabor, John, 231, 232
Tabor, Mary E., 42
Tacker, Ezekiel, 175
Tacket, Ezekiel, 180
Tacket, John, 181
Tackett, 170
Tackett, John, 166
Taffanstedt, Isabelle, 221
Tailor, Matilda, 217
Talley & Procter, 104
Talley, H, P., 193
Talley, H. H., 225
Talley, J. H., 98
Talley, John, 77
Talley, M., 201
Tallman, James A., 113
Tankersley, J. F., 48
Tankersly, Daniel, 12
Tanter, James, 32
Tasker, C. E., 131
Tate, A. S., 235
Tate, A. W., 40
Tate, Aaron, 185
Tate, Altha, 40
Tate, Aron, 239
Tate, D. M., 40, 252
Tate, Early, 40
Tate, J. H., 166
Tate, John Ike, 134
Tate, John, 13
Tate, M. (W.), 231
Tate, Mabin, 142
Tate, Mayben, 166, 181
Tate, Robert, 185
Tate, S. H., 174
Tate, Wallace, 134
Tate, Willie, 40
Tatum, Ann, 21
Tatum, Bradford, 21
Tatum, E., 81
Tatum, Elisha, 80
Tatum, M. A. B., 58
Tatum, Pierce, 12
Tatum, R. H., 9
Tatum, Sam'l., 147
Tatum, Samuel, 146
Taylar, Elizabeth, 64
Tayler, B. G., 261
Tayler, T.N.F., 258
Taylor J. F., 240
Taylor, 229
Taylor, A. B., 122
Taylor, A. J., 260
Taylor, Allen, 232
Taylor, B. G., 260, 261
Taylor, B. H., 261
Taylor, Bruce, 135
Taylor, C. C. R., 59
Taylor, Carie J., 82
Taylor, Carry, 83
Taylor, D. G. C., 230
Taylor, Duncan G. C., 230
Taylor, E. N., 24, 221
Taylor, G. B., 251
Taylor, G., 166
Taylor, Green B., 135
Taylor, H. S., 235, 239, 240
Taylor, J. F., 235
Taylor, J. N., 110
Taylor, Jeremiah, 230
Taylor, Jesse, 11, 14
Taylor, John D., 215
Taylor, John, 55, 166, 171, 181, 239, 240
Taylor, Manah, 180
Taylor, R. M., 105
Taylor, Sam, 105
Taylor, Skelton, 166, 181
Taylor, Sol, 166
Taylor, Solomon, 174, 181
Taylor, Stephen, 166, 181
Taylor, T. A., 258
Taylor, T. E., 105
Taylor, Tabitha M., 230
Taylor, W. M., 103
Taylor, W. W., 102
Taylor, William, 237
Taylor, Zachary, 153
Teage, Isaac, 181
Teague, Albert, 194
Teague, Dora Cagle, 53
Teague, Dora, 53
Teague, Frank B., 237
Teague, Isaac, 166
Teague, J. M., 110
Teague, James M., 53
Teague, Joshua, 55
Teague, Mary, 250
Teague, Polly Hammock, 207
Teagues, Dorah, 53
Teets, 203
Teets, Mrs., 203
Temmemas?, Wm., 25
Templeton, Agatha Ann, 191
Templeton, J. A., 118
Templeton, J. C., 97
Templeton, J. F., 21
Templeton, J. L., 120, 190, 192
Templeton, John L., 118
Templeton, John, 199
Templeton, Levi, 223
Templeton, Ortha, 199
Templeton, Ortha/Martha, 199
Templeton, S. C., 103, 122
Tenis, Harper, 171
Tenn. Land Dev., 109
Terrell, T. J., 15
Thacker, John, 90
Thagog, R., 143
The Collinsville Courier, 120
The Coosa River News, 64
The Currier, 188
The DeKalb Co. Hotel, 131
The DeKalb Record, 103, 140, 207, 213
The DeKalb Times, 84, 125, 135
The Fort Payne Journal, 46, 84, 125, 131, 139, 148, 210, 227
The Marshall Banner, 84
The Sand Mountain News, 105
Therman, J. T., 60
Thiver, M. E., 58
Thomas, Alex, 233
Thomas, Bell, 76

Thomas, Berry J., 250
Thomas, D. A., 104
Thomas, E. B., 222, 226, 247
Thomas, George, 188
Thomas, J. R., MD, 62
Thomas, J. W., 243
Thomas, Jack, 239
Thomas, James, 79, 220
Thomas, John, 80, 84, 217
Thomas, M., 235
Thomas, Martha, 113
Thomas, Mont, 193
Thomas, Ped, 101
Thomas, Permelia C., 81
Thomas, Permelia Crabtree, 80
Thomas, Permelia Jane, 81
Thomas, R. L., 74, 75, 76
Thomas, Rich, 75
Thomas, W. A., 180
Thomas, Wm. A., 166
Thomasen, J. F., 149
Thomason, D., 170
Thomason, G., 33
Thomason, J. F., 70
Thomason, John F., 207
Thomason, John, 248
Thomason, Mary E., 207
Thomason, Mary Elizabeth, 207
Thomason, T., 184
Thomason, Z., 104
Thompson, 55
Thompson, A. W., 123
Thompson, B. C., 247
Thompson, D. B., 53
Thompson, D. J., 208
Thompson, D. R., 53
Thompson, Darthula, 208
Thompson, Frank, 208
Thompson, Henry, 174
Thompson, J. D., 44
Thompson, J. F., 191, 193
Thompson, J. J. F., 256
Thompson, J. J., Jr., 256
Thompson, J. L., 133, 218
Thompson, J. T., 230
Thompson, J. W., 16
Thompson, Jeremiah J. F., 255
Thompson, Jno., 193
Thompson, John F., 56
Thompson, John L., 55, 166, 181, 238, 255
Thompson, Joshua, 166, 181
Thompson, L. T., 80
Thompson, Letha Ann Crabtree, 79
Thompson, Letha Ann, 81
Thompson, W. F., 16
Thomson, J. L., 221
Thomson, John C., 251
Thomson, W. M., 191
Thornberry, William, 143
Thornburg, William, 248
Thrasher, Elias, 218
Thrasher, G. W., 102
Thrasher, T. J., 100
Thurman, 171
Thurman, B. R., 153
Thurman, I. S. N., 15
Thurman, J. L., 197
Thurman, Mary, 238
Thurman, Palmer, 81
Thurman, S., 224
Thurman, W. J., 128
Tibbitts, Florence, 105
Tibbitts, G. W., 105
Tibbitts, W. G., 105
Tickett, Ezekiel, 166
Tidmon, A. B., 201
Tidmon, Jere, 200
Tidmons, Tom, 91
Tidmore, 200, 202
Tidmore, A. B., 195, 201, 202, 203, 204, 205
Tidmore, A., 200, 203
Tidmore, C. B., 261
Tidmore, Casey, 202
Tidmore, D. H., 200
Tidmore, E. C., 260
Tidmore, Emmer Van, 66
Tidmore, Emmer, 66
Tidmore, H. J., 195, 202
Tidmore, H., 195, 202
Tidmore, Hence, 202
Tidmore, Henry, 204
Tidmore, J. A., 192
Tidmore, J. C., 195
Tidmore, J. H., 121
Tidmore, J. H., 195, 200, 201, 202, 204
Tidmore, J. M., 202, 261
Tidmore, J. P., 66
Tidmore, Jas. W., 66
Tidmore, Jere, 194, 201, 204, 205
Tidmore, M. J., Mrs., 73
Tidmore, M. M., 195, 202, 205
Tidmore, Mollie, 66
Tidmore, W. H., 66
Tidmore, W. J., 121, 261
Tidmore, William H., 66
Tidmore, Wm., 200, 201, 203
Tidwell, 193
Tidwell, C. N., 58, 77
Tidwell, C. W., 77
Tidwell, D., 194
Tidwell, Elenor, 166
Tidwell, Ellenor, 181
Tidwell, J. C., 58
Tidwell, J. W., 66
Tidwell, W. J., 66
Tidwell, William, 77, 180
Tidwell, Wm., 166
Tiege, Delila, 10
Tims, Harrison, 166, 181
Tims, M. C., 181
Tims, Mrs., 166
Tiner, Caroline, 149, 152, 155
Tiner, Caroline, Infant, 152
Tiner, Charles George, 155
Tiner, F? J., 151
Tiner, G. J., 150, 154
Tiner, J. C., 69, 236
Tiner, J. J., 151
Tiner, James A., 69
Tiner, James C., 28, 68
Tiner, James, 78
Tiner, Jas. C., 236
Tiner, Rachael, Mrs., 22
Tiner, S. J., 150, 155, 175, 240
Tiner, Stephen J., 180
Tiner, William, 181
Tinker, B., 34
Tinker, Benj., 233
Tinker, Benjamin, 233
Tinker, Cobb, 183, 184
Tinker, M. V., 2
Tinker, Malvina, 2
Tinn, W. E., Dr., 131
Tinnons, Levi, 123
Tipton, T. C., 60
Tobert, Wesley, 166
Todd, J. W., 253
Todd, John H., 60
Toins, Harvey, 170
Tolbert, J. J., 81
Tolbert, Wesley, 181
Toliver, L. M., 202
Tow, John, 55
Towers, Wm., 60
Tracey, Minnie, 40
Trafensted, Mary, 166
Traffanstedt, J. G., 194
Traffanstedt, Jas., 194
Traffanstedt, Joseph, 181
Traffanstedt, W. J., 222
Traffinsteet, 91
Train, A. W., 54
Train, Annie V., 54
Traylor, G. R., 1, 31, 140
Traylor, T. M., 2
Treadway, Arrie E., 189
Tribble, Alma, 226
Tribble, David, 226
Tribble, Wm., 226
Trible, M. F., 74, 76
Trible, M. H., 74
Trible, W. H., 74, 76
Trible, W. W., 226
Triffe, W. H., 249
Triplett, J. F., 122
Trout, J. G., 166
Trout, J., 175
Troutt, John, 112
Troxtel, J. R., 18
Truce, Baylus, 73
True, J. L., 186
Trump, Mandy, 217
Trusler, Hammack Thomas, 141
Trussell, A. L., 97
Trussell, Hester, 82
Tuck, T., 156
Tuck, Thomas, 158, 166, 181
Tuck/Luck/Turk, 157
Tucker, G. W., 209, 210
Tucker, Inez, Mrs., 43
Tucker, J. M., 43
Tucker, J. W., 91
Tucker, James, 113, 145, 223, 224
Tucker, Jas., 225
Tucker, R., 128
Tufton, Mary E., 166
Tuggle, Jessee, 7
Tuggle, Will, 7
Tulley, S., 11
Tumlin, J. M., 91
Tumlin, J. Noah, 128
Tumlin, T. J., 74, 75
Turinten, D. C., 251
Turk, Robert M., 151
Turk, Thomas, 151
Turk, Thos., 154
Turk/Luck/Tuck
Turner, Alfred, 136
Turner, E. J., 105
Turner, J. E., Mrs., 104
Turner, J. W., 99
Turner, J., 136
Turner, Jane Denton, 104
Turner, John T., 228
Turner, L. C., 104
Turner, R. J., 98
Turner, Susan, 123
Turner, W. A., 90, 91
Turner, W. C., 90
Turnery & Beeson, 148
Turney, M. J., 155
Turnipseed, W. E., 94

Turnley, M. J., 69, 149, 153, 155, 207
Tusculossa Female College, 110
Tutton, Mary E., Mrs., 181
Twitty, J. W., 41
Tygert, Wm., 112
Tyler, W. W., 67
Tyner, Caroline, 155
Tyner, Jack, 170, 171
Tyner, L. J., 172
Tyner, S. J., 154, 156, 166, 235
Tyner, S., 93
Tyner, Stephen I., 115
Tyner, Stephen J., 23, 154, 157, 158
Tyner, Steve J., 115
Tyner, Wm., 166
U S Fidelity & Guaranty, 120
U. S. Fidelity & Guar. Co., 41, 117
Ueasy, Corinna Tate, 40
Underwood, D. M., 82
Underwood, G. W., 99
Underwood, Tom, 122
Union Newspaper, Gadsden, 206
Uptain, David, 76
Uptain, R. L., 98, 101
Uptan, David, 74
Upton, D., 186
Upton, Henry, 257
Upton, Robert, 17
US Fidelity & Guaranty, 106, 209
V.R.R., 167
Valley Head Mercantile, 254
Vanderbirgh, John, 60
Vandergriff, Eva, 61
Vandergriff, T. M., 174
Vandergriff, Thos., 167
Vanderworker, John, 60
Vann Hall Grave Yard, 95
Vann, A. G., 154, 237
Vann, A. J., 28, 94, 156, 157, 167, 175, 200, 236, 253, 257, 263
Vann, A. M., 156
Vann, Dr., 256
Vann, L. S., Mrs., 188
Vann, S. J., 73, 193
Vannevar, Hattie M., 240
Vantanden, J. E., 59
Vaughn, Chessie, 93
Vaughn, James, 55
Vaun, A. P., 68
Venable, Isaac, 149, 185, 261
Venable, J., 149, 250
Ventuas, Thomas, 47
Vicent, W. A., 232
Vincent, Henry, 250
Vinson, E. R., 218
Vinson, S. G., 81
Vinson, W. A., 251
Violette, Benjamin, 34
W. D. Webster Co., 41
W. E. Lucy Co., 252
W. W. Dobbs Gen Hdwe., 110
Waddell, W. C., 167
Waddle, B. B., 228
Waddle, Wm. C., 181
Wade House & Land, 89
Wade, C. C., 221
Wade, H. E., 131
Wade, Henry, 74, 111
Wade, J. T., 122
Wade, L. H., 122
Wade, Marie, 2
Wade, Mary, 111
Wade, R. P., 13
Wade, T. L., 122
Wadkins, John A., 22
Wagencroft, L. L., 102
Wagon, C., 218
Walden & McSpadden, 142, 263
Walden, Geo. S., 141
Walden, George, Sr., 136
Walden, J. B., 23, 52, 84, 96, 135, 141, 149, 150, 154-156, 167, 170, 207, 214, 216, 218, 220, 230, 249, 253, 255, 263
Walden, J. D., 154, 235
Walden, J. V., 194
Walden, Jno. B., 223
Walden, John B., 113, 136, 158, 166, 174, 221, 224
Walden, Jos., 170
Walden, L. B., 42
Walden, N. L., 119
Walden, O. P., 119
Walden, Pearl, Mrs., 119
Walden, W. B., 129, 216, 249
Walden, W., 220
Walder, J. B., 21, 42
Waldon, J. B., 136
Waldorf, Dalas, 194
Waldrop Property, 127
Waldrop, Dovie, 238
Waldrop, R. L., 191
Waldrop, S., 250
Waldrop, Samuel, 87
Waldrop, Telitha, 127
Waldrop, W. D., 195
Wales, C. F. M., 149
Walice, S. W., 100
Walker, _ J., 151
Walker, Ben, 171
Walker, Betsy, 250
Walker, E. J., 17
Walker, G. W., 100
Walker, J. C., 250
Walker, J. N., 101, 141, 148
Walker, J. W., 99, 100, 102, 231
Walker, Jeremiah, 55, 56, 217, 230, 231, 232, 250
Walker, John, 167, 170, 172, 181, 256
Walker, M., 42
Walker, P. J. 153, 170, 221, 225
Walker, Peter J., 155, 171, 224
Walker, Peter T., 22
Walker, S. E., 141
Walker, S. W., 47
Walker, Susan E., 140
Walker, Susan, 148
Walker, W. A., 214
Walker, W. C., 220
Walker, W. J., 144
Walker, William, 181
Walker, Wm., 106, 167, 214, 235
Wall, Barksdale, 191
Wall, Fred, 120
Wall, J. L., 90
Wall, Jesse , 88, 90
Wall, William, 173
Wallace, E. L., 191
Wallace, Ella, 50, 51
Wallace, Ella, Mrs., 49
Wallace, J. O., 62
Wallace, J. S., 99, 103
Wallace, James P., 186
Wallace, John, 186
Wallace, L. P., 101
Wallace, S. J., 102
Wallace, S. M., 58
Wallace, S. W., 99
Wallace, William, 144
Wallace, Wm., 146
Wallas, Ella, Mrs., 49
Waller, C. J. M., 97
Waller, E. M., 38
Waller, Edgar M., 85
Waller, John, 73
Waller, P. J. M., 100
Wallis, John, 89
Wallis, L. M., 99, 102
Walls, B., 22
Walls, Bundy, 225
Walls, Burd, 167
Walls, L. K., 98, 101
Walls, Wm., 167
Walraven, Andy, 122
Walter, 48
Walter, C. J. M., 103
Walters, R., 46
Walthall, S. L., 134
Walton, J. B., 253
Walton, Janice/Jennie, 228
Walton, Raymond, 228
Wammock/Wommack, 42
Ward & Darby, 89, 90
Ward & Edwards, 255
Ward & Loyd, 89, 90
Ward & Penn, 126
Ward & Pickens, 88
Ward, A. F., 245
Ward, A. I., 22
Ward, A. J., 114, 130, 155, 156, 158, 167, 181,
Ward, A. W., 253
Ward, Andrew J., 248
Ward, Andrew, 223
Ward, Andy, 170
Ward, B. J., 250
Ward, C. G., 241
Ward, C. G., 7, 88, 89
Ward, C. P., 247
Ward, C. W., 256
Ward, Caroline, 244, 247
Ward, Darby & Loyd, 90
Ward, Isaac G., 23, 158
Ward, Isaac Y., 172
Ward, Isaac, 166, 181
Ward, J. D., 150, 154, 156
Ward, J. G., 157, 170, 251
Ward, J. R., 194
Ward, J. S., 193
Ward, J. W., 175
Ward, James B., 246
Ward, Jas. S., 130
Ward, John B., 167
Ward, John D., 21, 22, 23, 93, 153, 155, 223
Ward, John, 43, 146, 231
Ward, Kate, 243, 248
Ward, L. P., 55, 56, 126, 238, 254
Ward, Lewis P., 84
Ward, M. B., 120
Ward, Malinda, 167, 168, 245
Ward, Malinda, Mrs., 181
Ward, Mary, 167, 181
Ward, Mrs., 120

Ward, N. A., 42
Ward, N. W., 28, 118, 120, 148, 245
Ward, Noah W., 245, 248
Ward, O. M., 150
Ward, O. W., 55, 64, 148, 151, 155, 166, 168, 181, 249, 253, 256
Ward, Obadiah W., 148
Ward, S. T., 256
Ward, S., 22
Ward, Sam, 234
Ward, T. G., 144, 174
Ward, W. W., 120
Wards, John D., 167
Ware, Beulah Lacy, 63
Warner-Smiley Co., 131
Warnock, H., 60
Warnock, Robt., 108
Warren, Ara, 59
Warren, C. W., 64, 182, 183
Warren, Charles, 10
Warren, Clayton, 243
Warren, Edward, 22, 157, 158
Warren, Eliza, 59
Warren, F. M., 52, 63, 66, 73, 74, 80, 81, 94, 105, 106, 112, 187, 190
Warren, H. L., 190
Warren, Henry, 223
Warren, James, 122, 243, 245
Warren, John, 13, 59
Warren, Joseph, 10
Warren, L. D., 150
Warren, Lot, 14, 182
Warren, N. M., 8, 155
Warren, R. I. (R.J.), 11
Warren, R. J., 11, 148
Warren, Rebecca, 59
Warren, Reuben, 59
Warren, S. D., 66, 123, 144
Warren, Sam, 158
Warren, Saml., Jr., 166
Warren, Samuel D., 155
Warren, Samuel, 13, 145, 158
Warren, W. D., Dr., 20
Warren, W. E., 21, 74
Warren, William, 59
Warren, Wm., 11
Wasa, John, 43
Washburn, J. B., 167
Washburn, T. S., 98
Waterman, A. J., 64
Waters, W. R., 16
Waters, William R., 16
Watkins, John A., 167
Watkins, Strong, 181
Watley, Wm., 174
Watson, A. W., 232
Watson, G. M., 66, 69, 236
Watson, James, 167, 174
Watson, Jesse, 256, 257
Watson, John, 135, 192
Watson, Junken, 210
Watson, Luther, 261
Watson, Missouri, 210
Watt, 181
Watt, Louisa, 13
Watts & Fisher, 167
Watts, Benj., 156
Watts, Berry, 158
Watts, Fortune, 177
Watts, G. M., 99
Watts, H., 238
Watts, Jesse, 170
Watts, L. B., 68, 130, 202, 236
Watts, Moses, 235
Watts, S. T., 166, 175
Watts, Thos. B., 167, 181
Watts, W. J., 153, 166, 168, 181
Wauldin, J. B., 217
Wazencraft, L. L., 103
Wean, Walter, 73
Wear, Suear, 99
Wearthy, A. C., 57
Wearthy, W. C., 57
Weatherford, J. G., 168, 172
Weatherton, John T., 127
Weathington, J. T., 219
Weaver, D., 151
Weaver, F. A., 215
Weaver, J. R., 183, 184
Webb, Brunston W., 141
Webb, D. H., 228
Webb, E. B., 142, 143, 144, 146, 167, 174, 232
Webb, E. W., 142
Webb, Elias B., 147
Webb, G. M., 246
Webb, G. W., 24, 26, 48, 92, 141, 234, 242
Webb, Garrett W., 82, 141, 144, 147, 208
Webb, Henry, 65
Webb, J. M., 37
Webb, J. W., 41
Webb, Jane, 141, 144
Webb, Laura Cagle, 54
Webb, Laura, 53
Webb, Laura, Mrs., 53
Webb, Lavica Garrett, 144
Webb, Lavice Garrett, 141
Webb, Lavicey Garrett, 147
Webb, Lavina, Mrs., 53
Webb, Lovica Garrett, 141
Webb, S. N, Jr., 53
Webb, Sarah Jane, 141, 147
Webb, W. G., 207
Webb, Washington, 91
Wedgworth, H. C., 7
Welborn, 256
Welborn, D. R., 256
Welborn, John F., 149
Welch, Geo. W., 214
Welch, George, 213
Welch, Mary A., 213
Welch, P. L., 71
Welch, Samuel, 12
Welch, Thomas, 151
Weldon, 185
Weldon, George, 35
Weldon, Laura, 35
Weldon, Lula, 35
Weldon, Sandford, 35
Wellborn, D. A., 60
Wellborn, R. G., 83
Wells, Andrew, 18, 19
Wells, Bird, 181
Wells, Franklin, 18
Wells, J. F., 183
Wells, M. H., 228
Wells, Marion/Myron, 227
Wells, Myron H., 227
Wells, Myron, 229
Wells, Sarah, 46
Wells, W. L., 248
Wells, William, 181
Wern?, John, 181
Wesser, W. P., 98
Wesson, 205
Wesson, J. M., 218
Wesson, J. W., 93, 193-195, 200, 201-205, 235, 239
Wesson, J., 203
Wesson, King J., 217
Wesson, Mr., 167
Wesson, Mrs., 181
Wesson, W. A., 191
Wesson, W. J., 197, 200
West, Isaac G., 233
West, J. L., 233
West, J. R., 101
West, James, 7, 39, 182, 183, 184, 209
West, Jas., 24, 134
West, Tom, 194
Westbrooks, Wiley H., 188
Wester, F. H., 101
Wester, Thomas, 90, 91
Wester, W. P., 101, 102
Whaley, W. W., 247
Whatley, Burrel, 246
Whatley, Harriett, 40
Whatley, William, 166
Whatley, Wm., 167, 175
Wheeler, 100
Wheeler, 143
Wheeler, Benj., 182
Wheeler, Drura, 146
Wheeler, Drury C., 142
Wheeler, Drury, 144
Wheeler, Lilla Valentine, Mrs., 67
Wheeler, T. D., 93, 94
Wheeler, Thos. D., 94
Wheler, Drurye C., 143
Whit, 181
White Star Market, 74
White, E., 131
White, Fannie, 62
White, Fannie, Mrs., 62
White, George, 126, 167, 196, 257
White, George, Dr., 181
White, H. R., 62
White, I. L., 18
White, J. B., 62
White, J. G., 5
White, J. H., 53
White, J. L., 19
White, J. M., 121, 254
White, J. T., 48
White, James H., 53
White, James T., 48
White, Jno, 194
White, John C., 231
White, John L., 121
White, John S., 32
White, Joseph A., 112
White, L. W., 18
White, M. G., 87
White, M. J., Mrs., 240
White, M. P., 205
White, Mary E., 9
White, Mrs., 109
White, S. M., 84, 126, 152, 153, 217 237, 255
White, T. H., 98
White, Thomas H., 9
White, Thomas, 23
White, W. C., 121
White, W. T., 260
White, W., 26
White, William, 232
White, Wm. H., 5
White, Wm., 231

White/Whitt, 237
Whited, Abraham, 12
Whited, Frances, 37
Whited, James, 13
Whited, Jas. P., 213
Whited, John, 37, 38
Whited, Maranda F., 37
Whited, William, 35
Whitehead, John G., 10
Whitehead, M. Frances, 38
Whiteside, W. W., 49
Whitman, Blanton, 129
Whitmire, J. G., 30
Whitt (White), Eliza, 47
Whitt, Caroline Horton, 237
Whitt, Caroline, 237
Whitt, S. M., 238
Whitt, Shade M., 237
Whitt, Shade, 167
Whitt, W. P., 167
Whitt, Wm. T., 84
Whitten, Inman, 167
Whitten, Jurene, 181
Whittle, J. W., 109
Whitton, S. M., 219
Whitty, M., 257
Whitty, N. M., 256
Whorton, Jesse, 181
Wiggins, Joseph F., 44
Wiggins, R. W., 153
Wiggs, Henry, 167
Wilbanks, 260
Wilbanks, E., 10
Wilbanks, James, 65
Wilbanks, W. A., 219, 260
Wilbanks, W. C., 92
Wilborn, J. L., 149
Wilborn, James S., 182
Wilborn, T. A., 182
Wilborn, Thomas, 137
Wilburn, Alfred, 13
Wilburn, L. D., 220
Wilburn, Mary, Mrs., 181
Wilburn, Seburn, 238
Wilch, Jas., 170
Wilder, J. T., 123
Wilder, Jesse, 167, 173, 174
Wilder, M., 167
Wilder, Malina, 166
Wilder, Malissa, 181
Wiley, Banks & Co., 167
Wilkenson, E. R., 167
Wilkerson, Benjakin, 248
Wilkerson, E. R., 174
Wilkerson, Elizabeth, 248
Wilkerson, James, 248
Wilkerson, John B., 248
Wilkerson, John, 248
Wilkerson, Kathy, 248
Wilkerson, Lewis, 248
Wilkerson, Wm., 11
Wilkes, Minor, 181, 182
Wilkes, R. W., 22, 222
Wilkes, Washington, 181
Wilkinson, Malinda, 248
Wilkinson, Wm., 10
Wilks, H. J., 167, 172
Wilks, J. T., 74, 76
Wilks, Minor, 167
Wilks, R. W., 225
Wilks, Wash., 167
Wilks, Washington B., 21
William, P. J.(F.), 58
Williams & Tiner, 74
Williams, J. A., 9
Williams, __, 135
Williams, 223
Williams, 260
Williams, 90
Williams, C. D., 89
Williams, C. H., 100
Williams, Charles, 240
Williams, Charley, 235, 239
Williams, Cora, 261
Williams, D. C., 7, 68, 69, 77, 190, 195, 200, 236
Williams, Daniel L., 236
Williams, DeWitt C., 7, 68
Williams, Dorothy L., 36
Williams, E. W., 98
Williams, Earnest, 119
Williams, Elias, 115
Williams, Emma, 36
Williams, Estelle, 36
Williams, G. B., 226
Williams, Geo.C., Jr., 36
Williams, Grace, 36
Williams, H. B., 74
Williams, Harriet, 67
Williams, Henry B., 245
Williams, Henry, 22, 167, 181
Williams, Irvin, 186
Williams, J. D., 1
Williams, J. H., 73, 75
Williams, J. L., 122
Williams, J. M., 250
Williams, J. T., 88, 91
Williams, J. W., 99, 101
Williams, James H., 74
Williams, James, 114, 142, 144, 146, 147, 166, 170, 181, 221, 261
Williams, Jas., 22, 115,141, 146
Williams, Jennie, 243, 245
Williams, John E., 221
Williams, L. I. (T.), 97
Williams, Mary A., 44
Williams, Mattie, 74
Williams, Morgan, 171
Williams, Nena Nicholson, 58
Williams, Neviah, 248
Williams, P., 119
Williams, R. D. R., 231
Williams, R., 232
Williams, Ruth E., 119
Williams, Ruthy, 28
Williams, S. A., 191
Williams, S., 99
Williams, Sampson, 60
Williams, Stephen, 101
Williams, Thomas R., 230, 231, 232
Williams, Thomas, 28
Williams, Tom, 131
Williams, W. B., 183, 184
Williams, W. G., 56
Williams, W. H., 156
Williams, W. J., 91, 101
Williams, W. N., 155, 156
Williams, W. W. N., 156
Williams, W. W., 156
Williams, William G., 56
Williams, Yancy, 181
Williams, Zilmon, 80, 81
Williamson, D. C., 55
Williamson, E. G., 98
Williamson, J. H., 99
Williamson, J. W., 98
Willimson, E. G., 97
Willis, Green, 38
Willis, Mark, 144
Willis, W. F., 27, 167
Willis, W. G., 38
Willoughby, Hammack, 147
Willoughby, J. F., 144
Willoughby, J. H., 143
Willoughby, J. O., 57
Willoughby, T. A., 89
Wills Creek, 79
Wills Valley Railroad, 141
Wills Valley RR, 142
Wills, J. Walter, 135
Wills, J., 104
Willson, Andrew, 250, 252
Willson, H., 60
Willson, Joseph, 250, 252
Willson/Wilson, 250, 252
Wilson, Alex, 199
Wilson, Andrew, 251
Wilson, Benj., 229
Wilson, Bertha A Bruce, 45
Wilson, D. W., MD, 260
Wilson, Elijah, 167
Wilson, Eliza, 174
Wilson, H. B., 76
Wilson, Hattie, 199
Wilson, Hattie/Hettie, 199
Wilson, Henry, 199
Wilson, Hiram, 199
Wilson, J. M., 166, 181
Wilson, J. M., 257
Wilson, James, 230, 231
Wilson, Jesse, 231
Wilson, John P., 10
Wilson, John, 13, 199, 250, 252
Wilson, Joseph, 231, 232, 250, 251,
Wilson, Joshua, 199
Wilson, M. M., 29, 210
Wilson, Mack, 29
Wilson, Martha, 199
Wilson, Martha, Mrs., 191
Wilson, R. D., 144
Wilson, R. F., 166
Wilson, Thos., 257
Wilson, William, 22, 199, 223
Wilson, Wm., 23
Wimpee, F. M., 207
Wimpee, J. A., 172
Wimpey, John H., 181
Wimpsy, T. W., 207
Windsor, Billy, 100
Windsor, H. H., 99, 100
Windsor, H., 98
Windsor, N. E., Mrs., 40
Windsor, W. F., 99
Wingfield, M. A., 13
Winoche, Geo., 112
Winply, J. N., 166
Winsor, H. H., 191
Winston & Finley, 153
Winston & George, 129, 144
Winston & Hoge, 114, 129
Winston & Poe, 167
Winston & Son, 167
Winston, Ed, 221, 247
Winston, Edward, 143, 221
Winston, H. H., 193
Winston, J. G. & Co., 244
Winston, J. G., 56, 95, 96, 114, 115, 147, 167, 172, 221, 225, 243,

Winston, J. J., 150
Winston, J. M., MD, 68
Winston, J. N., 92, 170, 228
Winston, J. N., Dr., 52, 229
Winston, J. N., MD, 258
Winston, J. S., 244
Winston, J. W., 227
Winston, John G., 21, 56, 114, 130, 136, 167, 181, 222, 225,
Winston, John N., 154
Winston, John W., 70, 114
Winston, W. O., 153, 168
Winston, William O., 56
Winston, William, 147
Winston, Wm. O., 21, 142, 167
Winters, J. W., 12
Wistan, W. H., 40
Withrow, Jane, 225
Withrow, Martha, 166
Withrow, Mary A., 23
Withrow, Mary, 166
Withrow, Nancy, 21
Withrow, Rich, Jr., 224
Withrow, Rich, Sr., 224
Witt, A., 174, 257
Witt, Abner, 167
Witt, R., 257
Witt, Robt., 254
Wolf, Alice M., 226
Wolf, Alice, 226
Wolf, E. R., 105
Wolf, S. A., 226
Wolfes, C. A., 39, 133
Wommack, Nancy C., 42
Wommack, R. J., 42
Wood, B. F., 167, 181
Wood, Benj. F., 175
Wood, Emma, 7
Wood, G. W., 10
Wood, J. H., 137
Wood, J. N., 101
Wood, J. W., 261
Wood, J. Y., 123
Wood, John, 195
Wood, Pluma, 17
Wood, T. J., 7
Wood, William, 7
Wood, Wm. B., 130
Woodall, A. J., 19
Woodall, Andrew, 10
Woodall, Georga, 13
Woodall, T. I., 18
Woods, Ed, 133
Woodward, E. L., 231, 232
Woodward, Robert, 108
Woodward, W. K., 95
Wooten, J. J., 1
Wooten, W. I (J.), 26
Wooten, W., 26
Word, J. D., 150
Word, J. J. & O. B., 187
Word/Ward, 155, 194
Work, N., 84
Work, Nelson, 83
Work, O. B., 187
Workman, G. D., 236
Workman, S. D., 1, 31, 140, 208
Workman, S. J., 139
Workman, Samuel D., 31
Works, W., 45
Works, Wm., 167
Worley, Lank, 13
Worley, S. R., 99, 100, 101, 102
Worley, T. H., 102
Worley, W. L., 100
Worley, Winston, 13
Worthington, L., 64
Worthington, Mr., 225
Worthy, B. J., 106
Worthy, Clifford, 57
Wright, C. W., 209
Wright, C. W., MD, 210
Wright, Dr., 149
Wright, Edgar, 122
Wright, Elizabeth, 8
Wright, Freeman, 22
Wright, Geo., 167
Wright, George, 174, 181
Wright, Hallatine, 253
Wright, Hannah, 253
Wright, Haseltine, 253
Wright, J. F., 167, 174
Wright, J. N., 122
Wright, J. T., 171
Wright, J. W. J., 76
Wright, J. W., 17, 91, 228
Wright, James C., 167
Wright, James, 174
Wright, Jas. W., 68
Wright, Jas., 120
Wright, John, 255
Wright, Joseph, 253
Wright, Kittie, 210
Wright, L. T., 39
Wright, Lucy, 253
Wright, Mary Smith, 253
Wright, Mary, 221
Wright, O. W., 210
Wright, Rebecca, 253
Wright, W. H., 91
Wright, W. I. (Dr.), 5
Wright, W. I., 88, 89, 91
Wright, W. I., Dr., 88, 91, 105
Wright, W. J., 88
Wright, W. J., Dr., 187
Wright, W. T., Dr., 260
Wright, Wallace, 122
Wyatt, J. J., 241
Yancey, Lewis, 181
Yancey, Wm. A., 175
Yancey, Wm., 167
Yancy, A. W., 253
Yancy, Andrew W., 253
Yancy, Delana, 74
Yancy, Delana, 76
Yancy, J. E., 97, 100, 102
Yancy, J. L., 108
Yancy, M. E., 253
Yancy, Margaret Johnson, 253
Yancy, Margaret, 253
Yancy, R. J., 193
Yancy, T. P., 75
Yancy, W. J., 57
Yancy, W., 156
Yancy, William A., 158
Yancy, Williams, 181
Yancy, Wm. A., 55, 168, 256
Yarberry, Jas., 256
Yarbrough, J. C., 56, 188
Yarbrough, J. L., 187
Yarbrough, J. L., Sr., 186
Yarbrough, J. T., 36
Yarbrough, J. W., 68, 154
Yarbrough, W. C., 57
Yarbrough, W. R., 186
Yarbry, James, 238
Yarny, Ida, 110
Yates, Jesse A., 86
Yeagin, Jasper, 230
Yeagin, Mary Holcomb, 230
Yearan, Newton, 218
Yeargan, Harriett, 250
Yeargan, John B., 250
Yeargan, Joseph, 251
Yeargan, M. N., 250, 251
Yeargan, Memory N., 250
Yeargen, M. N., 251
Yeargen/Yeargin, 230
Yeargen/Yeargin/Yeargan, 250
Yeargin, J. B., 231
Yeargin, Jasper, 230, 232
Yeargin, Joseph, 230
Yeargin, M. N., 251
Yering, Rebeca, 252
Yeuell, Claris, 103
Yeuell, Claris, 84, 135, 140
York, Elijah, 43
York, Enoch, 32
York, F. J., 123
York, F. M., 38, 83, 123, 215
York, John C., 37, 38
York, John G., 189
York, John, 15, 215
York, Moses, 35, 36
York, Rosa, 36
York, W. E., 81
Young & Hughes, 251
Young, A., 207
Young, B. B., 75
Young, B. F., 31
Young, Ben, 183, 184
Young, Benjamin, 13
Young, Bird, 105
Young, C. H., 209
Young, Fayette, 251
Young, G. L., 4
Young, G. T., 73
Young, J. B., 75
Young, J. W., 2, 3
Young, James F., 144
Young, John, 167, 181
Young, Lafayette F., 195
Young, Lewis, 167
Young, M. D., Mrs., 106
Young, M., 10
Young, Margaret D., 105
Young, Nancy, 15
Young, R. M., 126
Young, Rebecca, 252
Young, Robert, 251
Young, Rueben, 191
Young, S. C., 10
Young, Samuel, 14, 15
Young, W. H., 137, 227
Young, W., 10
Young, Wm. C., 252
Youngblood, M., 188
Zimmerman, Henry, 60

www.ingramcontent.com/pod-product-compliance
Lightning Source LLC
Chambersburg PA
CBHW071836270326
41929CB00013B/2015

* 9 7 8 0 8 0 6 3 5 4 8 8 0 *